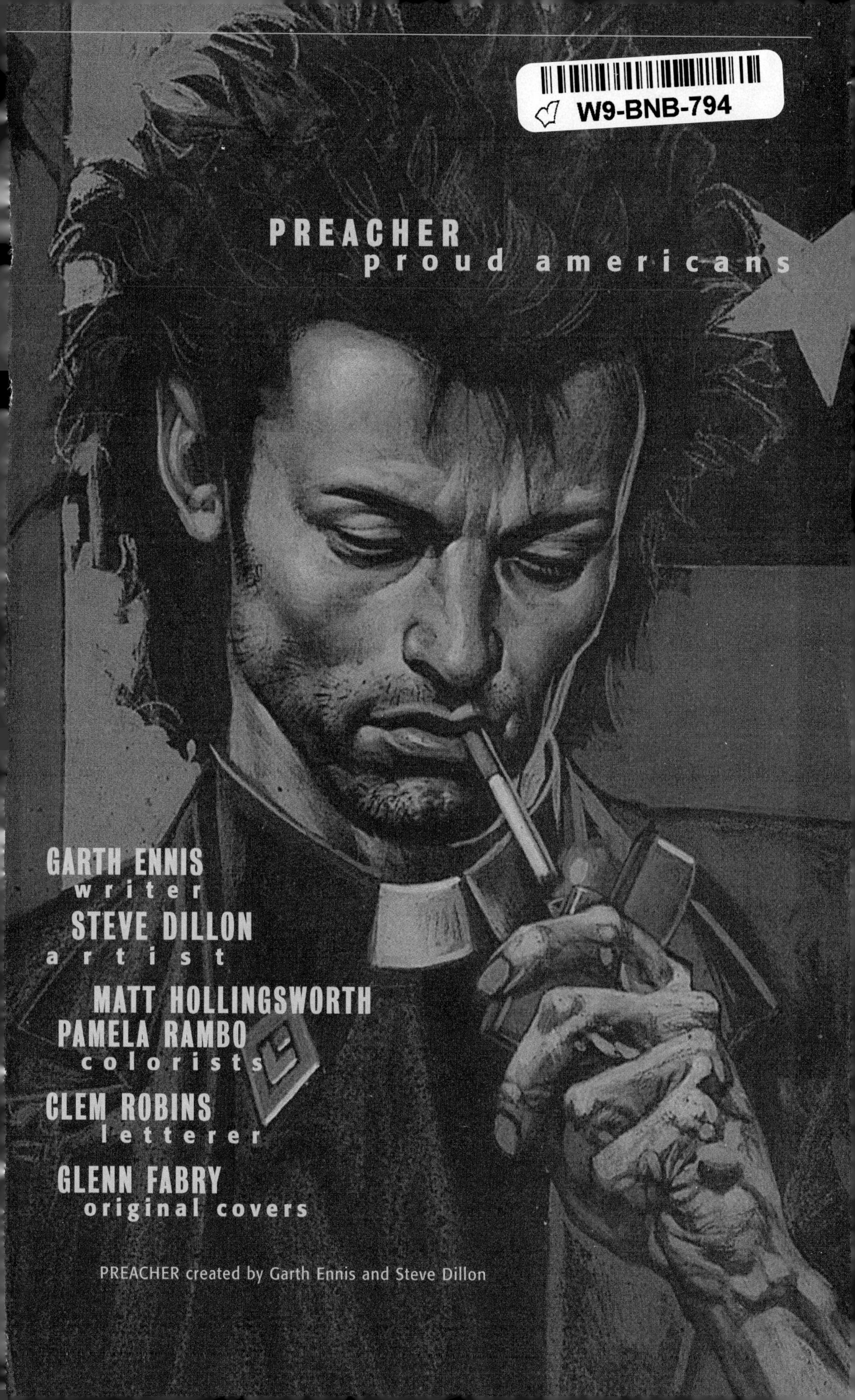

PREACHER
proud americans

GARTH ENNIS
writer

STEVE DILLON
artist

MATT HOLLINGSWORTH
PAMELA RAMBO
colorists

CLEM ROBINS
letterer

GLENN FABRY
original covers

PREACHER created by Garth Ennis and Steve Dillon

JENETTE KAHN
president & editor-in-chief

PAUL LEVITZ
executive vice president & publisher

KAREN BERGER
executive editor

AXEL ALONSO
editor-original series

BOB KAHAN
editor-collected edition

JIM SPIVEY
associate editor-collected edition

GEORG BREWER
design director

ROBBIN BROSTERMAN
art director

RICHARD BRUNING
vp-creative director

PATRICK CALDON
vp-finance & operations

DOROTHY CROUCH
vp-licensed publishing

TERRI CUNNINGHAM
vp-managing editor

JOEL EHRLICH
senior vp-advertising & promotions

LILLIAN LASERSON
vp & general counsel

BOB ROZAKIS
executive director-production

Special thanks to James Rochelle, Ryan Stirling and Scott Dunbier,
without whose generosity and help this volume would not have happened.

introduction

by PENN JILLETTE

Why would I read a comic book called PREACHER?
It sounds like some sort of *Chick Tract*? (Well, that's not a good example, because I do read *Chick Tracts*. There's really nothing funnier than mentally ill Jack Chick with his groovy sexy hell panic—but you know what I mean.)

Here's how it happened:
my love and I were in our friendly Las Vegas comic book shop and the proprietor, a guy like us, said something to the effect of, "Hey, Penn, man, have you seen this, man? It's really the fucking, most fucked-up, fucking thing I've fucking seen. I mean it's **Ennis** and **Dillon**, so it's really well written, the art is beautiful—but it's really fucked up. It's fucking great, man."

...THE PACKAGE HAD EVËRYTHING I HATE— ANGELS, GOD, MIRACLES, MYSTIC POWERS, DEVILS...

He handed me one of the PREACHER issues that was reprinted in the last trade paperback. It was the one that started with the "SEX INVESTIGATORS." I thumbed through: vampires bursting into flames, anal rape, hookers, and a cat in a toilet—what more could we want? My local comic-book dealer then gushed that he "never" wrote "those stupid fucking fan letters in the back of comics," but "I had to for this one, man. I just wrote them a blowjob, man, and at a signing, I even stood in fucking line to get an autograph, man. It's fucking really fucking great."

He had sold me (I think it was the penultimate participial adjective that really did it), but he didn't sell me; he gave me the comic for free. (This gentleman loves comics more than commerce.) We jumped into my car, Pink Death, and I drove through Sin City, while my girlfriend read PREACHER aloud and described the pictures **(sorry, Steve)** to me. She was doing accents **(sorry, Garth)** where they were called for, and it was killing us dead. I kind of forgot about the title and the hated collar—it just sounded good. When I got home I read it with only my lips moving. It looked g o o d ,   t o o .

...IT ALSO HAD ALL THE THINGS I LOVE— TITS, FUCKING, AND THINGS BLOWING UP.

As much as I loved it, I didn't keep up with it. I just don't get into my local comic shop as often as I should. A few months later, DC Comics asked me to write an intro for an entirely unrelated comic. The thinking was that since it was nominally concerned with "magic," and that's kinda sorta my day job, I'd be perfect. I wrote a preachy little something about how it was good to make believe about "magic" in comics and shows, but man, don't get nutty in the real world. But, it turned out to be not so perfect a match. So, I was fired from the intro writing gig, and the DC people said they felt awful.

A bit later, they asked me to write an intro for another trade paperback. I was skeptical. They promised I could write whatever I wanted. I was skeptical. They were sure they had found the perfect match. I'm a skeptical guy. B u t, when they said it was

PREACHER, my ears pricked up. "Yeah, I saw an issue, I really liked it. It is called PREACHER, though. Are you sure the cheeses won't be offended? Are you sure they don't believe in anything? Are we setting up ourselves for another problem?" They were confident. I was skeptical, but what the hey, it's free comics.

They gave me the whole PREACHER package—the first two collections, plus all the individual comics that are collected here in your hot little hands, and they bought me a fancy lunch. The package had everything I hate—angels, god, miracles, mystic powers, devils, even a protagonist with the initials "J.C." (Get it?). But it also had all the things I love—tits, fucking, and things blowing up. And good or bad, everything was beautiful and rich.

Now, some would say that putting some of the backbones of Western religion into a comic book blasphemes. It actually has the opposite effect on me. Seeing those religious symbols used in this context without the constant, obsessive, anti-science, anti-freedom, anti-sex, woman-bashing, gay-bashing, racist, delusional, politically manipulative babbling of a bunch of ancient, psycho McVeigh-types was wonderfully refreshing. It seems some of the images of religion could be pretty entertaining.

It gave me a different view of the Bible; maybe the old hate book was really written with the good-natured, rollicking fun of PREACHER and over the millennia, well, it just got a bit preverted (and I use that word here, oddly for me, as a pejorative). And maybe, after a few more millennia have passed, someone will find copies of these comic books in a cave somewhere (I'm sure some of us keep our copies in caves somewhere), mistake great art for bad philosophy, and start an evil religion with this great comic book. Hey, Cassidy is better than the Holy Ghost and Tulip kicks the ass of both momma-Madonnas on every front.

Here's hoping PREACHER is simply remembered forever as a great comic, but if it does get co-opted—at least they'll have better pictures.

ENJOY THESE LIKE HOLY HELL,
penn jillette
(waiting to be fired again)

Penn Jillette is more than half, by weight, of Penn & Teller.

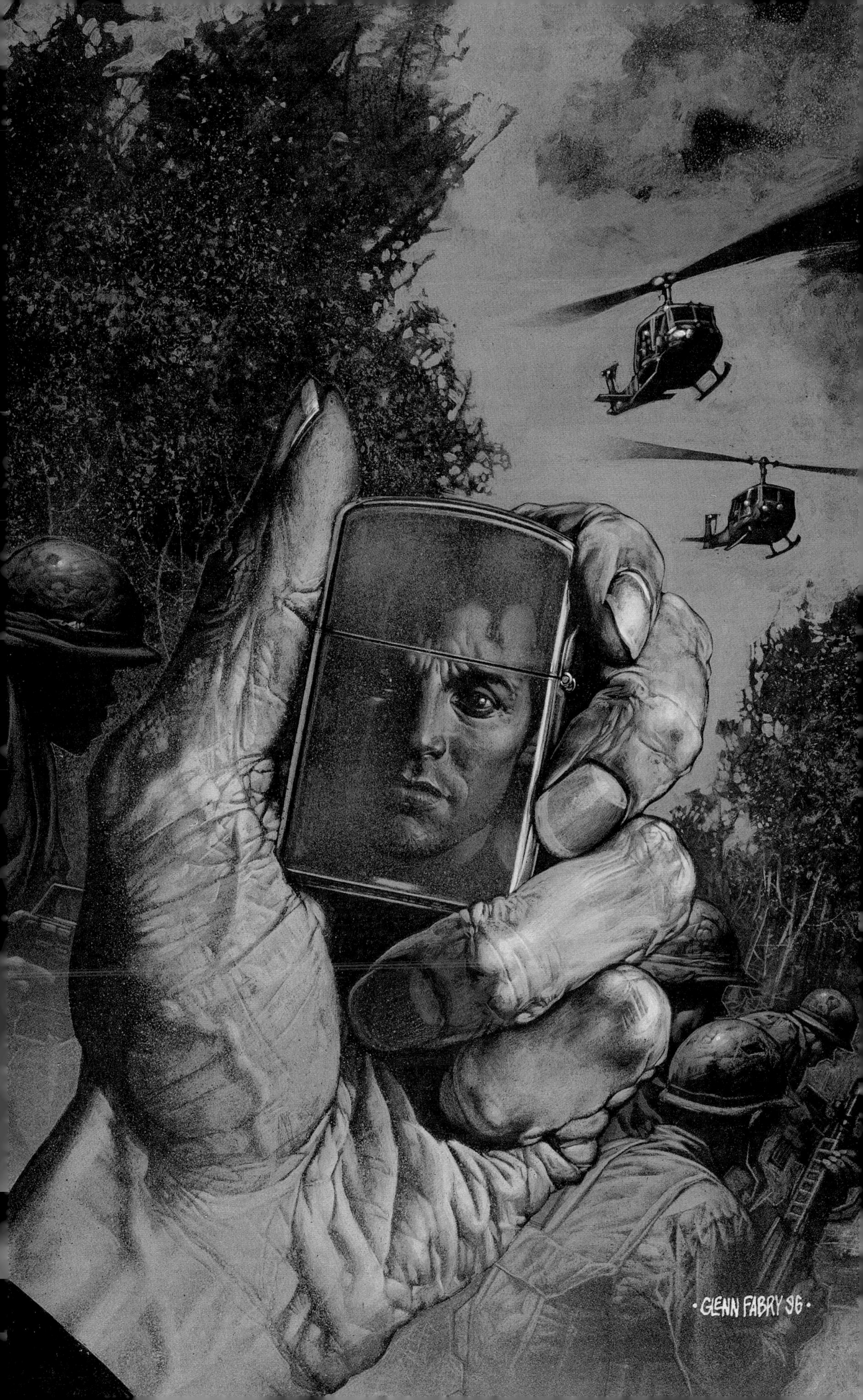
·GLENN FABRY 96·

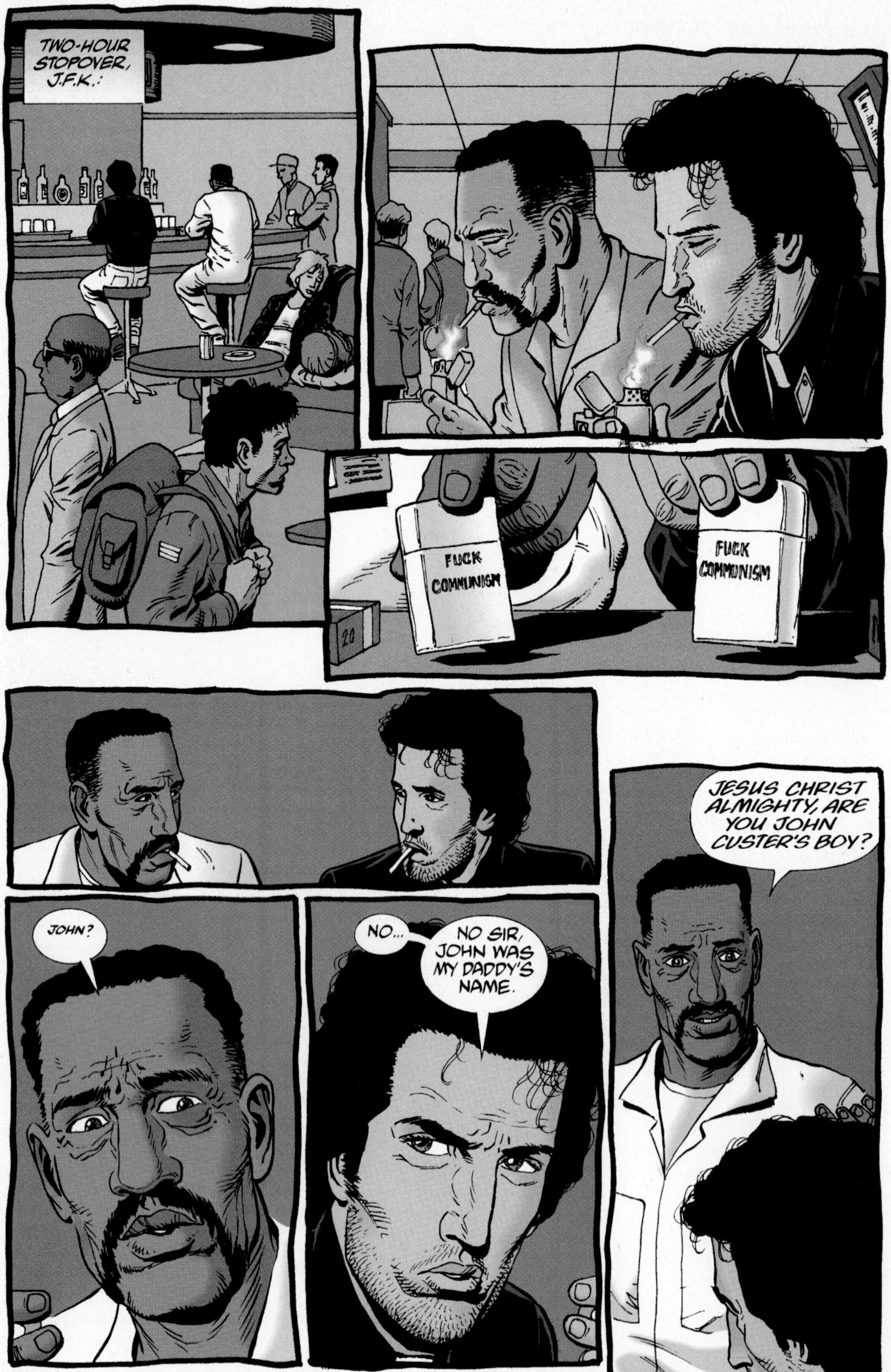

TWO-HOUR STOPOVER, J.F.K.:
FUCK COMMUNISM
FUCK COMMUNISM
JESUS CHRIST ALMIGHTY, ARE YOU JOHN CUSTER'S BOY?
JOHN?
NO...
NO SIR, JOHN WAS MY DADDY'S NAME.

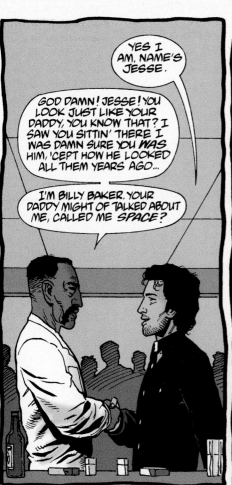

YES I AM. NAME'S JESSE.

GOD DAMN! JESSE! YOU LOOK JUST LIKE YOUR DADDY, YOU KNOW THAT? I SAW YOU SITTIN' THERE I WAS DAMN SURE YOU WAS HIM, 'CEPT HOW HE LOOKED ALL THEM YEARS AGO...

I'M BILLY BAKER. YOUR DADDY MIGHT OF TALKED ABOUT ME, CALLED ME SPACE?

IF HE DID, I DON'T RECALL. IT'S BEEN A WHILE SINCE WE TALKED.

YOU AIN'T CLOSE?

HE DIED IN NINETEEN SEVENTY-FOUR.

I'M REAL SORRY.

WE WAS BUDDIES IN VIETNAM. HE WAS A GOOD FRIEND, YOU KNOW? I ALWAYS WONDERED WHY HE NEVER CALLED ME UP.

I GUESS THAT'S WHY.

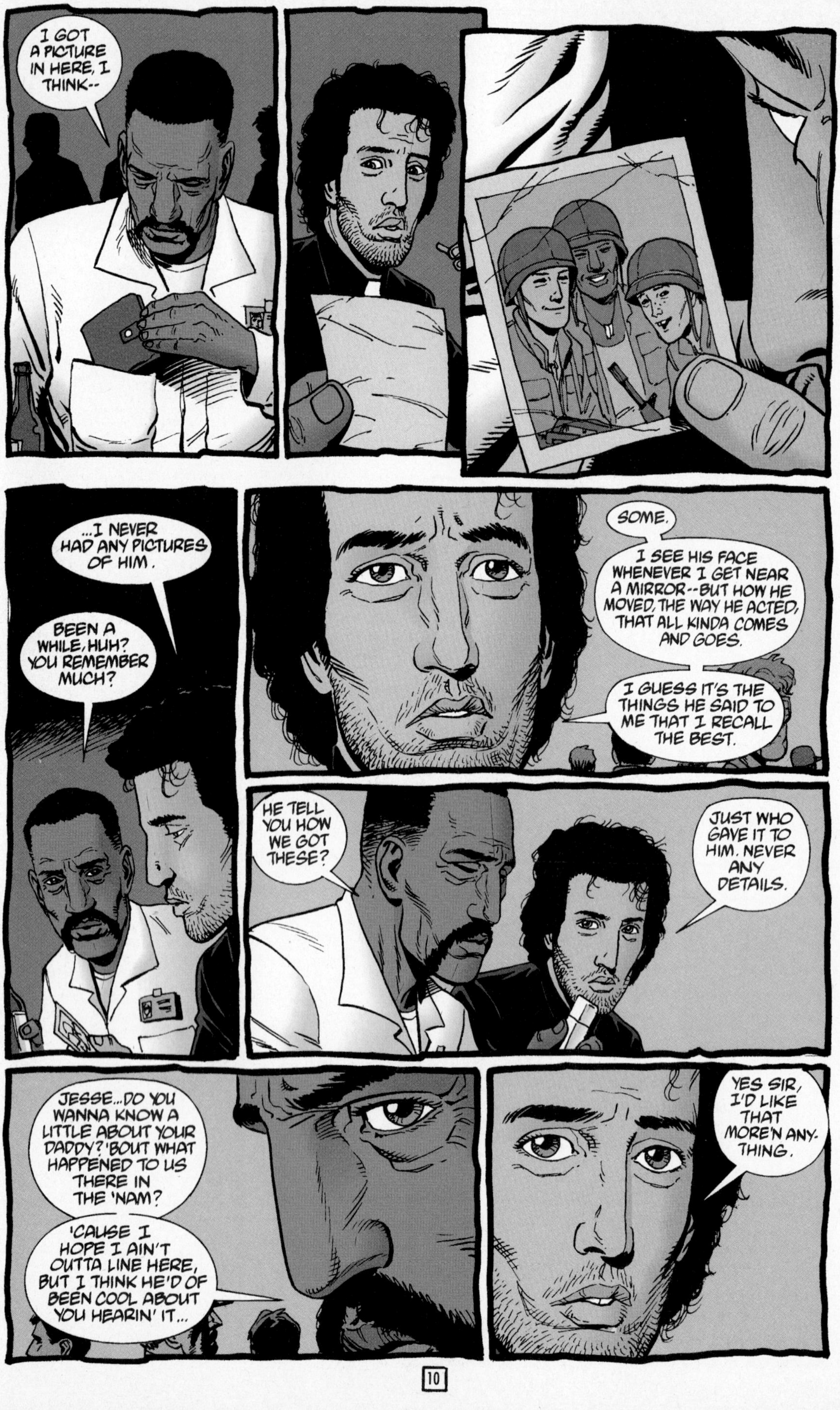
I GOT A PICTURE IN HERE, I THINK--
...I NEVER HAD ANY PICTURES OF HIM.
BEEN A WHILE, HUH? YOU REMEMBER MUCH?
SOME.
I SEE HIS FACE WHENEVER I GET NEAR A MIRROR--BUT HOW HE MOVED, THE WAY HE ACTED, THAT ALL KINDA COMES AND GOES.
I GUESS IT'S THE THINGS HE SAID TO ME THAT I RECALL THE BEST.
HE TELL YOU HOW WE GOT THESE?
JUST WHO GAVE IT TO HIM. NEVER ANY DETAILS.
JESSE...DO YOU WANNA KNOW A LITTLE ABOUT YOUR DADDY? 'BOUT WHAT HAPPENED TO US THERE IN THE 'NAM?
'CAUSE I HOPE I AIN'T OUTTA LINE HERE, BUT I THINK HE'D OF BEEN COOL ABOUT YOU HEARIN' IT...
YES SIR, I'D LIKE THAT MORE'N ANY-THING.

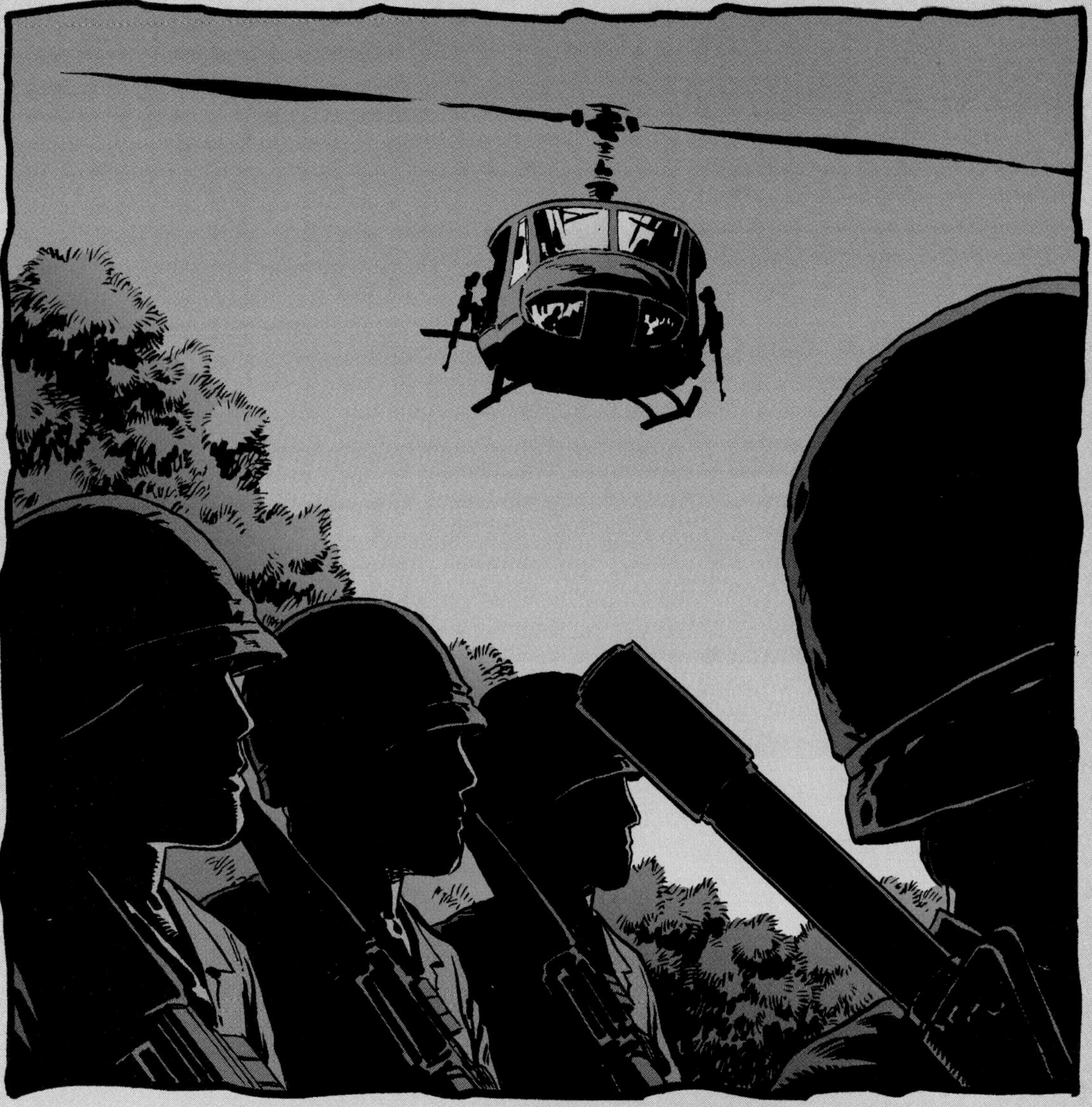

TEXAS AND THE SPACEMAN

GARTH ENNIS - Writer STEVE DILLON - Artist

MATT HOLLINGSWORTH - Colorist

CLEM ROBINS - Letterer AXEL ALONSO - Editor

PREACHER created by GARTH ENNIS and STEVE DILLON

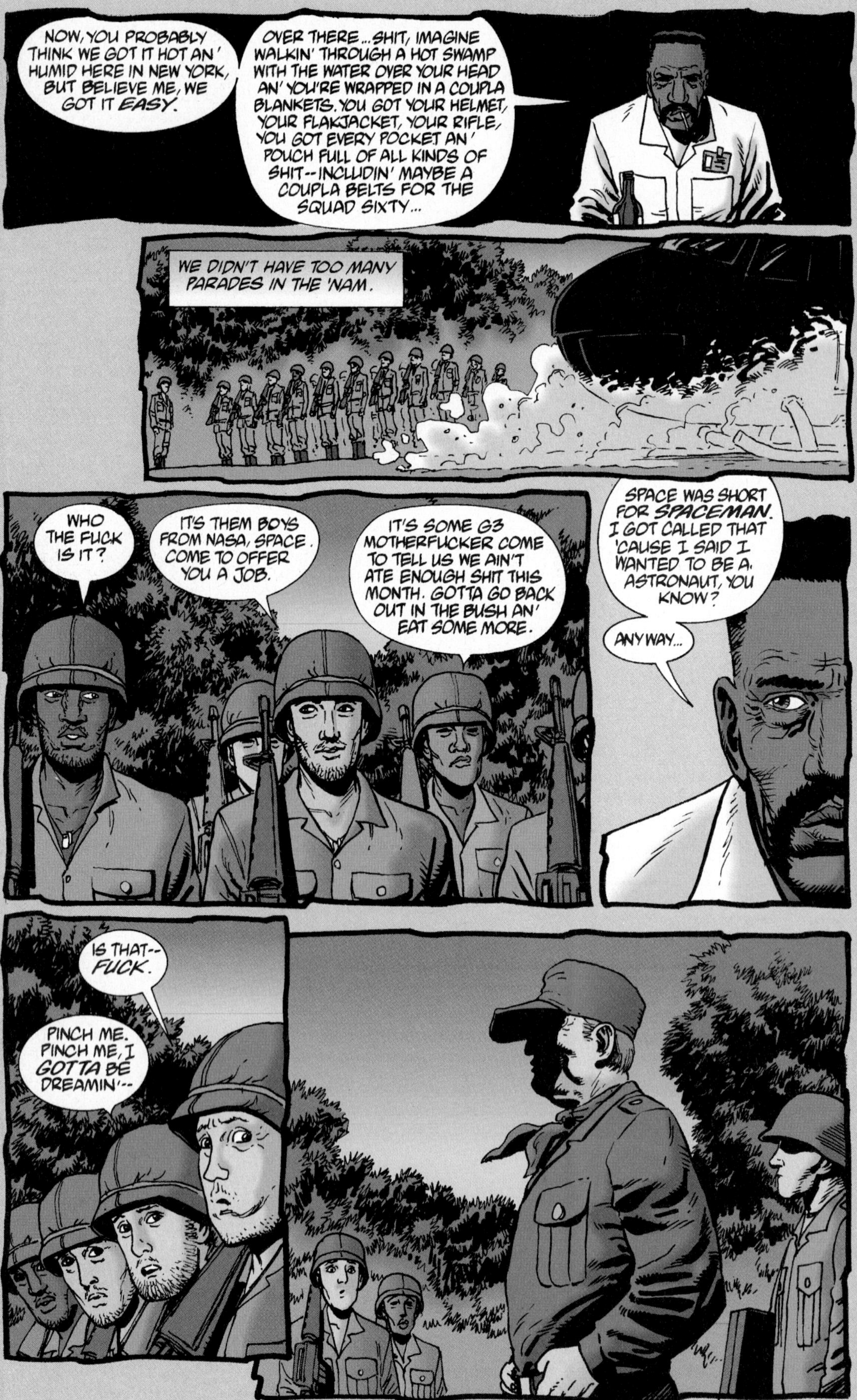
NOW, YOU PROBABLY THINK WE GOT IT HOT AN' HUMID HERE IN NEW YORK, BUT BELIEVE ME, WE GOT IT *EASY*.
OVER THERE... SHIT, IMAGINE WALKIN' THROUGH A HOT SWAMP WITH THE WATER OVER YOUR HEAD AN' YOU'RE WRAPPED IN A COUPLA BLANKETS. YOU GOT YOUR HELMET, YOUR FLAKJACKET, YOUR RIFLE, YOU GOT EVERY POCKET AN' POUCH FULL OF ALL KINDS OF SHIT--INCLUDIN' MAYBE A COUPLA BELTS FOR THE SQUAD SIXTY...
WE DIDN'T HAVE TOO MANY PARADES IN THE 'NAM.
WHO THE FUCK IS IT?
IT'S THEM BOYS FROM NASA, SPACE. COME TO OFFER YOU A JOB.
IT'S SOME G3 MOTHERFUCKER COME TO TELL US WE AIN'T ATE ENOUGH SHIT THIS MONTH. GOTTA GO BACK OUT IN THE BUSH AN' EAT SOME MORE.
SPACE WAS SHORT FOR *SPACEMAN*. I GOT CALLED THAT 'CAUSE I SAID I WANTED TO BE A. ASTRONAUT, YOU KNOW?
ANYWAY...
IS THAT-- *FUCK*.
PINCH ME. PINCH ME, I *GOTTA* BE DREAMIN'--

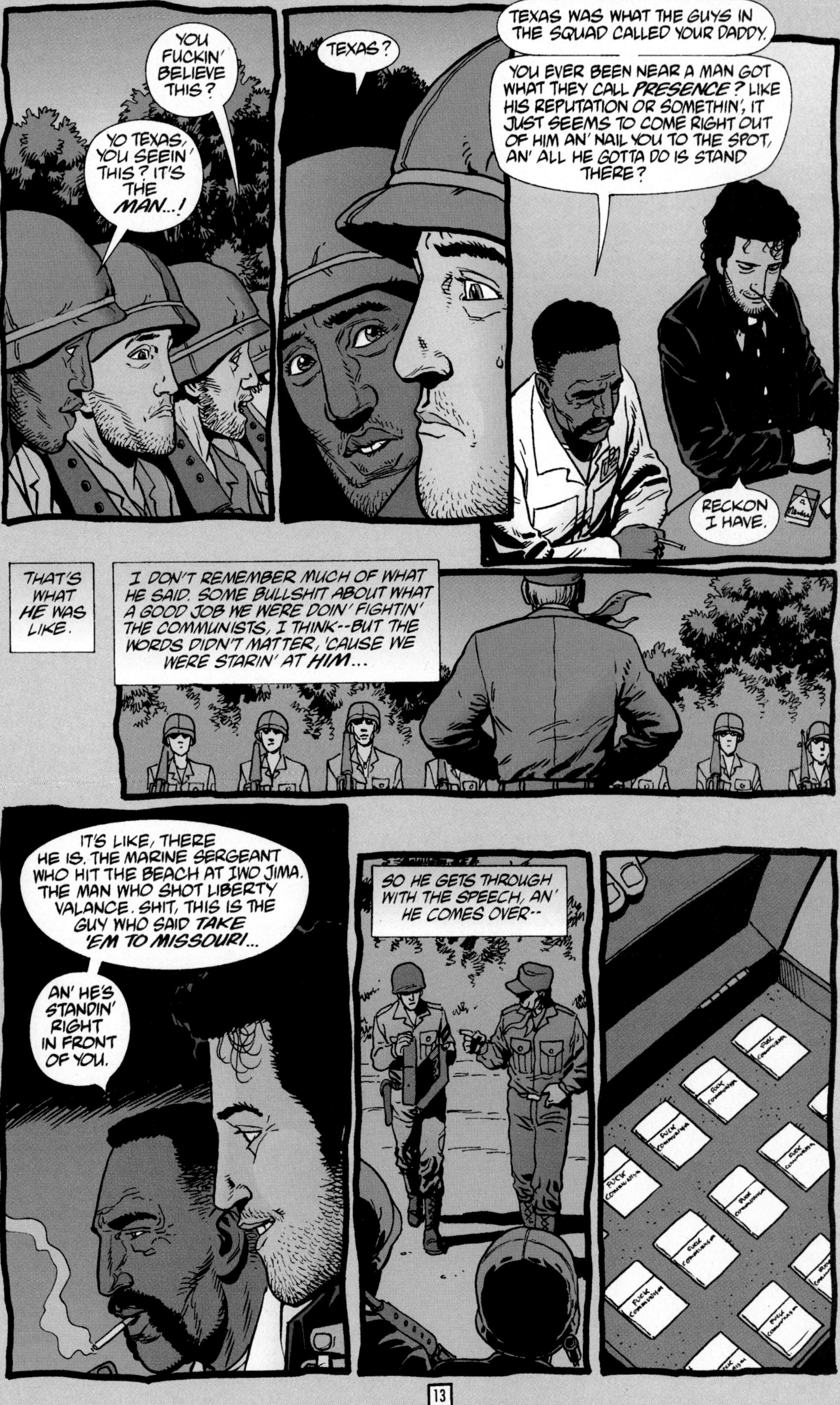

YOU FUCKIN' BELIEVE THIS?
YO TEXAS, YOU SEEIN' THIS? IT'S THE MAN...!
TEXAS?
TEXAS WAS WHAT THE GUYS IN THE SQUAD CALLED YOUR DADDY.
YOU EVER BEEN NEAR A MAN GOT WHAT THEY CALL PRESENCE? LIKE HIS REPUTATION OR SOMETHIN', IT JUST SEEMS TO COME RIGHT OUT OF HIM AN' NAIL YOU TO THE SPOT, AN' ALL HE GOTTA DO IS STAND THERE?
RECKON I HAVE.
THAT'S WHAT HE WAS LIKE.
I DON'T REMEMBER MUCH OF WHAT HE SAID. SOME BULLSHIT ABOUT WHAT A GOOD JOB WE WERE DOIN' FIGHTIN' THE COMMUNISTS, I THINK--BUT THE WORDS DIDN'T MATTER, 'CAUSE WE WERE STARIN' AT HIM...
IT'S LIKE, THERE HE IS. THE MARINE SERGEANT WHO HIT THE BEACH AT IWO JIMA. THE MAN WHO SHOT LIBERTY VALANCE. SHIT, THIS IS THE GUY WHO SAID TAKE 'EM TO MISSOURI...
AN' HE'S STANDIN' RIGHT IN FRONT OF YOU.
SO HE GETS THROUGH WITH THE SPEECH, AN' HE COMES OVER--

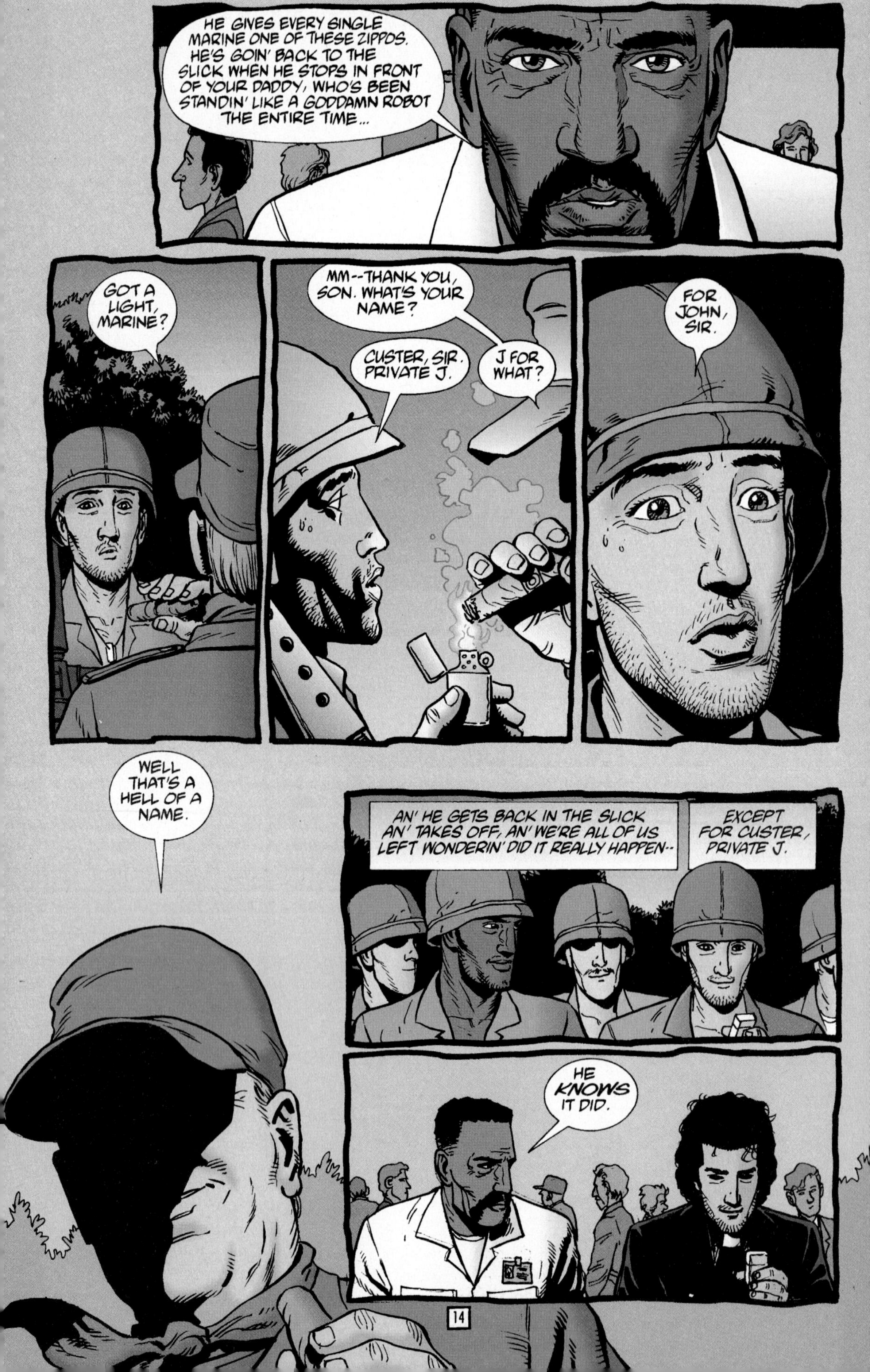
HE GIVES EVERY SINGLE MARINE ONE OF THESE ZIPPOS. HE'S GOIN' BACK TO THE SLICK WHEN HE STOPS IN FRONT OF YOUR DADDY, WHO'S BEEN STANDIN' LIKE A GODDAMN ROBOT THE ENTIRE TIME...
GOT A LIGHT, MARINE?
MM--THANK YOU, SON. WHAT'S YOUR NAME?
CUSTER, SIR. PRIVATE J.
J FOR WHAT?
FOR JOHN, SIR.
WELL THAT'S A HELL OF A NAME.
AN' HE GETS BACK IN THE SLICK AN' TAKES OFF, AN' WE'RE ALL OF US LEFT WONDERIN' DID IT REALLY HAPPEN--
EXCEPT FOR CUSTER, PRIVATE J.
HE KNOWS IT DID.

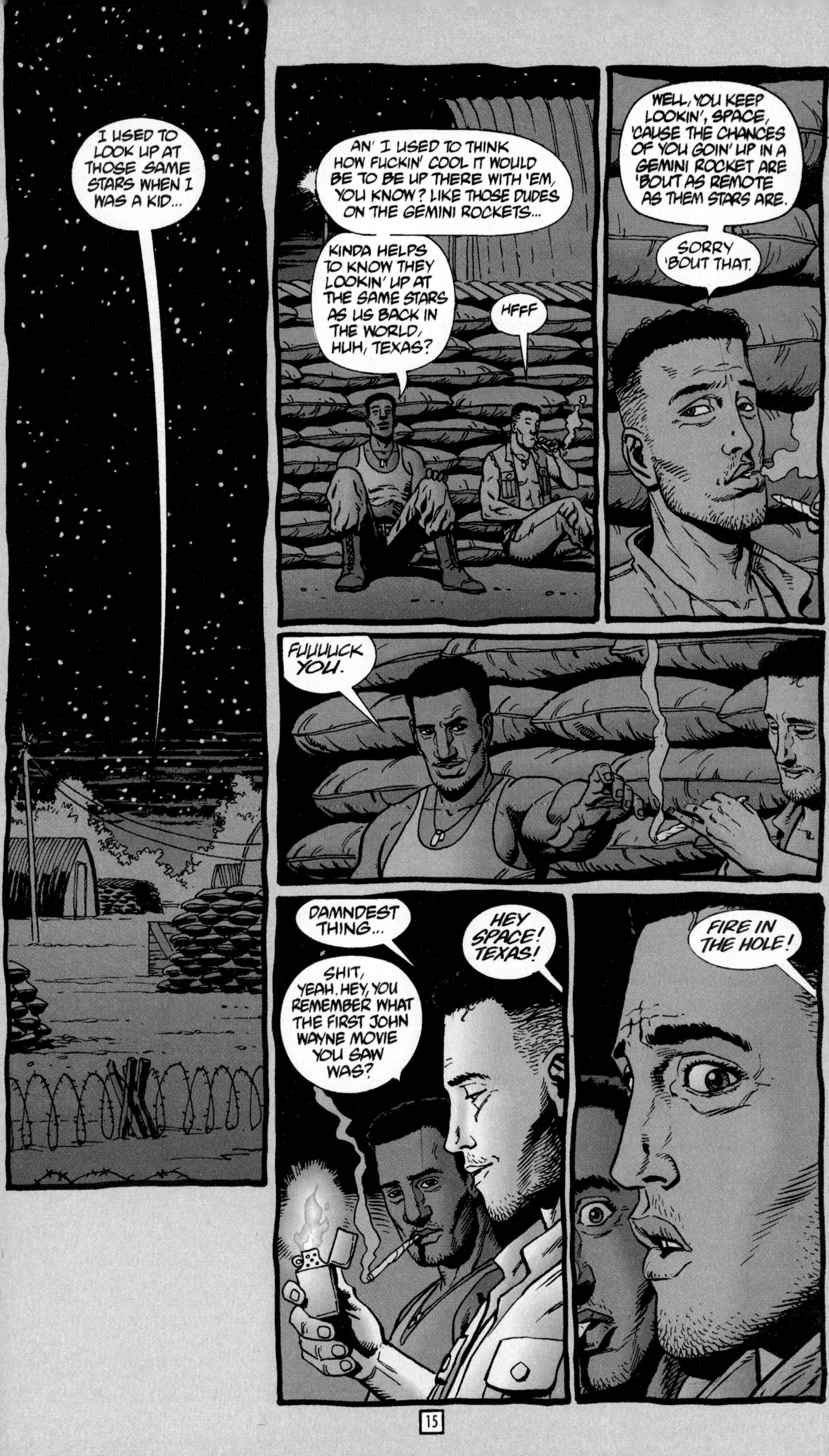
I USED TO LOOK UP AT THOSE SAME STARS WHEN I WAS A KID...
AN' I USED TO THINK HOW FUCKIN' COOL IT WOULD BE TO BE UP THERE WITH 'EM, YOU KNOW? LIKE THOSE DUDES ON THE GEMINI ROCKETS...
KINDA HELPS TO KNOW THEY LOOKIN' UP AT THE SAME STARS AS US BACK IN THE WORLD, HUH, TEXAS?
HFFF
WELL, YOU KEEP LOOKIN', SPACE, 'CAUSE THE CHANCES OF YOU GOIN' UP IN A GEMINI ROCKET ARE 'BOUT AS REMOTE AS THEM STARS ARE.
SORRY 'BOUT THAT.
FUUUUCK YOU.
DAMNDEST THING...
SHIT, YEAH. HEY, YOU REMEMBER WHAT THE FIRST JOHN WAYNE MOVIE YOU SAW WAS?
HEY SPACE! TEXAS!
FIRE IN THE HOLE!

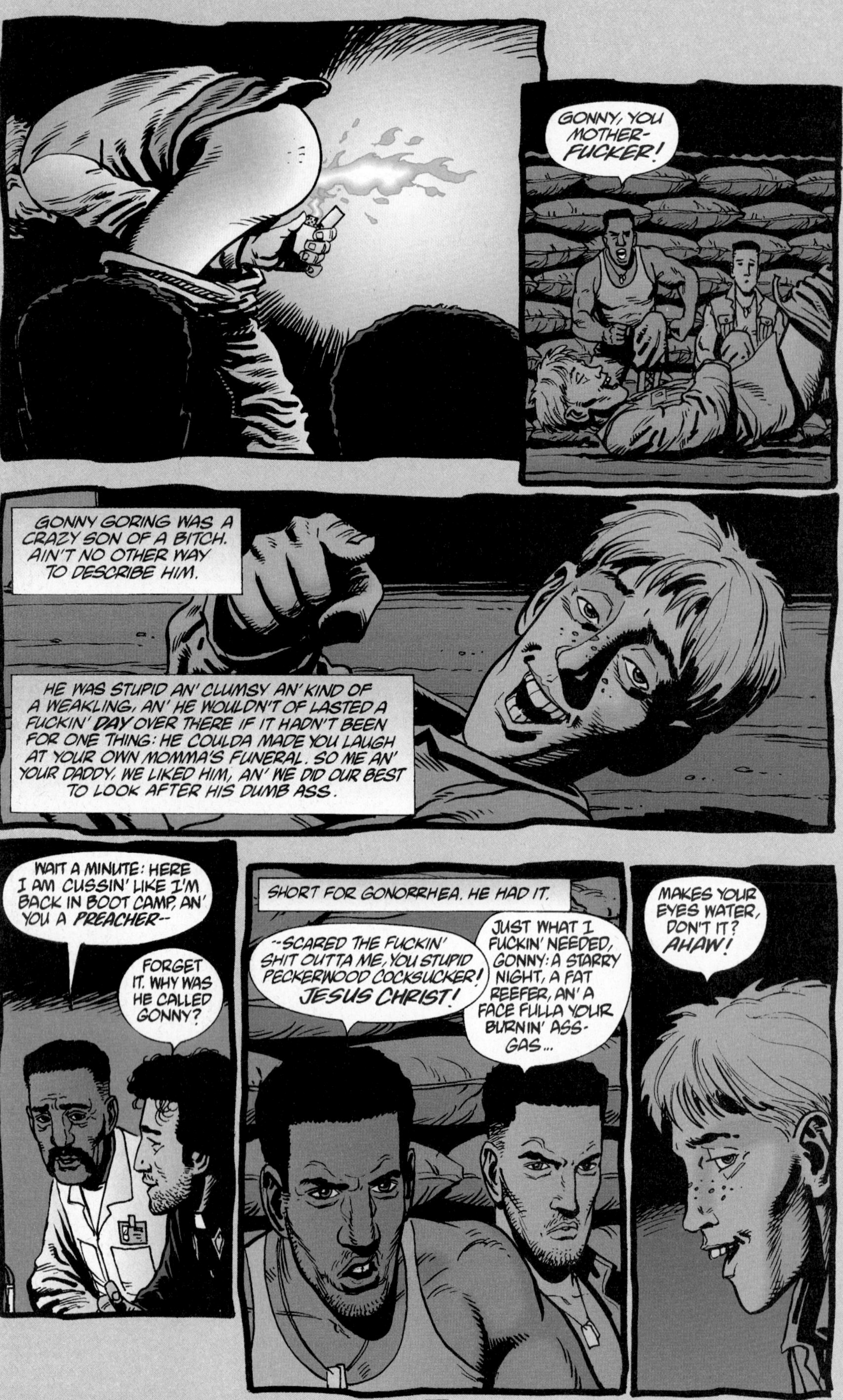
GONNY, YOU MOTHER-FUCKER!
GONNY GORING WAS A CRAZY SON OF A BITCH. AIN'T NO OTHER WAY TO DESCRIBE HIM.
HE WAS STUPID AN' CLUMSY AN' KIND OF A WEAKLING, AN' HE WOULDN'T OF LASTED A FUCKIN' DAY OVER THERE IF IT HADN'T BEEN FOR ONE THING: HE COULDA MADE YOU LAUGH AT YOUR OWN MOMMA'S FUNERAL. SO ME AN' YOUR DADDY, WE LIKED HIM, AN' WE DID OUR BEST TO LOOK AFTER HIS DUMB ASS.
WAIT A MINUTE: HERE I AM CUSSIN' LIKE I'M BACK IN BOOT CAMP, AN' YOU A PREACHER--
FORGET IT. WHY WAS HE CALLED GONNY?
SHORT FOR GONORRHEA. HE HAD IT.
--SCARED THE FUCKIN' SHIT OUTTA ME, YOU STUPID PECKERWOOD COCKSUCKER! JESUS CHRIST!
JUST WHAT I FUCKIN' NEEDED, GONNY: A STARRY NIGHT, A FAT REEFER, AN' A FACE FULLA YOUR BURNIN' ASS-GAS...
MAKES YOUR EYES WATER, DON'T IT? AHAW!

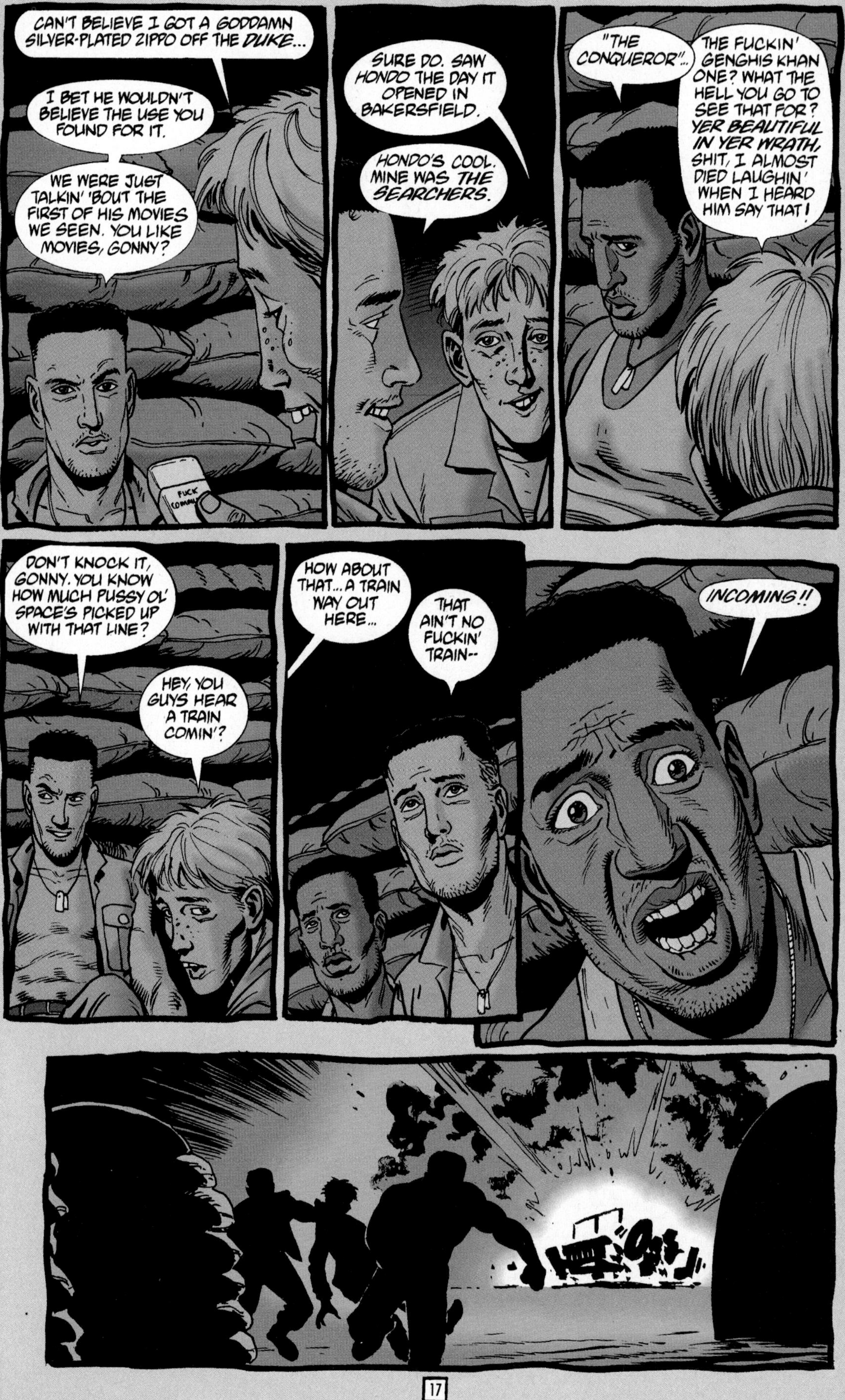
CAN'T BELIEVE I GOT A GODDAMN SILVER-PLATED ZIPPO OFF THE *DUKE*...
I BET HE WOULDN'T BELIEVE THE USE YOU FOUND FOR IT.
WE WERE JUST TALKIN' 'BOUT THE FIRST OF HIS MOVIES WE SEEN. YOU LIKE MOVIES, GONNY?
SURE DO. SAW *HONDO* THE DAY IT OPENED IN BAKERSFIELD.
HONDO'S COOL. MINE WAS *THE SEARCHERS*.
"THE CONQUEROR"...
THE FUCKIN' GENGHIS KHAN ONE? WHAT THE HELL YOU GO TO SEE THAT FOR? ***YER BEAUTIFUL IN YER WRATH,*** SHIT, I ALMOST DIED LAUGHIN' WHEN I HEARD HIM SAY THAT!
DON'T KNOCK IT, GONNY. YOU KNOW HOW MUCH PUSSY OL' SPACE'S PICKED UP WITH THAT LINE?
HEY, YOU GUYS HEAR A TRAIN COMIN'?
HOW ABOUT THAT... A TRAIN WAY OUT HERE...
THAT AIN'T NO FUCKIN' TRAIN--
INCOMING!!

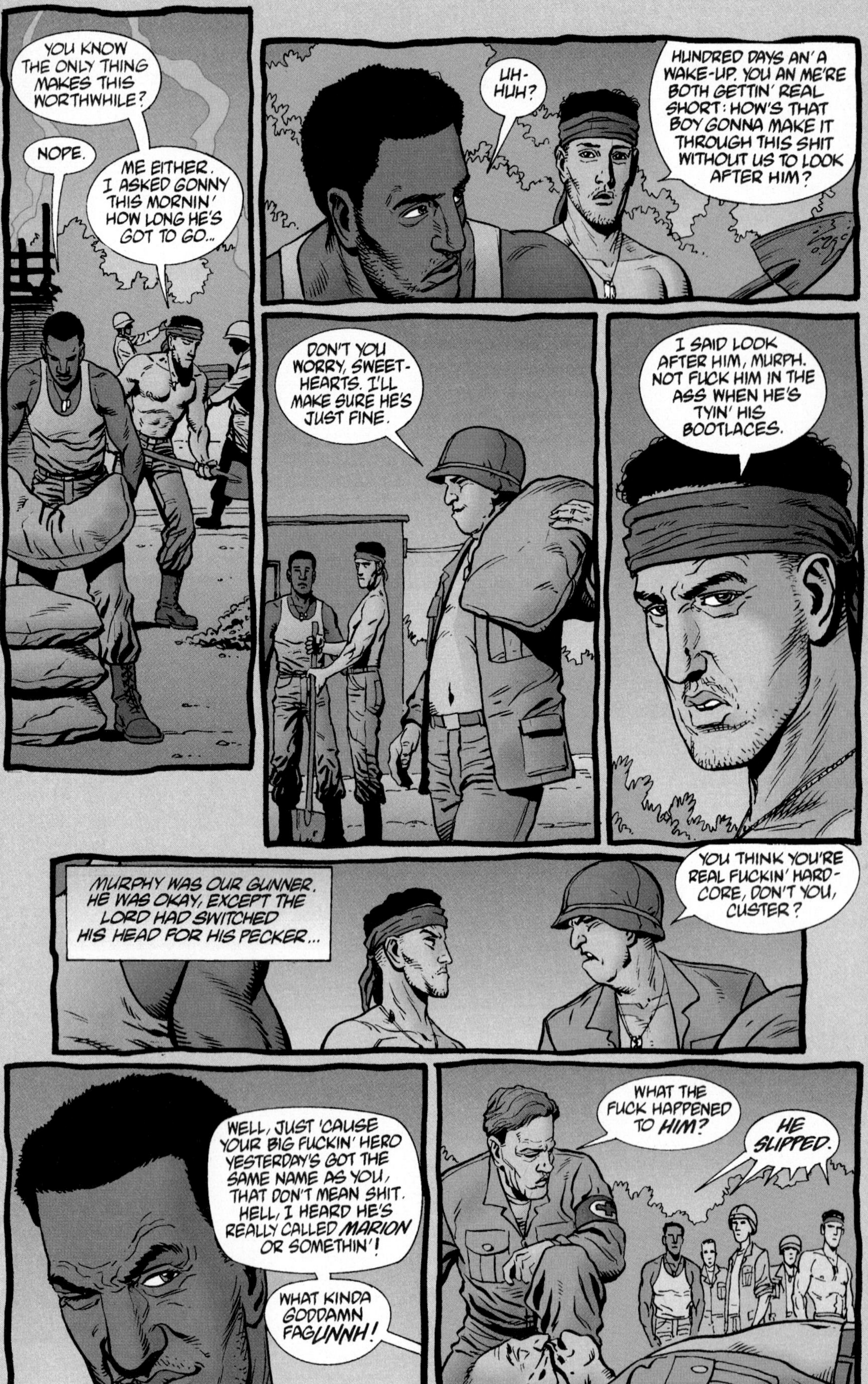
YOU KNOW THE ONLY THING MAKES THIS WORTHWHILE?
NOPE.
ME EITHER. I ASKED GONNY THIS MORNIN' HOW LONG HE'S GOT TO GO...
UH-HUH?
HUNDRED DAYS AN' A WAKE-UP. YOU AN ME'RE BOTH GETTIN' REAL SHORT: HOW'S THAT BOY GONNA MAKE IT THROUGH THIS SHIT WITHOUT US TO LOOK AFTER HIM?
DON'T YOU WORRY, SWEET-HEARTS. I'LL MAKE SURE HE'S JUST FINE.
I SAID LOOK AFTER HIM, MURPH. NOT FUCK HIM IN THE ASS WHEN HE'S TYIN' HIS BOOTLACES.
MURPHY WAS OUR GUNNER. HE WAS OKAY, EXCEPT THE LORD HAD SWITCHED HIS HEAD FOR HIS PECKER...
YOU THINK YOU'RE REAL FUCKIN' HARD-CORE, DON'T YOU, CUSTER?
WELL, JUST 'CAUSE YOUR BIG FUCKIN' HERO YESTERDAY'S GOT THE SAME NAME AS YOU, THAT DON'T MEAN SHIT. HELL, I HEARD HE'S REALLY CALLED MARION OR SOMETHIN'!
WHAT KINDA GODDAMN FAGUNNH!
WHAT THE FUCK HAPPENED TO HIM?
HE SLIPPED.

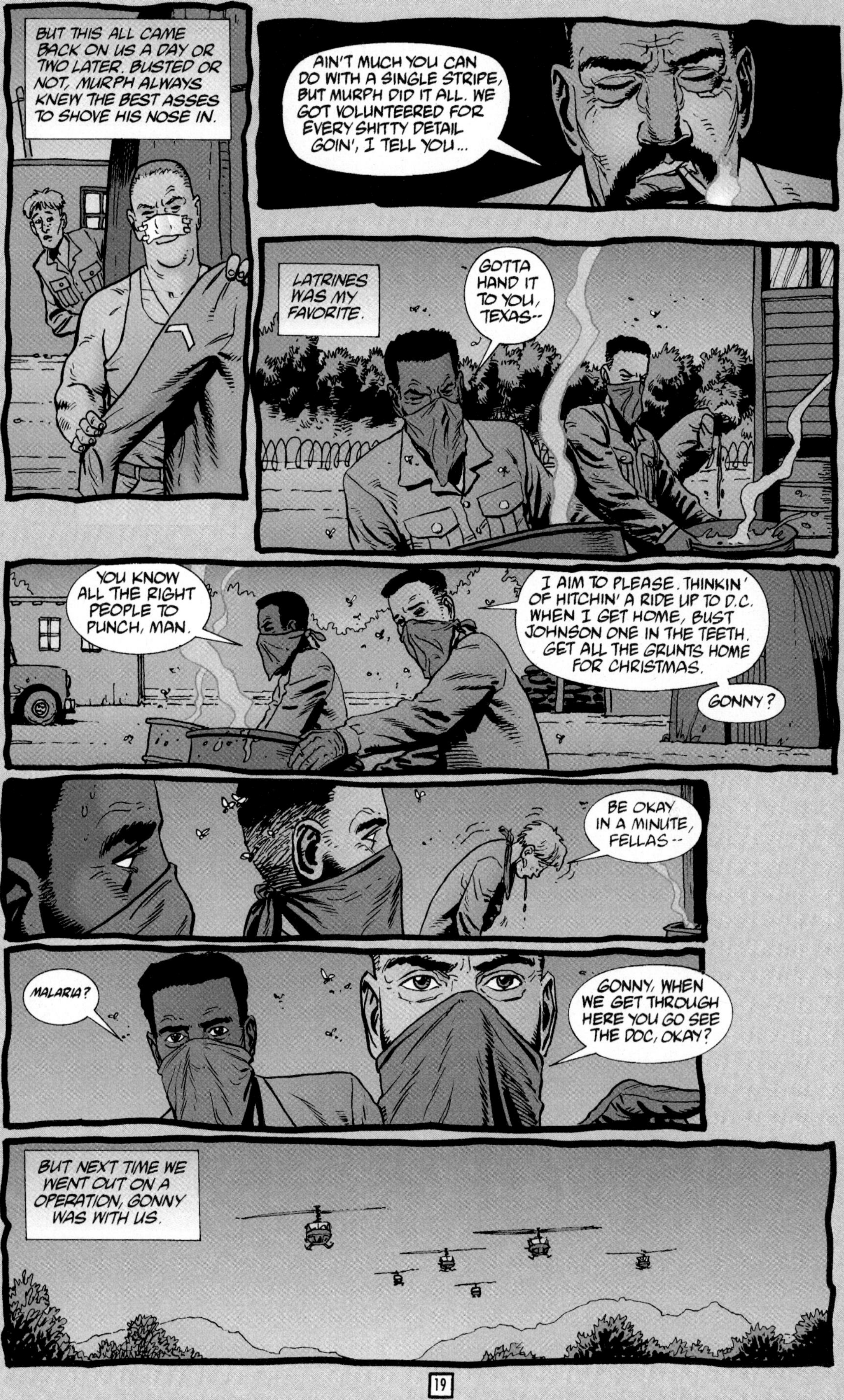
BUT THIS ALL CAME BACK ON US A DAY OR TWO LATER. BUSTED OR NOT, MURPH ALWAYS KNEW THE BEST ASSES TO SHOVE HIS NOSE IN.
AIN'T MUCH YOU CAN DO WITH A SINGLE STRIPE, BUT MURPH DID IT ALL. WE GOT VOLUNTEERED FOR EVERY SHITTY DETAIL GOIN', I TELL YOU...
LATRINES WAS MY FAVORITE.
GOTTA HAND IT TO YOU, TEXAS--
YOU KNOW ALL THE RIGHT PEOPLE TO PUNCH, MAN.
I AIM TO PLEASE. THINKIN' OF HITCHIN' A RIDE UP TO D.C. WHEN I GET HOME, BUST JOHNSON ONE IN THE TEETH. GET ALL THE GRUNTS HOME FOR CHRISTMAS.
GONNY?
BE OKAY IN A MINUTE, FELLAS--
MALARIA?
GONNY, WHEN WE GET THROUGH HERE YOU GO SEE THE DOC, OKAY?
BUT NEXT TIME WE WENT OUT ON A OPERATION, GONNY WAS WITH US.

GONNY! GONNY, YOU SEE THE DOC LIKE I TOLD YOU?

FORGOT.

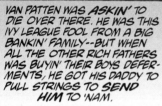

WELL, WE AIN'T GONE FAR FROM THE L.Z. WHEN MURPHY'S A-GUNNER, NETTLES, HE STEPS ON A MINE AN' TAKES LEEMING AN' HALF OF McCOSKER UP WITH HIM. BY THE TIME THE MEDEVAC CHOPPER GETS THERE, McCOSKER'S DEAD AN' WE'RE A HALF-HOUR BEHIND THE REST OF THE SQUAD.

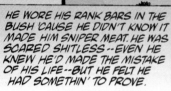

GONNY, ME, YOUR DADDY, MURPH AN' LIEUTENANT VAN PATTEN.

VAN PATTEN WAS *ASKIN'* TO DIE OVER THERE. HE WAS THIS IVY LEAGUE FOOL FROM A BIG BANKIN' FAMILY--BUT WHEN ALL THE OTHER RICH FATHERS WAS BUYIN' THEIR BOYS DEFERMENTS, HE GOT HIS DADDY TO PULL STRINGS TO *SEND HIM* TO 'NAM.

HE WORE HIS RANK BARS IN THE BUSH 'CAUSE HE DIDN'T KNOW IT MADE HIM SNIPER MEAT. HE WAS SCARED SHITLESS--EVEN HE KNEW HE'D MADE THE MISTAKE OF HIS LIFE--BUT HE FELT HE HAD SOMETHIN' TO PROVE.

ONE DANGEROUS MOTHERFUCKER.

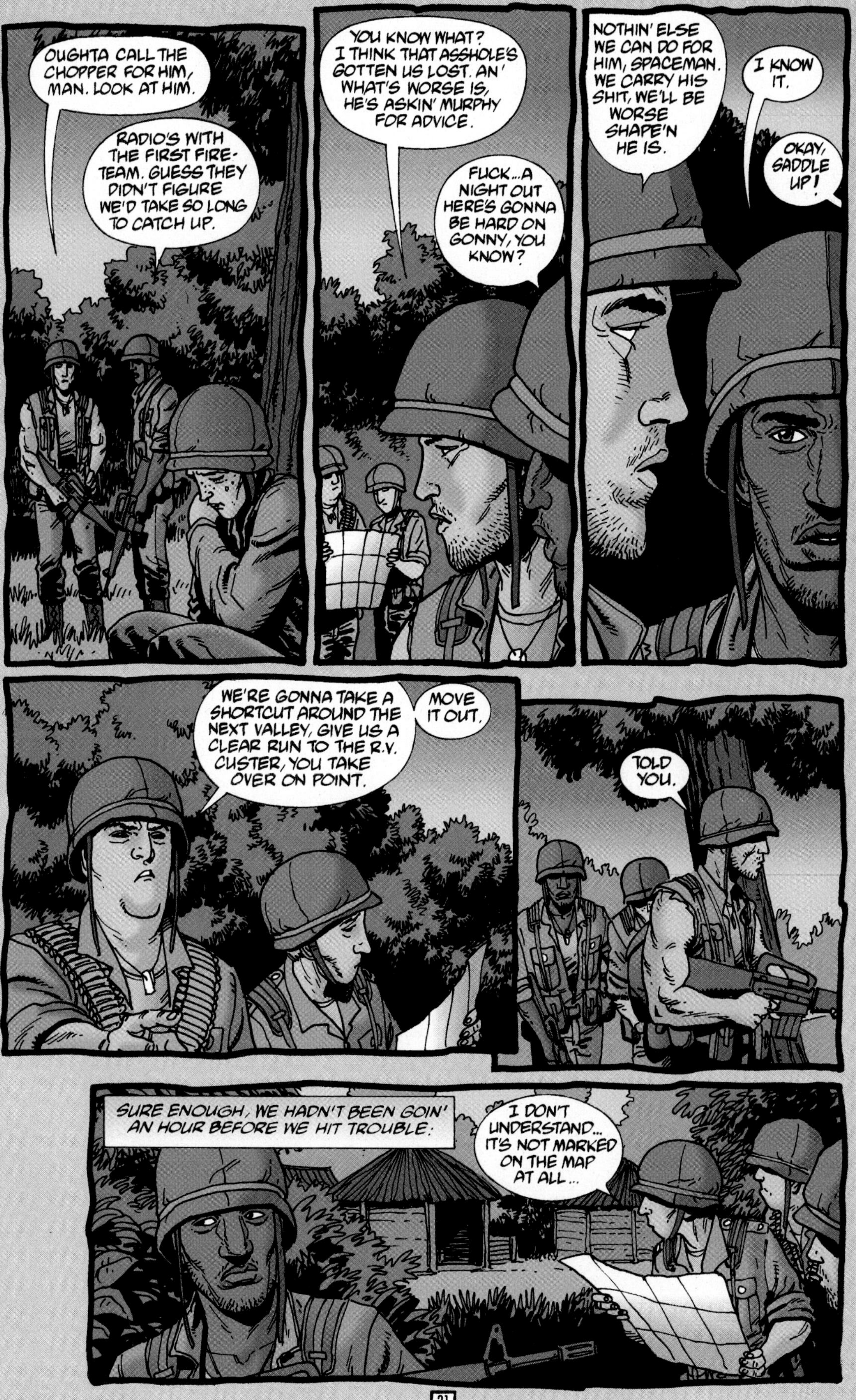
OUGHTA CALL THE CHOPPER FOR HIM, MAN. LOOK AT HIM.
RADIO'S WITH THE FIRST FIRE-TEAM. GUESS THEY DIDN'T FIGURE WE'D TAKE SO LONG TO CATCH UP.
YOU KNOW WHAT? I THINK THAT ASSHOLE'S GOTTEN US LOST. AN' WHAT'S WORSE IS, HE'S ASKIN' MURPHY FOR ADVICE.
FUCK...A NIGHT OUT HERE'S GONNA BE HARD ON GONNY, YOU KNOW?
NOTHIN' ELSE WE CAN DO FOR HIM, SPACEMAN. WE CARRY HIS SHIT, WE'LL BE WORSE SHAPE'N HE IS.
I KNOW IT.
OKAY, SADDLE UP!
WE'RE GONNA TAKE A SHORTCUT AROUND THE NEXT VALLEY, GIVE US A CLEAR RUN TO THE R.V. CUSTER, YOU TAKE OVER ON POINT.
MOVE IT OUT.
TOLD YOU.
SURE ENOUGH, WE HADN'T BEEN GOIN' AN HOUR BEFORE WE HIT TROUBLE:
I DON'T UNDERSTAND... IT'S NOT MARKED ON THE MAP AT ALL...

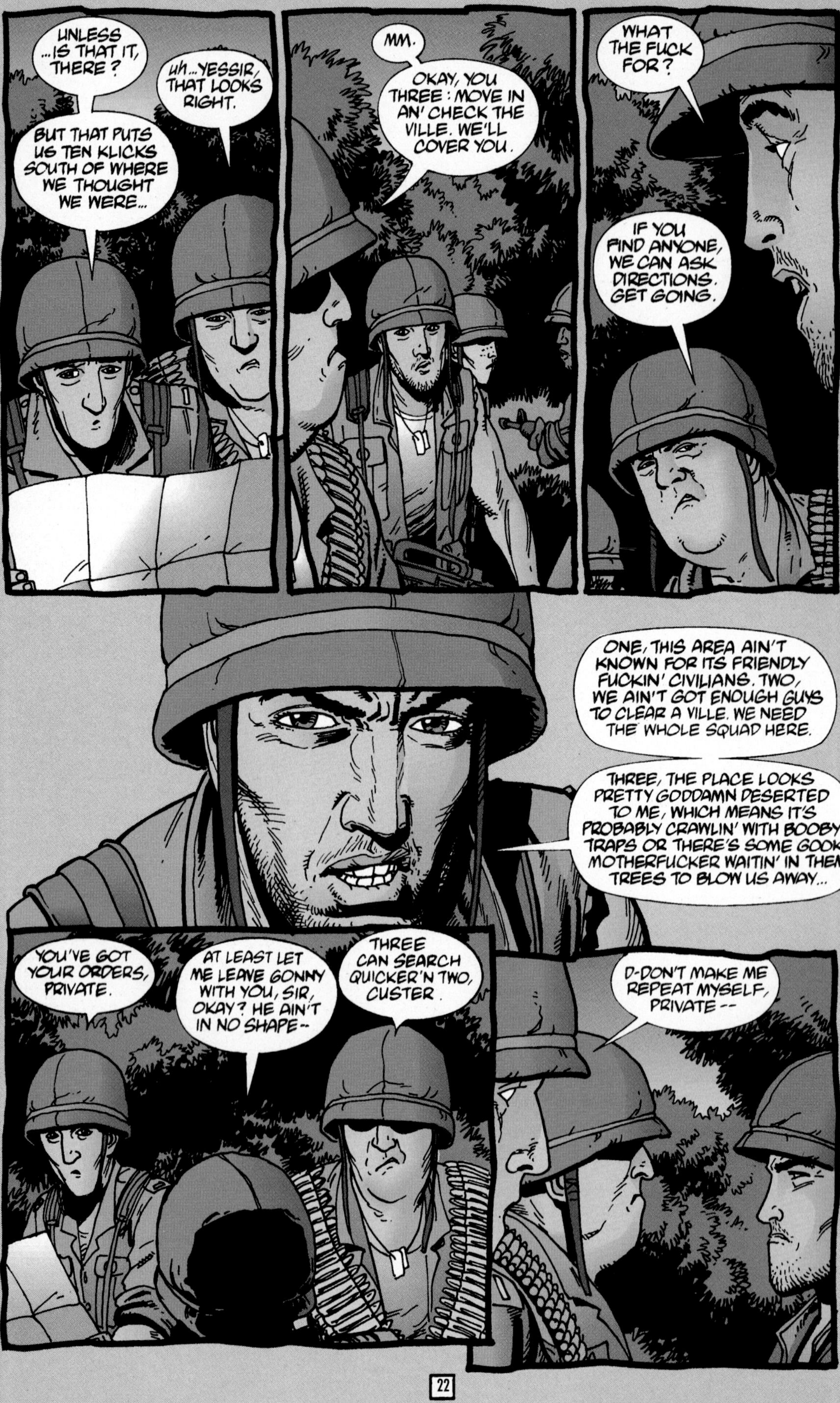
UNLESS ...IS THAT IT, THERE?
BUT THAT PUTS US TEN KLICKS SOUTH OF WHERE WE THOUGHT WE WERE...
UH...YESSIR, THAT LOOKS RIGHT.
MM.
OKAY, YOU THREE: MOVE IN AN' CHECK THE VILLE. WE'LL COVER YOU.
WHAT THE FUCK FOR?
IF YOU FIND ANYONE, WE CAN ASK DIRECTIONS. GET GOING.
ONE, THIS AREA AIN'T KNOWN FOR ITS FRIENDLY FUCKIN' CIVILIANS. TWO, WE AIN'T GOT ENOUGH GUYS TO CLEAR A VILLE. WE NEED THE WHOLE SQUAD HERE.
THREE, THE PLACE LOOKS PRETTY GODDAMN DESERTED TO ME, WHICH MEANS IT'S PROBABLY CRAWLIN' WITH BOOBY-TRAPS OR THERE'S SOME GOOK MOTHERFUCKER WAITIN' IN THEM TREES TO BLOW US AWAY...
YOU'VE GOT YOUR ORDERS, PRIVATE.
AT LEAST LET ME LEAVE GONNY WITH YOU, SIR, OKAY? HE AIN'T IN NO SHAPE--
THREE CAN SEARCH QUICKER'N TWO, CUSTER.
D-DON'T MAKE ME REPEAT MYSELF, PRIVATE--

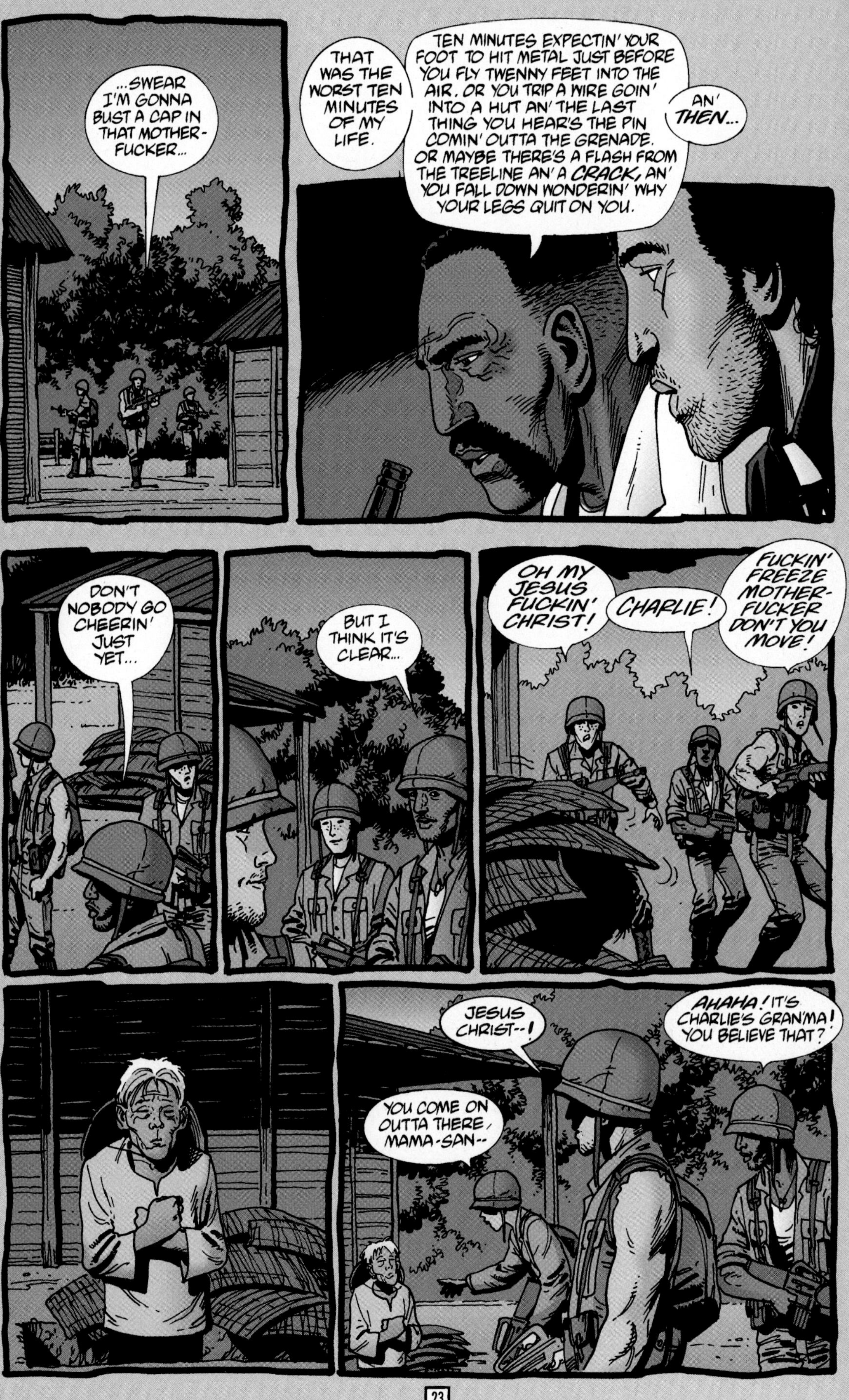
...SWEAR I'M GONNA BUST A CAP IN THAT MOTHER-FUCKER...
THAT WAS THE WORST TEN MINUTES OF MY LIFE.
TEN MINUTES EXPECTIN' YOUR FOOT TO HIT METAL JUST BEFORE YOU FLY TWENNY FEET INTO THE AIR. OR YOU TRIP A WIRE GOIN' INTO A HUT AN' THE LAST THING YOU HEAR'S THE PIN COMIN' OUTTA THE GRENADE. OR MAYBE THERE'S A FLASH FROM THE TREELINE AN' A CRACK, AN' YOU FALL DOWN WONDERIN' WHY YOUR LEGS QUIT ON YOU.
AN' THEN...
DON'T NOBODY GO CHEERIN' JUST YET...
BUT I THINK IT'S CLEAR...
OH MY JESUS FUCKIN' CHRIST!
CHARLIE!
FUCKIN' FREEZE MOTHER-FUCKER DON'T YOU MOVE!
JESUS CHRIST--!
AHAHA! IT'S CHARLIE'S GRAN'MA! YOU BELIEVE THAT?
YOU COME ON OUTTA THERE, MAMA-SAN--

WELL...

AT FIRST I CAN'T HEAR NOTHIN' EXCEPT THIS BUZZIN', AN' THAT TURNS INTO YOUR DADDY, YELLIN' LIKE A CRAZY MAN.

I LOOK UP AN' I CAN'T SEE GONNY OR THE MAMA-SAN ANYWHERE. THEN I LOOK OVER AT TEXAS AN' DOWN AT MYSELF AN' I SEE WHY.

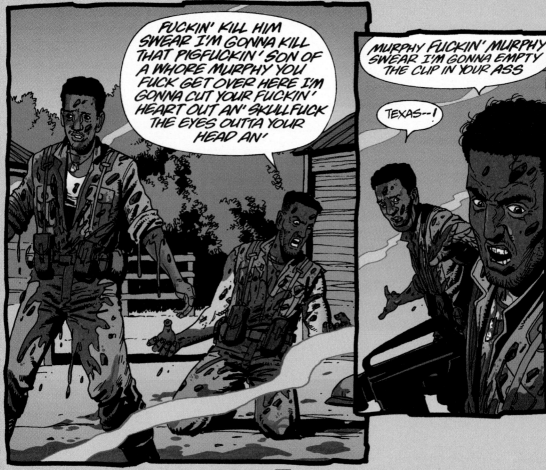

FUCKIN' KILL HIM SWEAR I'M GONNA KILL THAT PIGFUCKIN' SON OF A WHORE MURPHY YOU FUCK GET OVER HERE I'M GONNA CUT YOUR FUCKIN' HEART OUT AN' SKULLFUCK THE EYES OUTTA YOUR HEAD AN'

MURPHY FUCKIN' MURPHY SWEAR I'M GONNA EMPTY THE CLIP IN YOUR ASS

TEXAS--!

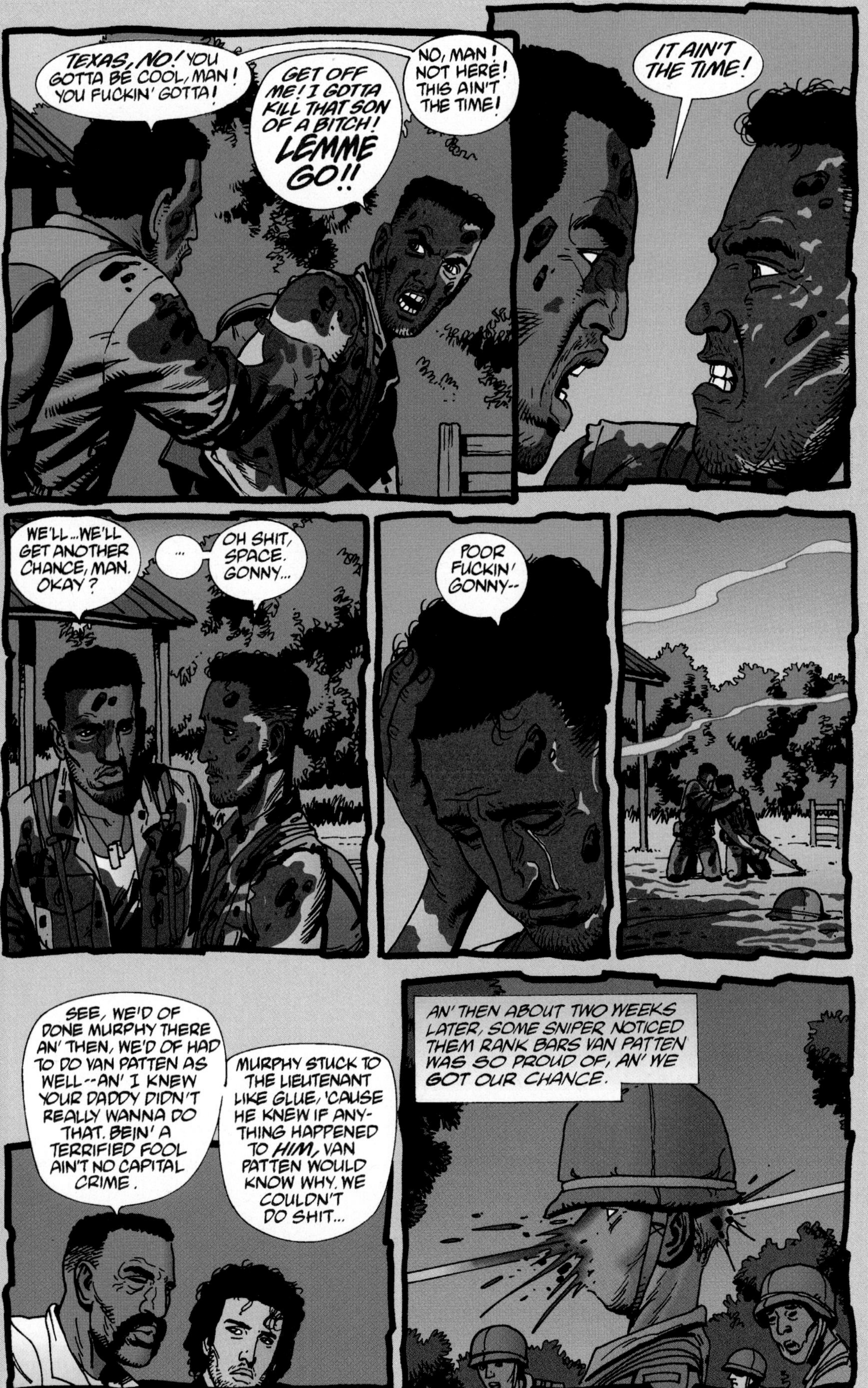
TEXAS, NO! YOU GOTTA BE COOL, MAN! YOU FUCKIN' GOTTA!
GET OFF ME! I GOTTA KILL THAT SON OF A BITCH! LEMME GO!!
NO, MAN! NOT HERE! THIS AIN'T THE TIME!
IT AIN'T THE TIME!
WE'LL...WE'LL GET ANOTHER CHANCE, MAN. OKAY?
...
OH SHIT, SPACE. GONNY...
POOR FUCKIN' GONNY--
SEE, WE'D OF DONE MURPHY THERE AN' THEN, WE'D OF HAD TO DO VAN PATTEN AS WELL--AN' I KNEW YOUR DADDY DIDN'T REALLY WANNA DO THAT. BEIN' A TERRIFIED FOOL AIN'T NO CAPITAL CRIME.
MURPHY STUCK TO THE LIEUTENANT LIKE GLUE, 'CAUSE HE KNEW IF ANY-THING HAPPENED TO HIM, VAN PATTEN WOULD KNOW WHY. WE COULDN'T DO SHIT...
AN' THEN ABOUT TWO WEEKS LATER, SOME SNIPER NOTICED THEM RANK BARS VAN PATTEN WAS SO PROUD OF, AN' WE GOT OUR CHANCE.

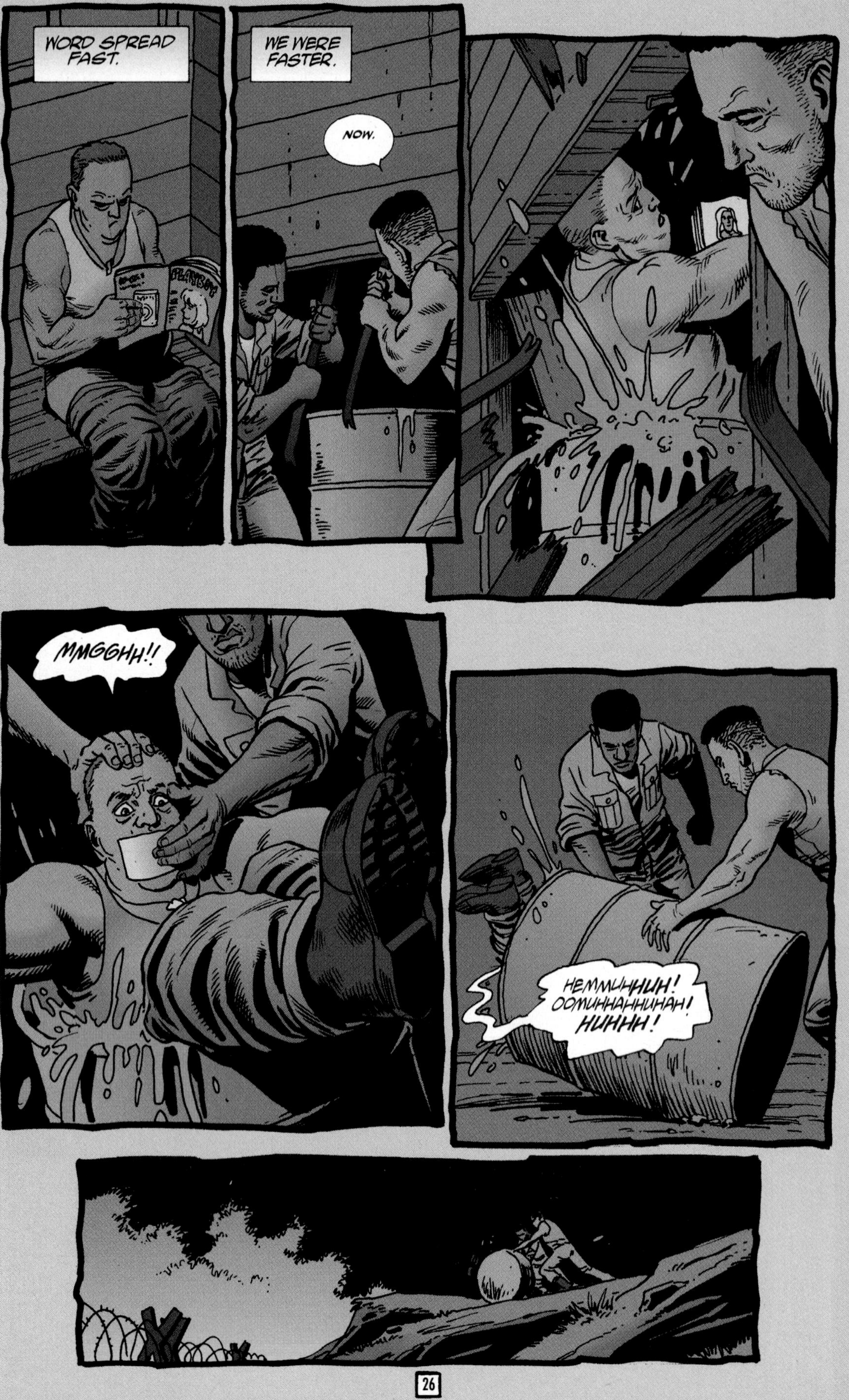
WORD SPREAD FAST.
WE WERE FASTER.
NOW.
MMGGHH!!
HEMMUHHUH! OOMUHHAHHUHAH! HUHHH!

THIS IS WHAT HAPPENS, MOTHER-FUCKER.

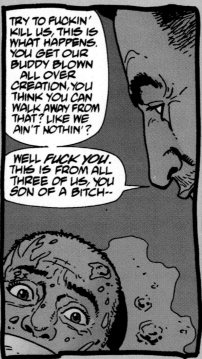

TRY TO FUCKIN' KILL US, THIS IS WHAT HAPPENS. YOU GET OUR BUDDY BLOWN ALL OVER CREATION, YOU THINK YOU CAN WALK AWAY FROM THAT? LIKE WE AIN'T NOTHIN'?

WELL FUCK YOU. THIS IS FROM ALL THREE OF US, YOU SON OF A BITCH--

THIS IS WHAT YOU GET.

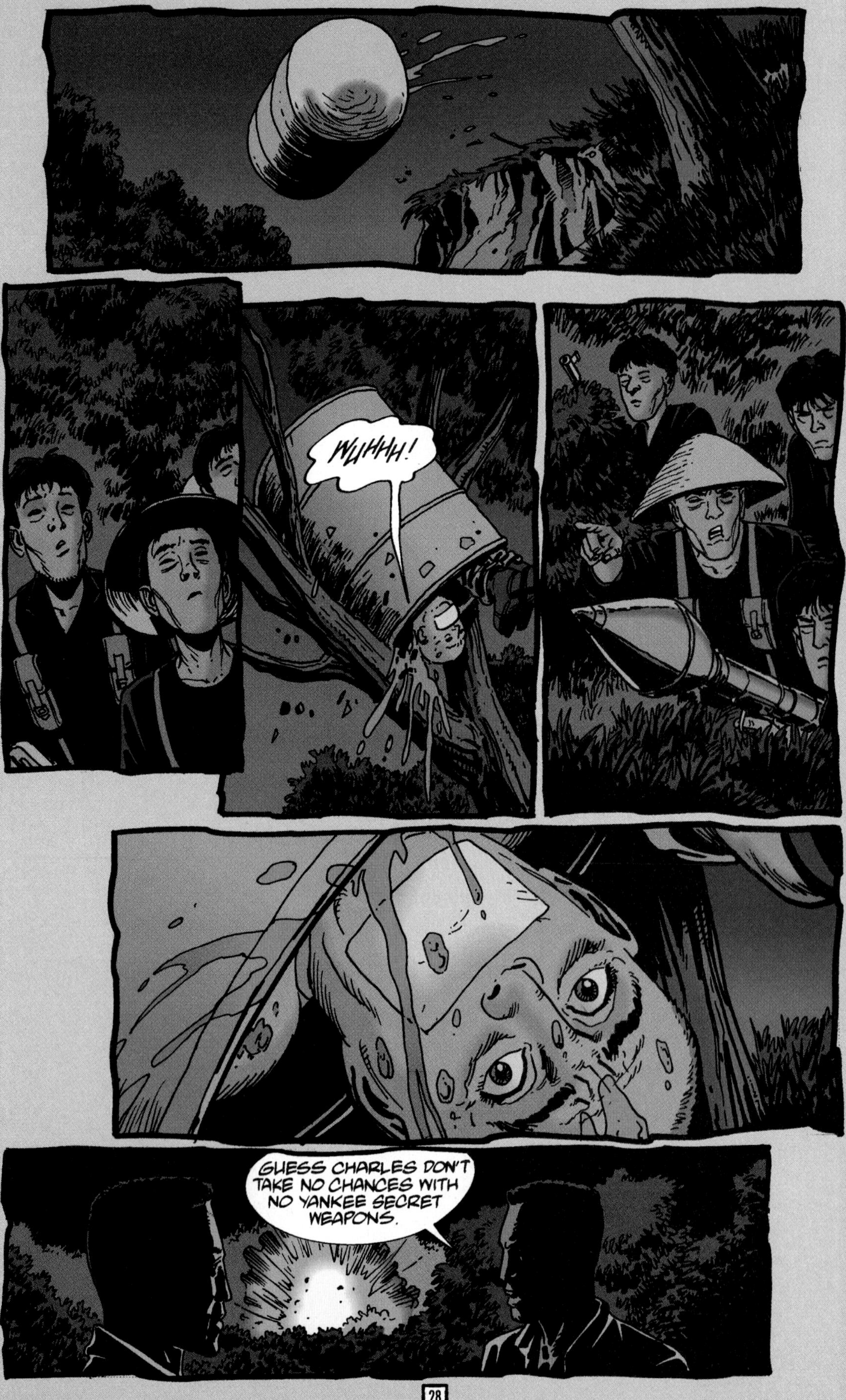
WUHHH!
GUESS CHARLES DON'T TAKE NO CHANCES WITH NO YANKEE SECRET WEAPONS.

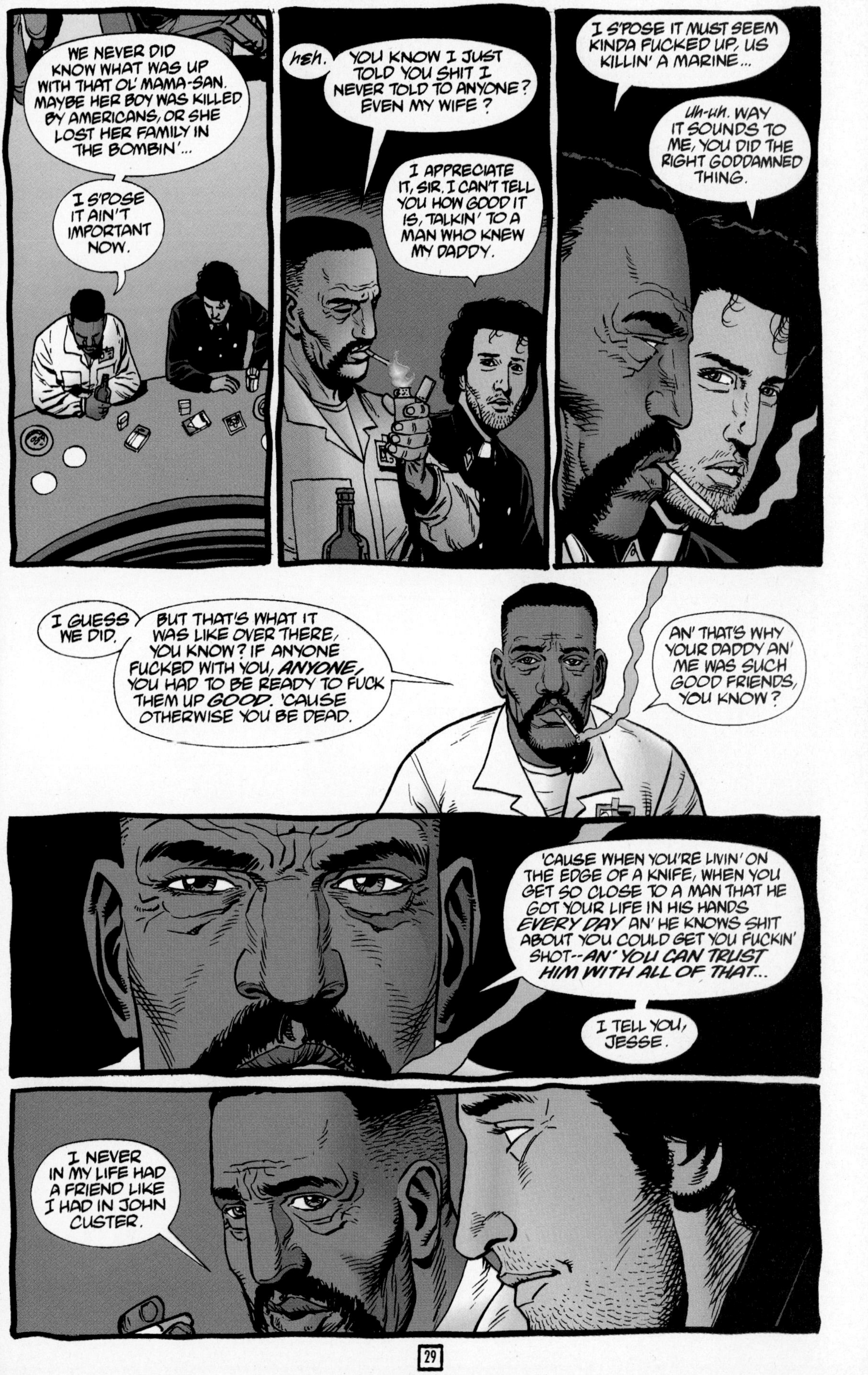
WE NEVER DID KNOW WHAT WAS UP WITH THAT OL' MAMA-SAN. MAYBE HER BOY WAS KILLED BY AMERICANS, OR SHE LOST HER FAMILY IN THE BOMBIN'...
I S'POSE IT AIN'T IMPORTANT NOW.
heh.
YOU KNOW I JUST TOLD YOU SHIT I NEVER TOLD TO ANYONE? EVEN MY WIFE?
I APPRECIATE IT, SIR. I CAN'T TELL YOU HOW GOOD IT IS, TALKIN' TO A MAN WHO KNEW MY DADDY.
I S'POSE IT MUST SEEM KINDA FUCKED UP, US KILLIN' A MARINE...
Uh-uh. WAY IT SOUNDS TO ME, YOU DID THE RIGHT GODDAMNED THING.
I GUESS WE DID.
BUT THAT'S WHAT IT WAS LIKE OVER THERE, YOU KNOW? IF ANYONE FUCKED WITH YOU, ANYONE, YOU HAD TO BE READY TO FUCK THEM UP GOOD. 'CAUSE OTHERWISE YOU BE DEAD.
AN' THAT'S WHY YOUR DADDY AN' ME WAS SUCH GOOD FRIENDS, YOU KNOW?
'CAUSE WHEN YOU'RE LIVIN' ON THE EDGE OF A KNIFE, WHEN YOU GET SO CLOSE TO A MAN THAT HE GOT YOUR LIFE IN HIS HANDS EVERY DAY AN' HE KNOWS SHIT ABOUT YOU COULD GET YOU FUCKIN' SHOT--AN' YOU CAN TRUST HIM WITH ALL OF THAT...
I TELL YOU, JESSE.
I NEVER IN MY LIFE HAD A FRIEND LIKE I HAD IN JOHN CUSTER.

AN' THEN, YOU KNOW, YOU COME BACK HERE AN' YOU FIND OUT YOU WERE FIGHTIN' FOR POLITICIANS AN' THE MOTHERFUCKERS IN ARMS INDUSTRY, AN' YOU CAN FORGET ABOUT FOLKS SAYIN' YOU A HERO. YOU AIN'T SHIT.

YOU THINK, FUCK, WE GOT EACH OTHER THROUGH 'NAM AN' IT'S ALL BEEN FOR NOTHIN'.

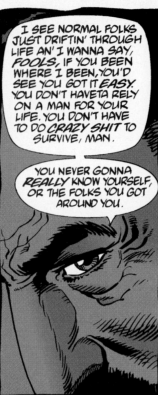

I SEE NORMAL FOLKS JUST DRIFTIN' THROUGH LIFE AN' I WANNA SAY, FOOLS, IF YOU BEEN WHERE I BEEN, YOU'D SEE YOU GOT IT EASY. YOU DON'T HAVETA RELY ON A MAN FOR YOUR LIFE. YOU DON'T HAVE TO DO CRAZY SHIT TO SURVIVE, MAN.

YOU NEVER GONNA REALLY KNOW YOURSELF, OR THE FOLKS YOU GOT AROUND YOU.

SHIT, LISTEN TO ME.

WOULD ALL UNITED AIRLINES PASSENGERS BOUND FOR PARIS PLEASE EXTINGUISH ALL CIGARETTES AND MAKE THEIR WAY TO BOARDING GATE NUMBER NINE...

GODDAMMIT, THAT'S MY FLIGHT.

HERE'S YOUR PICTURE.

uh-uh. YOU KEEP IT.

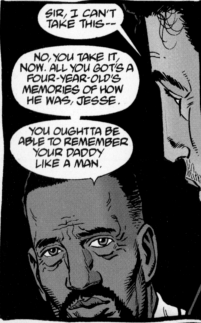

SIR, I CAN'T TAKE THIS--

NO, YOU TAKE IT, NOW. ALL YOU GOT'S A FOUR-YEAR-OLD'S MEMORIES OF HOW HE WAS, JESSE.

YOU OUGHTTA BE ABLE TO REMEMBER YOUR DADDY LIKE A MAN.

"Thinking about Vietnam once in a while, in a crazy kind of way, I wish that just for a while I could be there. And then be transported back."

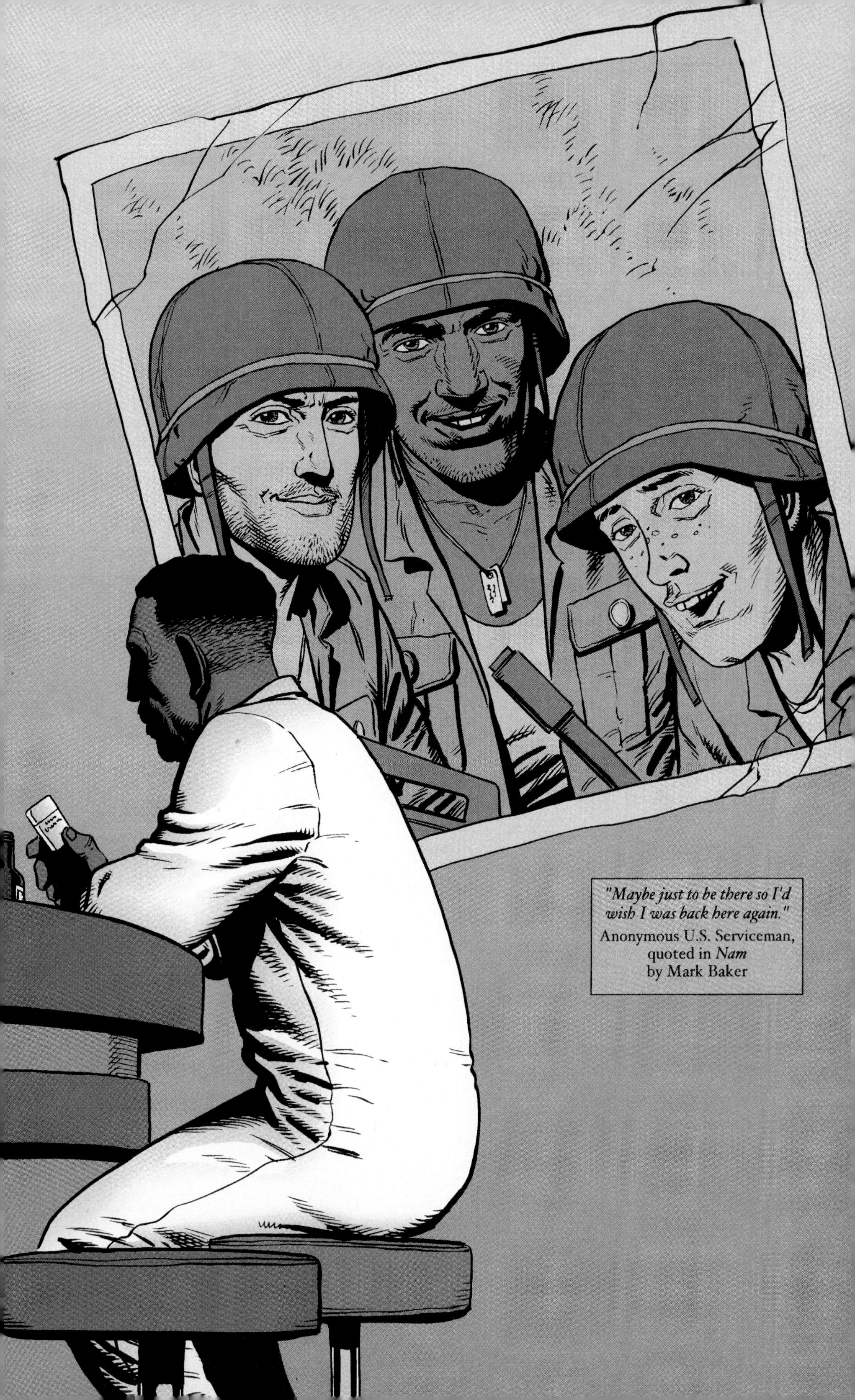
"Maybe just to be there so I'd wish I was back here again."
Anonymous U.S. Serviceman, quoted in *Nam* by Mark Baker

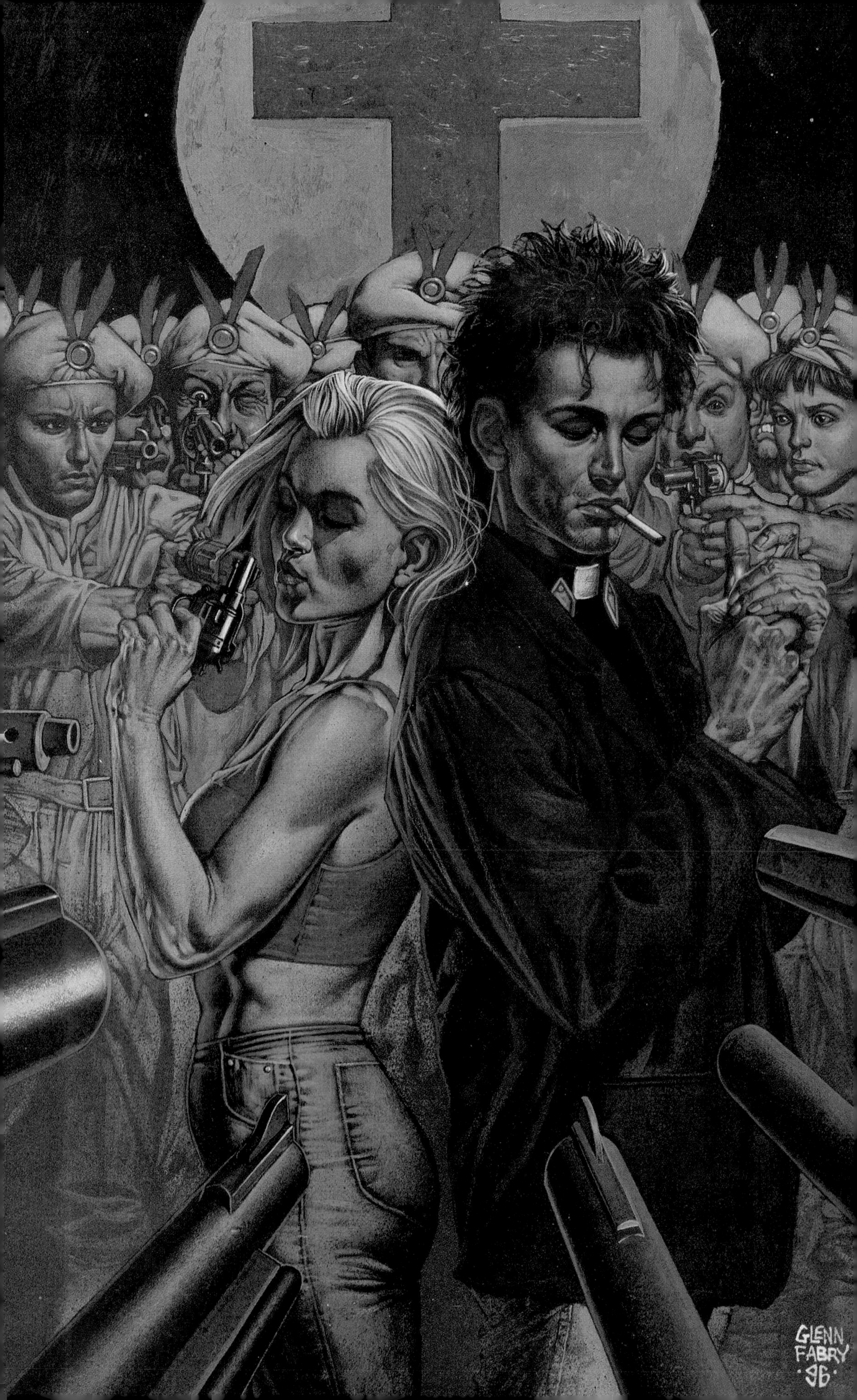
GLENN
FABRY
·96·

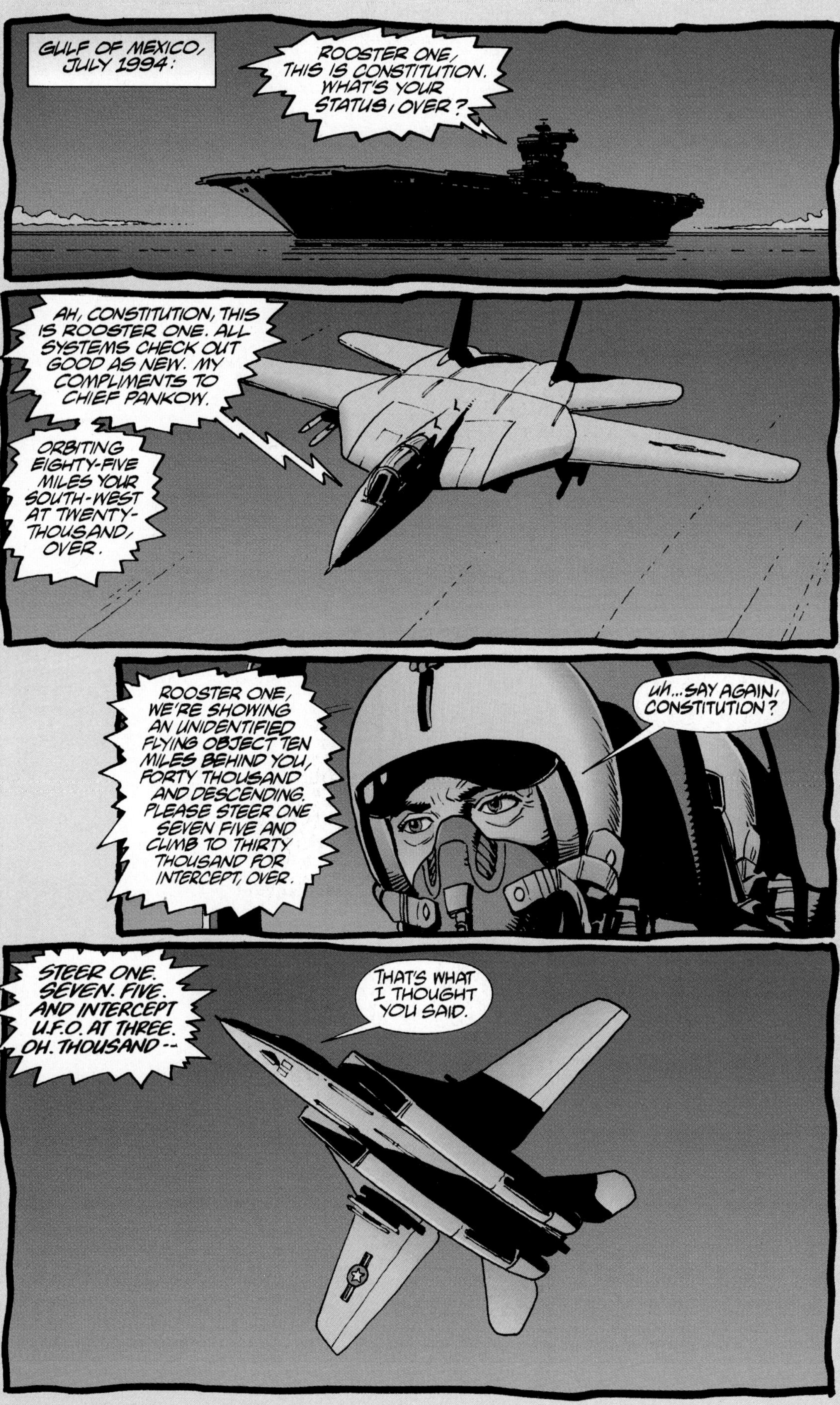
GULF OF MEXICO, JULY 1994:
ROOSTER ONE, THIS IS CONSTITUTION. WHAT'S YOUR STATUS, OVER?
AH, CONSTITUTION, THIS IS ROOSTER ONE. ALL SYSTEMS CHECK OUT GOOD AS NEW. MY COMPLIMENTS TO CHIEF PANKOW.
ORBITING EIGHTY-FIVE MILES YOUR SOUTH-WEST AT TWENTY-THOUSAND, OVER.
ROOSTER ONE, WE'RE SHOWING AN UNIDENTIFIED FLYING OBJECT TEN MILES BEHIND YOU, FORTY THOUSAND AND DESCENDING. PLEASE STEER ONE SEVEN FIVE AND CLIMB TO THIRTY THOUSAND FOR INTERCEPT, OVER.
uh...SAY AGAIN, CONSTITUTION?
STEER ONE. SEVEN. FIVE. AND INTERCEPT U.F.O. AT THREE. OH. THOUSAND --
THAT'S WHAT I THOUGHT YOU SAID.

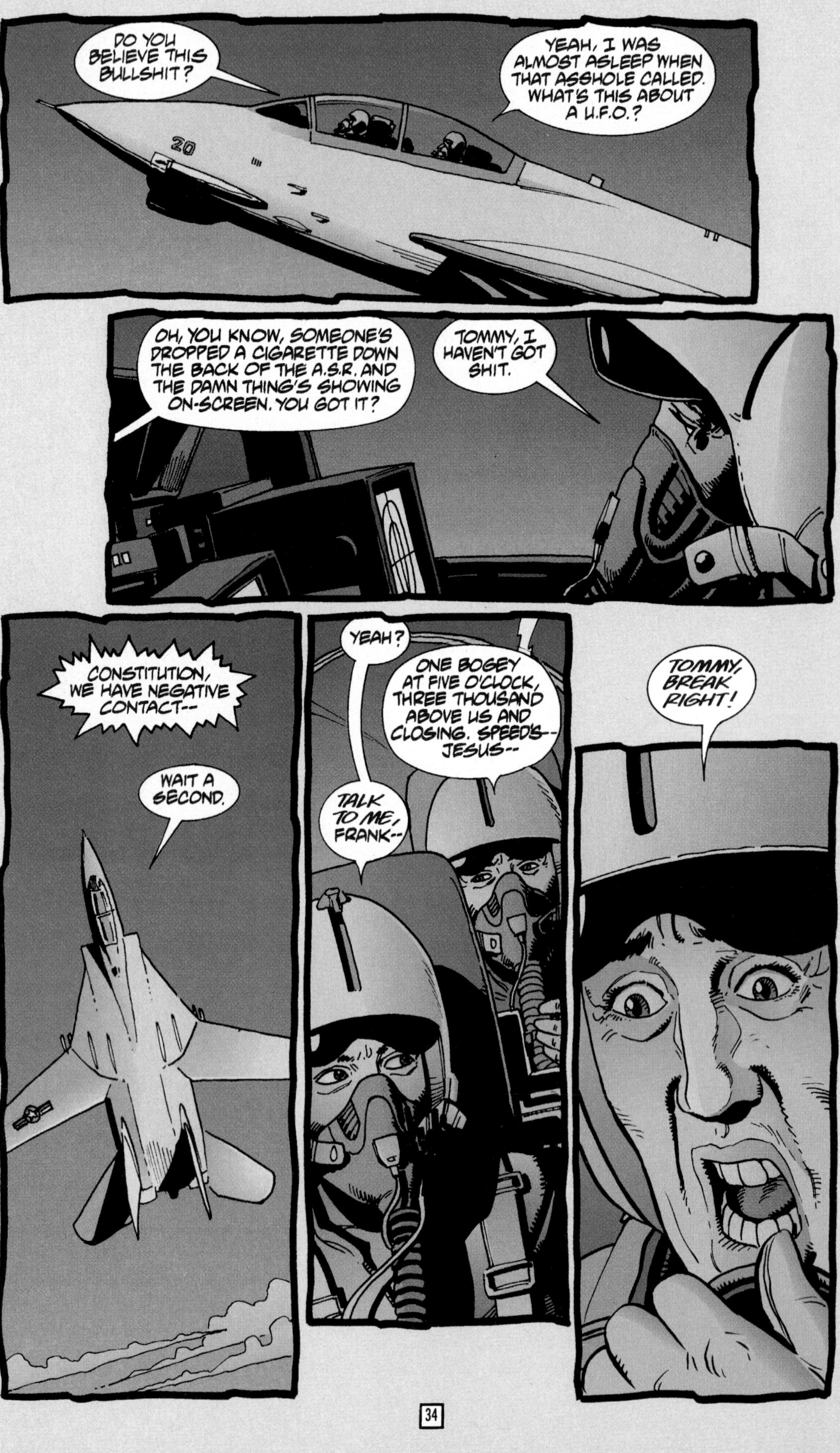
DO YOU BELIEVE THIS BULLSHIT?
YEAH, I WAS ALMOST ASLEEP WHEN THAT ASSHOLE CALLED. WHAT'S THIS ABOUT A U.F.O.?
OH, YOU KNOW, SOMEONE'S DROPPED A CIGARETTE DOWN THE BACK OF THE A.S.R. AND THE DAMN THING'S SHOWING ON-SCREEN. YOU GOT IT?
TOMMY, I HAVEN'T GOT SHIT.
CONSTITUTION, WE HAVE NEGATIVE CONTACT--
WAIT A SECOND.
YEAH?
ONE BOGEY AT FIVE O'CLOCK, THREE THOUSAND ABOVE US AND CLOSING. SPEED'S-- JESUS--
TALK TO ME, FRANK--
TOMMY, BREAK RIGHT!

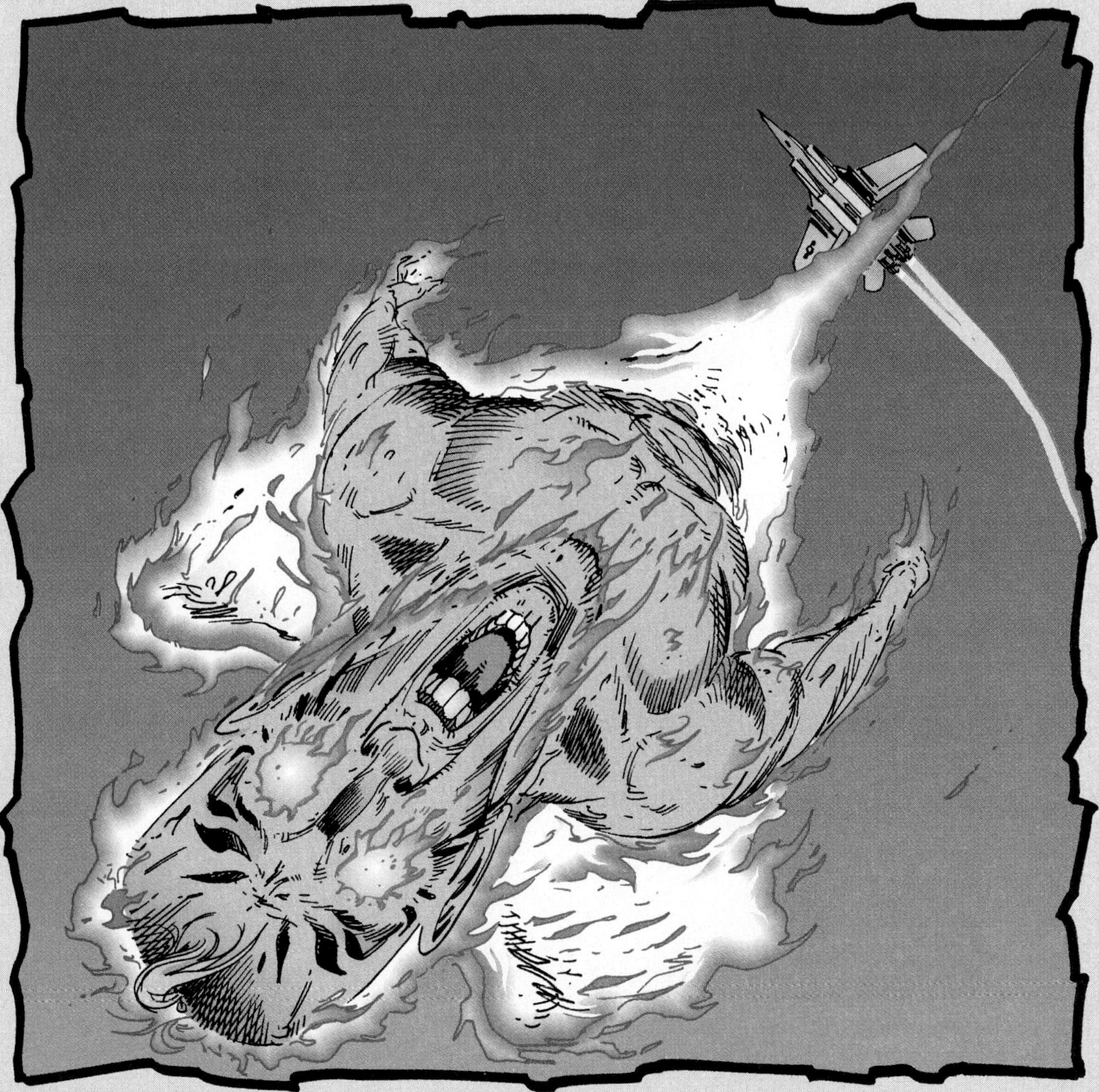

OF THINGS TO COME

GARTH ENNIS - Writer STEVE DILLON - Artist
MATT HOLLINGSWORTH - Colorist
CLEM ROBINS - Letterer AXEL ALONSO - Editor

PREACHER created by GARTH ENNIS and STEVE DILLON

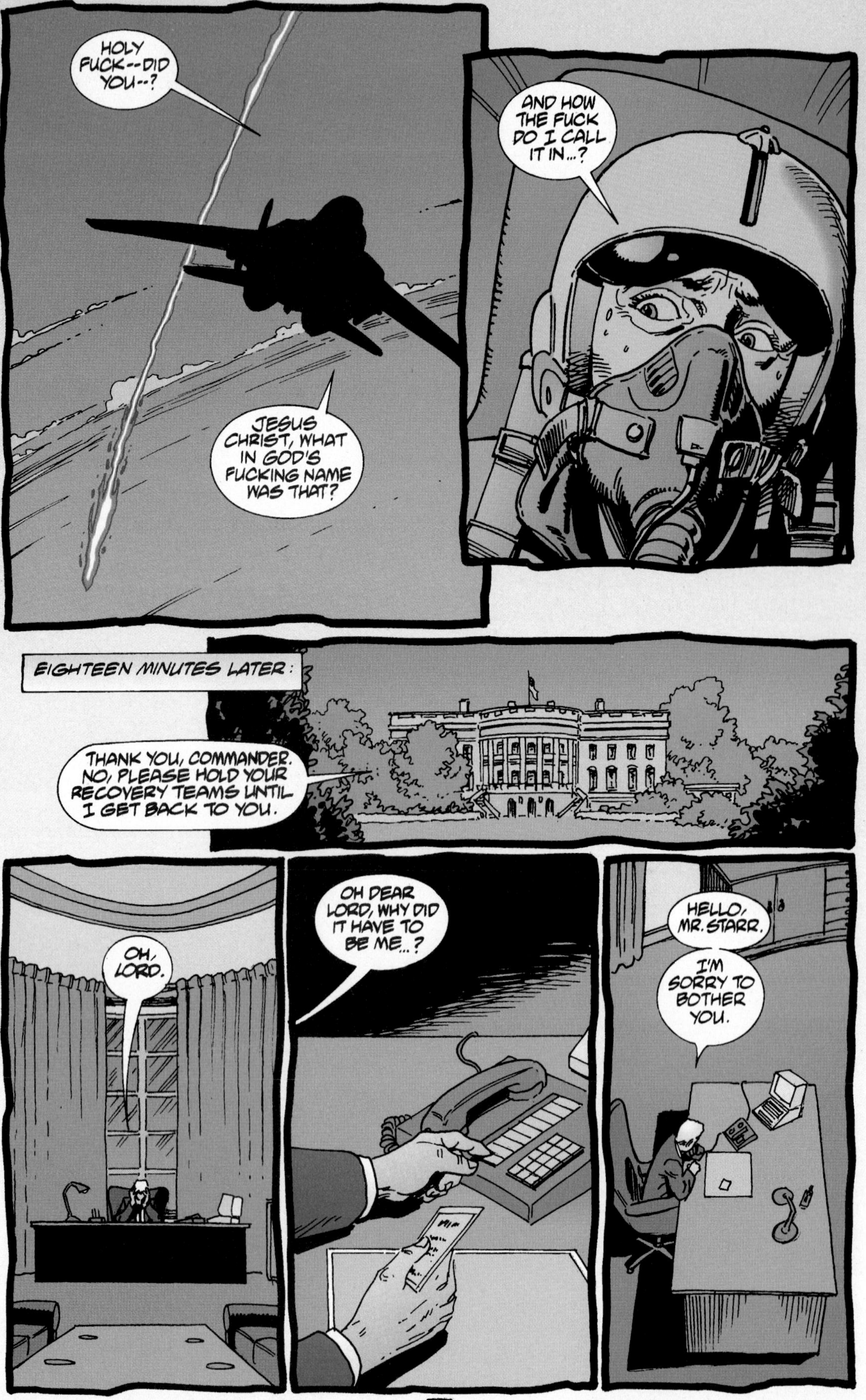
HOLY FUCK--DID YOU--?
JESUS CHRIST, WHAT IN GOD'S FUCKING NAME WAS THAT?
AND HOW THE FUCK DO I CALL IT IN...?
EIGHTEEN MINUTES LATER:
THANK YOU, COMMANDER. NO, PLEASE HOLD YOUR RECOVERY TEAMS UNTIL I GET BACK TO YOU.
OH, LORD.
OH DEAR LORD, WHY DID IT HAVE TO BE ME...?
HELLO, MR. STARR.
I'M SORRY TO BOTHER YOU.

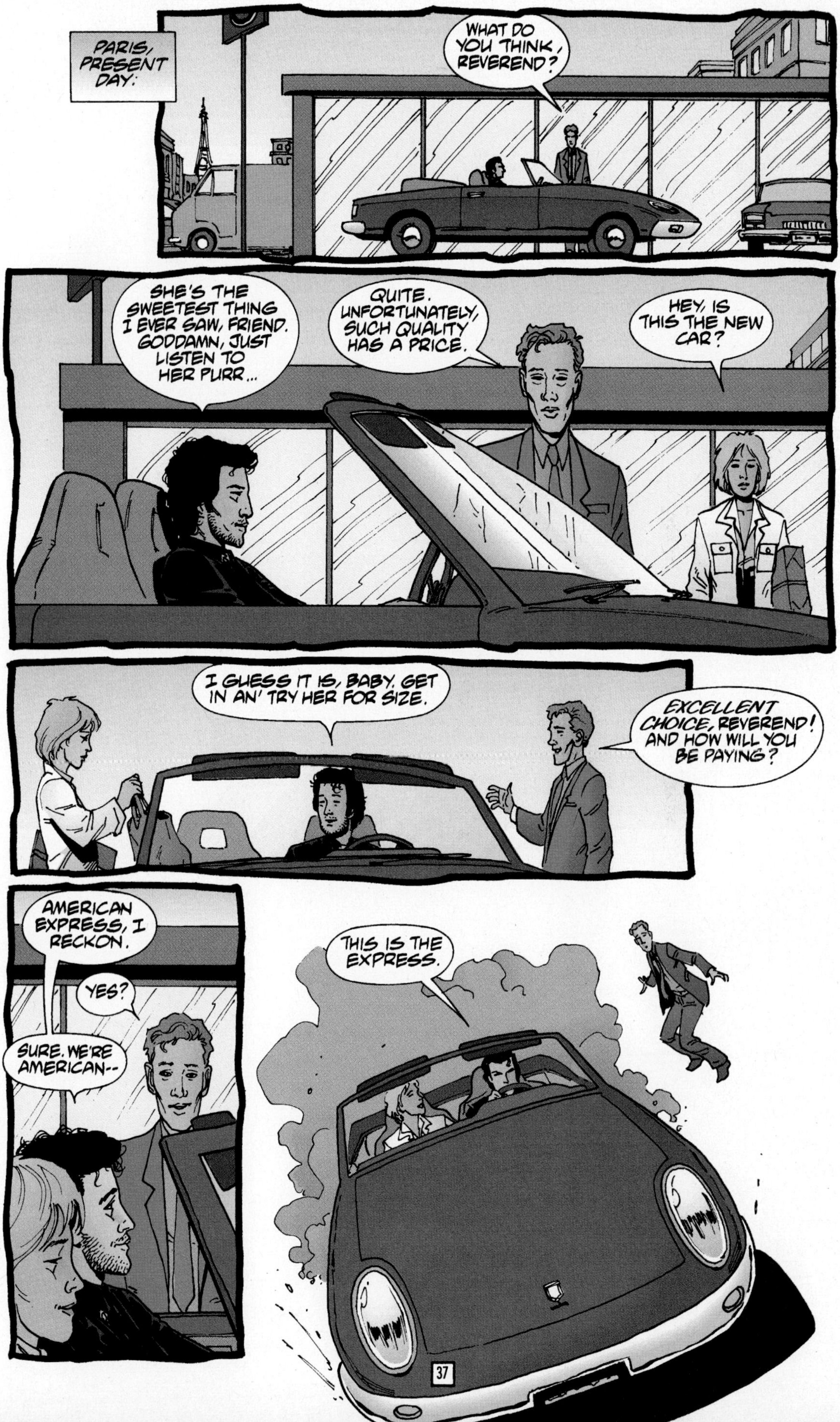
PARIS, PRESENT DAY:
WHAT DO YOU THINK, REVEREND?
SHE'S THE SWEETEST THING I EVER SAW, FRIEND. GODDAMN, JUST LISTEN TO HER PURR...
QUITE. UNFORTUNATELY, SUCH QUALITY HAS A PRICE.
HEY, IS THIS THE NEW CAR?
I GUESS IT IS, BABY. GET IN AN' TRY HER FOR SIZE.
EXCELLENT CHOICE, REVEREND! AND HOW WILL YOU BE PAYING?
AMERICAN EXPRESS, I RECKON.
YES?
SURE. WE'RE AMERICAN--
THIS IS THE EXPRESS.

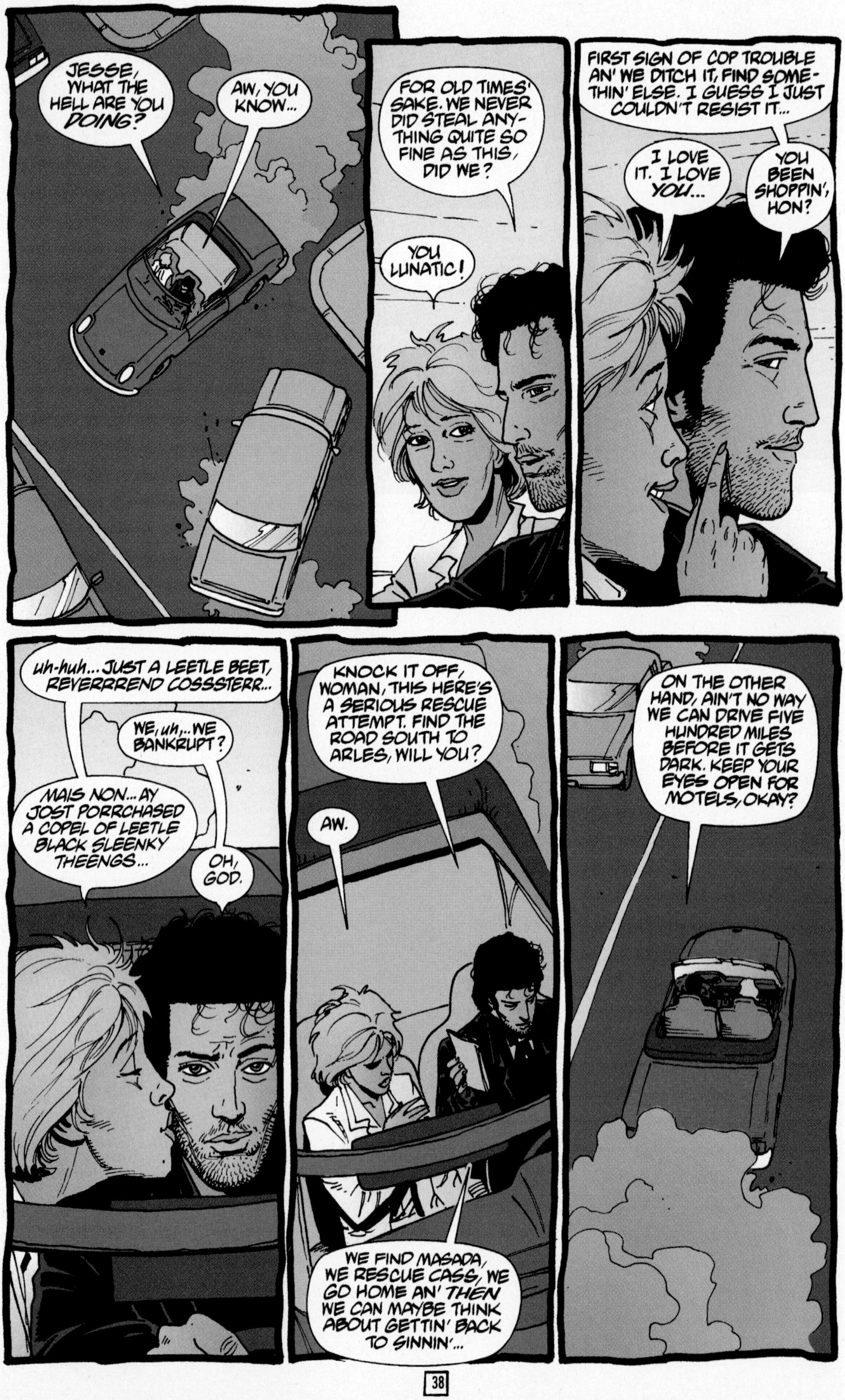
JESSE, WHAT THE HELL ARE YOU *DOING*?
AW, YOU KNOW...
FOR OLD TIMES' SAKE. WE NEVER DID STEAL ANYTHING QUITE SO FINE AS THIS, DID WE?
YOU LUNATIC!
FIRST SIGN OF COP TROUBLE AN' WE DITCH IT, FIND SOMETHIN' ELSE. I GUESS I JUST COULDN'T RESIST IT...
I LOVE IT. I LOVE *YOU*...
YOU BEEN SHOPPIN', HON?
uh-huh... JUST A LEETLE BEET, REVERRREND COSSSTERR...
WE, uh... WE BANKRUPT?
MAIS NON... AY JOST PORRCHASED A COPEL OF LEETLE BLACK SLEENKY THEENGS...
OH, GOD.
KNOCK IT OFF, WOMAN, THIS HERE'S A SERIOUS RESCUE ATTEMPT. FIND THE ROAD SOUTH TO ARLES, WILL YOU?
AW.
WE FIND MASADA, WE RESCUE CASS, WE GO HOME AN' *THEN* WE CAN MAYBE THINK ABOUT GETTIN' BACK TO SINNIN'...
ON THE OTHER HAND, AIN'T NO WAY WE CAN DRIVE FIVE HUNDRED MILES BEFORE IT GETS DARK. KEEP YOUR EYES OPEN FOR MOTELS, OKAY?

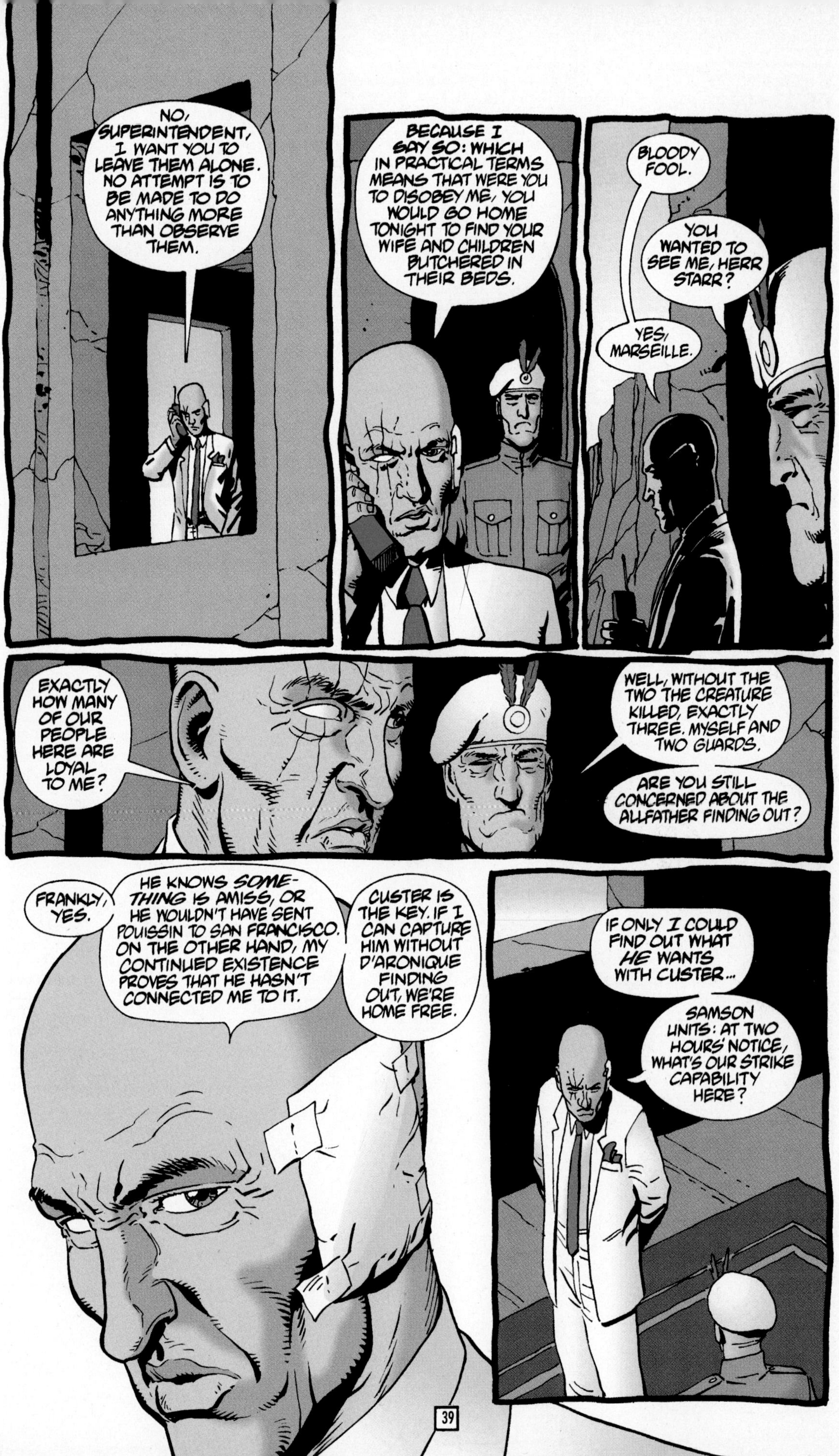
NO, SUPERINTENDENT, I WANT YOU TO LEAVE THEM ALONE. NO ATTEMPT IS TO BE MADE TO DO ANYTHING MORE THAN OBSERVE THEM.
BECAUSE I SAY SO: WHICH IN PRACTICAL TERMS MEANS THAT WERE YOU TO DISOBEY ME, YOU WOULD GO HOME TONIGHT TO FIND YOUR WIFE AND CHILDREN BUTCHERED IN THEIR BEDS.
BLOODY FOOL.
YOU WANTED TO SEE ME, HERR STARR?
YES, MARSEILLE.
EXACTLY HOW MANY OF OUR PEOPLE HERE ARE LOYAL TO ME?
WELL, WITHOUT THE TWO THE CREATURE KILLED, EXACTLY THREE. MYSELF AND TWO GUARDS.
ARE YOU STILL CONCERNED ABOUT THE ALLFATHER FINDING OUT?
FRANKLY, YES.
HE KNOWS *SOMETHING* IS AMISS, OR HE WOULDN'T HAVE SENT POUISSIN TO SAN FRANCISCO. ON THE OTHER HAND, MY CONTINUED EXISTENCE PROVES THAT HE HASN'T CONNECTED ME TO IT.
CUSTER IS THE KEY. IF I CAN CAPTURE HIM WITHOUT D'ARONIQUE FINDING OUT, WE'RE HOME FREE.
IF ONLY I COULD FIND OUT WHAT *HE* WANTS WITH CUSTER...
SAMSON UNITS: AT TWO HOURS' NOTICE, WHAT'S OUR STRIKE CAPABILITY HERE?

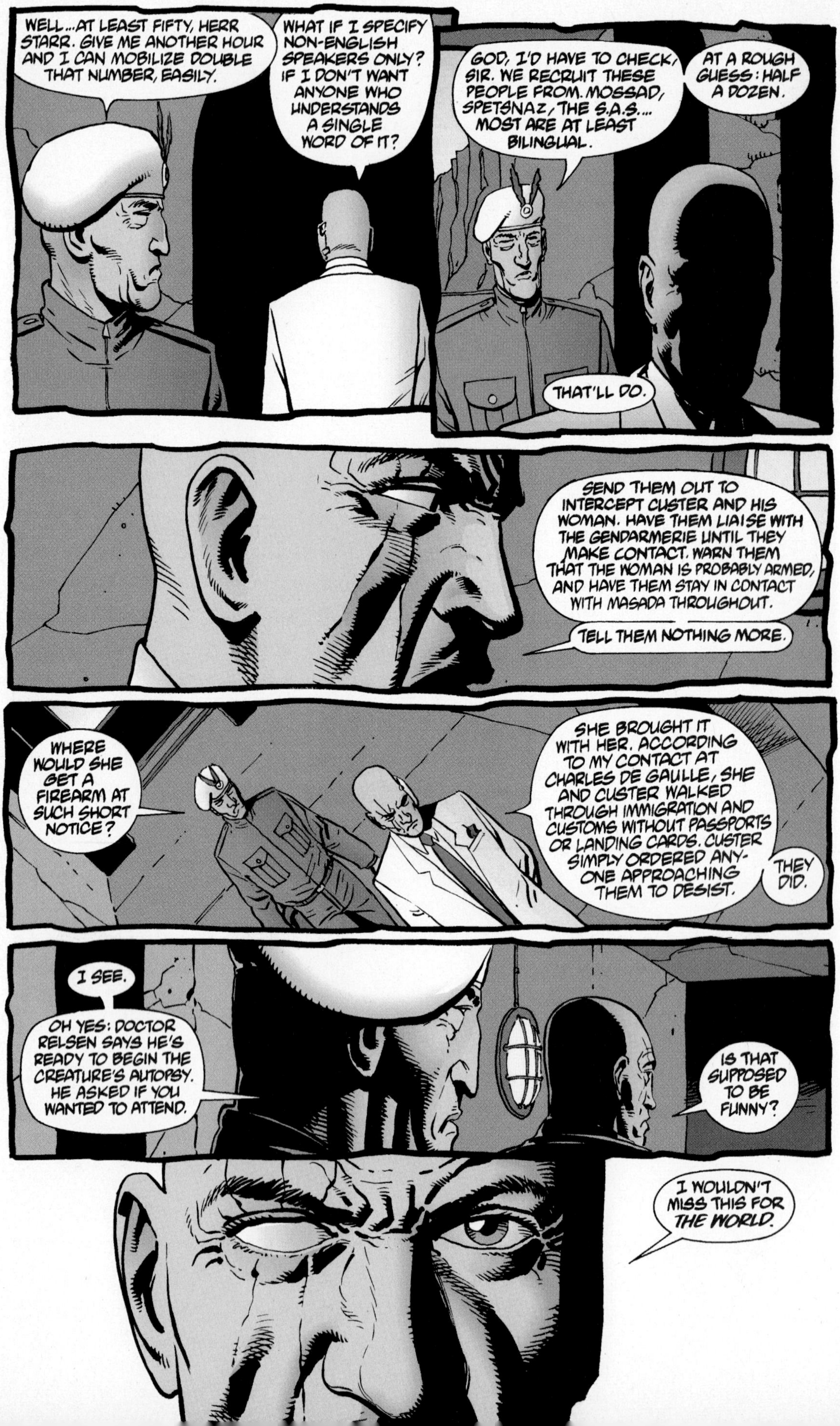
WELL...AT LEAST FIFTY, HERR STARR. GIVE ME ANOTHER HOUR AND I CAN MOBILIZE DOUBLE THAT NUMBER, EASILY.
WHAT IF I SPECIFY NON-ENGLISH SPEAKERS ONLY? IF I DON'T WANT ANYONE WHO UNDERSTANDS A SINGLE WORD OF IT?
GOD, I'D HAVE TO CHECK, SIR. WE RECRUIT THESE PEOPLE FROM MOSSAD, SPETSNAZ, THE S.A.S.... MOST ARE AT LEAST BILINGUAL.
AT A ROUGH GUESS: HALF A DOZEN.
THAT'LL DO.
SEND THEM OUT TO INTERCEPT CUSTER AND HIS WOMAN. HAVE THEM LIAISE WITH THE GENDARMERIE UNTIL THEY MAKE CONTACT. WARN THEM THAT THE WOMAN IS PROBABLY ARMED, AND HAVE THEM STAY IN CONTACT WITH MASADA THROUGHOUT.
TELL THEM NOTHING MORE.
WHERE WOULD SHE GET A FIREARM AT SUCH SHORT NOTICE?
SHE BROUGHT IT WITH HER. ACCORDING TO MY CONTACT AT CHARLES DE GAULLE, SHE AND CUSTER WALKED THROUGH IMMIGRATION AND CUSTOMS WITHOUT PASSPORTS OR LANDING CARDS. CUSTER SIMPLY ORDERED ANY-ONE APPROACHING THEM TO DESIST.
THEY DID.
I SEE.
OH YES: DOCTOR RELSEN SAYS HE'S READY TO BEGIN THE CREATURE'S AUTOPSY. HE ASKED IF YOU WANTED TO ATTEND.
IS THAT SUPPOSED TO BE FUNNY?
I WOULDN'T MISS THIS FOR *THE WORLD*.

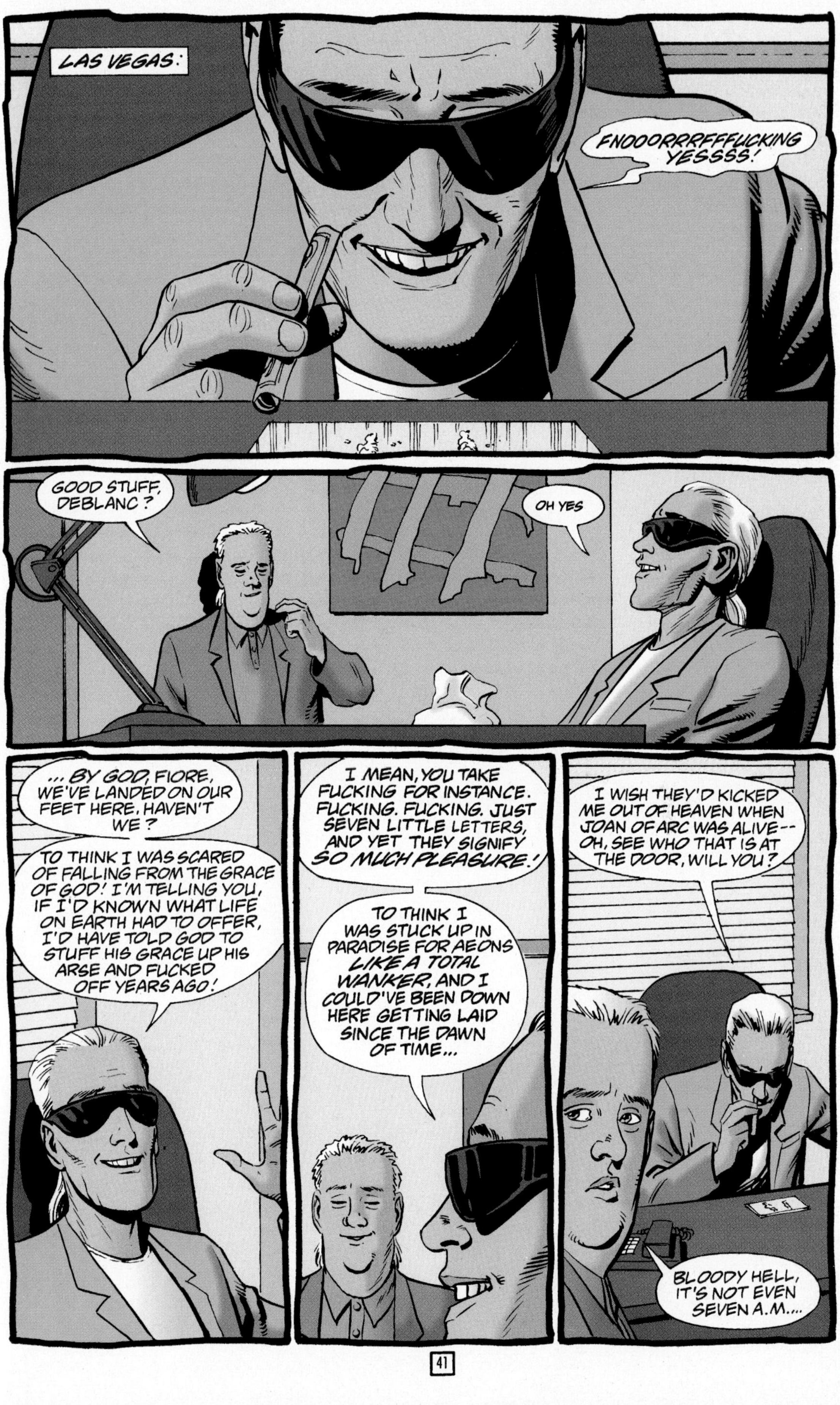
LAS VEGAS:
FNOOORRRFFFUCKING YESSSS!
GOOD STUFF, DEBLANC?
OH YES
...BY GOD, FIORE, WE'VE LANDED ON OUR FEET HERE, HAVEN'T WE?
TO THINK I WAS SCARED OF FALLING FROM THE GRACE OF GOD! I'M TELLING YOU, IF I'D KNOWN WHAT LIFE ON EARTH HAD TO OFFER, I'D HAVE TOLD GOD TO STUFF HIS GRACE UP HIS ARSE AND FUCKED OFF YEARS AGO!
I MEAN, YOU TAKE FUCKING FOR INSTANCE. FUCKING. FUCKING. JUST SEVEN LITTLE LETTERS, AND YET THEY SIGNIFY SO MUCH PLEASURE!
TO THINK I WAS STUCK UP IN PARADISE FOR AEONS LIKE A TOTAL WANKER, AND I COULD'VE BEEN DOWN HERE GETTING LAID SINCE THE DAWN OF TIME...
I WISH THEY'D KICKED ME OUT OF HEAVEN WHEN JOAN OF ARC WAS ALIVE--OH, SEE WHO THAT IS AT THE DOOR, WILL YOU?
BLOODY HELL, IT'S NOT EVEN SEVEN A.M....

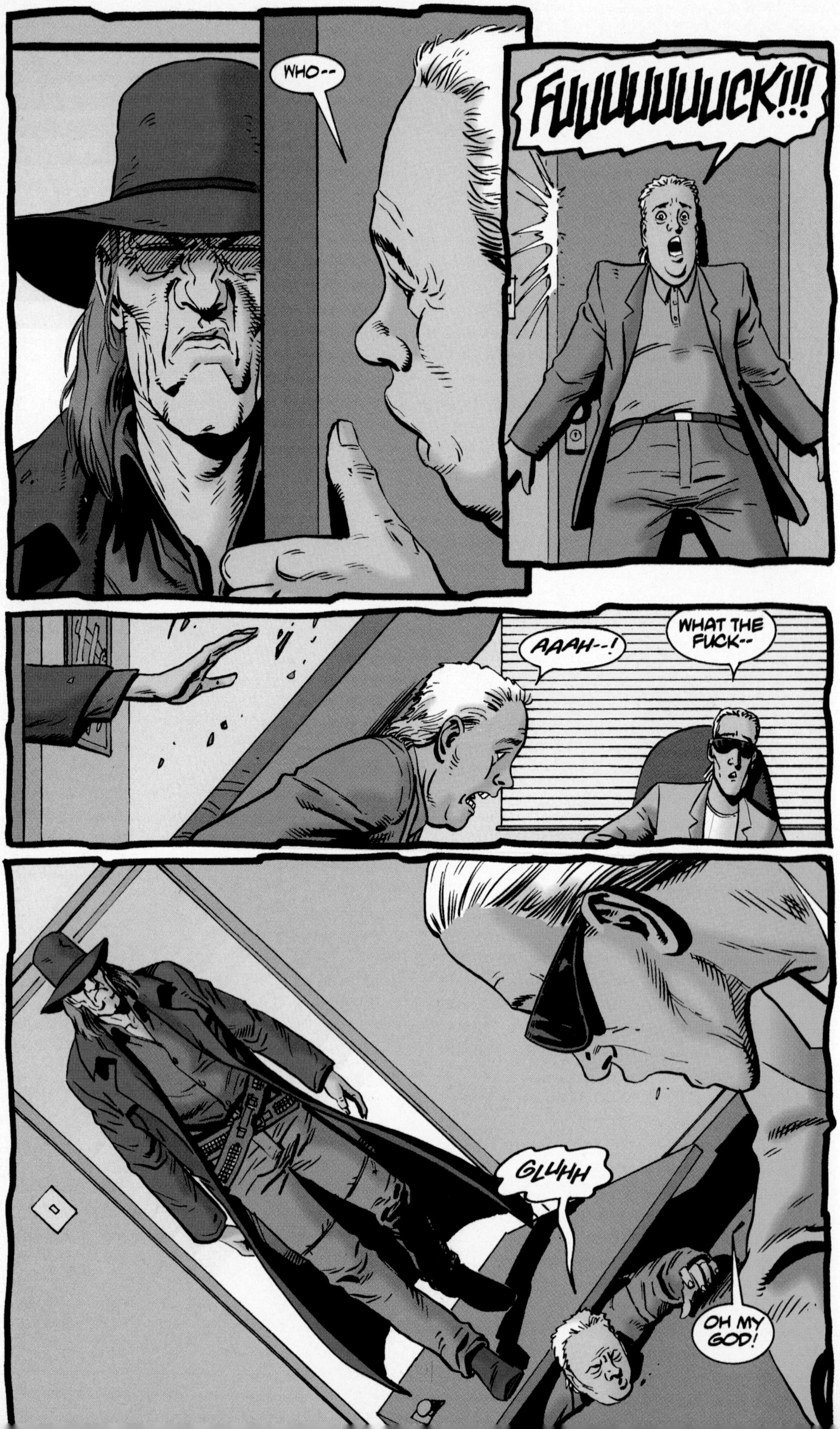
WHO--
FUUUUUUUUCK!!!
AAAH--!
WHAT THE FUCK--
GLUHH
OH MY GOD!

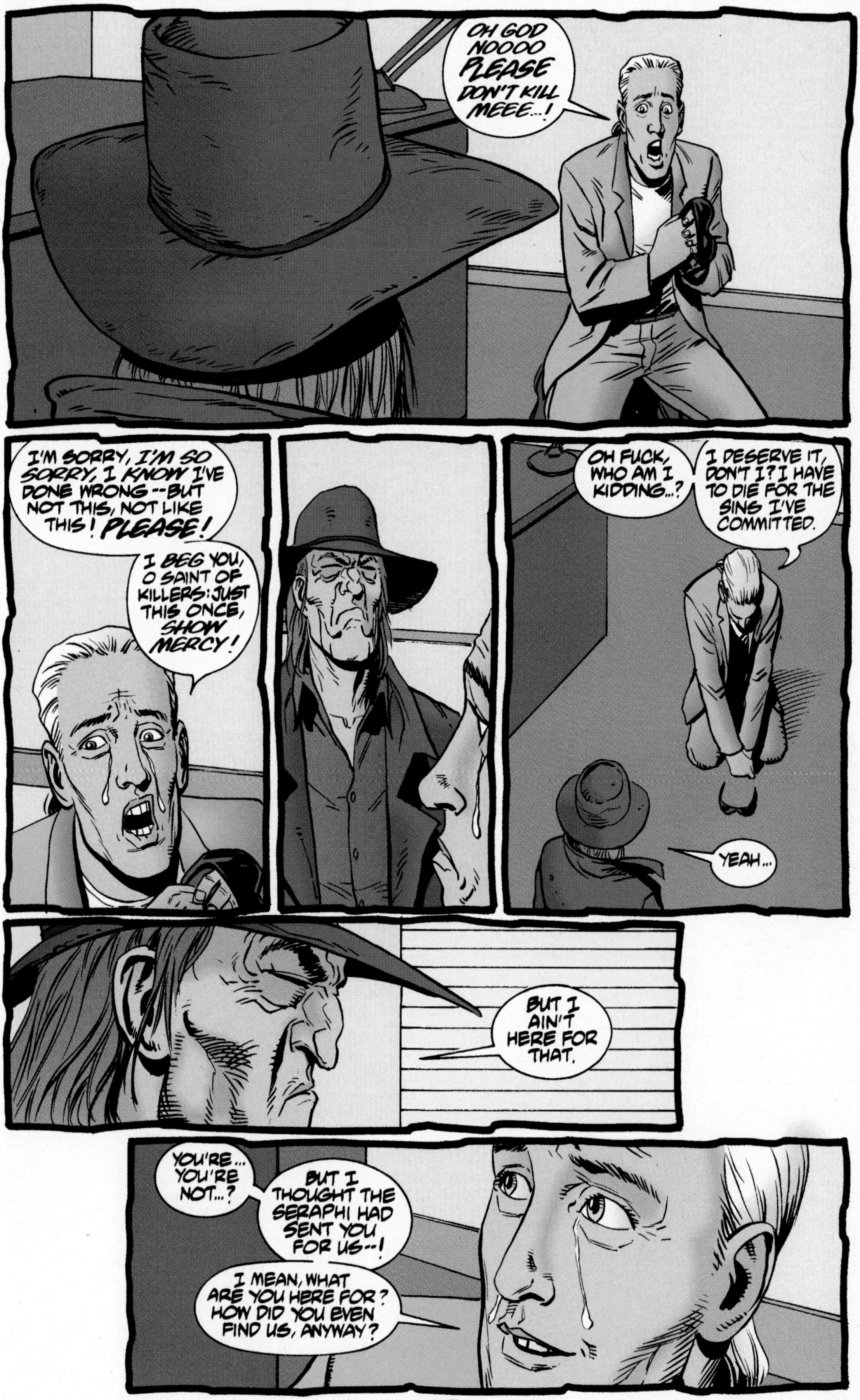
OH GOD NOOOO PLEASE DON'T KILL MEEE...!
I'M SORRY, I'M SO SORRY, I KNOW I'VE DONE WRONG--BUT NOT THIS, NOT LIKE THIS! PLEASE!
I BEG YOU, O SAINT OF KILLERS: JUST THIS ONCE, SHOW MERCY!
OH FUCK, WHO AM I KIDDING...?
I DESERVE IT, DON'T I? I HAVE TO DIE FOR THE SINS I'VE COMMITTED.
YEAH...
BUT I AIN'T HERE FOR THAT.
YOU'RE... YOU'RE NOT...?
BUT I THOUGHT THE SERAPHI HAD SENT YOU FOR US--!
I MEAN, WHAT ARE YOU HERE FOR? HOW DID YOU EVEN FIND US, ANYWAY?

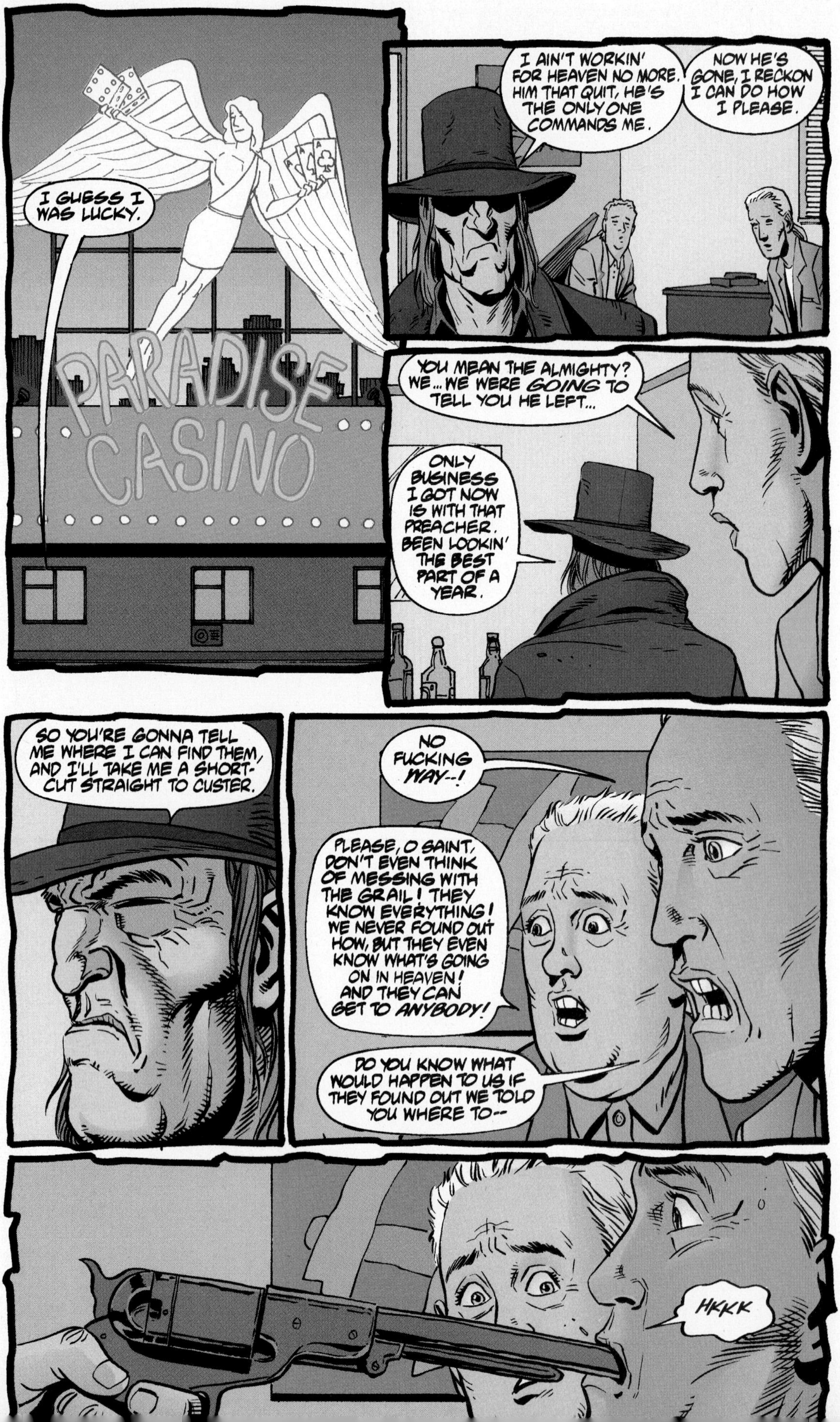
I GUESS I WAS LUCKY.
PARADISE CASINO
I AIN'T WORKIN' FOR HEAVEN NO MORE. HIM THAT QUIT, HE'S THE ONLY ONE COMMANDS ME.
NOW HE'S GONE, I RECKON I CAN DO HOW I PLEASE.
YOU MEAN THE ALMIGHTY? WE... WE WERE *GOING* TO TELL YOU HE LEFT...
ONLY BUSINESS I GOT NOW IS WITH THAT PREACHER. BEEN LOOKIN' THE BEST PART OF A YEAR.
SO YOU'RE GONNA TELL ME WHERE I CAN FIND THEM, AND I'LL TAKE ME A SHORT-CUT STRAIGHT TO CUSTER.
NO FUCKING *WAY*--!
PLEASE, O SAINT, DON'T EVEN THINK OF MESSING WITH THE GRAIL! THEY KNOW EVERYTHING! WE NEVER FOUND OUT HOW, BUT THEY EVEN KNOW WHAT'S GOING ON IN HEAVEN! AND THEY CAN GET TO *ANYBODY*!
DO YOU KNOW WHAT WOULD HAPPEN TO US IF THEY FOUND OUT WE TOLD YOU WHERE TO--
HKKK

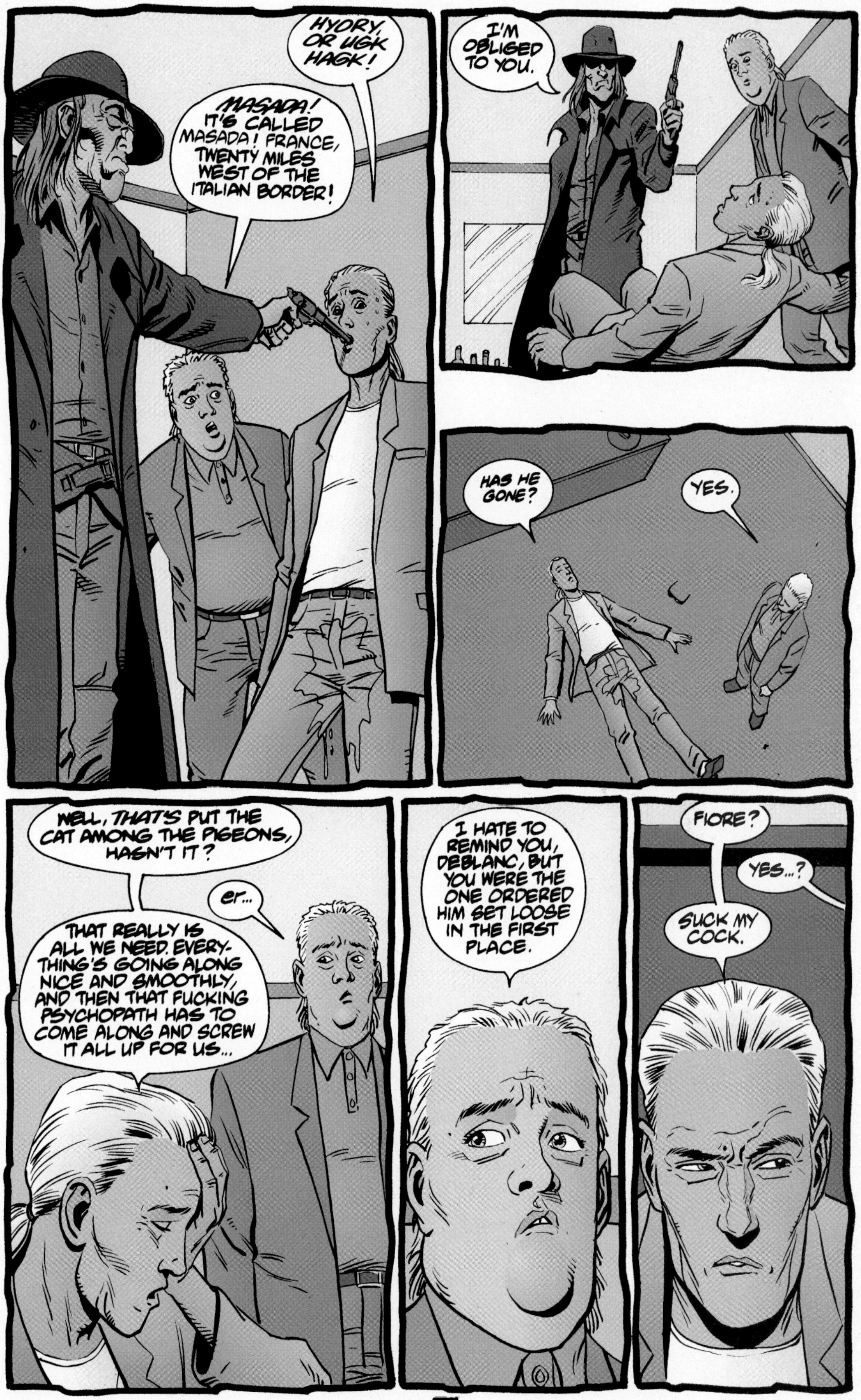
HYORY, OR UGK HAGK!
MASADA! IT'S CALLED MASADA! FRANCE, TWENTY MILES WEST OF THE ITALIAN BORDER!
I'M OBLIGED TO YOU.
HAS HE GONE?
YES.
WELL, THAT'S PUT THE CAT AMONG THE PIGEONS, HASN'T IT?
er...
THAT REALLY IS ALL WE NEED. EVERYTHING'S GOING ALONG NICE AND SMOOTHLY, AND THEN THAT FUCKING PSYCHOPATH HAS TO COME ALONG AND SCREW IT ALL UP FOR US...
I HATE TO REMIND YOU, DEBLANC, BUT YOU WERE THE ONE ORDERED HIM SET LOOSE IN THE FIRST PLACE.
FIORE?
YES...?
SUCK MY COCK.

PRELIMINARY EXAMINATION REVEALS NO HEARTBEAT OR RESPIRATORY FUNCTION.

CAUSE OF DEATH HAS BEEN DETERMINED AS MULTIPLE GUNSHOT WOUNDS...

FUCKING BRILLIANT, DOCTOR. I'D NEVER HAVE GUESSED.

HERR STARR, I'M TRYING TO DO THIS PROPERLY...

WHAT YOU'RE DOING IS DETERMINING WHAT THIS CREATURE IS, HOW IT WAS ABLE TO SURVIVE BEING SHOT TWENTY TIMES, WHY IT WAS STILL TWITCHING AFTER ANOTHER FORTY, AND IF IT IS IN FACT DEFINITELY DEAD.

WITHOUT FURTHER DELAY, DOCTOR.

VERY WELL, HERR STARR.

I'LL NEED TO REMOVE THE SUBJECT'S CLOTHING, BEGINNING WITH THE EYEWEAR...

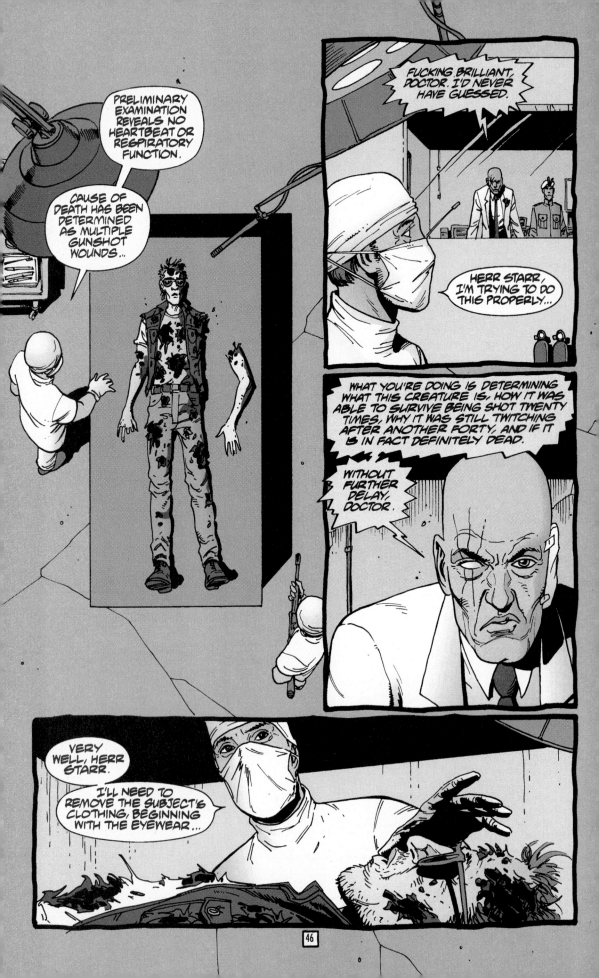

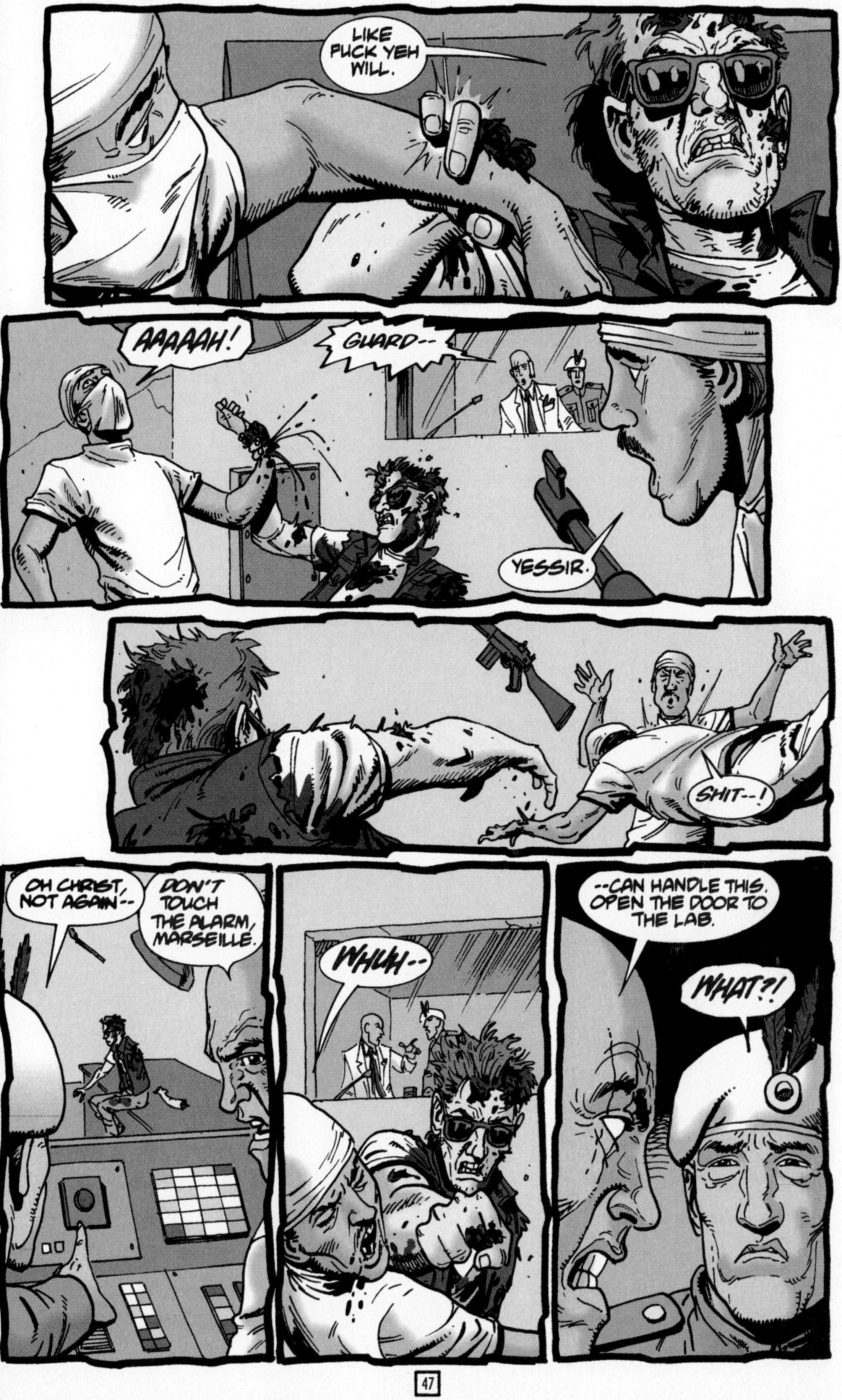
LIKE FUCK YEH WILL.
AAAAAH!
GUARD--
YESSIR.
SHIT--!
OH CHRIST, NOT AGAIN--
DON'T TOUCH THE ALARM, MARSEILLE.
WHUH--
--CAN HANDLE THIS. OPEN THE DOOR TO THE LAB.
WHAT?!

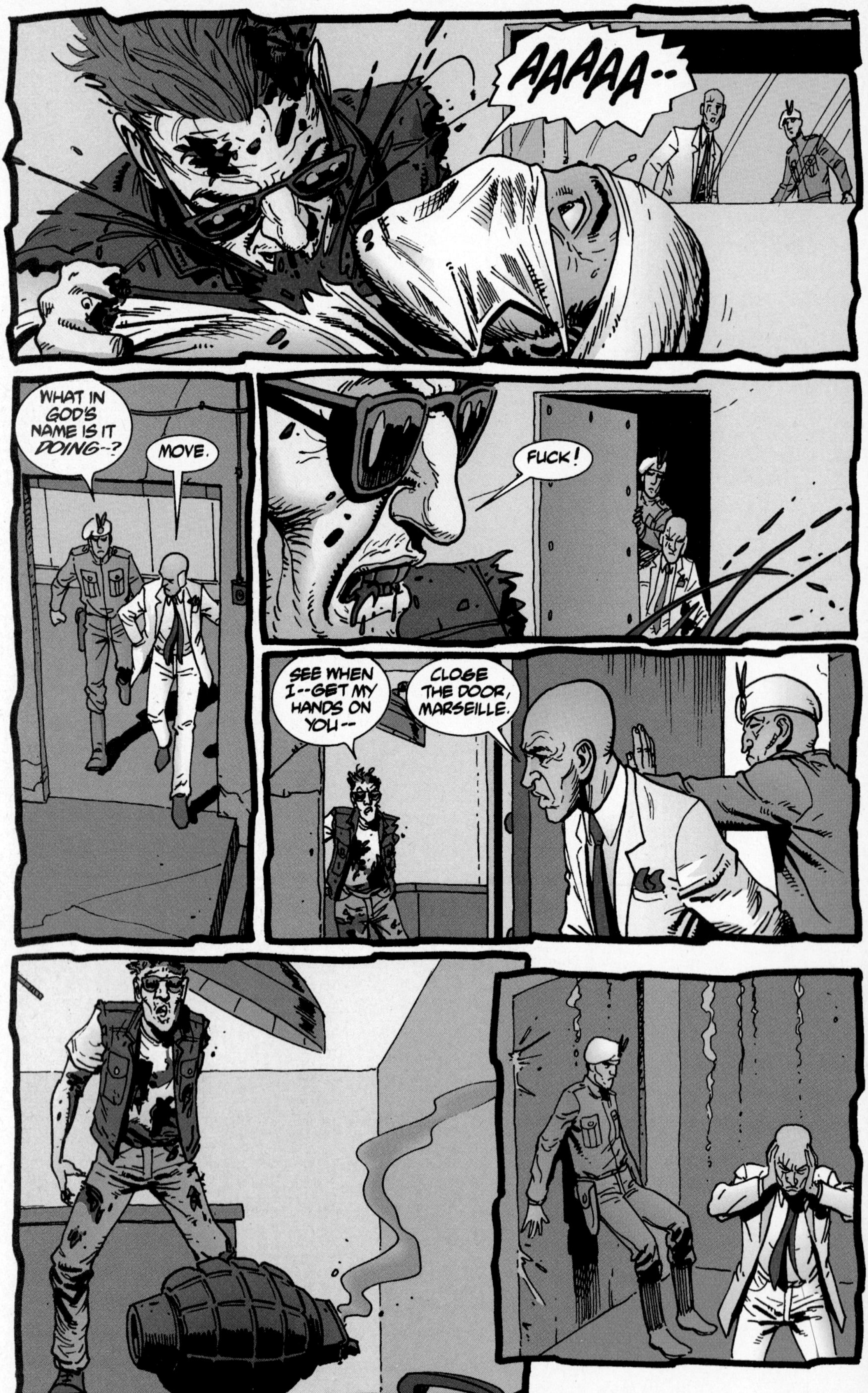
AAAAA--
WHAT IN GOD'S NAME IS IT DOING--?
MOVE.
FUCK!
SEE WHEN I--GET MY HANDS ON YOU--
CLOSE THE DOOR, MARSEILLE.

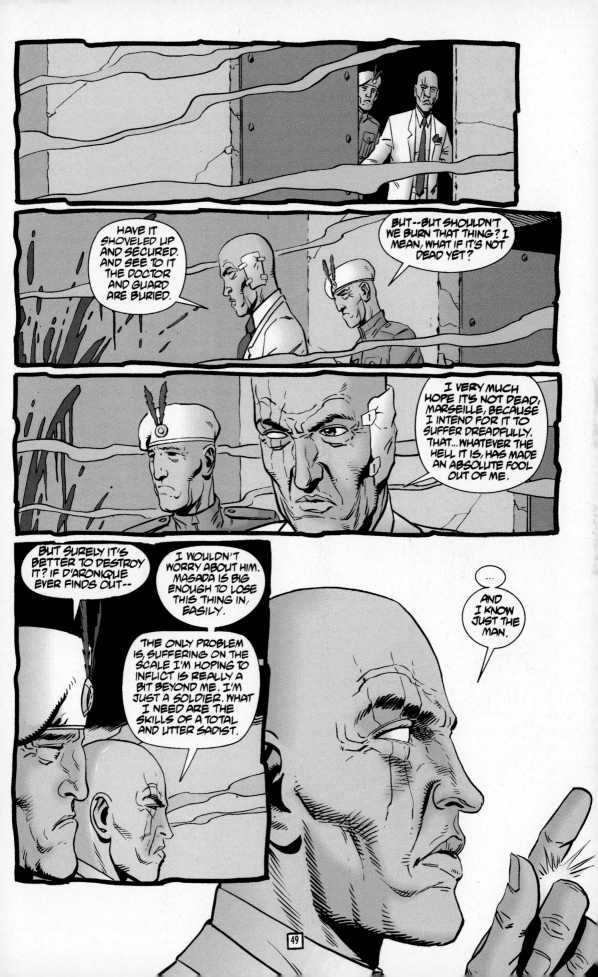

HAVE IT SHOVELED UP AND SECURED. AND SEE TO IT THE DOCTOR AND GUARD ARE BURIED.

BUT--BUT SHOULDN'T WE BURN THAT THING? I MEAN, WHAT IF IT'S NOT DEAD YET?

I VERY MUCH HOPE IT'S NOT DEAD, MARSEILLE, BECAUSE I INTEND FOR IT TO SUFFER DREADFULLY. THAT...WHATEVER THE HELL IT IS, HAS MADE AN ABSOLUTE FOOL OUT OF ME.

BUT SURELY IT'S BETTER TO DESTROY IT? IF D'ARONIQUE EVER FINDS OUT--

I WOULDN'T WORRY ABOUT HIM. MASADA IS BIG ENOUGH TO LOSE THIS THING IN, EASILY.

THE ONLY PROBLEM IS, SUFFERING ON THE SCALE I'M HOPING TO INFLICT IS REALLY A BIT BEYOND ME. I'M JUST A SOLDIER. WHAT I NEED ARE THE SKILLS OF A TOTAL AND UTTER SADIST.

...

AND I KNOW JUST THE MAN.

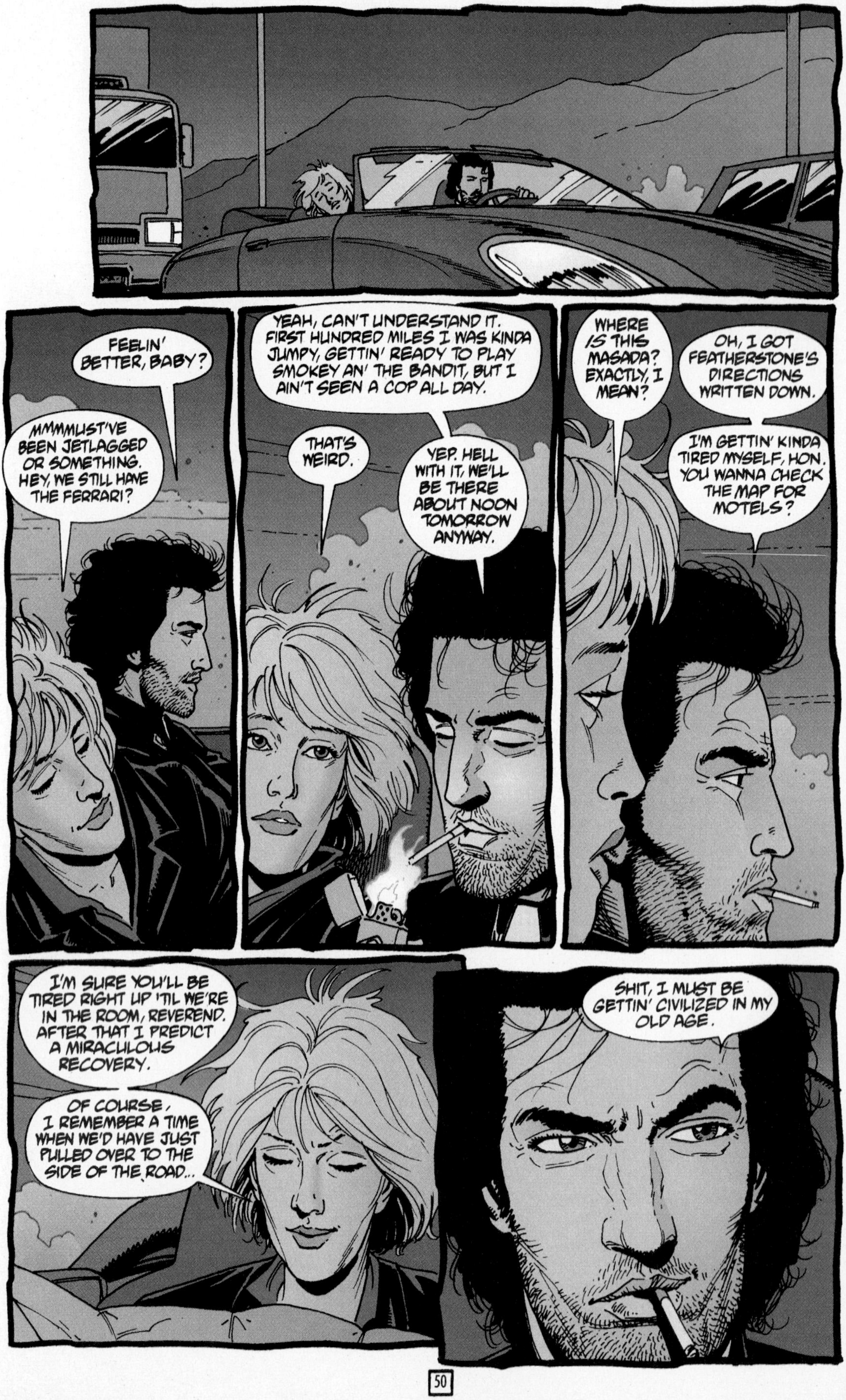
FEELIN' BETTER, BABY?
MMMMUST'VE BEEN JETLAGGED OR SOMETHING. HEY, WE STILL HAVE THE FERRARI?
YEAH, CAN'T UNDERSTAND IT. FIRST HUNDRED MILES I WAS KINDA JUMPY, GETTIN' READY TO PLAY SMOKEY AN' THE BANDIT, BUT I AIN'T SEEN A COP ALL DAY.
THAT'S WEIRD.
YEP. HELL WITH IT, WE'LL BE THERE ABOUT NOON TOMORROW ANYWAY.
WHERE IS THIS MASADA? EXACTLY, I MEAN?
OH, I GOT FEATHERSTONE'S DIRECTIONS WRITTEN DOWN.
I'M GETTIN' KINDA TIRED MYSELF, HON. YOU WANNA CHECK THE MAP FOR MOTELS?
I'M SURE YOU'LL BE TIRED RIGHT UP 'TIL WE'RE IN THE ROOM, REVEREND. AFTER THAT I PREDICT A MIRACULOUS RECOVERY.
OF COURSE, I REMEMBER A TIME WHEN WE'D HAVE JUST PULLED OVER TO THE SIDE OF THE ROAD...
SHIT, I MUST BE GETTIN' CIVILIZED IN MY OLD AGE.

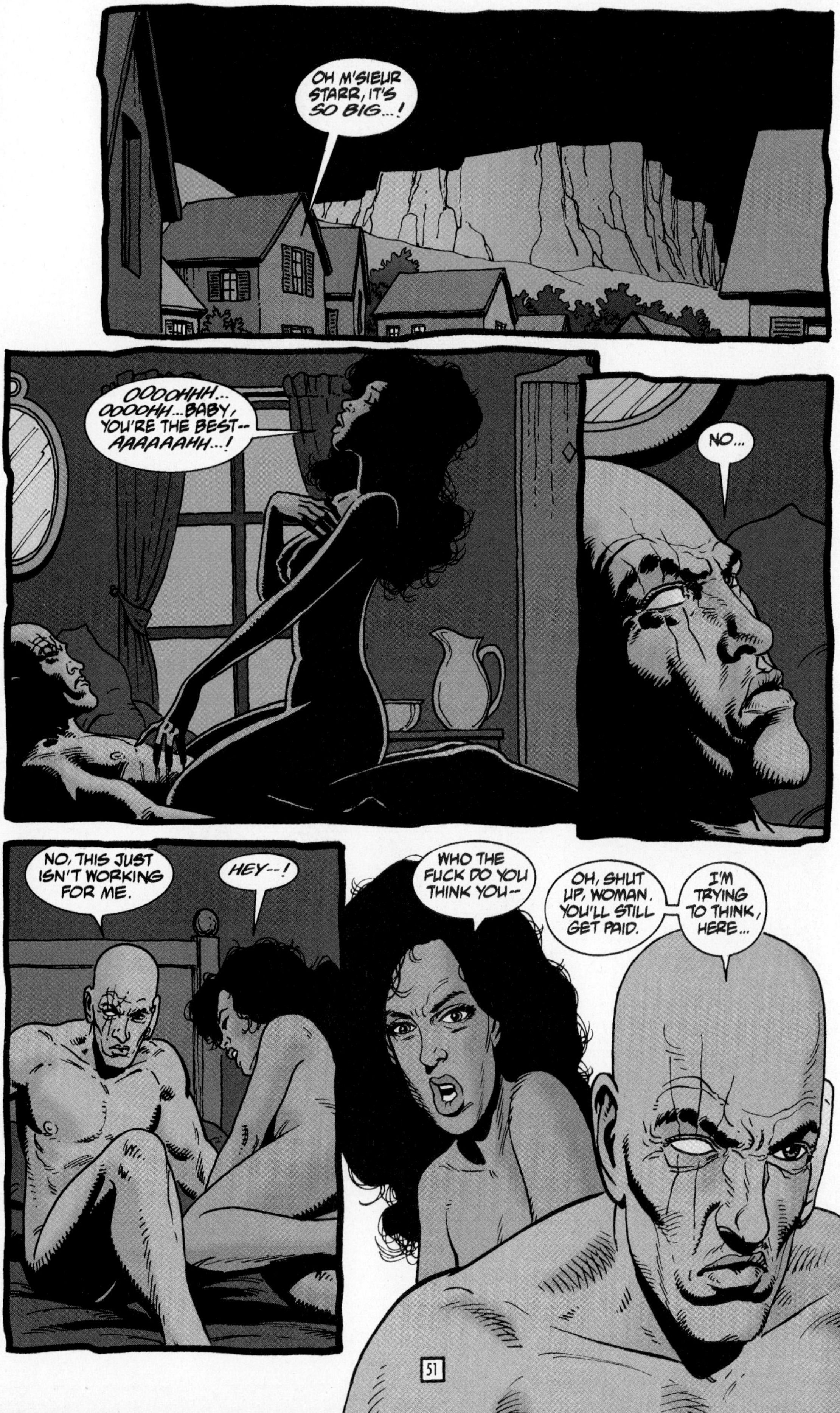
OH M'SIEUR STARR, IT'S SO BIG...!
OOOOHHH... OOOOHH...BABY, YOU'RE THE BEST-- AAAAAAHH...!
NO...
NO, THIS JUST ISN'T WORKING FOR ME.
HEY--!
WHO THE FUCK DO YOU THINK YOU--
OH, SHUT UP, WOMAN. YOU'LL STILL GET PAID.
I'M TRYING TO THINK, HERE...

I DID EVERYTHING YOU LIKE, M'SIEUR. I SAID THE THINGS YOU ALWAYS LIKE ME TO SAY...

NOT ANYMORE I DON'T. SOMETHING'S CHANGED, BUT I JUST CAN'T THINK WHAT IT--

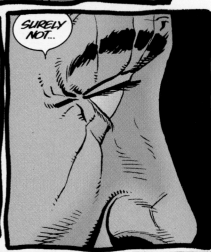

SURELY NOT...

M'SIEUR?

OH, WHAT NOW...

MARSEILLE? I TOLD YOU NOT TO CALL ME WHEN I'M HERE.

MY APOLOGIES, HERR STARR, BUT I THOUGHT YOU'D WANT TO KNOW THAT SAMSON TWO-FIVE HAVE CALLED IN. THEY'VE LOCATED CUSTER A HUNDRED MILES NORTH OF ARLES.

HAVE THEM PROCEED. I'M ON MY WAY BACK NOW. AND MARSEILLE?

SIR?

TELL THE CHIEF ARMOURER I'D LIKE A LITTLE WORD WITH HIM.

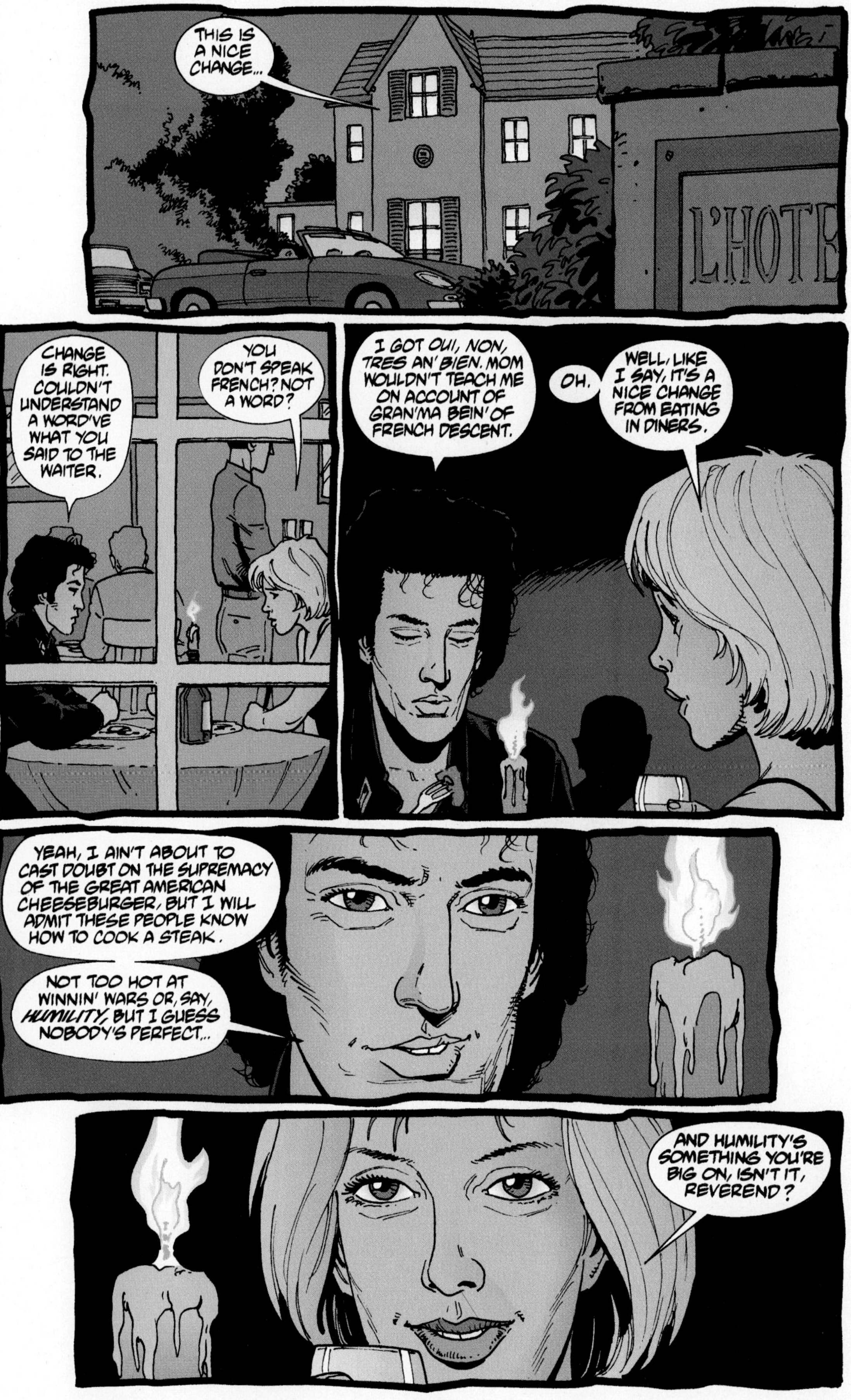
THIS IS A NICE CHANGE...
L'HOTE
CHANGE IS RIGHT. COULDN'T UNDERSTAND A WORD'VE WHAT YOU SAID TO THE WAITER.
YOU DON'T SPEAK FRENCH? NOT A WORD?
I GOT OUI, NON, TRES AN' BIEN. MOM WOULDN'T TEACH ME ON ACCOUNT OF GRAN'MA BEIN' OF FRENCH DESCENT.
OH.
WELL, LIKE I SAY, IT'S A NICE CHANGE FROM EATING IN DINERS.
YEAH, I AIN'T ABOUT TO CAST DOUBT ON THE SUPREMACY OF THE GREAT AMERICAN CHEESEBURGER, BUT I WILL ADMIT THESE PEOPLE KNOW HOW TO COOK A STEAK.
NOT TOO HOT AT WINNIN' WARS OR, SAY, *HUMILITY*, BUT I GUESS NOBODY'S PERFECT...
AND HUMILITY'S SOMETHING YOU'RE BIG ON, ISN'T IT, REVEREND?

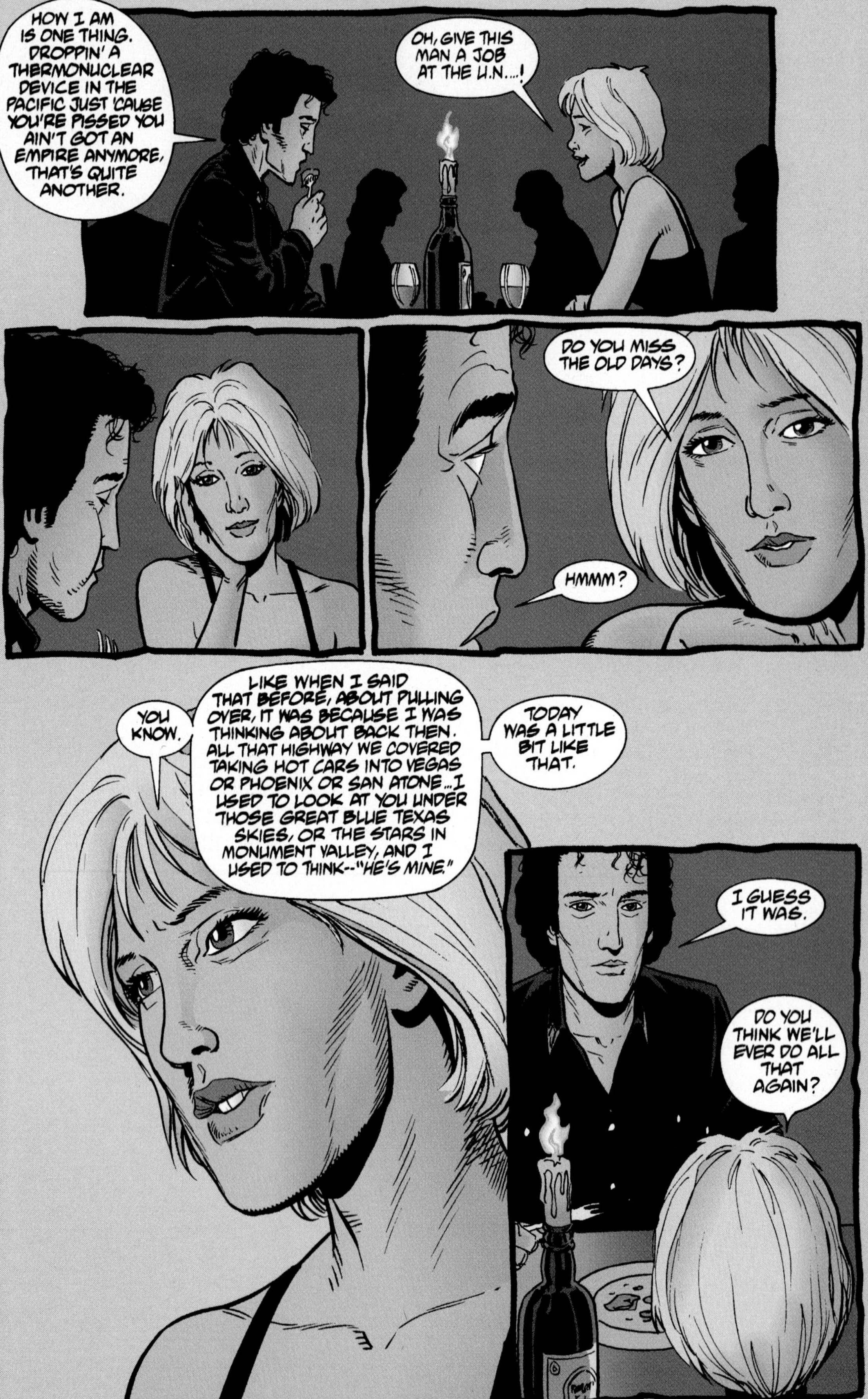
HOW I AM IS ONE THING. DROPPIN' A THERMONUCLEAR DEVICE IN THE PACIFIC JUST 'CAUSE YOU'RE PISSED YOU AIN'T GOT AN EMPIRE ANYMORE, THAT'S QUITE ANOTHER.
OH, GIVE THIS MAN A JOB AT THE U.N....!
DO YOU MISS THE OLD DAYS?
HMMM?
YOU KNOW.
LIKE WHEN I SAID THAT BEFORE, ABOUT PULLING OVER, IT WAS BECAUSE I WAS THINKING ABOUT BACK THEN. ALL THAT HIGHWAY WE COVERED TAKING HOT CARS INTO VEGAS OR PHOENIX OR SAN ATONE...I USED TO LOOK AT YOU UNDER THOSE GREAT BLUE TEXAS SKIES, OR THE STARS IN MONUMENT VALLEY, AND I USED TO THINK--"HE'S MINE."
TODAY WAS A LITTLE BIT LIKE THAT.
I GUESS IT WAS.
DO YOU THINK WE'LL EVER DO ALL THAT AGAIN?

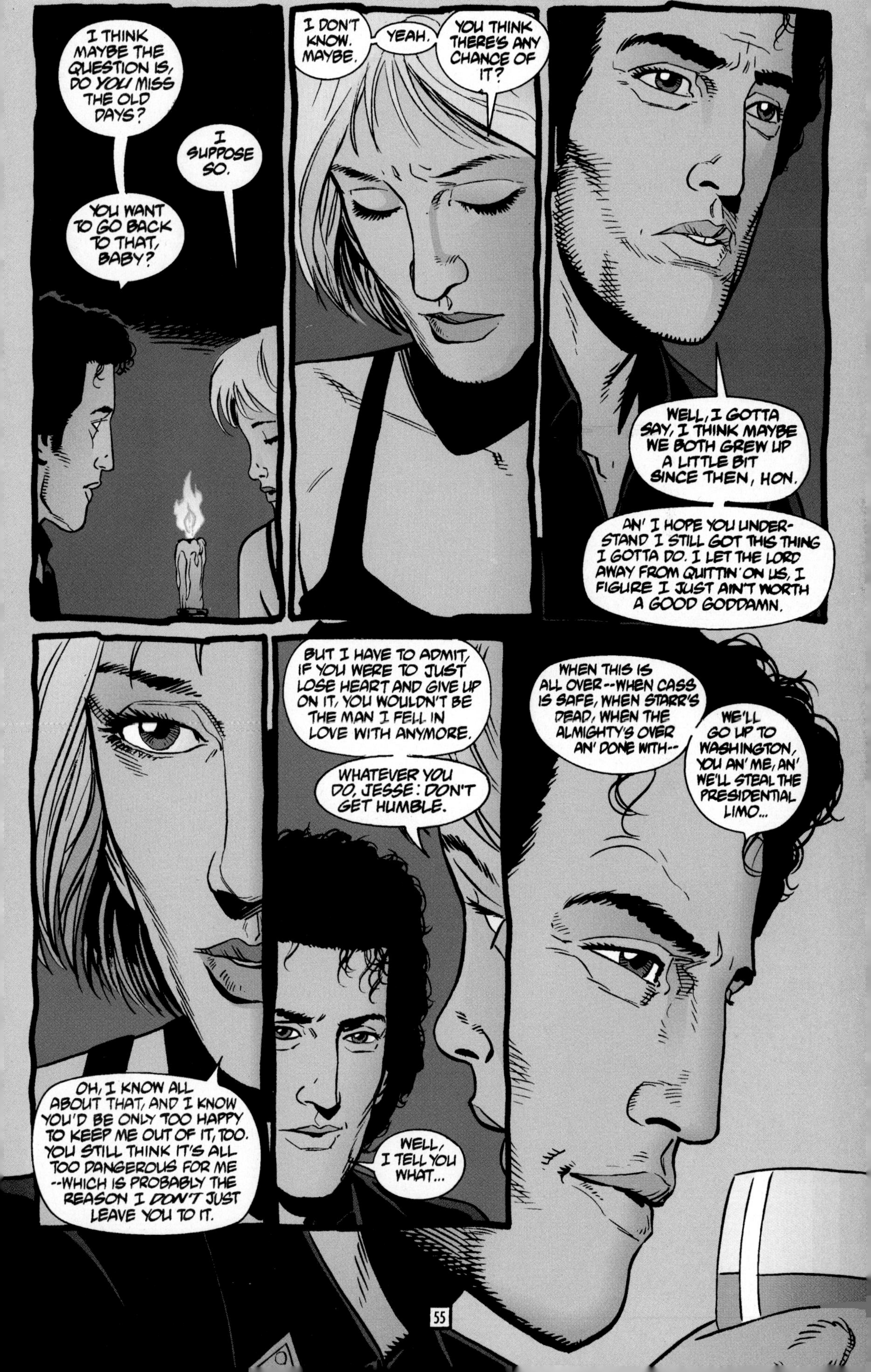
I THINK MAYBE THE QUESTION IS, DO YOU MISS THE OLD DAYS?
YOU WANT TO GO BACK TO THAT, BABY?
I SUPPOSE SO.
I DON'T KNOW. MAYBE.
YEAH.
YOU THINK THERE'S ANY CHANCE OF IT?
WELL, I GOTTA SAY, I THINK MAYBE WE BOTH GREW UP A LITTLE BIT SINCE THEN, HON.
AN' I HOPE YOU UNDERSTAND I STILL GOT THIS THING I GOTTA DO. I LET THE LORD AWAY FROM QUITTIN' ON US, I FIGURE I JUST AIN'T WORTH A GOOD GODDAMN.
OH, I KNOW ALL ABOUT THAT, AND I KNOW YOU'D BE ONLY TOO HAPPY TO KEEP ME OUT OF IT, TOO. YOU STILL THINK IT'S ALL TOO DANGEROUS FOR ME --WHICH IS PROBABLY THE REASON I DON'T JUST LEAVE YOU TO IT.
BUT I HAVE TO ADMIT, IF YOU WERE TO JUST LOSE HEART AND GIVE UP ON IT, YOU WOULDN'T BE THE MAN I FELL IN LOVE WITH ANYMORE.
WHATEVER YOU DO, JESSE: DON'T GET HUMBLE.
WELL, I TELL YOU WHAT...
WHEN THIS IS ALL OVER--WHEN CASS IS SAFE, WHEN STARR'S DEAD, WHEN THE ALMIGHTY'S OVER AN' DONE WITH--
WE'LL GO UP TO WASHINGTON, YOU AN' ME, AN' WE'LL STEAL THE PRESIDENTIAL LIMO...

AN' WE'LL DRIVE THAT SON OF A BITCH DOWN ROUTE SIXTY-SIX UNTIL THE GODDAMN WHEELS FALL OFF.

OR SOMETHING SIMILAR.

OR SOME-THIN' SIMILAR. C'MON NOW.

UNTIL THE END OF THE WORLD.

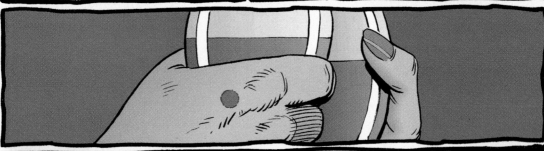

JESSE...

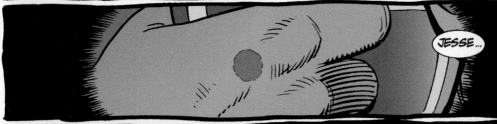

WHY WON'T YOU STOP, JESSE?

IF ONLY YOU'D LEAVE ME ALONE...

I'D DO THE SAME FOR YOU.

TO BE CONTINUED

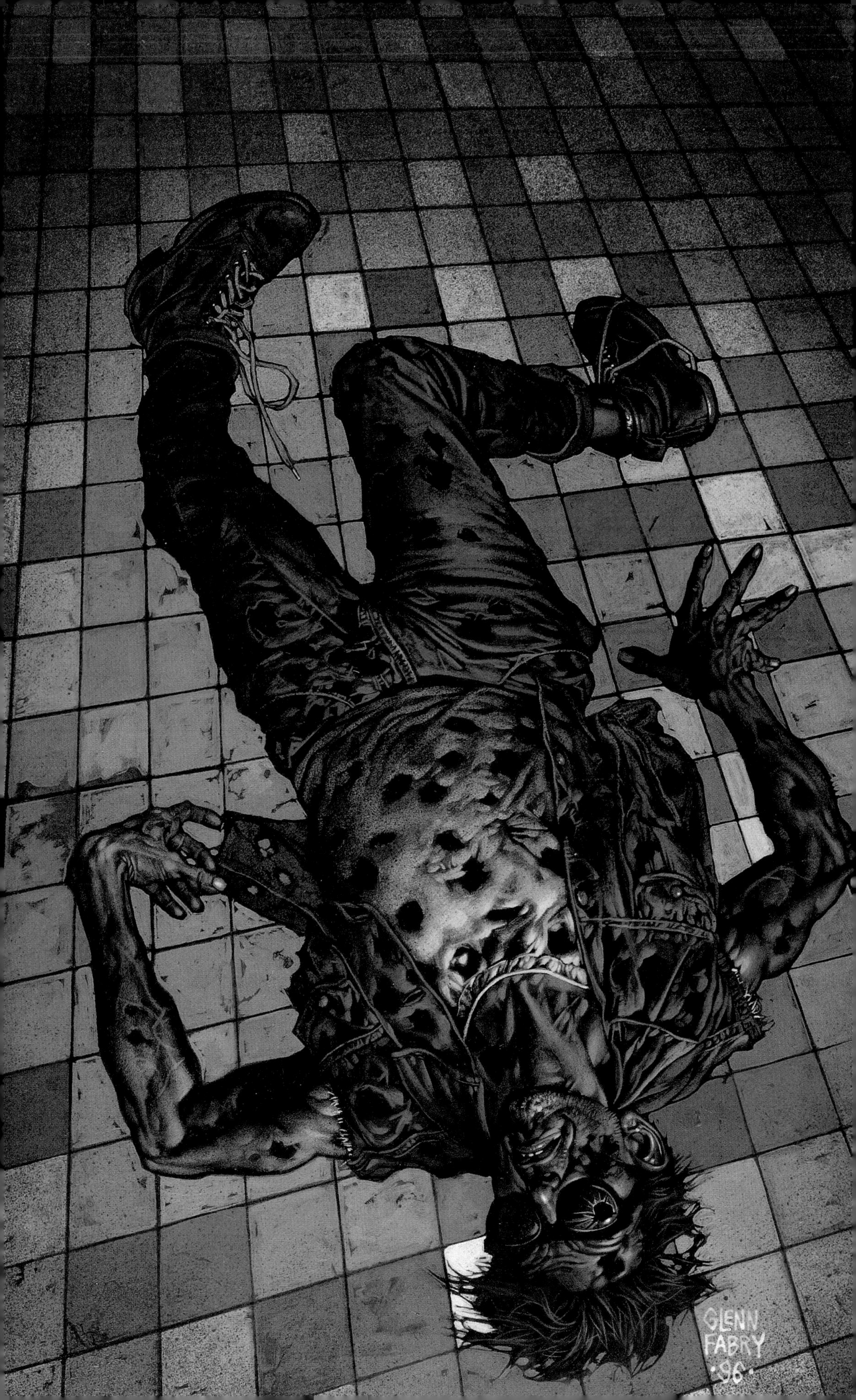
GLENN FABRY ·96·

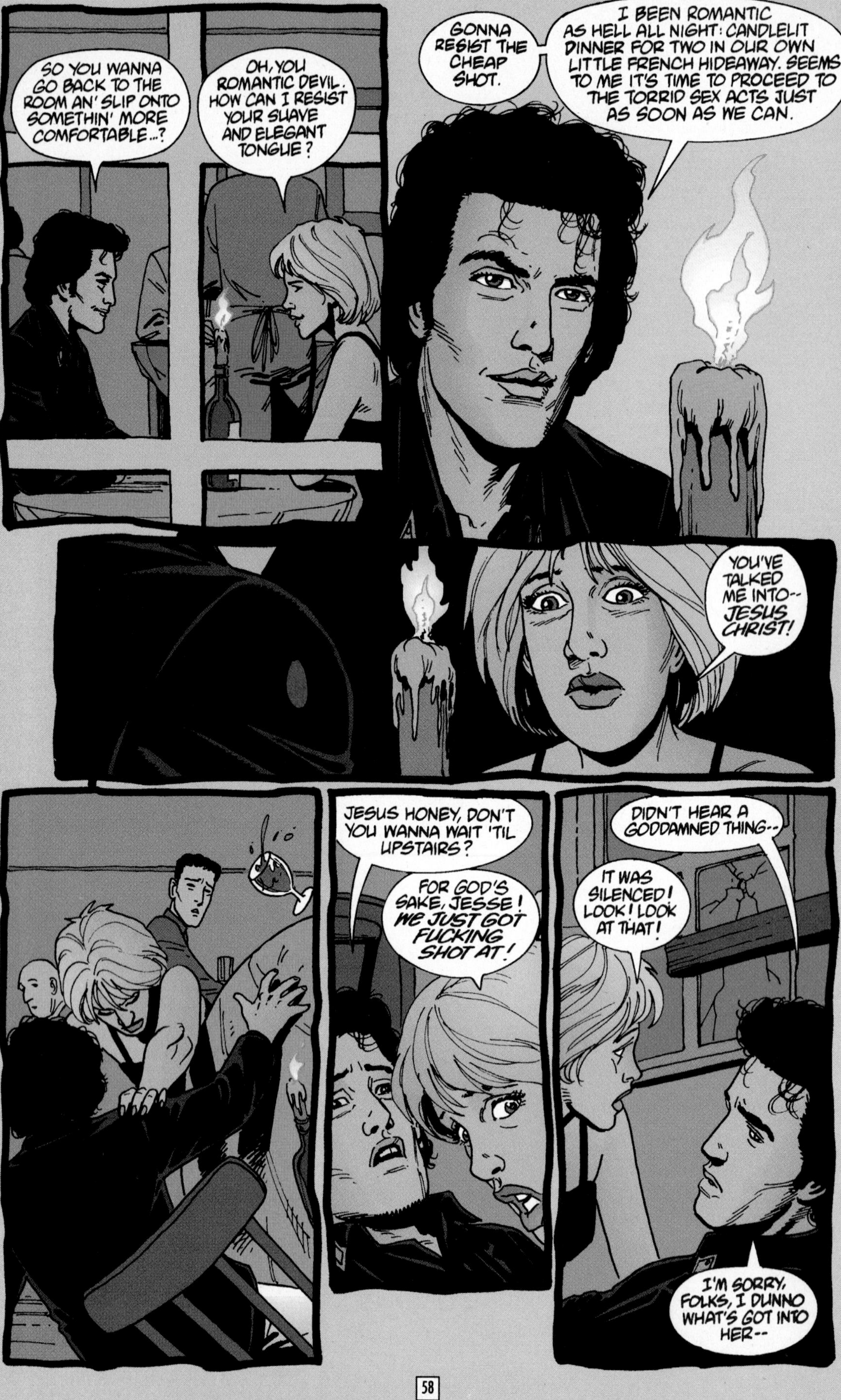
SO YOU WANNA GO BACK TO THE ROOM AN' SLIP ONTO SOMETHIN' MORE COMFORTABLE...?
OH, YOU ROMANTIC DEVIL. HOW CAN I RESIST YOUR SUAVE AND ELEGANT TONGUE?
GONNA RESIST THE CHEAP SHOT.
I BEEN ROMANTIC AS HELL ALL NIGHT: CANDLELIT DINNER FOR TWO IN OUR OWN LITTLE FRENCH HIDEAWAY. SEEMS TO ME IT'S TIME TO PROCEED TO THE TORRID SEX ACTS JUST AS SOON AS WE CAN.
YOU'VE TALKED ME INTO-- JESUS CHRIST!
JESUS HONEY, DON'T YOU WANNA WAIT 'TIL UPSTAIRS?
FOR GOD'S SAKE, JESSE! WE JUST GOT FUCKING SHOT AT!
DIDN'T HEAR A GODDAMNED THING--
IT WAS SILENCED! LOOK! LOOK AT THAT!
I'M SORRY, FOLKS, I DUNNO WHAT'S GOT INTO HER--

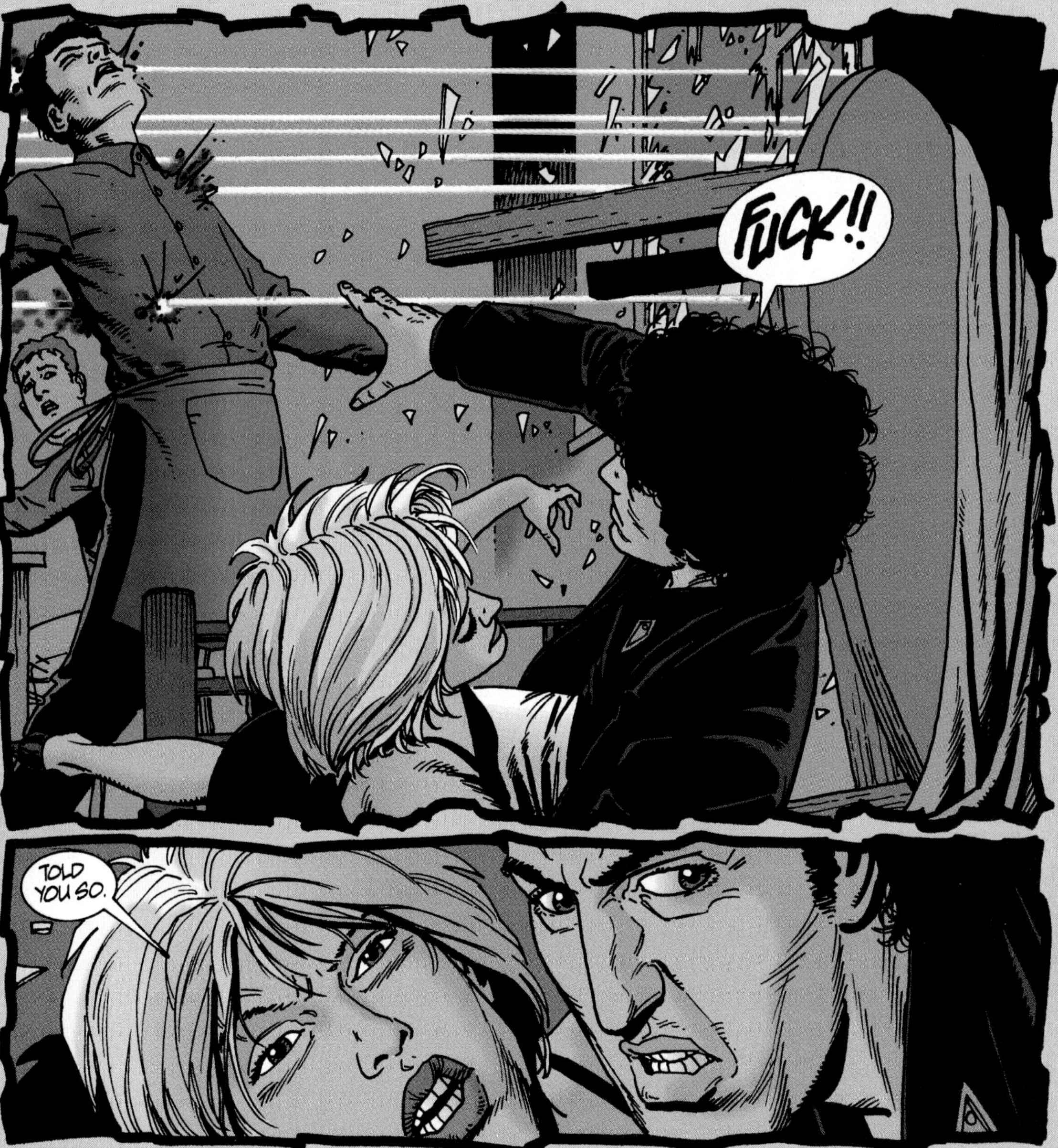
FUCK!!
TOLD YOU SO.

TOO MUCH GUN

GARTH ENNIS - Writer STEVE DILLON - Artist

MATT HOLLINGSWORTH - Colorist

CLEM ROBINS - Letterer AXEL ALONSO - Editor

PREACHER created by GARTH ENNIS and STEVE DILLON

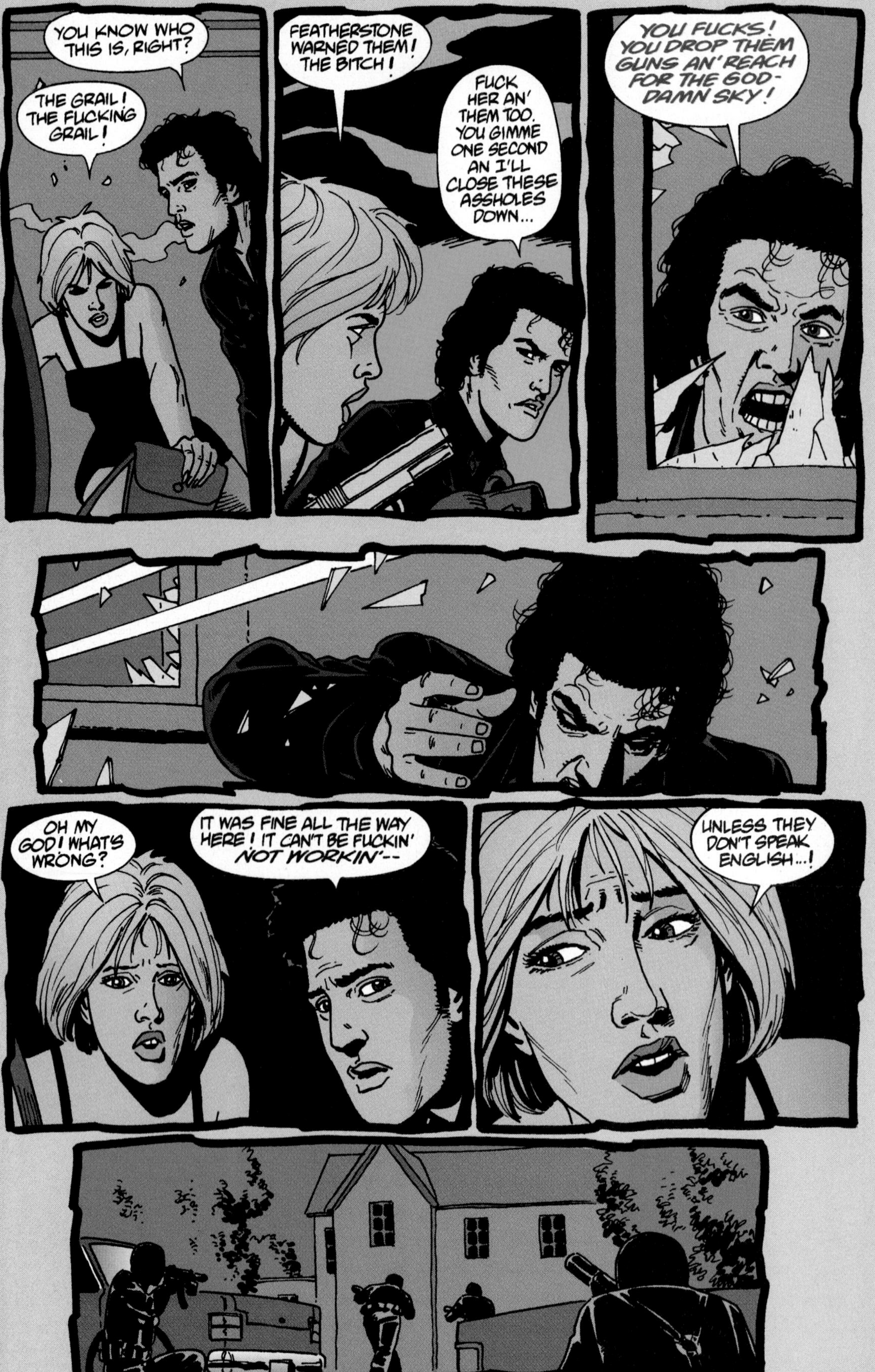
YOU KNOW WHO THIS IS, RIGHT?
THE GRAIL! THE FUCKING GRAIL!
FEATHERSTONE WARNED THEM! THE BITCH!
FUCK HER AN' THEM TOO. YOU GIMME ONE SECOND AN I'LL CLOSE THESE ASSHOLES DOWN...
YOU FUCKS! YOU DROP THEM GUNS AN' REACH FOR THE GOD-DAMN SKY!
OH MY GOD! WHAT'S WRONG?
IT WAS FINE ALL THE WAY HERE! IT CAN'T BE FUCKIN' *NOT WORKIN'*--
UNLESS THEY DON'T SPEAK ENGLISH...!

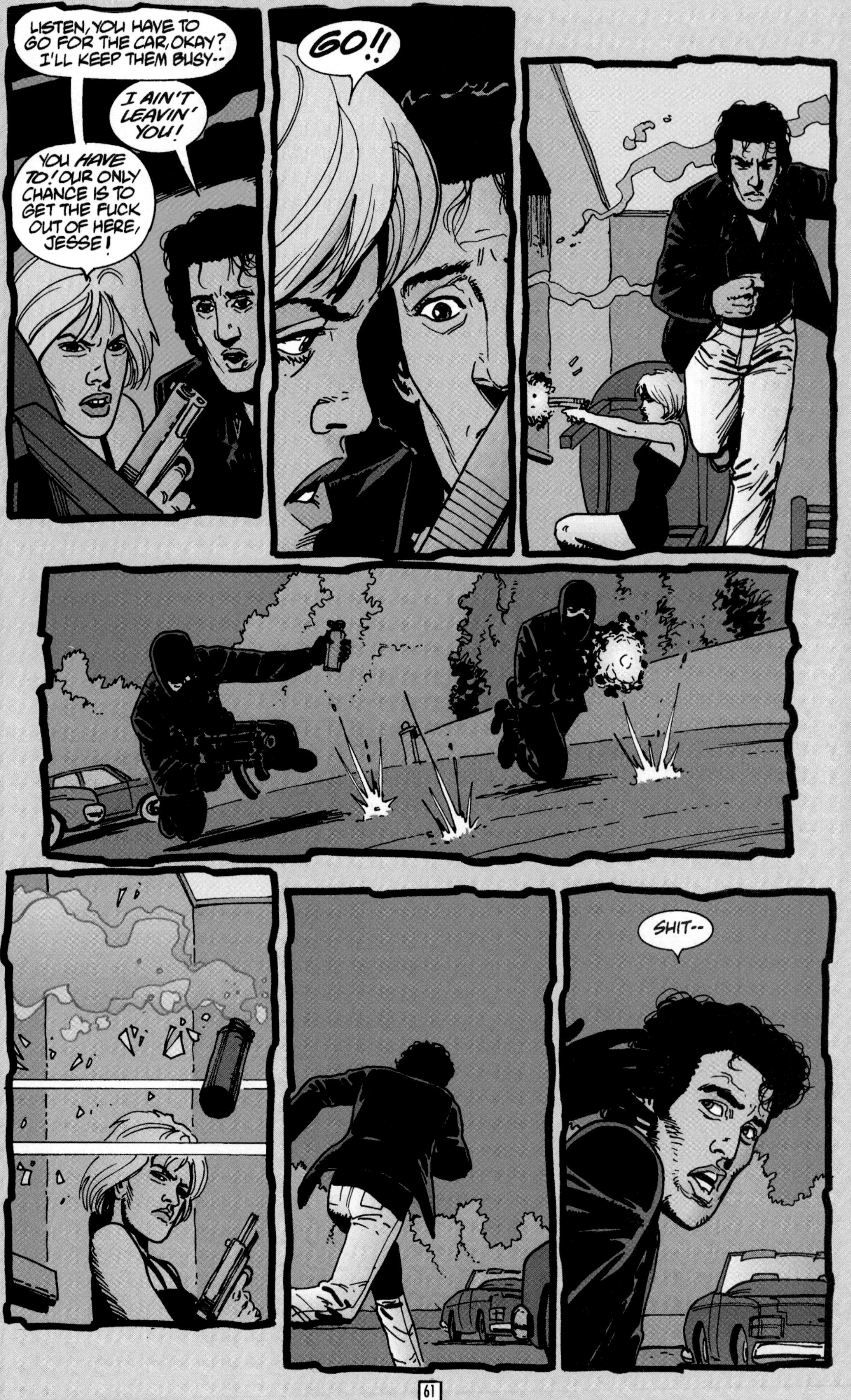
LISTEN, YOU HAVE TO GO FOR THE CAR, OKAY? I'LL KEEP THEM BUSY--
I AIN'T LEAVIN' YOU!
YOU HAVE TO! OUR ONLY CHANCE IS TO GET THE FUCK OUT OF HERE, JESSE!
GO!!
SHIT--

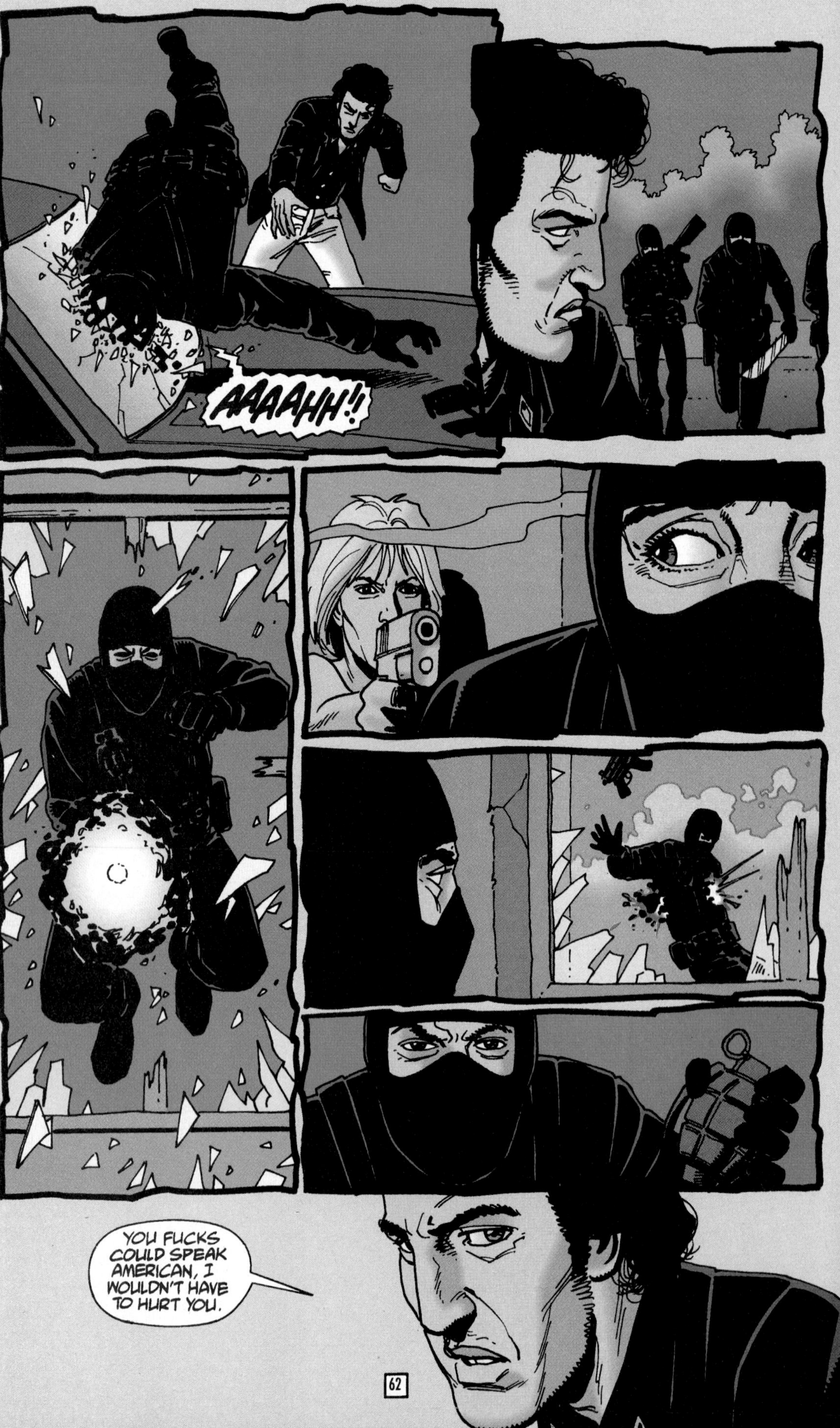
AAAAHH!!
YOU FUCKS COULD SPEAK AMERICAN, I WOULDN'T HAVE TO HURT YOU.

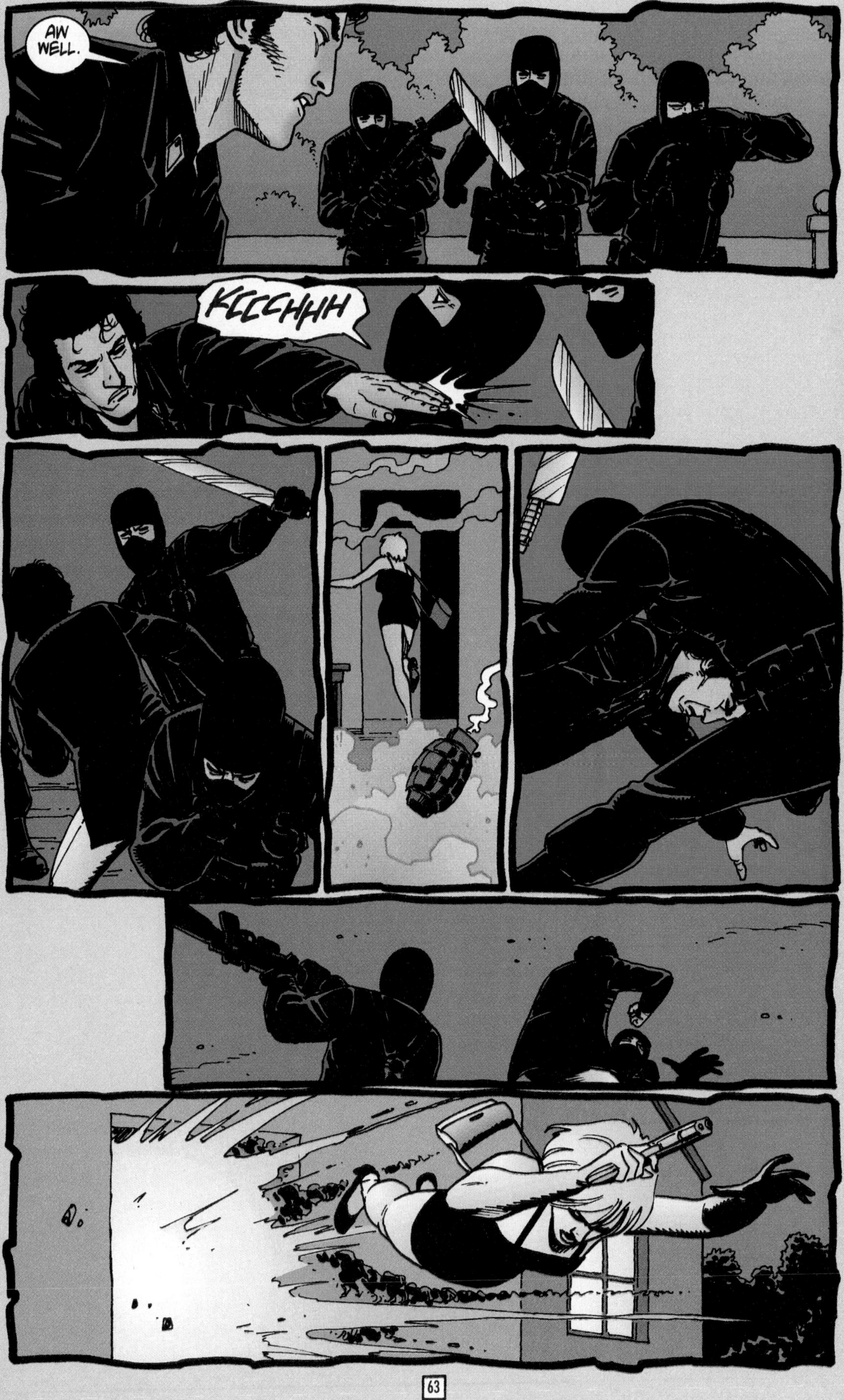
AW WELL.
KCCCHHH

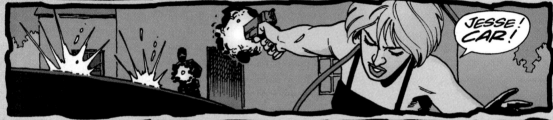

JESSE! CAR!

COMIN' NOW!

YEEEE AAGH!

GO!

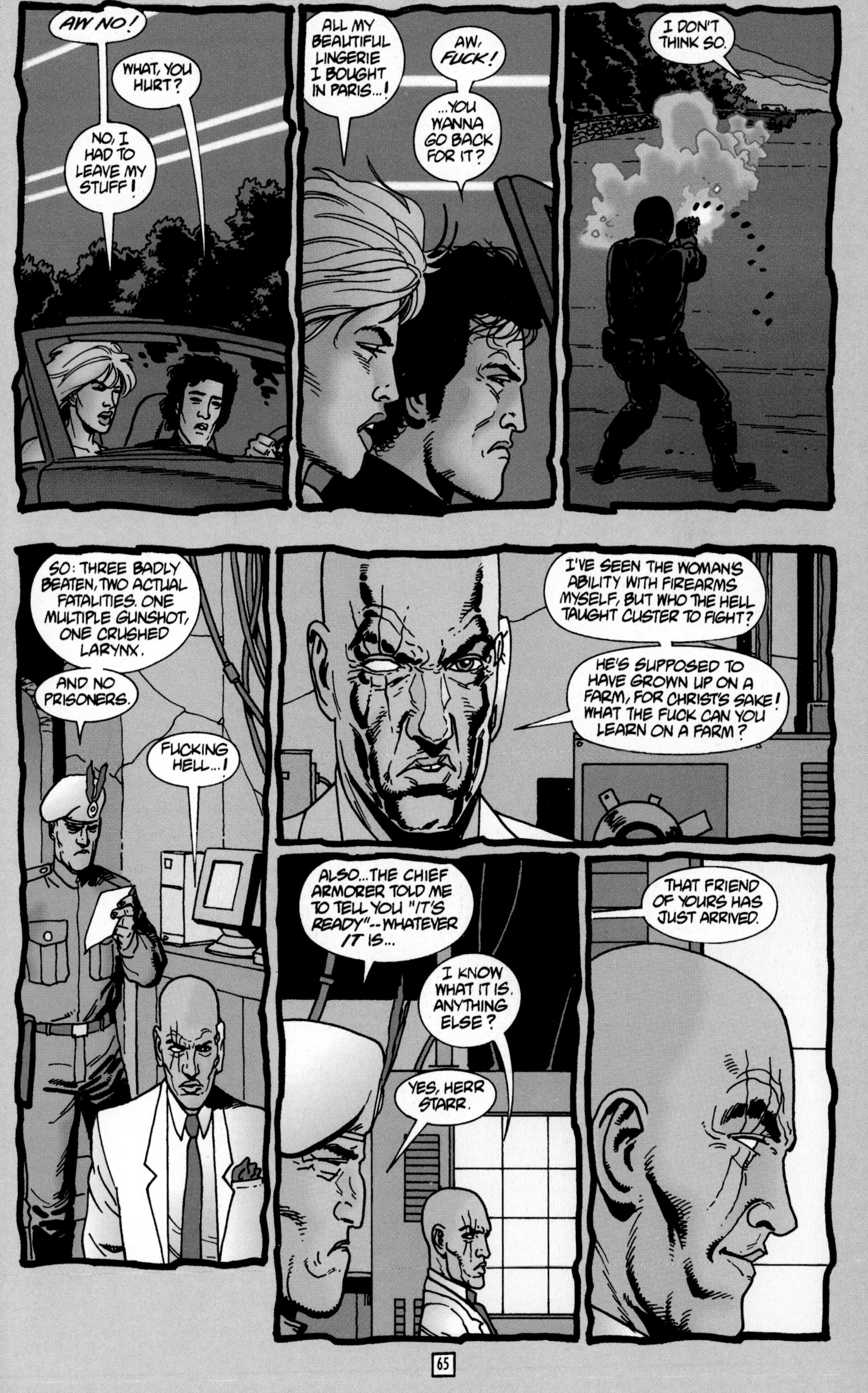
AW NO!
WHAT, YOU HURT?
NO, I HAD TO LEAVE MY STUFF!
ALL MY BEAUTIFUL LINGERIE I BOUGHT IN PARIS...!
AW, FUCK!
...YOU WANNA GO BACK FOR IT?
I DON'T THINK SO.
SO: THREE BADLY BEATEN, TWO ACTUAL FATALITIES. ONE MULTIPLE GUNSHOT, ONE CRUSHED LARYNX.
AND NO PRISONERS.
FUCKING HELL...!
I'VE SEEN THE WOMAN'S ABILITY WITH FIREARMS MYSELF, BUT WHO THE HELL TAUGHT CUSTER TO FIGHT?
HE'S SUPPOSED TO HAVE GROWN UP ON A FARM, FOR CHRIST'S SAKE! WHAT THE FUCK CAN YOU LEARN ON A FARM?
ALSO...THE CHIEF ARMORER TOLD ME TO TELL YOU "IT'S READY"--WHATEVER IT IS...
I KNOW WHAT IT IS. ANYTHING ELSE?
YES, HERR STARR.
THAT FRIEND OF YOURS HAS JUST ARRIVED.

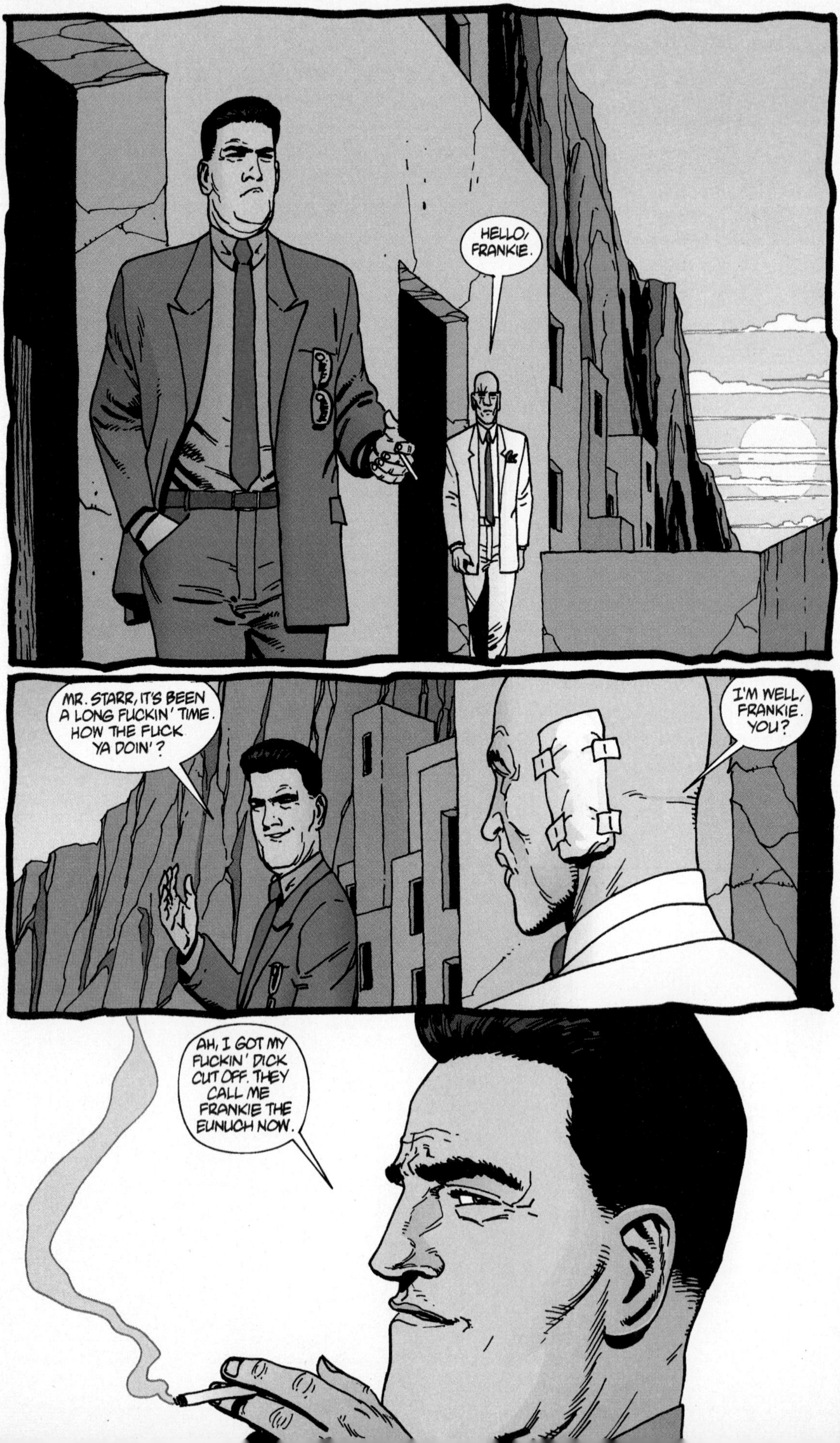
HELLO, FRANKIE.
MR. STARR, IT'S BEEN A LONG FUCKIN' TIME. HOW THE FUCK YA DOIN'?
I'M WELL, FRANKIE. YOU?
AH, I GOT MY FUCKIN' DICK CUT OFF. THEY CALL ME FRANKIE THE EUNUCH NOW.

I SEE...

YEAH, HOW ABOUT THAT, HUH? DON'T WORRY, I KNOW IT'S KIND OF A SHOCK. CAME AS A BIG FUCKIN' SHOCK TO ME, I TELL YA.

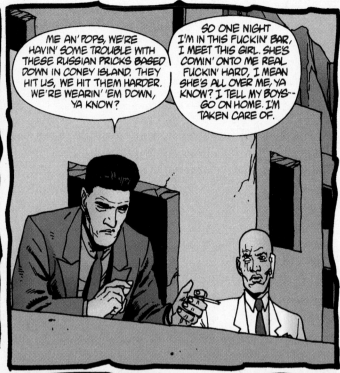

ME AN' POPS, WE'RE HAVIN' SOME TROUBLE WITH THESE RUSSIAN PRICKS BASED DOWN IN CONEY ISLAND. THEY HIT US, WE HIT THEM HARDER. WE'RE WEARIN' 'EM DOWN, YA KNOW?

SO ONE NIGHT I'M IN THIS FUCKIN' BAR, I MEET THIS GIRL. SHE'S COMIN' ONTO ME REAL FUCKIN' HARD, I MEAN SHE'S ALL OVER ME, YA KNOW? I TELL MY BOYS-- GO ON HOME. I'M TAKEN CARE OF.

NEVER A TRUER FUCKIN' WORD SPOKEN. WE GO BACK TO HER PLACE, SOME MOTHERFUCKER HITS ME WITH A TIRE IRON. LIGHTS OUT.

I WAKE UP TIED TO A CHAIR, NAKED AS THE DAY I WAS FUCKIN' BORN. THESE IVAN FUCKS ARE ALL AROUND ME. THEN THIS BIG ONE COMES OUT, GOT A BEARD, CRAZY FUCKIN' BIG LONG BEARD--WHAT YOU CALL THOSE RUSSIAN GUYS WITH BEARDS, SOUNDS KINDA LIKE COCKSUCKERS...?

COSSACKS?

COSSACKS, THAT'S RIGHT.

SO THIS GUY, THIS FUCKIN' COSSACK, HE GRINS AT ME AN' SAYS *FUCK YOUR YANKEE COCA-COLA, WE WIN THE COLD WAR.* ALL THESE OTHER FUCKS START LAUGHIN'.

THE COSSACK GETS OUT THIS PAIR OF FUCKIN' GARDENIN' SHEARS.

SNIP- SNIP.

FRANKIE THE EUNUCH.

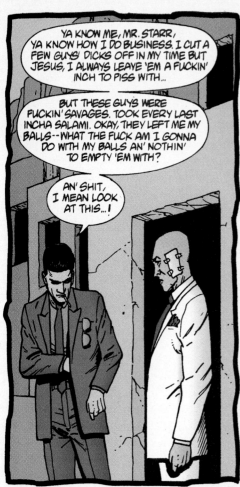

YA KNOW ME, MR. STARR, YA KNOW HOW I DO BUSINESS. I CUT A FEW GUYS' DICKS OFF IN MY TIME BUT JESUS, I ALWAYS LEAVE 'EM A FUCKIN' INCH TO PISS WITH...

BUT THESE GUYS WERE FUCKIN' SAVAGES. TOOK EVERY LAST INCHA SALAMI. OKAY, THEY LEFT ME MY BALLS--WHAT THE FUCK AM I GONNA DO WITH MY BALLS AN' NOTHIN' TO EMPTY 'EM WITH?

AN' SHIT, I MEAN LOOK AT THIS...!

WHAT THE FUCK IS THIS, HUH? I GOT THIS FUCKIN' BAG I GOTTA TAKE EVERYWHERE WITH ME. IT BURSTS, I RUIN MY SUIT, I...

YES...I ASSUME YOU AND THE DON EXACTED SUDDEN AND BLOODY VENGEANCE FOR THIS?

NO.

NO?

I GO TO SEE POPS AS SOON AS I GET OUTTA THE HOSPITAL. HE GIVES ME ALL THIS FUCKIN' BULLSHIT, YA KNOW? HOW THIS AIN'T THE TIME TO HIT THE IVANS, THEY'RE TOO STRONG, WE GOTTA WAIT...

I SAY POPS, COME ON. THINK WHAT YOU'RE FUCKIN' SAYIN' HERE. THE MOTHERFUCKERS CASTRATED ME. I DON'T GIVE A SHIT HOW STRONG THEY ARE, IF HULK FUCKIN' HOGAN CUT MY HOWITZER OFF I'D STILL BE OUT TO FUCK HIM UP...

SO YOU KNOW WHAT HE DOES THEN, MR. STARR?

I REALLY CAN'T IMAGINE.

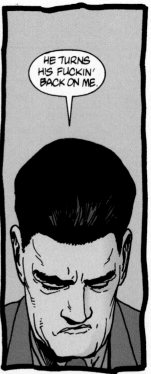

HE TURNS HIS FUCKIN' BACK ON ME.

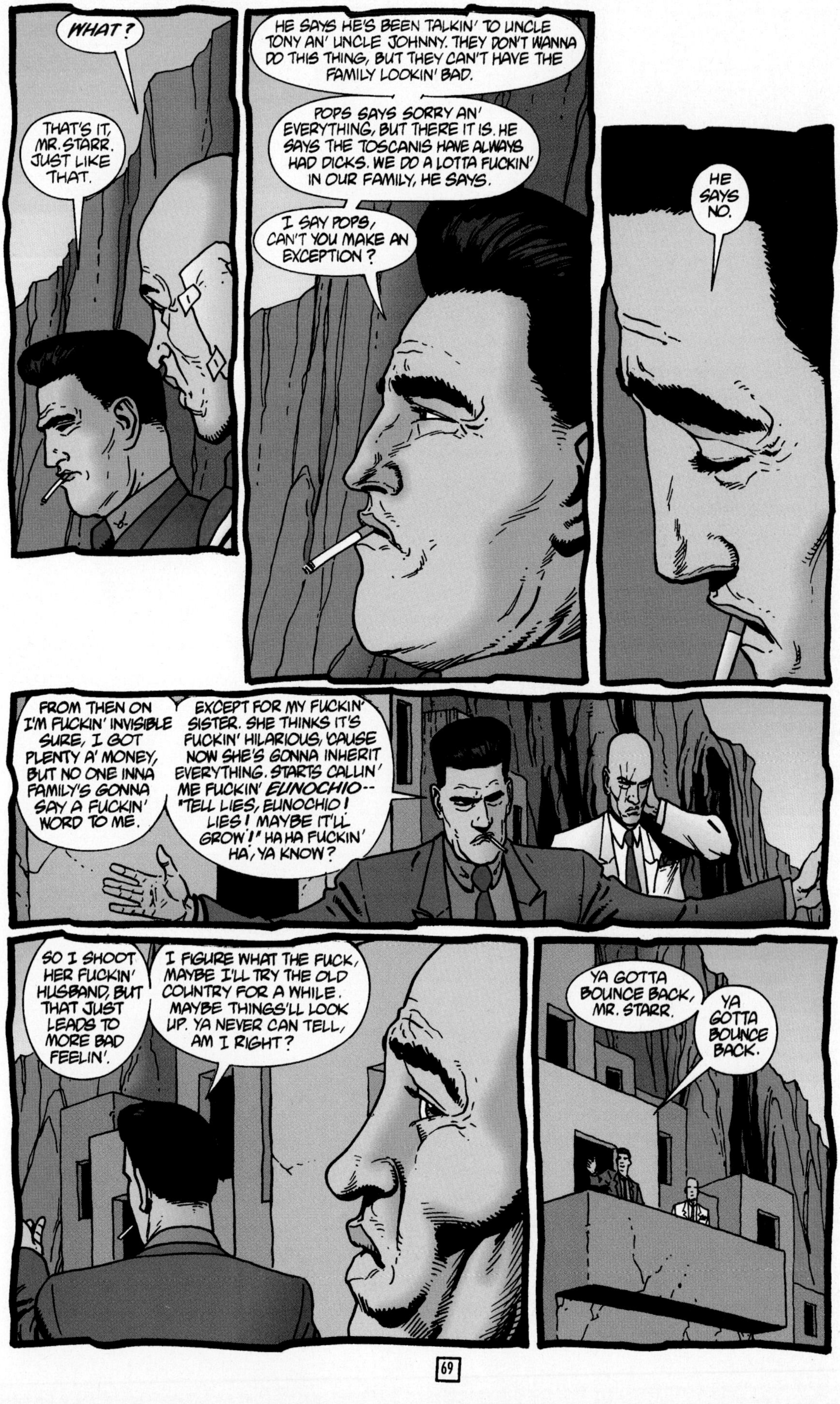
WHAT?
THAT'S IT, MR. STARR. JUST LIKE THAT.
HE SAYS HE'S BEEN TALKIN' TO UNCLE TONY AN' UNCLE JOHNNY. THEY DON'T WANNA DO THIS THING, BUT THEY CAN'T HAVE THE FAMILY LOOKIN' BAD.
POPS SAYS SORRY AN' EVERYTHING, BUT THERE IT IS. HE SAYS THE TOSCANIS HAVE ALWAYS HAD DICKS. WE DO A LOTTA FUCKIN' IN OUR FAMILY, HE SAYS.
I SAY POPS, CAN'T YOU MAKE AN EXCEPTION?
HE SAYS NO.
FROM THEN ON I'M FUCKIN' INVISIBLE SURE, I GOT PLENTY A' MONEY, BUT NO ONE INNA FAMILY'S GONNA SAY A FUCKIN' WORD TO ME.
EXCEPT FOR MY FUCKIN' SISTER. SHE THINKS IT'S FUCKIN' HILARIOUS, 'CAUSE NOW SHE'S GONNA INHERIT EVERYTHING. STARTS CALLIN' ME FUCKIN' *EUNOCHIO*-- "TELL LIES, EUNOCHIO! LIES! MAYBE IT'LL GROW!" HA HA FUCKIN' HA, YA KNOW?
SO I SHOOT HER FUCKIN' HUSBAND, BUT THAT JUST LEADS TO MORE BAD FEELIN'.
I FIGURE WHAT THE FUCK, MAYBE I'LL TRY THE OLD COUNTRY FOR A WHILE. MAYBE THINGS'LL LOOK UP. YA NEVER CAN TELL, AM I RIGHT?
YA GOTTA BOUNCE BACK, MR. STARR.
YA GOTTA BOUNCE BACK.

HMM.

...

SO WHAT'S THIS JOB YOU GOT FOR ME, HUH?

WELL, YOU'VE SEEN THE TAPE?

YEAH, I WATCHED IT ON THE HELICOPTER. YOU'VE GOT THIS FUCKIN' GUY IT'S IMPOSSIBLE TO KILL: YOU WANT ME TO KILL HIM?

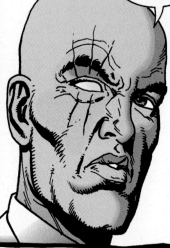

NOT RIGHT AWAY.

AS YOU'LL HAVE SEEN, THE CREATURE'S CAPABLE OF WITHSTANDING ENORMOUS PUNISHMENT, WHILE AT THE SAME TIME *REGENERATING* A CERTAIN AMOUNT OF DAMAGED TISSUE THROUGH CONSUMPTION OF--IN THIS INSTANCE--HUMAN BLOOD.

I WANT YOU TO USE THESE DEFENSIVE MECHANISMS AGAINST IT.

WE HAVE IT RESTRAINED IN A DEEP CELL. STARTING NOW, I WANT YOU TO KILL THAT BASTARD CREATION AS SLOWLY AS YOU CAN. I WANT YOU TO EMPLOY EVERY BIT OF THE SKILL AND INGENUITY THAT MADE FRANKIE TOSCANI A BYWORD FOR UNNECESSARILY PAINFUL DEATH.

WITH ITS CAPACITY TO SUSTAIN DAMAGE, I EXPECT YOU TO BE BUSY FOR A VERY LONG TIME.

AND SOMETHING TELLS ME YOU MIGHT HAVE A CERTAIN AMOUNT OF FRUSTRATION TO GET RID OF...

MR. STARR, I GOT A BIG BAG A' PISS IN MY POCKET, AN' WHENEVER I SEE A BEAUTIFUL GIRL I GET A FUNNY LITTLE ITCH WHERE I OUGHTA HAVE A TEN-INCH FUCKIN' BONER.

I THINK I GOT SOME FRUSTRATION TO GET RID OF, ALL RIGHT.

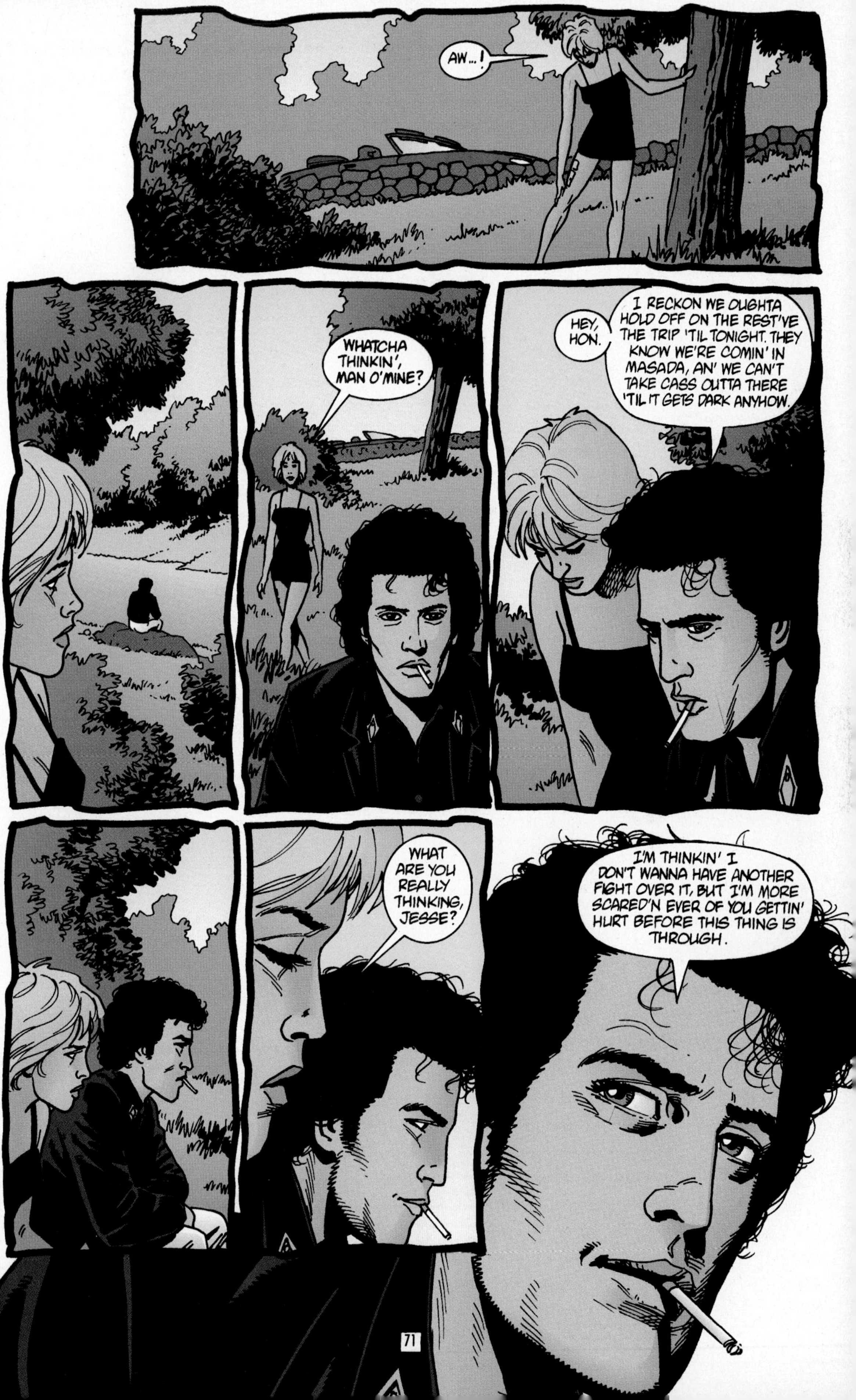
AW...!
WHATCHA THINKIN', MAN O'MINE?
HEY, HON.
I RECKON WE OUGHTA HOLD OFF ON THE REST'VE THE TRIP 'TIL TONIGHT. THEY KNOW WE'RE COMIN' IN MASADA, AN' WE CAN'T TAKE CASS OUTTA THERE 'TIL IT GETS DARK ANYHOW.
WHAT ARE YOU REALLY THINKING, JESSE?
I'M THINKIN' I DON'T WANNA HAVE ANOTHER FIGHT OVER IT, BUT I'M MORE SCARED'N EVER OF YOU GETTIN' HURT BEFORE THIS THING IS THROUGH.

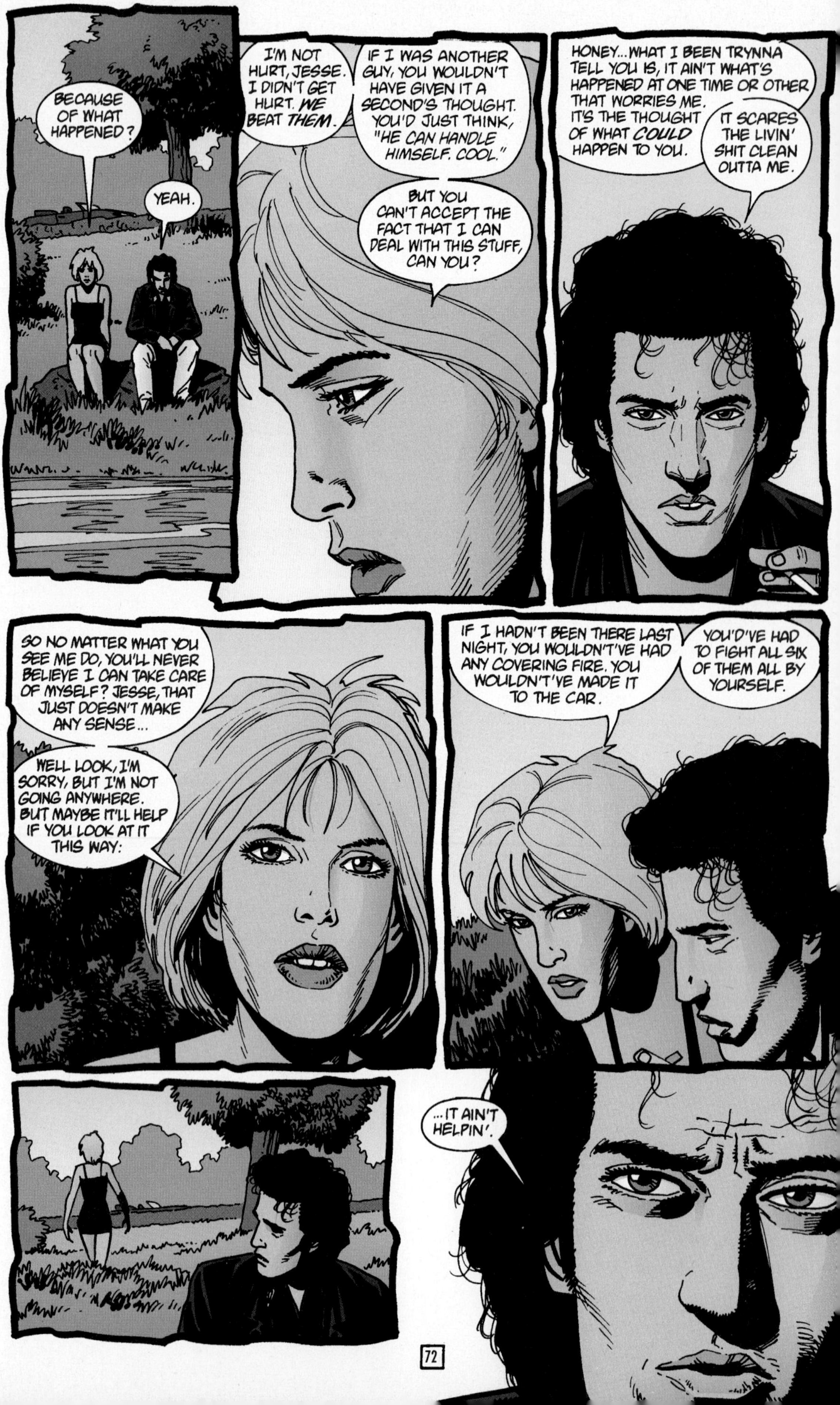
BECAUSE OF WHAT HAPPENED?
YEAH.
I'M NOT HURT, JESSE. I DIDN'T GET HURT. WE BEAT THEM.
IF I WAS ANOTHER GUY, YOU WOULDN'T HAVE GIVEN IT A SECOND'S THOUGHT. YOU'D JUST THINK, "HE CAN HANDLE HIMSELF. COOL."
BUT YOU CAN'T ACCEPT THE FACT THAT I CAN DEAL WITH THIS STUFF, CAN YOU?
HONEY... WHAT I BEEN TRYNNA TELL YOU IS, IT AIN'T WHAT'S HAPPENED AT ONE TIME OR OTHER THAT WORRIES ME. IT'S THE THOUGHT OF WHAT COULD HAPPEN TO YOU.
IT SCARES THE LIVIN' SHIT CLEAN OUTTA ME.
SO NO MATTER WHAT YOU SEE ME DO, YOU'LL NEVER BELIEVE I CAN TAKE CARE OF MYSELF? JESSE, THAT JUST DOESN'T MAKE ANY SENSE...
WELL LOOK, I'M SORRY, BUT I'M NOT GOING ANYWHERE. BUT MAYBE IT'LL HELP IF YOU LOOK AT IT THIS WAY:
IF I HADN'T BEEN THERE LAST NIGHT, YOU WOULDN'T'VE HAD ANY COVERING FIRE. YOU WOULDN'T'VE MADE IT TO THE CAR.
YOU'D'VE HAD TO FIGHT ALL SIX OF THEM ALL BY YOURSELF.
...IT AIN'T HELPIN'.

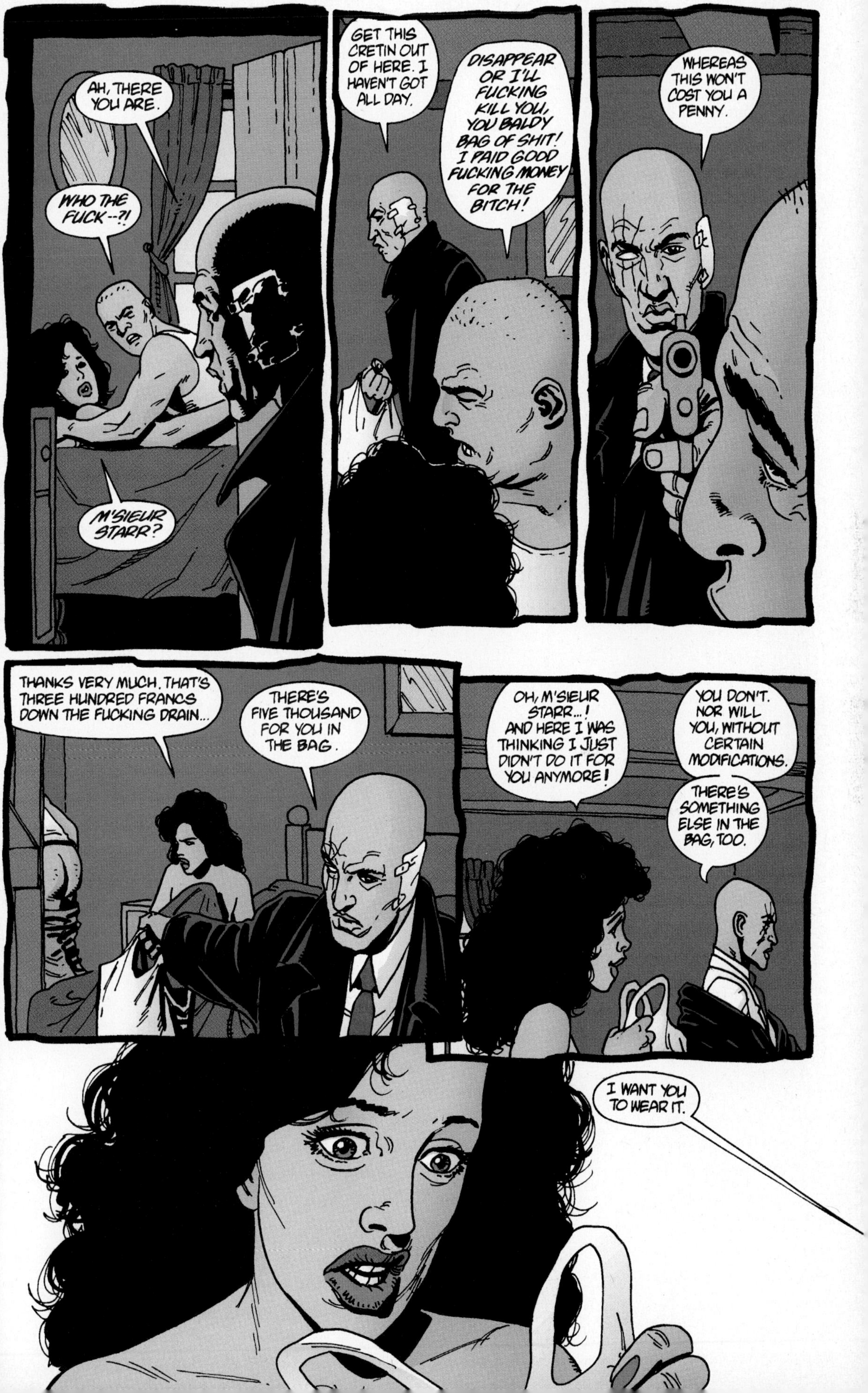
AH, THERE YOU ARE.
WHO THE FUCK--?!
M'SIEUR STARR?
GET THIS CRETIN OUT OF HERE. I HAVEN'T GOT ALL DAY.
DISAPPEAR OR I'LL FUCKING KILL YOU, YOU BALDY BAG OF SHIT! I PAID GOOD FUCKING MONEY FOR THE BITCH!
WHEREAS THIS WON'T COST YOU A PENNY.
THANKS VERY MUCH. THAT'S THREE HUNDRED FRANCS DOWN THE FUCKING DRAIN...
THERE'S FIVE THOUSAND FOR YOU IN THE BAG.
OH, M'SIEUR STARR...! AND HERE I WAS THINKING I JUST DIDN'T DO IT FOR YOU ANYMORE!
YOU DON'T. NOR WILL YOU, WITHOUT CERTAIN MODIFICATIONS.
THERE'S SOMETHING ELSE IN THE BAG, TOO.
I WANT YOU TO WEAR IT.

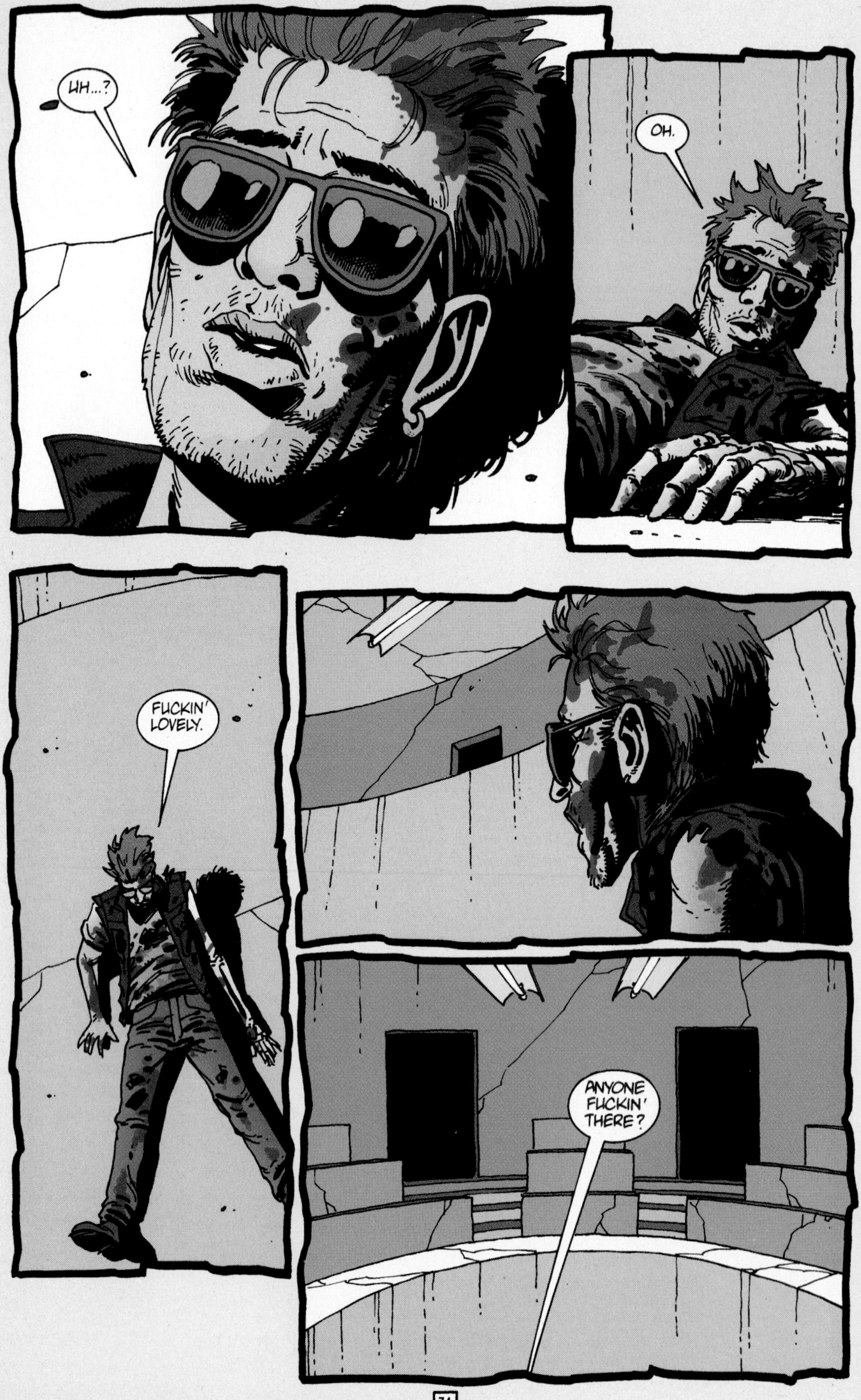
UH...?
OH.
FUCKIN' LOVELY.
ANYONE FUCKIN' THERE?

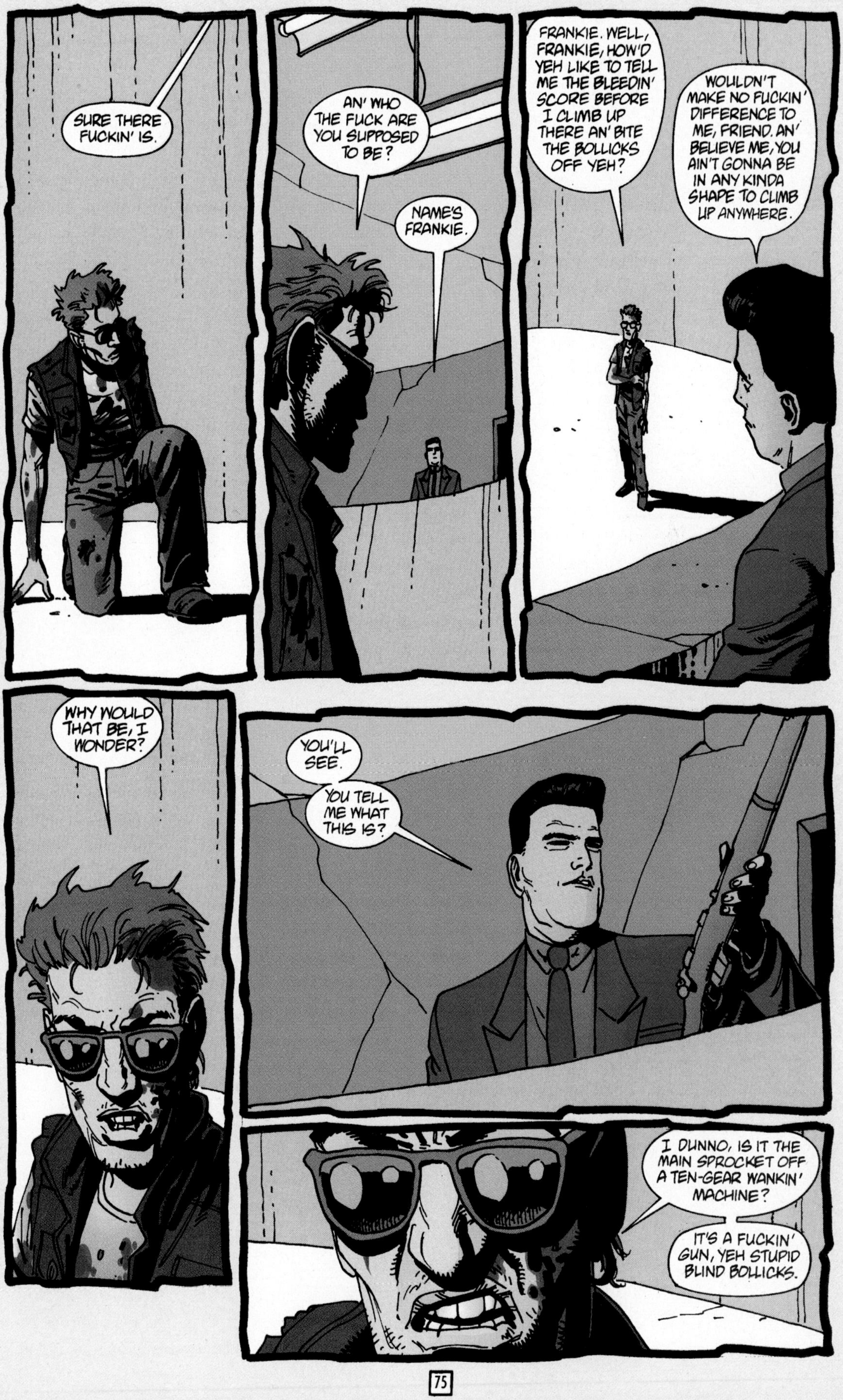
SURE THERE FUCKIN' IS.
AN' WHO THE FUCK ARE YOU SUPPOSED TO BE?
NAME'S FRANKIE.
FRANKIE. WELL, FRANKIE, HOW'D YEH LIKE TO TELL ME THE BLEEDIN' SCORE BEFORE I CLIMB UP THERE AN' BITE THE BOLLICKS OFF YEH?
WOULDN'T MAKE NO FUCKIN' DIFFERENCE TO ME, FRIEND. AN' BELIEVE ME, YOU AIN'T GONNA BE IN ANY KINDA SHAPE TO CLIMB UP ANYWHERE.
WHY WOULD THAT BE, I WONDER?
YOU'LL SEE.
YOU TELL ME WHAT THIS IS?
I DUNNO, IS IT THE MAIN SPROCKET OFF A TEN-GEAR WANKIN' MACHINE?
IT'S A FUCKIN' GUN, YEH STUPID BLIND BOLLICKS.

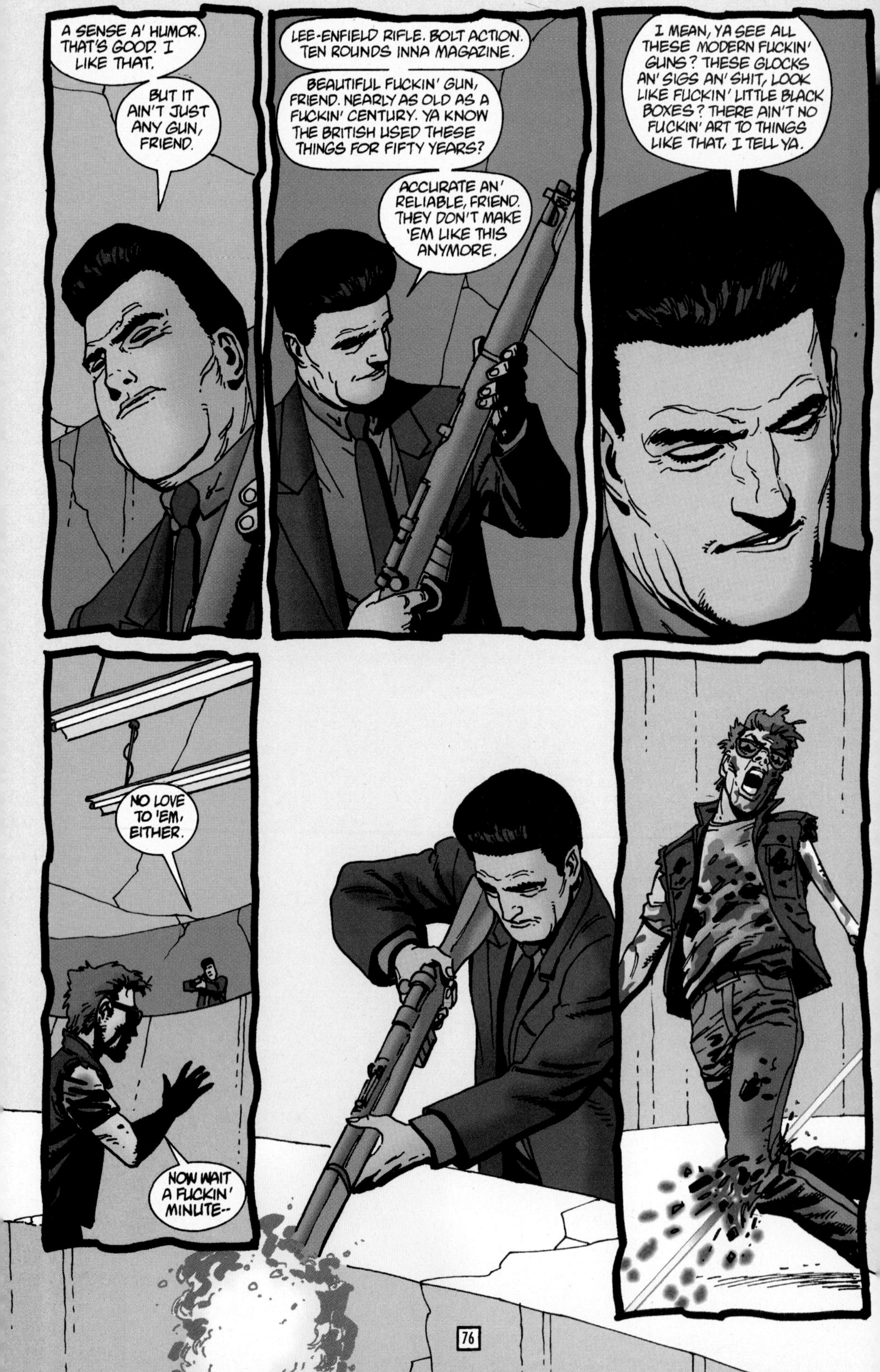
A SENSE A' HUMOR. THAT'S GOOD. I LIKE THAT.
BUT IT AIN'T JUST ANY GUN, FRIEND.
LEE-ENFIELD RIFLE. BOLT ACTION. TEN ROUNDS INNA MAGAZINE.
BEAUTIFUL FUCKIN' GUN, FRIEND. NEARLY AS OLD AS A FUCKIN' CENTURY. YA KNOW THE BRITISH USED THESE THINGS FOR FIFTY YEARS?
ACCURATE AN' RELIABLE, FRIEND. THEY DON'T MAKE 'EM LIKE THIS ANYMORE.
I MEAN, YA SEE ALL THESE MODERN FUCKIN' GUNS? THESE GLOCKS AN' SIGS AN' SHIT, LOOK LIKE FUCKIN' LITTLE BLACK BOXES? THERE AIN'T NO FUCKIN' ART TO THINGS LIKE THAT, I TELL YA.
NO LOVE TO 'EM, EITHER.
NOW WAIT A FUCKIN' MINUTE--

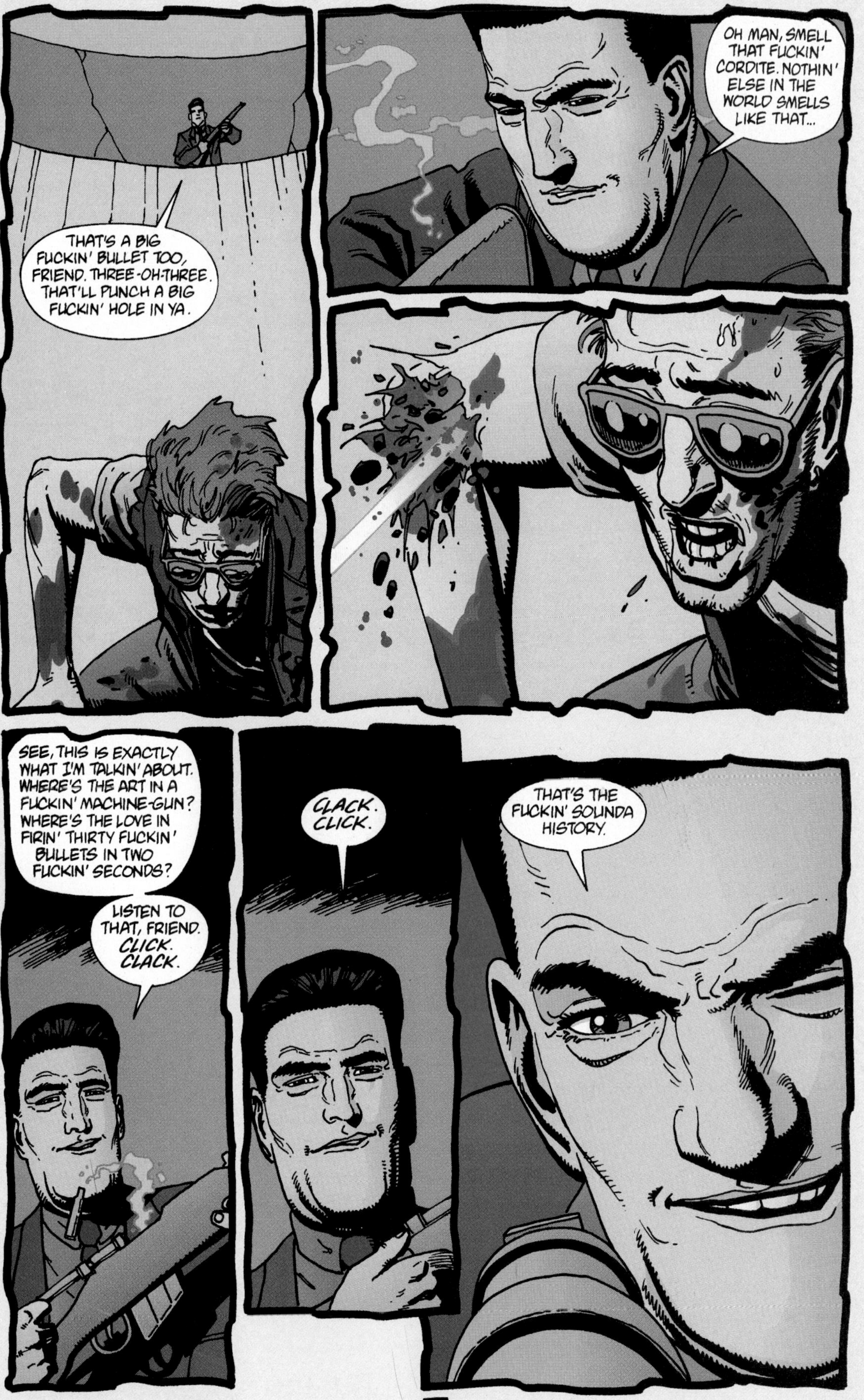
THAT'S A BIG FUCKIN' BULLET TOO, FRIEND. THREE-OH-THREE. THAT'LL PUNCH A BIG FUCKIN' HOLE IN YA.
OH MAN, SMELL THAT FUCKIN' CORDITE. NOTHIN' ELSE IN THE WORLD SMELLS LIKE THAT...
SEE, THIS IS EXACTLY WHAT I'M TALKIN' ABOUT. WHERE'S THE ART IN A FUCKIN' MACHINE-GUN? WHERE'S THE LOVE IN FIRIN' THIRTY FUCKIN' BULLETS IN TWO FUCKIN' SECONDS?
LISTEN TO THAT, FRIEND. *CLICK. CLACK.*
CLACK. CLICK.
THAT'S THE FUCKIN' SOUNDA HISTORY.

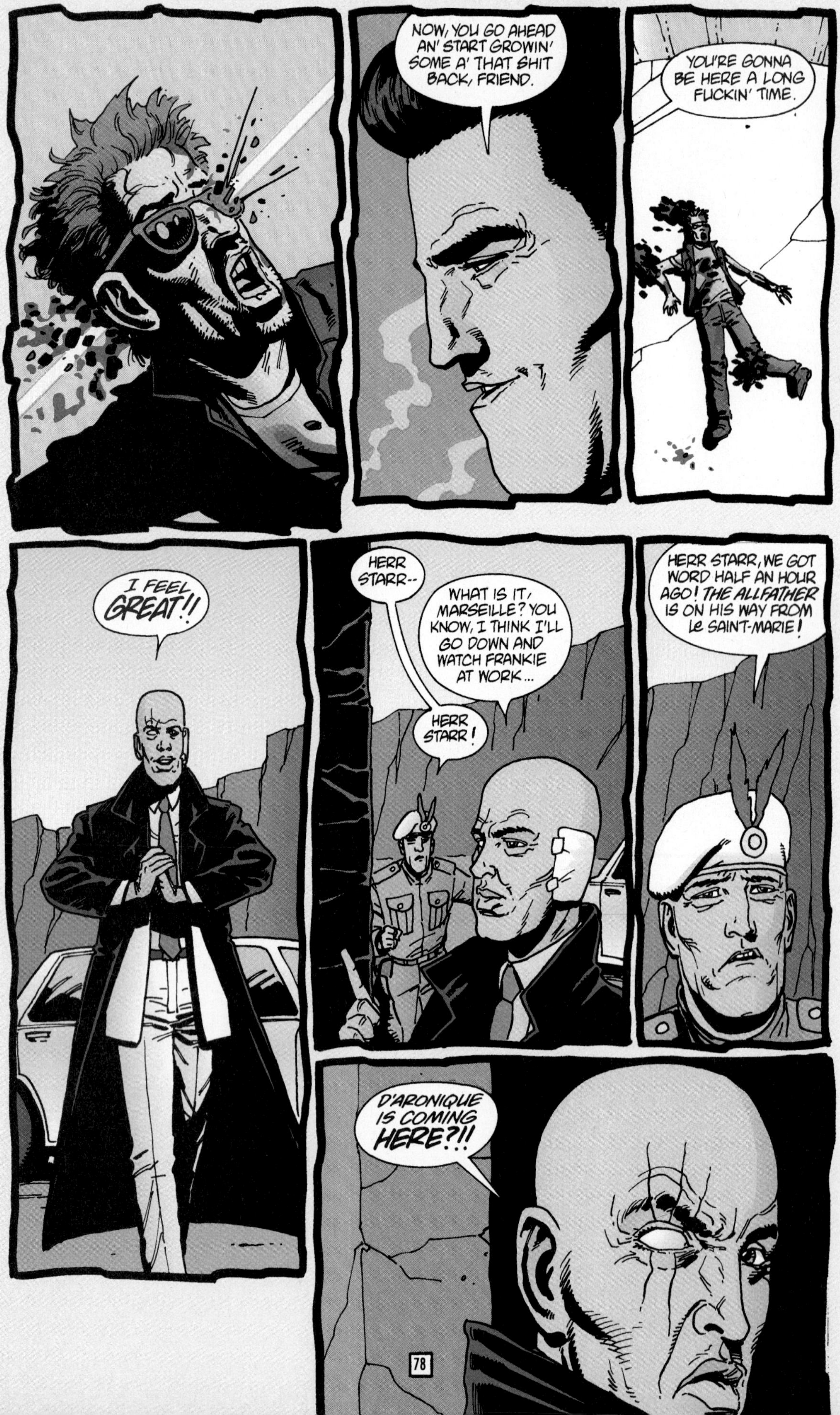
NOW, YOU GO AHEAD AN' START GROWIN' SOME A' THAT SHIT BACK, FRIEND.
YOU'RE GONNA BE HERE A LONG FUCKIN' TIME.
I FEEL GREAT!!
HERR STARR--
WHAT IS IT, MARSEILLE? YOU KNOW, I THINK I'LL GO DOWN AND WATCH FRANKIE AT WORK...
HERR STARR!
HERR STARR, WE GOT WORD HALF AN HOUR AGO! THE ALLFATHER IS ON HIS WAY FROM le SAINT-MARIE!
D'ARONIQUE IS COMING HERE?!!

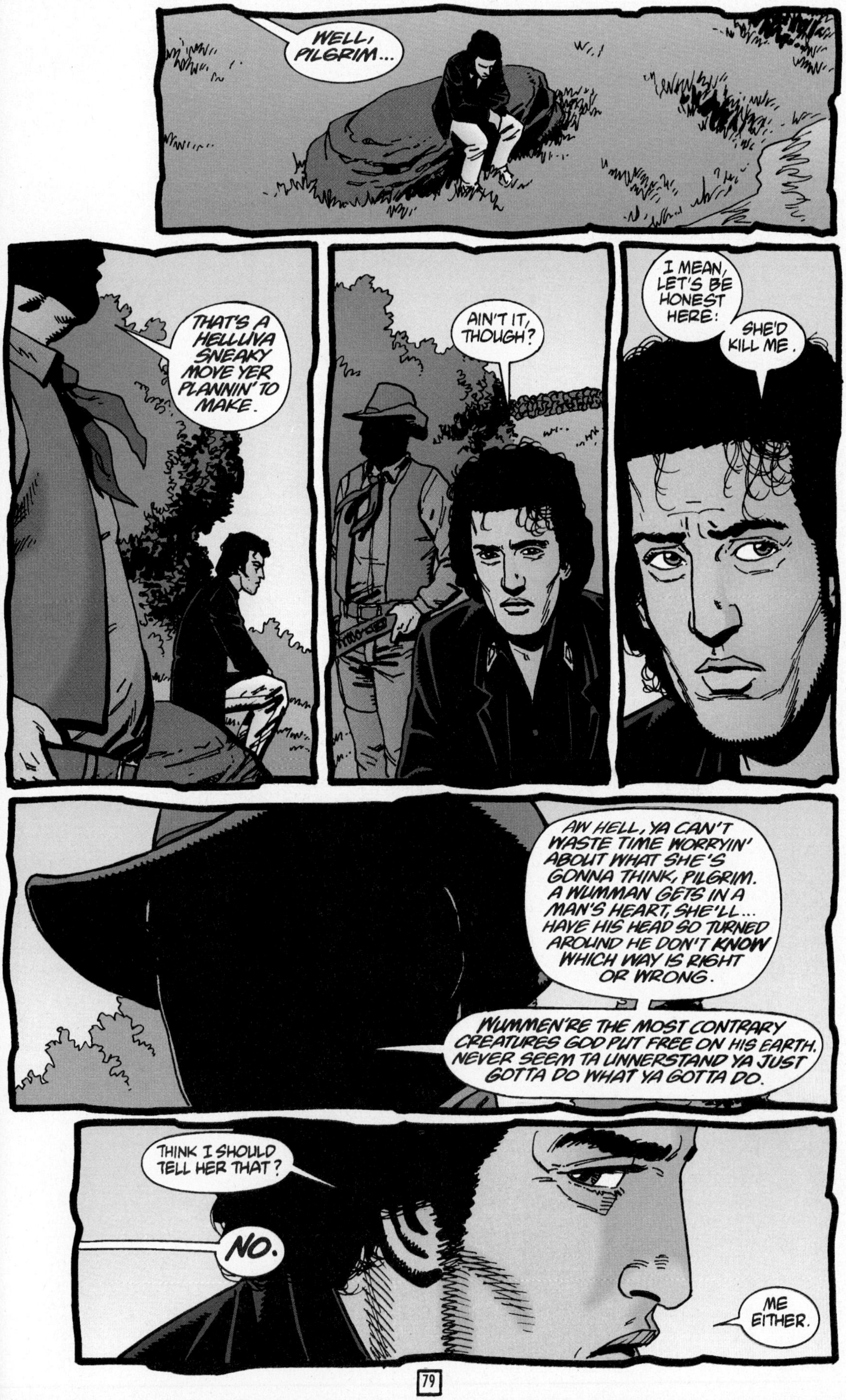
WELL, PILGRIM...
THAT'S A HELLUVA SNEAKY MOVE YER PLANNIN' TO MAKE.
AIN'T IT, THOUGH?
I MEAN, LET'S BE HONEST HERE:
SHE'D KILL ME.
AW HELL, YA CAN'T WASTE TIME WORRYIN' ABOUT WHAT SHE'S GONNA THINK, PILGRIM. A WUMMAN GETS IN A MAN'S HEART, SHE'LL... HAVE HIS HEAD SO TURNED AROUND HE DON'T KNOW WHICH WAY IS RIGHT OR WRONG.
WUMMEN'RE THE MOST CONTRARY CREATURES GOD PUT FREE ON HIS EARTH. NEVER SEEM TA UNNERSTAND YA JUST GOTTA DO WHAT YA GOTTA DO.
THINK I SHOULD TELL HER THAT?
NO.
ME EITHER.

AND DON'T BE SURPRISED IF I LOVE YOU, FOR ALL THAT ♪ YOU ARE... ♪

I COULDN'T HELP IT...♪

IT'S ALL YOUR FAU-UUULLT...♪

MM--TROUBLE IS, SHE'S GOT A POINT. IT AIN'T RIGHT FOR ME TO BE THIS WAY WITH HER.

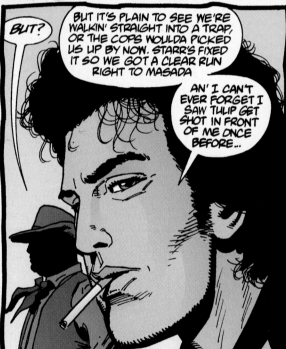

BUT?

BUT IT'S PLAIN TO SEE WE'RE WALKIN' STRAIGHT INTO A TRAP, OR THE COPS WOULDA PICKED US UP BY NOW. STARR'S FIXED IT SO WE GOT A CLEAR RUN RIGHT TO MASADA

AN' I CAN'T EVER FORGET I SAW TULIP GET SHOT IN FRONT OF ME ONCE BEFORE...

AN' SEEIN' THAT WAS LIKE SEEIN' THE GOOD GO OUTTA THE WORLD FOREVER.

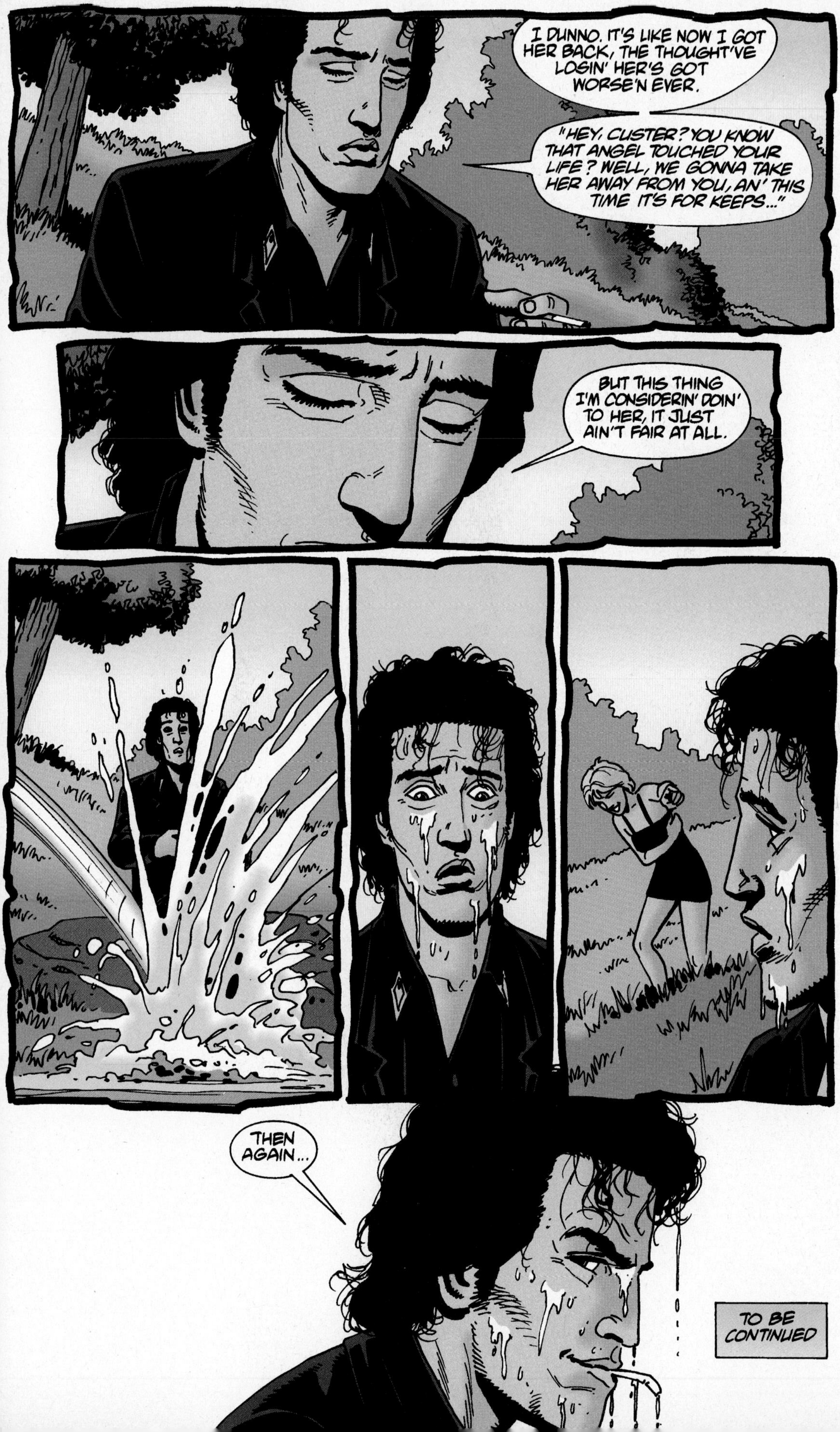
I DUNNO. IT'S LIKE NOW I GOT HER BACK, THE THOUGHT'VE LOSIN' HER'S GOT WORSE'N EVER.
"HEY, CUSTER? YOU KNOW THAT ANGEL TOUCHED YOUR LIFE? WELL, WE GONNA TAKE HER AWAY FROM YOU, AN' THIS TIME IT'S FOR KEEPS..."
BUT THIS THING I'M CONSIDERIN' DOIN' TO HER, IT JUST AIN'T FAIR AT ALL.
THEN AGAIN...
TO BE CONTINUED

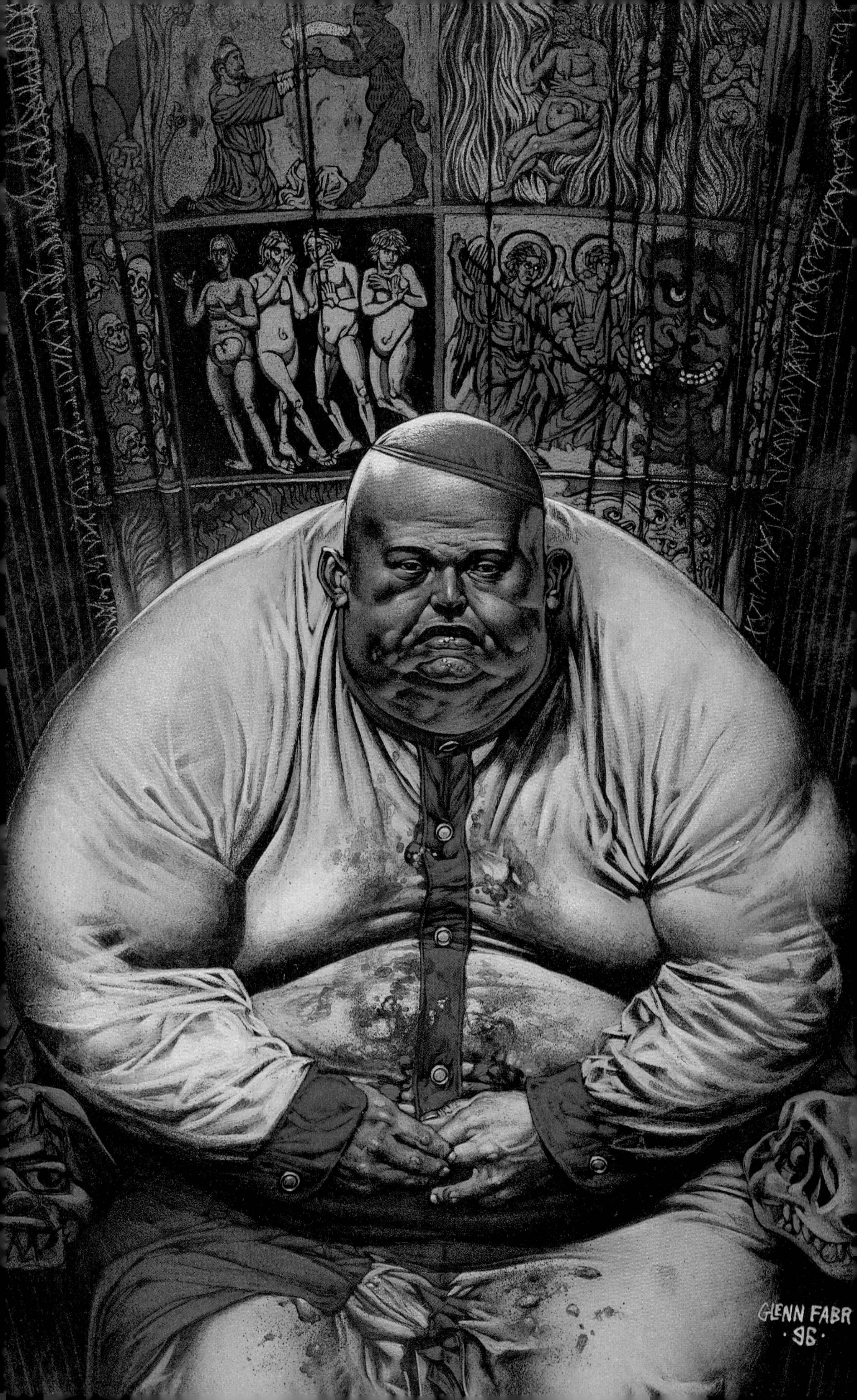
GLENN FABR
·96·

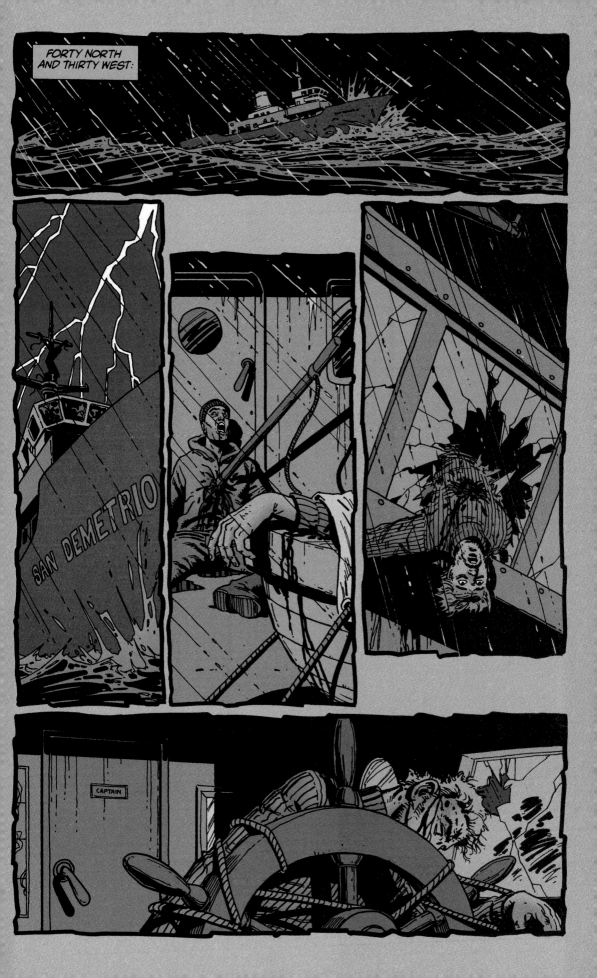

FORTY NORTH
AND THIRTY WEST:

SAN DEMETRIO

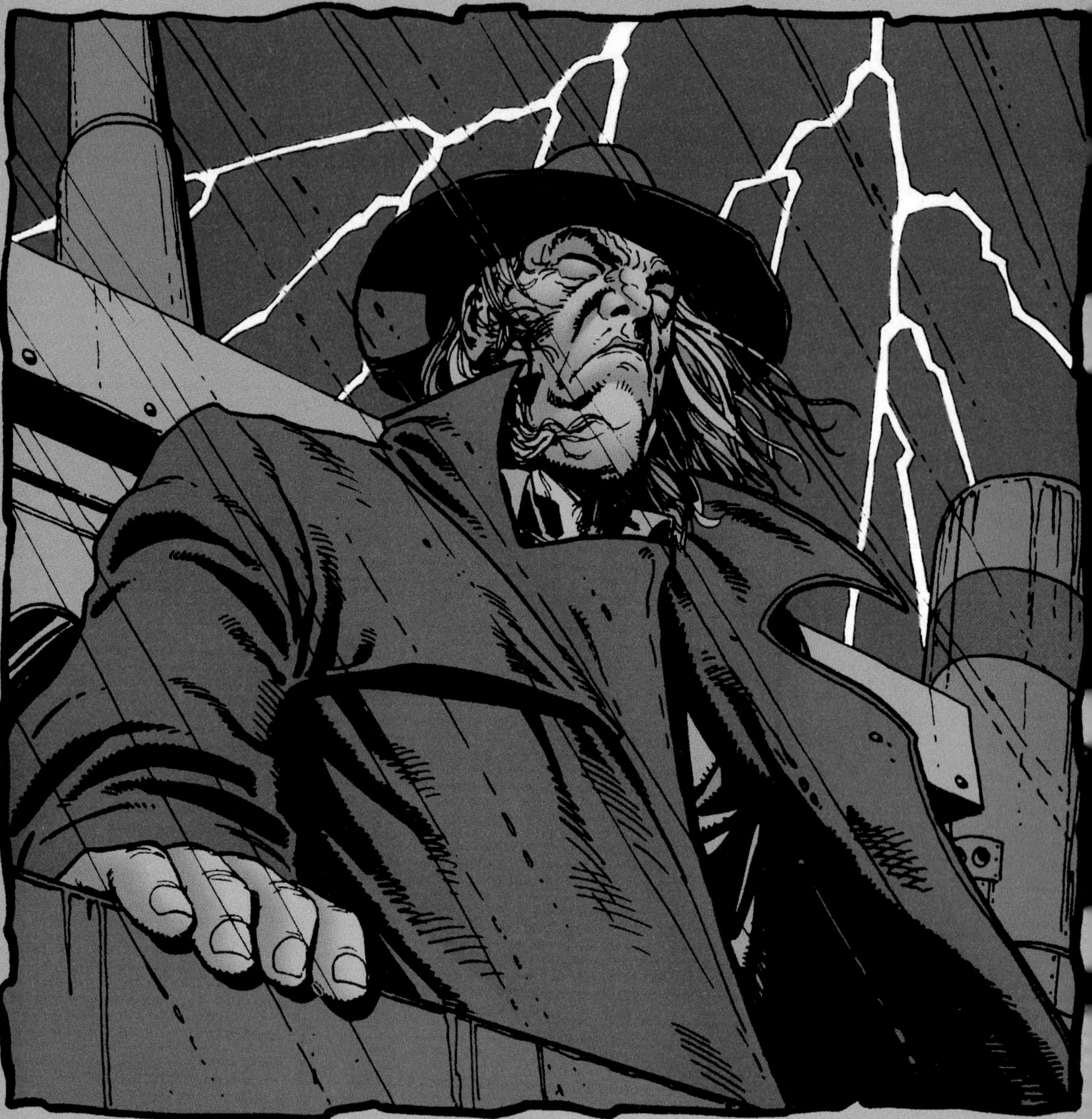

STORMBRINGERS

GARTH ENNIS - Writer STEVE DILLON - Artist
PAMELA RAMBO - Guest Colorist
CLEM ROBINS - Letterer AXEL ALONSO - Editor

PREACHER created by GARTH ENNIS and STEVE DILLON

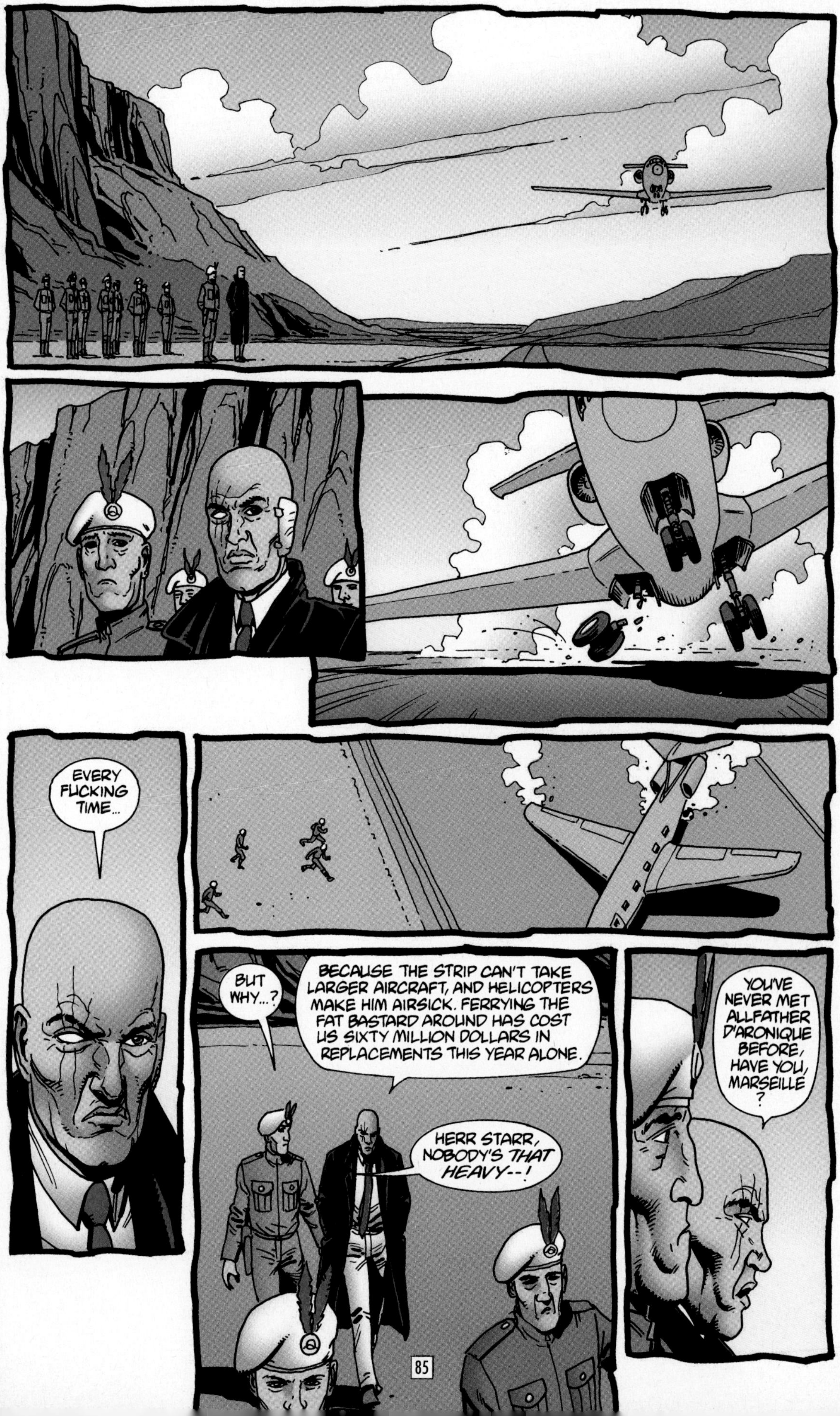
EVERY FUCKING TIME...
BUT WHY...?
BECAUSE THE STRIP CAN'T TAKE LARGER AIRCRAFT, AND HELICOPTERS MAKE HIM AIRSICK. FERRYING THE FAT BASTARD AROUND HAS COST US SIXTY MILLION DOLLARS IN REPLACEMENTS THIS YEAR ALONE.
HERR STARR, NOBODY'S *THAT HEAVY*--!
YOU'VE NEVER MET ALLFATHER D'ARONIQUE BEFORE, HAVE YOU, MARSEILLE?

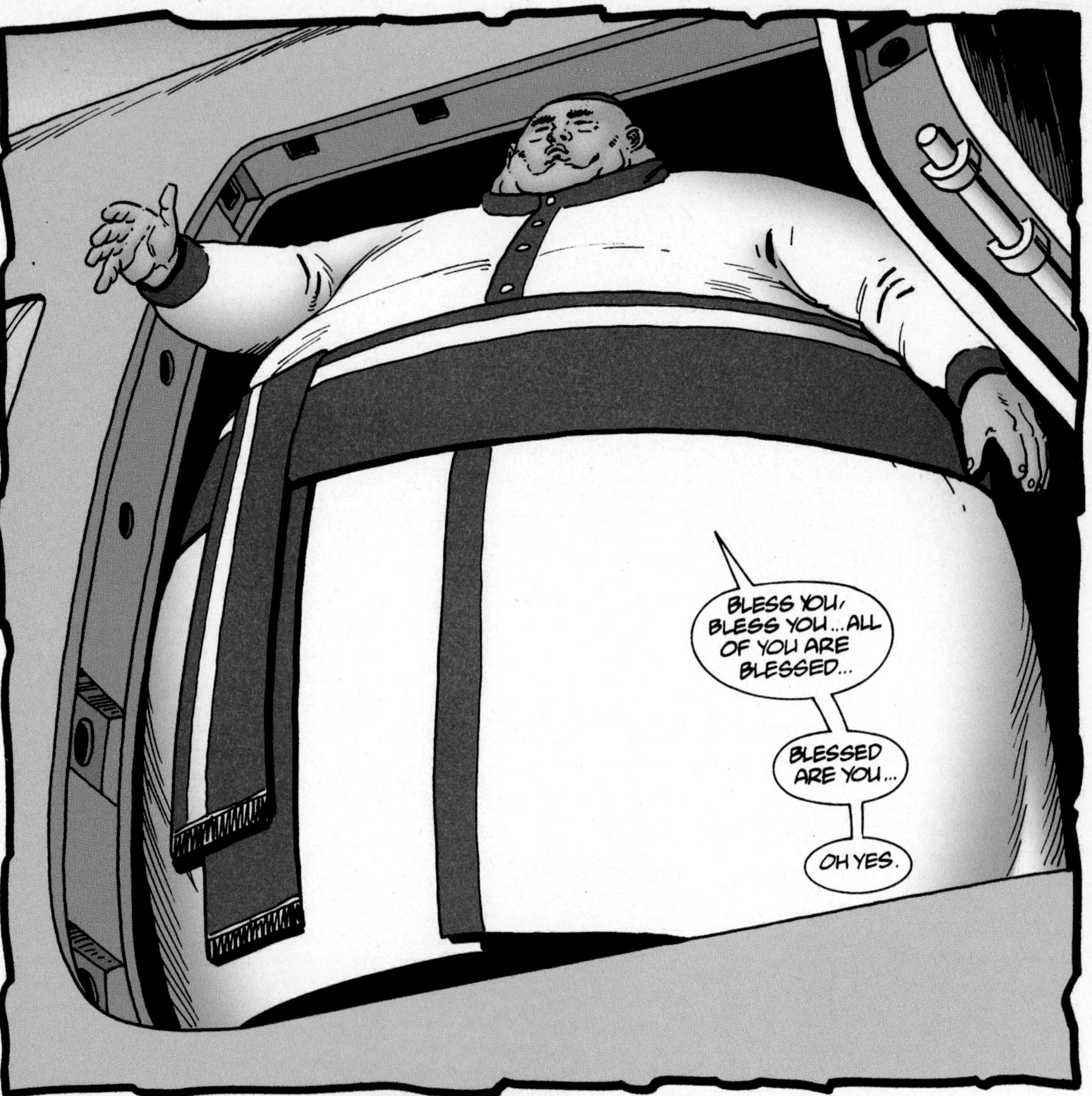
BLESS YOU, BLESS YOU...ALL OF YOU ARE BLESSED...
BLESSED ARE YOU...
OH YES.

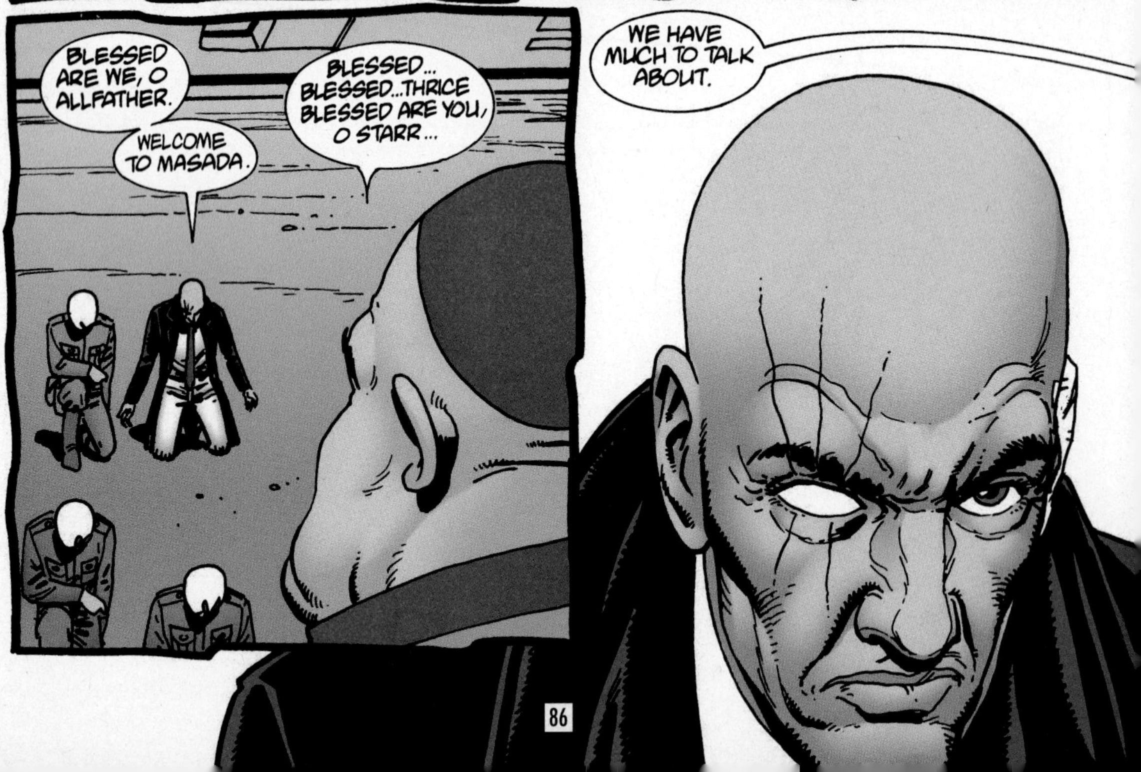
BLESSED ARE WE, O ALLFATHER.
WELCOME TO MASADA.
BLESSED... BLESSED...THRICE BLESSED ARE YOU, O STARR...
WE HAVE MUCH TO TALK ABOUT.

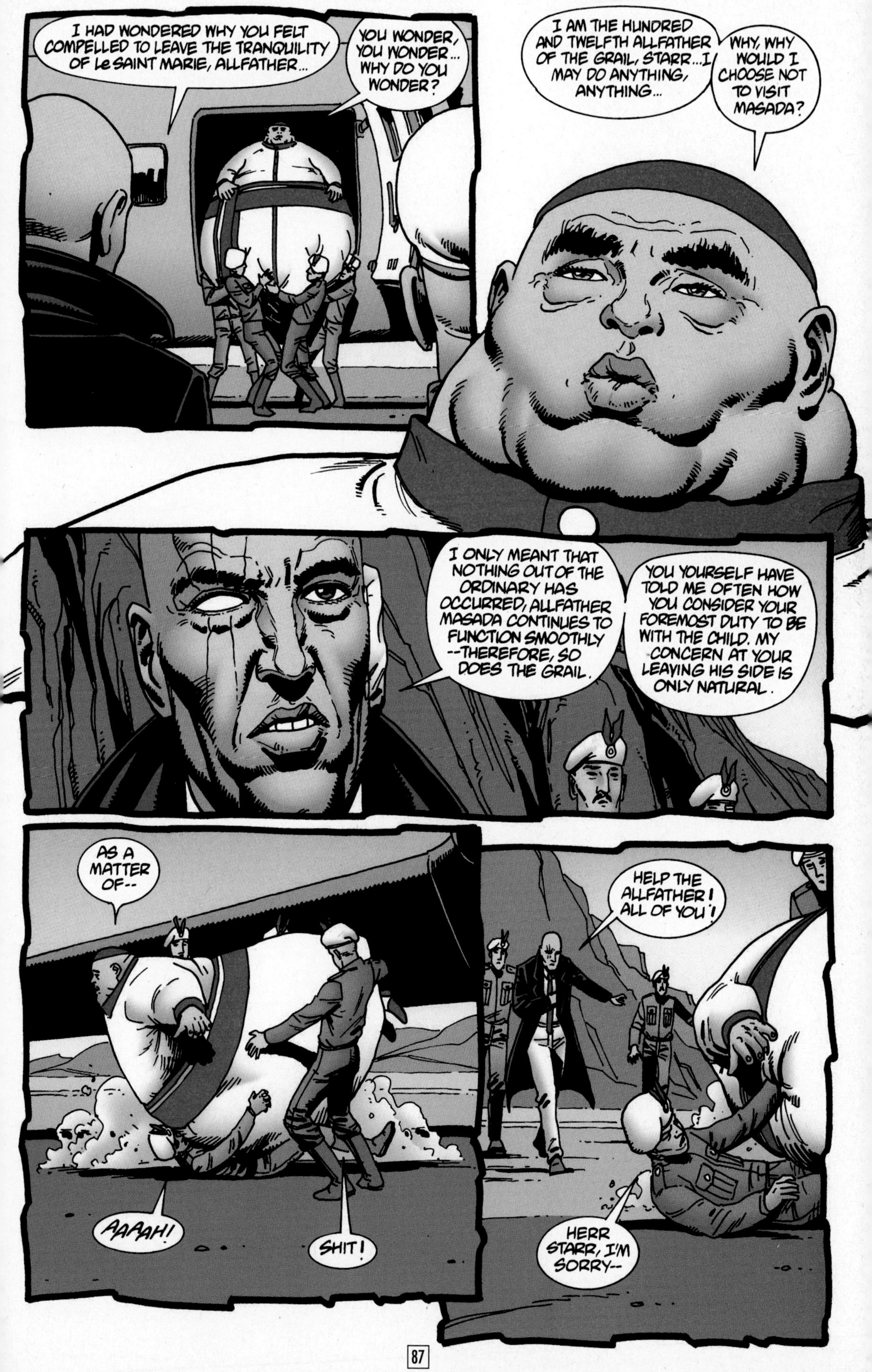

I HAD WONDERED WHY YOU FELT COMPELLED TO LEAVE THE TRANQUILITY OF Le SAINT MARIE, ALLFATHER...
YOU WONDER, YOU WONDER... WHY DO YOU WONDER?
I AM THE HUNDRED AND TWELFTH ALLFATHER OF THE GRAIL, STARR...I MAY DO ANYTHING, ANYTHING...
WHY, WHY WOULD I CHOOSE NOT TO VISIT MASADA?
I ONLY MEANT THAT NOTHING OUT OF THE ORDINARY HAS OCCURRED, ALLFATHER. MASADA CONTINUES TO FUNCTION SMOOTHLY --THEREFORE, SO DOES THE GRAIL.
YOU YOURSELF HAVE TOLD ME OFTEN HOW YOU CONSIDER YOUR FOREMOST DUTY TO BE WITH THE CHILD. MY CONCERN AT YOUR LEAVING HIS SIDE IS ONLY NATURAL.
AS A MATTER OF--
AAAAH!
SHIT!
HELP THE ALLFATHER! ALL OF YOU!
HERR STARR, I'M SORRY--

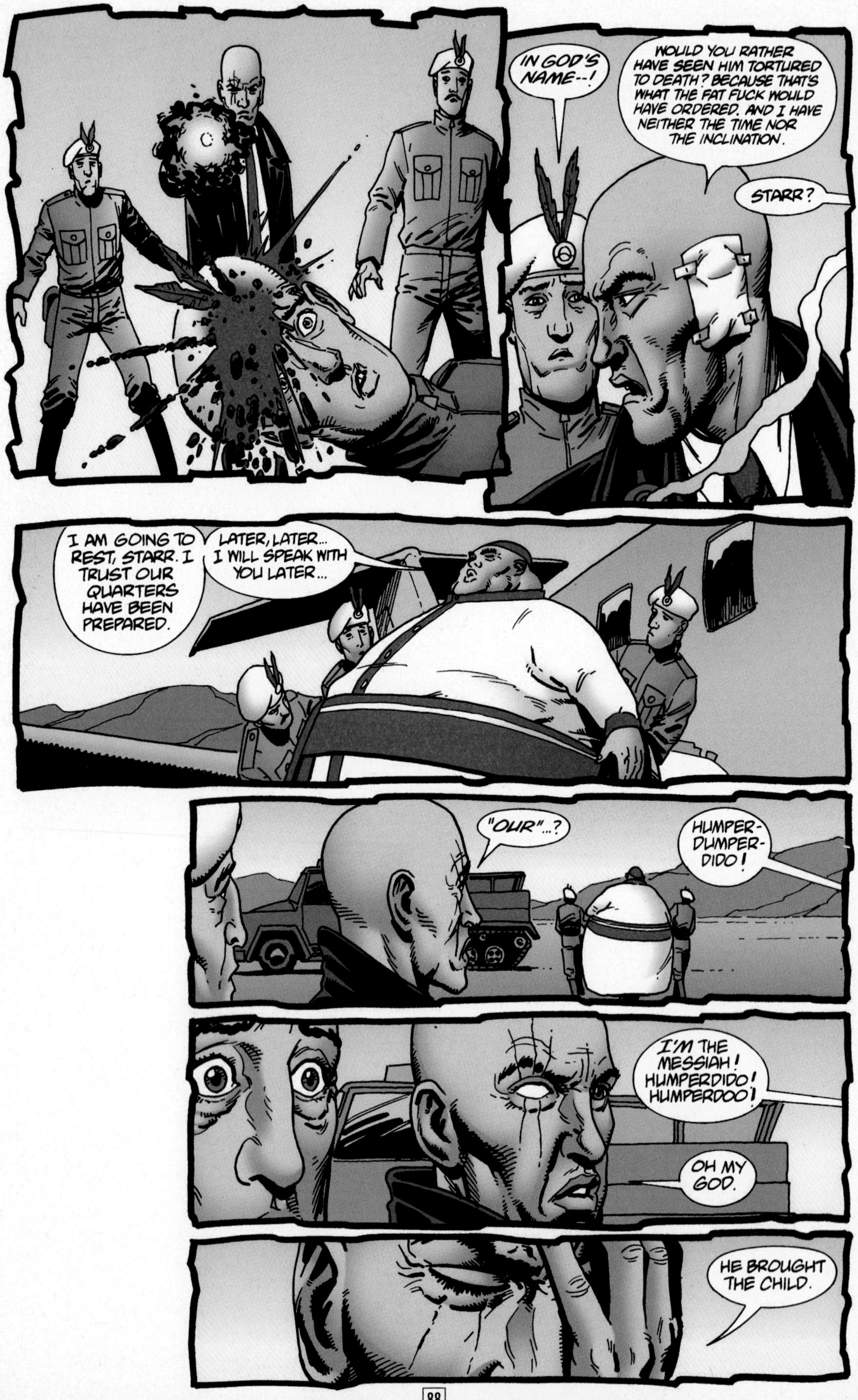
IN GOD'S NAME--!
WOULD YOU RATHER HAVE SEEN HIM TORTURED TO DEATH? BECAUSE THAT'S WHAT THE FAT FUCK WOULD HAVE ORDERED. AND I HAVE NEITHER THE TIME NOR THE INCLINATION.
STARR?
I AM GOING TO REST, STARR. I TRUST OUR QUARTERS HAVE BEEN PREPARED.
LATER, LATER... I WILL SPEAK WITH YOU LATER...
"OUR"...?
HUMPER-DUMPER-DIDO!
I'M THE MESSIAH! HUMPERDIDO! HUMPERDOO!
OH MY GOD.
HE BROUGHT THE CHILD.

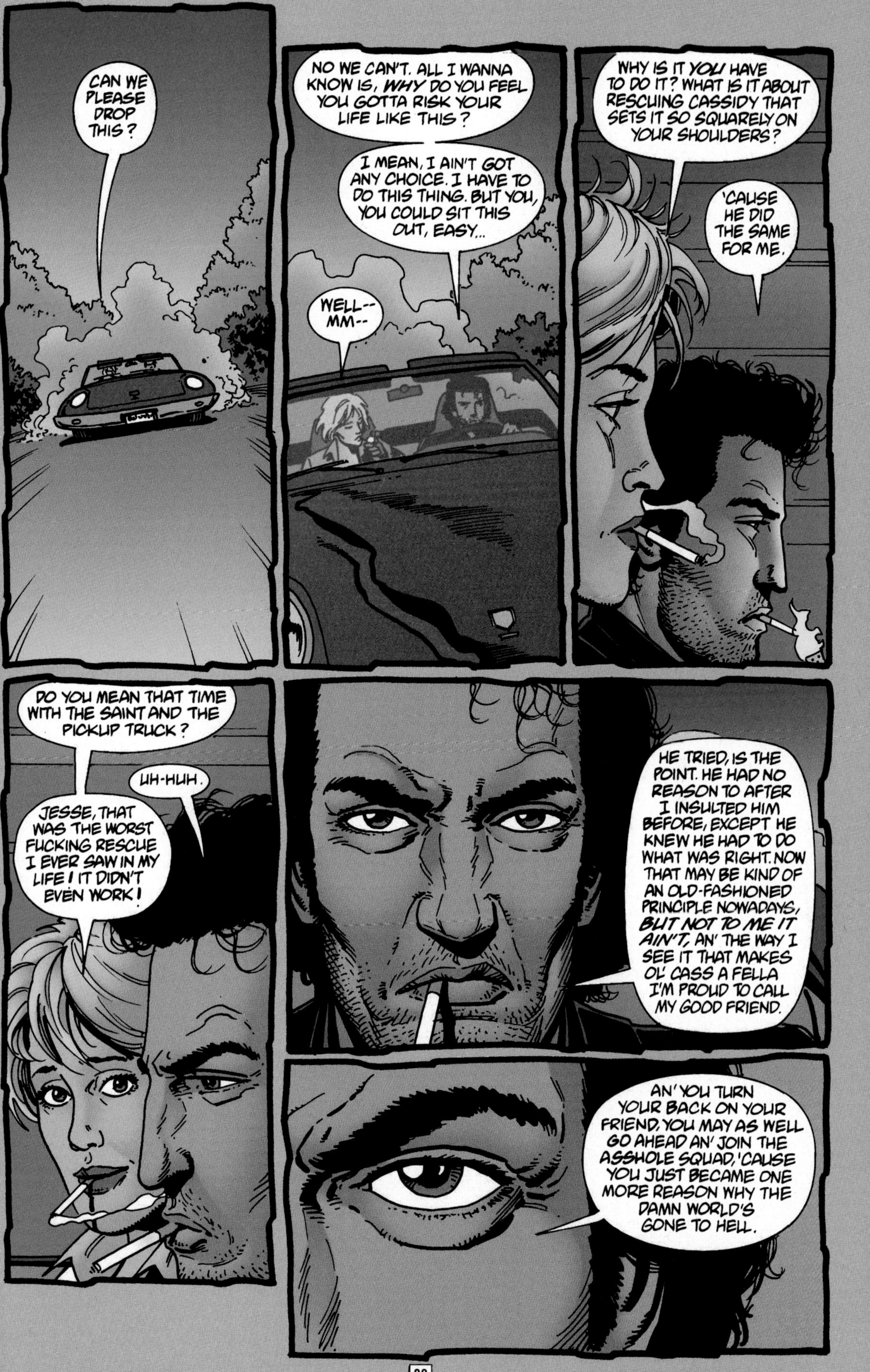
CAN WE PLEASE DROP THIS?
NO WE CAN'T. ALL I WANNA KNOW IS, WHY DO YOU FEEL YOU GOTTA RISK YOUR LIFE LIKE THIS?
I MEAN, I AIN'T GOT ANY CHOICE. I HAVE TO DO THIS THING. BUT YOU, YOU COULD SIT THIS OUT, EASY...
WELL-- MM--
WHY IS IT YOU HAVE TO DO IT? WHAT IS IT ABOUT RESCUING CASSIDY THAT SETS IT SO SQUARELY ON YOUR SHOULDERS?
'CAUSE HE DID THE SAME FOR ME.
DO YOU MEAN THAT TIME WITH THE SAINT AND THE PICKUP TRUCK?
UH-HUH.
JESSE, THAT WAS THE WORST FUCKING RESCUE I EVER SAW IN MY LIFE! IT DIDN'T EVEN WORK!
HE TRIED, IS THE POINT. HE HAD NO REASON TO AFTER I INSULTED HIM BEFORE, EXCEPT HE KNEW HE HAD TO DO WHAT WAS RIGHT. NOW THAT MAY BE KIND OF AN OLD-FASHIONED PRINCIPLE NOWADAYS, BUT NOT TO ME IT AIN'T, AN' THE WAY I SEE IT THAT MAKES OL' CASS A FELLA I'M PROUD TO CALL MY GOOD FRIEND.
AN' YOU TURN YOUR BACK ON YOUR FRIEND, YOU MAY AS WELL GO AHEAD AN' JOIN THE ASSHOLE SQUAD, 'CAUSE YOU JUST BECAME ONE MORE REASON WHY THE DAMN WORLD'S GONE TO HELL.

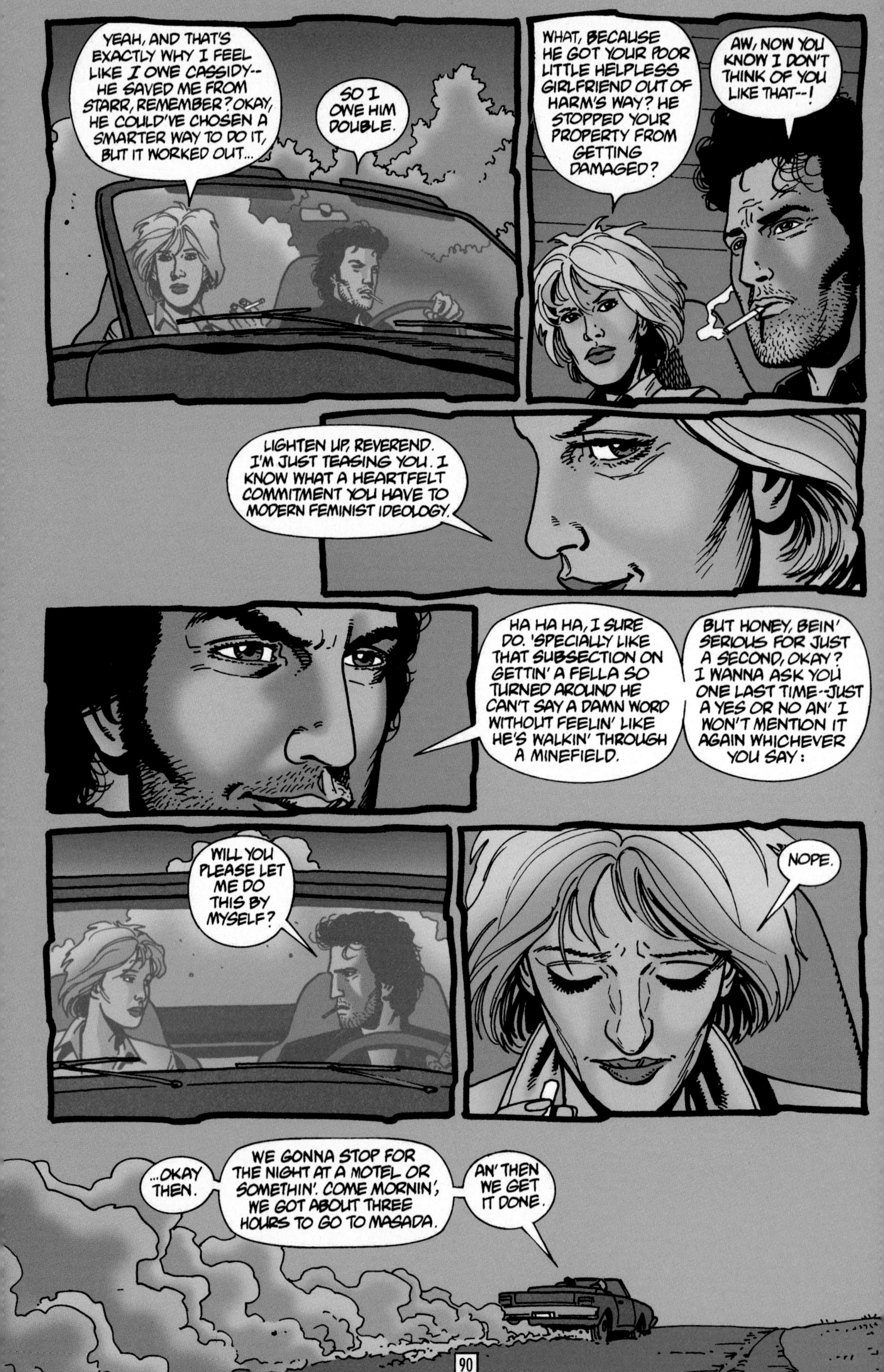
YEAH, AND THAT'S EXACTLY WHY I FEEL LIKE *I* OWE CASSIDY-- HE SAVED ME FROM STARR, REMEMBER? OKAY, HE COULD'VE CHOSEN A SMARTER WAY TO DO IT, BUT IT WORKED OUT...
SO I OWE HIM DOUBLE.
WHAT, BECAUSE HE GOT YOUR POOR LITTLE HELPLESS GIRLFRIEND OUT OF HARM'S WAY? HE STOPPED YOUR PROPERTY FROM GETTING DAMAGED?
AW, NOW YOU KNOW I DON'T THINK OF YOU LIKE THAT--!
LIGHTEN UP, REVEREND. I'M JUST TEASING YOU. I KNOW WHAT A HEARTFELT COMMITMENT YOU HAVE TO MODERN FEMINIST IDEOLOGY.
HA HA HA, I SURE DO. 'SPECIALLY LIKE THAT SUBSECTION ON GETTIN' A FELLA SO TURNED AROUND HE CAN'T SAY A DAMN WORD WITHOUT FEELIN' LIKE HE'S WALKIN' THROUGH A MINEFIELD.
BUT HONEY, BEIN' SERIOUS FOR JUST A SECOND, OKAY? I WANNA ASK YOU ONE LAST TIME--JUST A YES OR NO AN' I WON'T MENTION IT AGAIN WHICHEVER YOU SAY:
WILL YOU PLEASE LET ME DO THIS BY MYSELF?
NOPE.
...OKAY THEN.
WE GONNA STOP FOR THE NIGHT AT A MOTEL OR SOMETHIN'. COME MORNIN', WE GOT ABOUT THREE HOURS TO GO TO MASADA.
AN' THEN WE GET IT DONE.

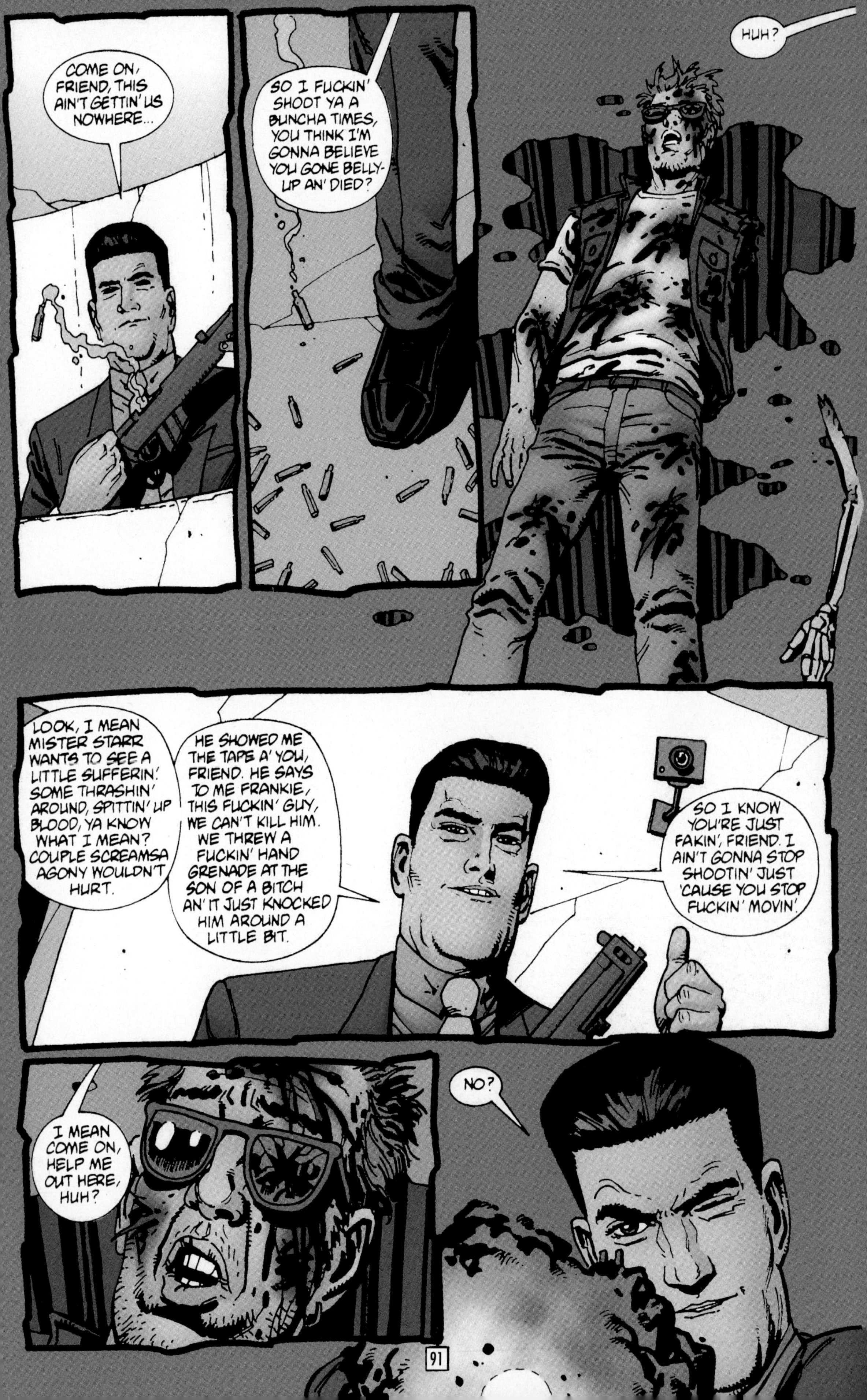
COME ON, FRIEND, THIS AIN'T GETTIN' US NOWHERE...
SO I FUCKIN' SHOOT YA A BUNCHA TIMES, YOU THINK I'M GONNA BELIEVE YOU GONE BELLY-UP AN' DIED?
HUH?
LOOK, I MEAN MISTER STARR WANTS TO SEE A LITTLE SUFFERIN'. SOME THRASHIN' AROUND, SPITTIN' UP BLOOD, YA KNOW WHAT I MEAN? COUPLE SCREAMSA AGONY WOULDN'T HURT.
HE SHOWED ME THE TAPE A' YOU, FRIEND. HE SAYS TO ME FRANKIE, THIS FUCKIN' GUY, WE CAN'T KILL HIM. WE THREW A FUCKIN' HAND GRENADE AT THE SON OF A BITCH AN' IT JUST KNOCKED HIM AROUND A LITTLE BIT.
SO I KNOW YOU'RE JUST FAKIN', FRIEND. I AIN'T GONNA STOP SHOOTIN' JUST 'CAUSE YOU STOP FUCKIN' MOVIN'.
I MEAN COME ON, HELP ME OUT HERE, HUH?
NO?

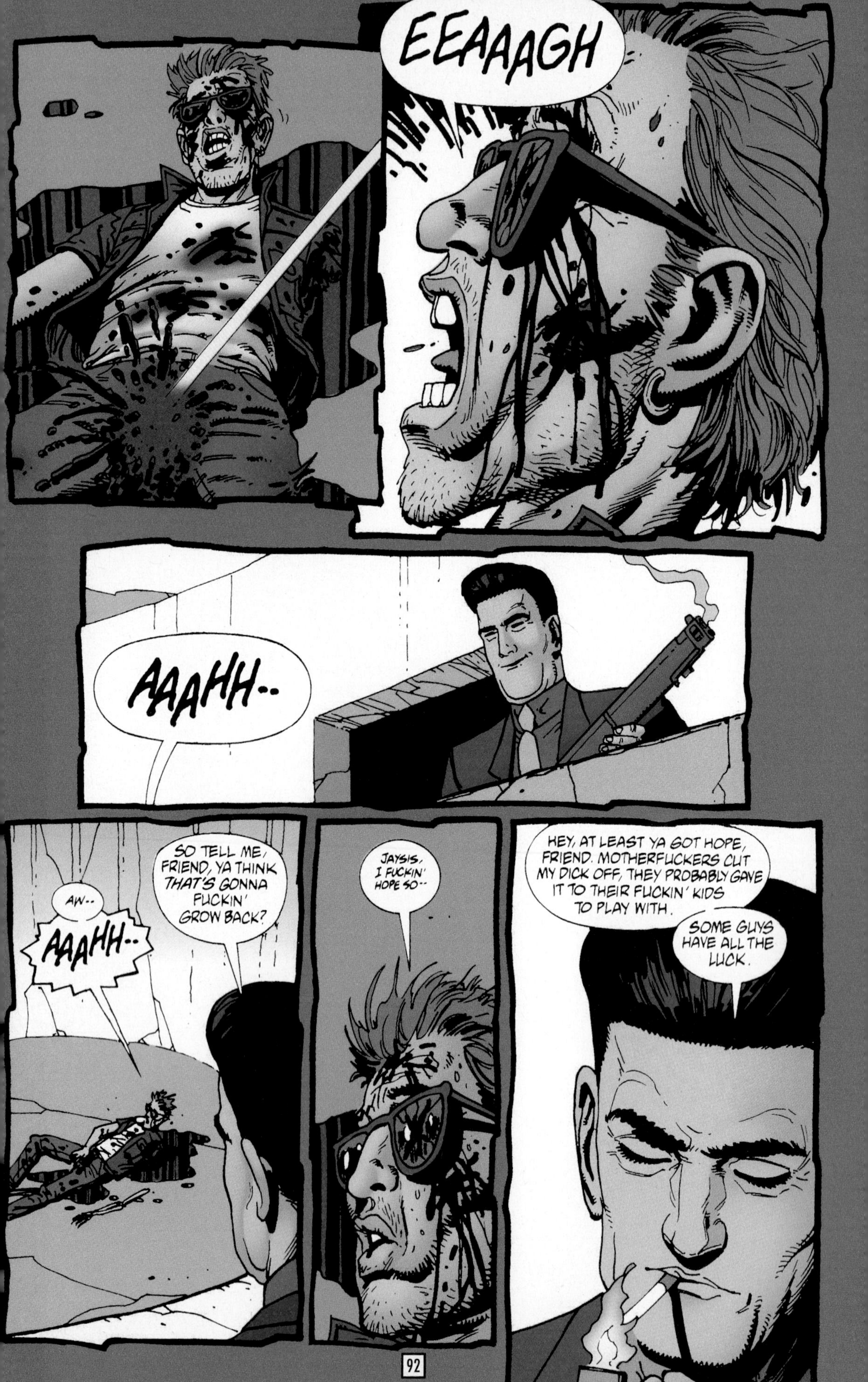
EEAAAGH
AAAHH--
AW--
AAAHH--
SO TELL ME, FRIEND, YA THINK THAT'S GONNA FUCKIN' GROW BACK?
JAYSIS, I FUCKIN' HOPE SO--
HEY, AT LEAST YA GOT HOPE, FRIEND. MOTHERFUCKERS CUT MY DICK OFF, THEY PROBABLY GAVE IT TO THEIR FUCKIN' KIDS TO PLAY WITH.
SOME GUYS HAVE ALL THE LUCK.

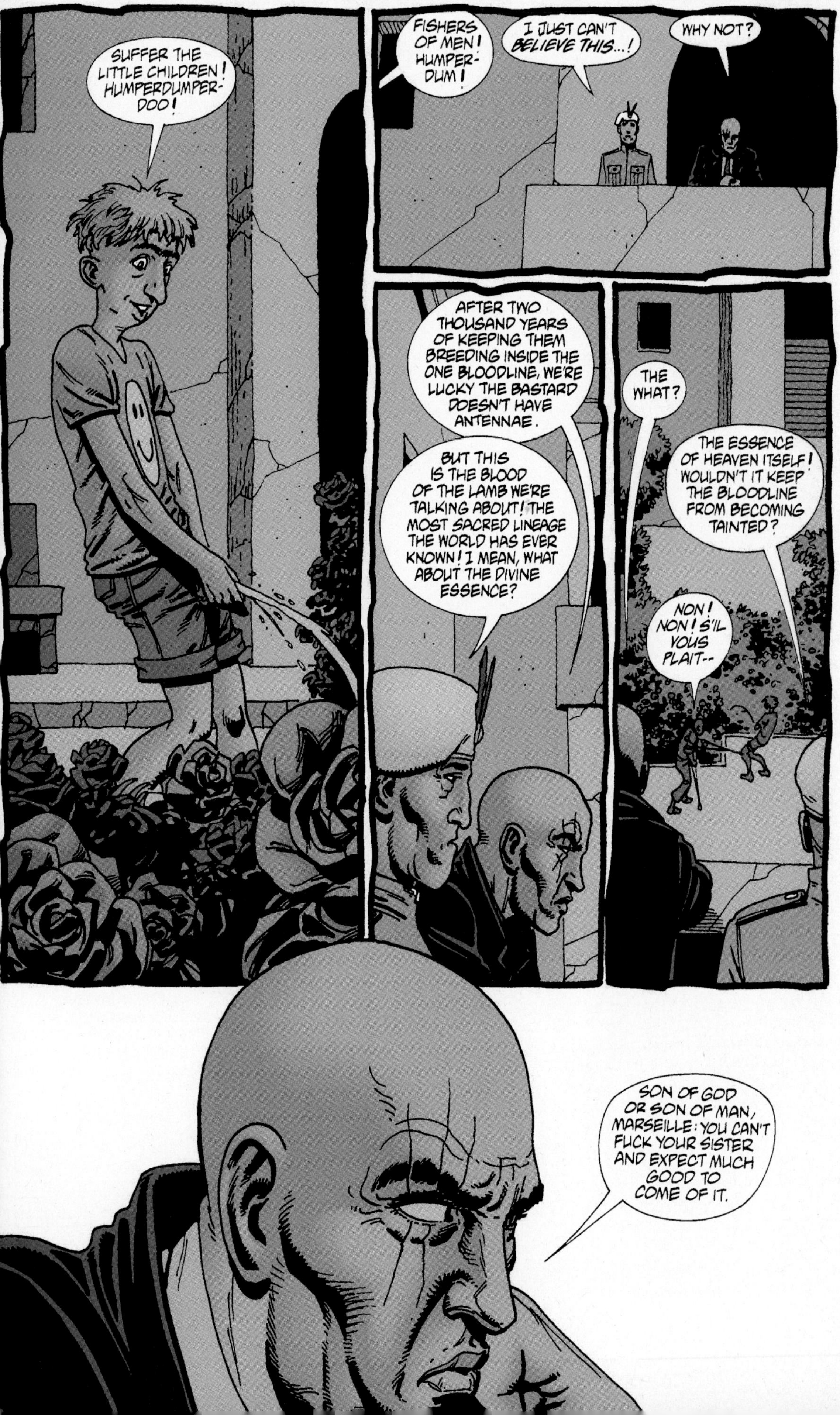
SUFFER THE LITTLE CHILDREN! HUMPERDUMPER-DOO!
FISHERS OF MEN! HUMPER-DUM!
I JUST CAN'T BELIEVE THIS...!
WHY NOT?
AFTER TWO THOUSAND YEARS OF KEEPING THEM BREEDING INSIDE THE ONE BLOODLINE, WE'RE LUCKY THE BASTARD DOESN'T HAVE ANTENNAE.
BUT THIS IS THE BLOOD OF THE LAMB WE'RE TALKING ABOUT! THE MOST SACRED LINEAGE THE WORLD HAS EVER KNOWN! I MEAN, WHAT ABOUT THE DIVINE ESSENCE?
THE WHAT?
THE ESSENCE OF HEAVEN ITSELF! WOULDN'T IT KEEP THE BLOODLINE FROM BECOMING TAINTED?
NON! NON! S'IL VOUS PLAIT--
SON OF GOD OR SON OF MAN, MARSEILLE: YOU CAN'T FUCK YOUR SISTER AND EXPECT MUCH GOOD TO COME OF IT.

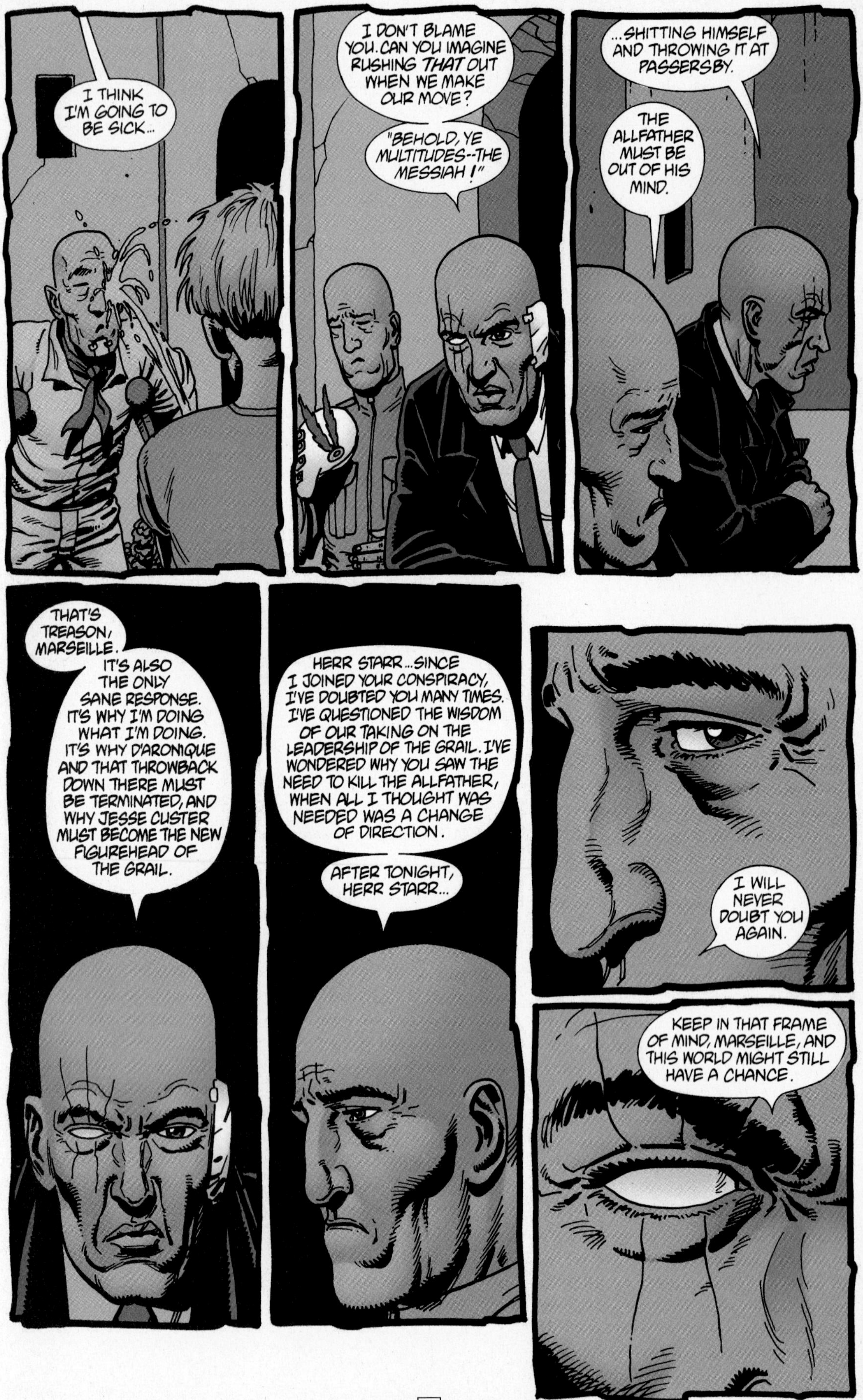
I THINK I'M GOING TO BE SICK...
I DON'T BLAME YOU. CAN YOU IMAGINE RUSHING *THAT* OUT WHEN WE MAKE OUR MOVE?
"BEHOLD, YE MULTITUDES--THE MESSIAH!"
...SHITTING HIMSELF AND THROWING IT AT PASSERSBY.
THE ALLFATHER MUST BE OUT OF HIS MIND.
THAT'S TREASON, MARSEILLE.
IT'S ALSO THE ONLY SANE RESPONSE. IT'S WHY I'M DOING WHAT I'M DOING. IT'S WHY D'ARONIQUE AND THAT THROWBACK DOWN THERE MUST BE TERMINATED, AND WHY JESSE CUSTER MUST BECOME THE NEW FIGUREHEAD OF THE GRAIL.
HERR STARR...SINCE I JOINED YOUR CONSPIRACY, I'VE DOUBTED YOU MANY TIMES. I'VE QUESTIONED THE WISDOM OF OUR TAKING ON THE LEADERSHIP OF THE GRAIL. I'VE WONDERED WHY YOU SAW THE NEED TO KILL THE ALLFATHER, WHEN ALL I THOUGHT WAS NEEDED WAS A CHANGE OF DIRECTION.
AFTER TONIGHT, HERR STARR...
I WILL NEVER DOUBT YOU AGAIN.
KEEP IN THAT FRAME OF MIND, MARSEILLE, AND THIS WORLD MIGHT STILL HAVE A CHANCE.

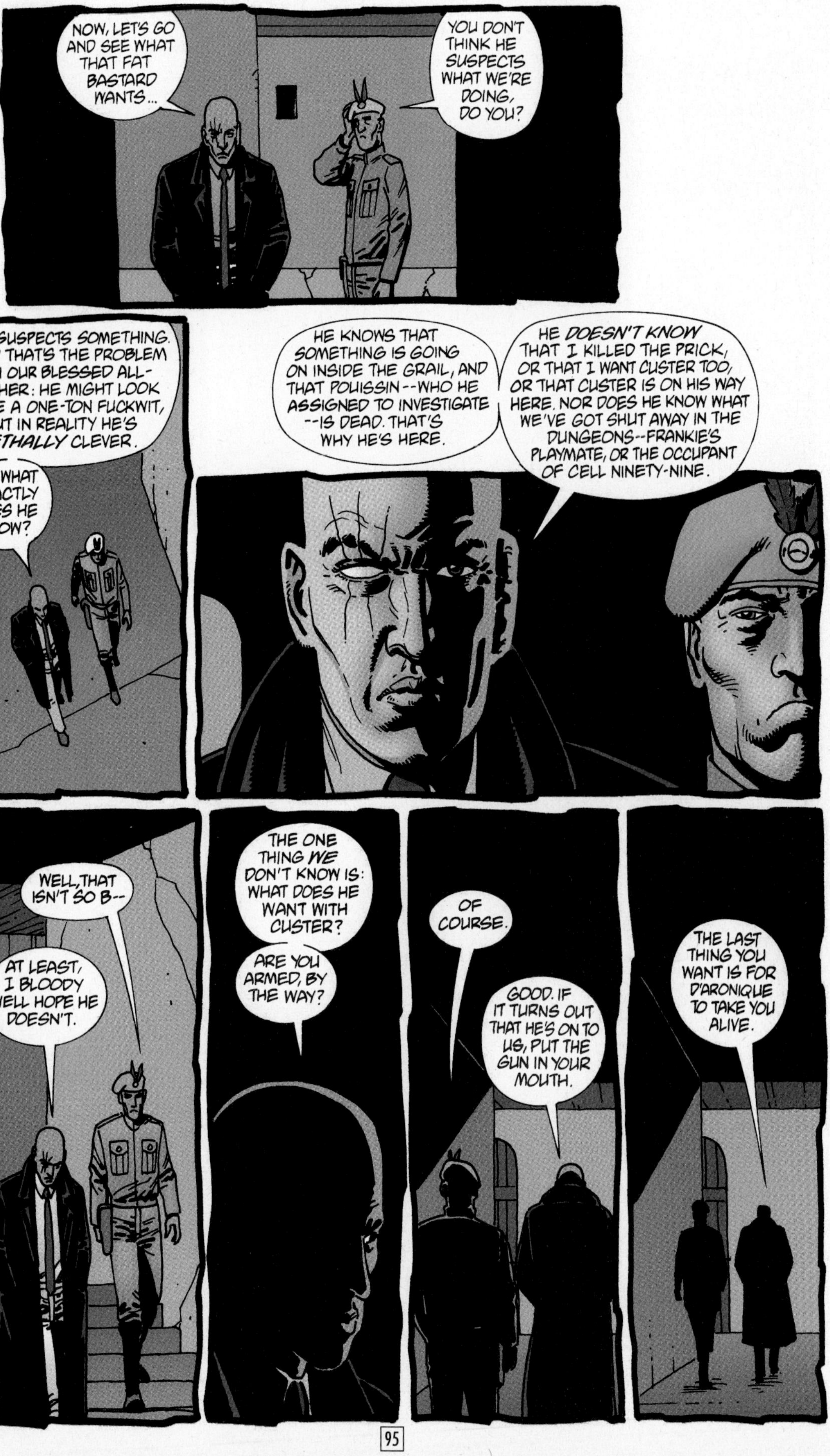
NOW, LET'S GO AND SEE WHAT THAT FAT BASTARD WANTS...
YOU DON'T THINK HE SUSPECTS WHAT WE'RE DOING, DO YOU?
HE SUSPECTS SOMETHING. AND THAT'S THE PROBLEM WITH OUR BLESSED ALL-FATHER: HE MIGHT LOOK LIKE A ONE-TON FUCKWIT, BUT IN REALITY HE'S *LETHALLY* CLEVER.
SO WHAT EXACTLY DOES HE KNOW?
HE KNOWS THAT SOMETHING IS GOING ON INSIDE THE GRAIL, AND THAT POUISSIN--WHO HE ASSIGNED TO INVESTIGATE--IS DEAD. THAT'S WHY HE'S HERE.
HE *DOESN'T KNOW* THAT I KILLED THE PRICK, OR THAT I WANT CUSTER TOO, OR THAT CUSTER IS ON HIS WAY HERE. NOR DOES HE KNOW WHAT WE'VE GOT SHUT AWAY IN THE DUNGEONS--FRANKIE'S PLAYMATE, OR THE OCCUPANT OF CELL NINETY-NINE.
WELL, THAT ISN'T SO B--
AT LEAST, I BLOODY WELL HOPE HE DOESN'T.
THE ONE THING *WE* DON'T KNOW IS: WHAT DOES HE WANT WITH CUSTER?
ARE YOU ARMED, BY THE WAY?
OF COURSE.
GOOD. IF IT TURNS OUT THAT HE'S ON TO US, PUT THE GUN IN YOUR MOUTH.
THE LAST THING YOU WANT IS FOR D'ARONIQUE TO TAKE YOU ALIVE.

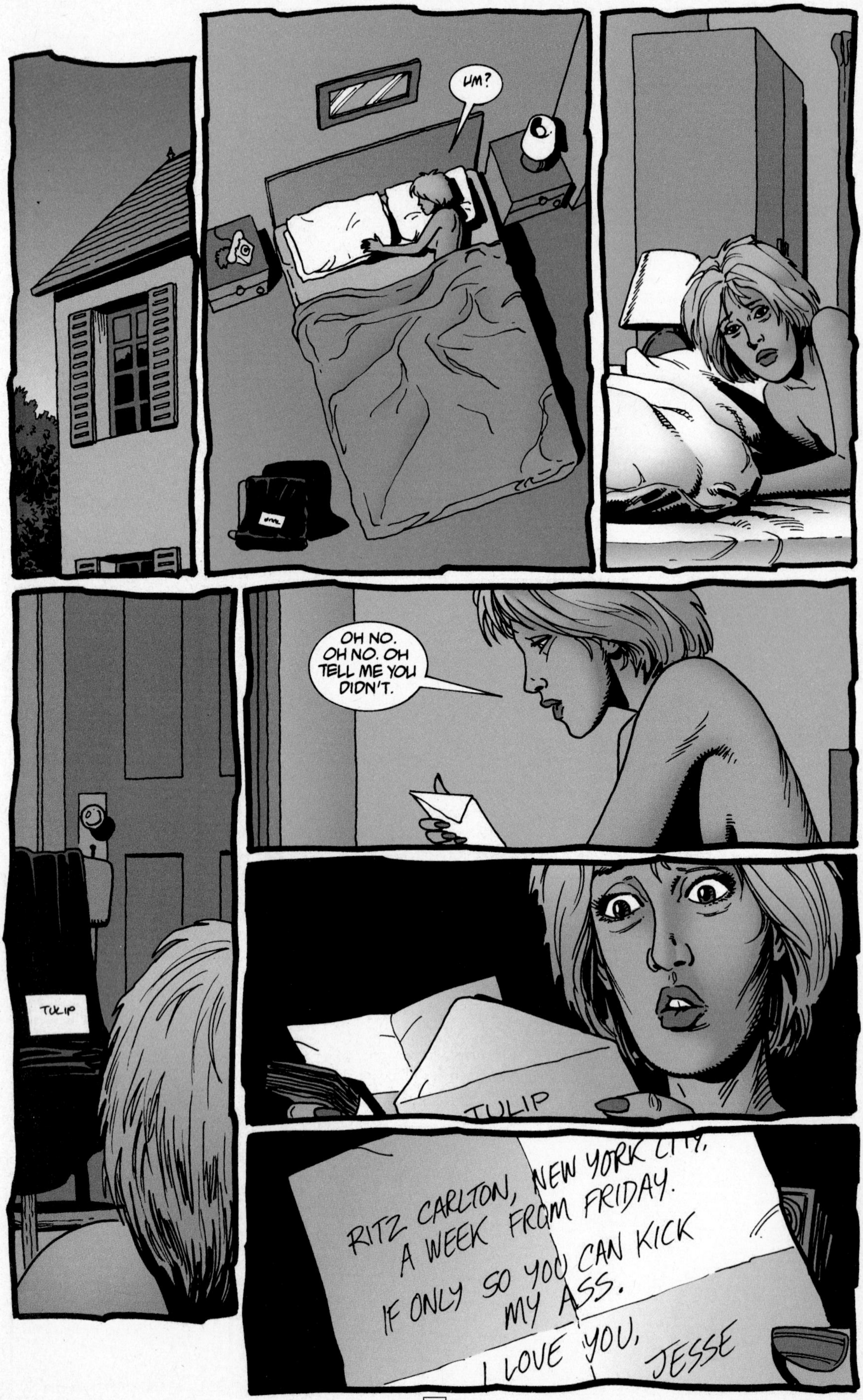
UM?
TULIP
OH NO. OH NO. OH TELL ME YOU DIDN'T.
TULIP
RITZ CARLTON, NEW YORK CITY, A WEEK FROM FRIDAY.
IF ONLY SO YOU CAN KICK MY ASS.
I LOVE YOU,
JESSE

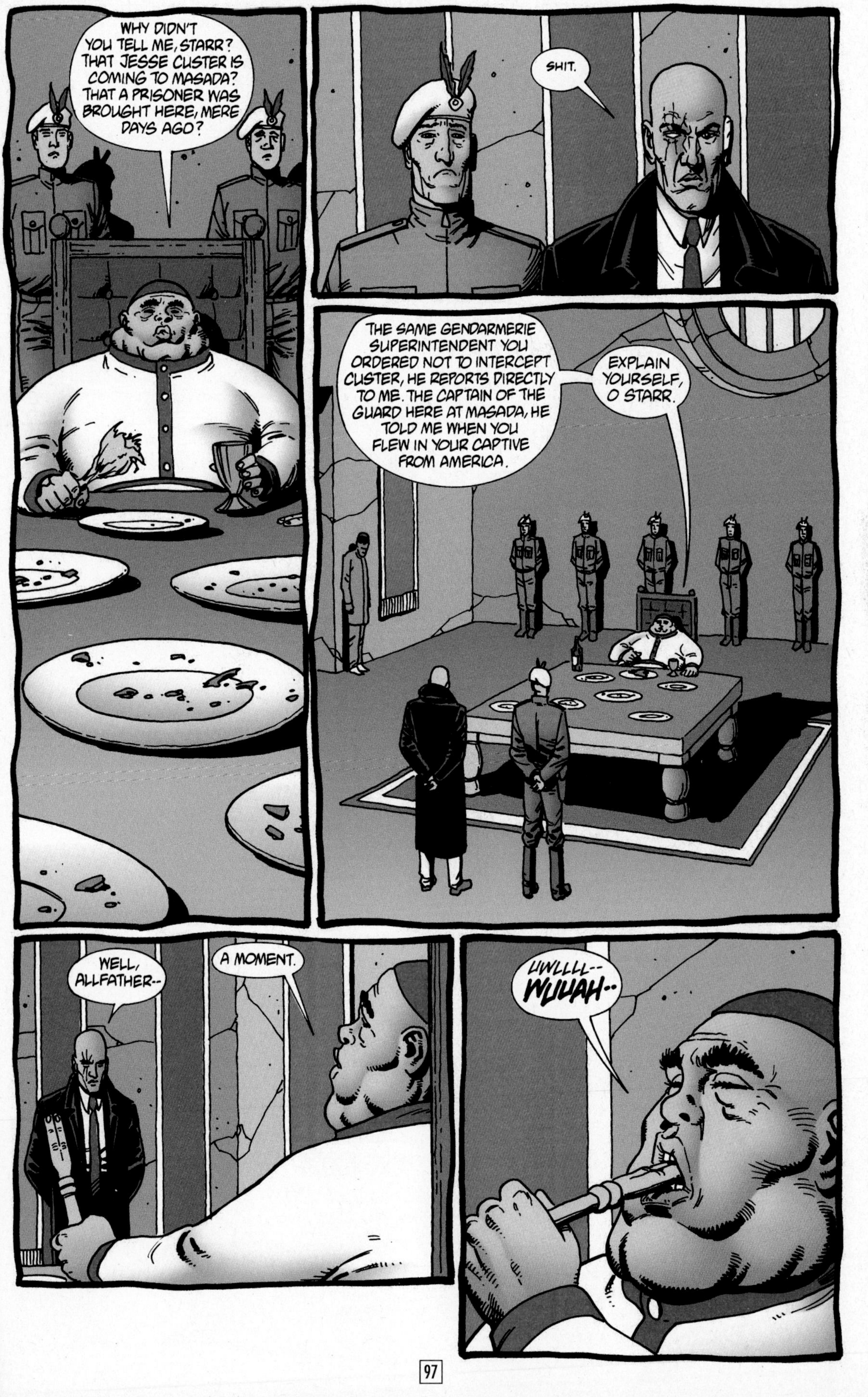

WHY DIDN'T YOU TELL ME, STARR? THAT JESSE CUSTER IS COMING TO MASADA? THAT A PRISONER WAS BROUGHT HERE, MERE DAYS AGO?
SHIT.
EXPLAIN YOURSELF, O STARR.
THE SAME GENDARMERIE SUPERINTENDENT YOU ORDERED NOT TO INTERCEPT CUSTER, HE REPORTS DIRECTLY TO ME. THE CAPTAIN OF THE GUARD HERE AT MASADA, HE TOLD ME WHEN YOU FLEW IN YOUR CAPTIVE FROM AMERICA.
WELL, ALLFATHER--
A MOMENT.
UWLLLL-- WUUAH--

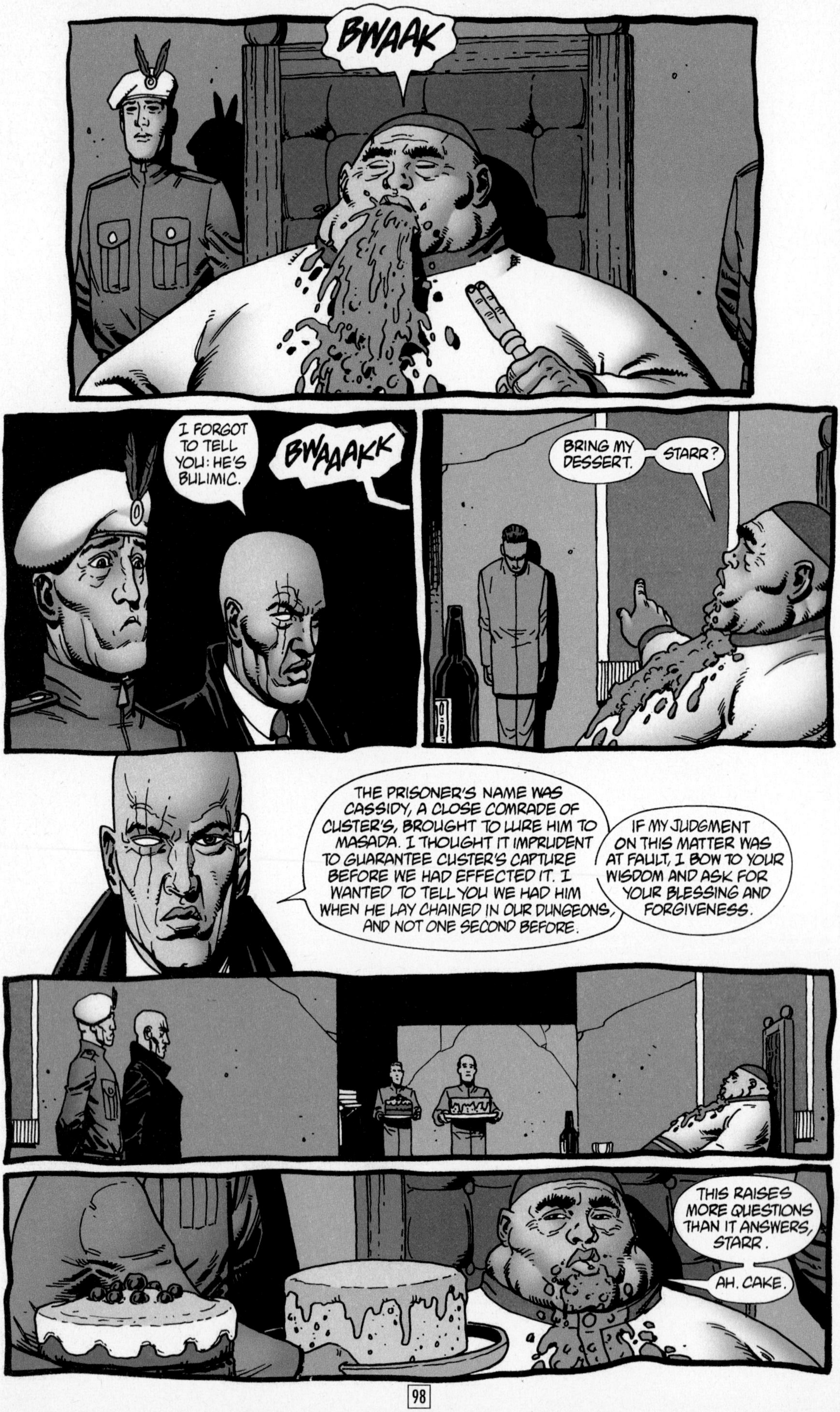
BWAAK
I FORGOT TO TELL YOU: HE'S BULIMIC.
BWAAAKK
BRING MY DESSERT.
STARR?
THE PRISONER'S NAME WAS CASSIDY, A CLOSE COMRADE OF CUSTER'S, BROUGHT TO LURE HIM TO MASADA. I THOUGHT IT IMPRUDENT TO GUARANTEE CUSTER'S CAPTURE BEFORE WE HAD EFFECTED IT. I WANTED TO TELL YOU WE HAD HIM WHEN HE LAY CHAINED IN OUR DUNGEONS, AND NOT ONE SECOND BEFORE.
IF MY JUDGMENT ON THIS MATTER WAS AT FAULT, I BOW TO YOUR WISDOM AND ASK FOR YOUR BLESSING AND FORGIVENESS.
THIS RAISES MORE QUESTIONS THAN IT ANSWERS, STARR.
AH. CAKE.

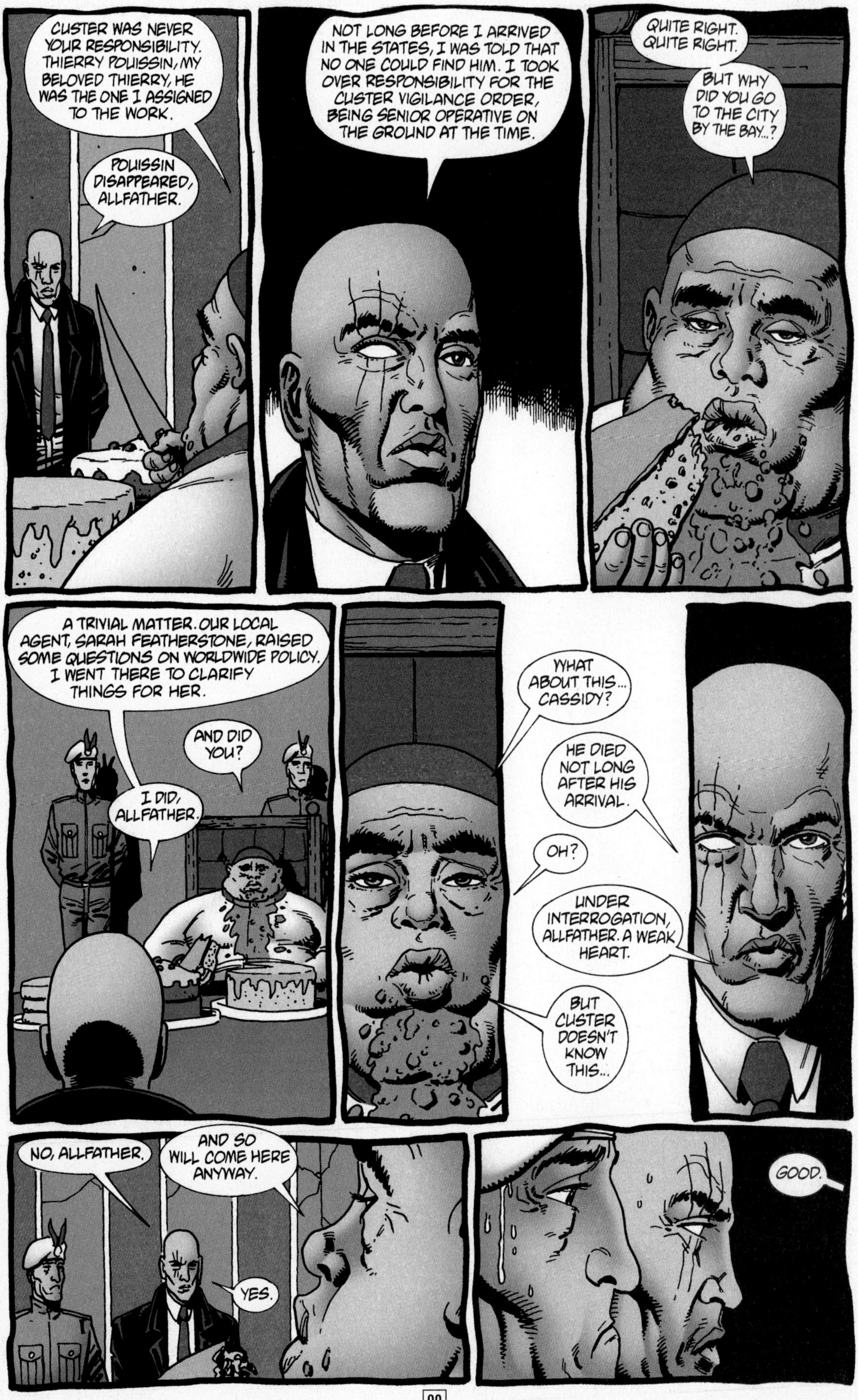
CUSTER WAS NEVER YOUR RESPONSIBILITY. THIERRY POUISSIN, MY BELOVED THIERRY, HE WAS THE ONE I ASSIGNED TO THE WORK.
POUISSIN DISAPPEARED, ALLFATHER.
NOT LONG BEFORE I ARRIVED IN THE STATES, I WAS TOLD THAT NO ONE COULD FIND HIM. I TOOK OVER RESPONSIBILITY FOR THE CUSTER VIGILANCE ORDER, BEING SENIOR OPERATIVE ON THE GROUND AT THE TIME.
QUITE RIGHT. QUITE RIGHT.
BUT WHY DID YOU GO TO THE CITY BY THE BAY...?
A TRIVIAL MATTER. OUR LOCAL AGENT, SARAH FEATHERSTONE, RAISED SOME QUESTIONS ON WORLDWIDE POLICY. I WENT THERE TO CLARIFY THINGS FOR HER.
AND DID YOU?
I DID, ALLFATHER.
WHAT ABOUT THIS... CASSIDY?
HE DIED NOT LONG AFTER HIS ARRIVAL.
OH?
UNDER INTERROGATION, ALLFATHER. A WEAK HEART.
BUT CUSTER DOESN'T KNOW THIS...
NO, ALLFATHER.
AND SO WILL COME HERE ANYWAY.
YES.
GOOD.

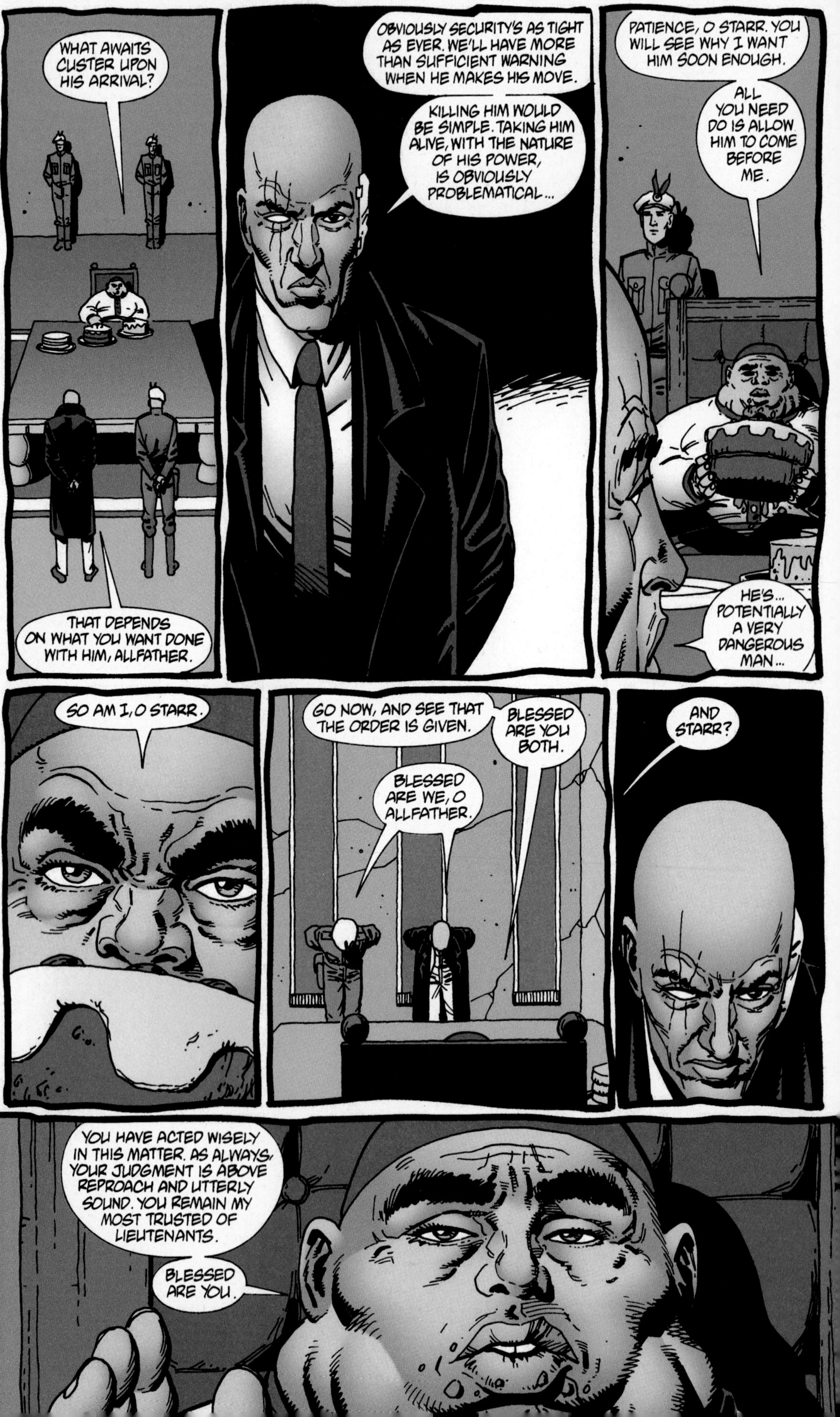
WHAT AWAITS CUSTER UPON HIS ARRIVAL?
THAT DEPENDS ON WHAT YOU WANT DONE WITH HIM, ALLFATHER.
OBVIOUSLY SECURITY'S AS TIGHT AS EVER. WE'LL HAVE MORE THAN SUFFICIENT WARNING WHEN HE MAKES HIS MOVE.
KILLING HIM WOULD BE SIMPLE. TAKING HIM ALIVE, WITH THE NATURE OF HIS POWER, IS OBVIOUSLY PROBLEMATICAL...
PATIENCE, O STARR. YOU WILL SEE WHY I WANT HIM SOON ENOUGH.
ALL YOU NEED DO IS ALLOW HIM TO COME BEFORE ME.
HE'S... POTENTIALLY A VERY DANGEROUS MAN...
SO AM I, O STARR.
GO NOW, AND SEE THAT THE ORDER IS GIVEN.
BLESSED ARE YOU BOTH.
BLESSED ARE WE, O ALLFATHER.
AND STARR?
YOU HAVE ACTED WISELY IN THIS MATTER. AS ALWAYS, YOUR JUDGMENT IS ABOVE REPROACH AND UTTERLY SOUND. YOU REMAIN MY MOST TRUSTED OF LIEUTENANTS.
BLESSED ARE YOU.

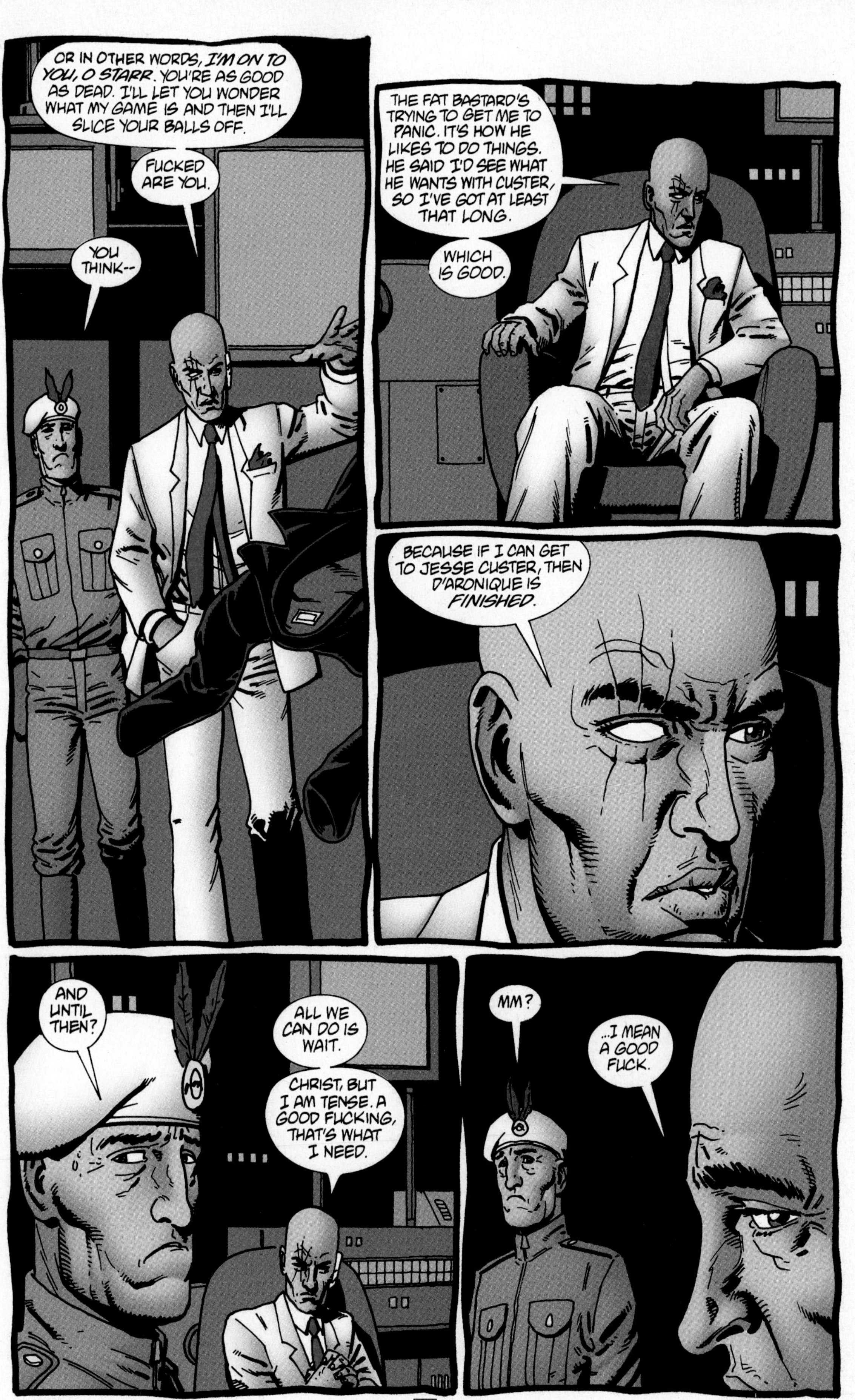
OR IN OTHER WORDS, I'M ON TO YOU, O STARR. YOU'RE AS GOOD AS DEAD. I'LL LET YOU WONDER WHAT MY GAME IS AND THEN I'LL SLICE YOUR BALLS OFF.
FUCKED ARE YOU.
YOU THINK--
THE FAT BASTARD'S TRYING TO GET ME TO PANIC. IT'S HOW HE LIKES TO DO THINGS. HE SAID I'D SEE WHAT HE WANTS WITH CUSTER, SO I'VE GOT AT LEAST THAT LONG.
WHICH IS GOOD.
BECAUSE IF I CAN GET TO JESSE CUSTER, THEN D'ARONIQUE IS FINISHED.
AND UNTIL THEN?
ALL WE CAN DO IS WAIT.
CHRIST, BUT I AM TENSE. A GOOD FUCKING, THAT'S WHAT I NEED.
MM?
...I MEAN A GOOD FUCK.

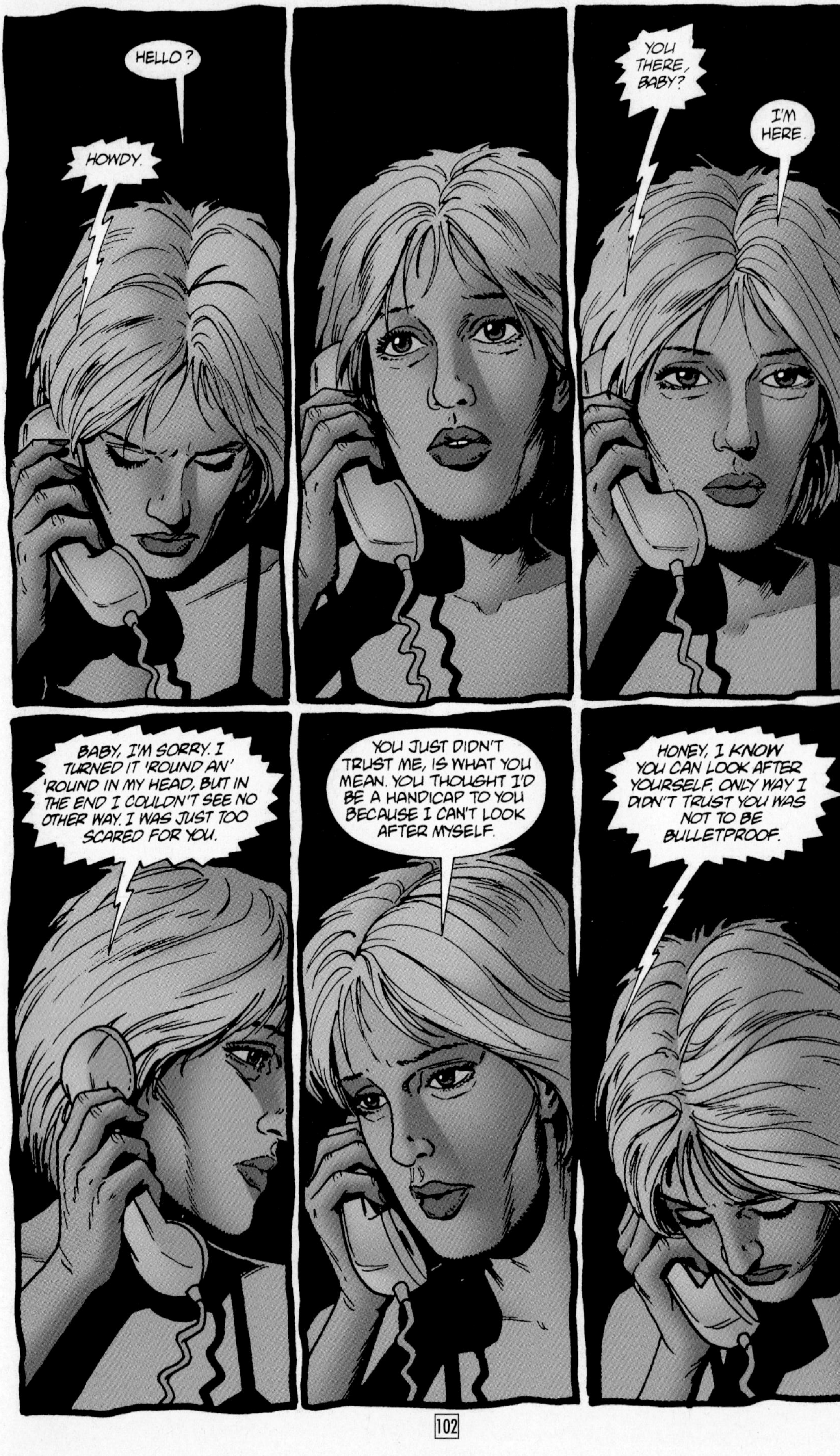
HELLO?
HOWDY.
YOU THERE, BABY?
I'M HERE.
BABY, I'M SORRY. I TURNED IT 'ROUND AN' 'ROUND IN MY HEAD, BUT IN THE END I COULDN'T SEE NO OTHER WAY. I WAS JUST TOO SCARED FOR YOU.
YOU JUST DIDN'T TRUST ME, IS WHAT YOU MEAN. YOU THOUGHT I'D BE A HANDICAP TO YOU BECAUSE I CAN'T LOOK AFTER MYSELF.
HONEY, I KNOW YOU CAN LOOK AFTER YOURSELF. ONLY WAY I DIDN'T TRUST YOU WAS NOT TO BE BULLETPROOF.

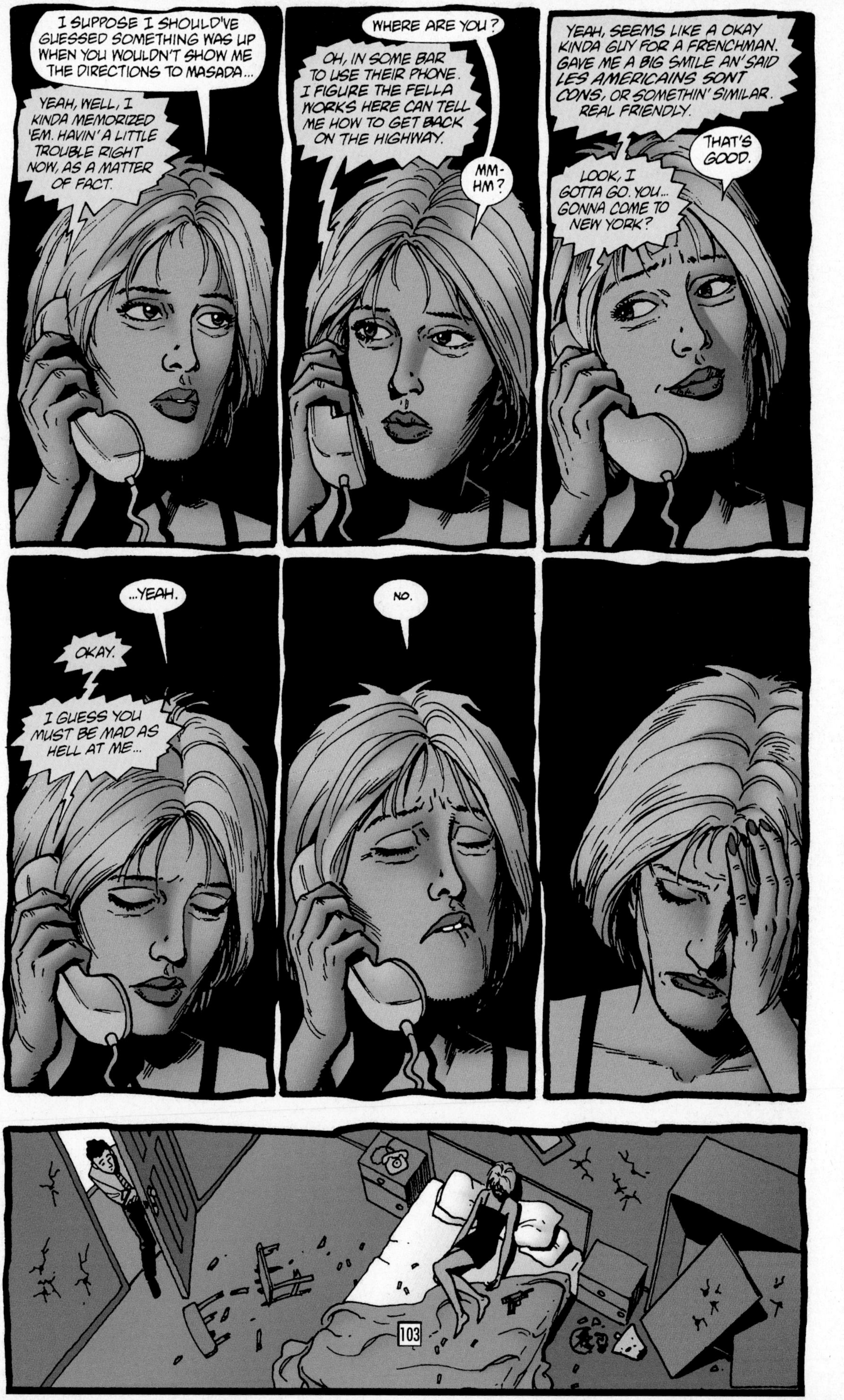
I SUPPOSE I SHOULD'VE GUESSED SOMETHING WAS UP WHEN YOU WOULDN'T SHOW ME THE DIRECTIONS TO MASADA...
YEAH, WELL, I KINDA MEMORIZED 'EM. HAVIN' A LITTLE TROUBLE RIGHT NOW, AS A MATTER OF FACT.
WHERE ARE YOU?
OH, IN SOME BAR TO USE THEIR PHONE. I FIGURE THE FELLA WORKS HERE CAN TELL ME HOW TO GET BACK ON THE HIGHWAY.
MM-HM?
YEAH, SEEMS LIKE A OKAY KINDA GUY FOR A FRENCHMAN. GAVE ME A BIG SMILE AN' SAID LES AMERICAINS SONT CONS, OR SOMETHIN' SIMILAR. REAL FRIENDLY.
THAT'S GOOD.
LOOK, I GOTTA GO. YOU... GONNA COME TO NEW YORK?
...YEAH.
OKAY.
I GUESS YOU MUST BE MAD AS HELL AT ME...
NO.

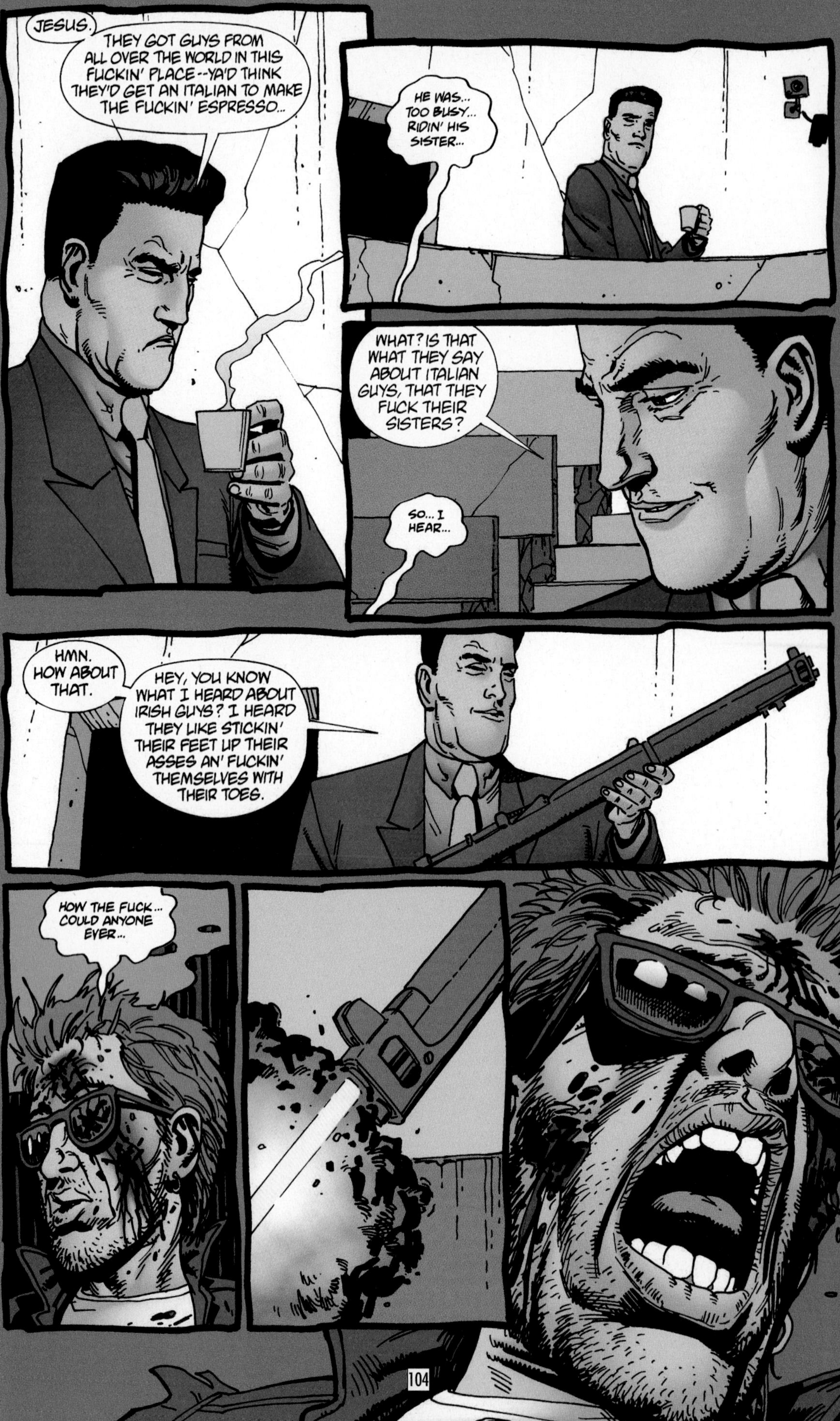
JESUS.
THEY GOT GUYS FROM ALL OVER THE WORLD IN THIS FUCKIN' PLACE--YA'D THINK THEY'D GET AN ITALIAN TO MAKE THE FUCKIN' ESPRESSO...
HE WAS... TOO BUSY... RIDIN' HIS SISTER...
WHAT? IS THAT WHAT THEY SAY ABOUT ITALIAN GUYS, THAT THEY FUCK THEIR SISTERS?
SO... I HEAR...
HMN. HOW ABOUT THAT.
HEY, YOU KNOW WHAT I HEARD ABOUT IRISH GUYS? I HEARD THEY LIKE STICKIN' THEIR FEET UP THEIR ASSES AN' FUCKIN' THEMSELVES WITH THEIR TOES.
HOW THE FUCK... COULD ANYONE EVER...

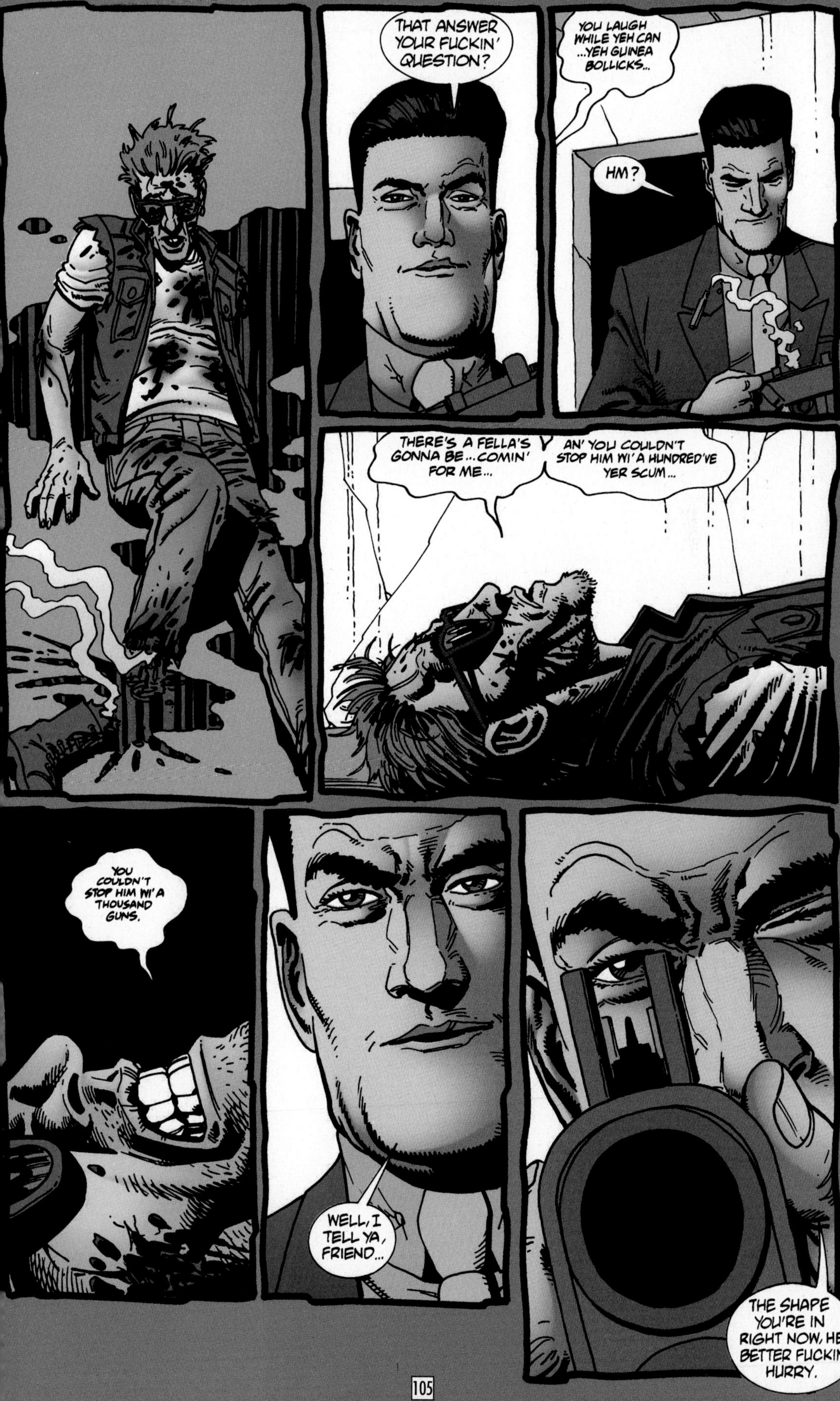
THAT ANSWER YOUR FUCKIN' QUESTION?
YOU LAUGH WHILE YEH CAN ...YEH GUINEA BOLLICKS...
HM?
THERE'S A FELLA'S GONNA BE... COMIN' FOR ME...
AN' YOU COULDN'T STOP HIM WI' A HUNDRED'VE YER SCUM...
YOU COULDN'T STOP HIM WI' A THOUSAND GUNS.
WELL, I TELL YA, FRIEND...
THE SHAPE YOU'RE IN RIGHT NOW, HE BETTER FUCKIN' HURRY.

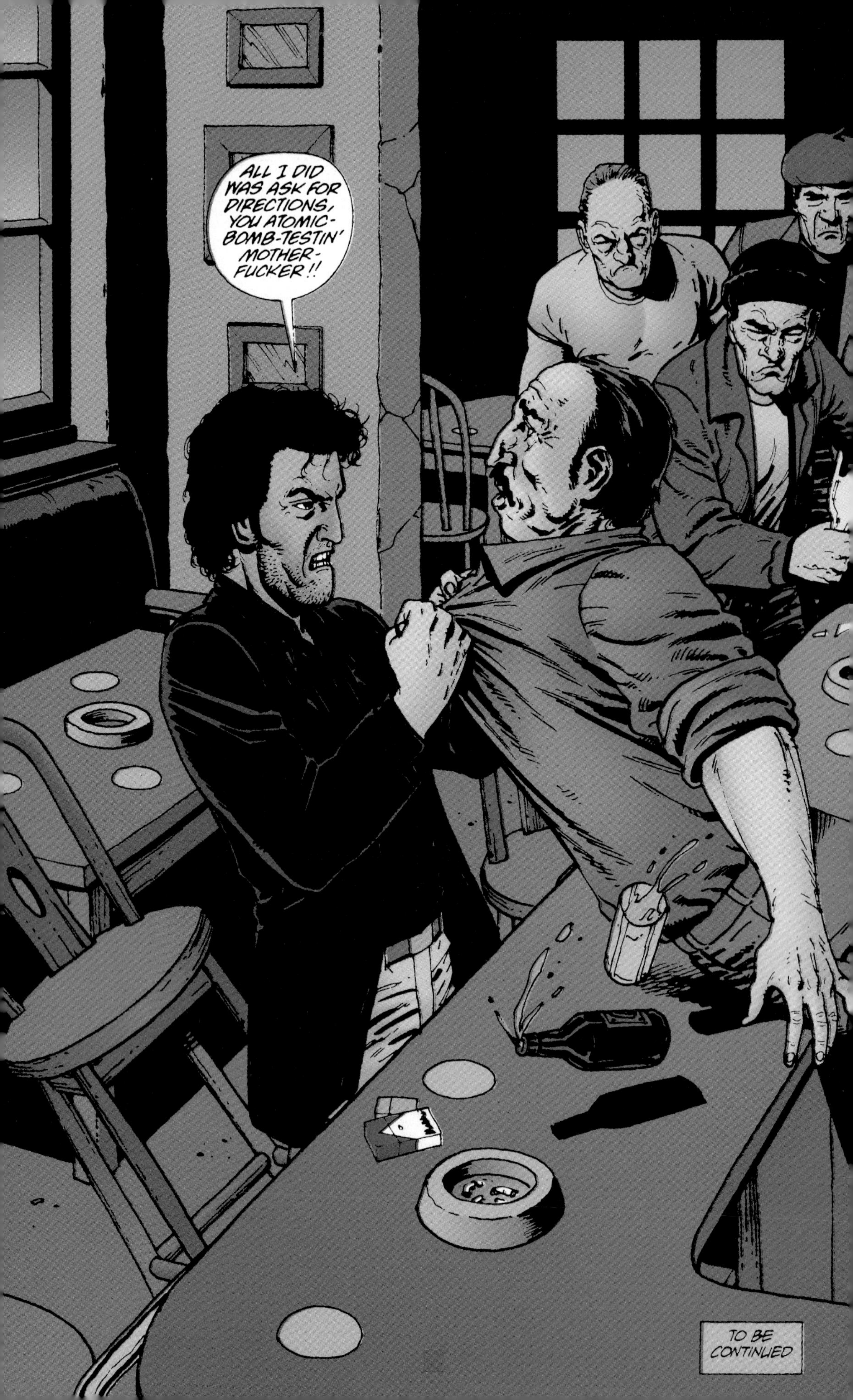
ALL I DID WAS ASK FOR DIRECTIONS, YOU ATOMIC-BOMB-TESTIN' MOTHER-FUCKER!!
TO BE CONTINUED

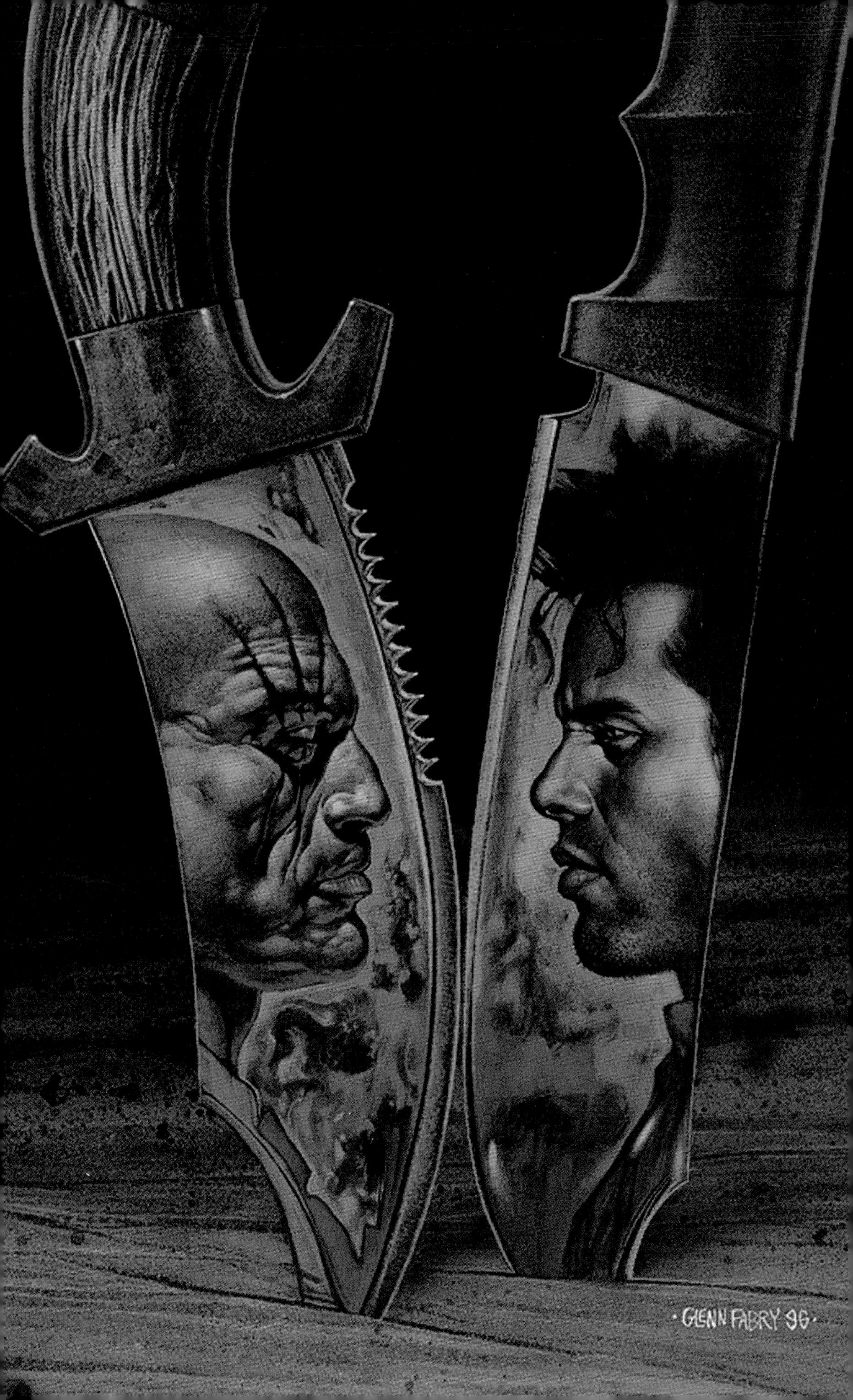
·GLENN FABRY 96·

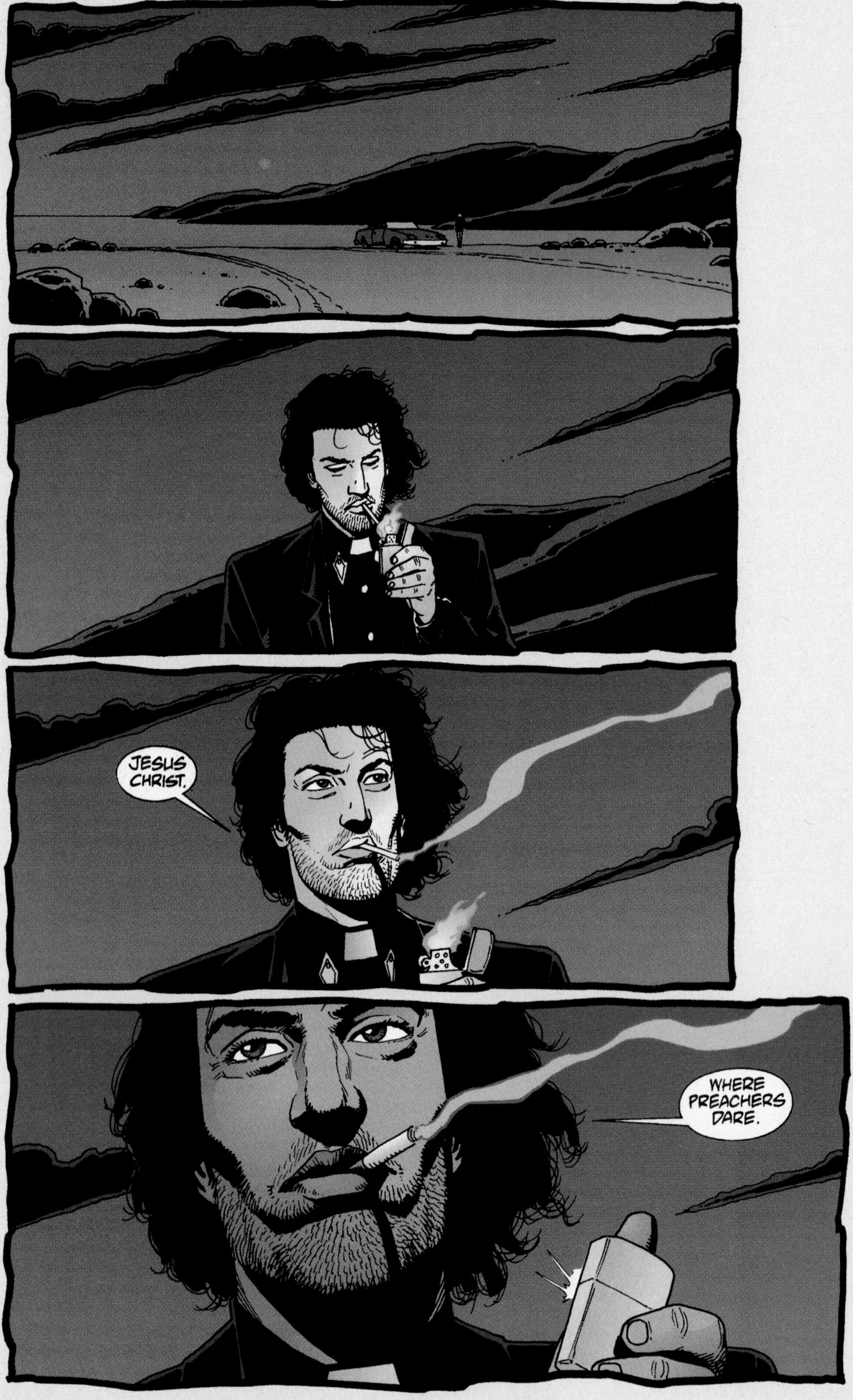
JESUS CHRIST.
WHERE PREACHERS DARE.

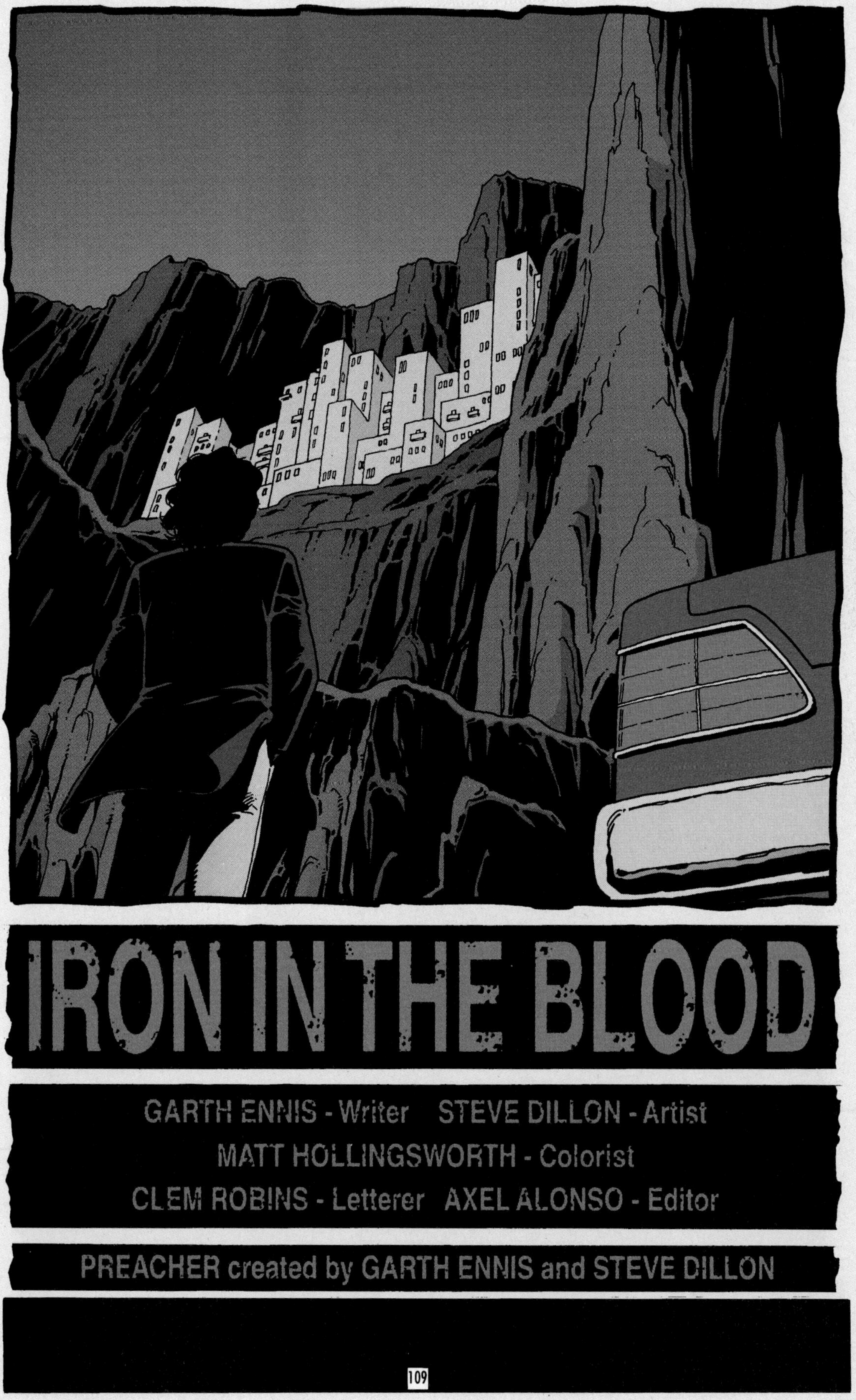

IRON IN THE BLOOD

GARTH ENNIS - Writer STEVE DILLON - Artist
MATT HOLLINGSWORTH - Colorist
CLEM ROBINS - Letterer AXEL ALONSO - Editor

PREACHER created by GARTH ENNIS and STEVE DILLON

FRANKIE, IS THAT THING STILL ALIVE DOWN THERE?

GIMME A SECOND--

YEAH, HE'S FINE. I WAS GONNA GIVE HIM AN HOUR OR TWO OFF, YA KNOW? I MEAN, I KEEP GOIN' LIKE I HAVE BEEN, THERE AIN'T GONNA BE NOTHIN' LEFT TO SHOOT AT...

RIGHT, WELL HOLD FIRE UNTIL I GET BACK TO YOU. IT'S JUST BARELY CONCEIVABLE THAT WE'RE GOING TO NEED THE FUCKER.

YAAAH--!

NOTHING?

ALL GATES STILL CHECKING IN NEGATIVE. WE DID GET ONE STRANGE REPORT FROM A WIDE PATROL...

SAMSON FOUR-FOUR WAS ASSIGNED THE COAST ROAD WEST. THEY CALLED IN TEN MINUTES AGO, SAID THERE WAS A SHIP RUN AGROUND ON THE POINT.

A SHIP?

AN OLD FREIGHTER, SAN SOMETHING-OR-OTHER. FOUR-FOUR SAID THEY WERE BOARDING HER, THEN WENT OFF THE AIR.

LOOK, CUSTER WON'T BE COMING ON A FUCKING BANANA BOAT. LET'S JUST CONCENTRATE ON STAYING ALIVE UNTIL HIS ARRIVAL, SHALL WE?

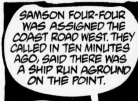

GOD, THAT MONSTER SICKENS ME. LOOK AT HIM ...WHAT DO YOU SUPPOSE HE'S THINKING ABOUT?

HIS FAVORITE SUBJECTS, I'D IMAGINE.

MASS MURDER AND BIG PIES.

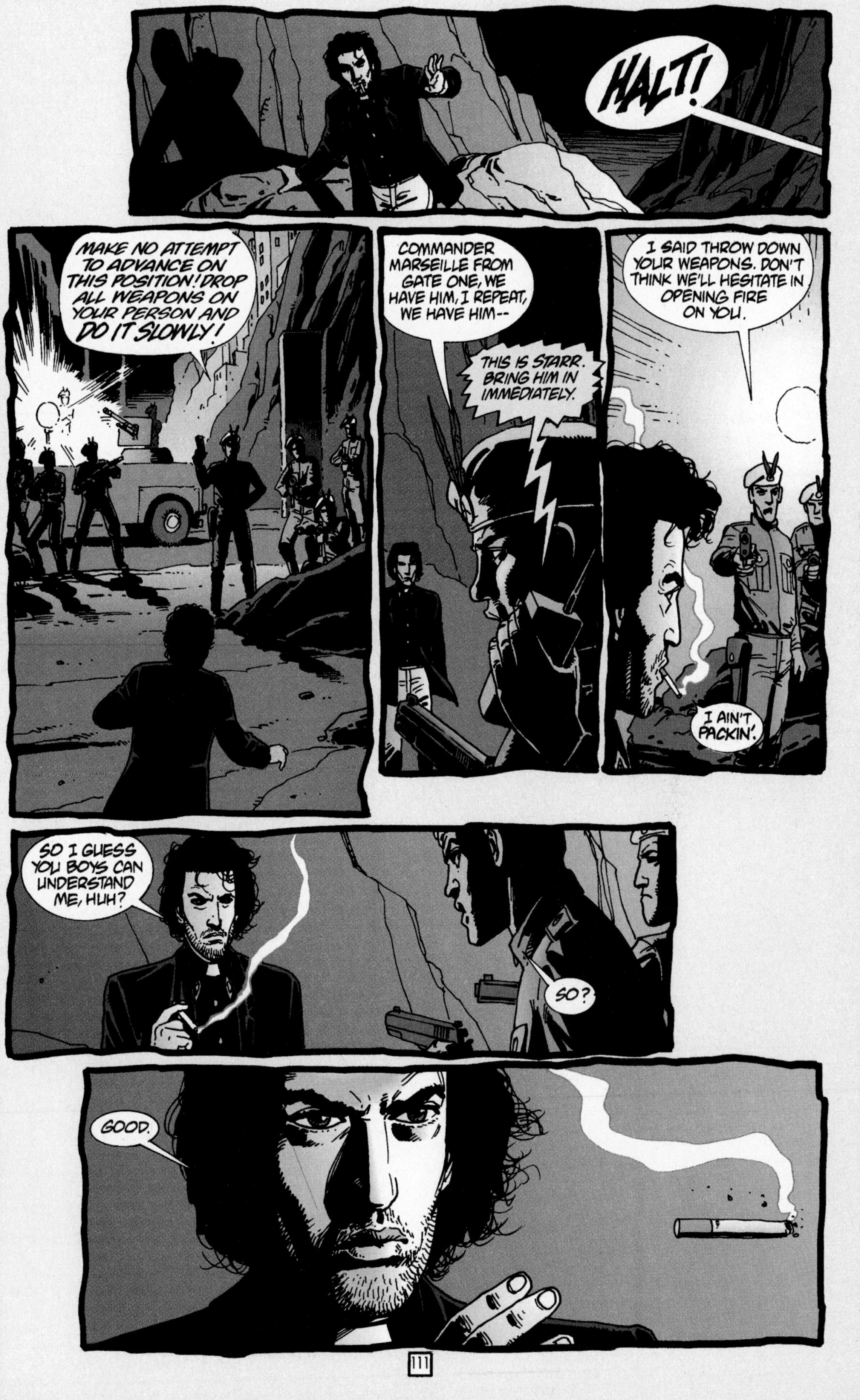
HALT!
MAKE NO ATTEMPT TO ADVANCE ON THIS POSITION! DROP ALL WEAPONS ON YOUR PERSON AND DO IT SLOWLY!
COMMANDER MARSEILLE FROM GATE ONE, WE HAVE HIM, I REPEAT, WE HAVE HIM--
THIS IS STARR. BRING HIM IN IMMEDIATELY.
I SAID THROW DOWN YOUR WEAPONS. DON'T THINK WE'LL HESITATE IN OPENING FIRE ON YOU.
I AIN'T PACKIN'.
SO I GUESS YOU BOYS CAN UNDERSTAND ME, HUH?
SO?
GOOD.

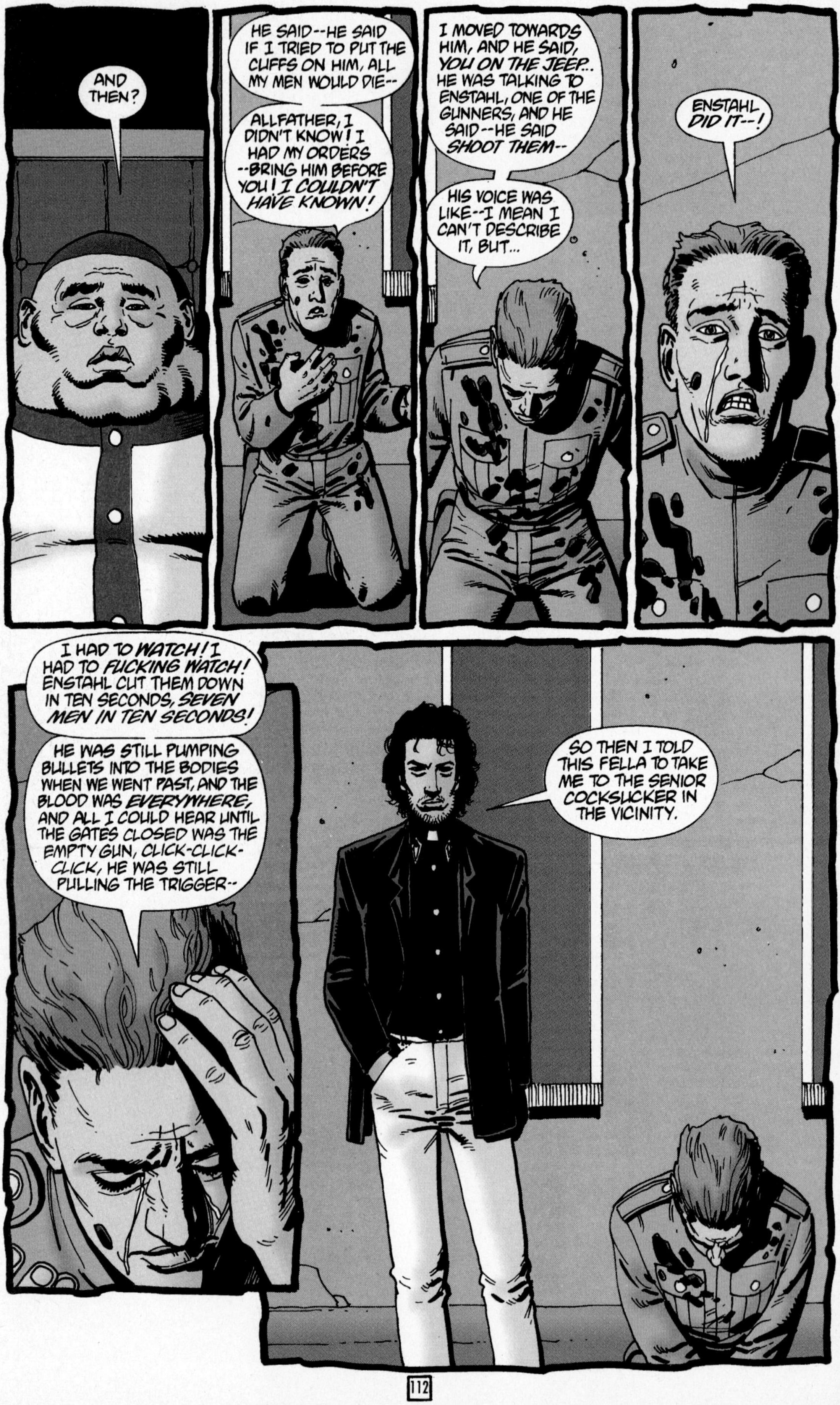
AND THEN?
HE SAID--HE SAID IF I TRIED TO PUT THE CUFFS ON HIM, ALL MY MEN WOULD DIE--
ALLFATHER, I DIDN'T KNOW! I HAD MY ORDERS --BRING HIM BEFORE YOU! I COULDN'T HAVE KNOWN!
I MOVED TOWARDS HIM, AND HE SAID, YOU ON THE JEEP.. HE WAS TALKING TO ENSTAHL, ONE OF THE GUNNERS, AND HE SAID--HE SAID SHOOT THEM--
HIS VOICE WAS LIKE--I MEAN I CAN'T DESCRIBE IT, BUT...
ENSTAHL DID IT--!
I HAD TO WATCH! I HAD TO FUCKING WATCH! ENSTAHL CUT THEM DOWN IN TEN SECONDS, SEVEN MEN IN TEN SECONDS!
HE WAS STILL PUMPING BULLETS INTO THE BODIES WHEN WE WENT PAST, AND THE BLOOD WAS EVERYWHERE, AND ALL I COULD HEAR UNTIL THE GATES CLOSED WAS THE EMPTY GUN, CLICK-CLICK-CLICK, HE WAS STILL PULLING THE TRIGGER--
SO THEN I TOLD THIS FELLA TO TAKE ME TO THE SENIOR COCKSUCKER IN THE VICINITY.

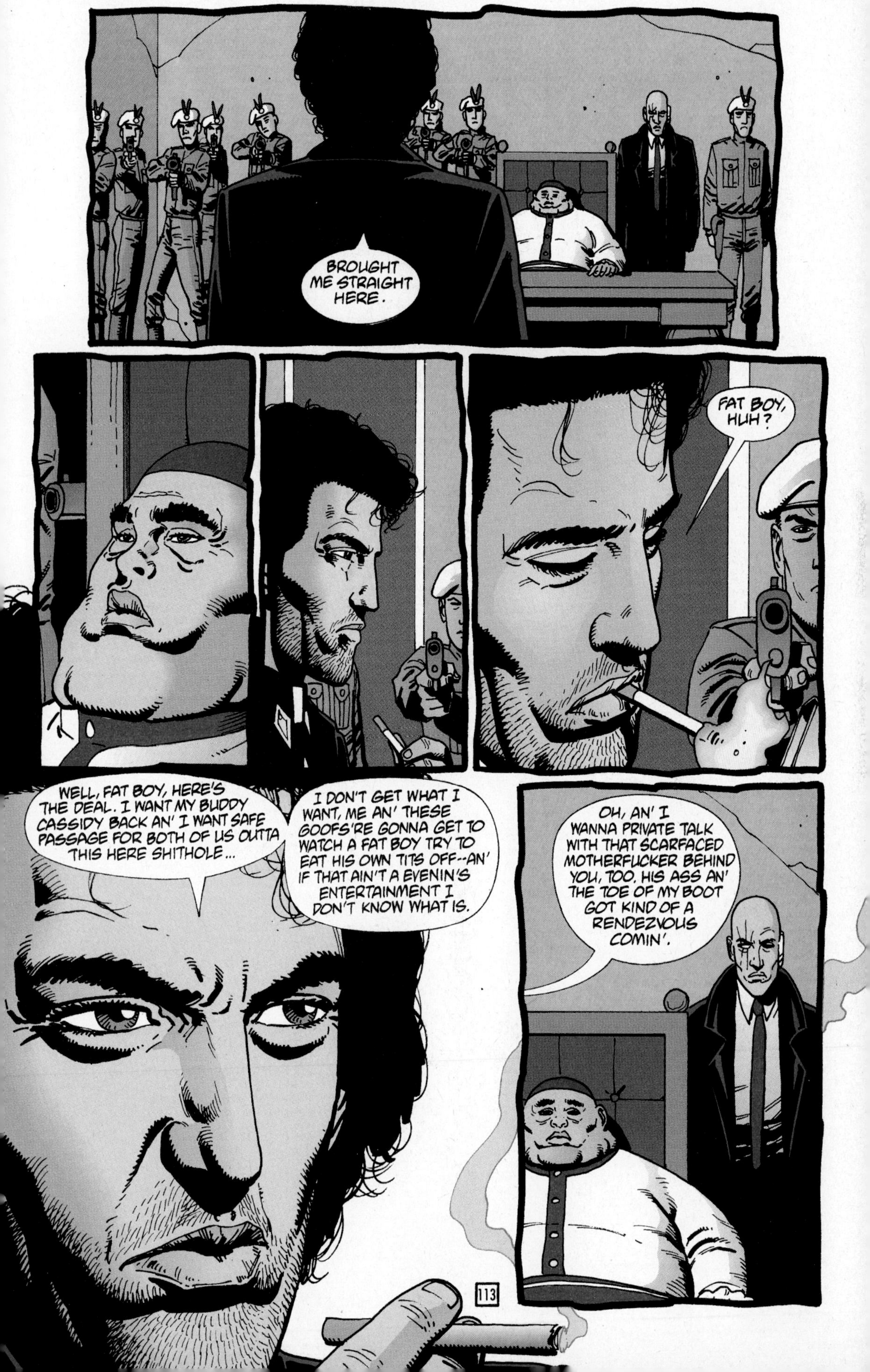
BROUGHT ME STRAIGHT HERE.
FAT BOY, HUH?
WELL, FAT BOY, HERE'S THE DEAL. I WANT MY BUDDY CASSIDY BACK AN' I WANT SAFE PASSAGE FOR BOTH OF US OUTTA THIS HERE SHITHOLE...
I DON'T GET WHAT I WANT, ME AN' THESE GOOFS'RE GONNA GET TO WATCH A FAT BOY TRY TO EAT HIS OWN TITS OFF--AN' IF THAT AIN'T A EVENIN'S ENTERTAINMENT I DON'T KNOW WHAT IS.
OH, AN' I WANNA PRIVATE TALK WITH THAT SCARFACED MOTHERFUCKER BEHIND YOU, TOO. HIS ASS AN' THE TOE OF MY BOOT GOT KIND OF A RENDEZVOUS COMIN'.

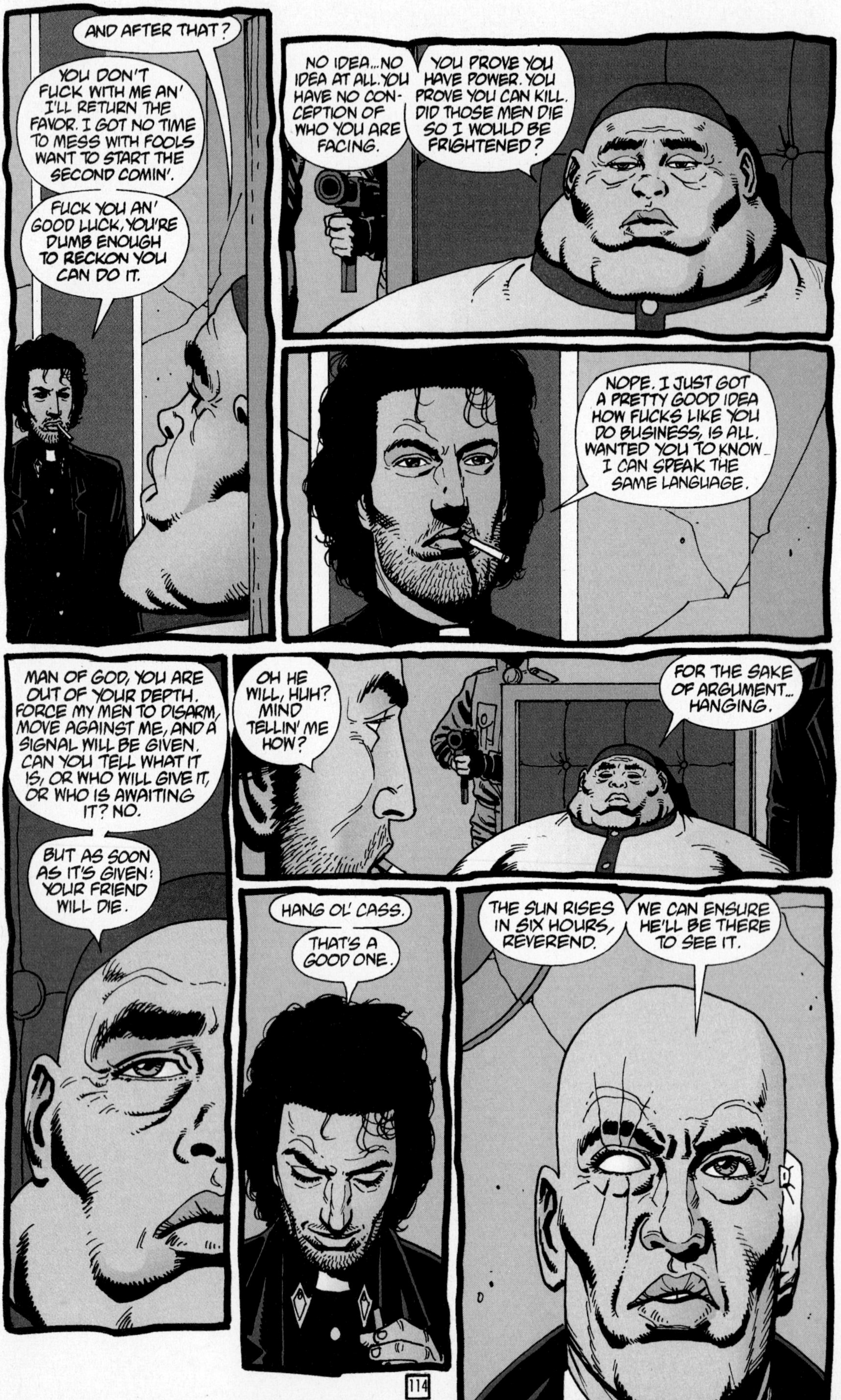
AND AFTER THAT?
YOU DON'T FUCK WITH ME AN' I'LL RETURN THE FAVOR. I GOT NO TIME TO MESS WITH FOOLS WANT TO START THE SECOND COMIN'.
FUCK YOU AN' GOOD LUCK, YOU'RE DUMB ENOUGH TO RECKON YOU CAN DO IT.
NO IDEA...NO IDEA AT ALL. YOU HAVE NO CONCEPTION OF WHO YOU ARE FACING.
YOU PROVE YOU HAVE POWER. YOU PROVE YOU CAN KILL. DID THOSE MEN DIE SO I WOULD BE FRIGHTENED?
NOPE. I JUST GOT A PRETTY GOOD IDEA HOW FUCKS LIKE YOU DO BUSINESS, IS ALL. WANTED YOU TO KNOW I CAN SPEAK THE SAME LANGUAGE.
MAN OF GOD, YOU ARE OUT OF YOUR DEPTH. FORCE MY MEN TO DISARM, MOVE AGAINST ME, AND A SIGNAL WILL BE GIVEN. CAN YOU TELL WHAT IT IS, OR WHO WILL GIVE IT, OR WHO IS AWAITING IT? NO.
BUT AS SOON AS IT'S GIVEN: YOUR FRIEND WILL DIE.
OH HE WILL, HUH? MIND TELLIN' ME HOW?
FOR THE SAKE OF ARGUMENT... HANGING.
HANG OL' CASS.
THAT'S A GOOD ONE.
THE SUN RISES IN SIX HOURS, REVEREND.
WE CAN ENSURE HE'LL BE THERE TO SEE IT.

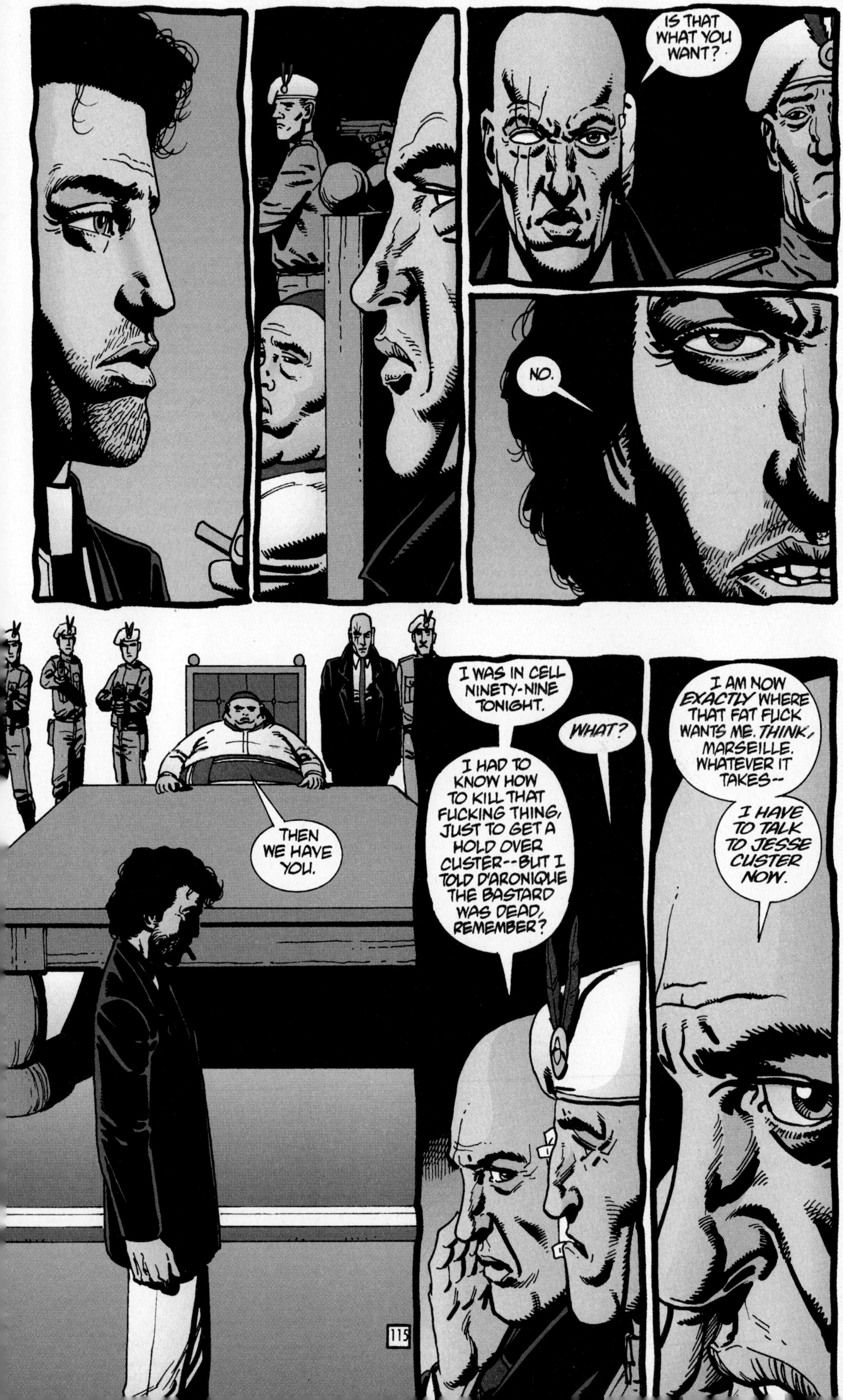
IS THAT WHAT YOU WANT?
NO.
THEN WE HAVE YOU.
I WAS IN CELL NINETY-NINE TONIGHT.
WHAT?
I HAD TO KNOW HOW TO KILL THAT FUCKING THING, JUST TO GET A HOLD OVER CUSTER--BUT I TOLD D'ARONIQUE THE BASTARD WAS DEAD, REMEMBER?
I AM NOW EXACTLY WHERE THAT FAT FUCK WANTS ME. THINK, MARSEILLE. WHATEVER IT TAKES--
I HAVE TO TALK TO JESSE CUSTER NOW.
115

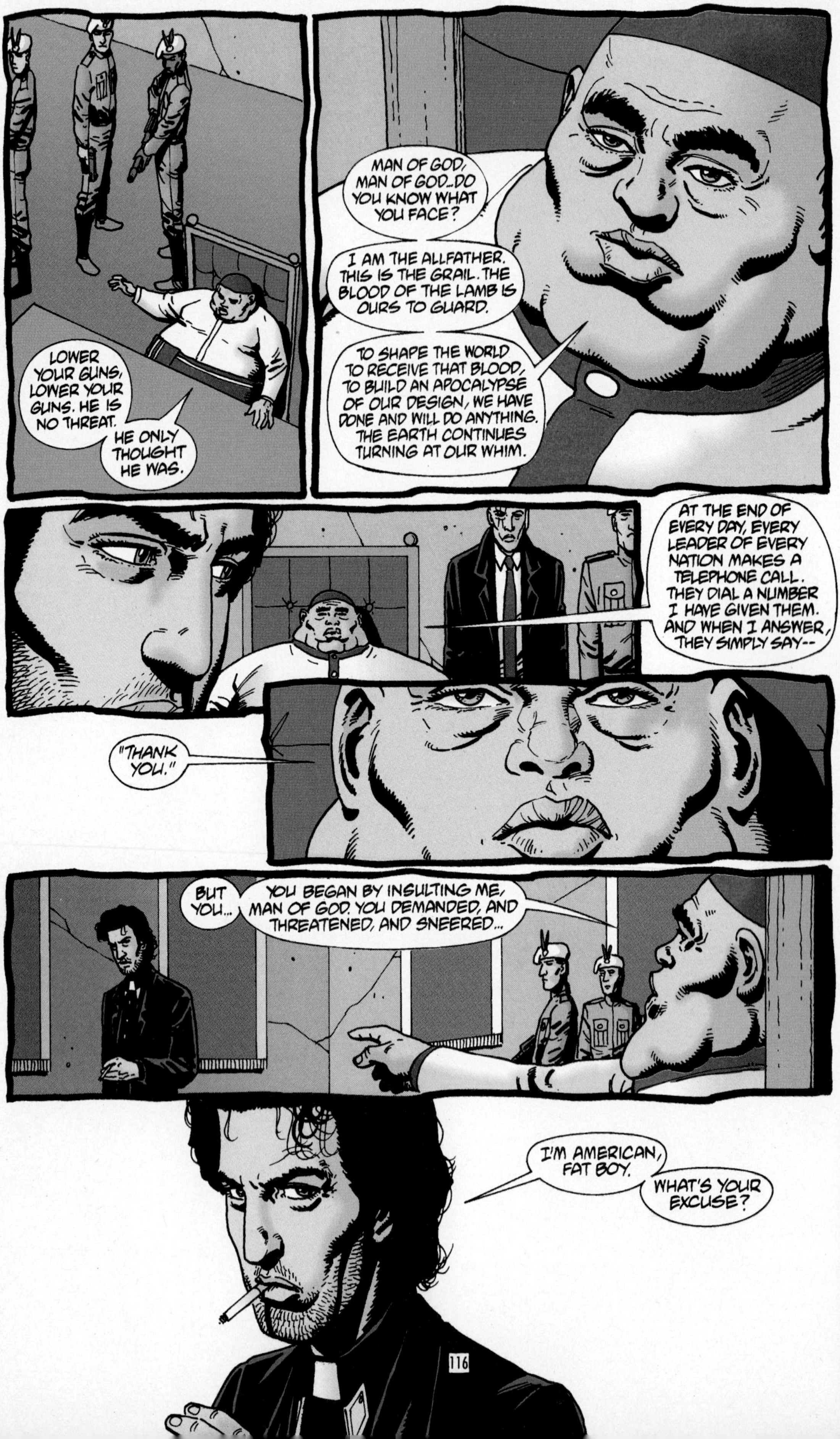
LOWER YOUR GUNS, LOWER YOUR GUNS. HE IS NO THREAT.
HE ONLY THOUGHT HE WAS.
MAN OF GOD, MAN OF GOD...DO YOU KNOW WHAT YOU FACE?
I AM THE ALLFATHER. THIS IS THE GRAIL. THE BLOOD OF THE LAMB IS OURS TO GUARD.
TO SHAPE THE WORLD TO RECEIVE THAT BLOOD, TO BUILD AN APOCALYPSE OF OUR DESIGN, WE HAVE DONE AND WILL DO ANYTHING. THE EARTH CONTINUES TURNING AT OUR WHIM.
AT THE END OF EVERY DAY, EVERY LEADER OF EVERY NATION MAKES A TELEPHONE CALL. THEY DIAL A NUMBER I HAVE GIVEN THEM. AND WHEN I ANSWER, THEY SIMPLY SAY--
"THANK YOU."
BUT YOU...
YOU BEGAN BY INSULTING ME, MAN OF GOD. YOU DEMANDED, AND THREATENED, AND SNEERED...
I'M AMERICAN, FAT BOY.
WHAT'S YOUR EXCUSE?

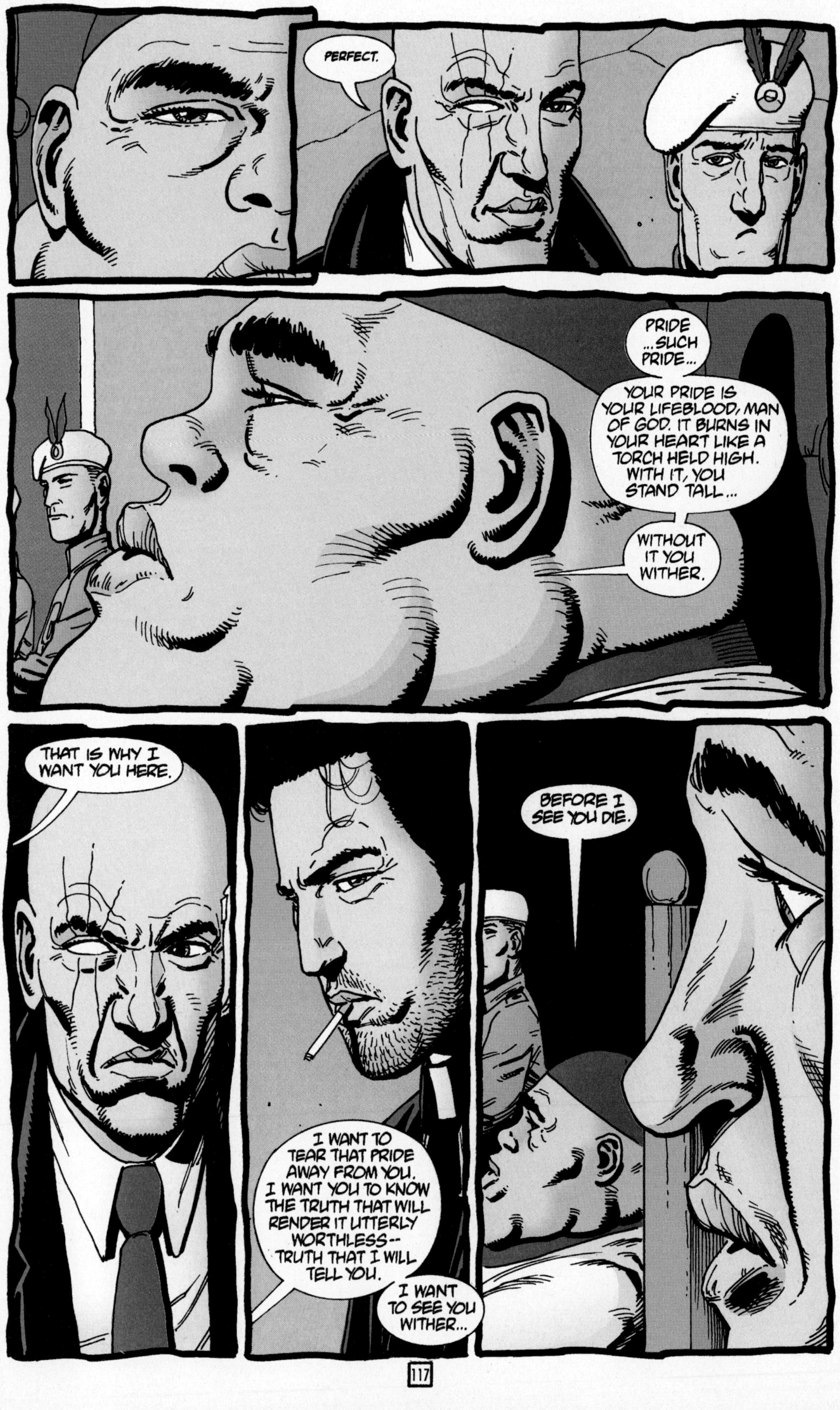
PERFECT.
PRIDE ...SUCH PRIDE...
YOUR PRIDE IS YOUR LIFEBLOOD, MAN OF GOD. IT BURNS IN YOUR HEART LIKE A TORCH HELD HIGH. WITH IT, YOU STAND TALL...
WITHOUT IT YOU WITHER.
THAT IS WHY I WANT YOU HERE.
I WANT TO TEAR THAT PRIDE AWAY FROM YOU. I WANT YOU TO KNOW THE TRUTH THAT WILL RENDER IT UTTERLY WORTHLESS-- TRUTH THAT I WILL TELL YOU.
I WANT TO SEE YOU WITHER...
BEFORE I SEE YOU DIE.

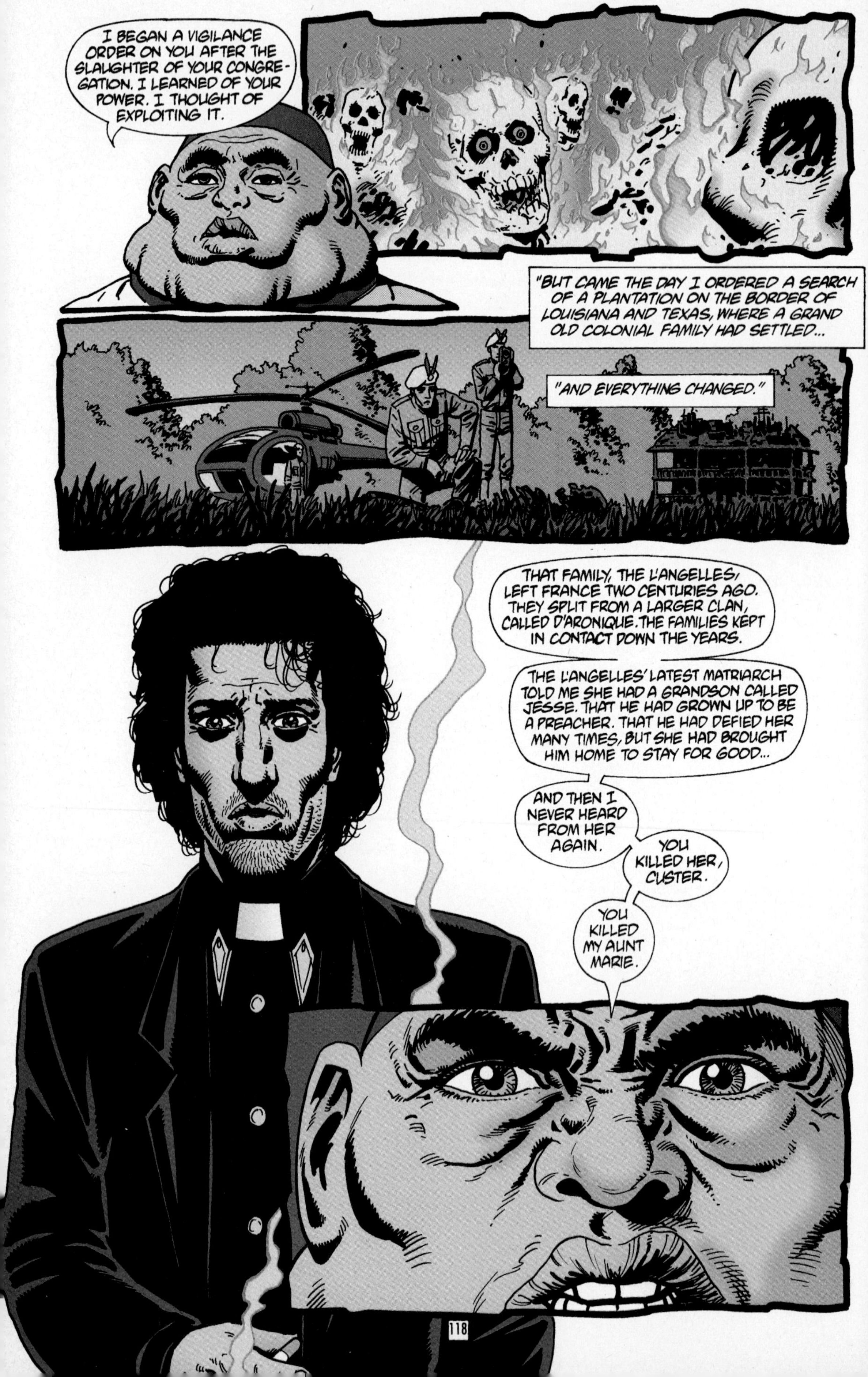
I BEGAN A VIGILANCE ORDER ON YOU AFTER THE SLAUGHTER OF YOUR CONGREGATION. I LEARNED OF YOUR POWER. I THOUGHT OF EXPLOITING IT.
"BUT CAME THE DAY I ORDERED A SEARCH OF A PLANTATION ON THE BORDER OF LOUISIANA AND TEXAS, WHERE A GRAND OLD COLONIAL FAMILY HAD SETTLED...
"AND EVERYTHING CHANGED."
THAT FAMILY, THE L'ANGELLES, LEFT FRANCE TWO CENTURIES AGO. THEY SPLIT FROM A LARGER CLAN, CALLED D'ARONIQUE. THE FAMILIES KEPT IN CONTACT DOWN THE YEARS.
THE L'ANGELLES' LATEST MATRIARCH TOLD ME SHE HAD A GRANDSON CALLED JESSE. THAT HE HAD GROWN UP TO BE A PREACHER. THAT HE HAD DEFIED HER MANY TIMES, BUT SHE HAD BROUGHT HIM HOME TO STAY FOR GOOD...
AND THEN I NEVER HEARD FROM HER AGAIN.
YOU KILLED HER, CUSTER.
YOU KILLED MY AUNT MARIE.

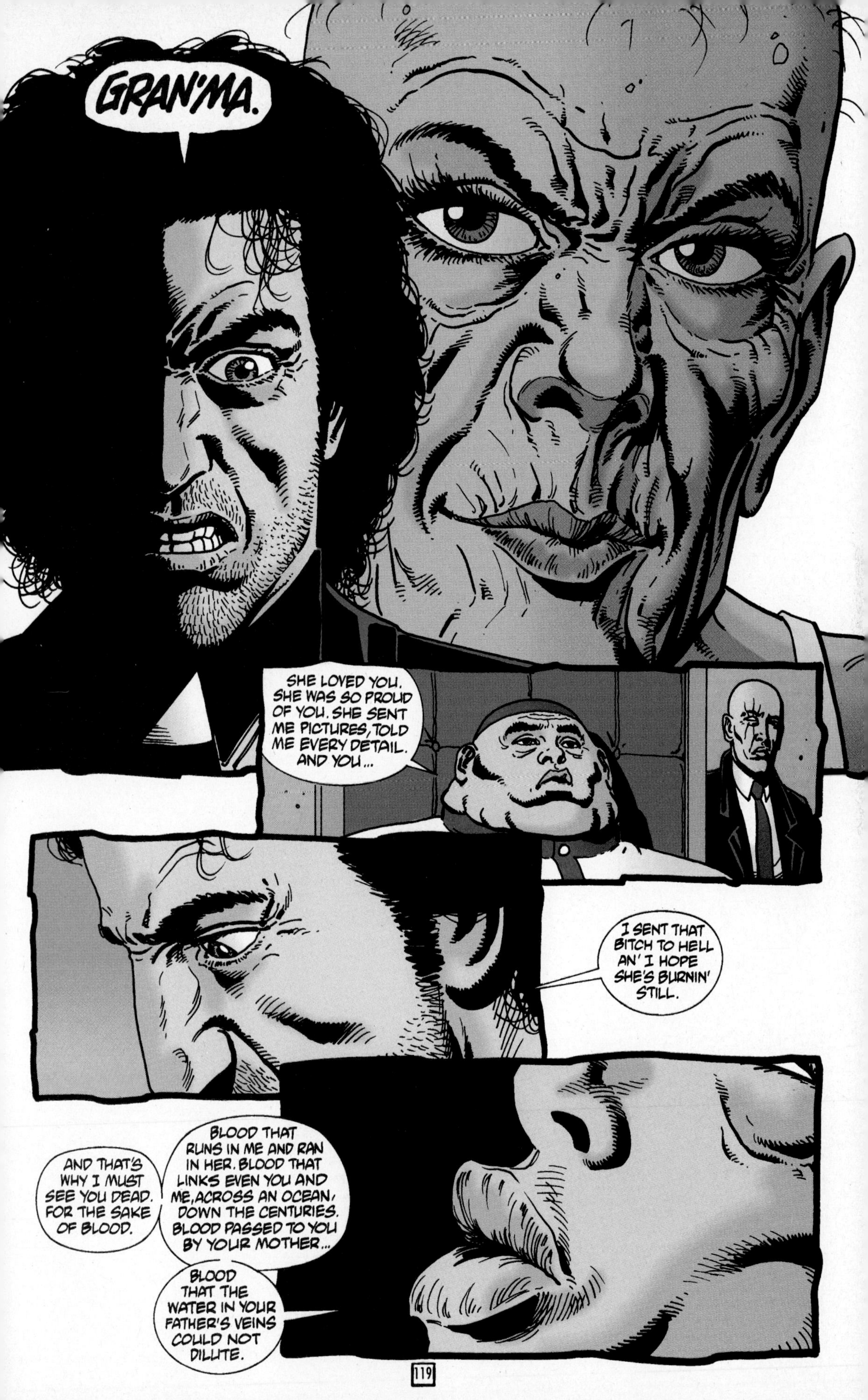
GRAN'MA.
SHE LOVED YOU. SHE WAS SO PROUD OF YOU. SHE SENT ME PICTURES, TOLD ME EVERY DETAIL. AND YOU...
I SENT THAT BITCH TO HELL AN' I HOPE SHE'S BURNIN' STILL.
BLOOD THAT RUNS IN ME AND RAN IN HER. BLOOD THAT LINKS EVEN YOU AND ME, ACROSS AN OCEAN, DOWN THE CENTURIES. BLOOD PASSED TO YOU BY YOUR MOTHER...
BLOOD THAT THE WATER IN YOUR FATHER'S VEINS COULD NOT DILUTE.
AND THAT'S WHY I MUST SEE YOU DEAD. FOR THE SAKE OF BLOOD.

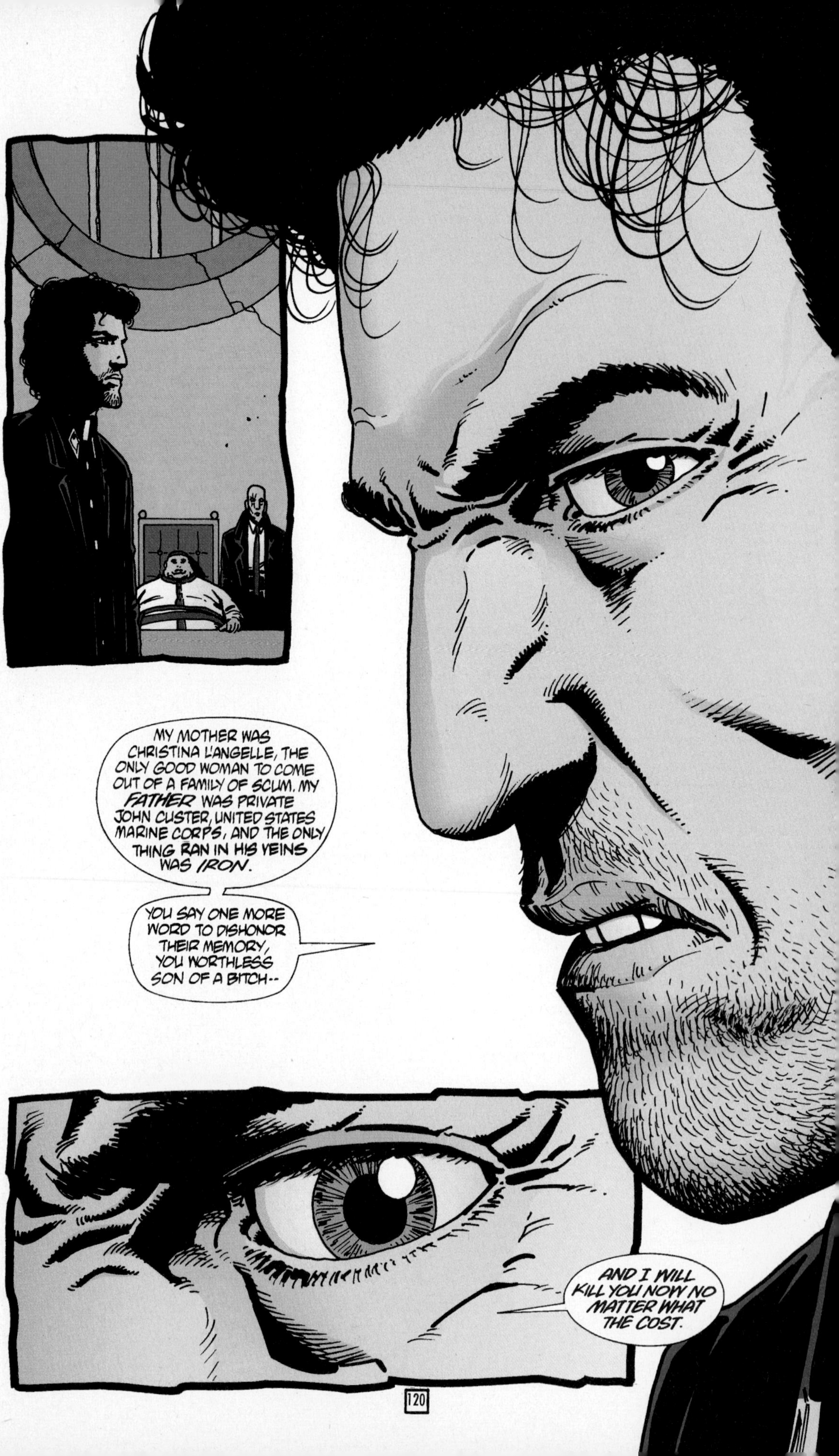
MY MOTHER WAS CHRISTINA L'ANGELLE, THE ONLY GOOD WOMAN TO COME OUT OF A FAMILY OF SCUM. MY *FATHER* WAS PRIVATE JOHN CUSTER, UNITED STATES MARINE CORPS, AND THE ONLY THING RAN IN HIS VEINS WAS *IRON*.
YOU SAY ONE MORE WORD TO DISHONOR THEIR MEMORY, YOU WORTHLESS SON OF A BITCH--
AND I WILL KILL YOU NOW NO MATTER WHAT THE COST.

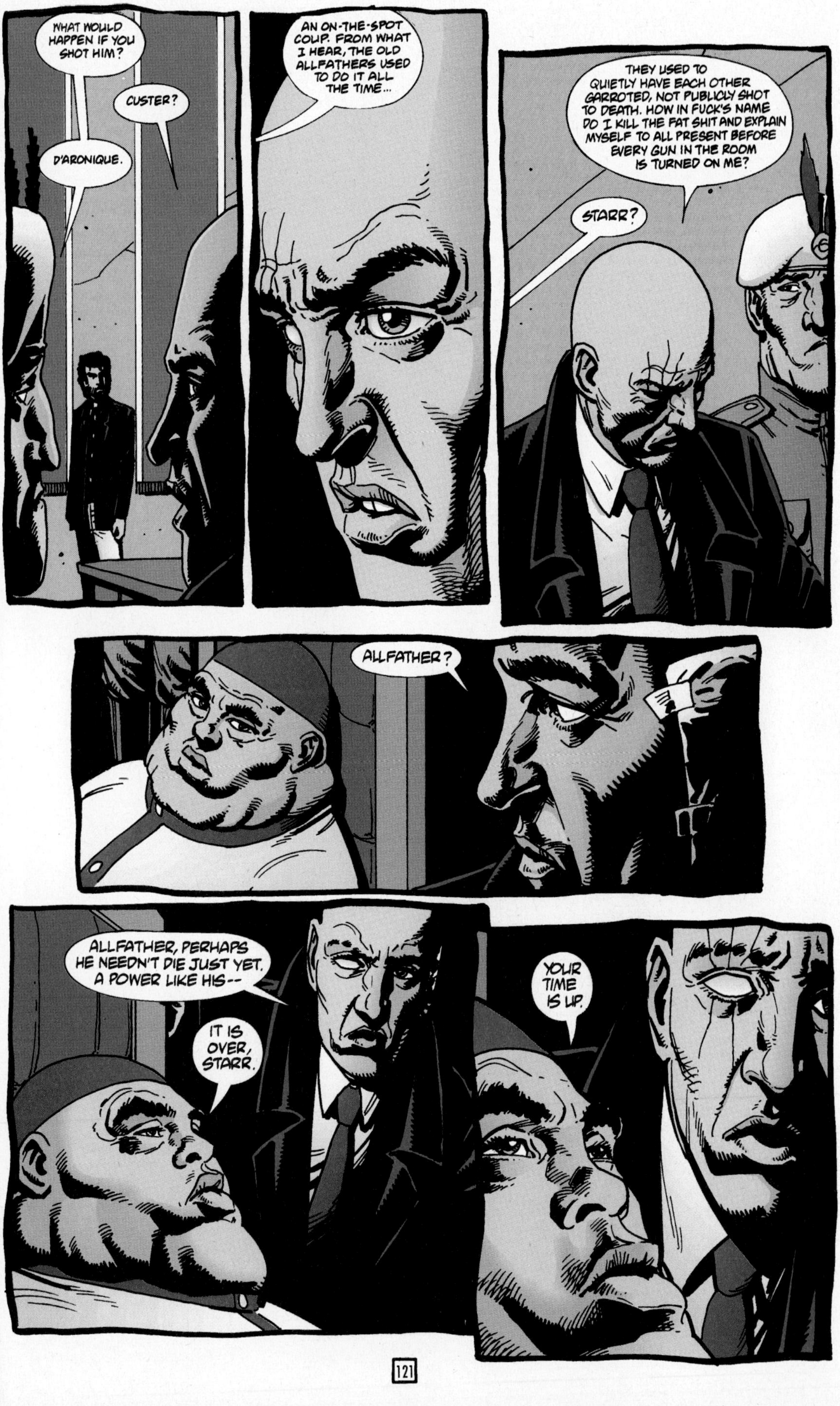
WHAT WOULD HAPPEN IF YOU SHOT HIM?
CUSTER?
D'ARONIQUE.
AN ON-THE-SPOT COUP. FROM WHAT I HEAR, THE OLD ALLFATHERS USED TO DO IT ALL THE TIME...
THEY USED TO QUIETLY HAVE EACH OTHER GARROTED, NOT PUBLICLY SHOT TO DEATH. HOW IN FUCK'S NAME DO I KILL THE FAT SHIT AND EXPLAIN MYSELF TO ALL PRESENT BEFORE EVERY GUN IN THE ROOM IS TURNED ON ME?
STARR?
ALLFATHER?
ALLFATHER, PERHAPS HE NEEDN'T DIE JUST YET. A POWER LIKE HIS--
IT IS OVER, STARR.
YOUR TIME IS UP.

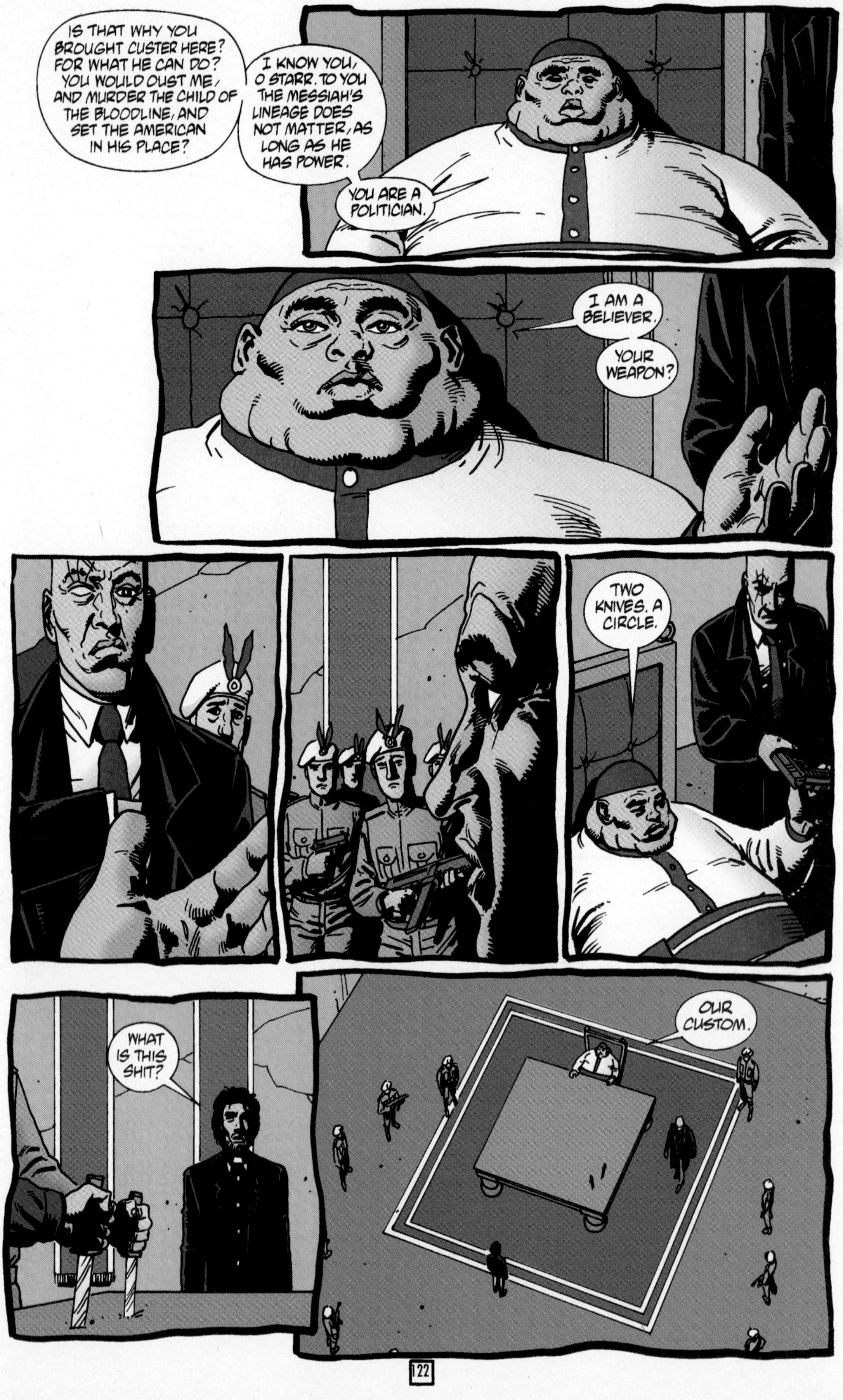
IS THAT WHY YOU BROUGHT CUSTER HERE? FOR WHAT HE CAN DO? YOU WOULD OUST ME, AND MURDER THE CHILD OF THE BLOODLINE, AND SET THE AMERICAN IN HIS PLACE?
I KNOW YOU, O STARR. TO YOU THE MESSIAH'S LINEAGE DOES NOT MATTER, AS LONG AS HE HAS POWER.
YOU ARE A POLITICIAN.
I AM A BELIEVER.
YOUR WEAPON?
TWO KNIVES. A CIRCLE.
WHAT IS THIS SHIT?
OUR CUSTOM.

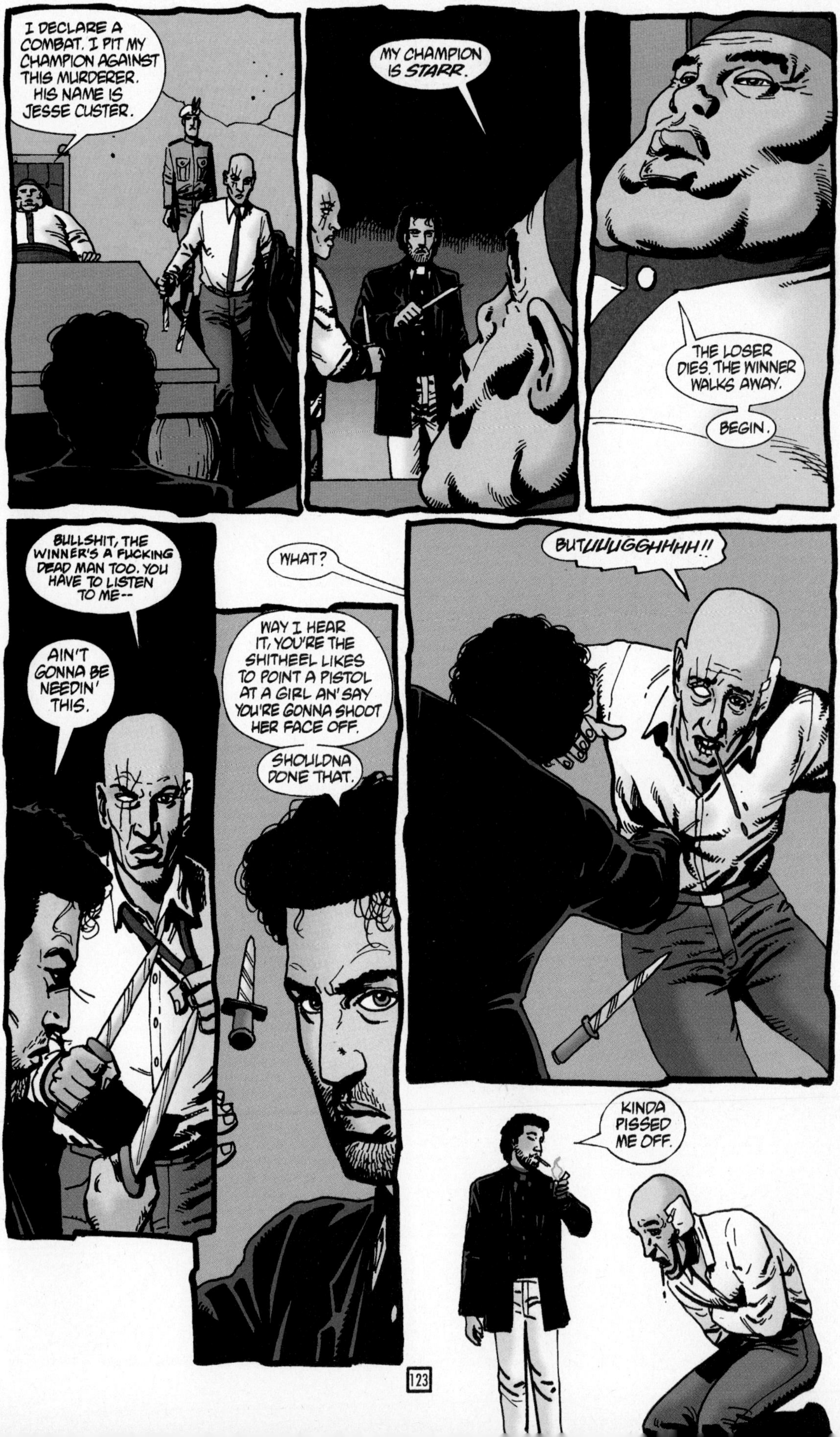
I DECLARE A COMBAT. I PIT MY CHAMPION AGAINST THIS MURDERER. HIS NAME IS JESSE CUSTER.
MY CHAMPION IS *STARR*.
THE LOSER DIES. THE WINNER WALKS AWAY.
BEGIN.
BULLSHIT, THE WINNER'S A FUCKING DEAD MAN TOO. YOU HAVE TO LISTEN TO ME--
AIN'T GONNA BE NEEDIN' THIS.
WHAT?
WAY I HEAR IT, YOU'RE THE SHITHEEL LIKES TO POINT A PISTOL AT A GIRL AN' SAY YOU'RE GONNA SHOOT HER FACE OFF.
SHOULDNA DONE THAT.
BUTUUUGGHHHH!!
KINDA PISSED ME OFF.

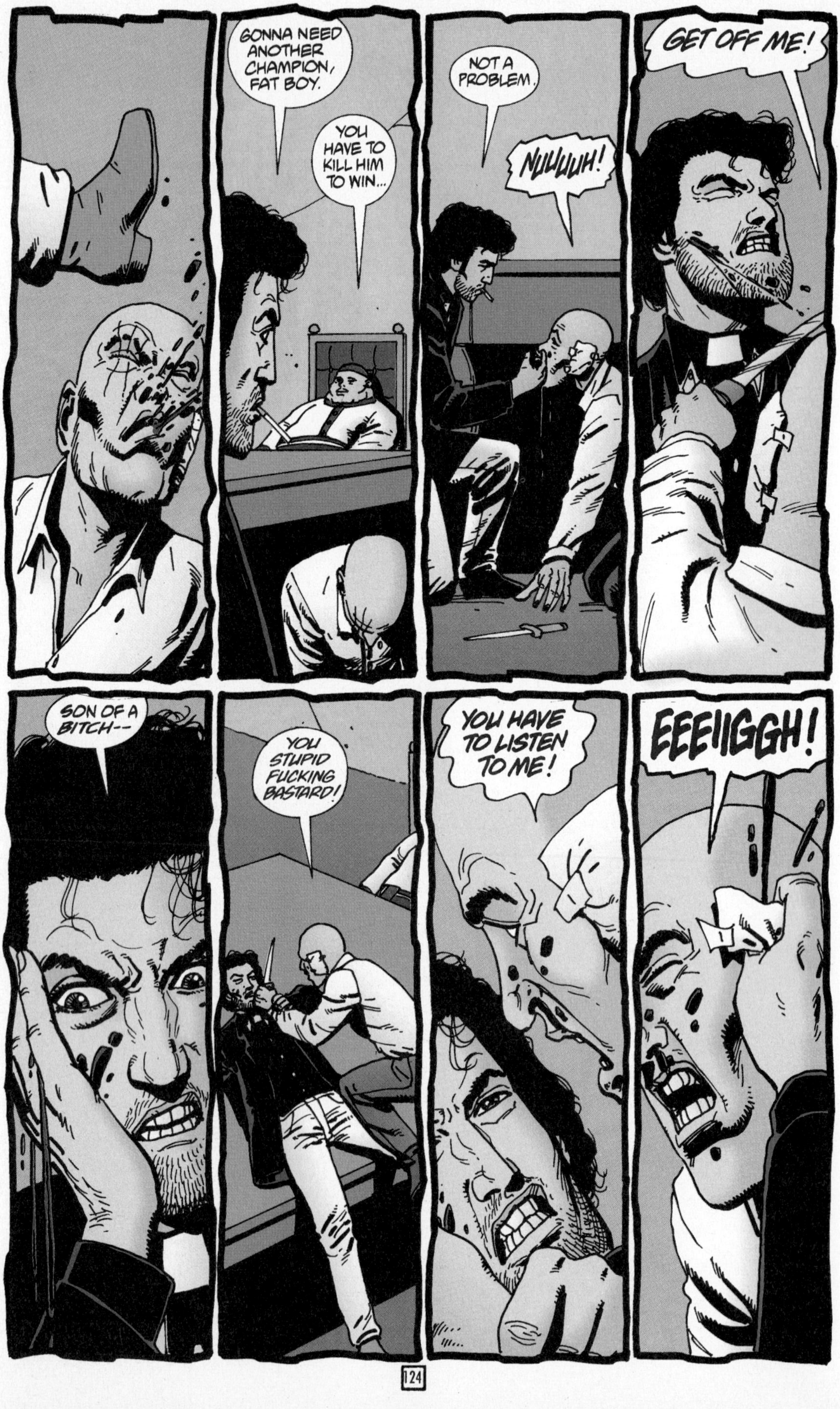
GONNA NEED ANOTHER CHAMPION, FAT BOY.
YOU HAVE TO KILL HIM TO WIN...
NOT A PROBLEM.
NUUUUH!
GET OFF ME!
SON OF A BITCH--
YOU STUPID FUCKING BASTARD!
YOU HAVE TO LISTEN TO ME!
EEEIIGGH!

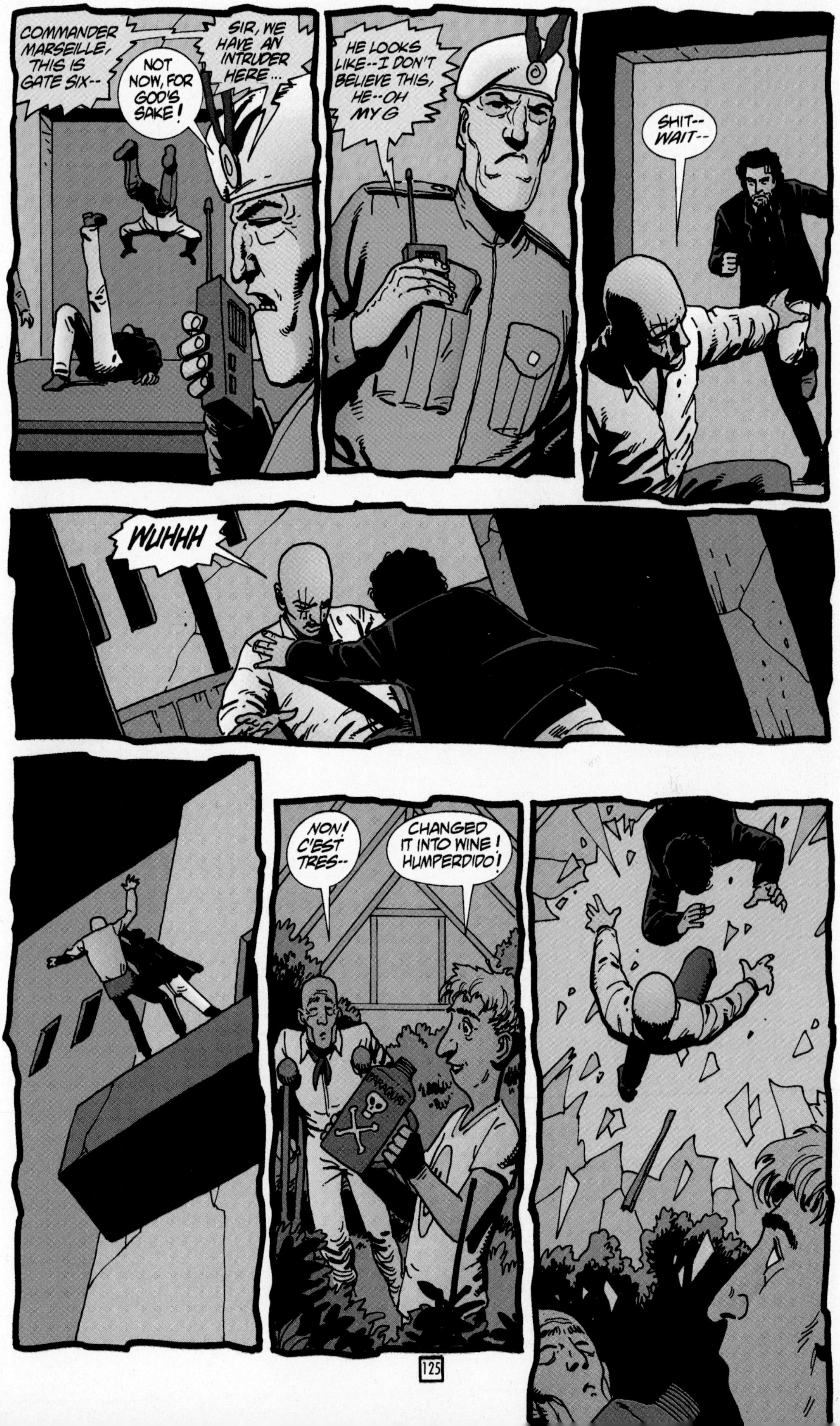
COMMANDER MARSEILLE, THIS IS GATE SIX--
SIR, WE HAVE AN INTRUDER HERE...
NOT NOW, FOR GOD'S SAKE!
HE LOOKS LIKE--I DON'T BELIEVE THIS, HE--OH MY G
SHIT-- WAIT--
WUHHH
NON! C'EST TRES--
CHANGED IT INTO WINE! HUMPERDIDO!
PARAQUAT

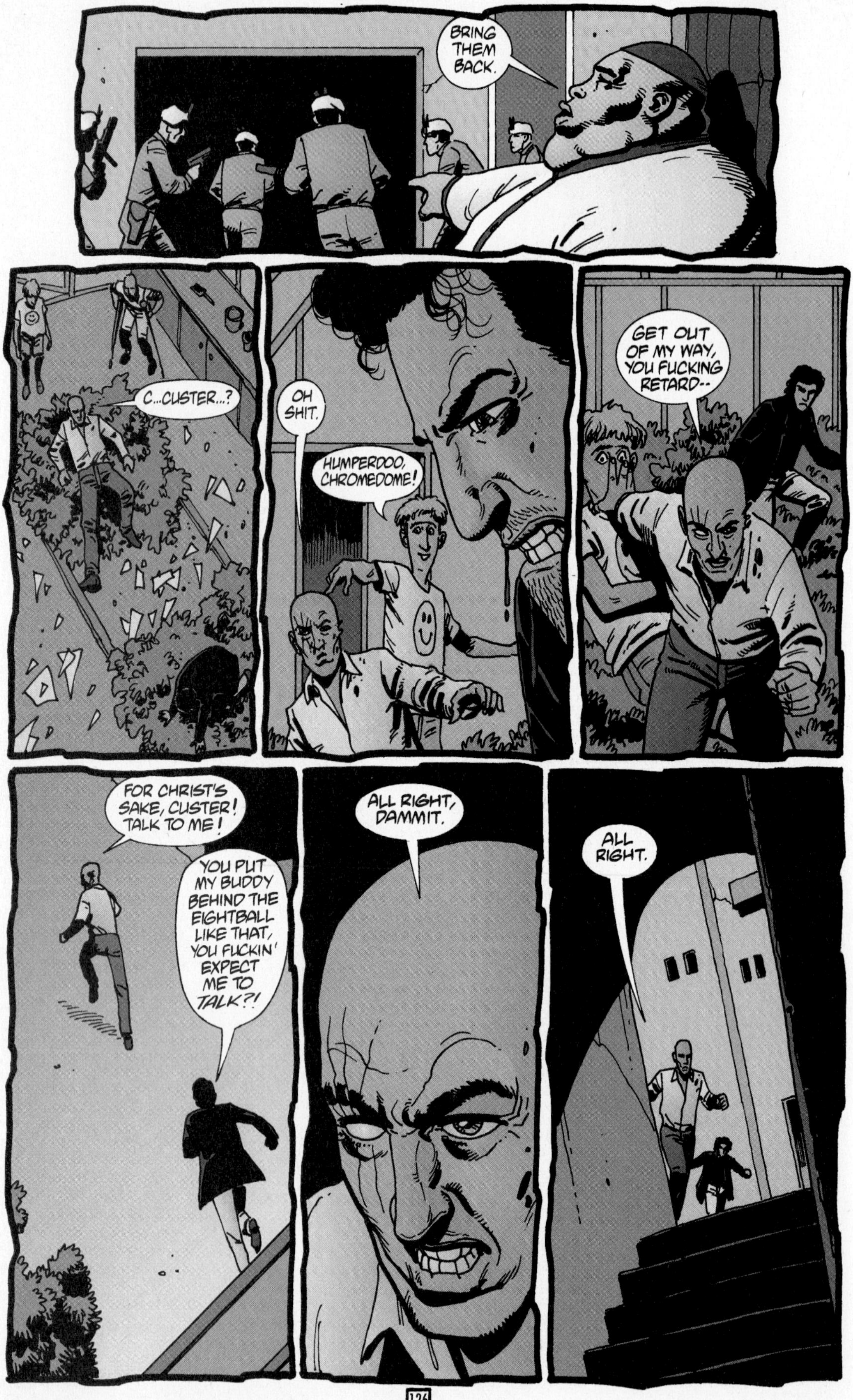
BRING THEM BACK.
C...CUSTER...?
OH SHIT.
HUMPERDOO, CHROMEDOME!
GET OUT OF MY WAY, YOU FUCKING RETARD--
FOR CHRIST'S SAKE, CUSTER! TALK TO ME!
YOU PUT MY BUDDY BEHIND THE EIGHTBALL LIKE THAT, YOU FUCKIN' EXPECT ME TO TALK?!
ALL RIGHT, DAMMIT.
ALL RIGHT.

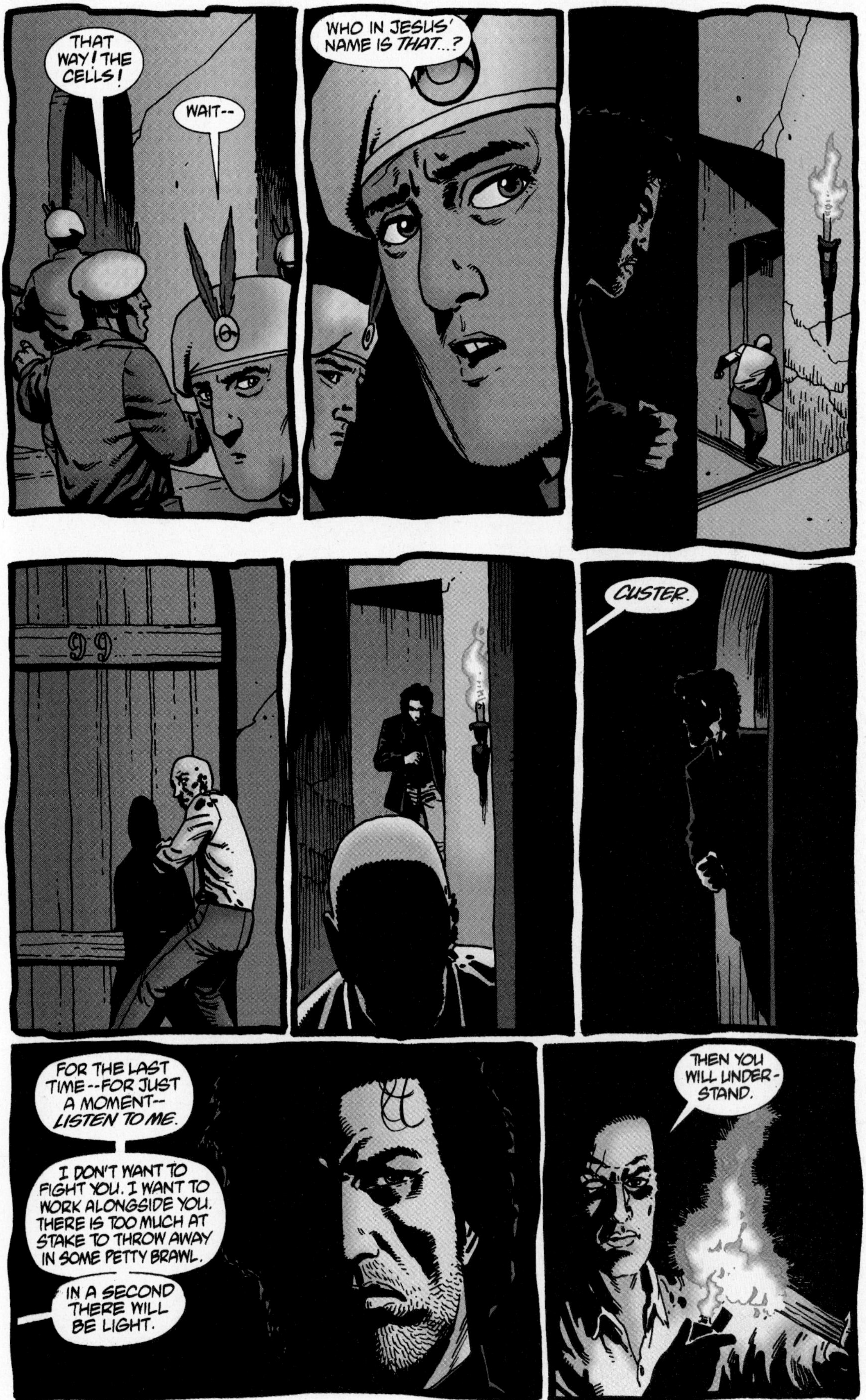
THAT WAY! THE CELLS!
WAIT--
WHO IN JESUS' NAME IS *THAT*...?
99
CUSTER.
FOR THE LAST TIME--FOR JUST A MOMENT-- *LISTEN TO ME.*
I DON'T WANT TO FIGHT YOU. I WANT TO WORK ALONGSIDE YOU. THERE IS TOO MUCH AT STAKE TO THROW AWAY IN SOME PETTY BRAWL.
IN A SECOND THERE WILL BE LIGHT.
THEN YOU WILL UNDER-STAND.

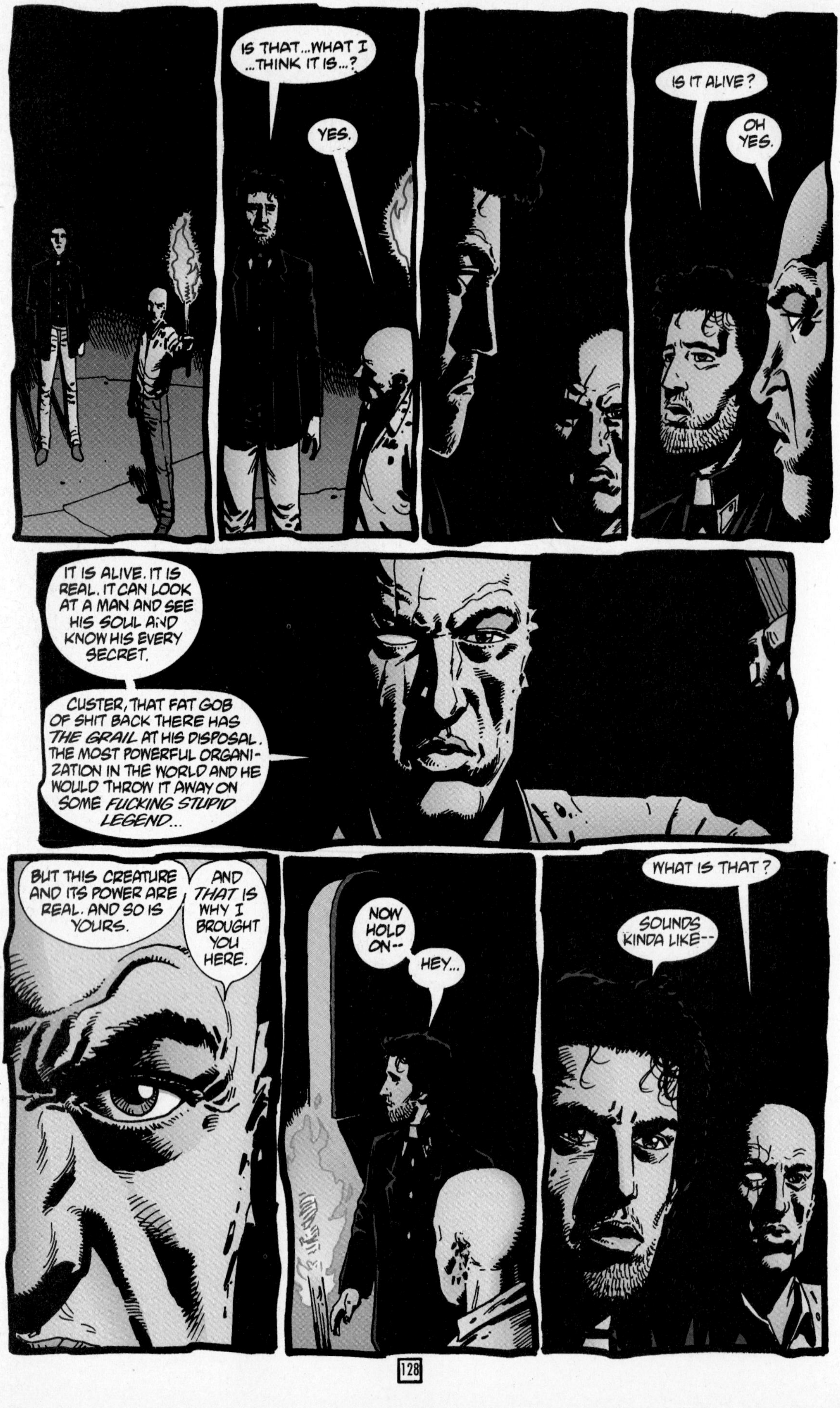
IS THAT...WHAT I ...THINK IT IS...?
YES.
IS IT ALIVE?
OH YES.
IT IS ALIVE. IT IS REAL. IT CAN LOOK AT A MAN AND SEE HIS SOUL AND KNOW HIS EVERY SECRET.
CUSTER, THAT FAT GOB OF SHIT BACK THERE HAS *THE GRAIL* AT HIS DISPOSAL. THE MOST POWERFUL ORGANIZATION IN THE WORLD AND HE WOULD THROW IT AWAY ON SOME *FUCKING STUPID LEGEND*...
BUT THIS CREATURE AND ITS POWER ARE REAL. AND SO IS YOURS.
AND *THAT* IS WHY I BROUGHT YOU HERE.
NOW HOLD ON--
HEY...
WHAT IS THAT?
SOUNDS KINDA LIKE--

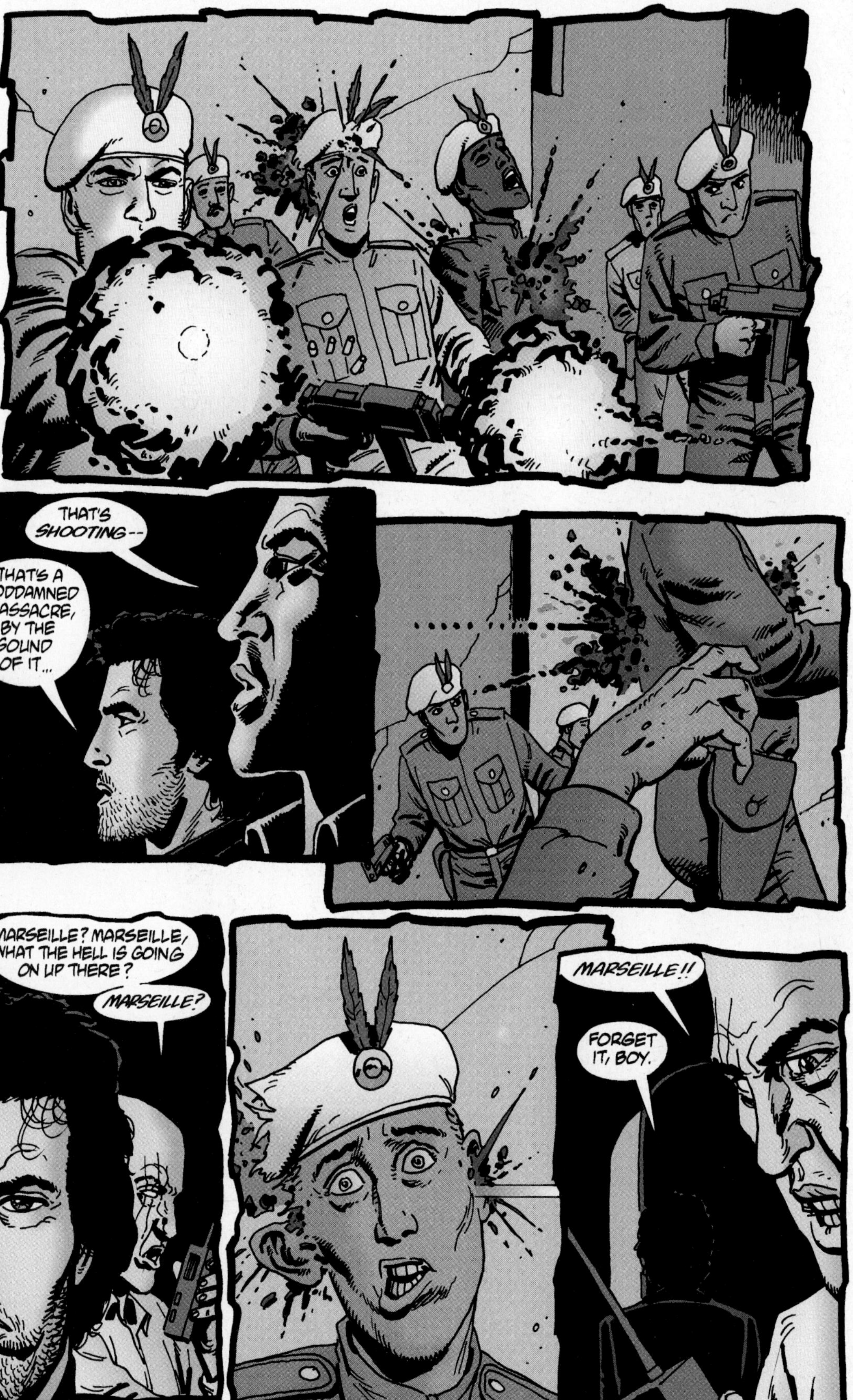
THAT'S *SHOOTING*--
THAT'S A GODDAMNED MASSACRE, BY THE SOUND OF IT...
MARSEILLE? MARSEILLE, WHAT THE HELL IS GOING ON UP THERE?
MARSEILLE?
MARSEILLE!!
FORGET IT, BOY.

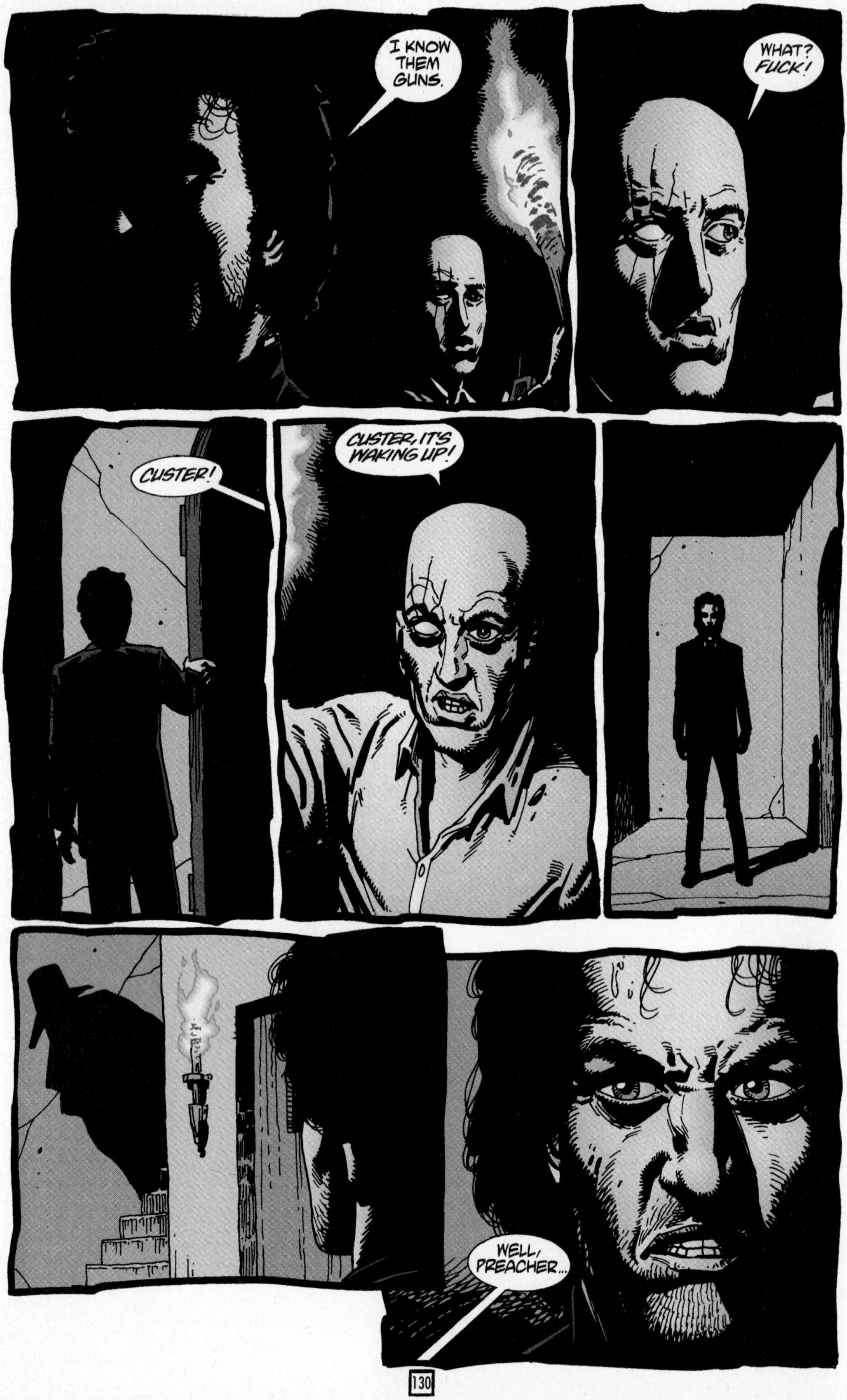
I KNOW THEM GUNS.
WHAT? FUCK!
CUSTER!
CUSTER, IT'S WAKING UP!
WELL, PREACHER...

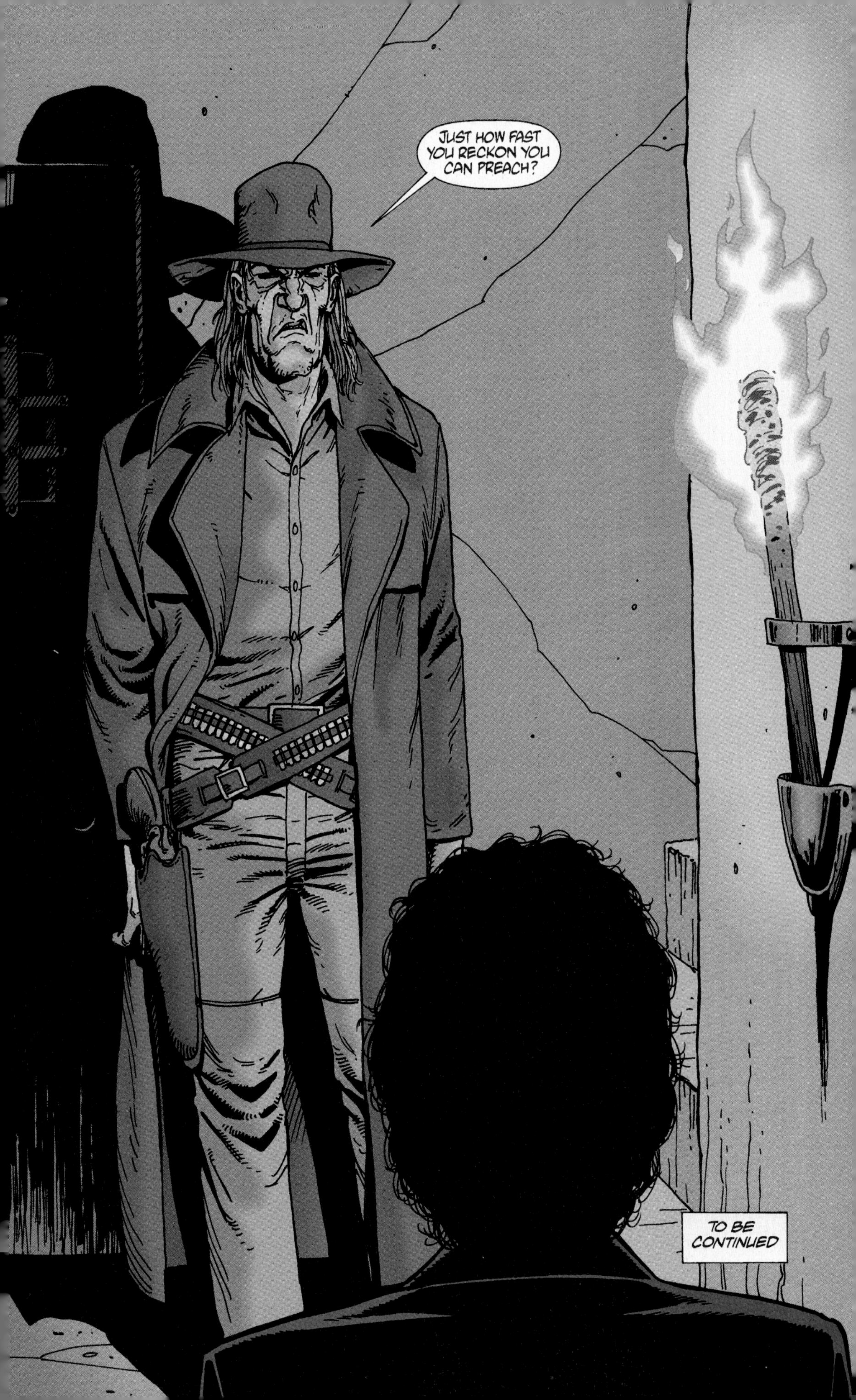
JUST HOW FAST YOU RECKON YOU CAN PREACH?
TO BE CONTINUED

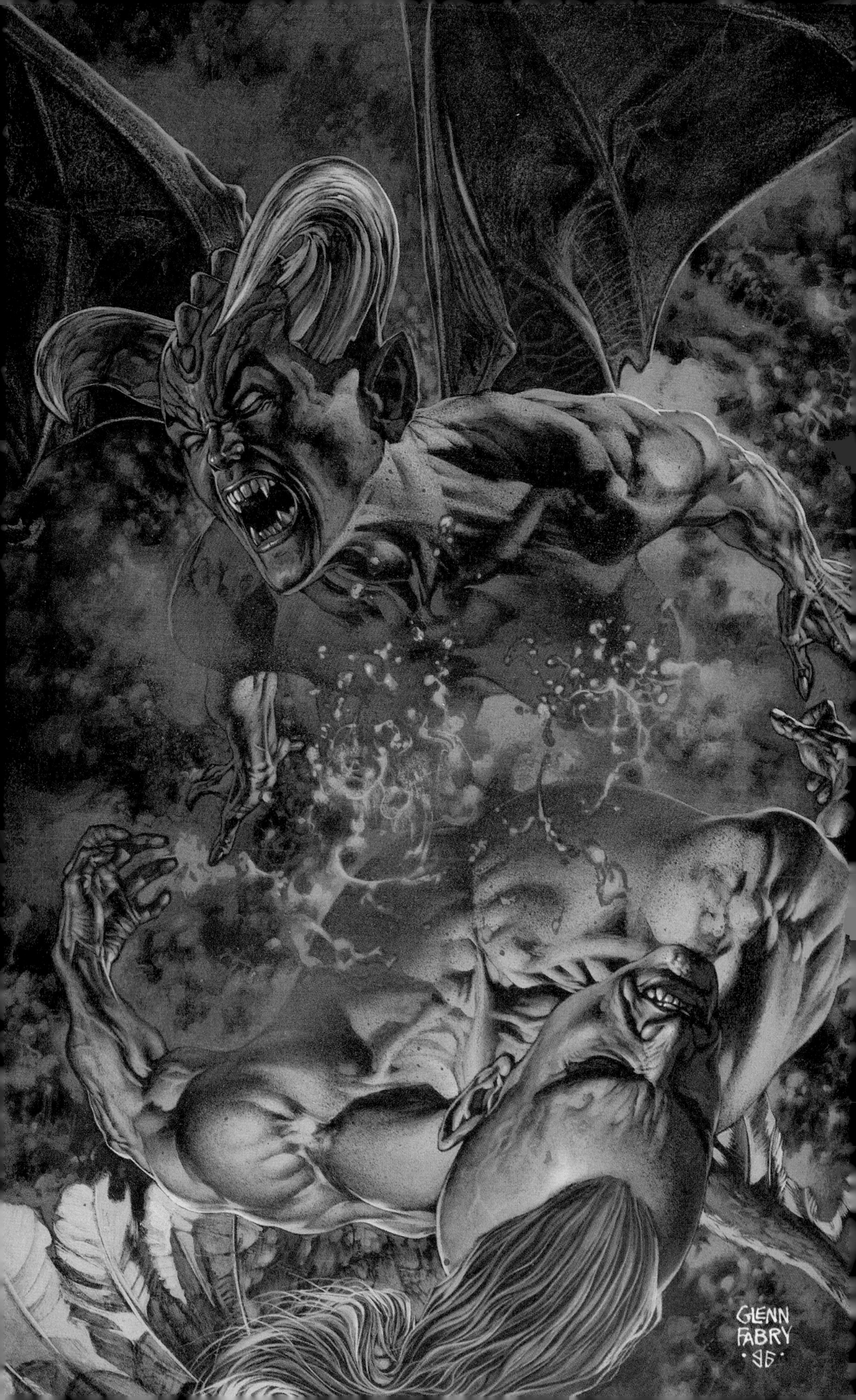
GLENN FABRY ·96·

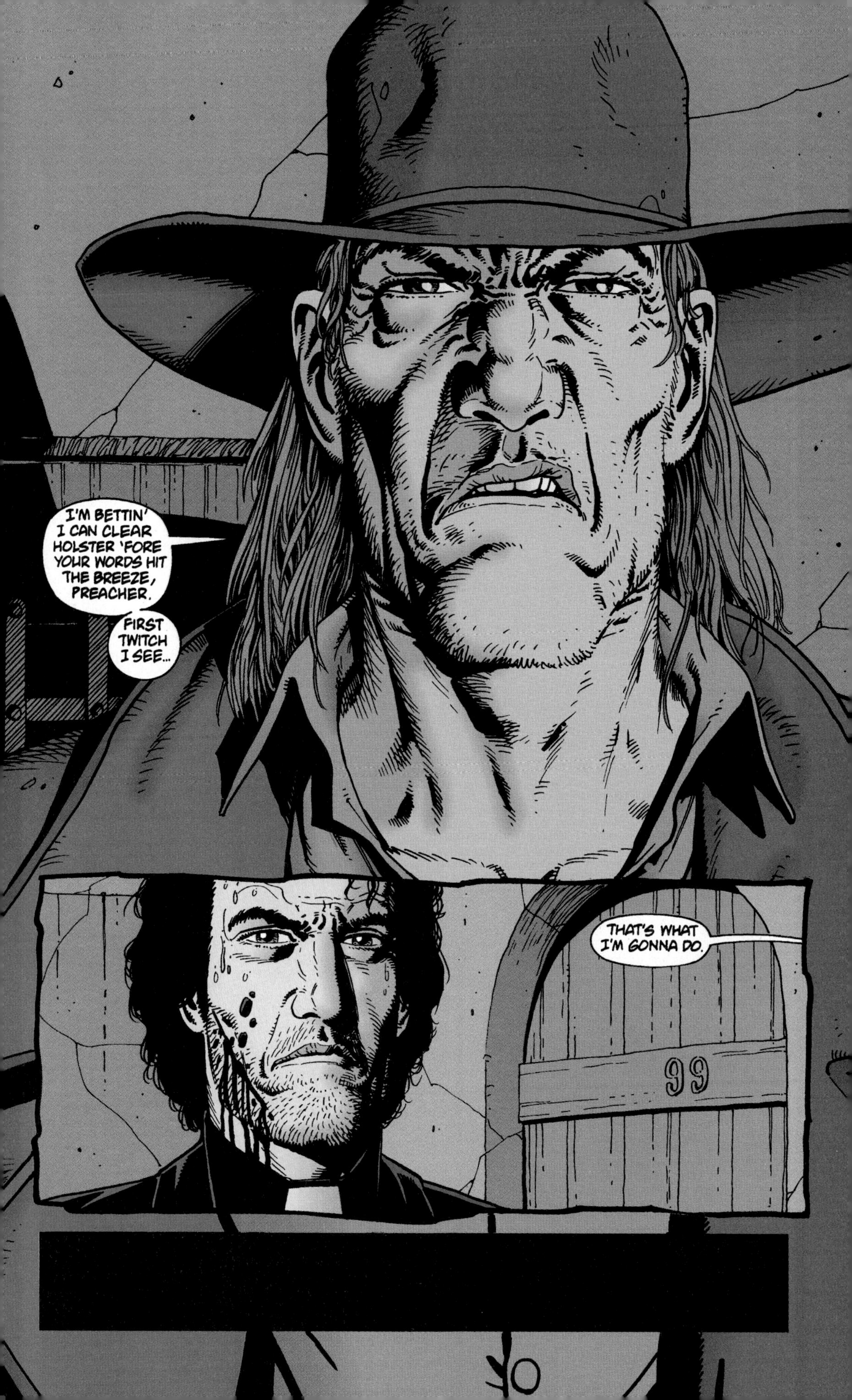
I'M BETTIN' I CAN CLEAR HOLSTER 'FORE YOUR WORDS HIT THE BREEZE, PREACHER.
FIRST TWITCH I SEE...
THAT'S WHAT I'M GONNA DO.

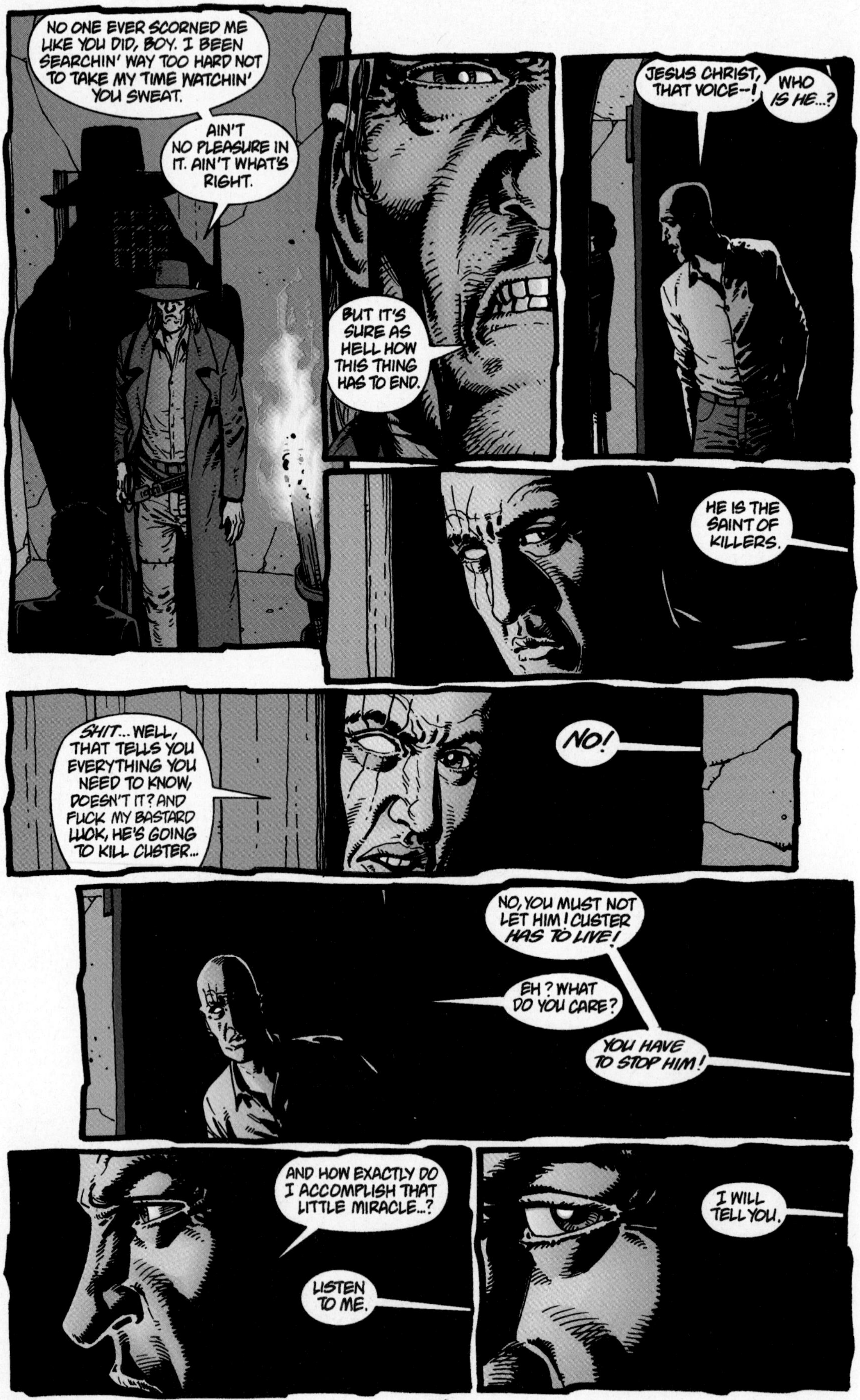
NO ONE EVER SCORNED ME LIKE YOU DID, BOY. I BEEN SEARCHIN' WAY TOO HARD NOT TO TAKE MY TIME WATCHIN' YOU SWEAT.
AIN'T NO PLEASURE IN IT. AIN'T WHAT'S RIGHT.
BUT IT'S SURE AS HELL HOW THIS THING HAS TO END.
JESUS CHRIST, THAT VOICE--!
WHO IS HE...?
HE IS THE SAINT OF KILLERS.
SHIT... WELL, THAT TELLS YOU EVERYTHING YOU NEED TO KNOW, DOESN'T IT? AND FUCK MY BASTARD LUCK, HE'S GOING TO KILL CUSTER...
NO!
NO, YOU MUST NOT LET HIM! CUSTER HAS TO LIVE!
EH? WHAT DO YOU CARE?
YOU HAVE TO STOP HIM!
AND HOW EXACTLY DO I ACCOMPLISH THAT LITTLE MIRACLE...?
LISTEN TO ME.
I WILL TELL YOU.

WHAT IS OCCURRING?

ALLFATHER!

WELL?

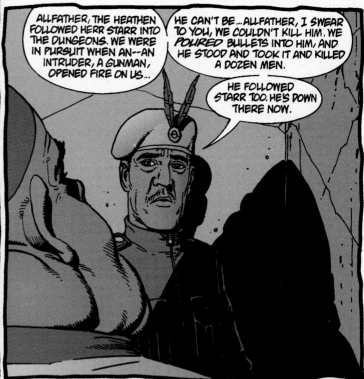

ALLFATHER, THE HEATHEN FOLLOWED HERR STARR INTO THE DUNGEONS. WE WERE IN PURSUIT WHEN AN--AN INTRUDER, A GUNMAN, OPENED FIRE ON US...

HE CAN'T BE... ALLFATHER, I SWEAR TO YOU, WE COULDN'T KILL HIM. WE POURED BULLETS INTO HIM, AND HE STOOD AND TOOK IT AND KILLED A DOZEN MEN.

HE FOLLOWED STARR TOO. HE'S DOWN THERE NOW.

TAKE HIM.

BUT--

RUSH HIM. SWAMP HIS GUNS WITH YOUR BODIES.

SACRIFICE AS MANY AS IT TAKES AND THEN BRING STARR AND CUSTER TO ME.

ALIVE.

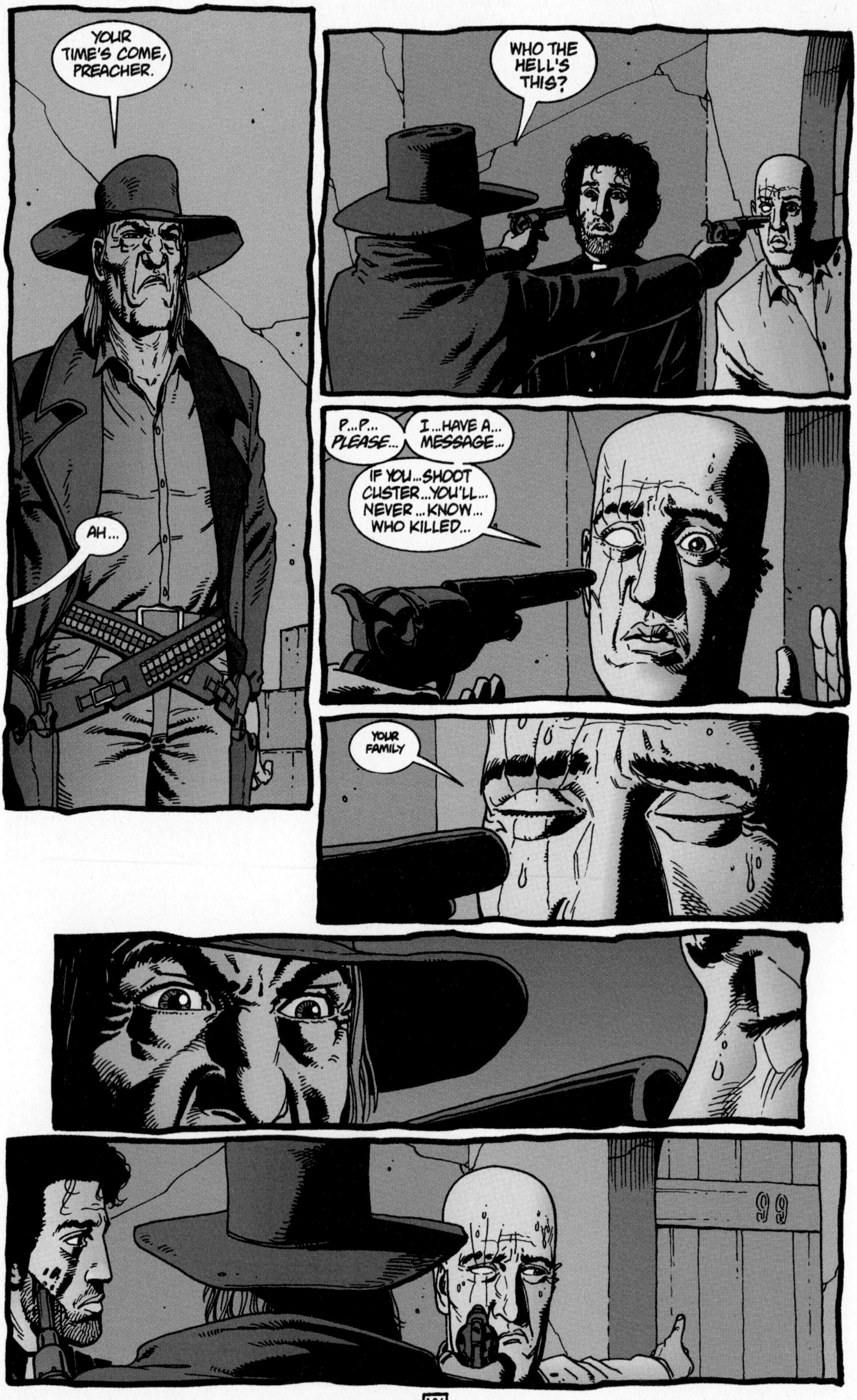
YOUR TIME'S COME, PREACHER.
AH...
WHO THE HELL'S THIS?
P...P... PLEASE...
I...HAVE A... MESSAGE...
IF YOU...SHOOT CUSTER...YOU'LL... NEVER...KNOW... WHO KILLED...
YOUR FAMILY
99

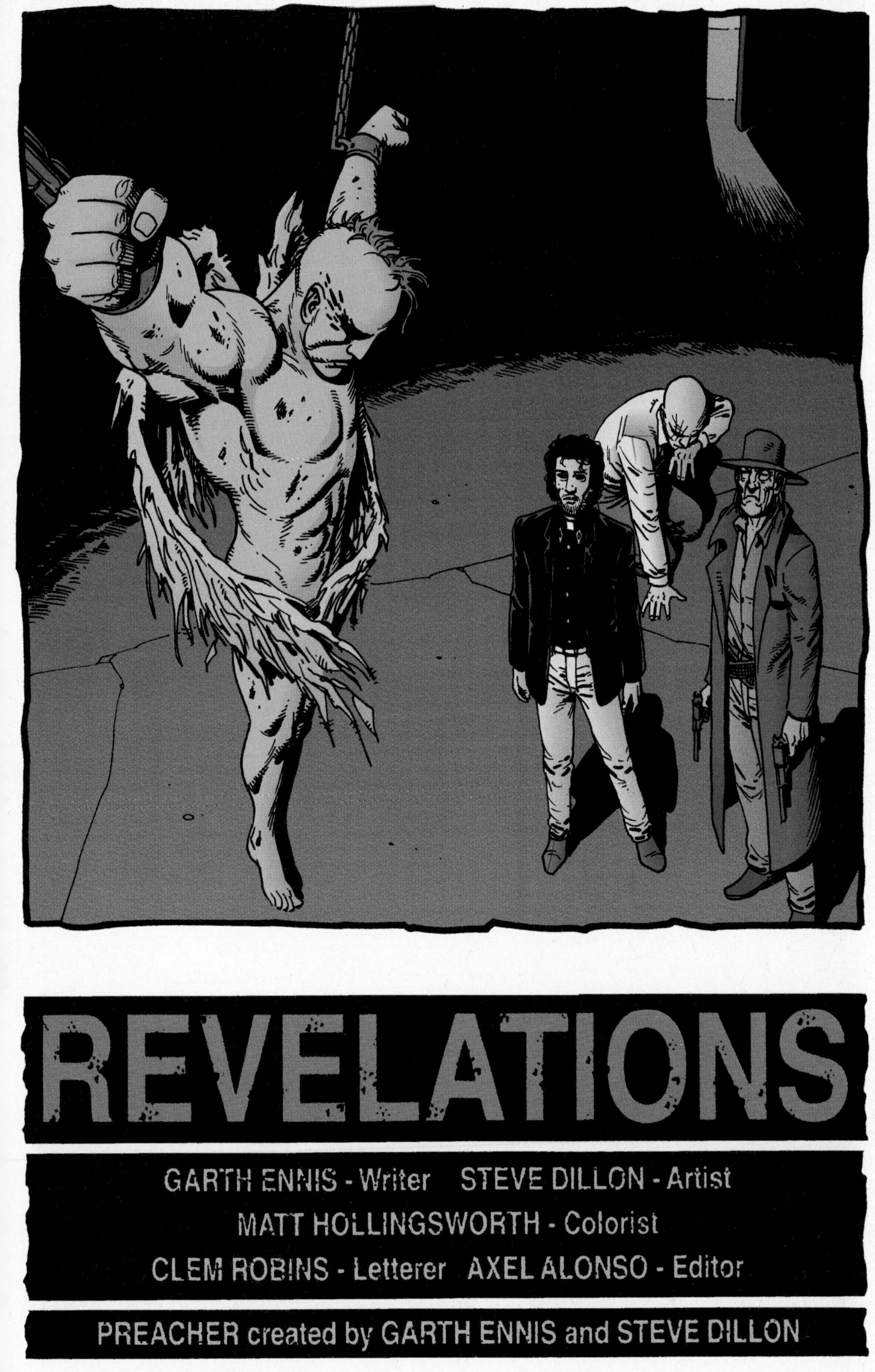

REVELATIONS

GARTH ENNIS - Writer STEVE DILLON - Artist

MATT HOLLINGSWORTH - Colorist

CLEM ROBINS - Letterer AXEL ALONSO - Editor

PREACHER created by GARTH ENNIS and STEVE DILLON

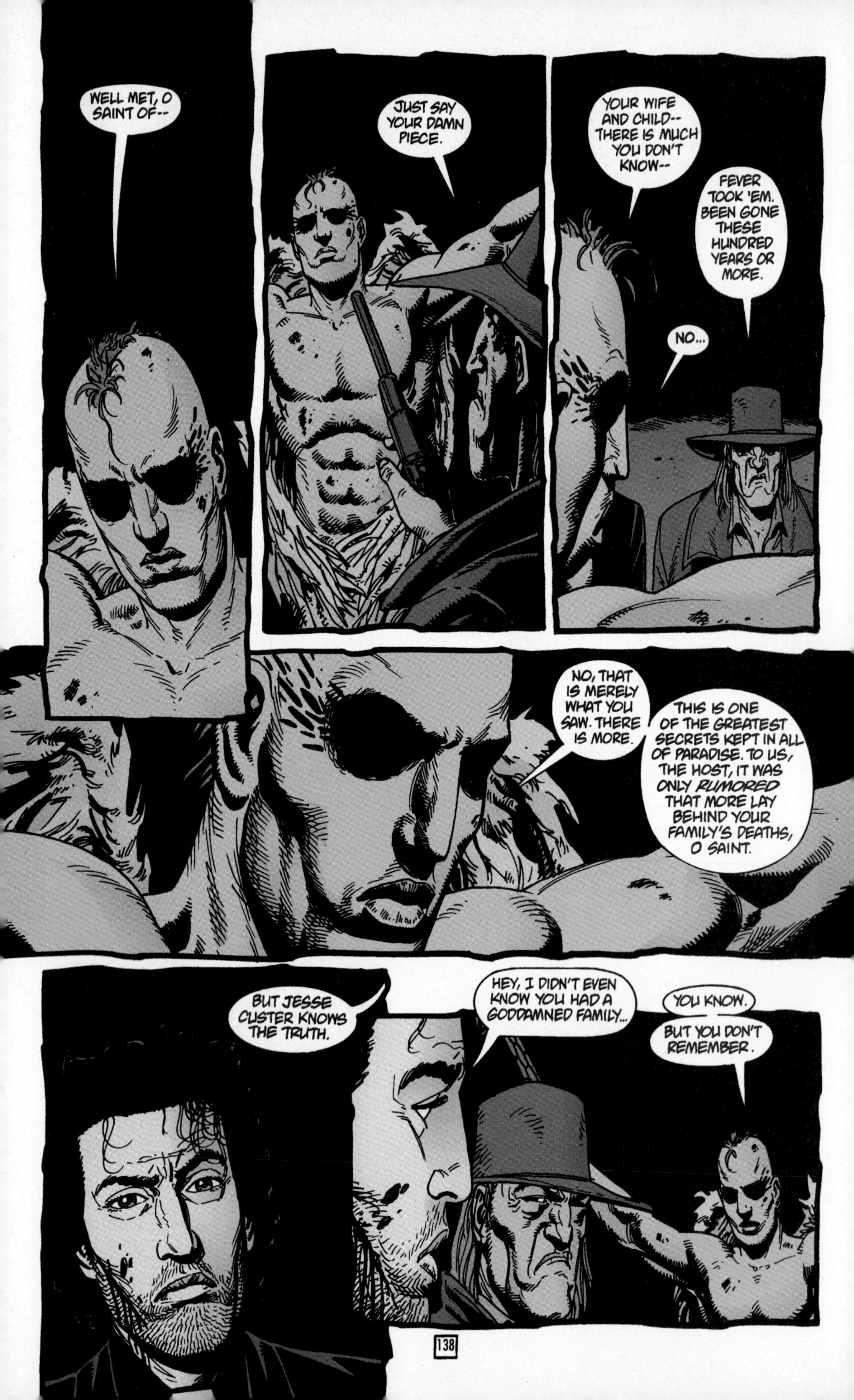

WELL MET, O SAINT OF--
JUST SAY YOUR DAMN PIECE.
YOUR WIFE AND CHILD-- THERE IS MUCH YOU DON'T KNOW--
FEVER TOOK 'EM. BEEN GONE THESE HUNDRED YEARS OR MORE.
NO...
NO, THAT IS MERELY WHAT YOU SAW. THERE IS MORE.
THIS IS ONE OF THE GREATEST SECRETS KEPT IN ALL OF PARADISE. TO US, THE HOST, IT WAS ONLY *RUMORED* THAT MORE LAY BEHIND YOUR FAMILY'S DEATHS, O SAINT.
BUT JESSE CUSTER KNOWS THE TRUTH.
HEY, I DIDN'T EVEN KNOW YOU HAD A GODDAMNED FAMILY...
YOU KNOW.
BUT YOU DON'T REMEMBER.

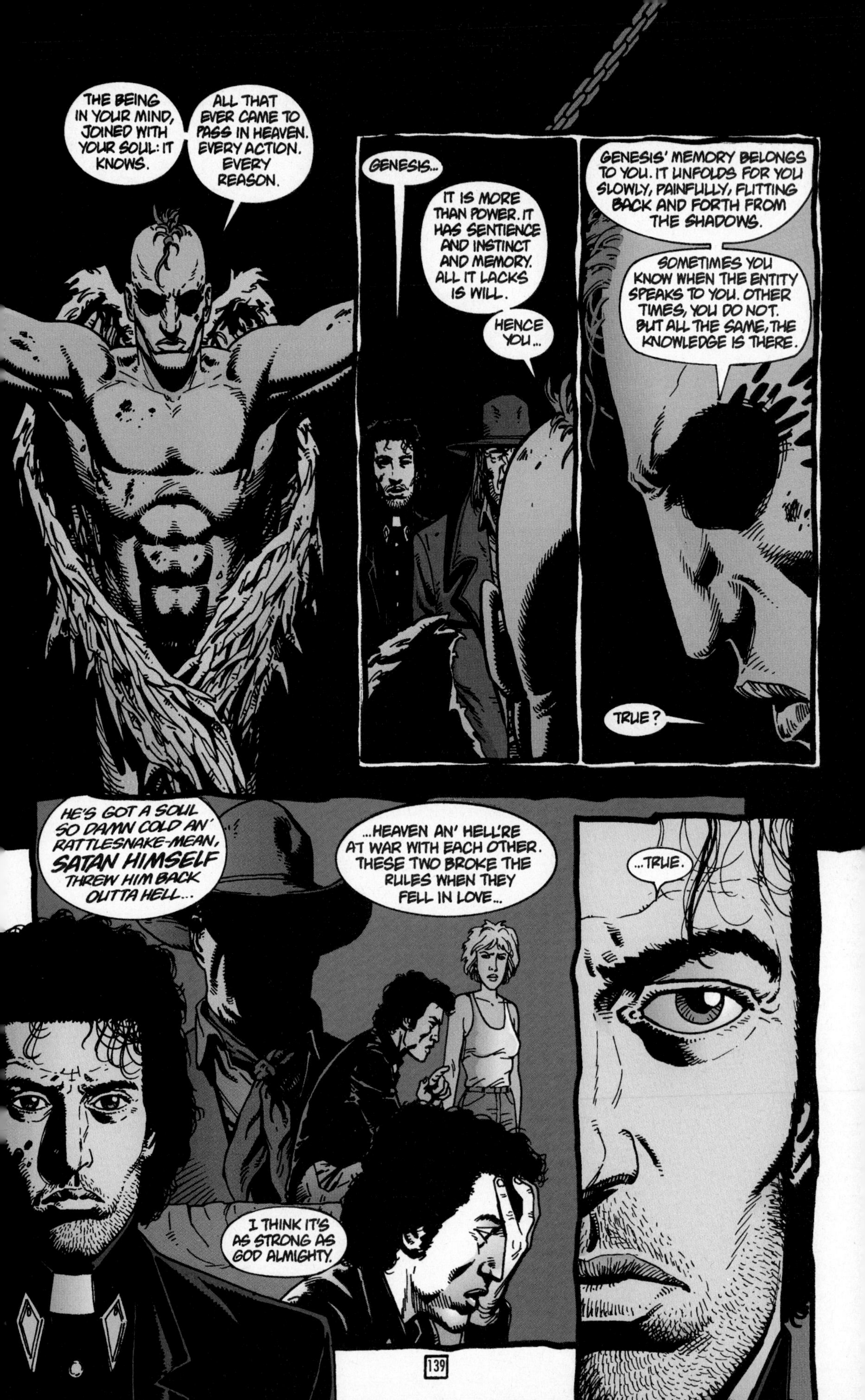
THE BEING IN YOUR MIND, JOINED WITH YOUR SOUL: IT KNOWS.
ALL THAT EVER CAME TO PASS IN HEAVEN. EVERY ACTION. EVERY REASON.
GENESIS...
IT IS MORE THAN POWER. IT HAS SENTIENCE AND INSTINCT AND MEMORY. ALL IT LACKS IS WILL.
HENCE YOU...
GENESIS' MEMORY BELONGS TO YOU. IT UNFOLDS FOR YOU SLOWLY, PAINFULLY, FLITTING BACK AND FORTH FROM THE SHADOWS.
SOMETIMES YOU KNOW WHEN THE ENTITY SPEAKS TO YOU. OTHER TIMES, YOU DO NOT. BUT ALL THE SAME, THE KNOWLEDGE IS THERE.
TRUE?
HE'S GOT A SOUL SO DAMN COLD AN' RATTLESNAKE-MEAN, SATAN HIMSELF THREW HIM BACK OUTTA HELL...
I THINK IT'S AS STRONG AS GOD ALMIGHTY.
...HEAVEN AN' HELL'RE AT WAR WITH EACH OTHER. THESE TWO BROKE THE RULES WHEN THEY FELL IN LOVE...
...TRUE.

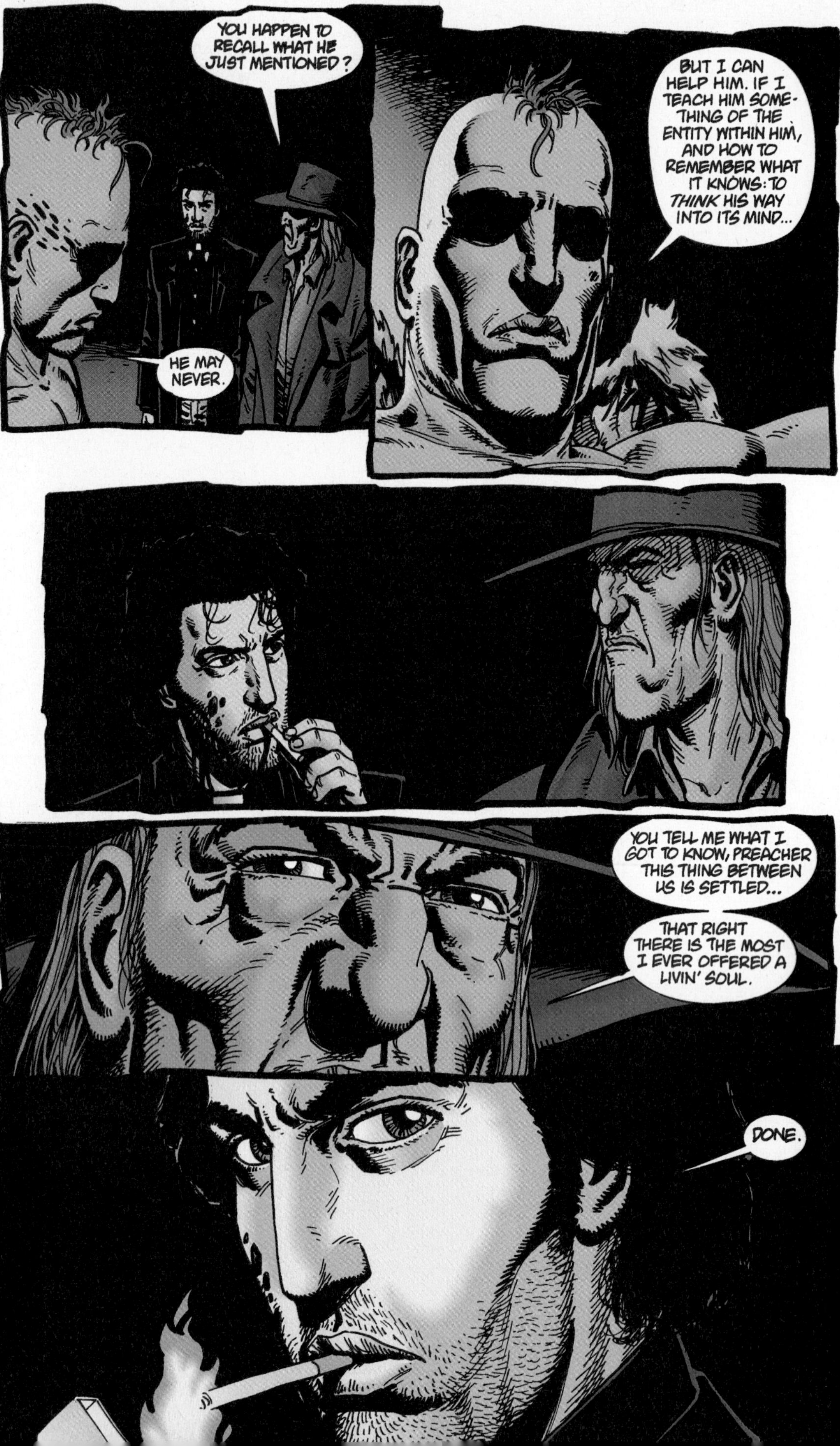
YOU HAPPEN TO RECALL WHAT HE JUST MENTIONED?
HE MAY NEVER.
BUT I CAN HELP HIM. IF I TEACH HIM SOMETHING OF THE ENTITY WITHIN HIM, AND HOW TO REMEMBER WHAT IT KNOWS: TO *THINK* HIS WAY INTO ITS MIND...
YOU TELL ME WHAT I GOT TO KNOW, PREACHER THIS THING BETWEEN US IS SETTLED...
THAT RIGHT THERE IS THE MOST I EVER OFFERED A LIVIN' SOUL.
DONE.

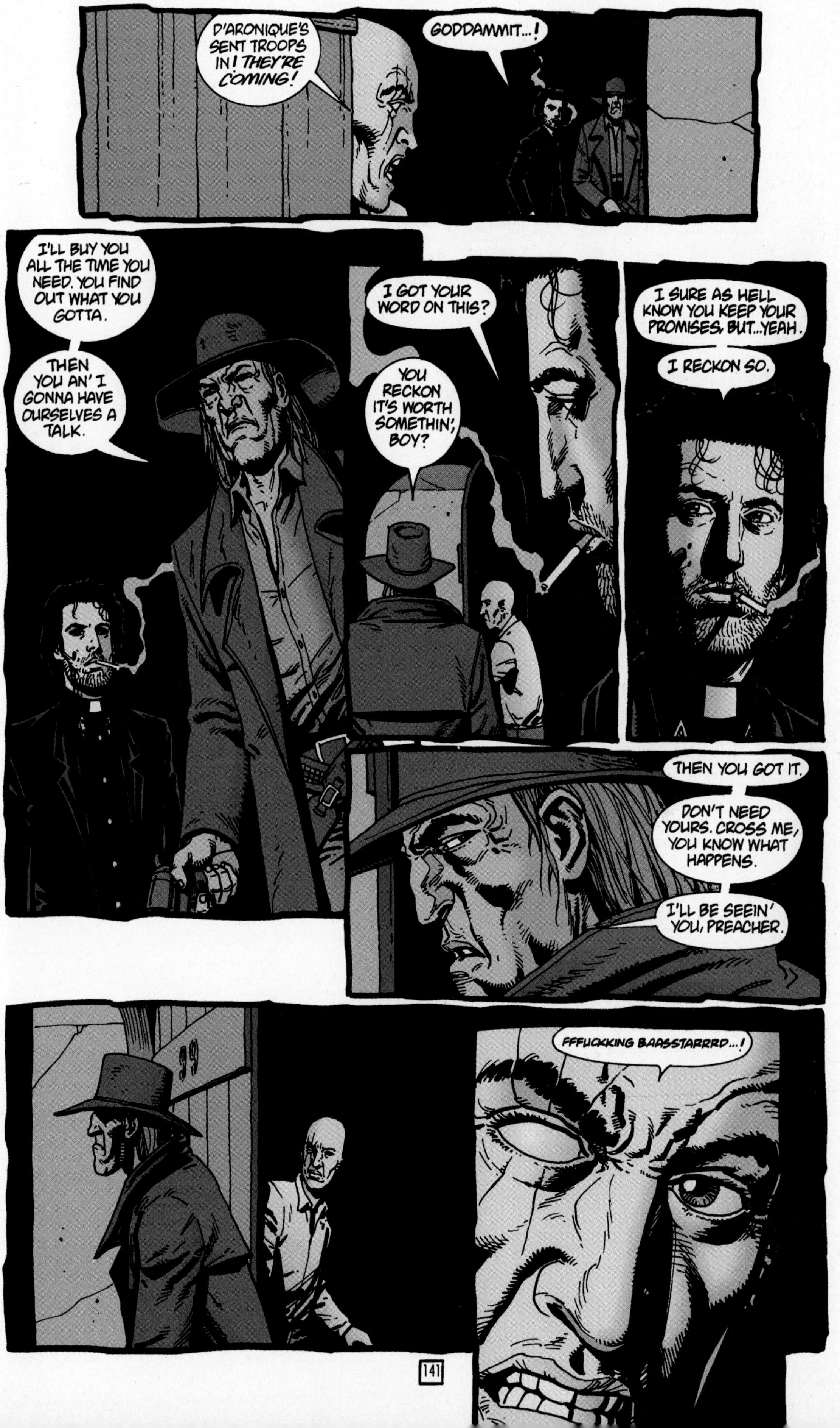
D'ARONIQUE'S SENT TROOPS IN! THEY'RE COMING!
GODDAMMIT...!
I'LL BUY YOU ALL THE TIME YOU NEED. YOU FIND OUT WHAT YOU GOTTA.
THEN YOU AN' I GONNA HAVE OURSELVES A TALK.
I GOT YOUR WORD ON THIS?
YOU RECKON IT'S WORTH SOMETHIN', BOY?
I SURE AS HELL KNOW YOU KEEP YOUR PROMISES, BUT...YEAH.
I RECKON SO.
THEN YOU GOT IT.
DON'T NEED YOURS. CROSS ME, YOU KNOW WHAT HAPPENS.
I'LL BE SEEIN' YOU, PREACHER.
FFFUCKKING BAASSTARRRD...!

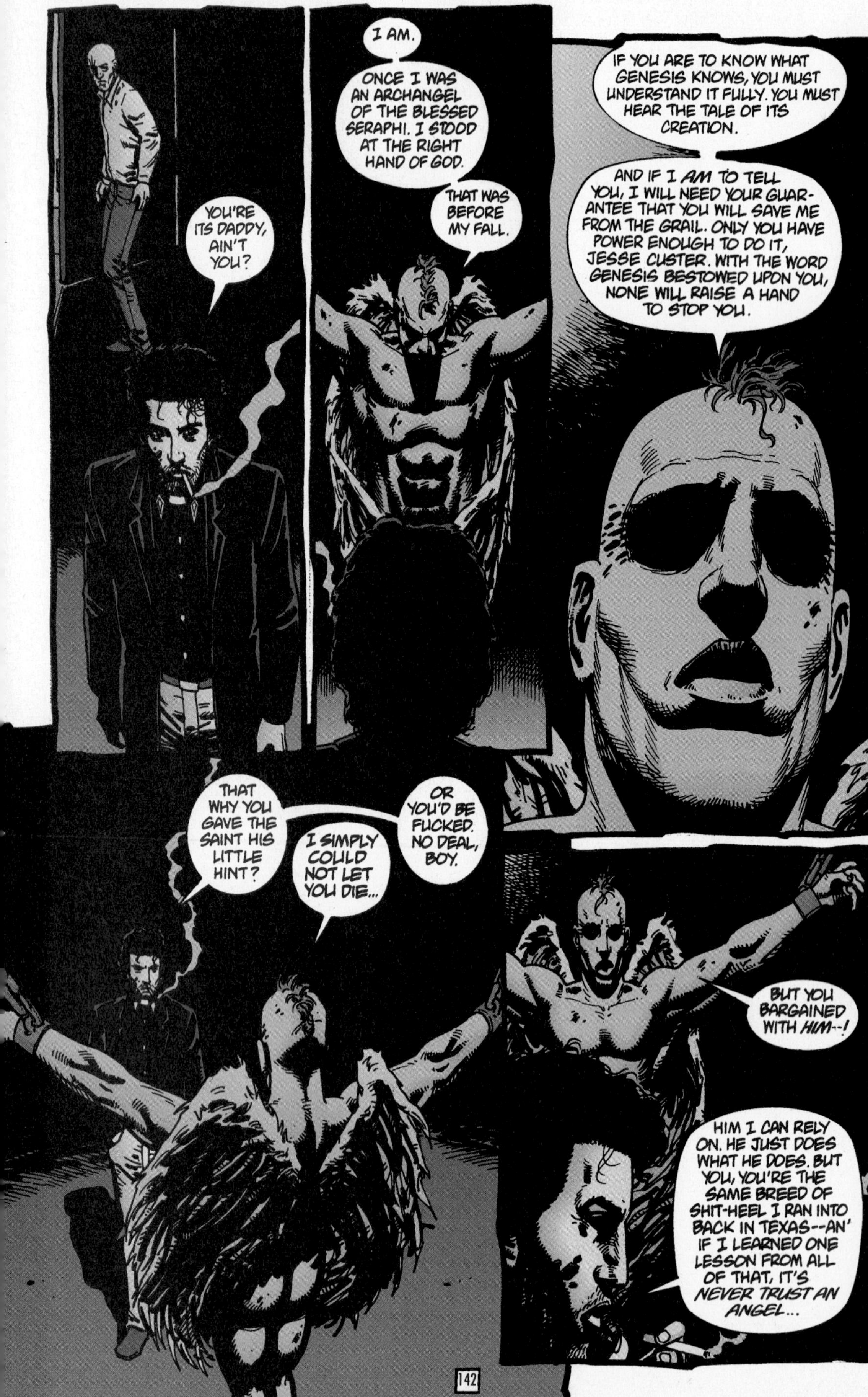
YOU'RE ITS DADDY, AIN'T YOU?
I AM.
ONCE I WAS AN ARCHANGEL OF THE BLESSED SERAPHI. I STOOD AT THE RIGHT HAND OF GOD.
THAT WAS BEFORE MY FALL.
IF YOU ARE TO KNOW WHAT GENESIS KNOWS, YOU MUST UNDERSTAND IT FULLY. YOU MUST HEAR THE TALE OF ITS CREATION.
AND IF I *AM* TO TELL YOU, I WILL NEED YOUR GUARANTEE THAT YOU WILL SAVE ME FROM THE GRAIL. ONLY YOU HAVE POWER ENOUGH TO DO IT, JESSE CUSTER. WITH THE WORD GENESIS BESTOWED UPON YOU, NONE WILL RAISE A HAND TO STOP YOU.
THAT WHY YOU GAVE THE SAINT HIS LITTLE HINT?
I SIMPLY COULD NOT LET YOU DIE...
OR YOU'D BE FUCKED. NO DEAL, BOY.
BUT YOU BARGAINED WITH *HIM*--!
HIM I CAN RELY ON. HE JUST DOES WHAT HE DOES. BUT YOU, YOU'RE THE SAME BREED OF SHIT-HEEL I RAN INTO BACK IN TEXAS--AN' IF I LEARNED ONE LESSON FROM ALL OF THAT, IT'S *NEVER TRUST AN ANGEL*...

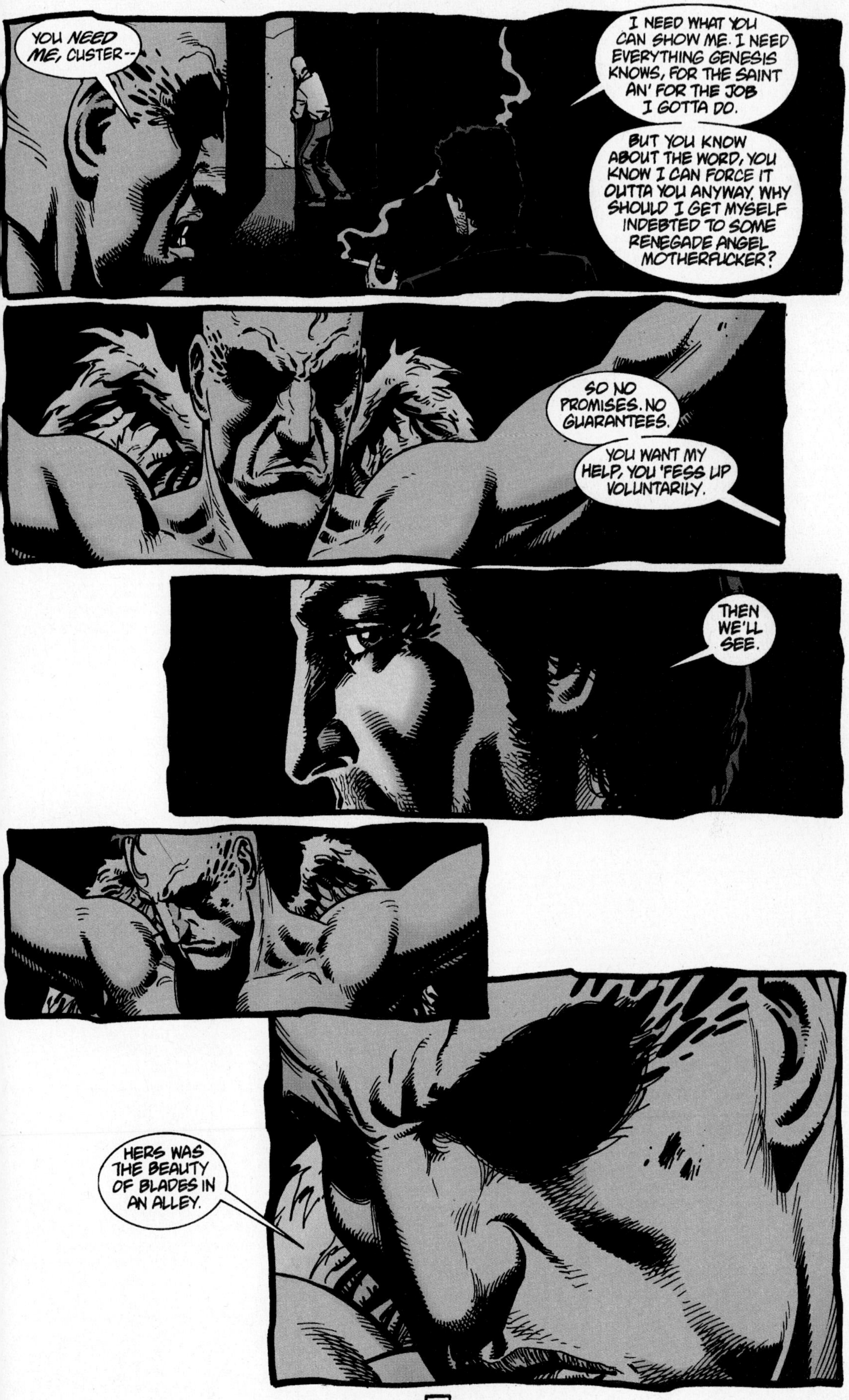
YOU NEED ME, CUSTER--
I NEED WHAT YOU CAN SHOW ME. I NEED EVERYTHING GENESIS KNOWS, FOR THE SAINT AN' FOR THE JOB I GOTTA DO.
BUT YOU KNOW ABOUT THE WORD, YOU KNOW I CAN FORCE IT OUTTA YOU ANYWAY. WHY SHOULD I GET MYSELF INDEBTED TO SOME RENEGADE ANGEL MOTHERFUCKER?
SO NO PROMISES. NO GUARANTEES.
YOU WANT MY HELP, YOU 'FESS UP VOLUNTARILY.
THEN WE'LL SEE.
HERS WAS THE BEAUTY OF BLADES IN AN ALLEY.

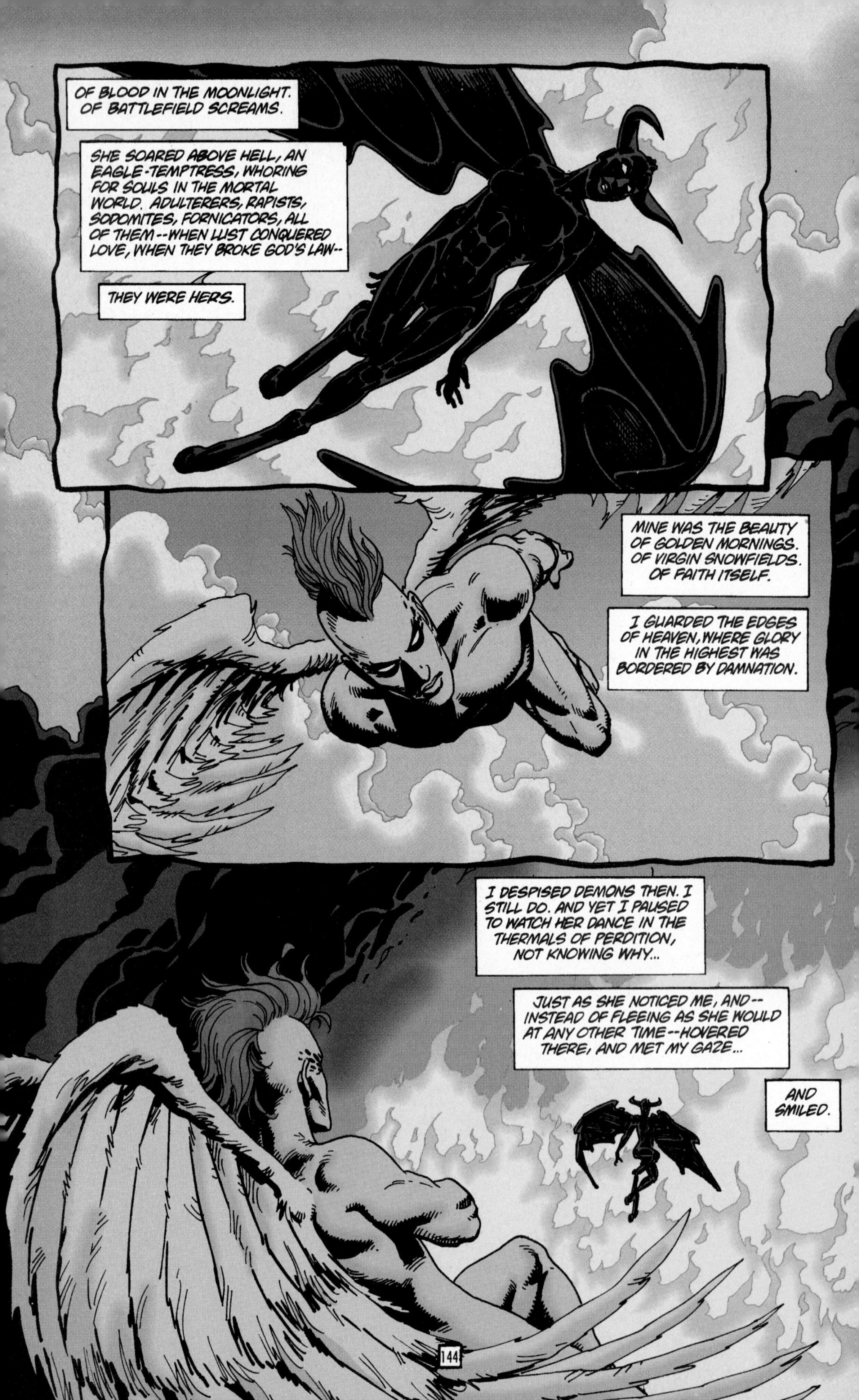

OF BLOOD IN THE MOONLIGHT. OF BATTLEFIELD SCREAMS.
SHE SOARED ABOVE HELL, AN EAGLE-TEMPTRESS, WHORING FOR SOULS IN THE MORTAL WORLD. ADULTERERS, RAPISTS, SODOMITES, FORNICATORS, ALL OF THEM--WHEN LUST CONQUERED LOVE, WHEN THEY BROKE GOD'S LAW--
THEY WERE HERS.
MINE WAS THE BEAUTY OF GOLDEN MORNINGS. OF VIRGIN SNOWFIELDS. OF FAITH ITSELF.
I GUARDED THE EDGES OF HEAVEN, WHERE GLORY IN THE HIGHEST WAS BORDERED BY DAMNATION.
I DESPISED DEMONS THEN. I STILL DO. AND YET I PAUSED TO WATCH HER DANCE IN THE THERMALS OF PERDITION, NOT KNOWING WHY...
JUST AS SHE NOTICED ME, AND--INSTEAD OF FLEEING AS SHE WOULD AT ANY OTHER TIME--HOVERED THERE, AND MET MY GAZE...
AND SMILED.

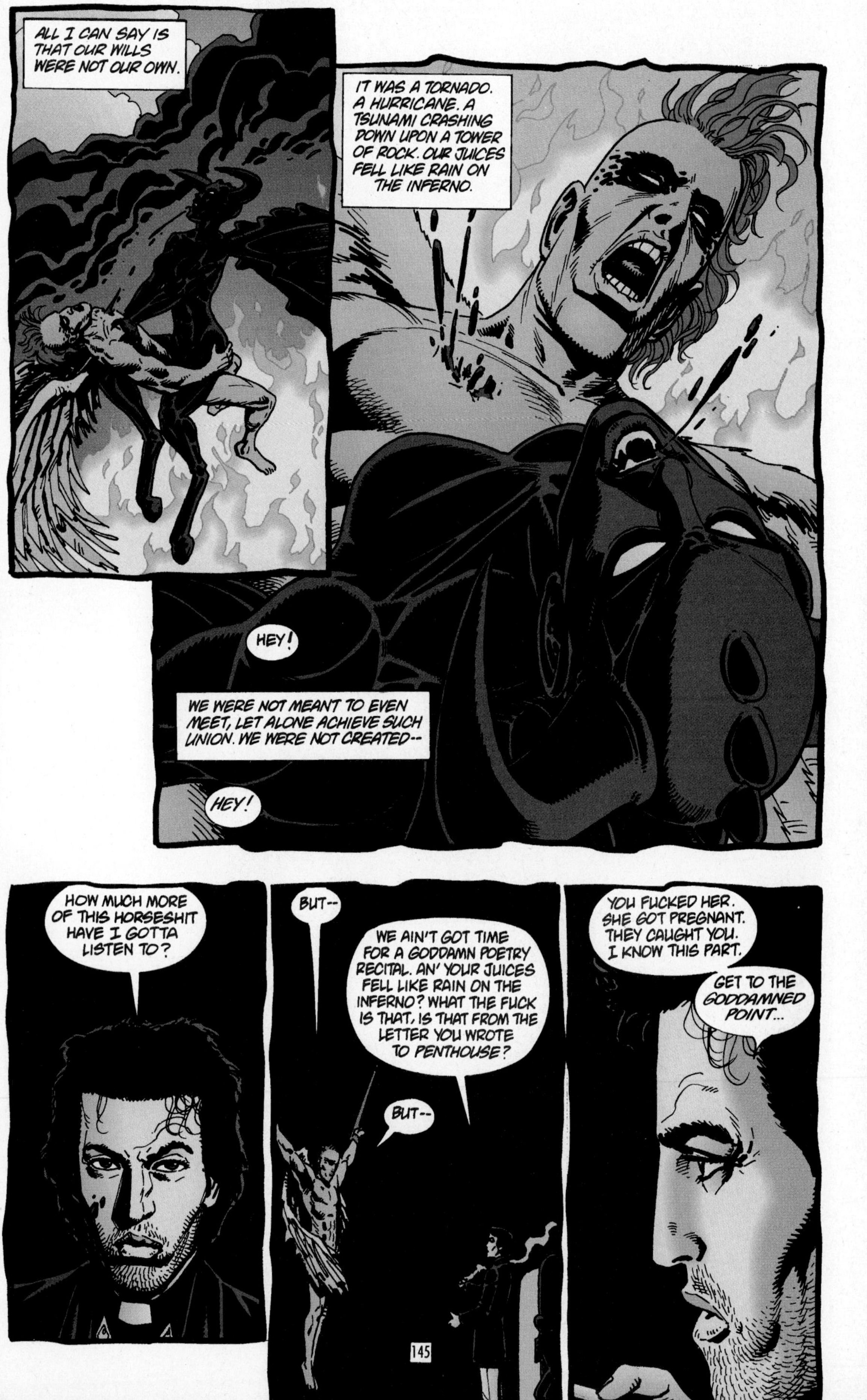
ALL I CAN SAY IS THAT OUR WILLS WERE NOT OUR OWN.
IT WAS A TORNADO. A HURRICANE. A TSUNAMI CRASHING DOWN UPON A TOWER OF ROCK. OUR JUICES FELL LIKE RAIN ON THE INFERNO.
HEY!
WE WERE NOT MEANT TO EVEN MEET, LET ALONE ACHIEVE SUCH UNION. WE WERE NOT CREATED--
HEY!
HOW MUCH MORE OF THIS HORSESHIT HAVE I GOTTA LISTEN TO?
BUT--
WE AIN'T GOT TIME FOR A GODDAMN POETRY RECITAL. AN' YOUR JUICES FELL LIKE RAIN ON THE INFERNO? WHAT THE FUCK IS THAT, IS THAT FROM THE LETTER YOU WROTE TO PENTHOUSE?
BUT--
YOU FUCKED HER. SHE GOT PREGNANT. THEY CAUGHT YOU. I KNOW THIS PART.
GET TO THE GODDAMNED POINT...

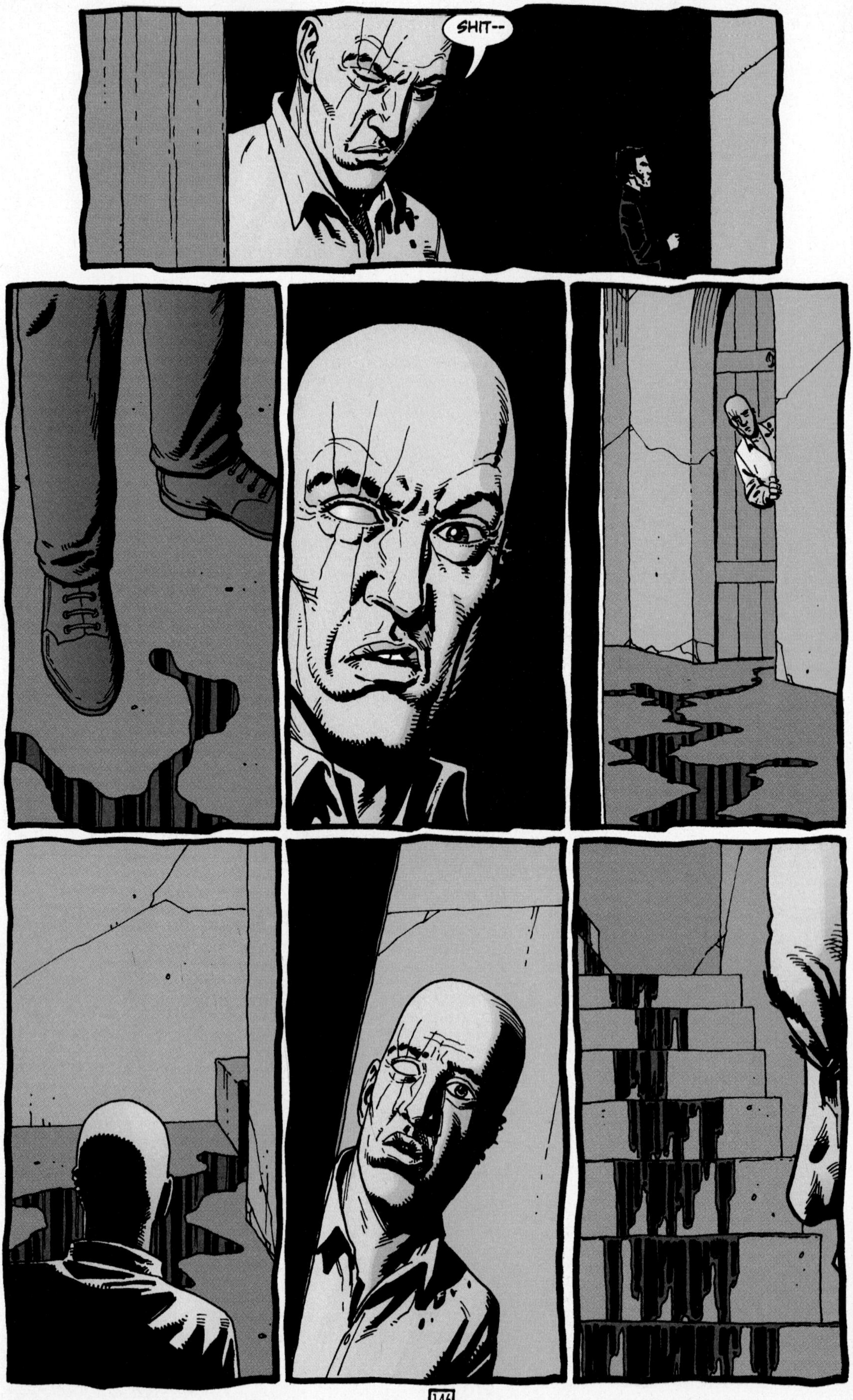
SHIT--

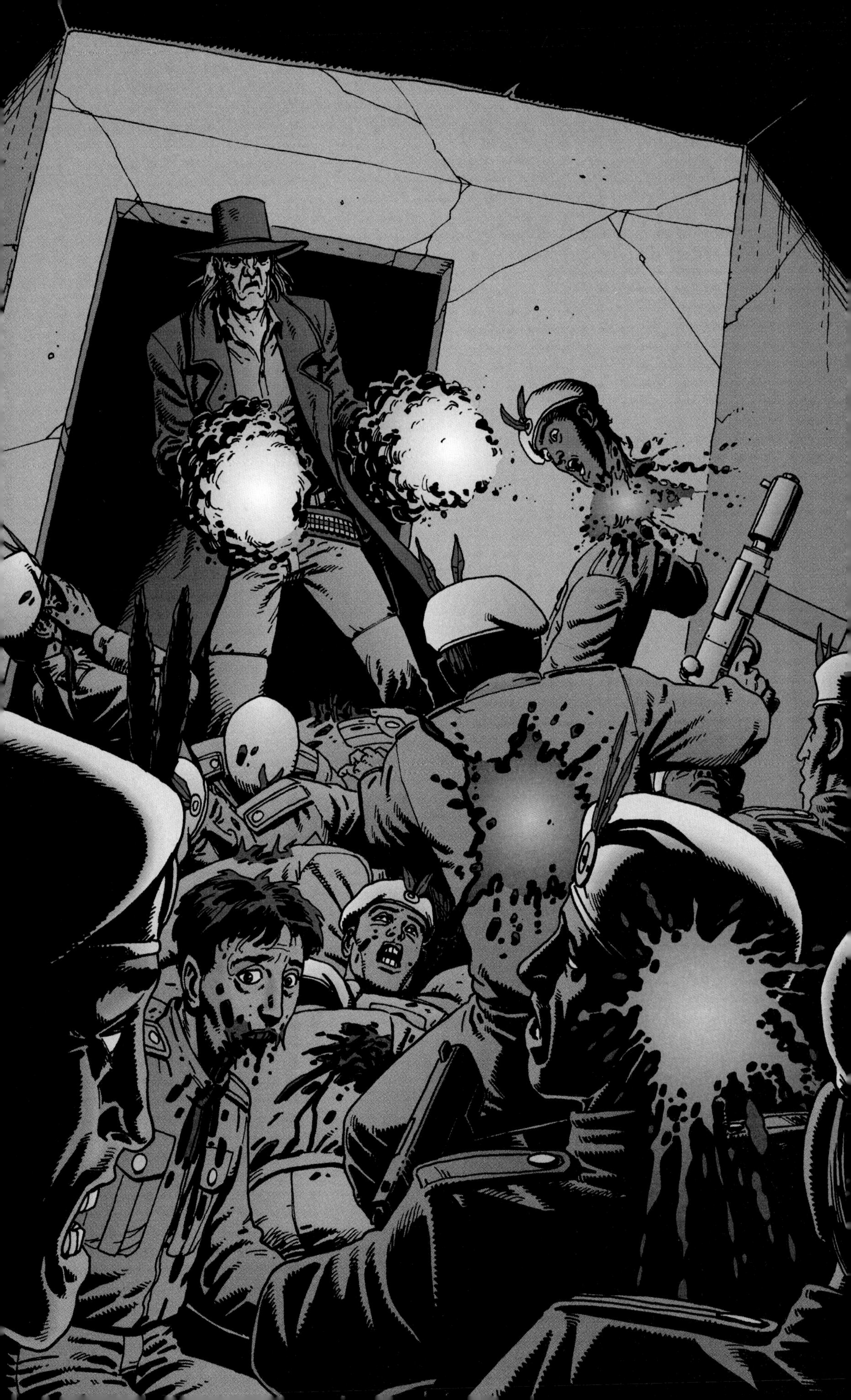

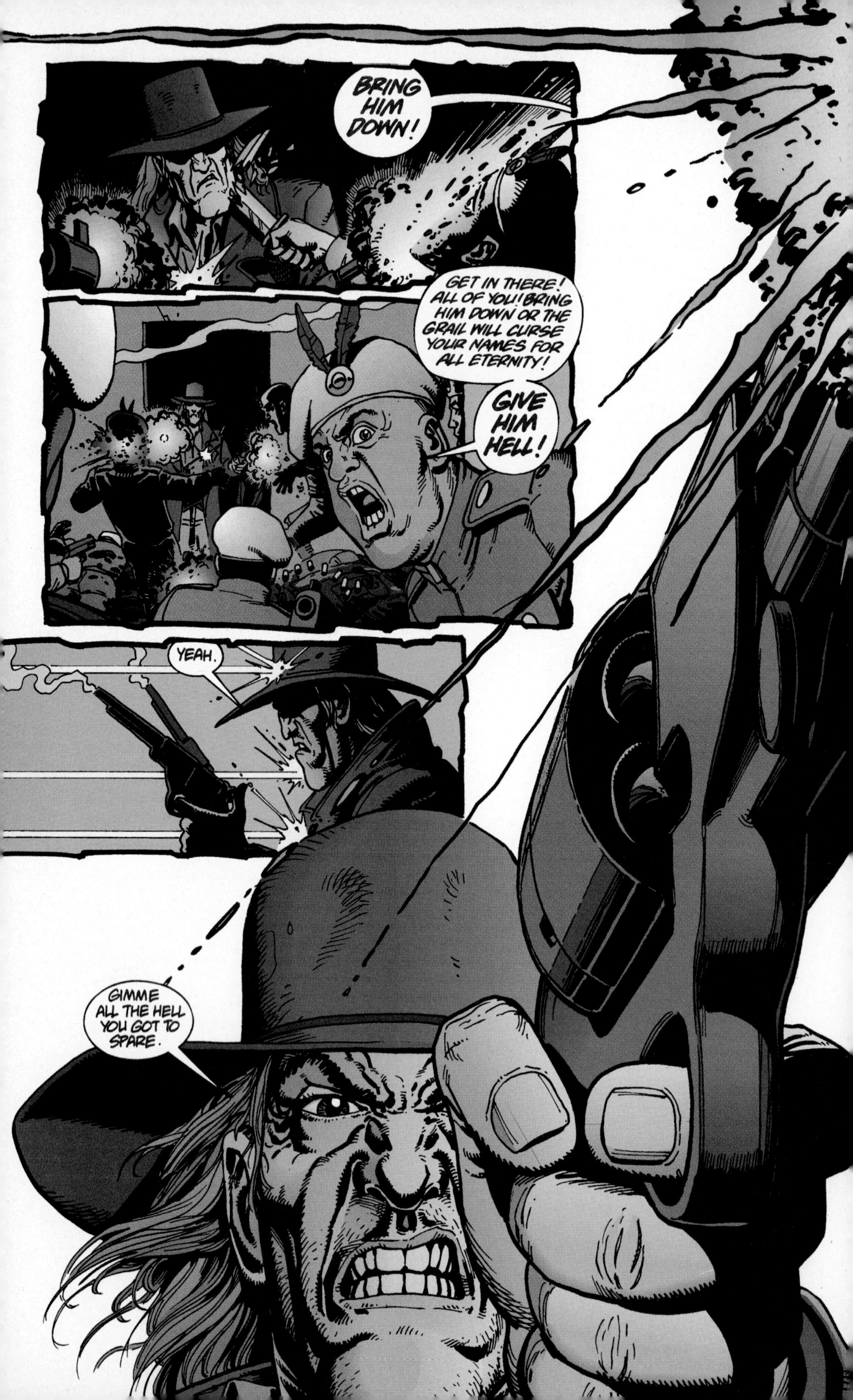
BRING HIM DOWN!
GET IN THERE! ALL OF YOU! BRING HIM DOWN OR THE GRAIL WILL CURSE YOUR NAMES FOR ALL ETERNITY!
GIVE HIM HELL!
YEAH.
GIMME ALL THE HELL YOU GOT TO SPARE.

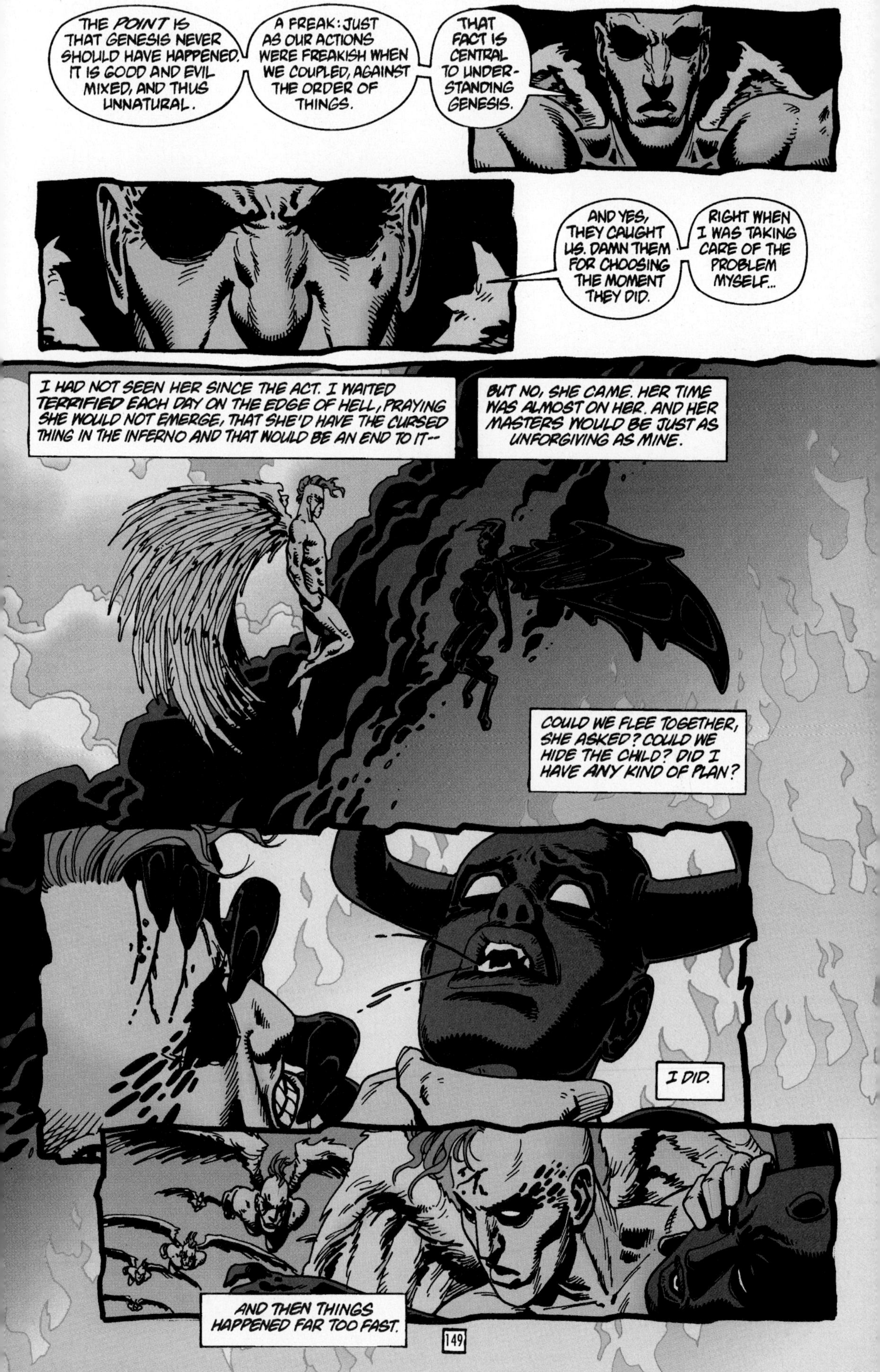
THE POINT IS THAT GENESIS NEVER SHOULD HAVE HAPPENED. IT IS GOOD AND EVIL MIXED, AND THUS UNNATURAL.
A FREAK: JUST AS OUR ACTIONS WERE FREAKISH WHEN WE COUPLED, AGAINST THE ORDER OF THINGS.
THAT FACT IS CENTRAL TO UNDER-STANDING GENESIS.
AND YES, THEY CAUGHT US. DAMN THEM FOR CHOOSING THE MOMENT THEY DID.
RIGHT WHEN I WAS TAKING CARE OF THE PROBLEM MYSELF...
I HAD NOT SEEN HER SINCE THE ACT. I WAITED TERRIFIED EACH DAY ON THE EDGE OF HELL, PRAYING SHE WOULD NOT EMERGE, THAT SHE'D HAVE THE CURSED THING IN THE INFERNO AND THAT WOULD BE AN END TO IT--
BUT NO, SHE CAME. HER TIME WAS ALMOST ON HER. AND HER MASTERS WOULD BE JUST AS UNFORGIVING AS MINE.
COULD WE FLEE TOGETHER, SHE ASKED? COULD WE HIDE THE CHILD? DID I HAVE ANY KIND OF PLAN?
I DID.
AND THEN THINGS HAPPENED FAR TOO FAST.

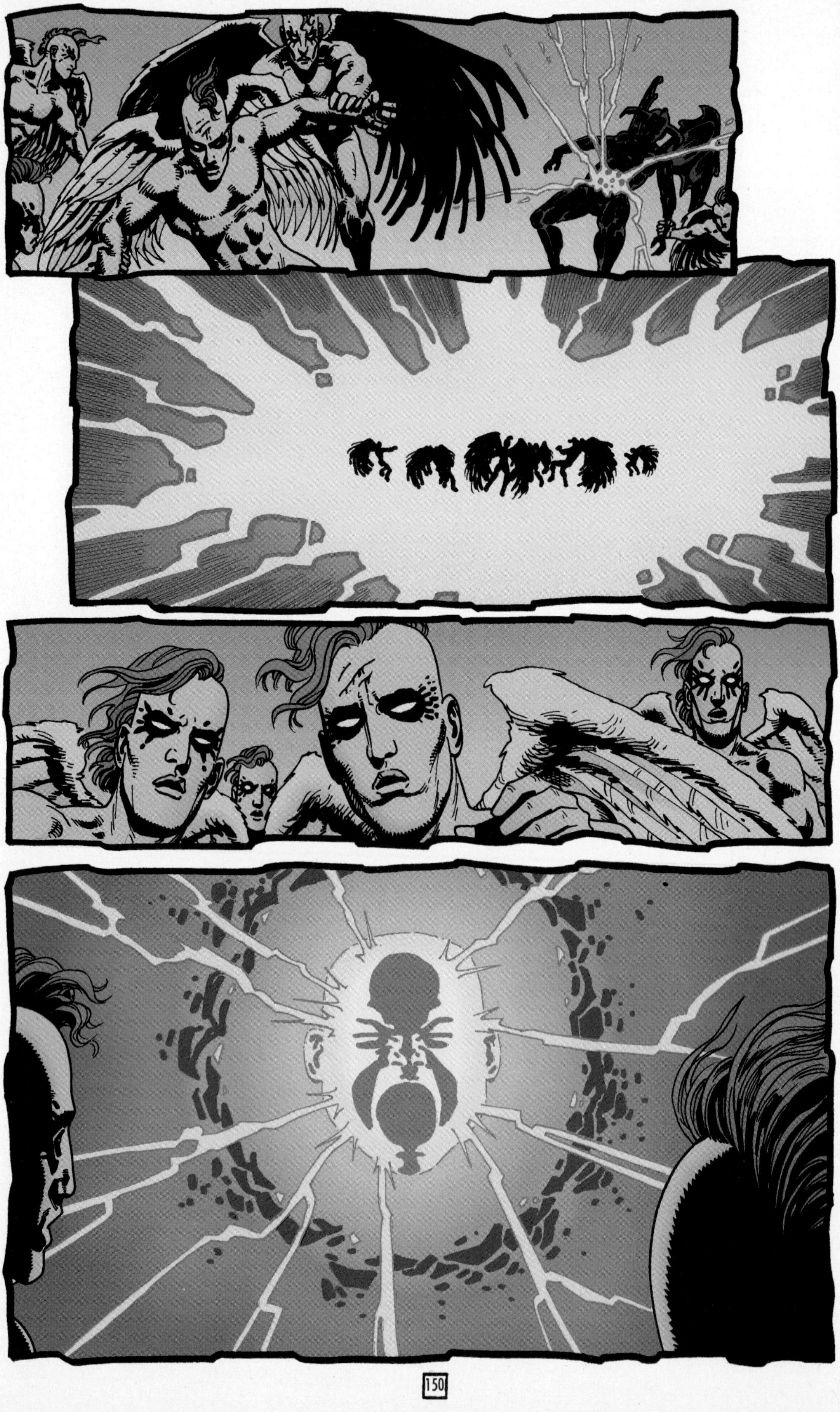

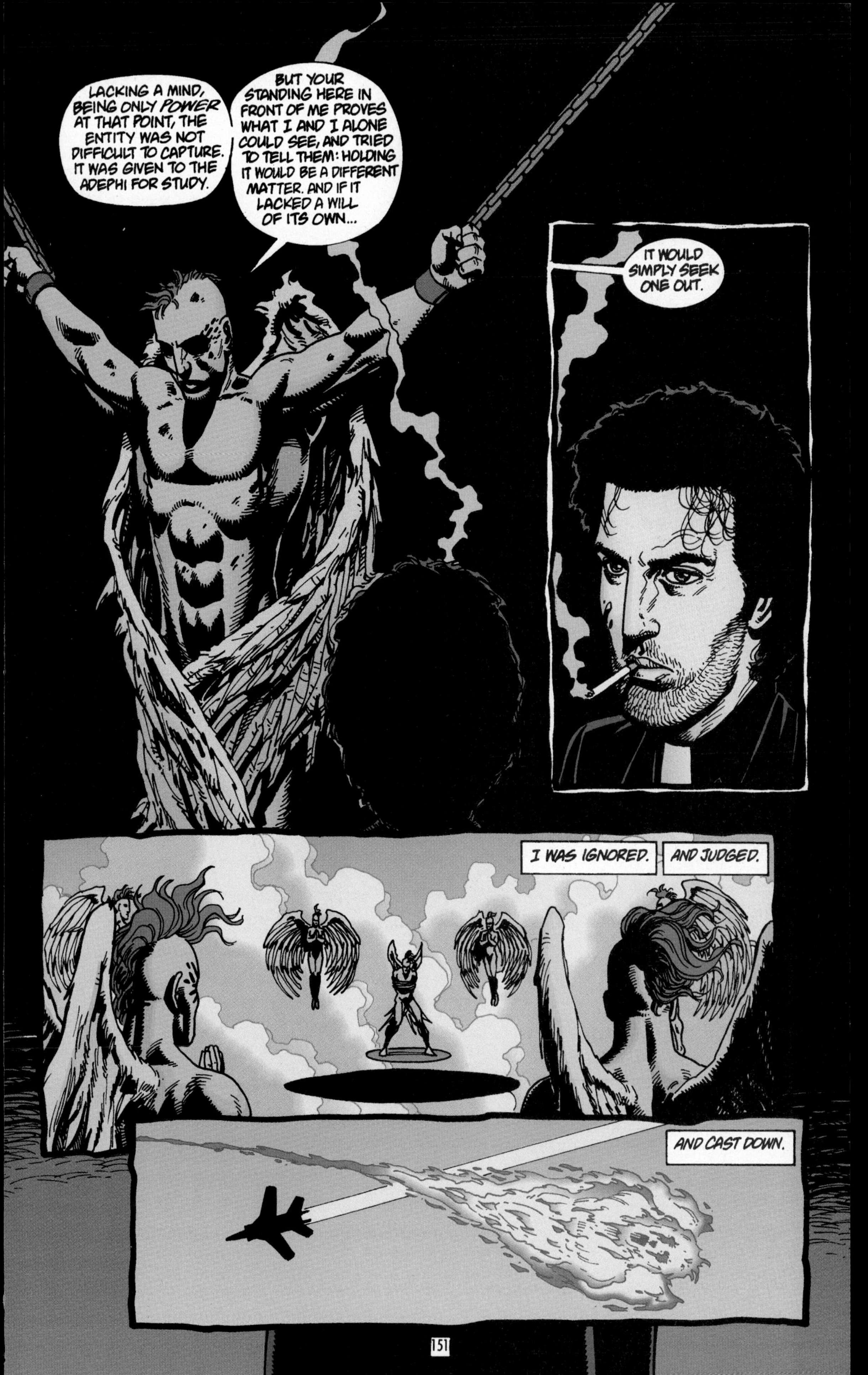
LACKING A MIND, BEING ONLY *POWER* AT THAT POINT, THE ENTITY WAS NOT DIFFICULT TO CAPTURE. IT WAS GIVEN TO THE ADEPHI FOR STUDY.
BUT YOUR STANDING HERE IN FRONT OF ME PROVES WHAT I AND I ALONE COULD SEE, AND TRIED TO TELL THEM: HOLDING IT WOULD BE A DIFFERENT MATTER. AND IF IT LACKED A WILL OF ITS OWN...
IT WOULD SIMPLY SEEK ONE OUT.
I WAS IGNORED.
AND JUDGED.
AND CAST DOWN.

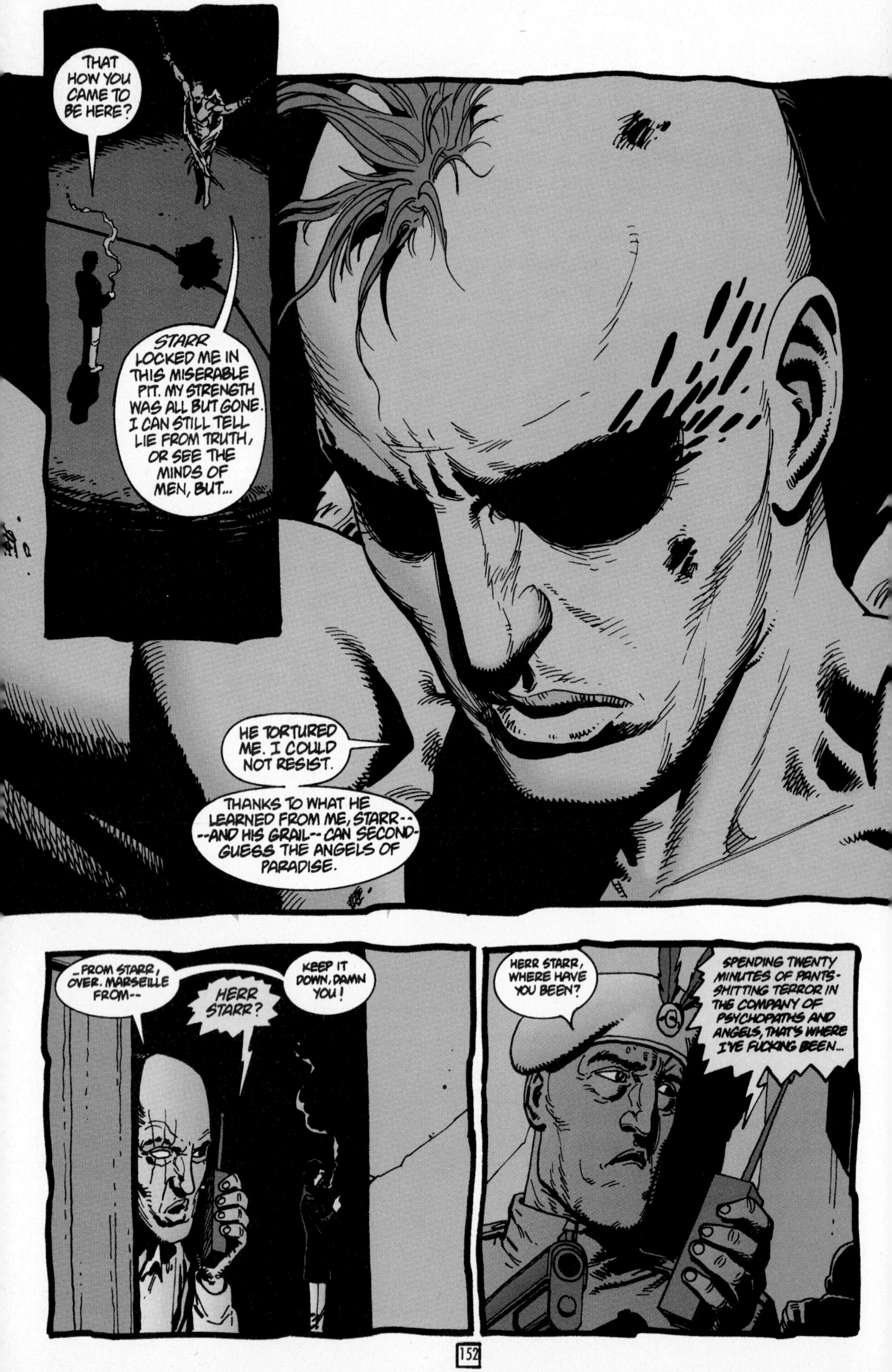
THAT HOW YOU CAME TO BE HERE?
STARR LOCKED ME IN THIS MISERABLE PIT. MY STRENGTH WAS ALL BUT GONE. I CAN STILL TELL LIE FROM TRUTH, OR SEE THE MINDS OF MEN, BUT...
HE TORTURED ME. I COULD NOT RESIST.
THANKS TO WHAT HE LEARNED FROM ME, STARR-- --AND HIS GRAIL--CAN SECOND-GUESS THE ANGELS OF PARADISE.
...FROM STARR, OVER. MARSEILLE FROM--
HERR STARR?
KEEP IT DOWN, DAMN YOU!
HERR STARR, WHERE HAVE YOU BEEN?
SPENDING TWENTY MINUTES OF PANTS-SHITTING TERROR IN THE COMPANY OF PSYCHOPATHS AND ANGELS, THAT'S WHERE I'VE FUCKING BEEN...

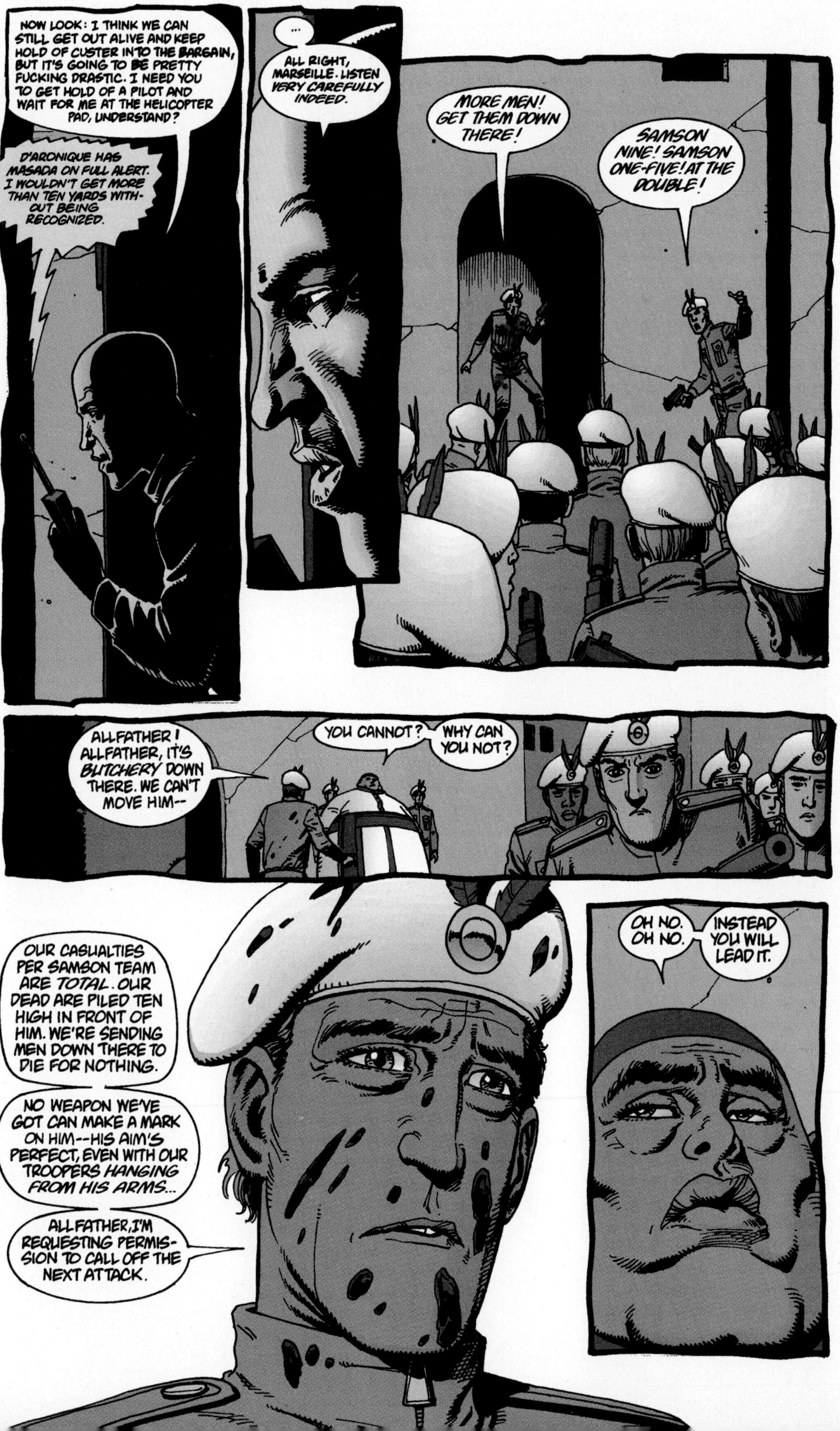
NOW LOOK: I THINK WE CAN STILL GET OUT ALIVE AND KEEP HOLD OF CUSTER INTO THE BARGAIN, BUT IT'S GOING TO BE PRETTY FUCKING DRASTIC. I NEED YOU TO GET HOLD OF A PILOT AND WAIT FOR ME AT THE HELICOPTER PAD, UNDERSTAND?
D'ARONIQUE HAS MASADA ON FULL ALERT. I WOULDN'T GET MORE THAN TEN YARDS WITHOUT BEING RECOGNIZED.
...
ALL RIGHT, MARSEILLE. LISTEN VERY CAREFULLY INDEED.
MORE MEN! GET THEM DOWN THERE!
SAMSON NINE! SAMSON ONE-FIVE! AT THE DOUBLE!
ALLFATHER! ALLFATHER, IT'S BUTCHERY DOWN THERE. WE CAN'T MOVE HIM--
YOU CANNOT?
WHY CAN YOU NOT?
OUR CASUALTIES PER SAMSON TEAM ARE TOTAL. OUR DEAD ARE PILED TEN HIGH IN FRONT OF HIM. WE'RE SENDING MEN DOWN THERE TO DIE FOR NOTHING.
NO WEAPON WE'VE GOT CAN MAKE A MARK ON HIM--HIS AIM'S PERFECT, EVEN WITH OUR TROOPERS HANGING FROM HIS ARMS...
ALLFATHER, I'M REQUESTING PERMISSION TO CALL OFF THE NEXT ATTACK.
OH NO. OH NO.
INSTEAD YOU WILL LEAD IT.

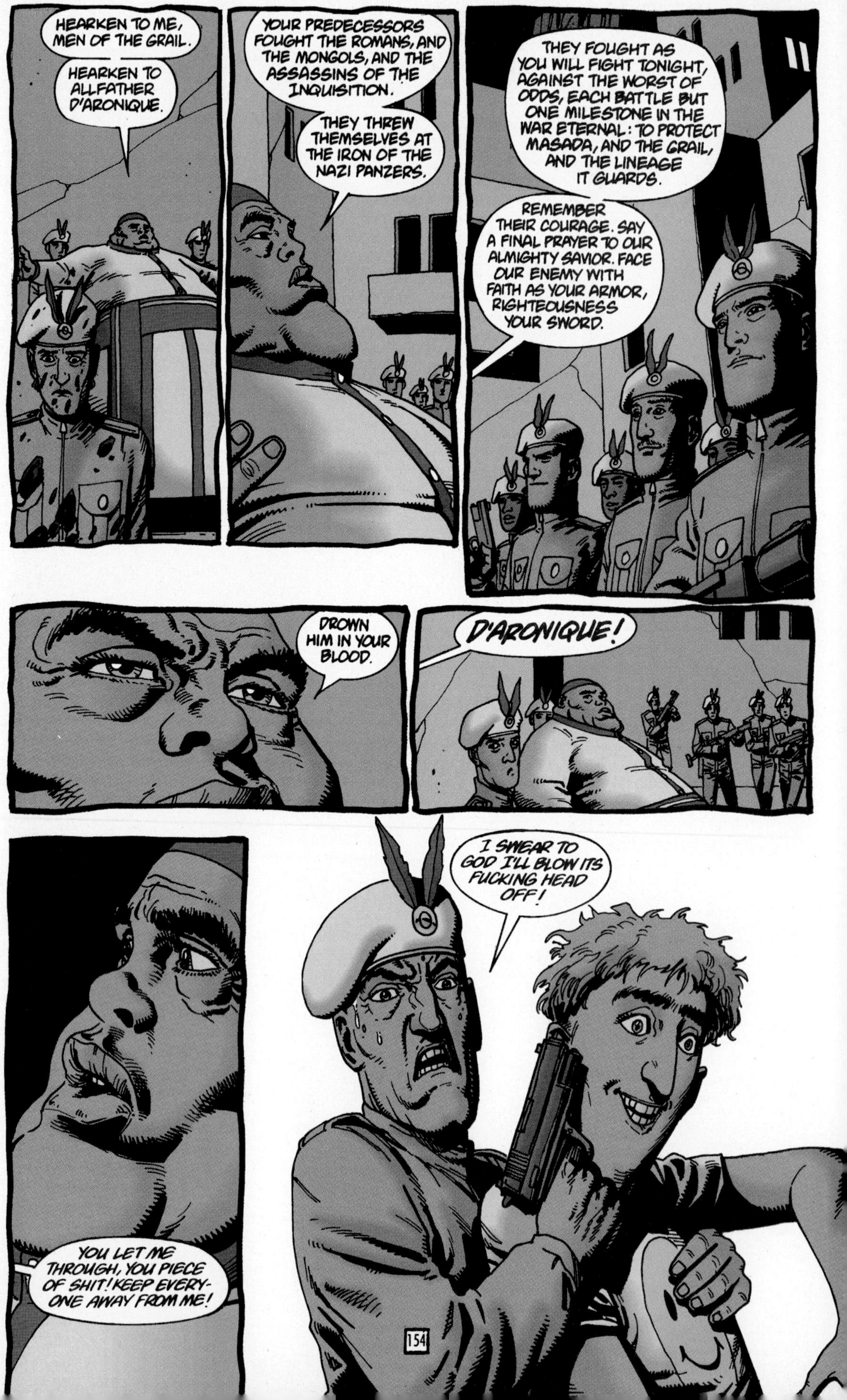
HEARKEN TO ME, MEN OF THE GRAIL.
HEARKEN TO ALLFATHER D'ARONIQUE.
YOUR PREDECESSORS FOUGHT THE ROMANS, AND THE MONGOLS, AND THE ASSASSINS OF THE INQUISITION.
THEY THREW THEMSELVES AT THE IRON OF THE NAZI PANZERS.
THEY FOUGHT AS YOU WILL FIGHT TONIGHT, AGAINST THE WORST OF ODDS, EACH BATTLE BUT ONE MILESTONE IN THE WAR ETERNAL: TO PROTECT MASADA, AND THE GRAIL, AND THE LINEAGE IT GUARDS.
REMEMBER THEIR COURAGE. SAY A FINAL PRAYER TO OUR ALMIGHTY SAVIOR. FACE OUR ENEMY WITH FAITH AS YOUR ARMOR, RIGHTEOUSNESS YOUR SWORD.
DROWN HIM IN YOUR BLOOD.
D'ARONIQUE!
YOU LET ME THROUGH, YOU PIECE OF SHIT! KEEP EVERY-ONE AWAY FROM ME!
I SWEAR TO GOD I'LL BLOW ITS FUCKING HEAD OFF!

LET'S GET DOWN TO CASES. WHERE IT CAME FROM, WHAT IT IS, WE BEEN THROUGH ALL THAT.

I NEED TO KNOW WHAT IT *KNOWS*...

STRICTLY SPEAKING, IT HAS BECOME YOU. ITS MEMORIES ARE YOURS. IT IS AS IF YOU HAVE FORGOTTEN SOMETHING *YOU* ONCE KNEW...

YEAH? SO? HOW DO I REMEMBER?

GENESIS RUNS DEEP WITHIN YOU.

JACK DANIEL'S?

ONLY OLDER WAYS FROM OLDER TIMES CAN BRING IT FORTH. YOU MUST ELEVATE THE SPIRIT. FORGET THE FLESH.

LOOK TO YOUR HOMELAND, CUSTER. TO THE FIRST AMERICANS. THE NAVAJO. THE HOPI.

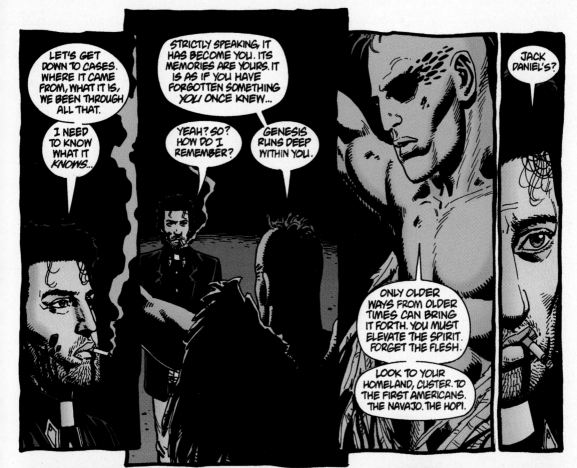

BUT NO MATTER WHICH OF THEM YOU GO TO, I BEG YOU TO UNDERSTAND--I PRAY MY WORDS HAVE SHOWN YOU--GENESIS SHOULD NOT EVEN *BE*. IT IS UNIQUE. IT IS *NEW*.

IT HAS POWER ENOUGH TO EQUAL THAT OF GOD: AND WHY HE HAS SUFFERED IT TO LIVE I CANNOT BEGIN TO IMAGINE.

KINDA BEHIND THE TIMES, AIN'T YOU? HE'S ALREADY RUNNIN' SCARED.

WHAT?

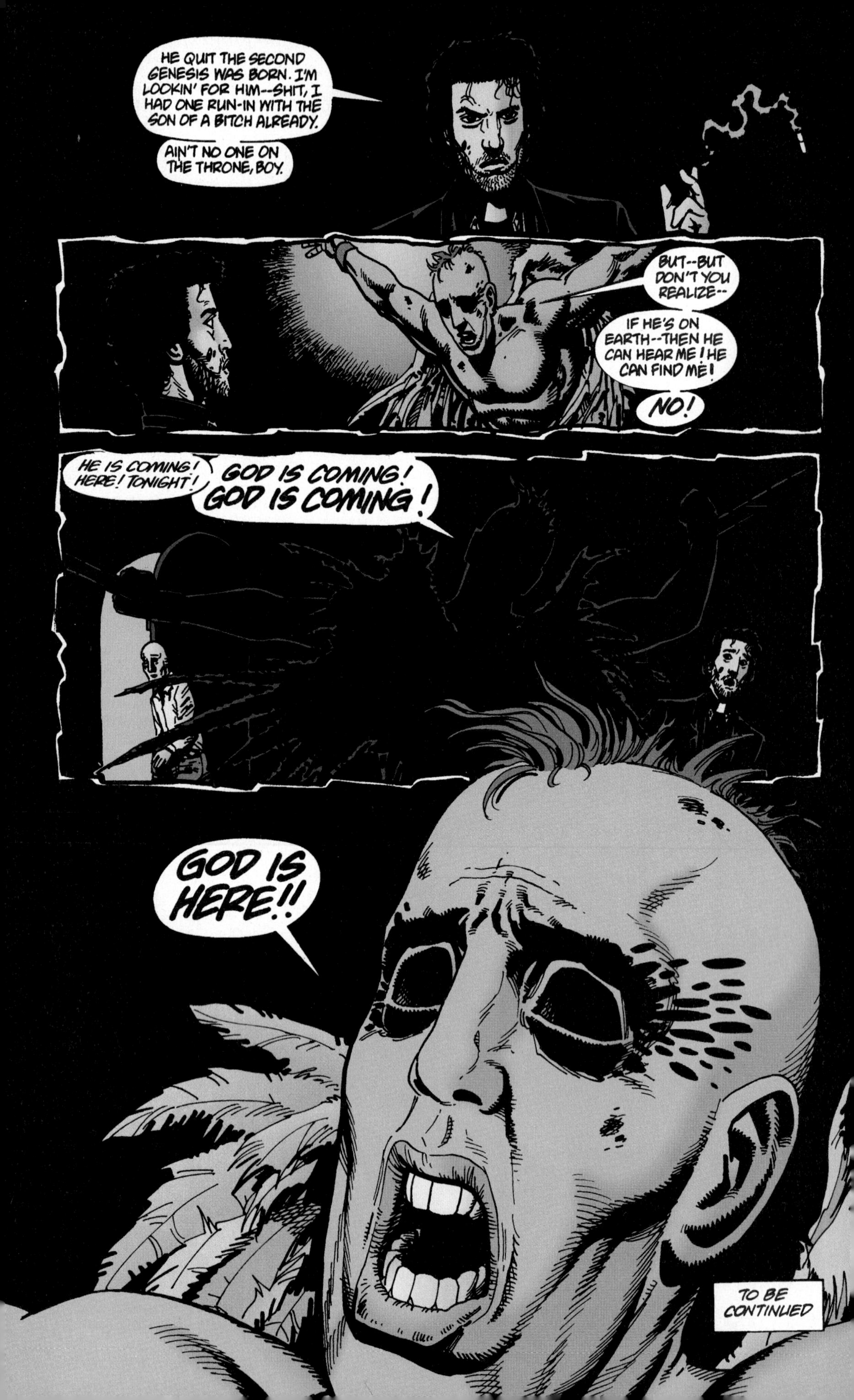
HE QUIT THE SECOND GENESIS WAS BORN. I'M LOOKIN' FOR HIM--SHIT, I HAD ONE RUN-IN WITH THE SON OF A BITCH ALREADY.
AIN'T NO ONE ON THE THRONE, BOY.
BUT--BUT DON'T YOU REALIZE--
IF HE'S ON EARTH--THEN HE CAN HEAR ME! HE CAN FIND ME!
NO!
HE IS COMING! HERE! TONIGHT!
GOD IS COMING! GOD IS COMING!
GOD IS HERE!!
TO BE CONTINUED

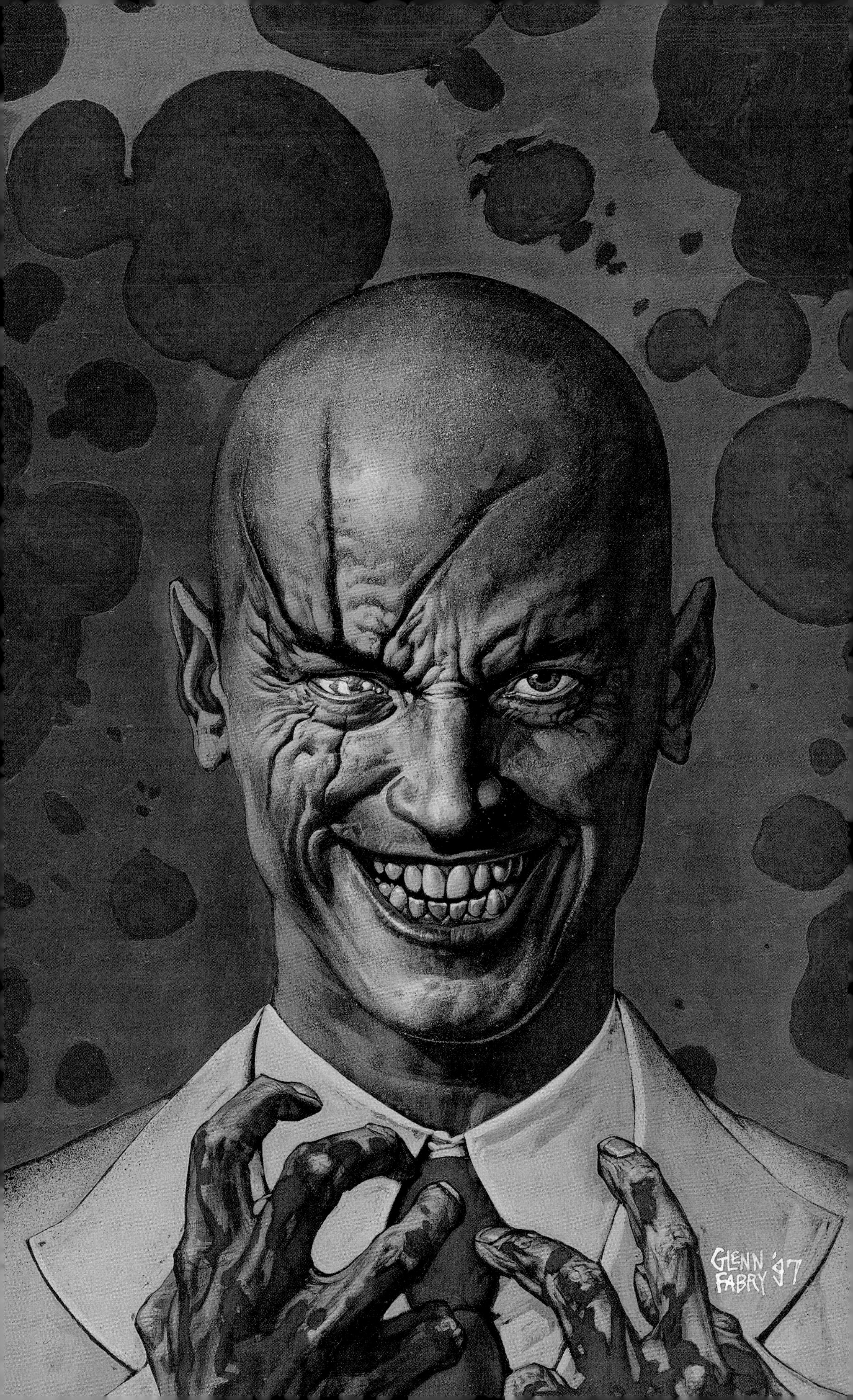
GLENN '97
FABRY

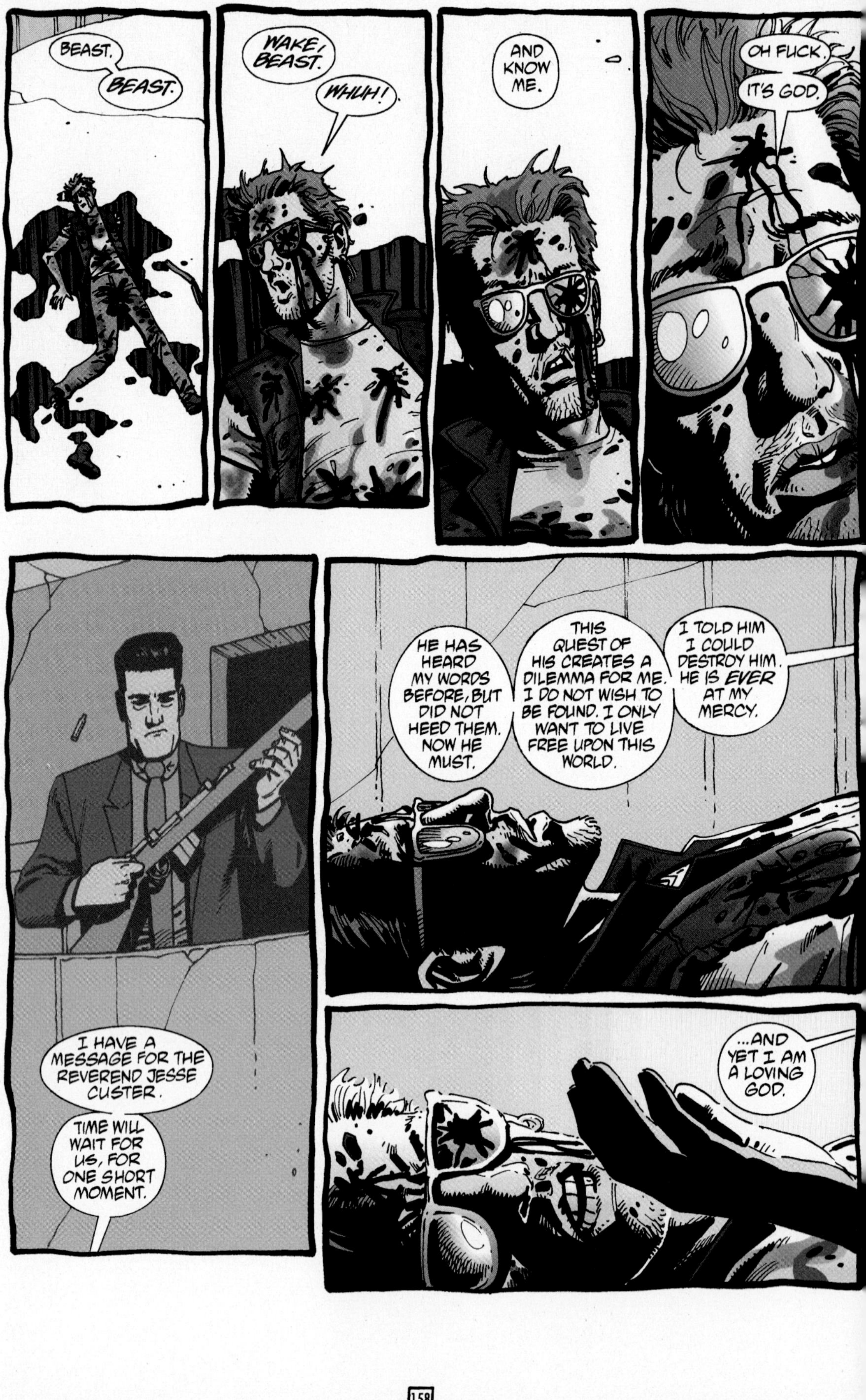
BEAST.
BEAST.
WAKE, BEAST.
WHUH!
AND KNOW ME.
OH FUCK.
IT'S GOD.
I HAVE A MESSAGE FOR THE REVEREND JESSE CUSTER.
TIME WILL WAIT FOR US, FOR ONE SHORT MOMENT.
HE HAS HEARD MY WORDS BEFORE, BUT DID NOT HEED THEM. NOW HE MUST.
THIS QUEST OF HIS CREATES A DILEMMA FOR ME. I DO NOT WISH TO BE FOUND. I ONLY WANT TO LIVE FREE UPON THIS WORLD.
I TOLD HIM I COULD DESTROY HIM. HE IS EVER AT MY MERCY.
...AND YET I AM A LOVING GOD.

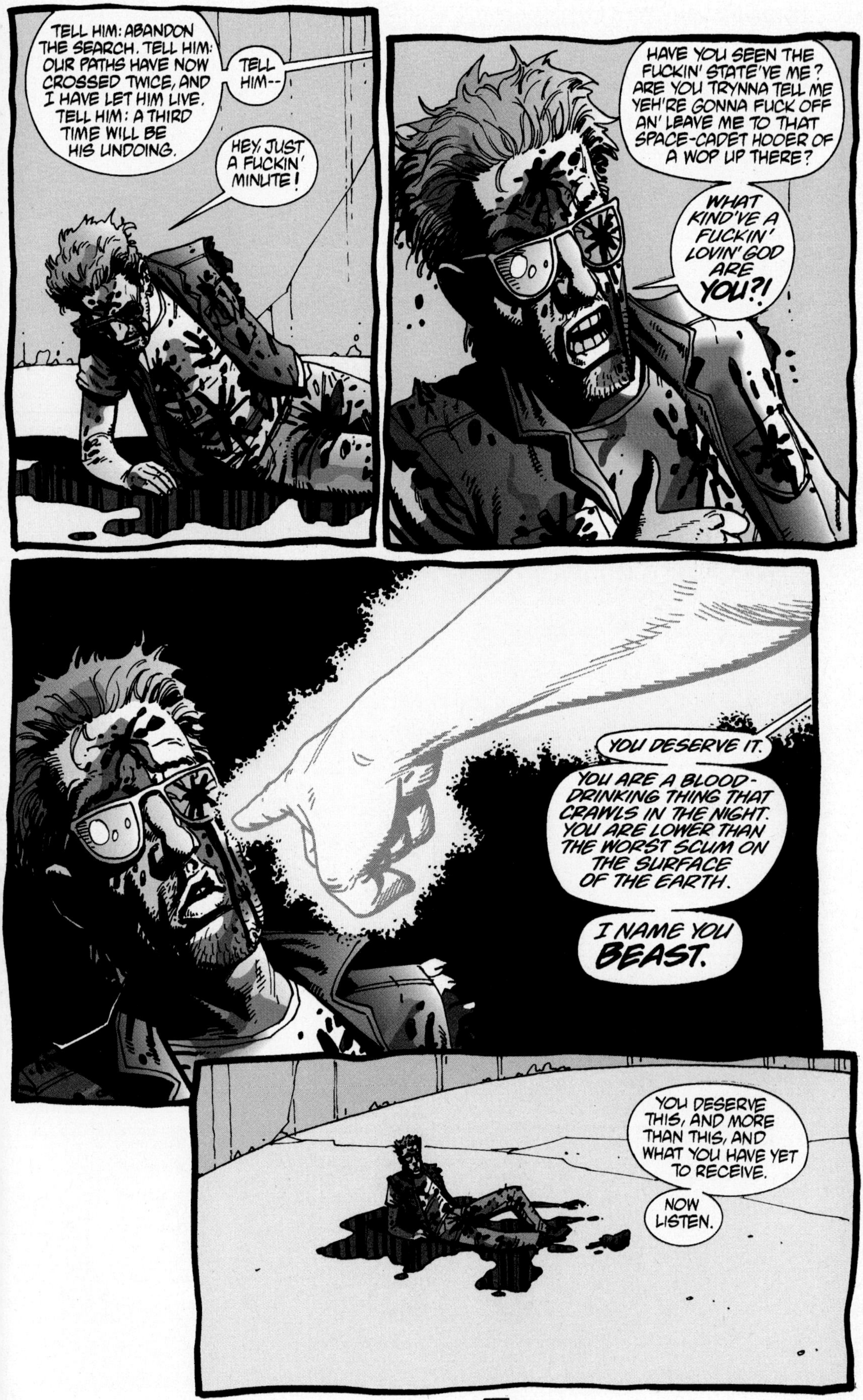
TELL HIM: ABANDON THE SEARCH. TELL HIM: OUR PATHS HAVE NOW CROSSED TWICE, AND I HAVE LET HIM LIVE. TELL HIM: A THIRD TIME WILL BE HIS UNDOING.
TELL HIM--
HEY, JUST A FUCKIN' MINUTE!
HAVE YOU SEEN THE FUCKIN' STATE'VE ME? ARE YOU TRYNNA TELL ME YEH'RE GONNA FUCK OFF AN' LEAVE ME TO THAT SPACE-CADET HOOER OF A WOP UP THERE?
WHAT KIND'VE A FUCKIN' LOVIN' GOD ARE YOU?!
YOU DESERVE IT.
YOU ARE A BLOOD-DRINKING THING THAT CRAWLS IN THE NIGHT. YOU ARE LOWER THAN THE WORST SCUM ON THE SURFACE OF THE EARTH.
I NAME YOU BEAST.
YOU DESERVE THIS, AND MORE THAN THIS, AND WHAT YOU HAVE YET TO RECEIVE.
NOW LISTEN.

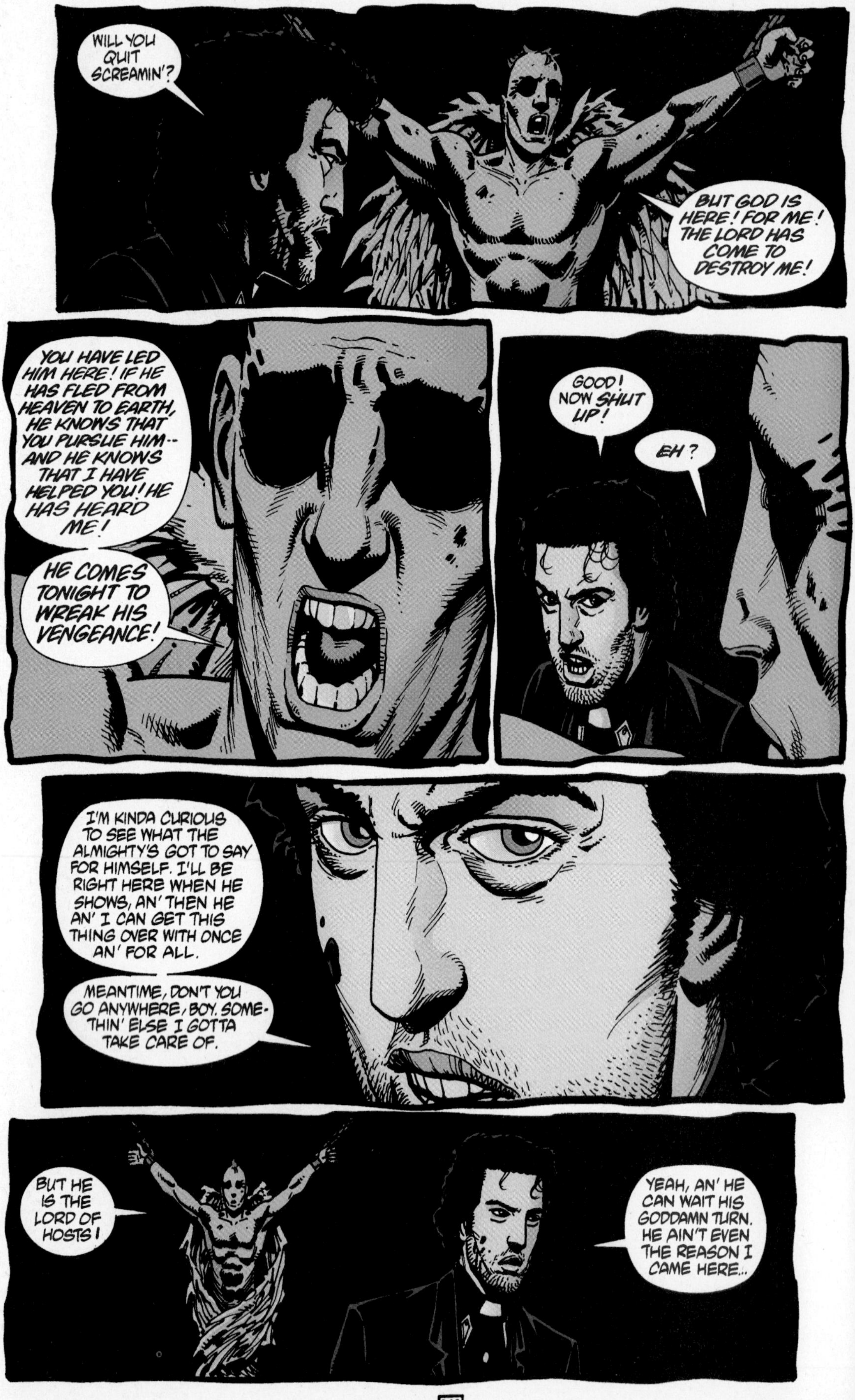
WILL YOU QUIT SCREAMIN'?
BUT GOD IS HERE! FOR ME! THE LORD HAS COME TO DESTROY ME!
YOU HAVE LED HIM HERE! IF HE HAS FLED FROM HEAVEN TO EARTH, HE KNOWS THAT YOU PURSUE HIM-- AND HE KNOWS THAT I HAVE HELPED YOU! HE HAS HEARD ME!
HE COMES TONIGHT TO WREAK HIS VENGEANCE!
GOOD! NOW SHUT UP!
EH?
I'M KINDA CURIOUS TO SEE WHAT THE ALMIGHTY'S GOT TO SAY FOR HIMSELF. I'LL BE RIGHT HERE WHEN HE SHOWS, AN' THEN HE AN' I CAN GET THIS THING OVER WITH ONCE AN' FOR ALL.
MEANTIME, DON'T YOU GO ANYWHERE, BOY. SOMETHIN' ELSE I GOTTA TAKE CARE OF.
BUT HE IS THE LORD OF HOSTS!
YEAH, AN' HE CAN WAIT HIS GODDAMN TURN. HE AIN'T EVEN THE REASON I CAME HERE...

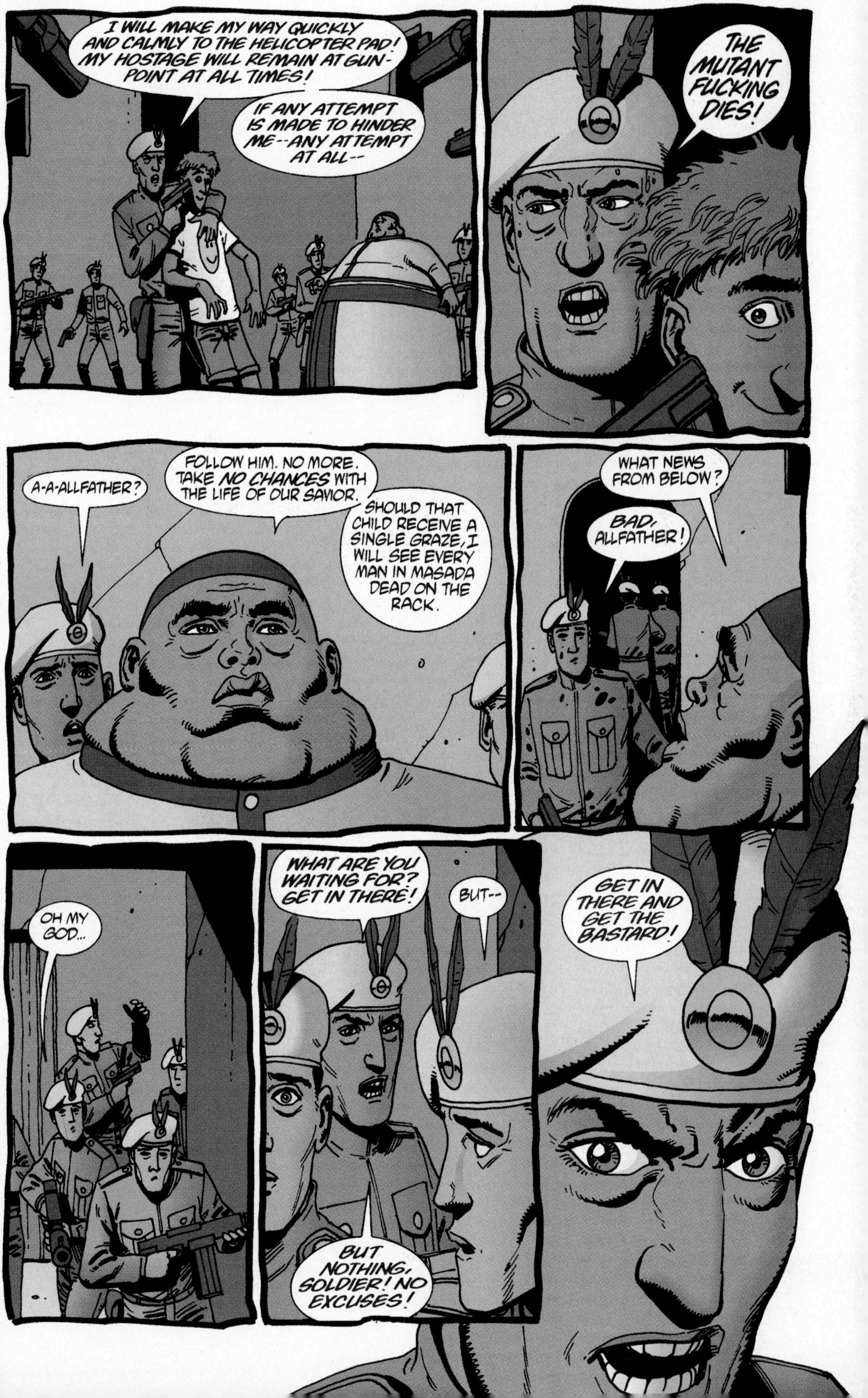
I WILL MAKE MY WAY QUICKLY AND CALMLY TO THE HELICOPTER PAD! MY HOSTAGE WILL REMAIN AT GUN-POINT AT ALL TIMES!
IF ANY ATTEMPT IS MADE TO HINDER ME--ANY ATTEMPT AT ALL--
THE MUTANT FUCKING DIES!
A-A-ALLFATHER?
FOLLOW HIM. NO MORE. TAKE NO CHANCES WITH THE LIFE OF OUR SAVIOR.
SHOULD THAT CHILD RECEIVE A SINGLE GRAZE, I WILL SEE EVERY MAN IN MASADA DEAD ON THE RACK.
WHAT NEWS FROM BELOW?
BAD, ALLFATHER!
OH MY GOD...
WHAT ARE YOU WAITING FOR? GET IN THERE!
BUT--
BUT NOTHING, SOLDIER! NO EXCUSES!
GET IN THERE AND GET THE BASTARD!

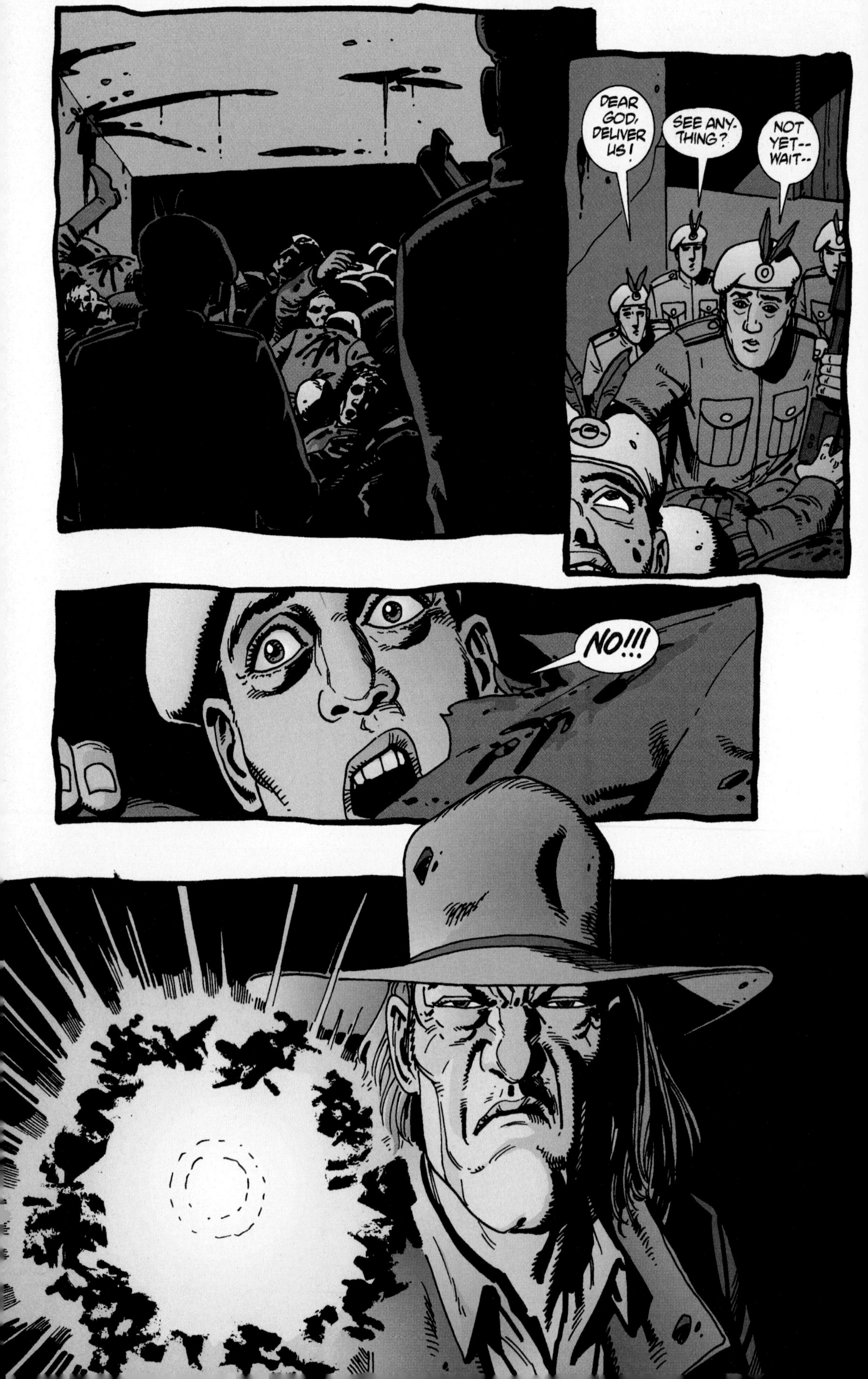
DEAR GOD, DELIVER US!
SEE ANYTHING?
NOT YET-- WAIT--
NO!!!

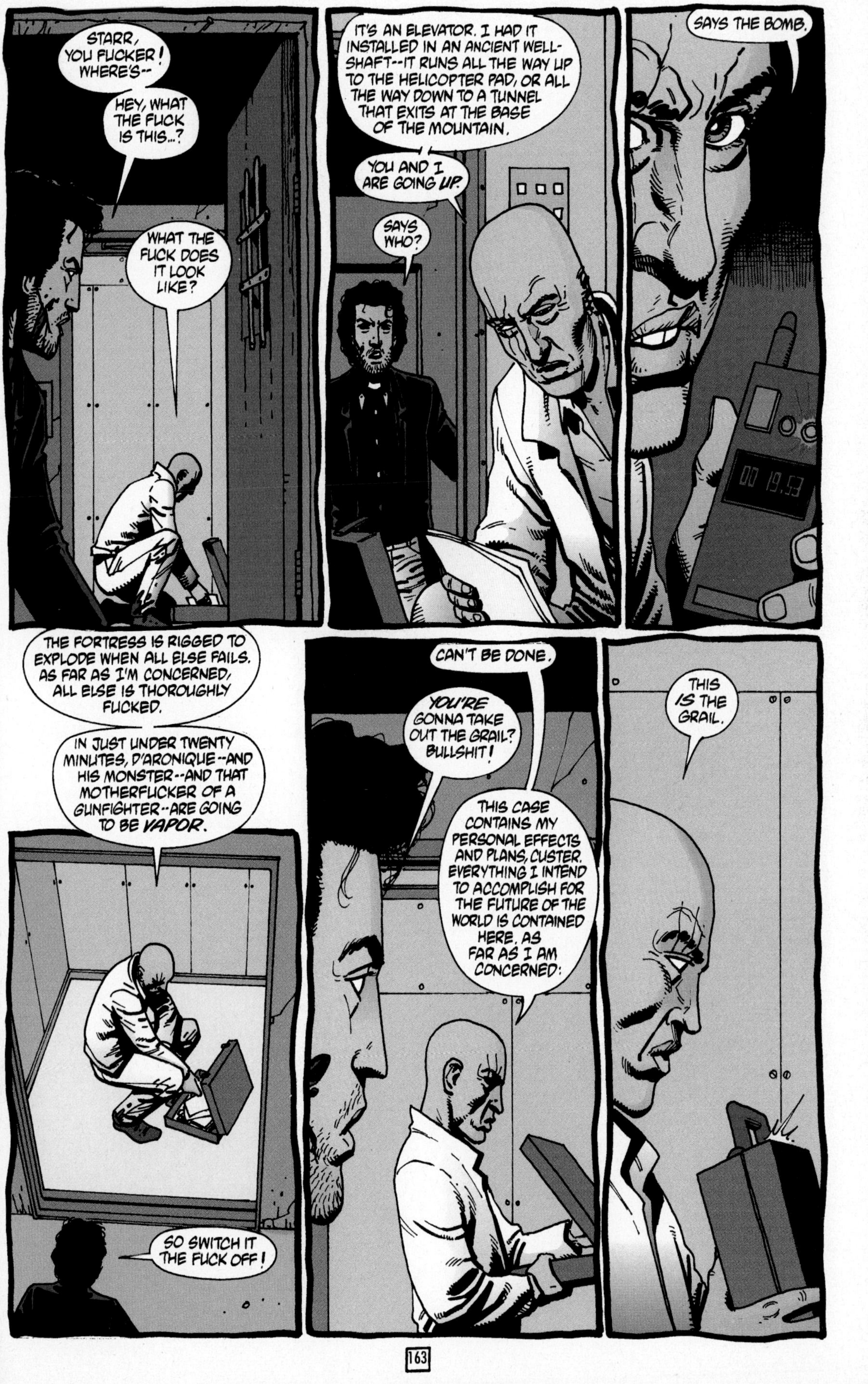

STARR, YOU FUCKER! WHERE'S--
HEY, WHAT THE FUCK IS THIS...?
WHAT THE FUCK DOES IT LOOK LIKE?
IT'S AN ELEVATOR. I HAD IT INSTALLED IN AN ANCIENT WELL-SHAFT--IT RUNS ALL THE WAY UP TO THE HELICOPTER PAD, OR ALL THE WAY DOWN TO A TUNNEL THAT EXITS AT THE BASE OF THE MOUNTAIN.
YOU AND I ARE GOING UP.
SAYS WHO?
SAYS THE BOMB.
THE FORTRESS IS RIGGED TO EXPLODE WHEN ALL ELSE FAILS. AS FAR AS I'M CONCERNED, ALL ELSE IS THOROUGHLY FUCKED.
IN JUST UNDER TWENTY MINUTES, D'ARONIQUE--AND HIS MONSTER--AND THAT MOTHERFUCKER OF A GUNFIGHTER--ARE GOING TO BE VAPOR.
SO SWITCH IT THE FUCK OFF!
CAN'T BE DONE.
YOU'RE GONNA TAKE OUT THE GRAIL? BULLSHIT!
THIS CASE CONTAINS MY PERSONAL EFFECTS AND PLANS, CUSTER. EVERYTHING I INTEND TO ACCOMPLISH FOR THE FUTURE OF THE WORLD IS CONTAINED HERE. AS FAR AS I AM CONCERNED:
THIS IS THE GRAIL.

LISTEN, ASSHOLE--

YOU LISTEN!

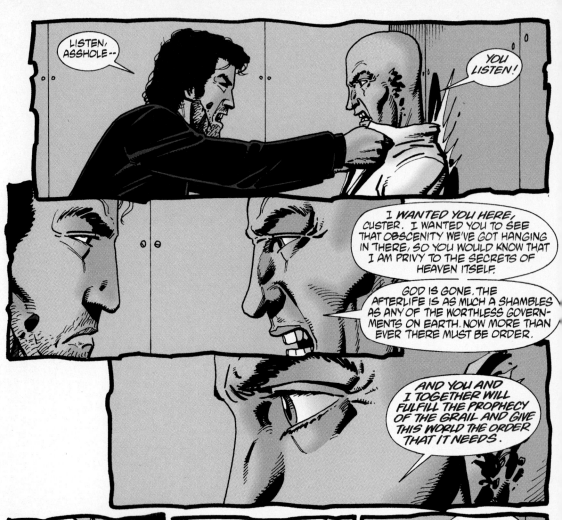

I WANTED YOU HERE, CUSTER. I WANTED YOU TO SEE THAT OBSCENITY WE'VE GOT HANGING IN THERE, SO YOU WOULD KNOW THAT I AM PRIVY TO THE SECRETS OF HEAVEN ITSELF.

GOD IS GONE. THE AFTERLIFE IS AS MUCH A SHAMBLES AS ANY OF THE WORTHLESS GOVERNMENTS ON EARTH. NOW MORE THAN EVER THERE MUST BE ORDER.

AND YOU AND I TOGETHER WILL FULFILL THE PROPHECY OF THE GRAIL AND GIVE THIS WORLD THE ORDER THAT IT NEEDS.

WHERE'S CASS?

WHAT?

MY BUDDY CASSIDY. I CAME HERE TO FETCH HIM BACK.

FOR CHRIST'S SAKE, THERE'S NO TIME FOR THAT NOW!

WHERE IS HE, STARR?

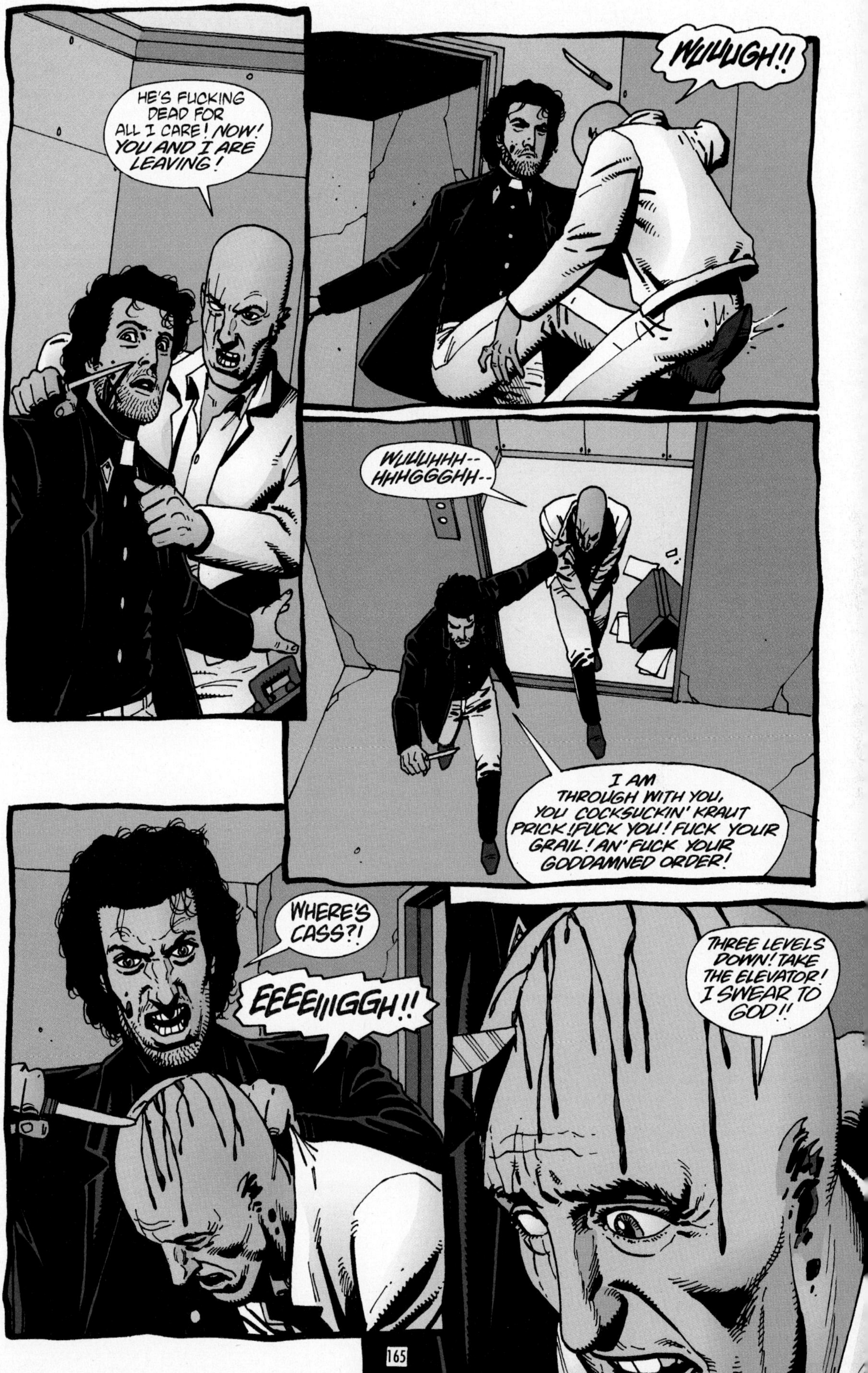
HE'S FUCKING DEAD FOR ALL I CARE! NOW! YOU AND I ARE LEAVING!
WUUUGH!!
WUUUHHH-- HHHGGGHH--
I AM THROUGH WITH YOU, YOU COCKSUCKIN' KRAUT PRICK! FUCK YOU! FUCK YOUR GRAIL! AN' FUCK YOUR GODDAMNED ORDER!
WHERE'S CASS?!
EEEEIIIGGH!!
THREE LEVELS DOWN! TAKE THE ELEVATOR! I SWEAR TO GOD!!

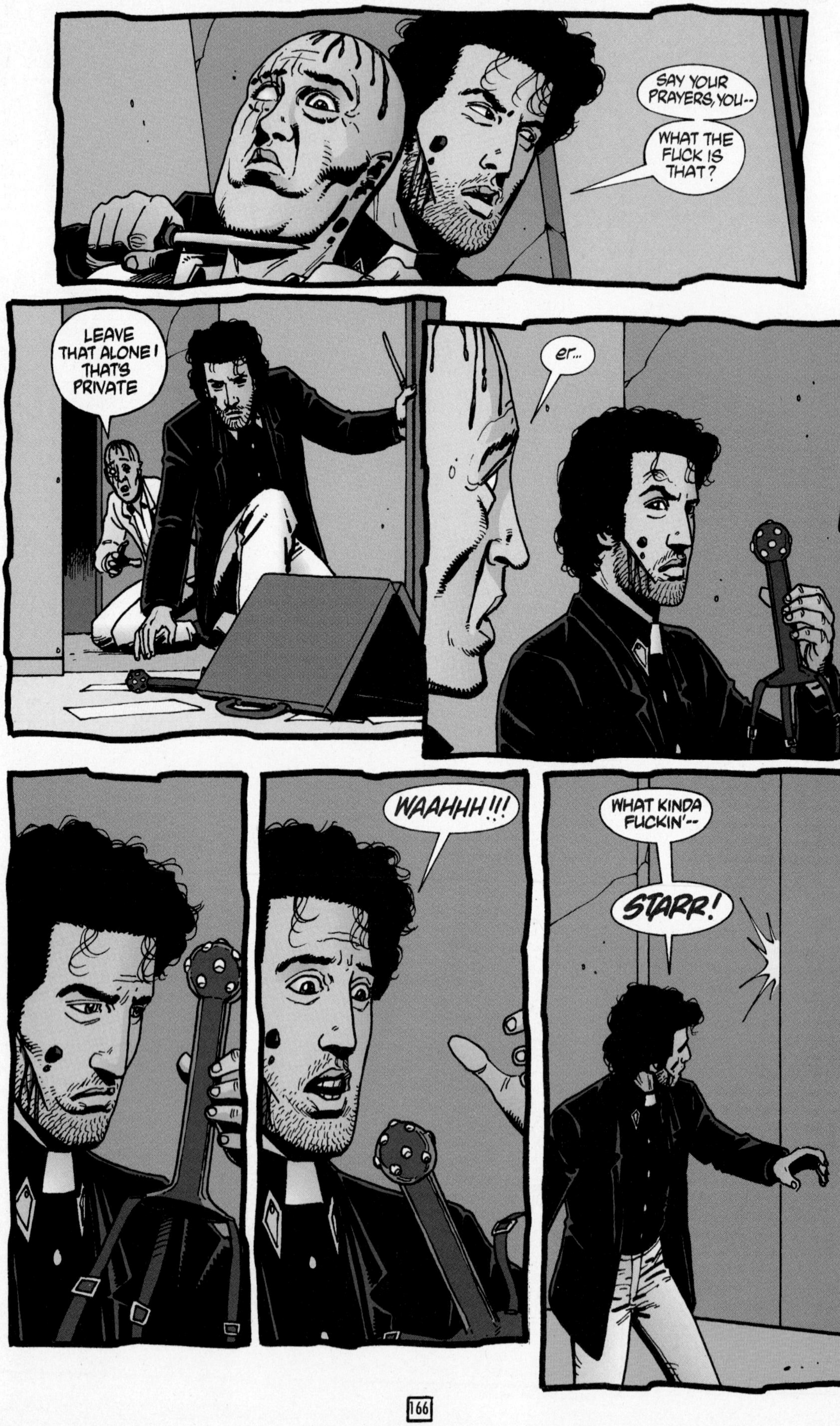
SAY YOUR PRAYERS, YOU--
WHAT THE FUCK IS THAT?
LEAVE THAT ALONE! THAT'S PRIVATE
er...
WAAHHH!!!
WHAT KINDA FUCKIN'--
STARR!

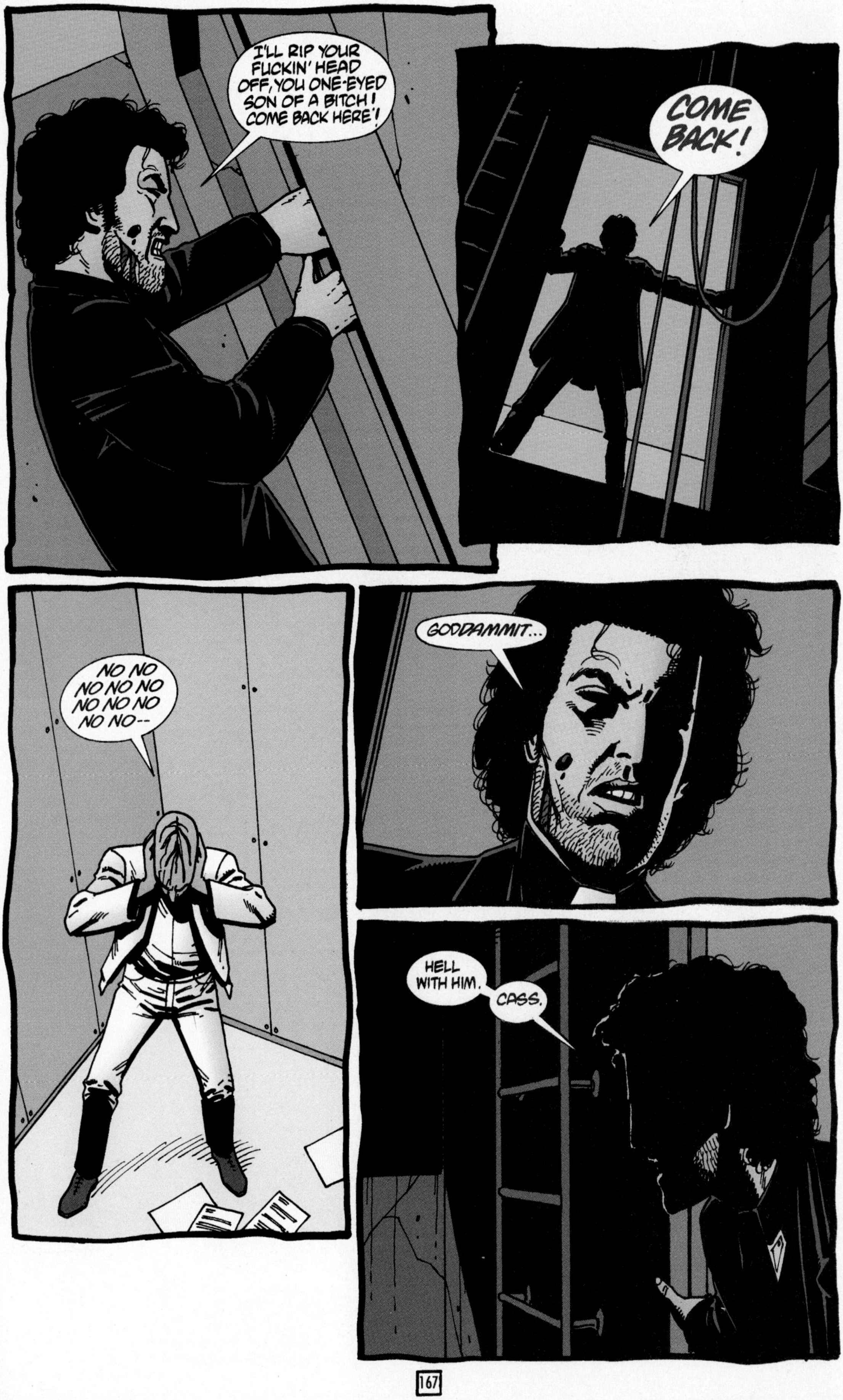
I'LL RIP YOUR FUCKIN' HEAD OFF, YOU ONE-EYED SON OF A BITCH! COME BACK HERE!
COME BACK!
NO NO NO NO NO NO NO NO NO NO--
GODDAMMIT...
HELL WITH HIM,
CASS.

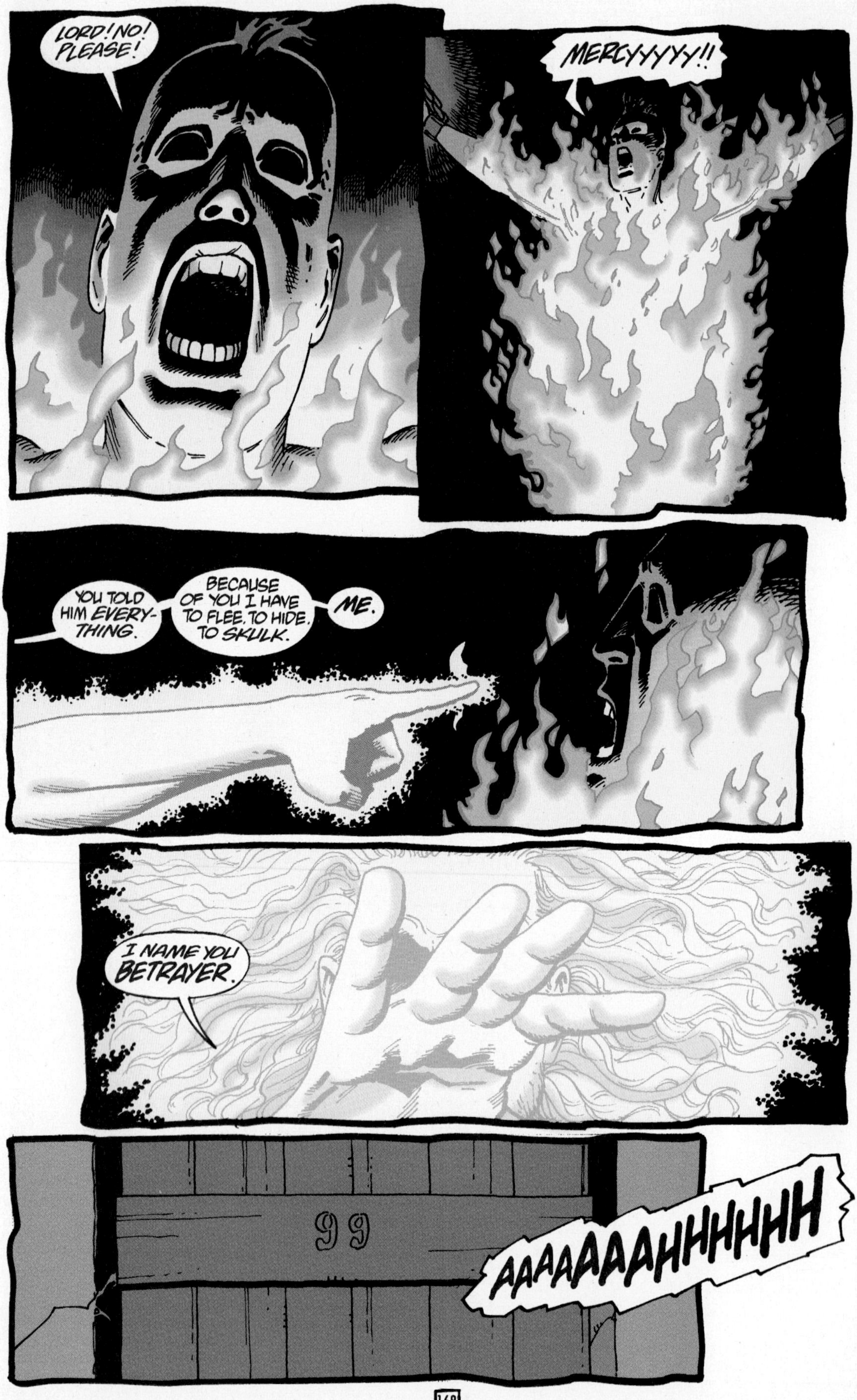
LORD! NO! PLEASE!
MERCYYYYY!!
YOU TOLD HIM EVERY-THING.
BECAUSE OF YOU I HAVE TO FLEE, TO HIDE, TO SKULK.
ME.
I NAME YOU BETRAYER.
99
AAAAAAAHHHHHHH

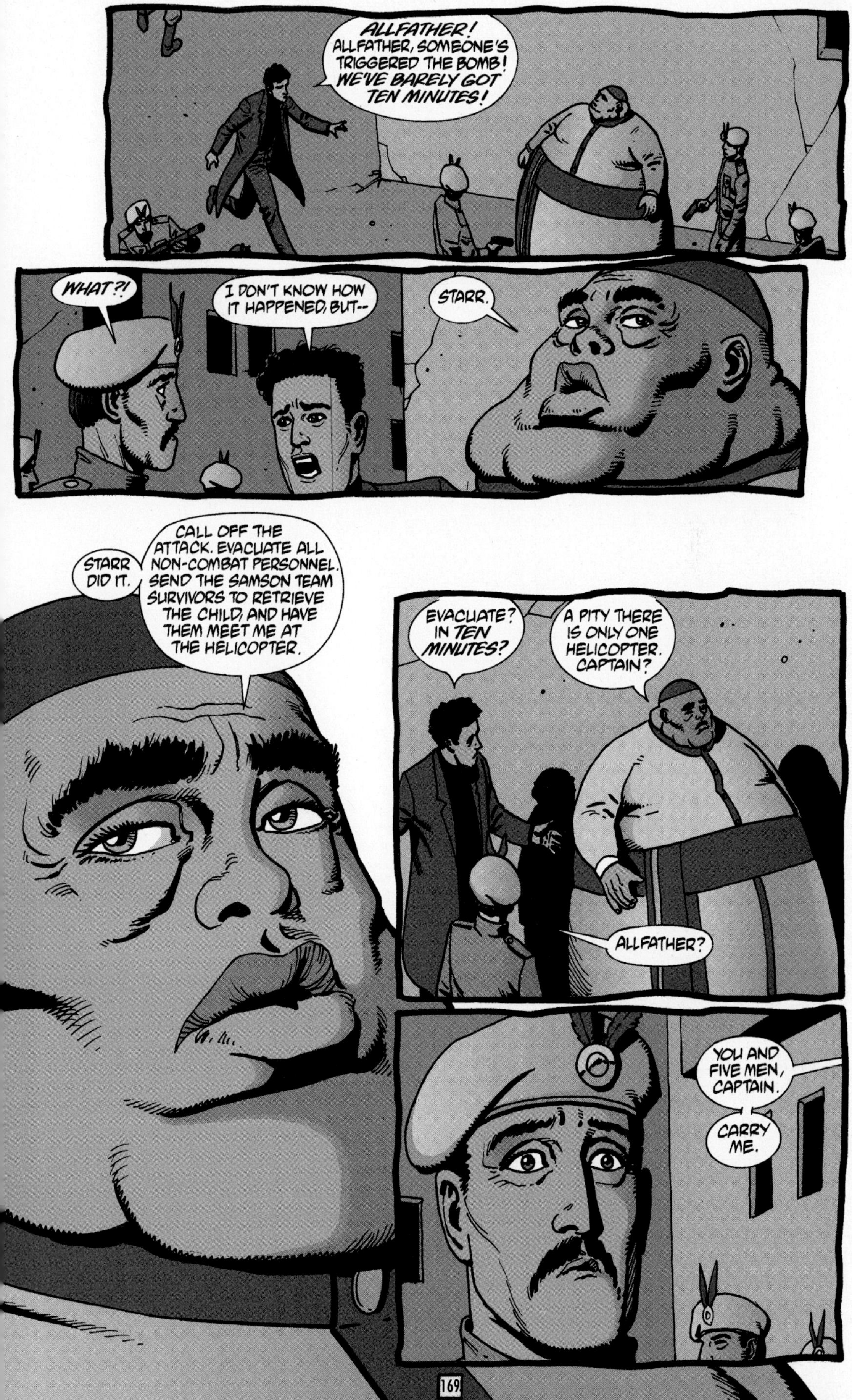
ALLFATHER! ALLFATHER, SOMEONE'S TRIGGERED THE BOMB! WE'VE BARELY GOT TEN MINUTES!
WHAT?!
I DON'T KNOW HOW IT HAPPENED, BUT--
STARR.
STARR DID IT.
CALL OFF THE ATTACK. EVACUATE ALL NON-COMBAT PERSONNEL. SEND THE SAMSON TEAM SURVIVORS TO RETRIEVE THE CHILD, AND HAVE THEM MEET ME AT THE HELICOPTER.
EVACUATE? IN TEN MINUTES?
A PITY THERE IS ONLY ONE HELICOPTER. CAPTAIN?
ALLFATHER?
YOU AND FIVE MEN, CAPTAIN.
CARRY ME.

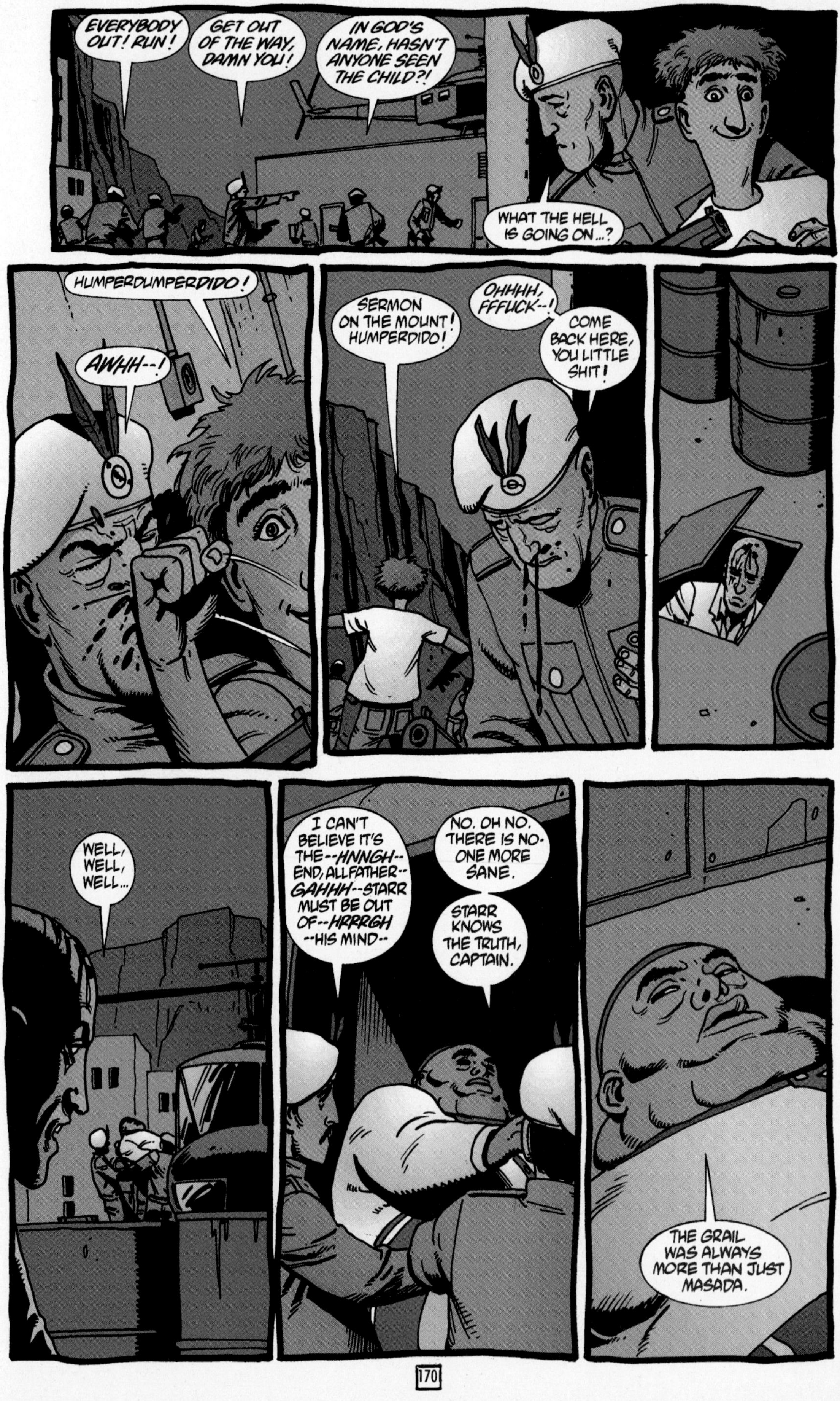
EVERYBODY OUT! RUN!
GET OUT OF THE WAY, DAMN YOU!
IN GOD'S NAME, HASN'T ANYONE SEEN THE CHILD?!
WHAT THE HELL IS GOING ON...?
HUMPERDUMPERDIDO!
AWHH--!
SERMON ON THE MOUNT! HUMPERDIDO!
OHHHH, FFFUCK--!
COME BACK HERE, YOU LITTLE SHIT!
WELL, WELL, WELL...
I CAN'T BELIEVE IT'S THE--HNNGH--END, ALLFATHER--GAHHH--STARR MUST BE OUT OF--HRRRGH--HIS MIND--
NO. OH NO. THERE IS NO ONE MORE SANE.
STARR KNOWS THE TRUTH, CAPTAIN.
THE GRAIL WAS ALWAYS MORE THAN JUST MASADA.

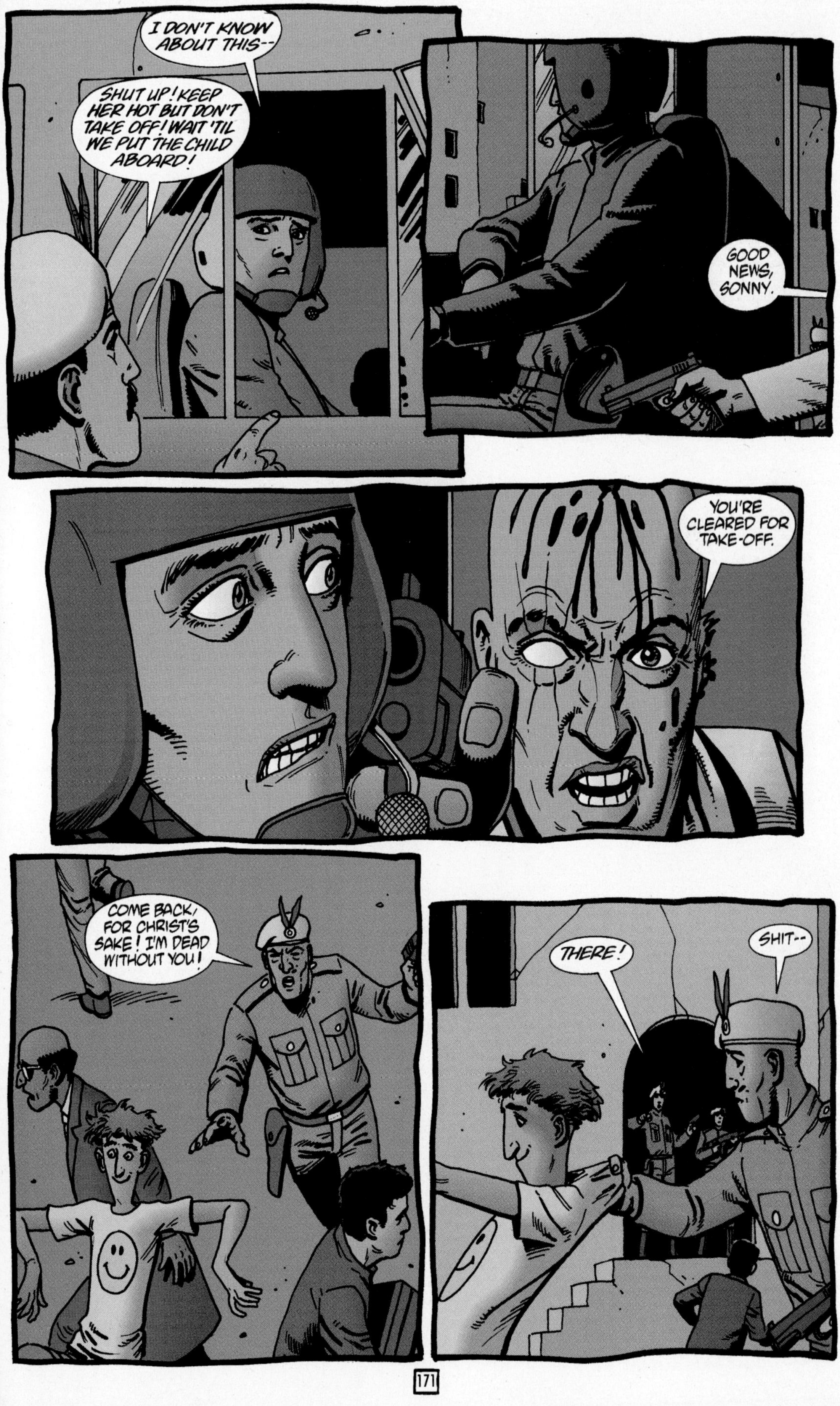
I DON'T KNOW ABOUT THIS--
SHUT UP! KEEP HER HOT BUT DON'T TAKE OFF! WAIT 'TIL WE PUT THE CHILD ABOARD!
GOOD NEWS, SONNY.
YOU'RE CLEARED FOR TAKE-OFF.
COME BACK, FOR CHRIST'S SAKE! I'M DEAD WITHOUT YOU!
THERE!
SHIT--

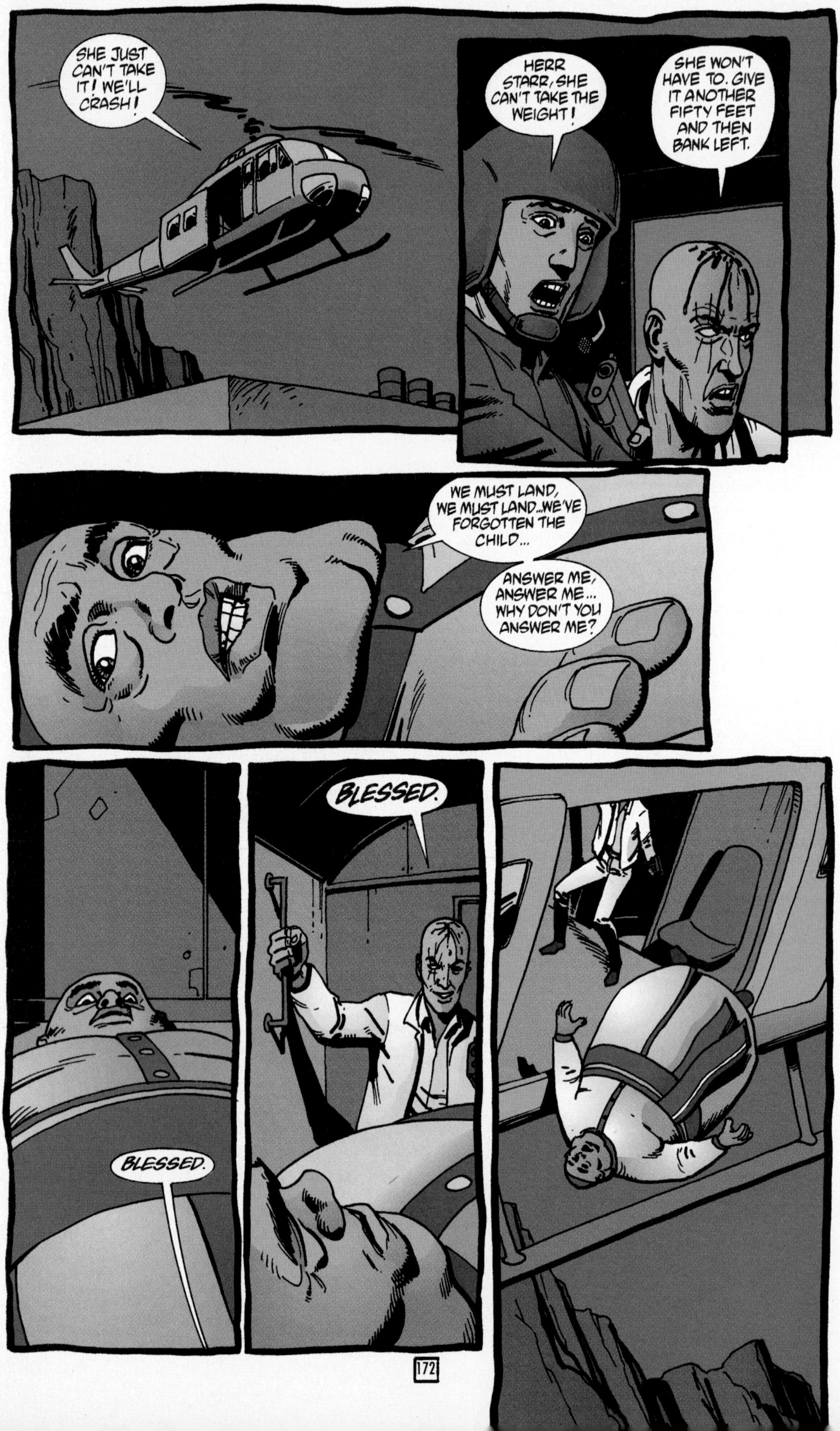
SHE JUST CAN'T TAKE IT! WE'LL CRASH!
HERR STARR, SHE CAN'T TAKE THE WEIGHT!
SHE WON'T HAVE TO. GIVE IT ANOTHER FIFTY FEET AND THEN BANK LEFT.
WE MUST LAND, WE MUST LAND...WE'VE FORGOTTEN THE CHILD...
ANSWER ME, ANSWER ME... WHY DON'T YOU ANSWER ME?
BLESSED.
BLESSED.

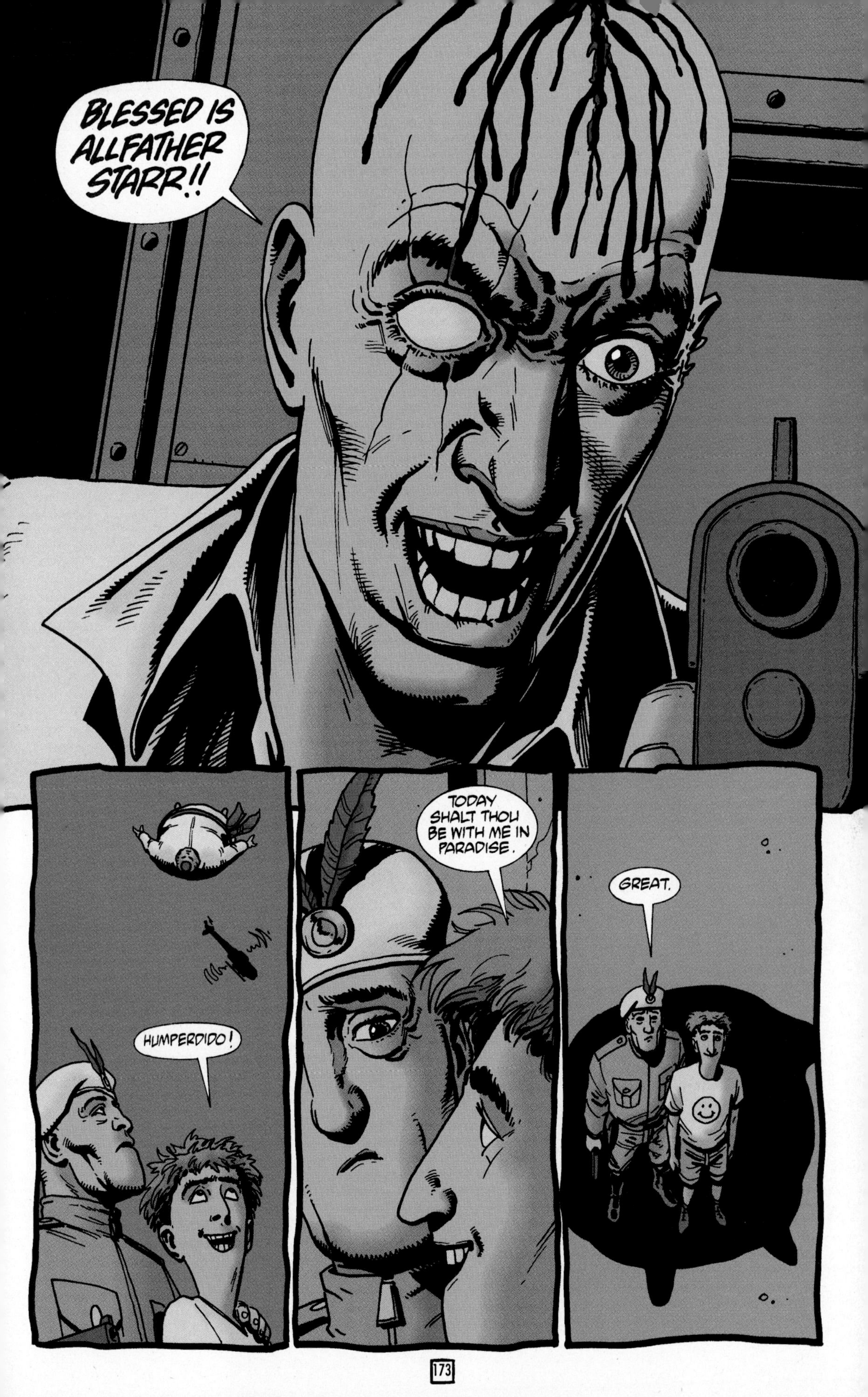
BLESSED IS ALLFATHER STARR!!
HUMPERDIDO!
TODAY SHALT THOU BE WITH ME IN PARADISE.
GREAT.

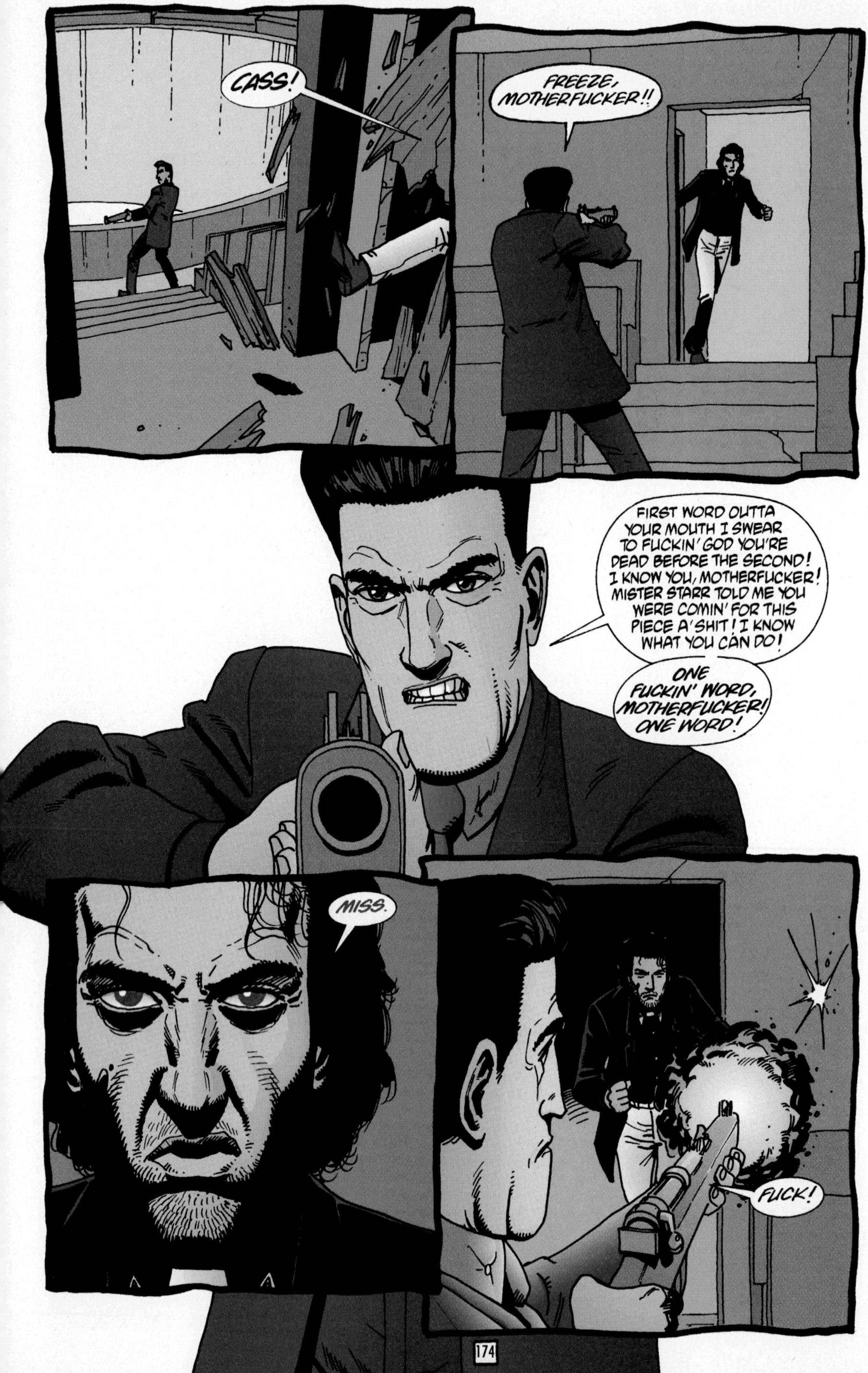
CASS!
FREEZE, MOTHERFUCKER!!
FIRST WORD OUTTA YOUR MOUTH I SWEAR TO FUCKIN' GOD YOU'RE DEAD BEFORE THE SECOND! I KNOW YOU, MOTHERFUCKER! MISTER STARR TOLD ME YOU WERE COMIN' FOR THIS PIECE A'SHIT! I KNOW WHAT YOU CAN DO!
ONE FUCKIN' WORD, MOTHERFUCKER! ONE WORD!
MISS.
FUCK!

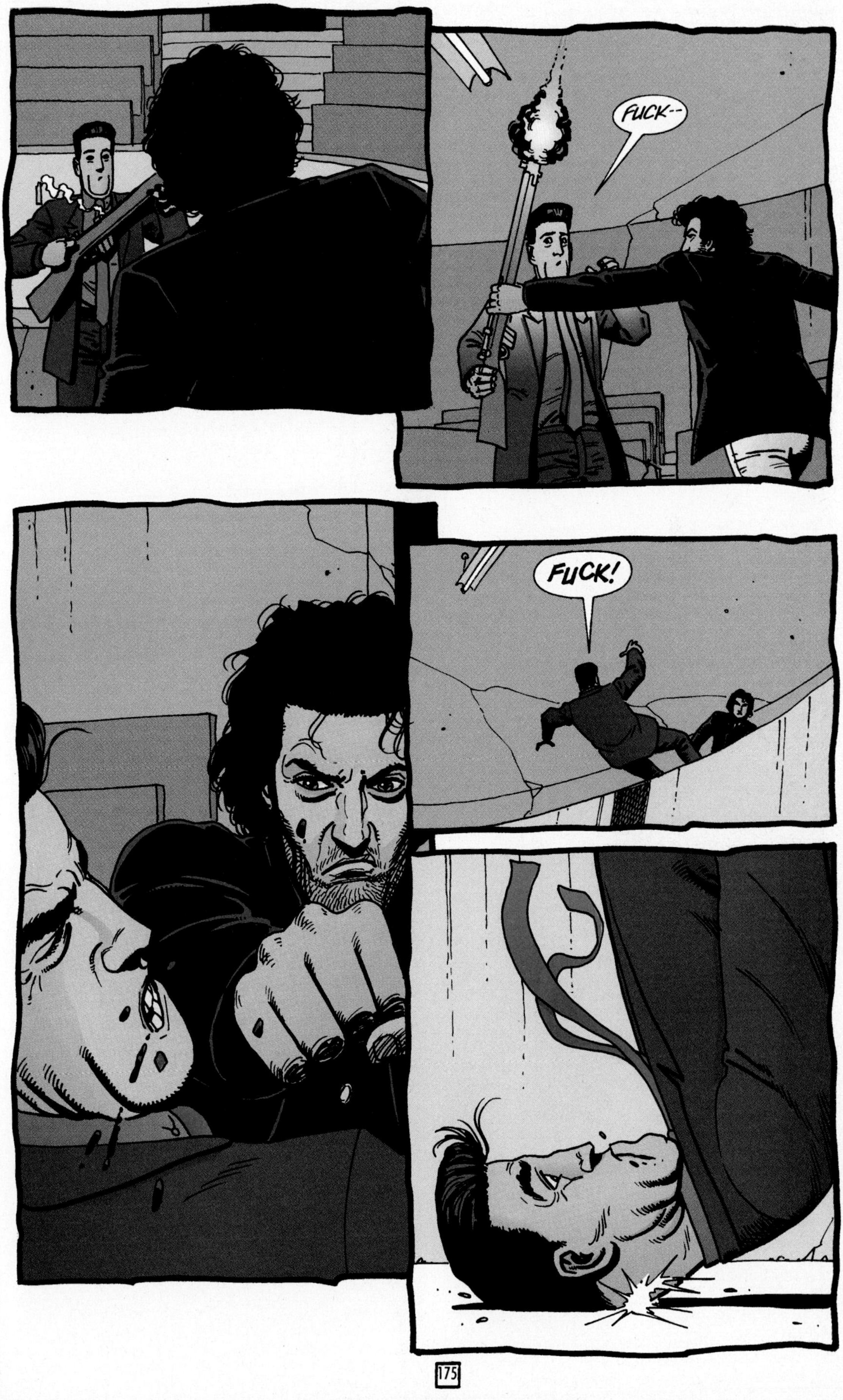
FUCK--
FUCK!

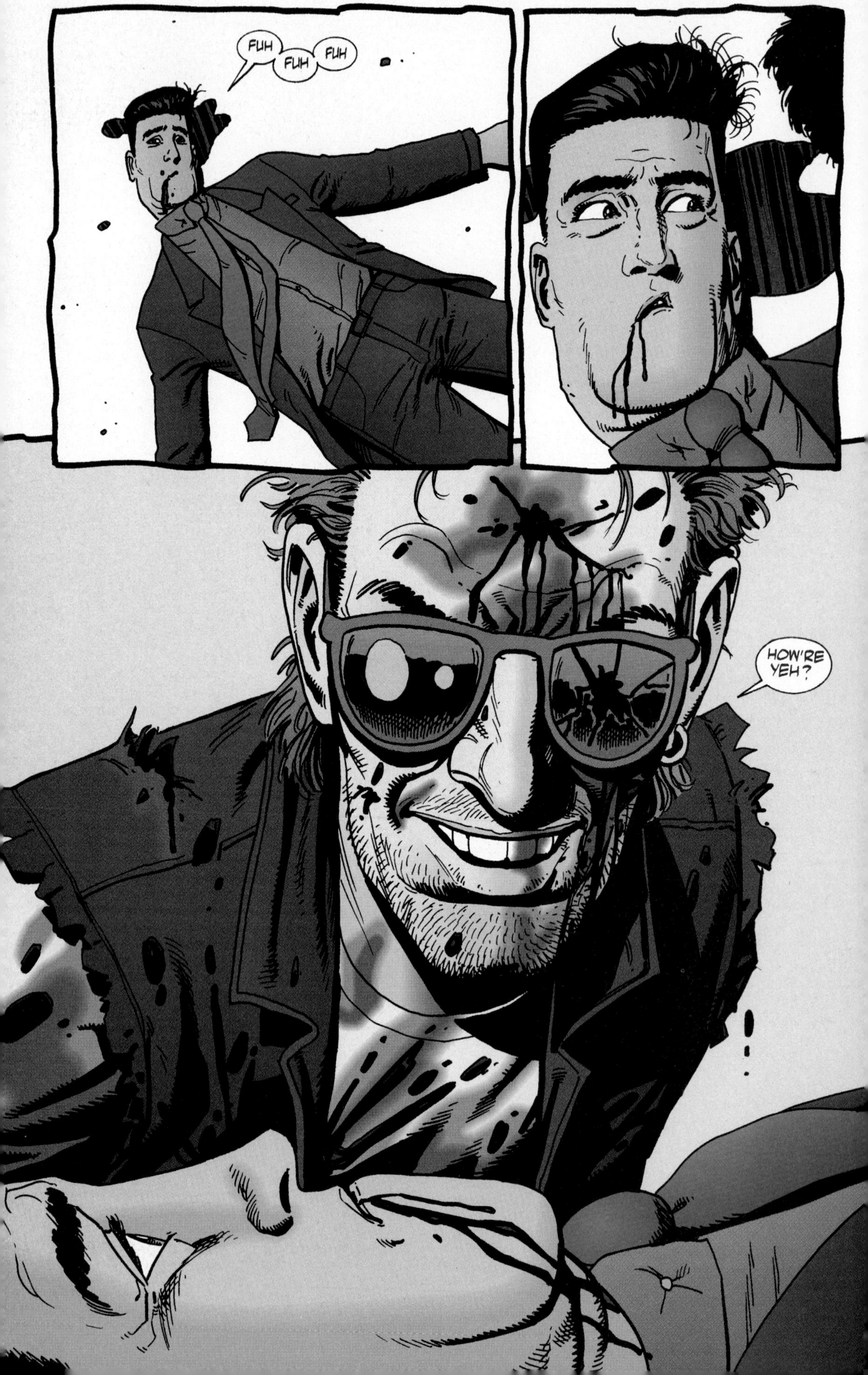
FUH
FUH
FUH
HOW'RE YEH?

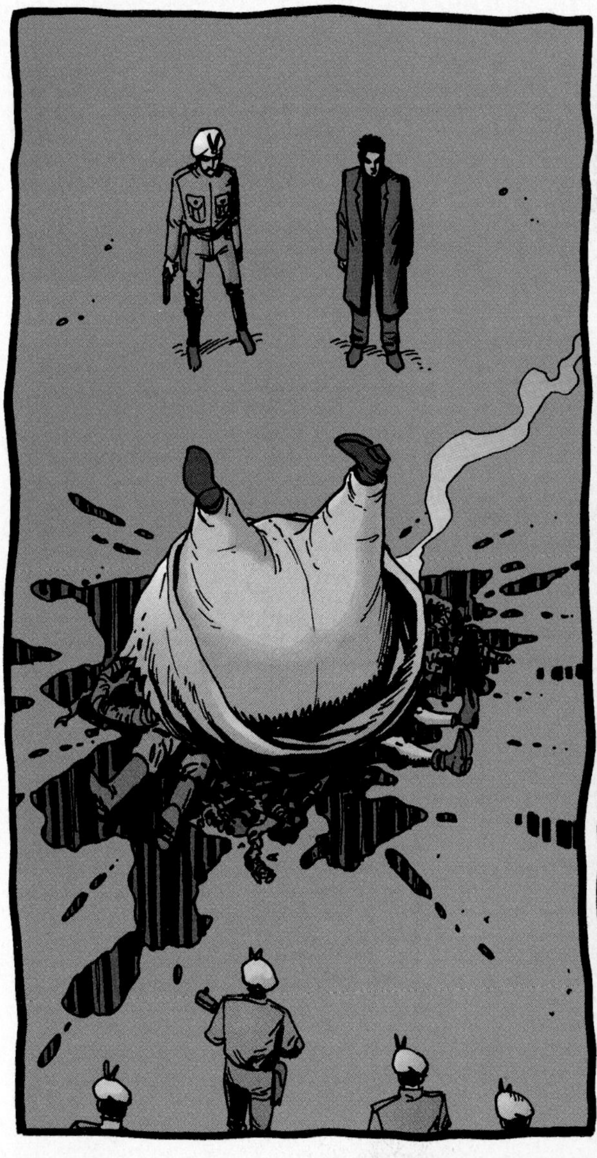
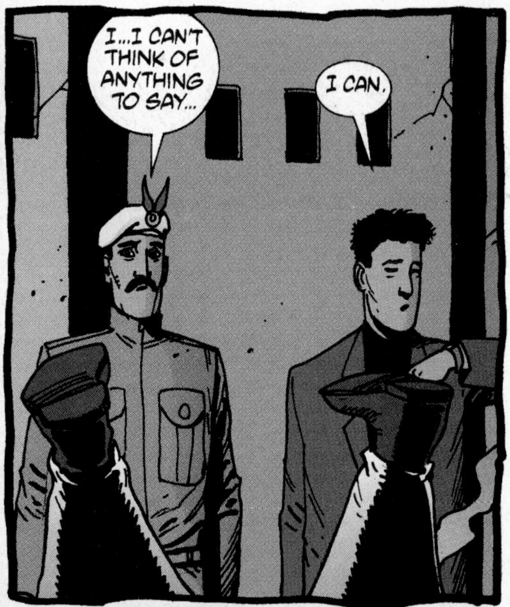
I...I CAN'T THINK OF ANYTHING TO SAY...
I CAN.
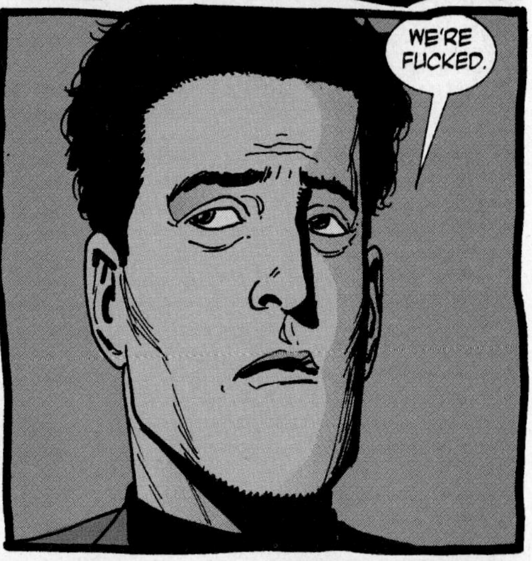
WE'RE FUCKED.
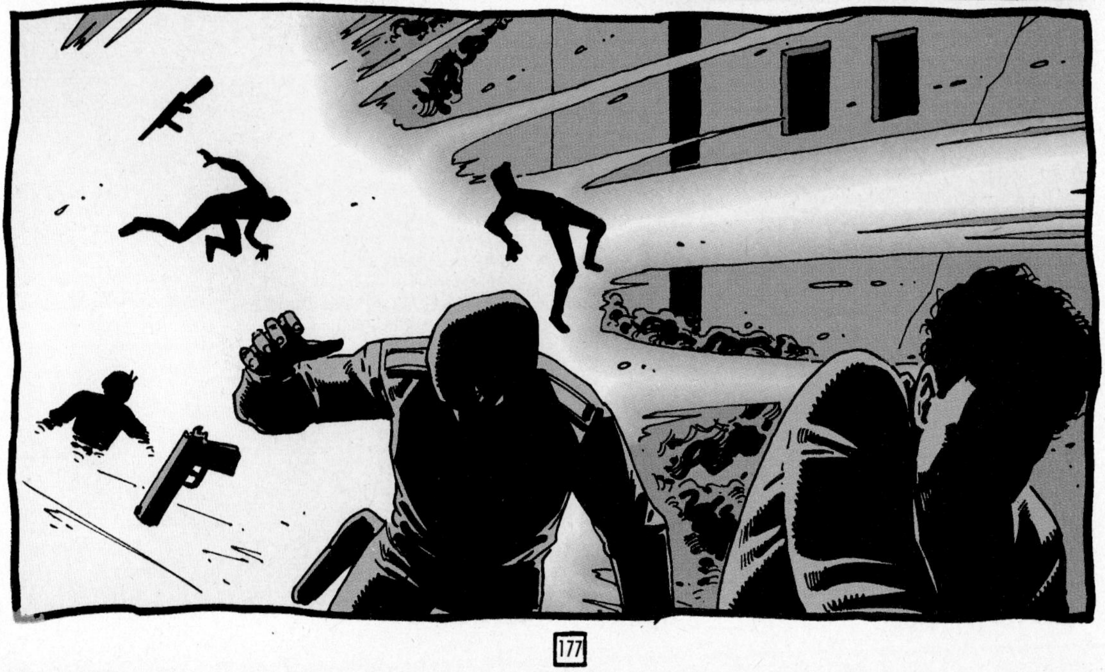

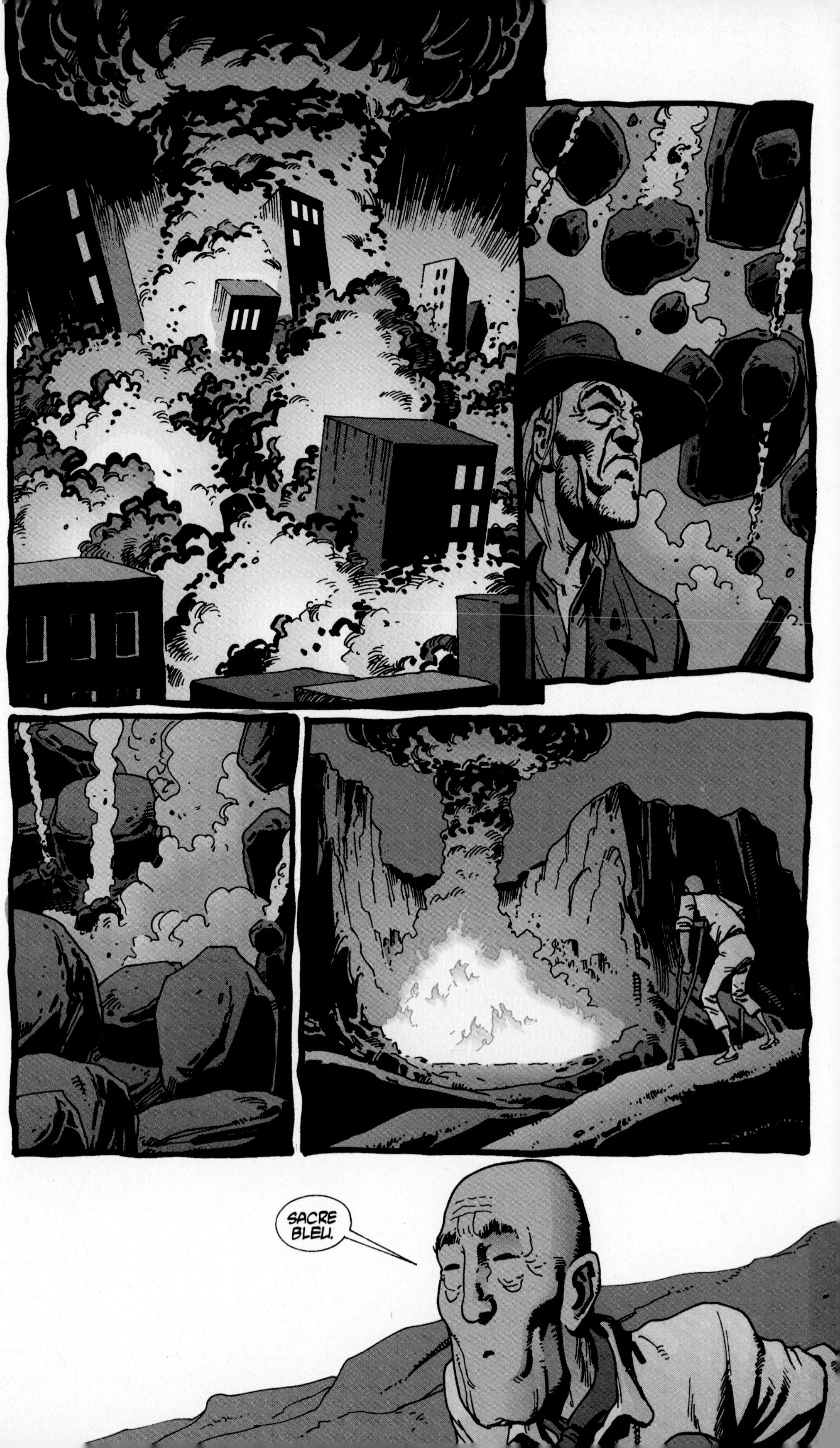
SACRE BLEU.

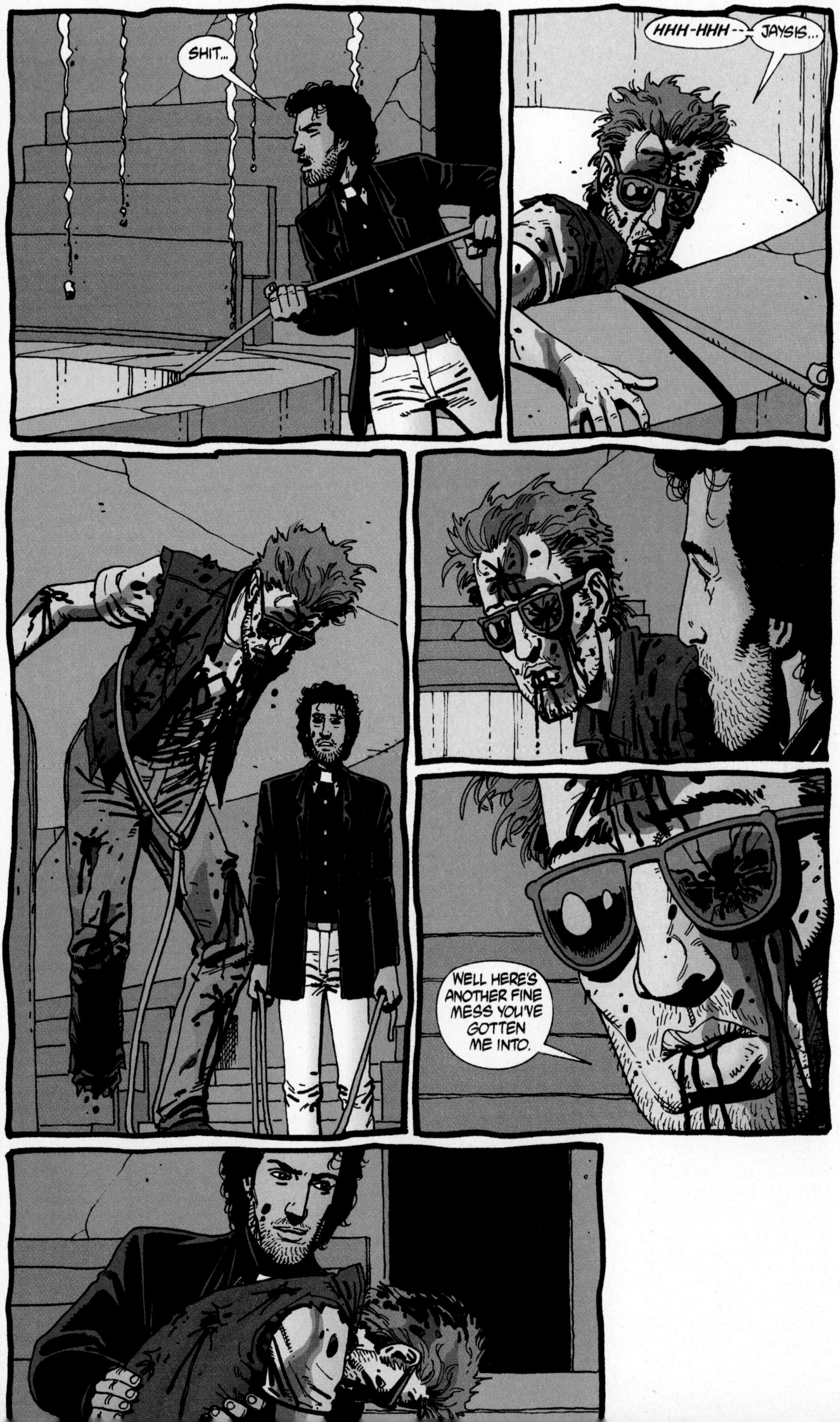
SHIT...
HHH-HHH--
JAYSIS...
WELL HERE'S ANOTHER FINE MESS YOU'VE GOTTEN ME INTO.

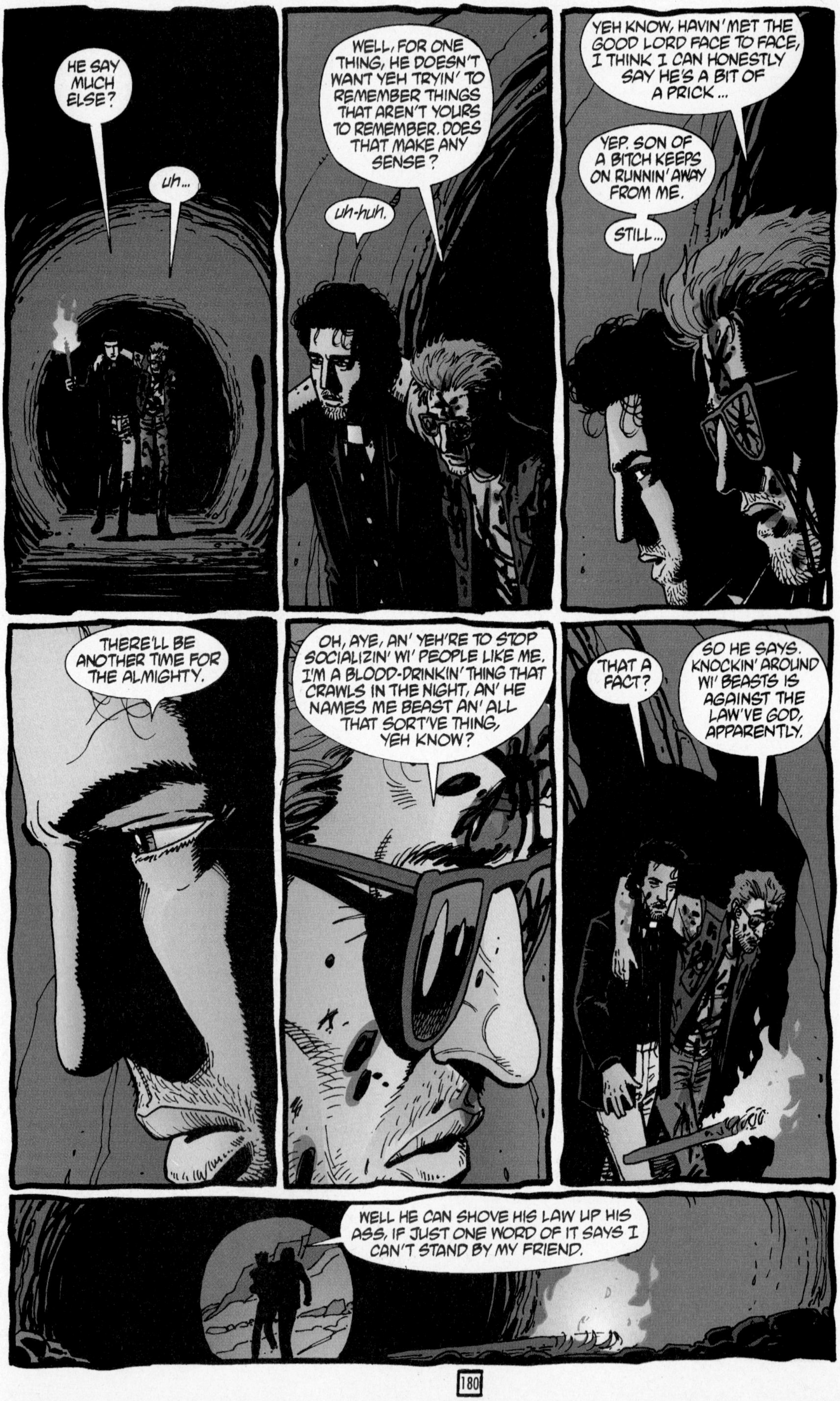
HE SAY MUCH ELSE?
uh...
WELL, FOR ONE THING, HE DOESN'T WANT YEH TRYIN' TO REMEMBER THINGS THAT AREN'T YOURS TO REMEMBER. DOES THAT MAKE ANY SENSE?
uh-huh.
YEH KNOW, HAVIN' MET THE GOOD LORD FACE TO FACE, I THINK I CAN HONESTLY SAY HE'S A BIT OF A PRICK...
YEP. SON OF A BITCH KEEPS ON RUNNIN' AWAY FROM ME.
STILL...
THERE'LL BE ANOTHER TIME FOR THE ALMIGHTY.
OH, AYE, AN' YEH'RE TO STOP SOCIALIZIN' WI' PEOPLE LIKE ME. I'M A BLOOD-DRINKIN' THING THAT CRAWLS IN THE NIGHT, AN' HE NAMES ME BEAST AN' ALL THAT SORT'VE THING, YEH KNOW?
THAT A FACT?
SO HE SAYS. KNOCKIN' AROUND WI' BEASTS IS AGAINST THE LAW'VE GOD, APPARENTLY.
WELL HE CAN SHOVE HIS LAW UP HIS ASS, IF JUST ONE WORD OF IT SAYS I CAN'T STAND BY MY FRIEND.

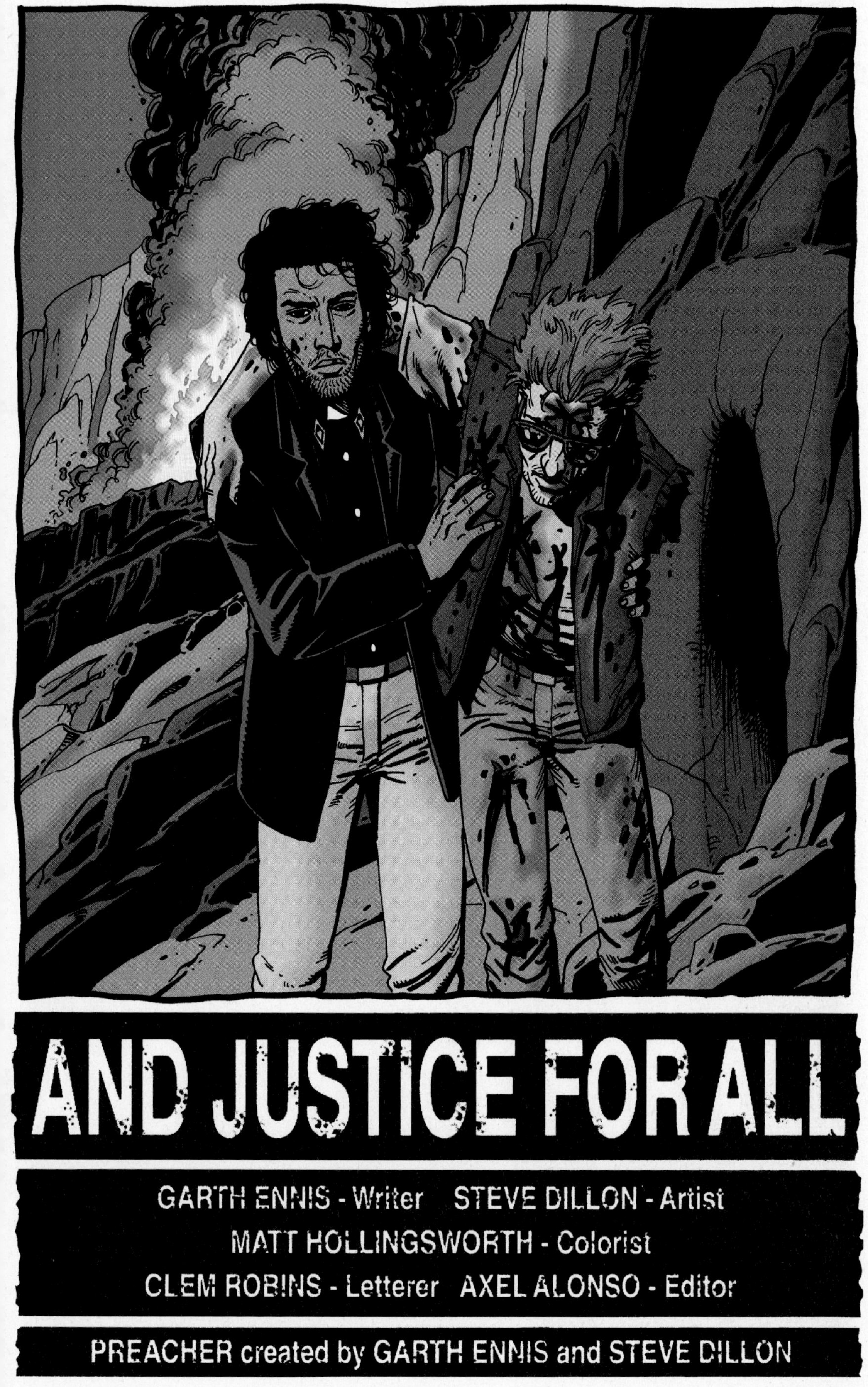

AND JUSTICE FOR ALL

GARTH ENNIS - Writer STEVE DILLON - Artist

MATT HOLLINGSWORTH - Colorist

CLEM ROBINS - Letterer AXEL ALONSO - Editor

PREACHER created by GARTH ENNIS and STEVE DILLON

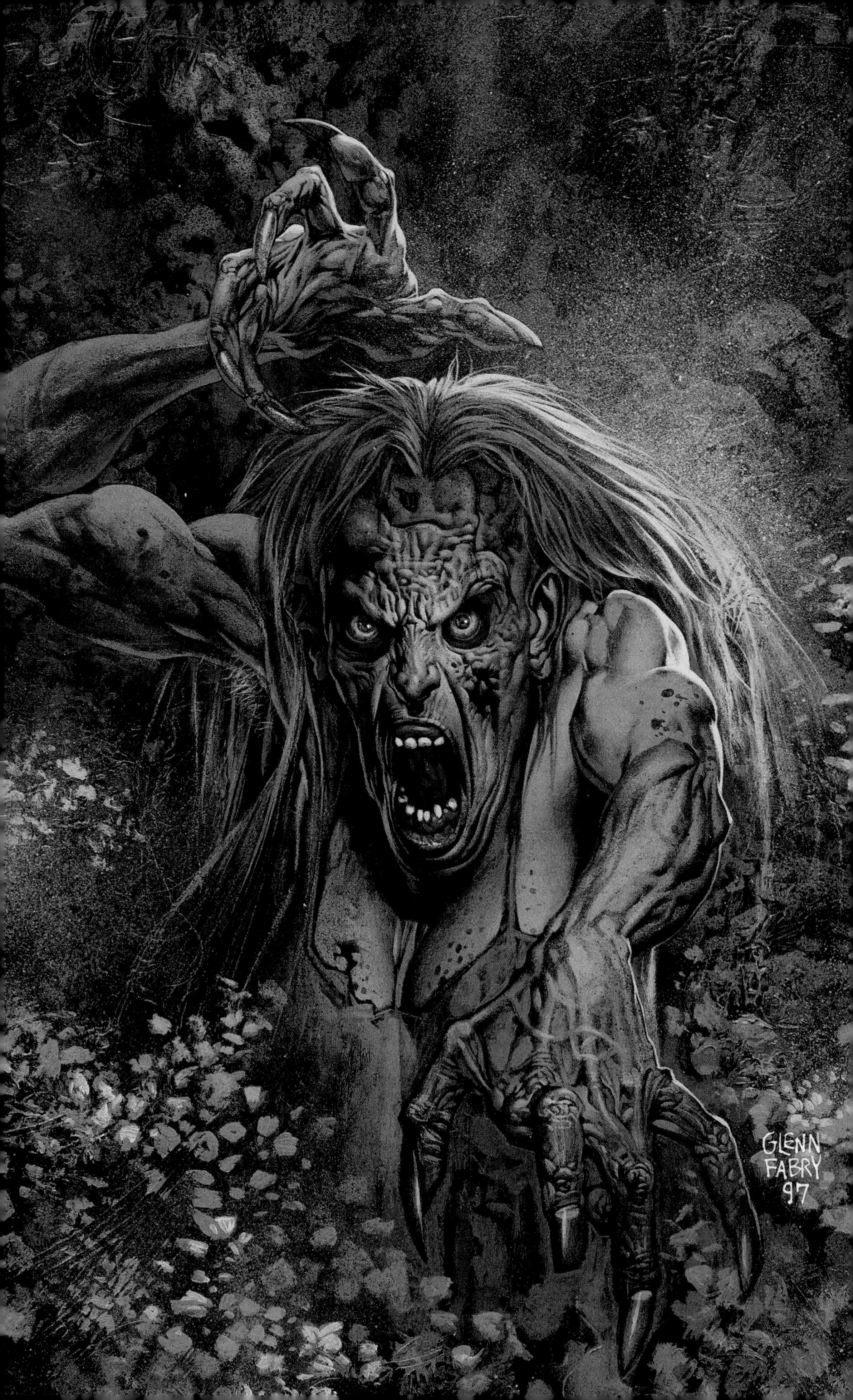
GLENN
FABRY
97

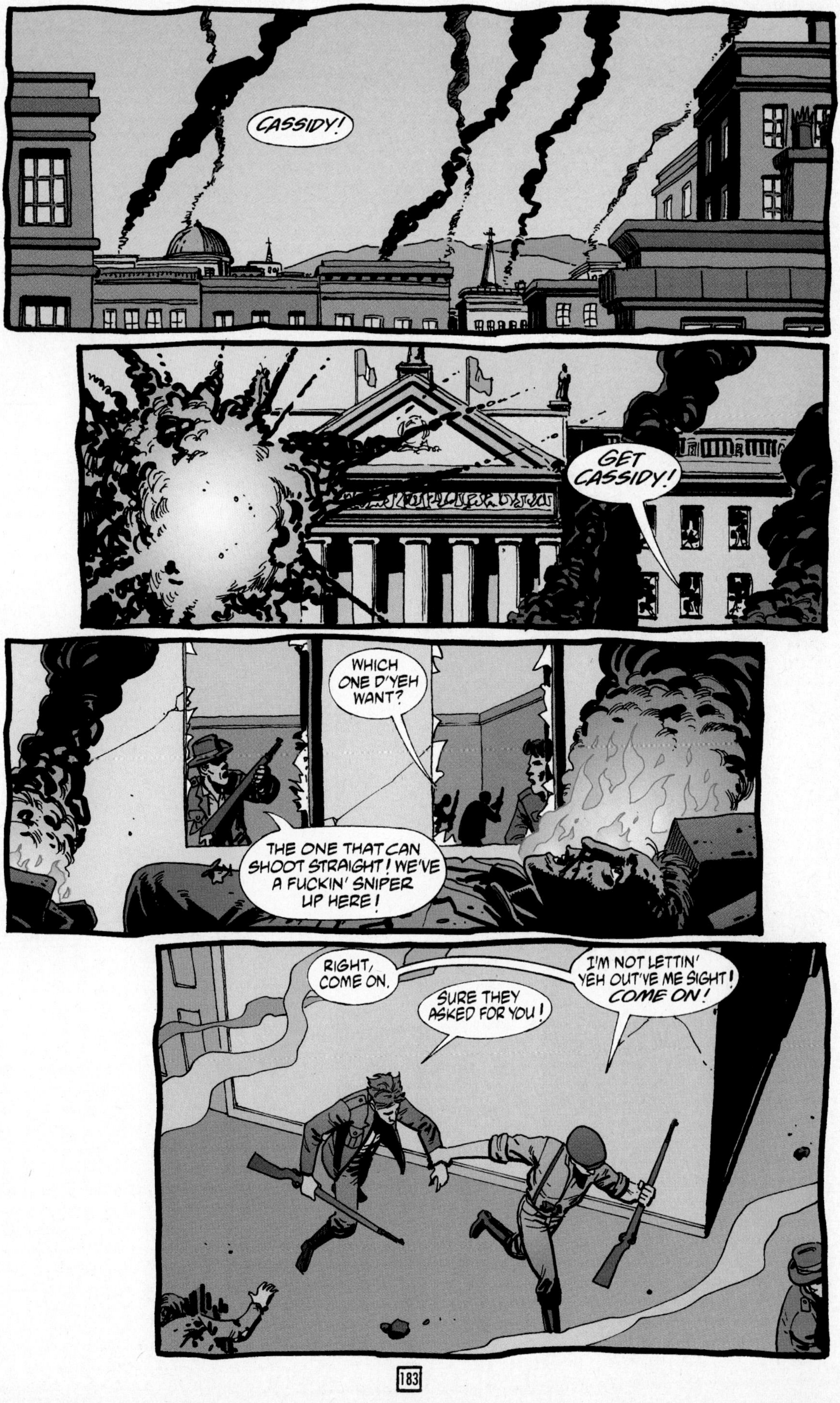
CASSIDY!
GET CASSIDY!
WHICH ONE D'YEH WANT?
THE ONE THAT CAN SHOOT STRAIGHT! WE'VE A FUCKIN' SNIPER UP HERE!
RIGHT, COME ON.
SURE THEY ASKED FOR YOU!
I'M NOT LETTIN' YEH OUT'VE ME SIGHT! COME ON!

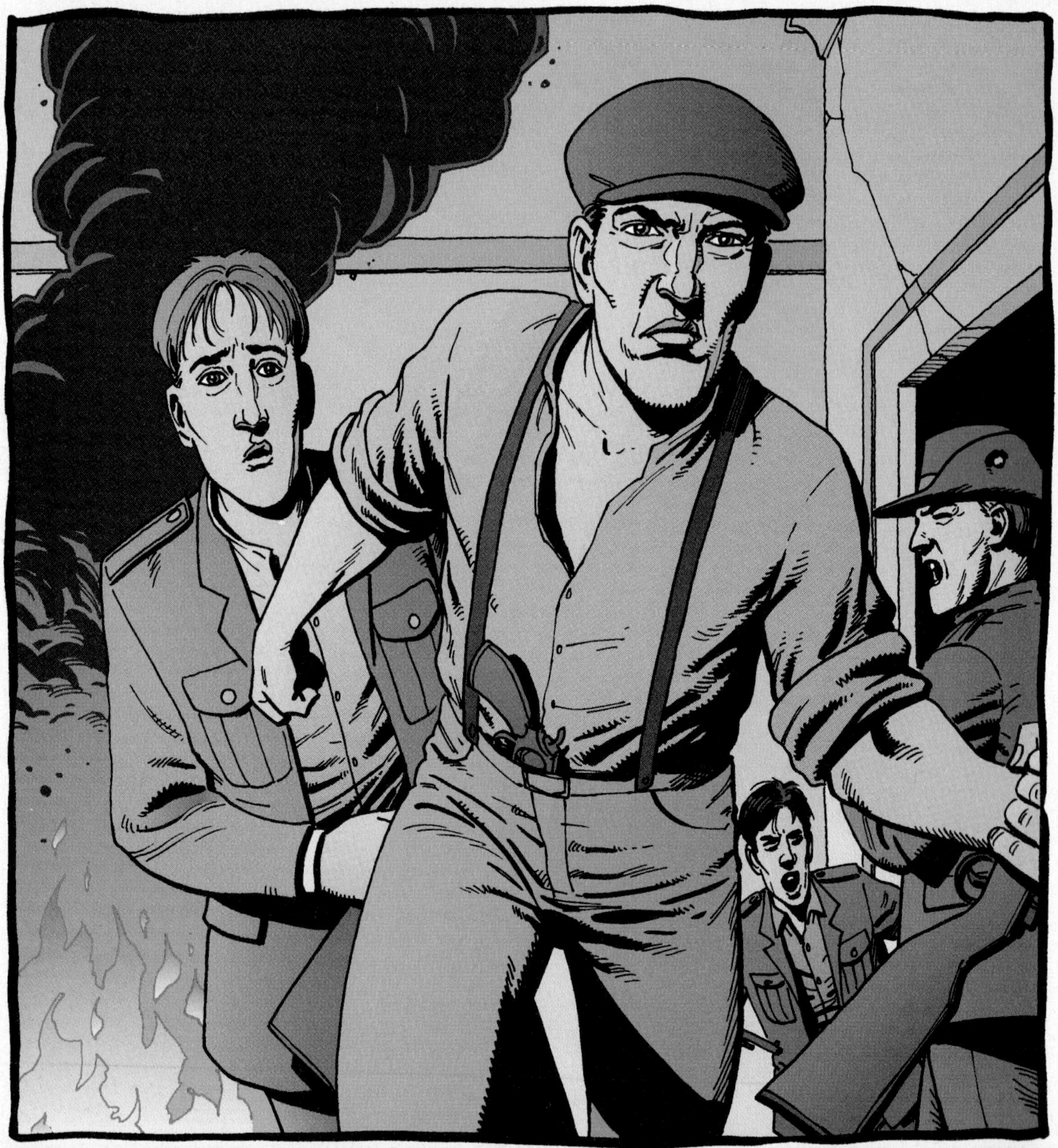

CRY BLOOD, CRY ERIN

GARTH ENNIS - Writer STEVE DILLON - Artist
MATT HOLLINGSWORTH - Colorist
CLEM ROBINS - Letterer AXEL ALONSO - Editor

PREACHER created by GARTH ENNIS and STEVE DILLON

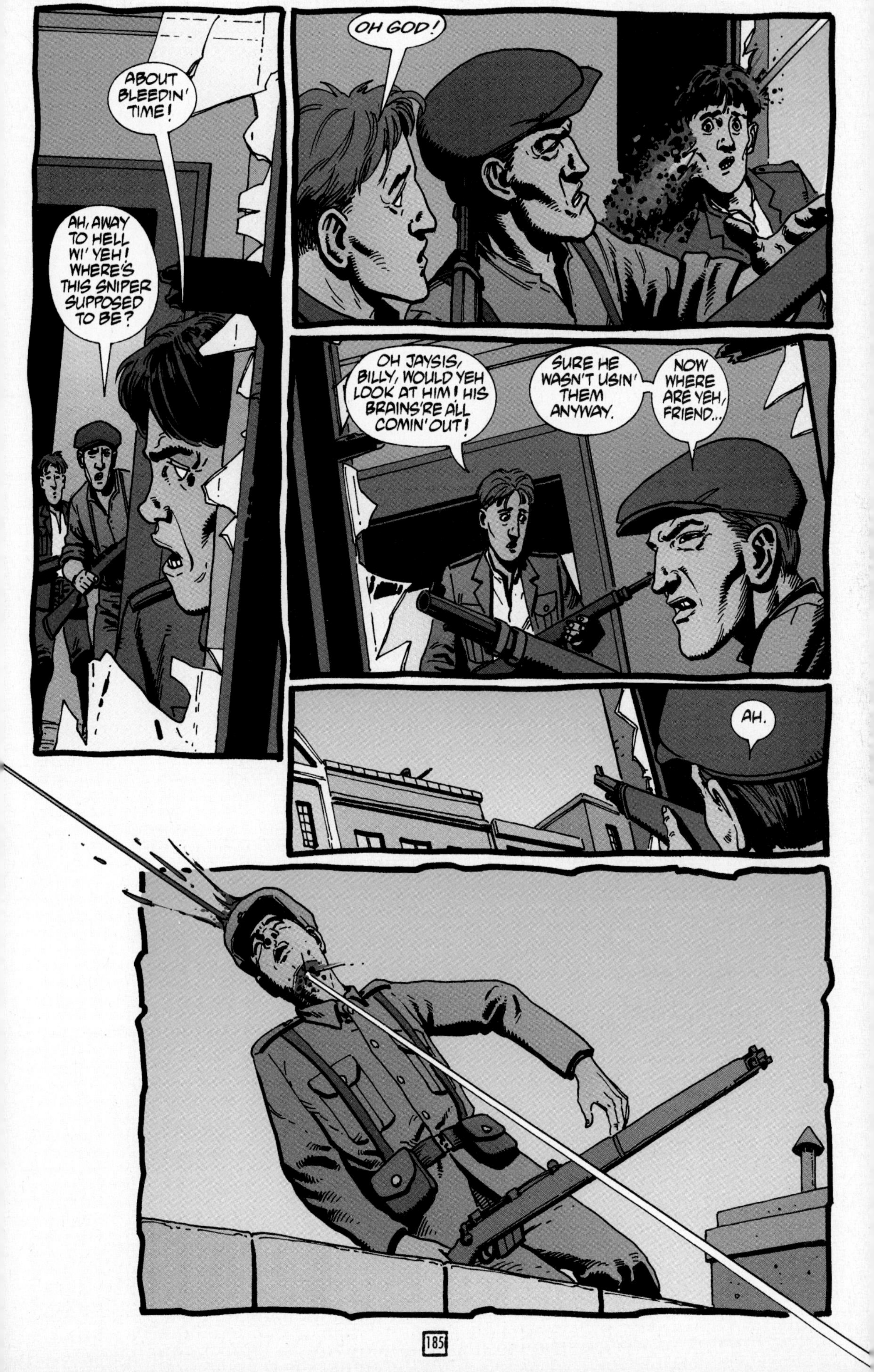
ABOUT BLEEDIN' TIME!
AH, AWAY TO HELL WI' YEH! WHERE'S THIS SNIPER SUPPOSED TO BE?
OH GOD!
OH JAYSIS, BILLY, WOULD YEH LOOK AT HIM! HIS BRAINS'RE ALL COMIN' OUT!
SURE HE WASN'T USIN' THEM ANYWAY.
NOW WHERE ARE YEH, FRIEND...
AH.

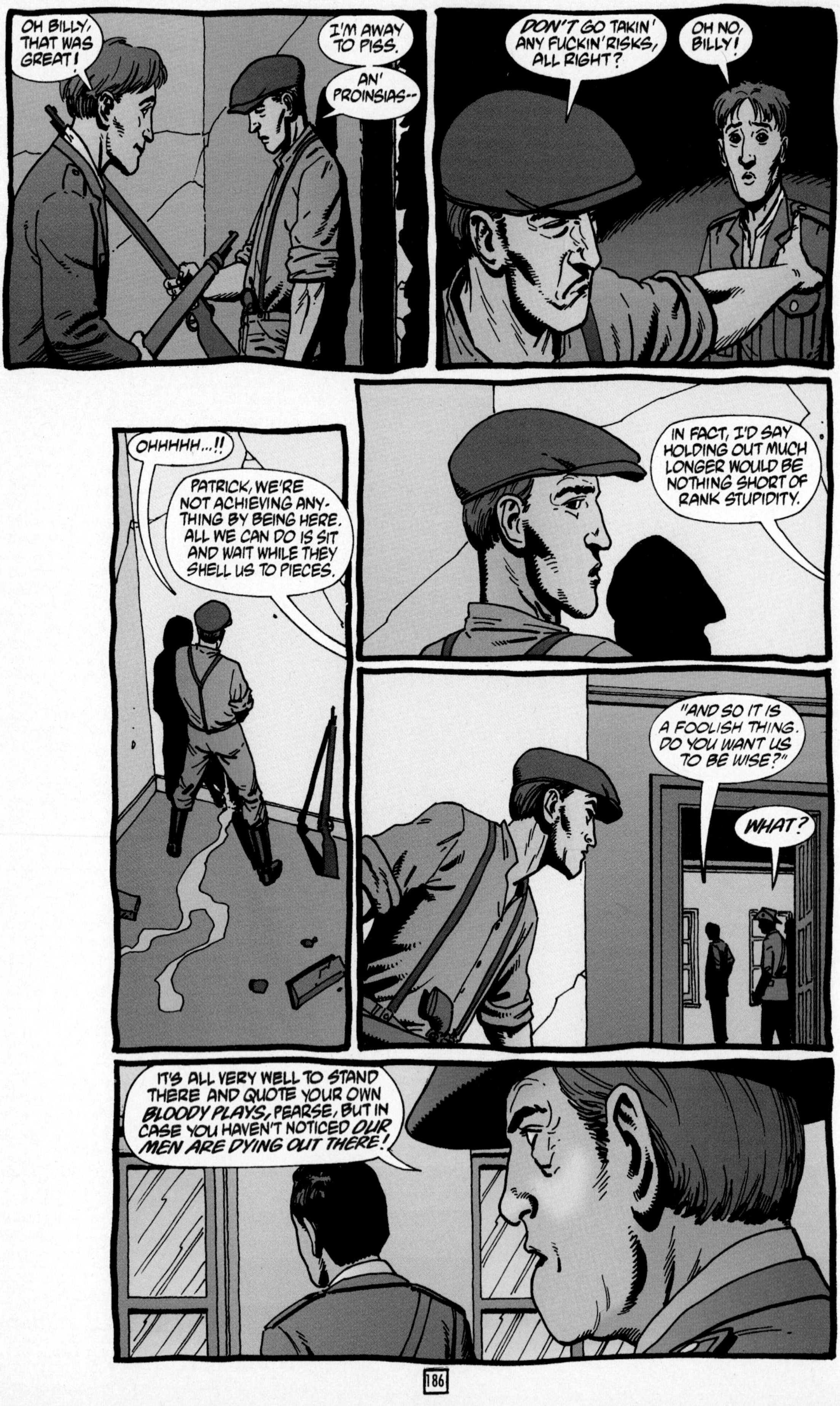
OH BILLY, THAT WAS GREAT!
I'M AWAY TO PISS.
AN' PROINSIAS--
DON'T GO TAKIN' ANY FUCKIN' RISKS, ALL RIGHT?
OH NO, BILLY!
OHHHHH...!!
PATRICK, WE'RE NOT ACHIEVING ANY-THING BY BEING HERE. ALL WE CAN DO IS SIT AND WAIT WHILE THEY SHELL US TO PIECES.
IN FACT, I'D SAY HOLDING OUT MUCH LONGER WOULD BE NOTHING SHORT OF RANK STUPIDITY.
"AND SO IT IS A FOOLISH THING. DO YOU WANT US TO BE WISE?"
WHAT?
IT'S ALL VERY WELL TO STAND THERE AND QUOTE YOUR OWN BLOODY PLAYS, PEARSE, BUT IN CASE YOU HAVEN'T NOTICED OUR MEN ARE DYING OUT THERE!

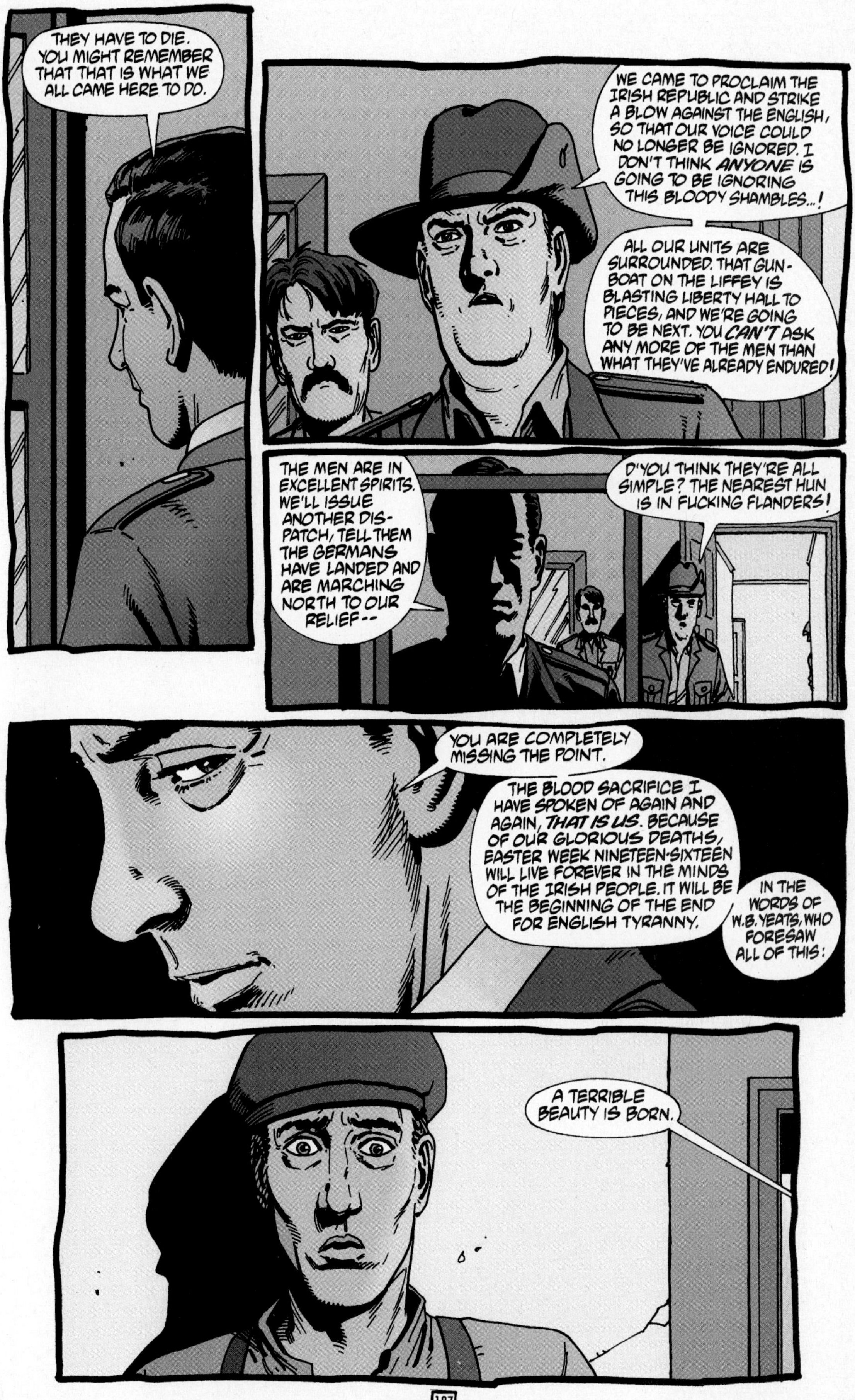
THEY HAVE TO DIE. YOU MIGHT REMEMBER THAT THAT IS WHAT WE ALL CAME HERE TO DO.
WE CAME TO PROCLAIM THE IRISH REPUBLIC AND STRIKE A BLOW AGAINST THE ENGLISH, SO THAT OUR VOICE COULD NO LONGER BE IGNORED. I DON'T THINK *ANYONE* IS GOING TO BE IGNORING THIS BLOODY SHAMBLES...!
ALL OUR UNITS ARE SURROUNDED. THAT GUN-BOAT ON THE LIFFEY IS BLASTING LIBERTY HALL TO PIECES, AND WE'RE GOING TO BE NEXT. YOU *CAN'T* ASK ANY MORE OF THE MEN THAN WHAT THEY'VE ALREADY ENDURED!
THE MEN ARE IN EXCELLENT SPIRITS. WE'LL ISSUE ANOTHER DIS-PATCH, TELL THEM THE GERMANS HAVE LANDED AND ARE MARCHING NORTH TO OUR RELIEF--
D'YOU THINK THEY'RE ALL SIMPLE? THE NEAREST HUN IS IN FUCKING FLANDERS!
YOU ARE COMPLETELY MISSING THE POINT.
THE BLOOD SACRIFICE I HAVE SPOKEN OF AGAIN AND AGAIN, *THAT IS US*. BECAUSE OF OUR GLORIOUS DEATHS, EASTER WEEK NINETEEN-SIXTEEN WILL LIVE FOREVER IN THE MINDS OF THE IRISH PEOPLE. IT WILL BE THE BEGINNING OF THE END FOR ENGLISH TYRANNY.
IN THE WORDS OF W.B. YEATS, WHO FORESAW ALL OF THIS:
A TERRIBLE BEAUTY IS BORN.

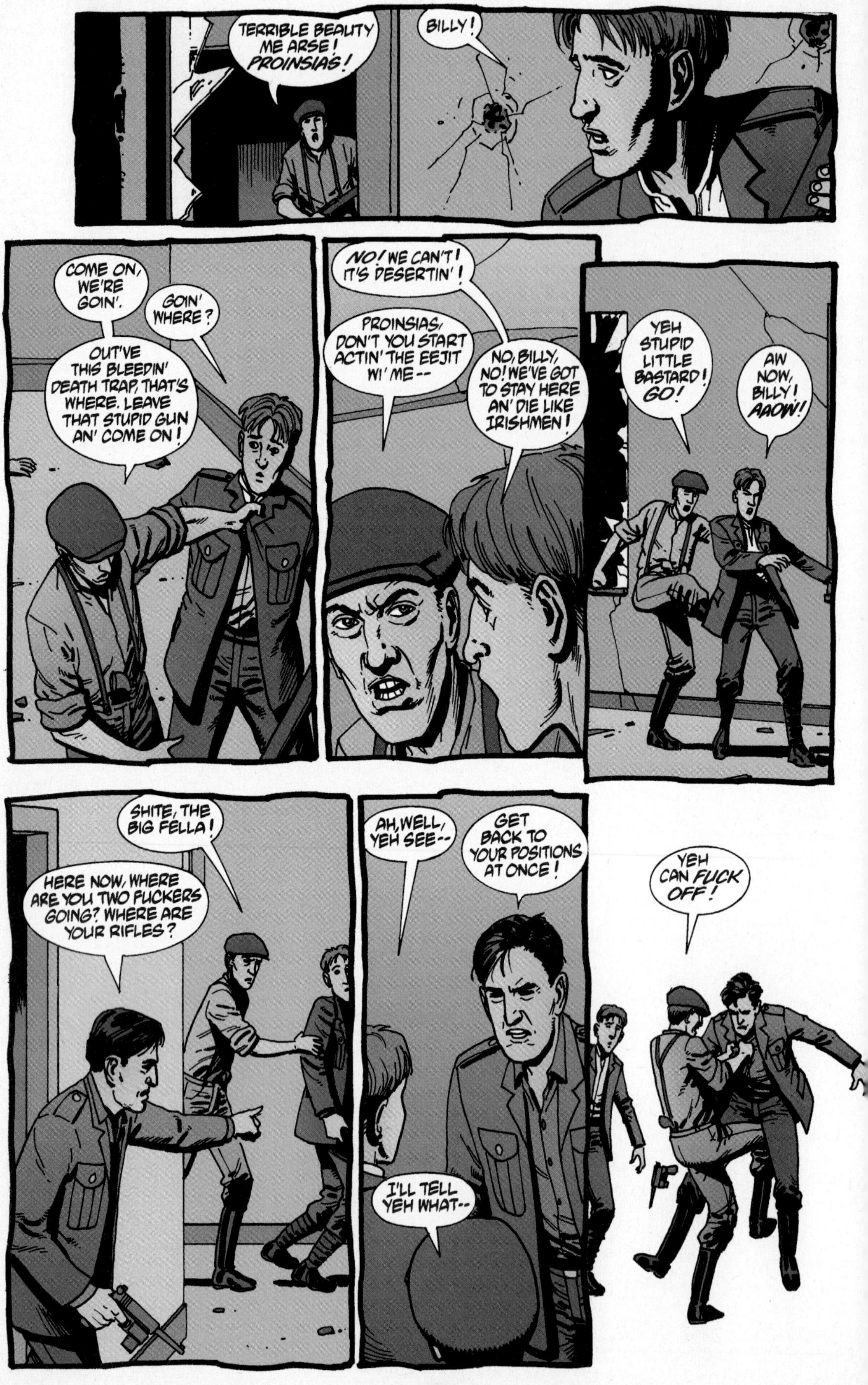
TERRIBLE BEAUTY ME ARSE! PROINSIAS!
BILLY!
COME ON, WE'RE GOIN'.
GOIN' WHERE?
OUT'VE THIS BLEEDIN' DEATH TRAP, THAT'S WHERE. LEAVE THAT STUPID GUN AN' COME ON!
NO! WE CAN'T! IT'S DESERTIN'!
PROINSIAS, DON'T YOU START ACTIN' THE EEJIT WI' ME--
NO, BILLY, NO! WE'VE GOT TO STAY HERE AN' DIE LIKE IRISHMEN!
YEH STUPID LITTLE BASTARD! GO!
AW NOW, BILLY! AAOW!
SHITE, THE BIG FELLA!
HERE NOW, WHERE ARE YOU TWO FUCKERS GOING? WHERE ARE YOUR RIFLES?
AH, WELL, YEH SEE--
GET BACK TO YOUR POSITIONS AT ONCE!
I'LL TELL YEH WHAT--
YEH CAN FUCK OFF!

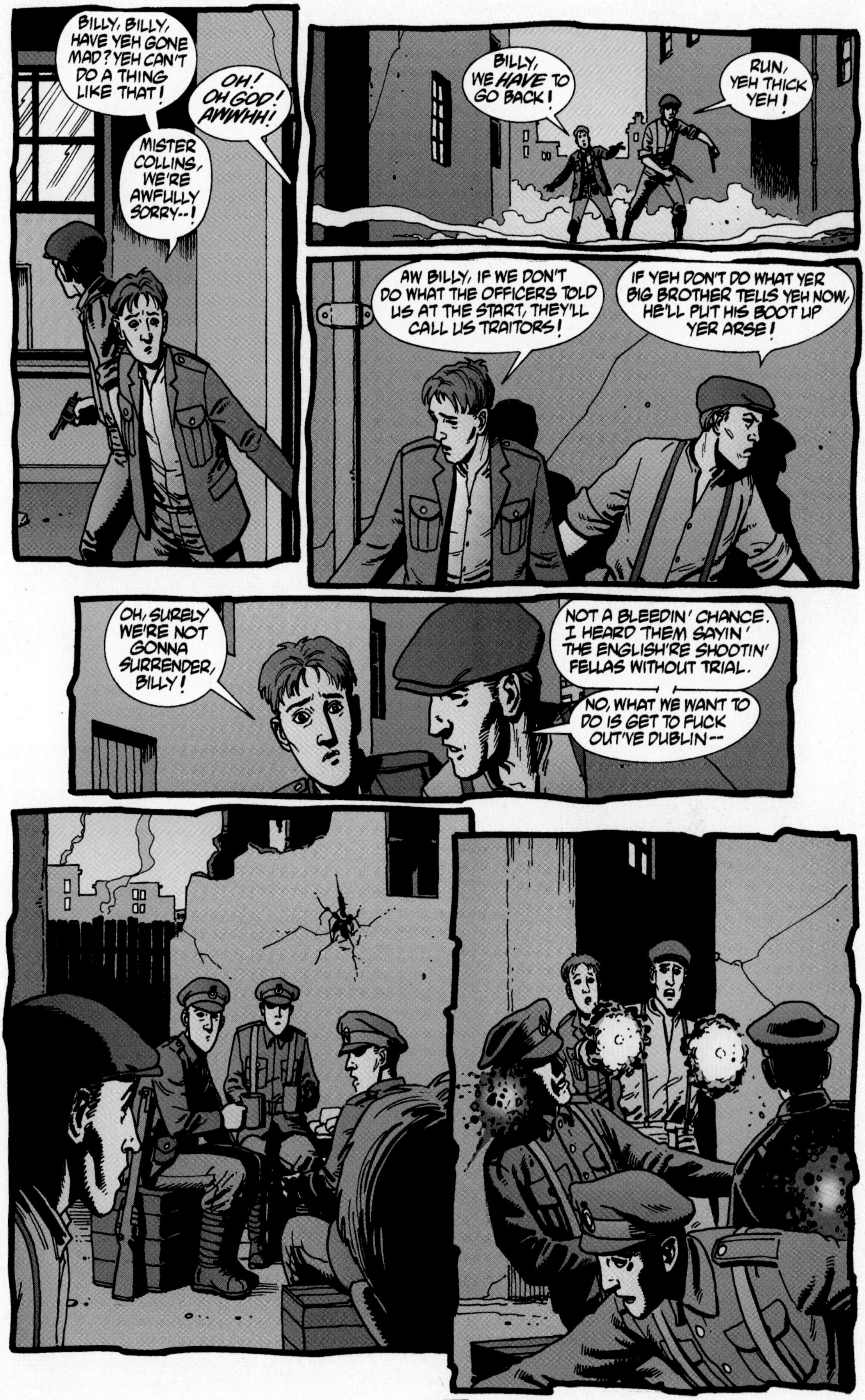
BILLY, BILLY, HAVE YEH GONE MAD? YEH CAN'T DO A THING LIKE THAT!
MISTER COLLINS, WE'RE AWFULLY SORRY--!
OH! OH GOD! AWWHH!
BILLY, WE HAVE TO GO BACK!
RUN, YEH THICK YEH!
AW BILLY, IF WE DON'T DO WHAT THE OFFICERS TOLD US AT THE START, THEY'LL CALL US TRAITORS!
IF YEH DON'T DO WHAT YER BIG BROTHER TELLS YEH NOW, HE'LL PUT HIS BOOT UP YER ARSE!
OH, SURELY WE'RE NOT GONNA SURRENDER, BILLY!
NOT A BLEEDIN' CHANCE. I HEARD THEM SAYIN' THE ENGLISH'RE SHOOTIN' FELLAS WITHOUT TRIAL.
NO, WHAT WE WANT TO DO IS GET TO FUCK OUT'VE DUBLIN--

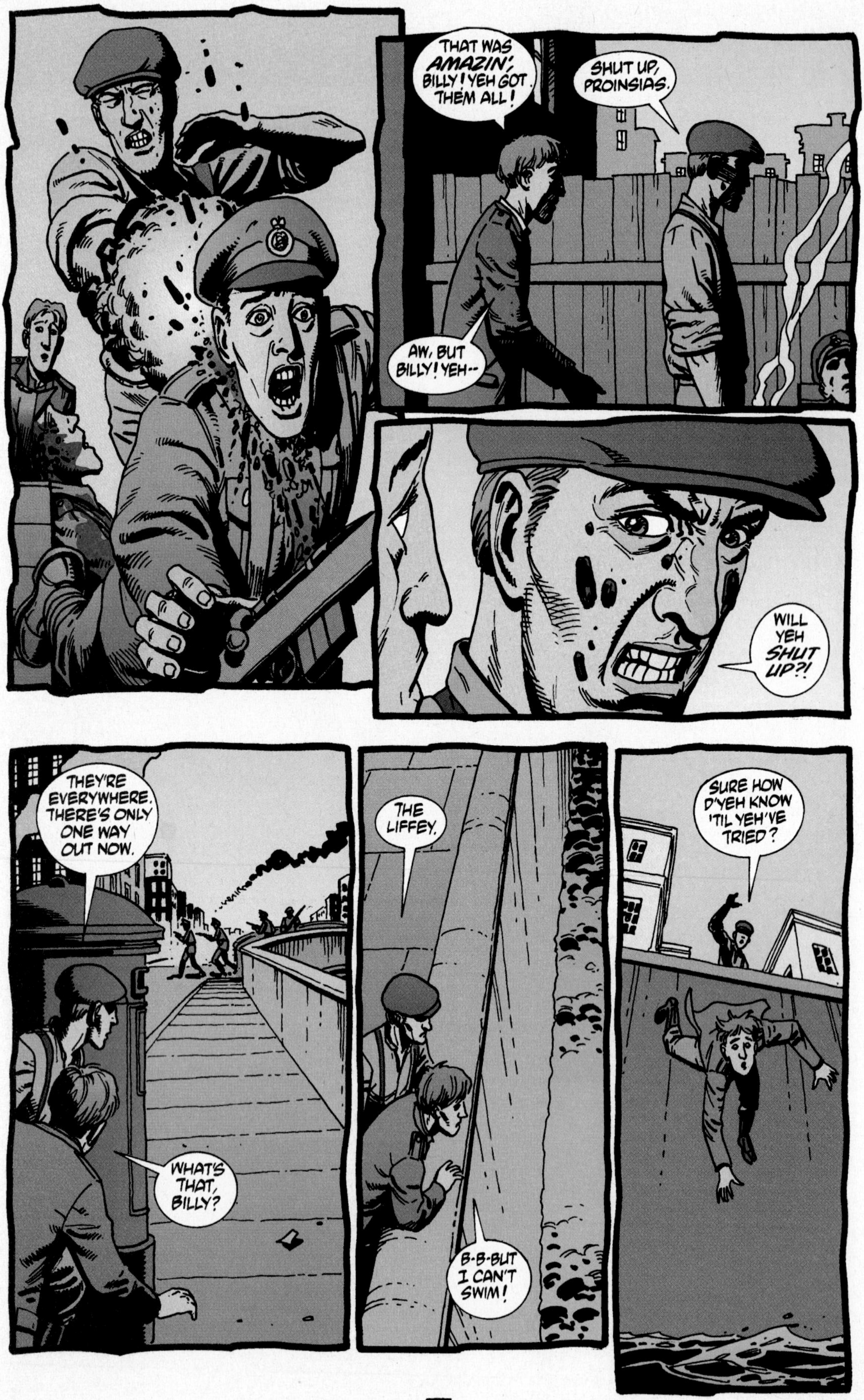
THAT WAS AMAZIN', BILLY! YEH GOT THEM ALL!
SHUT UP, PROINSIAS.
AW, BUT BILLY! YEH--
WILL YEH SHUT UP?!
THEY'RE EVERYWHERE. THERE'S ONLY ONE WAY OUT NOW.
WHAT'S THAT, BILLY?
THE LIFFEY.
B-B-BUT I CAN'T SWIM!
SURE HOW D'YEH KNOW 'TIL YEH'VE TRIED?

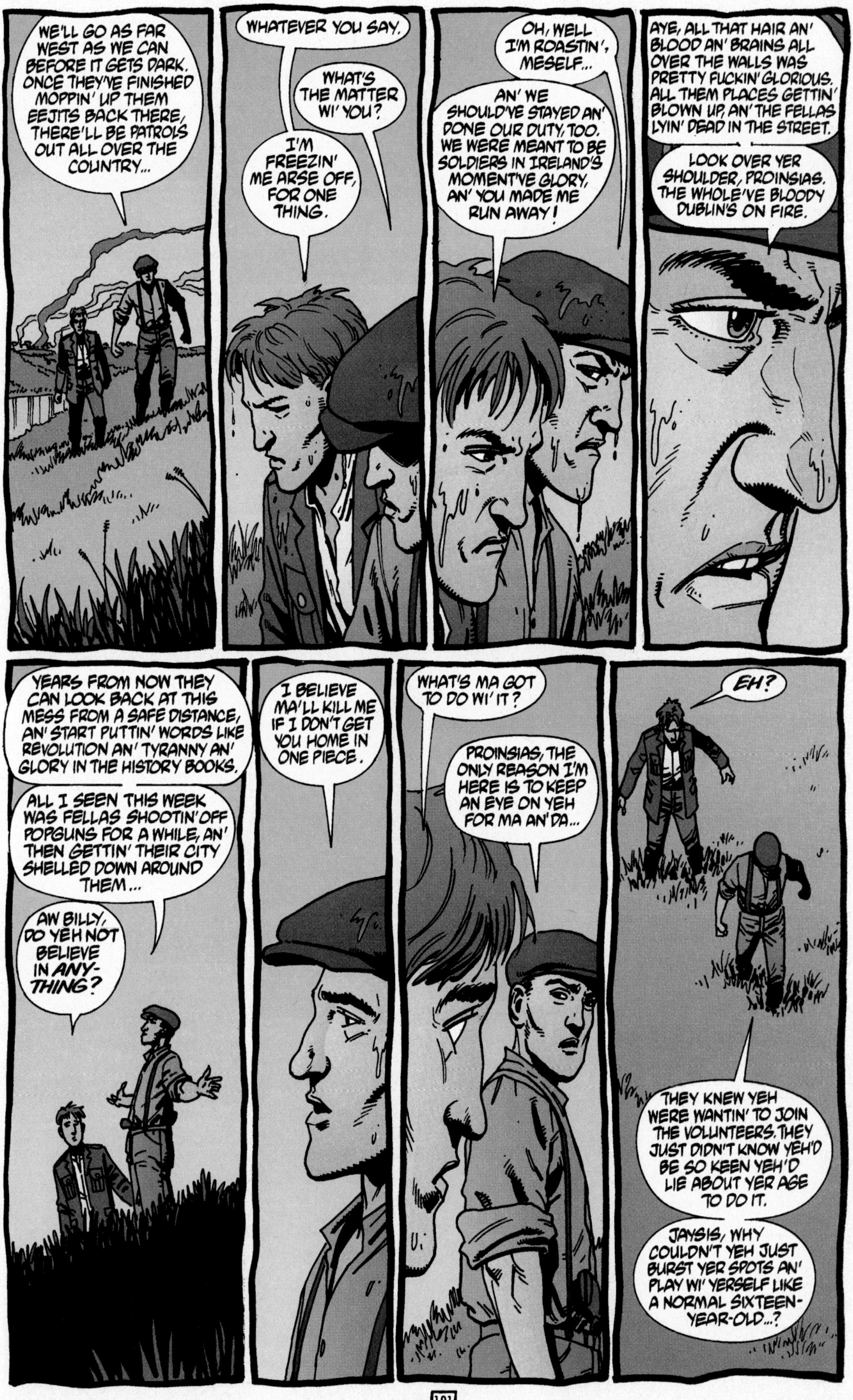
WE'LL GO AS FAR WEST AS WE CAN BEFORE IT GETS DARK. ONCE THEY'VE FINISHED MOPPIN' UP THEM EEJITS BACK THERE, THERE'LL BE PATROLS OUT ALL OVER THE COUNTRY...
WHATEVER YOU SAY.
WHAT'S THE MATTER WI' YOU?
I'M FREEZIN' ME ARSE OFF, FOR ONE THING.
OH, WELL I'M ROASTIN', MESELF...
AN' WE SHOULD'VE STAYED AN' DONE OUR DUTY, TOO. WE WERE MEANT TO BE SOLDIERS IN IRELAND'S MOMENT'VE GLORY, AN' YOU MADE ME RUN AWAY!
AYE, ALL THAT HAIR AN' BLOOD AN' BRAINS ALL OVER THE WALLS WAS PRETTY FUCKIN' GLORIOUS. ALL THEM PLACES GETTIN' BLOWN UP, AN' THE FELLAS LYIN' DEAD IN THE STREET.
LOOK OVER YER SHOULDER, PROINSIAS. THE WHOLE'VE BLOODY DUBLIN'S ON FIRE.
YEARS FROM NOW THEY CAN LOOK BACK AT THIS MESS FROM A SAFE DISTANCE, AN' START PUTTIN' WORDS LIKE REVOLUTION AN' TYRANNY AN' GLORY IN THE HISTORY BOOKS.
ALL I SEEN THIS WEEK WAS FELLAS SHOOTIN' OFF POPGUNS FOR A WHILE, AN' THEN GETTIN' THEIR CITY SHELLED DOWN AROUND THEM...
AW BILLY, DO YEH NOT BELIEVE IN *ANYTHING?*
I BELIEVE MA'LL KILL ME IF I DON'T GET YOU HOME IN ONE PIECE.
WHAT'S MA GOT TO DO WI' IT?
PROINSIAS, THE ONLY REASON I'M HERE IS TO KEEP AN EYE ON YEH FOR MA AN' DA...
EH?
THEY KNEW YEH WERE WANTIN' TO JOIN THE VOLUNTEERS. THEY JUST DIDN'T KNOW YEH'D BE SO KEEN YEH'D LIE ABOUT YER AGE TO DO IT.
JAYSIS, WHY COULDN'T YEH JUST BURST YER SPOTS AN' PLAY WI' YERSELF LIKE A NORMAL SIXTEEN-YEAR-OLD...?

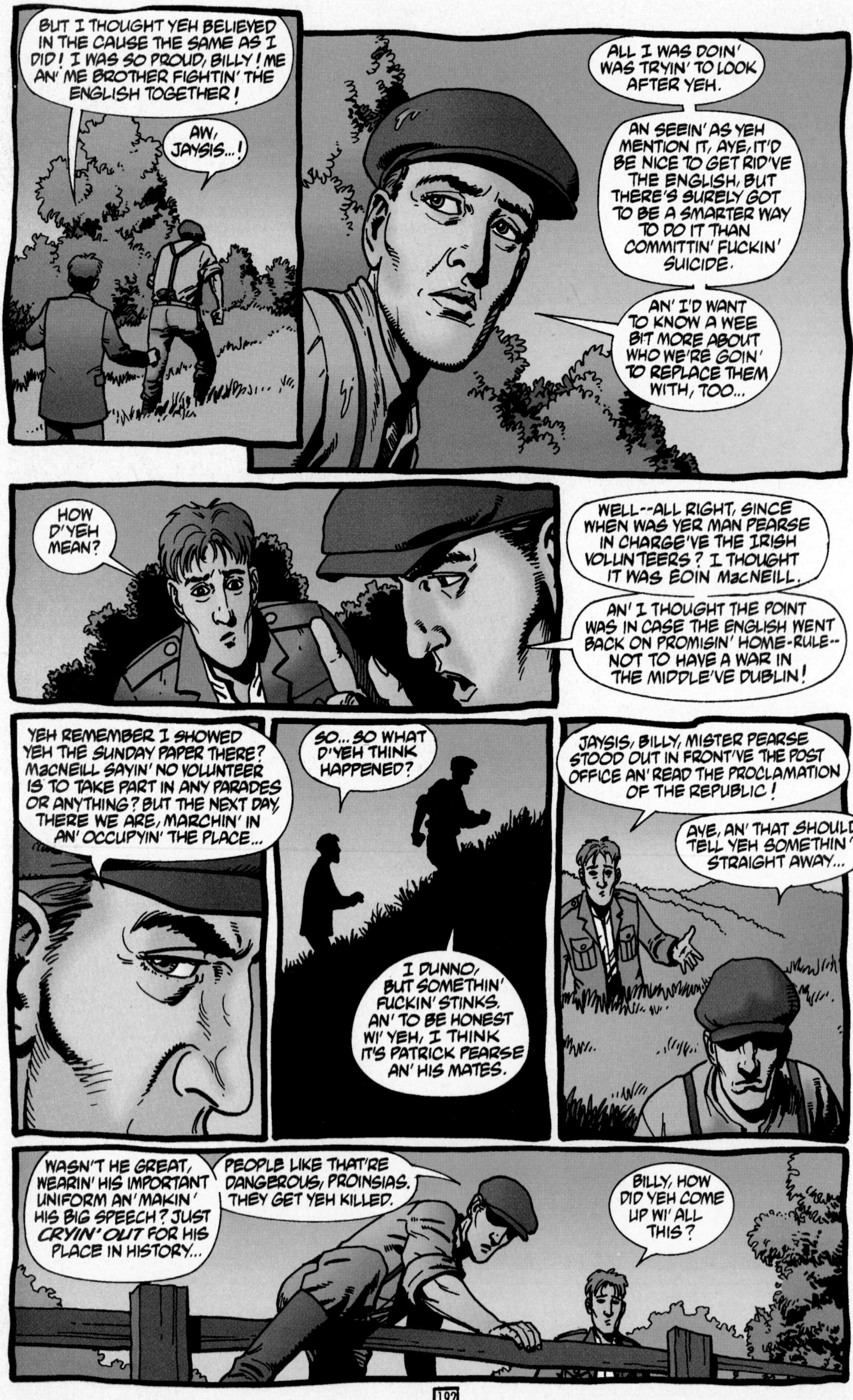
BUT I THOUGHT YEH BELIEVED IN THE CAUSE THE SAME AS I DID! I WAS SO PROUD, BILLY! ME AN' ME BROTHER FIGHTIN' THE ENGLISH TOGETHER!
AW, JAYSIS...!
ALL I WAS DOIN' WAS TRYIN' TO LOOK AFTER YEH.
AN SEEIN' AS YEH MENTION IT, AYE, IT'D BE NICE TO GET RID'VE THE ENGLISH, BUT THERE'S SURELY GOT TO BE A SMARTER WAY TO DO IT THAN COMMITTIN' FUCKIN' SUICIDE.
AN' I'D WANT TO KNOW A WEE BIT MORE ABOUT WHO WE'RE GOIN' TO REPLACE THEM WITH, TOO...
HOW D'YEH MEAN?
WELL--ALL RIGHT, SINCE WHEN WAS YER MAN PEARSE IN CHARGE'VE THE IRISH VOLUNTEERS? I THOUGHT IT WAS EOIN MacNEILL.
AN' I THOUGHT THE POINT WAS IN CASE THE ENGLISH WENT BACK ON PROMISIN' HOME-RULE--NOT TO HAVE A WAR IN THE MIDDLE'VE DUBLIN!
YEH REMEMBER I SHOWED YEH THE SUNDAY PAPER THERE? MacNEILL SAYIN' NO VOLUNTEER IS TO TAKE PART IN ANY PARADES OR ANYTHING? BUT THE NEXT DAY, THERE WE ARE, MARCHIN' IN AN' OCCUPYIN' THE PLACE...
SO... SO WHAT D'YEH THINK HAPPENED?
I DUNNO, BUT SOMETHIN' FUCKIN' STINKS. AN' TO BE HONEST WI' YEH, I THINK IT'S PATRICK PEARSE AN' HIS MATES.
JAYSIS, BILLY, MISTER PEARSE STOOD OUT IN FRONT'VE THE POST OFFICE AN' READ THE PROCLAMATION OF THE REPUBLIC!
AYE, AN' THAT SHOULD TELL YEH SOMETHIN' STRAIGHT AWAY...
WASN'T HE GREAT, WEARIN' HIS IMPORTANT UNIFORM AN' MAKIN' HIS BIG SPEECH? JUST *CRYIN' OUT* FOR HIS PLACE IN HISTORY...
PEOPLE LIKE THAT'RE DANGEROUS, PROINSIAS. THEY GET YEH KILLED.
BILLY, HOW DID YEH COME UP WI' ALL THIS?

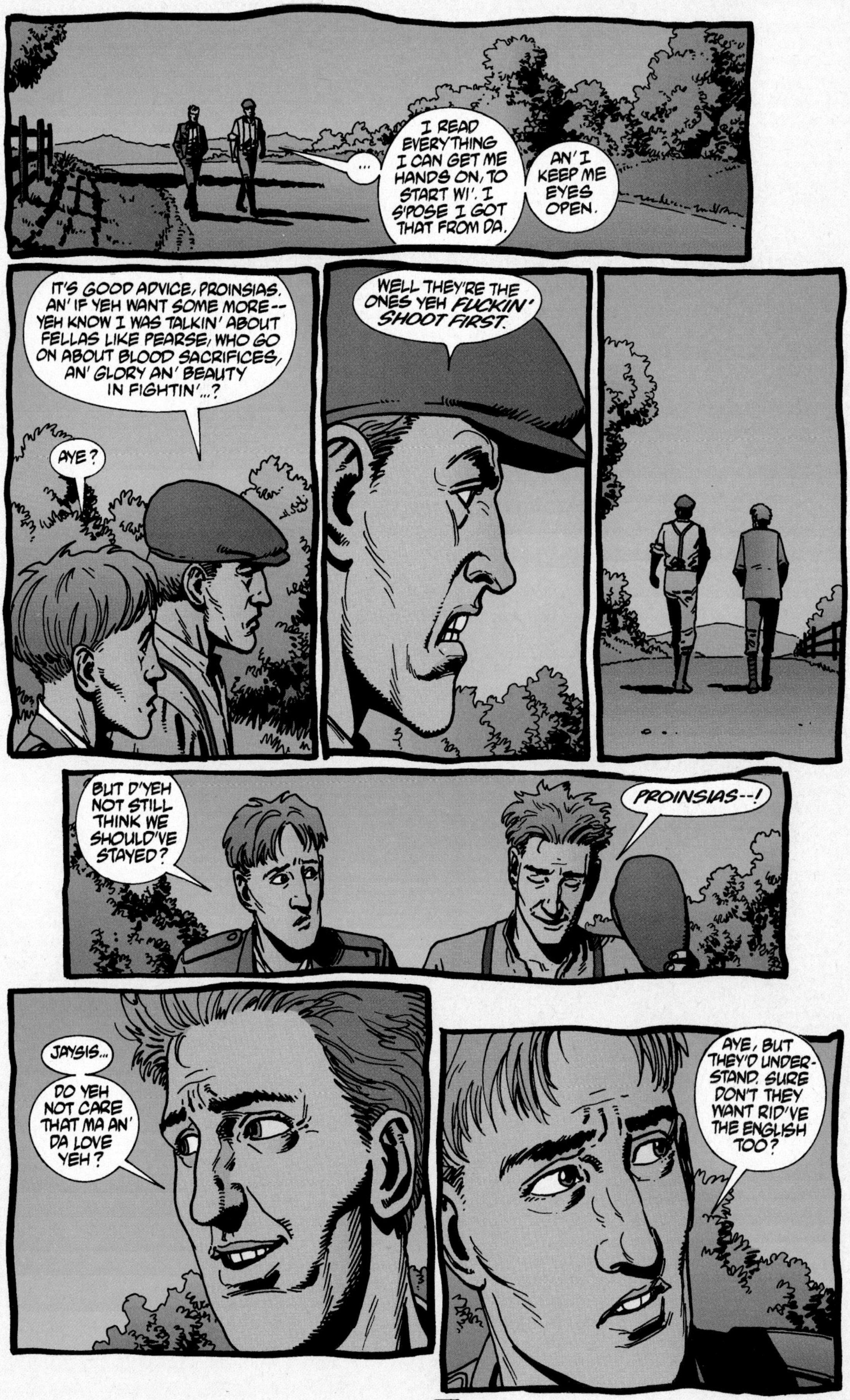
...
I READ EVERYTHING I CAN GET ME HANDS ON, TO START WI'. I S'POSE I GOT THAT FROM DA.
AN' I KEEP ME EYES OPEN.
IT'S GOOD ADVICE, PROINSIAS. AN' IF YEH WANT SOME MORE-- YEH KNOW I WAS TALKIN' ABOUT FELLAS LIKE PEARSE, WHO GO ON ABOUT BLOOD SACRIFICES, AN' GLORY AN' BEAUTY IN FIGHTIN'...?
AYE?
WELL THEY'RE THE ONES YEH FUCKIN' SHOOT FIRST.
BUT D'YEH NOT STILL THINK WE SHOULD'VE STAYED?
PROINSIAS--!
JAYSIS...
DO YEH NOT CARE THAT MA AN' DA LOVE YEH?
AYE, BUT THEY'D UNDER-STAND. SURE DON'T THEY WANT RID'VE THE ENGLISH TOO?

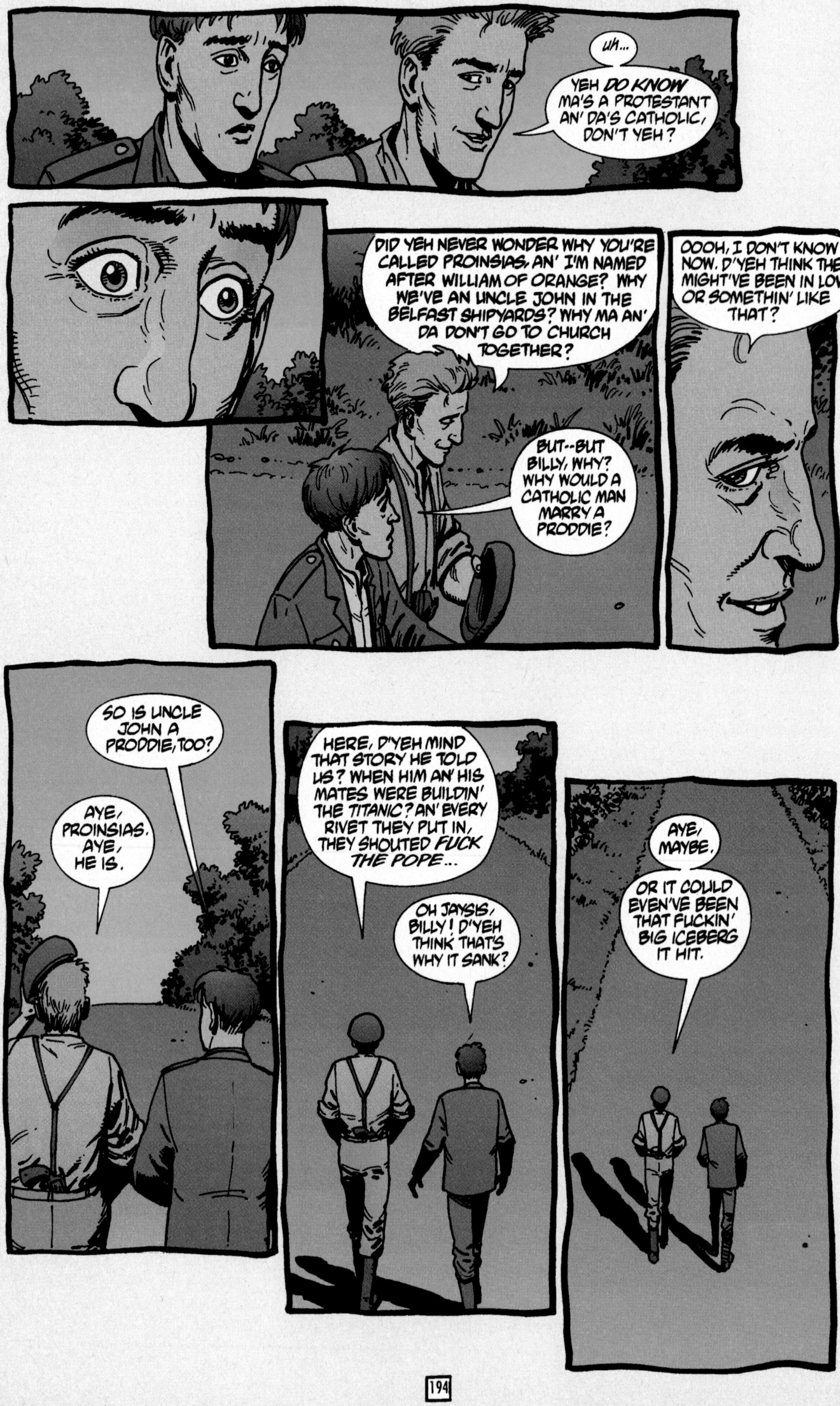
uh...
YEH DO KNOW MA'S A PROTESTANT AN' DA'S CATHOLIC, DON'T YEH?
DID YEH NEVER WONDER WHY YOU'RE CALLED PROINSIAS, AN' I'M NAMED AFTER WILLIAM OF ORANGE? WHY WE'VE AN UNCLE JOHN IN THE BELFAST SHIPYARDS? WHY MA AN' DA DON'T GO TO CHURCH TOGETHER?
BUT--BUT BILLY, WHY? WHY WOULD A CATHOLIC MAN MARRY A PRODDIE?
OOOH, I DON'T KNOW NOW. D'YEH THINK THEY MIGHT'VE BEEN IN LOVE OR SOMETHIN' LIKE THAT?
SO IS UNCLE JOHN A PRODDIE, TOO?
AYE, PROINSIAS. AYE, HE IS.
HERE, D'YEH MIND THAT STORY HE TOLD US? WHEN HIM AN' HIS MATES WERE BUILDIN' THE TITANIC? AN' EVERY RIVET THEY PUT IN, THEY SHOUTED FUCK THE POPE...
OH JAYSIS, BILLY! D'YEH THINK THAT'S WHY IT SANK?
AYE, MAYBE.
OR IT COULD EVEN'VE BEEN THAT FUCKIN' BIG ICEBERG IT HIT.

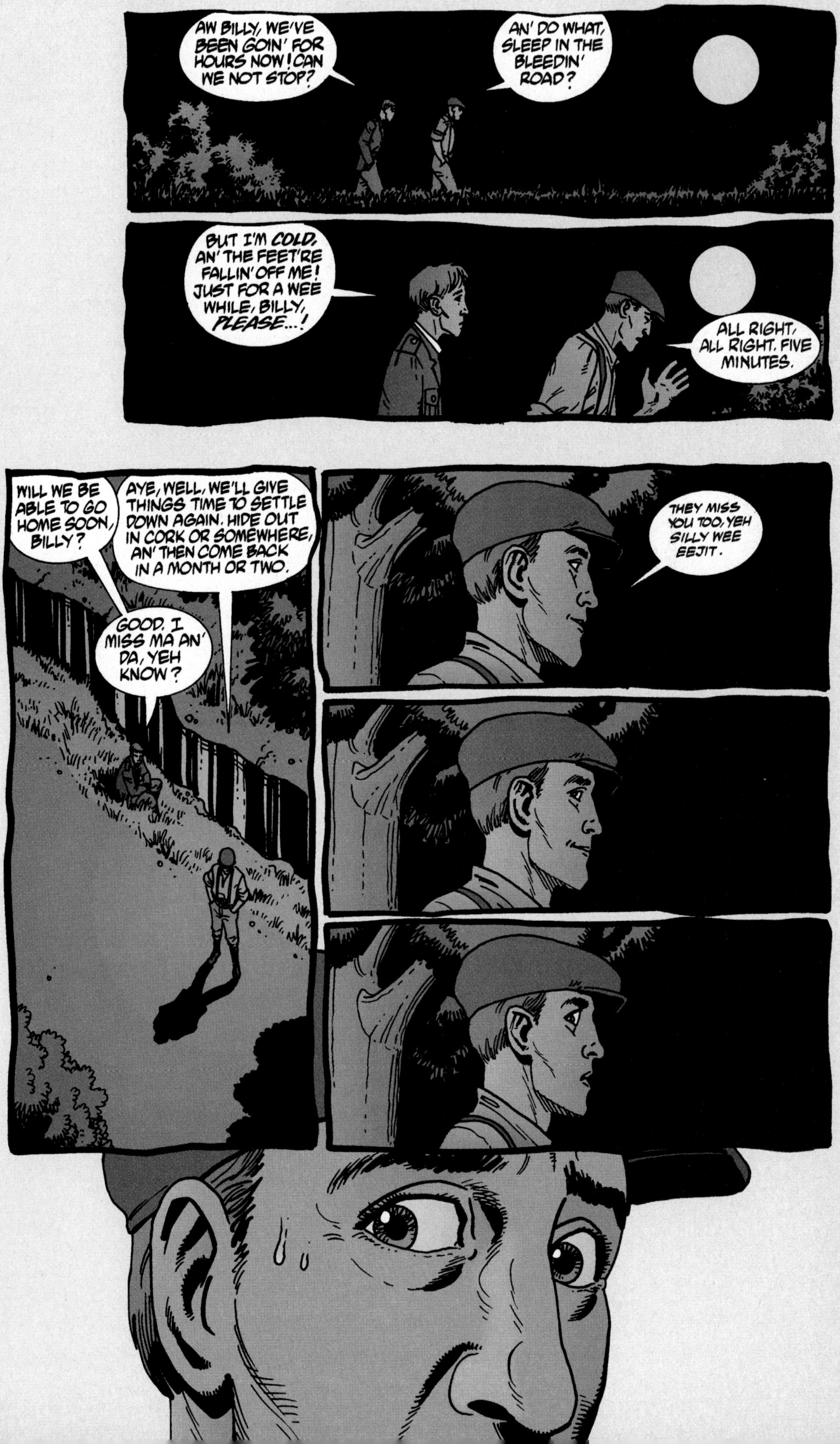
AW BILLY, WE'VE BEEN GOIN' FOR HOURS NOW! CAN WE NOT STOP?
AN' DO WHAT, SLEEP IN THE BLEEDIN' ROAD?
BUT I'M COLD, AN' THE FEET'RE FALLIN' OFF ME! JUST FOR A WEE WHILE, BILLY, PLEASE...!
ALL RIGHT, ALL RIGHT. FIVE MINUTES.
WILL WE BE ABLE TO GO HOME SOON, BILLY?
AYE, WELL, WE'LL GIVE THINGS TIME TO SETTLE DOWN AGAIN. HIDE OUT IN CORK OR SOMEWHERE, AN' THEN COME BACK IN A MONTH OR TWO.
GOOD. I MISS MA AN' DA, YEH KNOW?
THEY MISS YOU TOO, YEH SILLY WEE EEJIT.

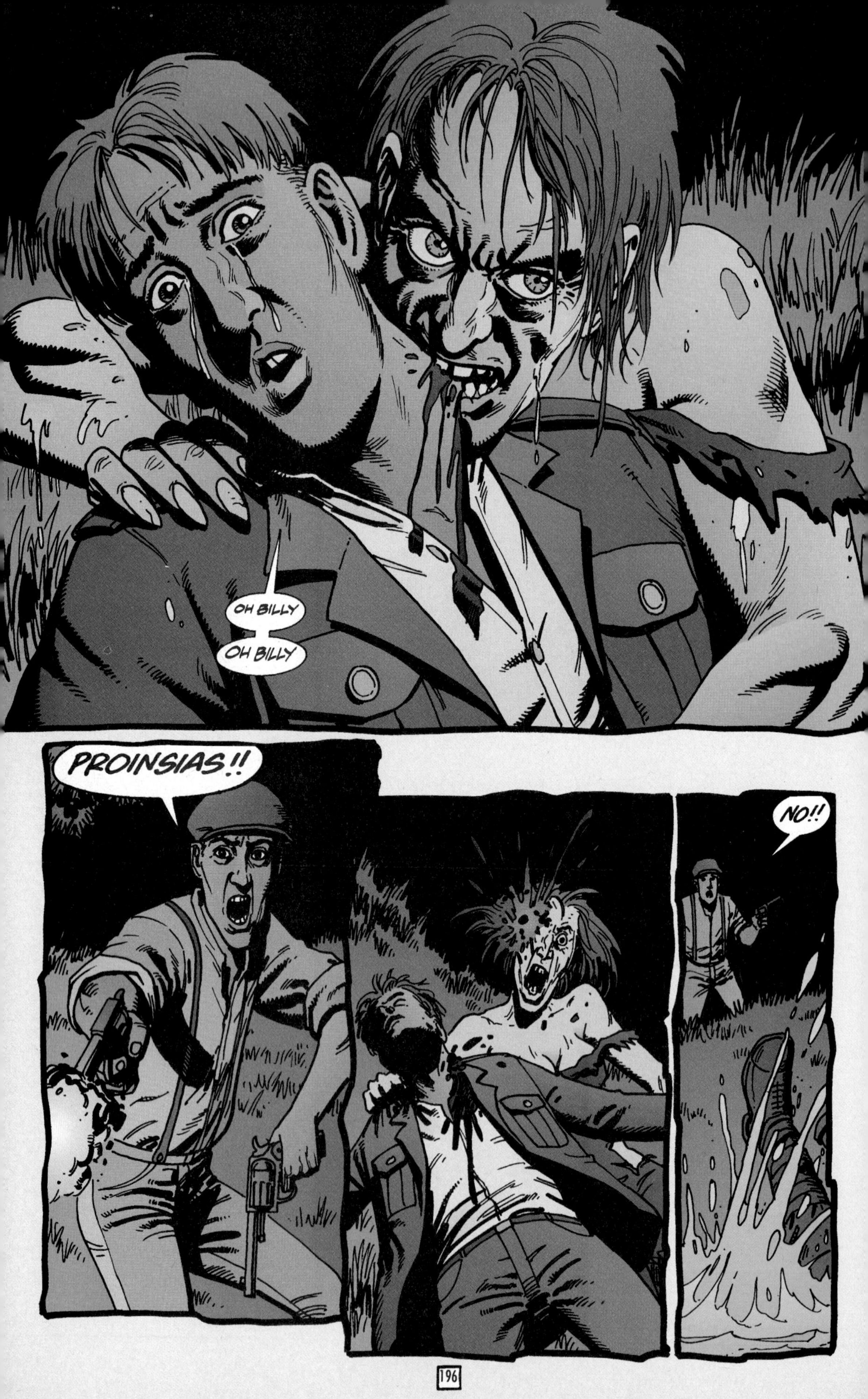
OH BILLY
OH BILLY
PROINSIAS!!
NO!!

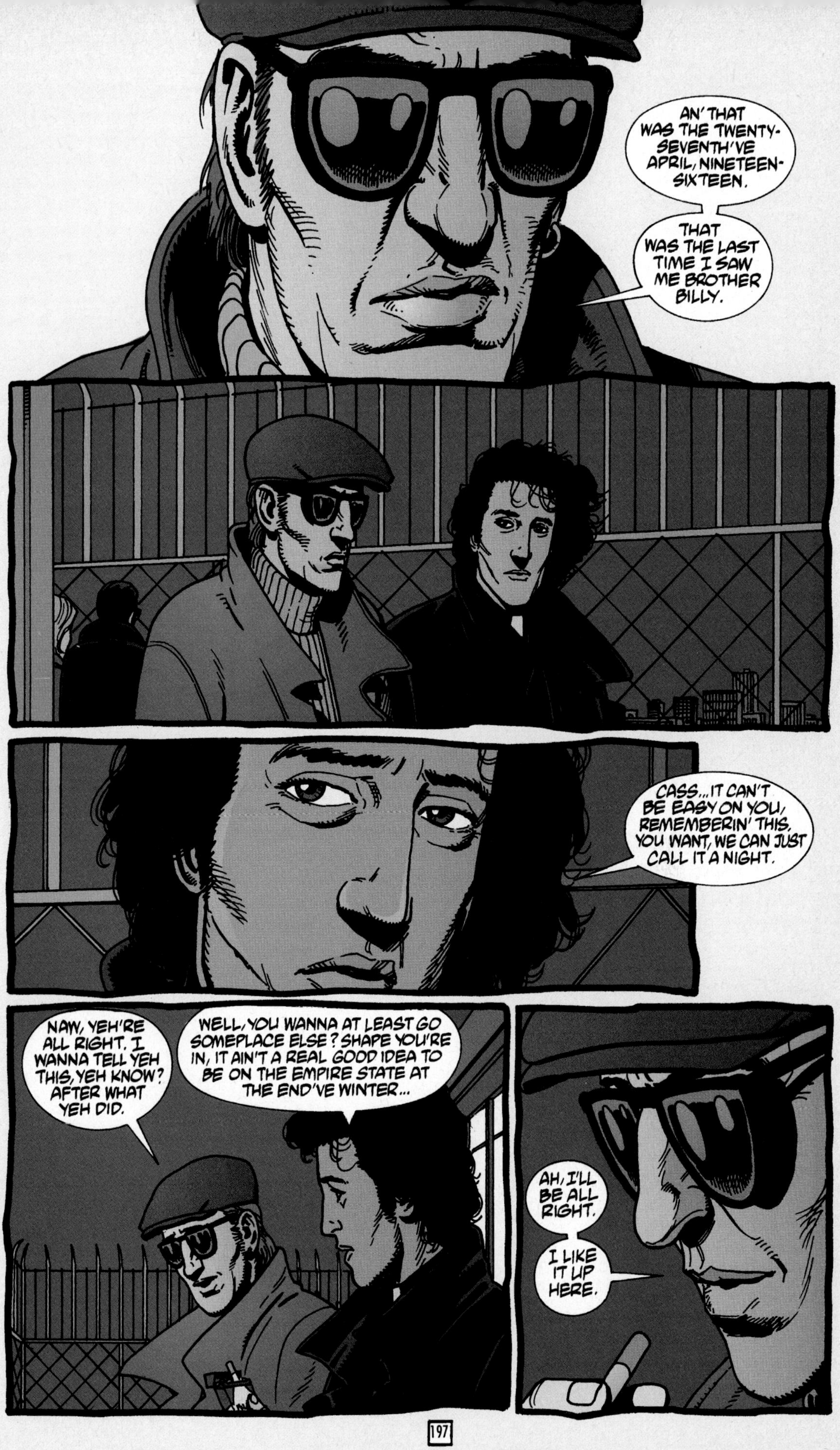
AN' THAT WAS THE TWENTY-SEVENTH'VE APRIL, NINETEEN-SIXTEEN.
THAT WAS THE LAST TIME I SAW ME BROTHER BILLY.
CASS... IT CAN'T BE EASY ON YOU, REMEMBERIN' THIS. YOU WANT, WE CAN JUST CALL IT A NIGHT.
NAW, YEH'RE ALL RIGHT. I WANNA TELL YEH THIS, YEH KNOW? AFTER WHAT YEH DID.
WELL, YOU WANNA AT LEAST GO SOMEPLACE ELSE? SHAPE YOU'RE IN, IT AIN'T A REAL GOOD IDEA TO BE ON THE EMPIRE STATE AT THE END'VE WINTER...
AH, I'LL BE ALL RIGHT.
I LIKE IT UP HERE.

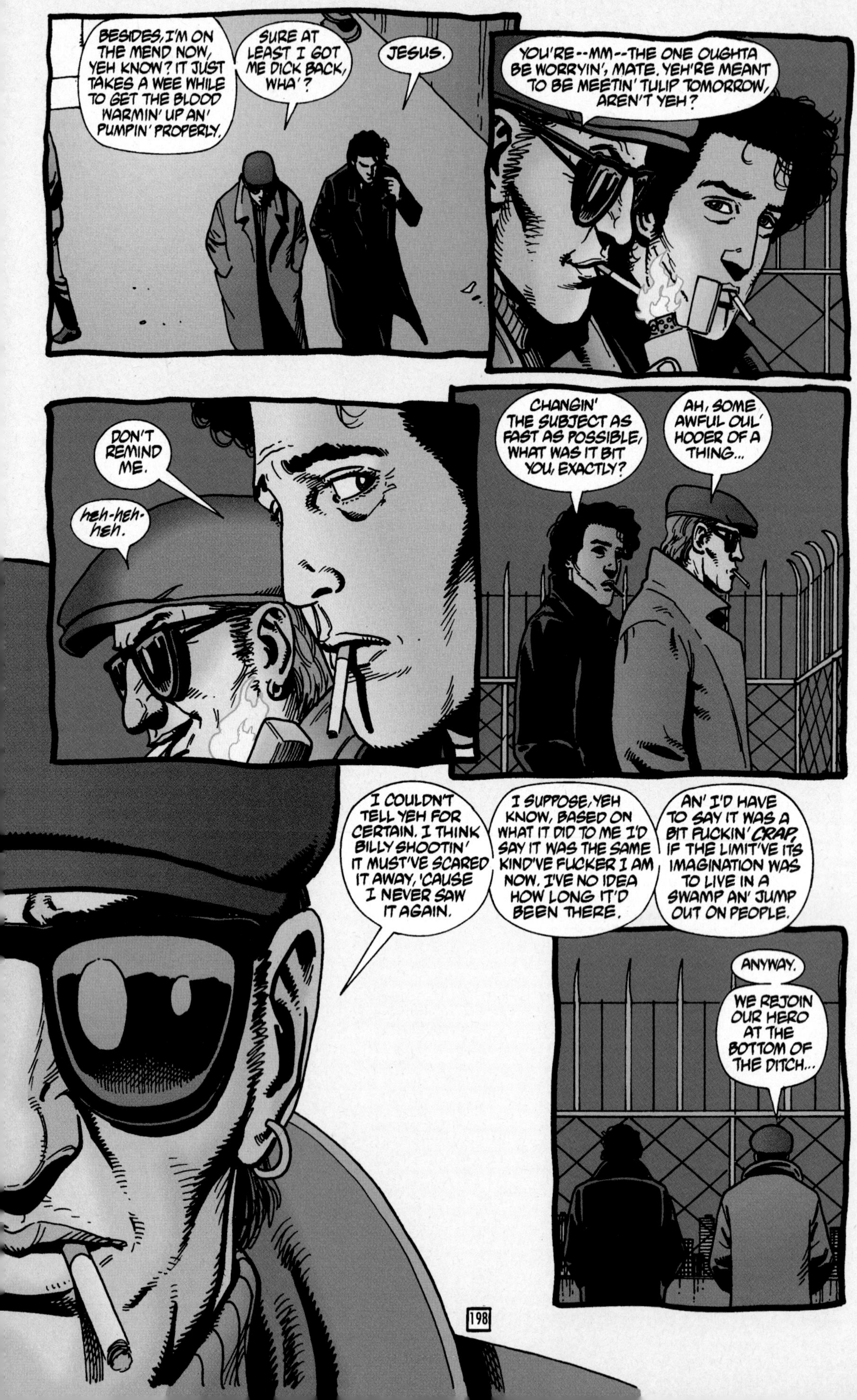
BESIDES, I'M ON THE MEND NOW, YEH KNOW? IT JUST TAKES A WEE WHILE TO GET THE BLOOD WARMIN' UP AN' PUMPIN' PROPERLY.
SURE AT LEAST I GOT ME DICK BACK, WHA'?
JESUS.
YOU'RE--MM--THE ONE OUGHTA BE WORRYIN', MATE. YEH'RE MEANT TO BE MEETIN' TULIP TOMORROW, AREN'T YEH?
DON'T REMIND ME.
heh-heh-heh.
CHANGIN' THE SUBJECT AS FAST AS POSSIBLE, WHAT WAS IT BIT YOU, EXACTLY?
AH, SOME AWFUL OUL' HOOER OF A THING...
I COULDN'T TELL YEH FOR CERTAIN. I THINK BILLY SHOOTIN' IT MUST'VE SCARED IT AWAY, 'CAUSE I NEVER SAW IT AGAIN.
I SUPPOSE, YEH KNOW, BASED ON WHAT IT DID TO ME I'D SAY IT WAS THE SAME KIND'VE FUCKER I AM NOW. I'VE NO IDEA HOW LONG IT'D BEEN THERE.
AN' I'D HAVE TO SAY IT WAS A BIT FUCKIN' CRAP, IF THE LIMIT'VE ITS IMAGINATION WAS TO LIVE IN A SWAMP AN' JUMP OUT ON PEOPLE.
ANYWAY.
WE REJOIN OUR HERO AT THE BOTTOM OF THE DITCH...

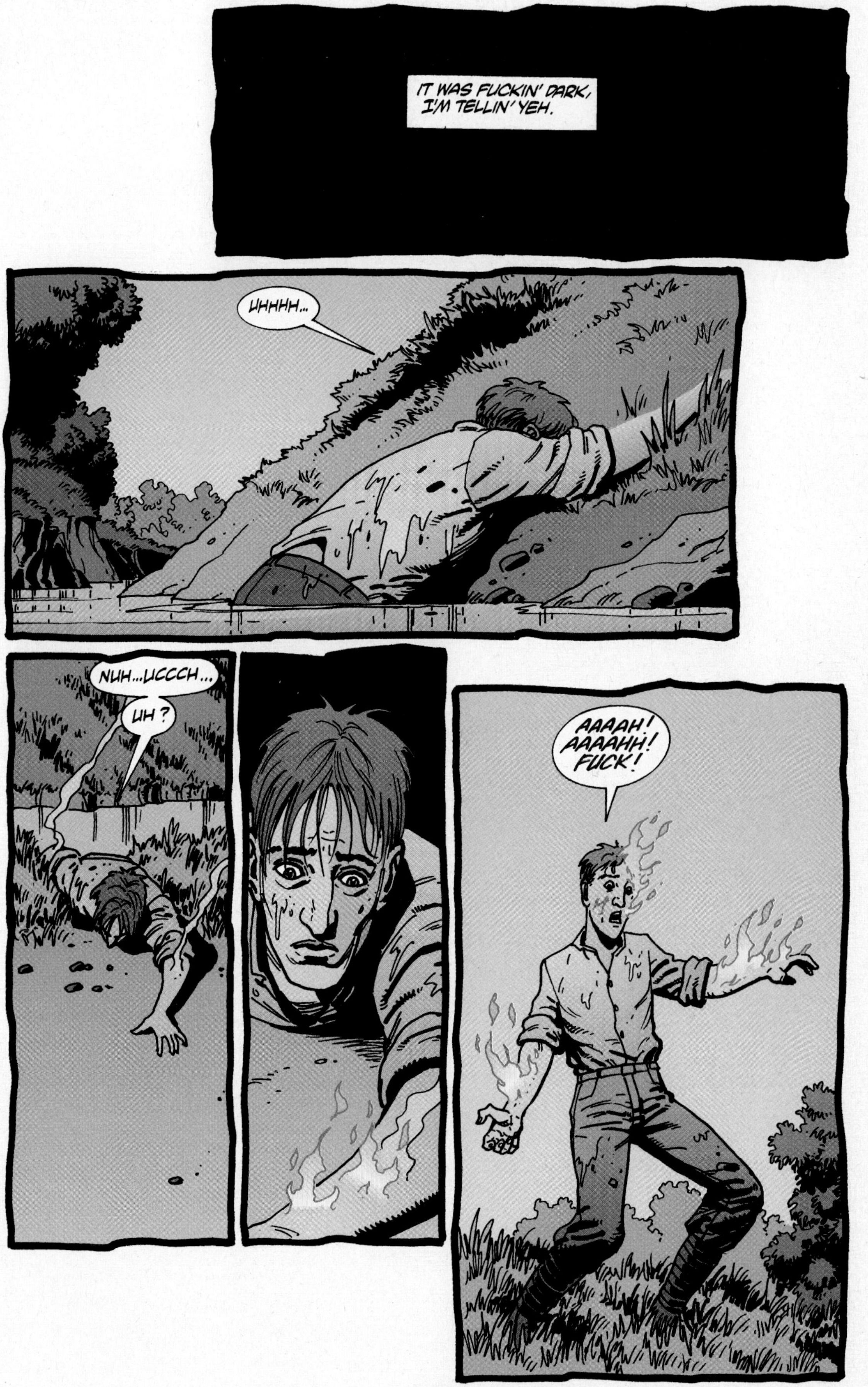
IT WAS FUCKIN' DARK, I'M TELLIN' YEH.
UHHHH...
NUH...UCCCH...
UH?
AAAAH! AAAAHH! FUCK!

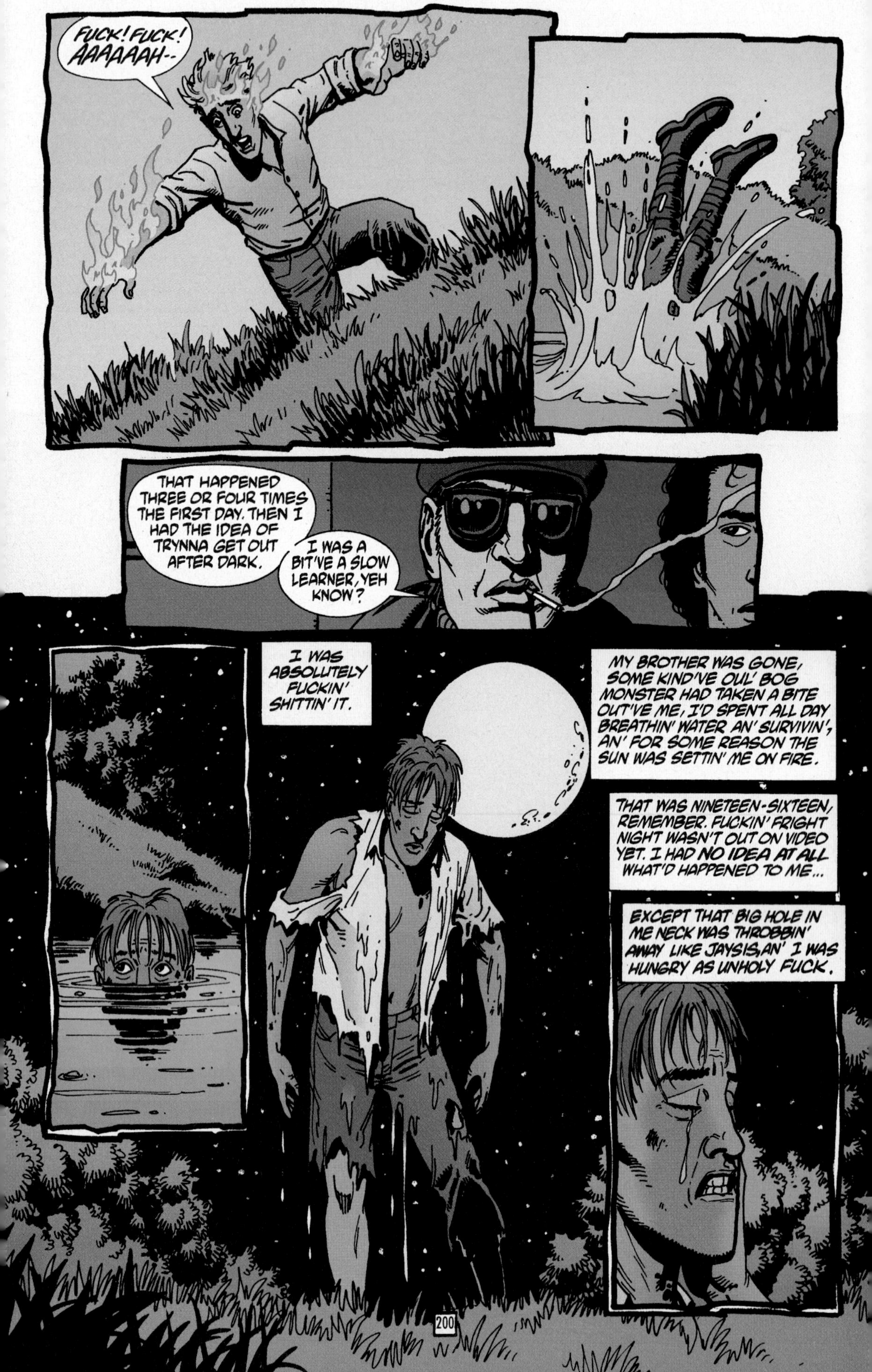
FUCK! FUCK! AAAAAAH--
THAT HAPPENED THREE OR FOUR TIMES THE FIRST DAY. THEN I HAD THE IDEA OF TRYNNA GET OUT AFTER DARK.
I WAS A BIT'VE A SLOW LEARNER, YEH KNOW?
I WAS ABSOLUTELY FUCKIN' SHITTIN' IT.
MY BROTHER WAS GONE, SOME KIND'VE OUL' BOG MONSTER HAD TAKEN A BITE OUT'VE ME, I'D SPENT ALL DAY BREATHIN' WATER AN' SURVIVIN', AN' FOR SOME REASON THE SUN WAS SETTIN' ME ON FIRE.
THAT WAS NINETEEN-SIXTEEN, REMEMBER. FUCKIN' FRIGHT NIGHT WASN'T OUT ON VIDEO YET. I HAD NO IDEA AT ALL WHAT'D HAPPENED TO ME...
EXCEPT THAT BIG HOLE IN ME NECK WAS THROBBIN' AWAY LIKE JAYSIS, AN' I WAS HUNGRY AS UNHOLY FUCK.

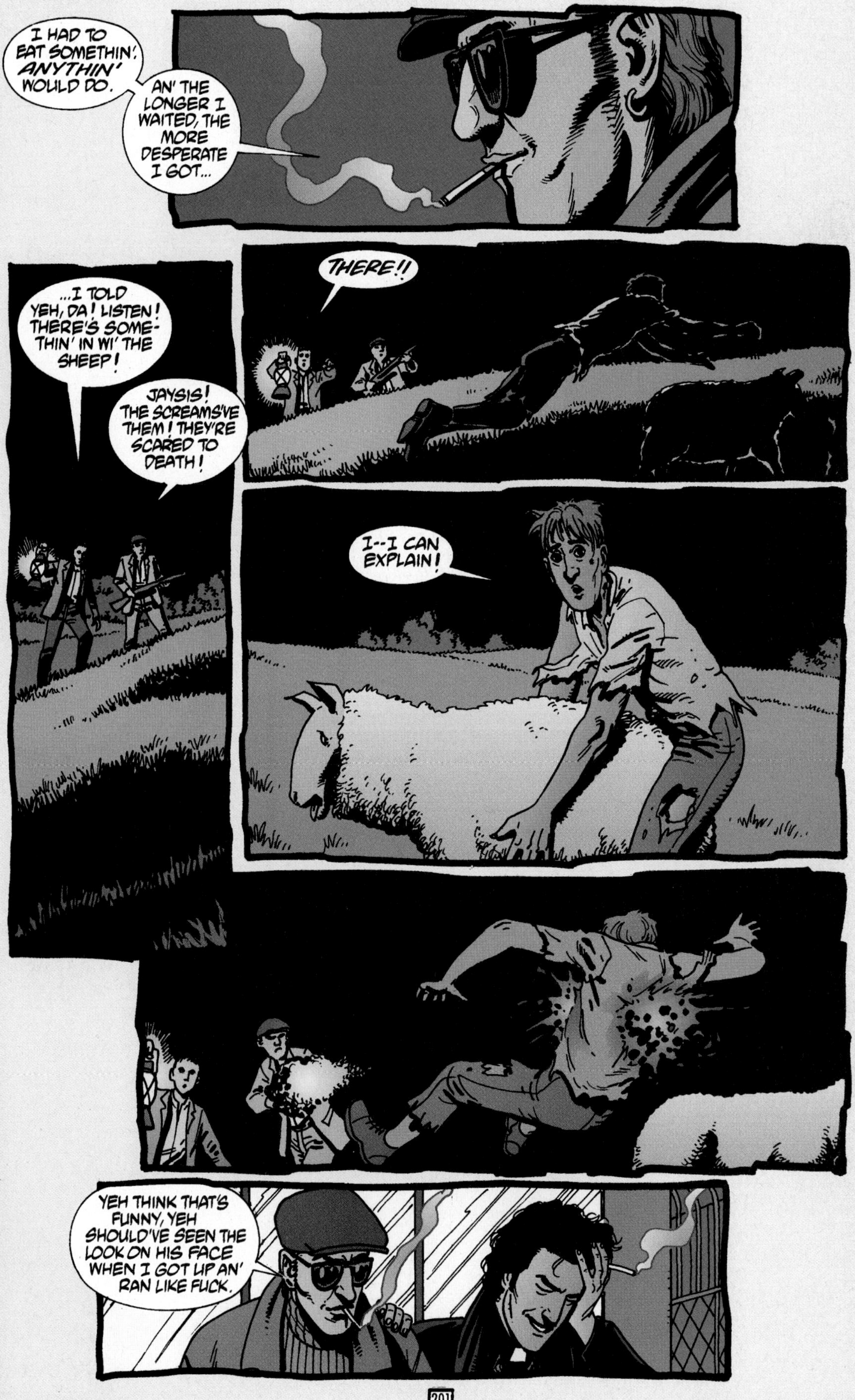
I HAD TO EAT SOMETHIN', ANYTHIN' WOULD DO.
AN' THE LONGER I WAITED, THE MORE DESPERATE I GOT...
...I TOLD YEH, DA! LISTEN! THERE'S SOMETHIN' IN WI' THE SHEEP!
JAYSIS! THE SCREAMS'VE THEM! THEY'RE SCARED TO DEATH!
THERE!!
I--I CAN EXPLAIN!
YEH THINK THAT'S FUNNY, YEH SHOULD'VE SEEN THE LOOK ON HIS FACE WHEN I GOT UP AN' RAN LIKE FUCK.

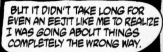

BUT IT DIDN'T TAKE LONG FOR EVEN AN EEJIT LIKE ME TO REALIZE I WAS GOING ABOUT THINGS COMPLETELY THE WRONG WAY.

ALL RIGHT, SO I COULDN'T GO OUT DURING THE DAY. BIG DEAL. NEITHER DO FELLAS WHO WORK THE NIGHT SHIFT.

IT DIDN'T MEAN I HAD TO LIVE ME LIFE LIKE THE STUPID FUCKER THAT BIT ME, THAT MUCH WAS OBVIOUS...

I COULD LOOK AND ACT AND TALK LIKE ANY OTHER TOSSER. I WAS TAKIN' IT EASY 'TIL I WORKED OUT WHAT TO DO, AN' I WAS STAYIN' *WELL* OUTTA DUBLIN, FOR REASONS THAT'LL SOON BECOME CLEAR.

YEH SEE, JESSE, IRELAND WAS NEVER THAT BIG A PLACE TO BEGIN WITH, YEH KNOW? AN' WHEN IT GOES MENTAL FROM TIME TO TIME, IT CAN GET EVEN SMALLER.

THE FIRST TIME IT HAPPENED, I WAS DRINKIN' IN A PUB IN COUNTY MONAGHAN...

PROINSIAS CASSIDY!

er...

YEH'RE PROINSIAS CASSIDY, FROM DUBLIN TOWN! YEH ARE NOW, YEH ARE, YEH ARE!

YEH'VE A BROTHER BILLY AN' OH, SURE DIDN'T HE TELL ME HIMSELF YEH DIED IN THE RISIN' LAST YEAR! HE WAS MISTAKEN, I'M SURE'VE IT! SURE DON'T I KNOW THE PAIR'VE YEZ, DIDN'T I USED TO SEE YEZ MARCHIN' WI' THE VOLUNTEERS!

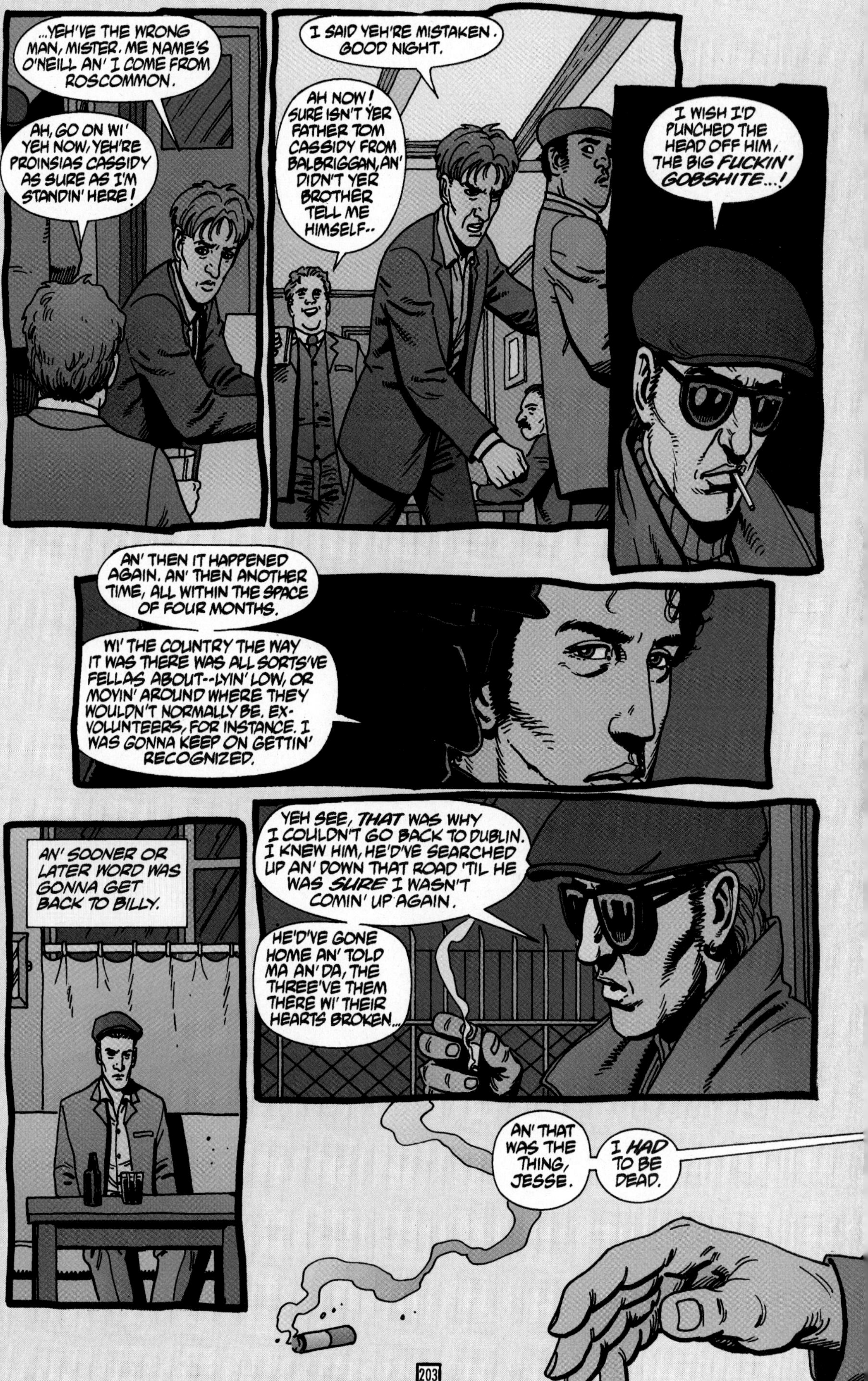

...YEH'VE THE WRONG MAN, MISTER. ME NAME'S O'NEILL AN' I COME FROM ROSCOMMON.
AH, GO ON WI' YEH NOW, YEH'RE PROINSIAS CASSIDY AS SURE AS I'M STANDIN' HERE!
I SAID YEH'RE MISTAKEN. GOOD NIGHT.
AH NOW! SURE ISN'T YER FATHER TOM CASSIDY FROM BALBRIGGAN, AN' DIDN'T YER BROTHER TELL ME HIMSELF..
I WISH I'D PUNCHED THE HEAD OFF HIM, THE BIG FUCKIN' GOBSHITE...!
AN' THEN IT HAPPENED AGAIN. AN' THEN ANOTHER TIME, ALL WITHIN THE SPACE OF FOUR MONTHS.
WI' THE COUNTRY THE WAY IT WAS THERE WAS ALL SORTS'VE FELLAS ABOUT--LYIN' LOW, OR MOVIN' AROUND WHERE THEY WOULDN'T NORMALLY BE. EX-VOLUNTEERS, FOR INSTANCE. I WAS GONNA KEEP ON GETTIN' RECOGNIZED.
AN' SOONER OR LATER WORD WAS GONNA GET BACK TO BILLY.
YEH SEE, THAT WAS WHY I COULDN'T GO BACK TO DUBLIN. I KNEW HIM, HE'D'VE SEARCHED UP AN' DOWN THAT ROAD 'TIL HE WAS SURE I WASN'T COMIN' UP AGAIN.
HE'D'VE GONE HOME AN' TOLD MA AN' DA, THE THREE'VE THEM THERE WI' THEIR HEARTS BROKEN...
AN' THAT WAS THE THING, JESSE.
I HAD TO BE DEAD.

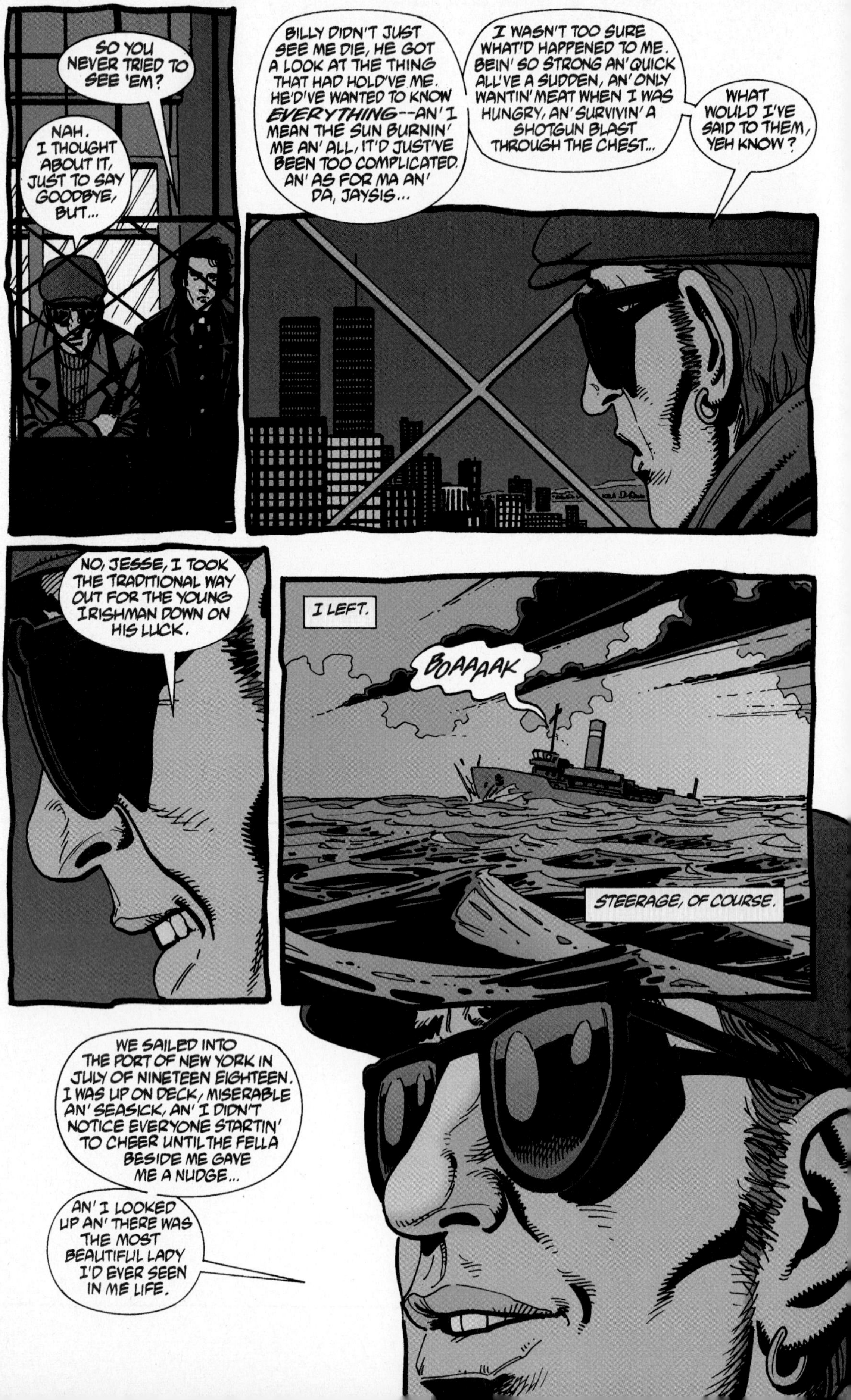
SO YOU NEVER TRIED TO SEE 'EM?
NAH. I THOUGHT ABOUT IT, JUST TO SAY GOODBYE, BUT...
BILLY DIDN'T JUST SEE ME DIE, HE GOT A LOOK AT THE THING THAT HAD HOLD'VE ME. HE'D'VE WANTED TO KNOW EVERYTHING--AN' I MEAN THE SUN BURNIN' ME AN' ALL, IT'D JUST'VE BEEN TOO COMPLICATED. AN' AS FOR MA AN' DA, JAYSIS...
I WASN'T TOO SURE WHAT'D HAPPENED TO ME. BEIN' SO STRONG AN' QUICK ALL'VE A SUDDEN, AN' ONLY WANTIN' MEAT WHEN I WAS HUNGRY, AN' SURVIVIN' A SHOTGUN BLAST THROUGH THE CHEST...
WHAT WOULD I'VE SAID TO THEM, YEH KNOW?
NO, JESSE, I TOOK THE TRADITIONAL WAY OUT FOR THE YOUNG IRISHMAN DOWN ON HIS LUCK.
I LEFT.
BOAAAAK
STEERAGE, OF COURSE.
WE SAILED INTO THE PORT OF NEW YORK IN JULY OF NINETEEN EIGHTEEN. I WAS UP ON DECK, MISERABLE AN' SEASICK, AN' I DIDN'T NOTICE EVERYONE STARTIN' TO CHEER UNTIL THE FELLA BESIDE ME GAVE ME A NUDGE...
AN' I LOOKED UP AN' THERE WAS THE MOST BEAUTIFUL LADY I'D EVER SEEN IN ME LIFE.

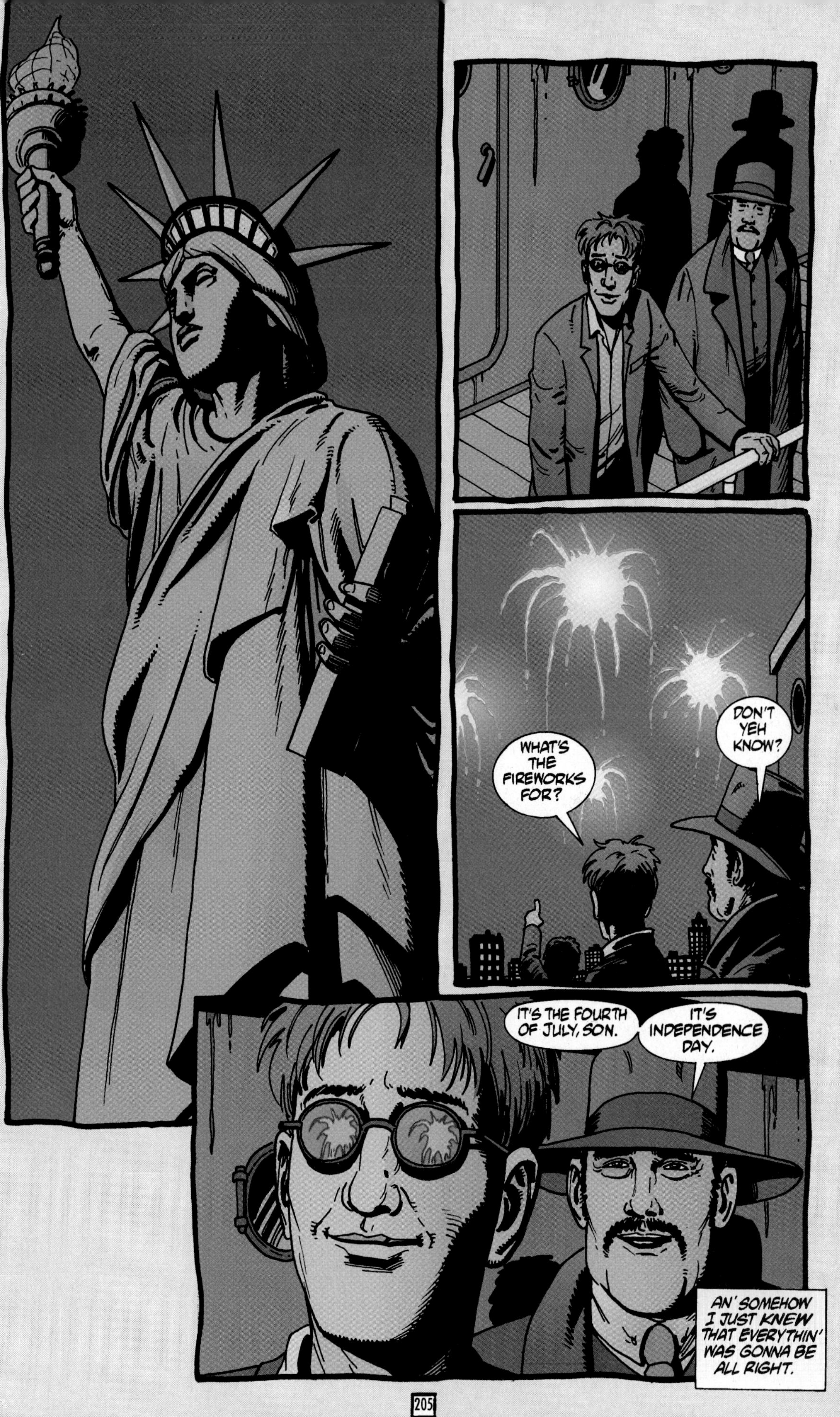
WHAT'S THE FIREWORKS FOR?
DON'T YEH KNOW?
IT'S THE FOURTH OF JULY, SON.
IT'S INDEPENDENCE DAY.
AN' SOMEHOW I JUST KNEW THAT EVERYTHIN' WAS GONNA BE ALL RIGHT.

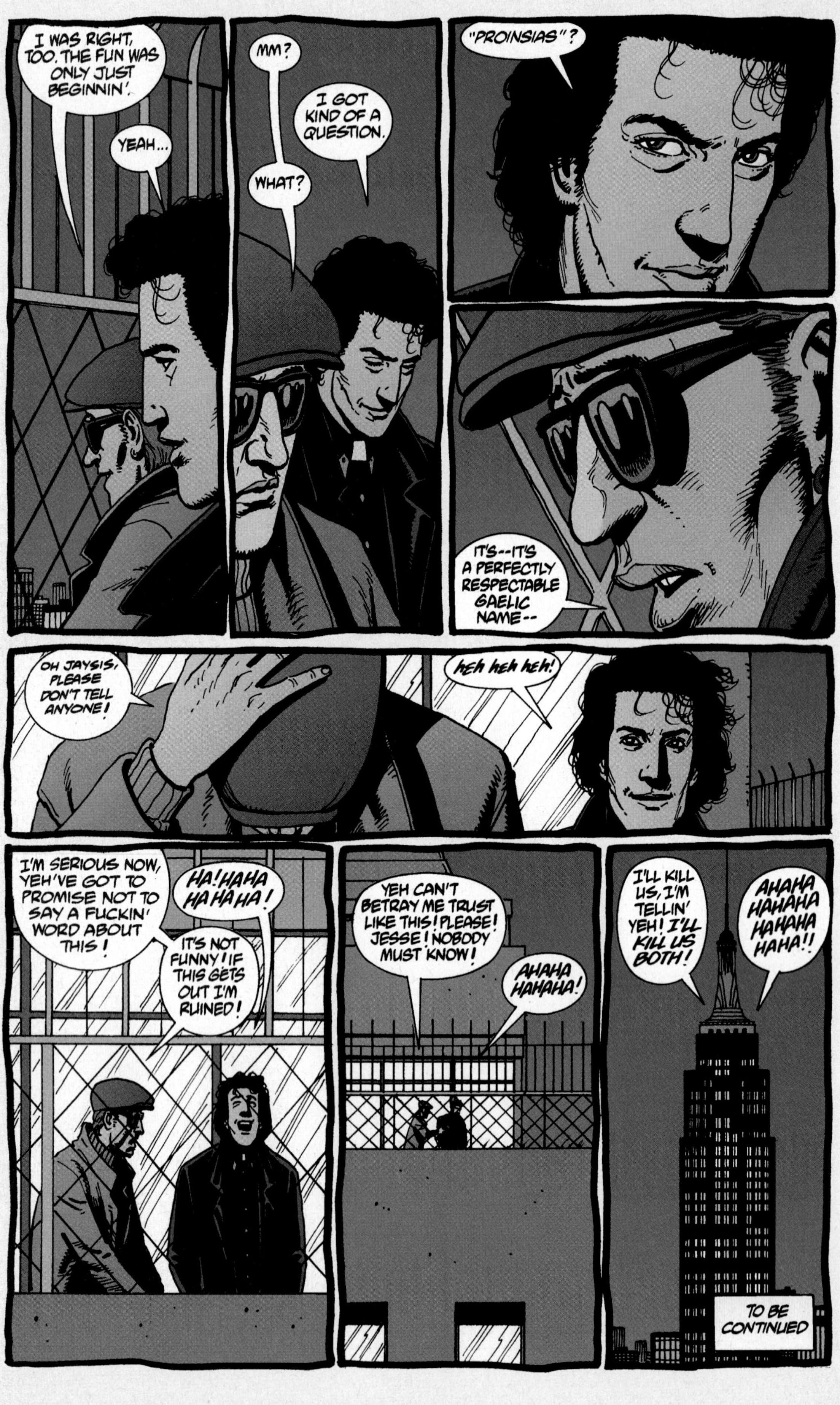
I WAS RIGHT, TOO. THE FUN WAS ONLY JUST BEGINNIN'.
YEAH...
MM?
I GOT KIND OF A QUESTION.
WHAT?
"PROINSIAS"?
IT'S--IT'S A PERFECTLY RESPECTABLE GAELIC NAME--
OH JAYSIS, PLEASE DON'T TELL ANYONE!
heh heh heh!
I'M SERIOUS NOW, YEH'VE GOT TO PROMISE NOT TO SAY A FUCKIN' WORD ABOUT THIS!
HA! HAHA HAHAHA!
IT'S NOT FUNNY! IF THIS GETS OUT I'M RUINED!
YEH CAN'T BETRAY ME TRUST LIKE THIS! PLEASE! JESSE! NOBODY MUST KNOW!
AHAHA HAHAHA!
I'LL KILL US, I'M TELLIN' YEH! I'LL KILL US BOTH!
AHAHA HAHAHA HAHAHA HAHA!!
TO BE CONTINUED

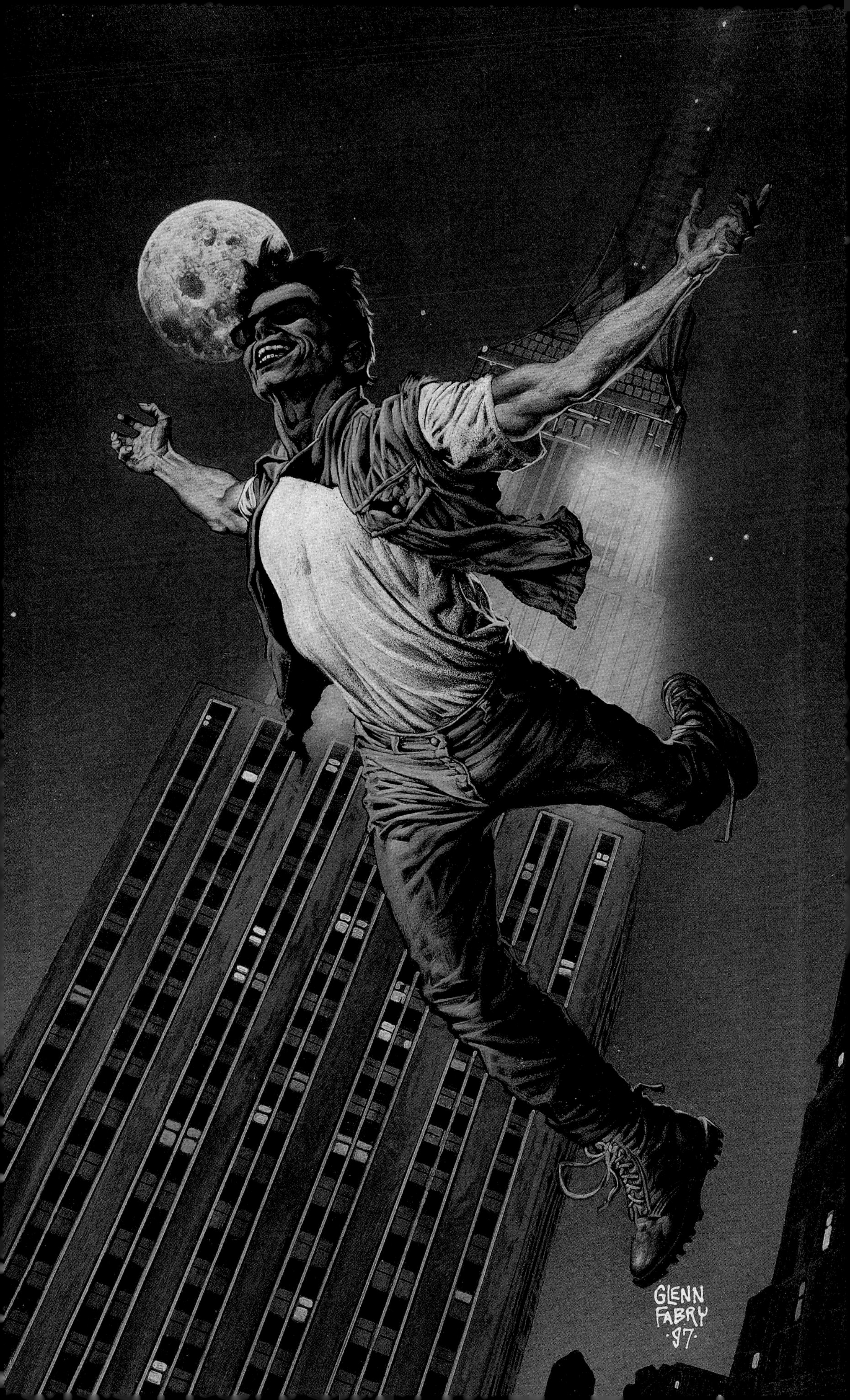
GLENN
FABRY
·97·

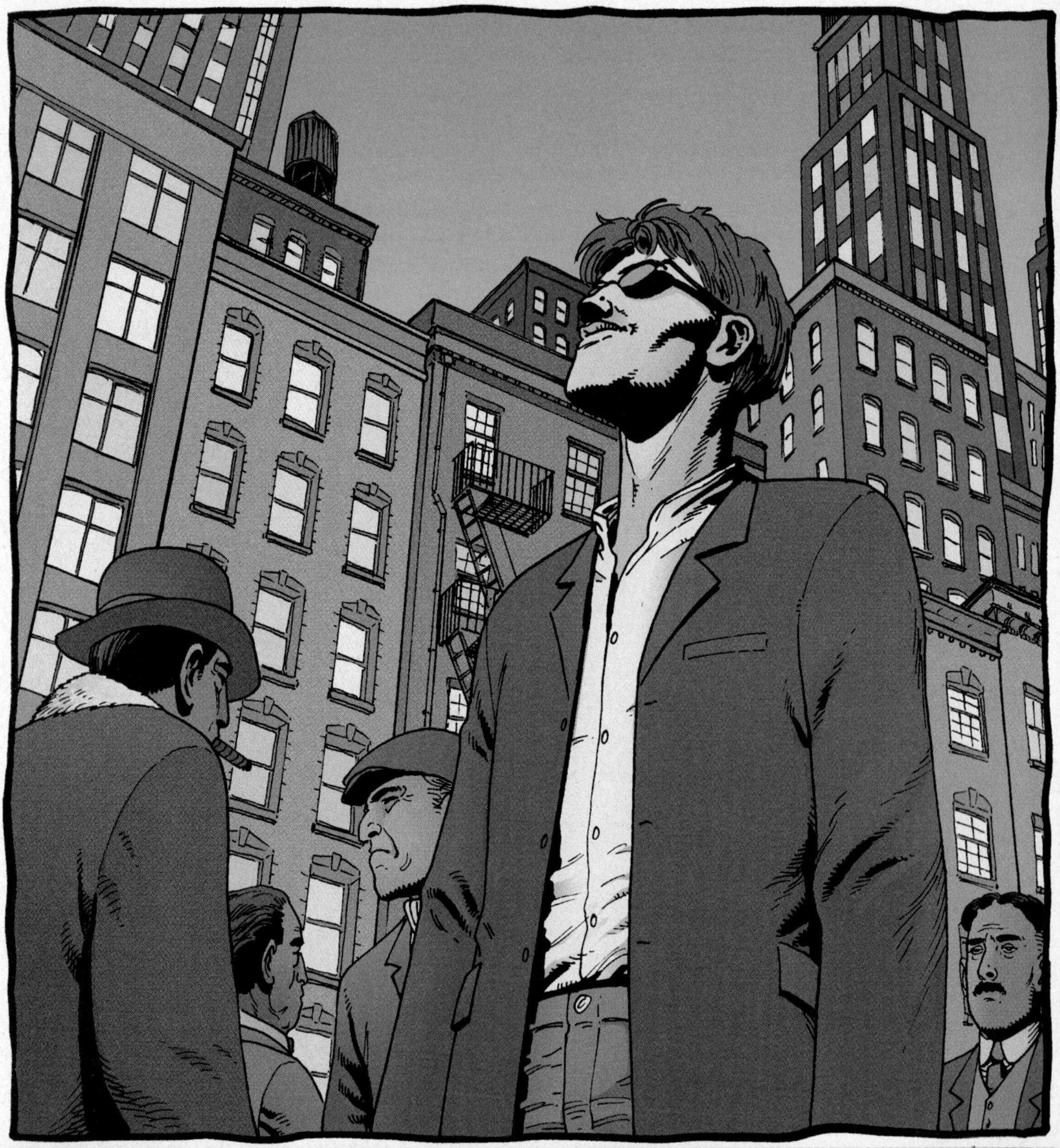

TO THE STREETS OF MANHATTAN I WANDERED AWAY

GARTH ENNIS - Writer STEVE DILLON - Artist

MATT HOLLINGSWORTH - Colorist

CLEM ROBINS - Letterer AXEL ALONSO - Editor

PREACHER created by GARTH ENNIS and STEVE DILLON

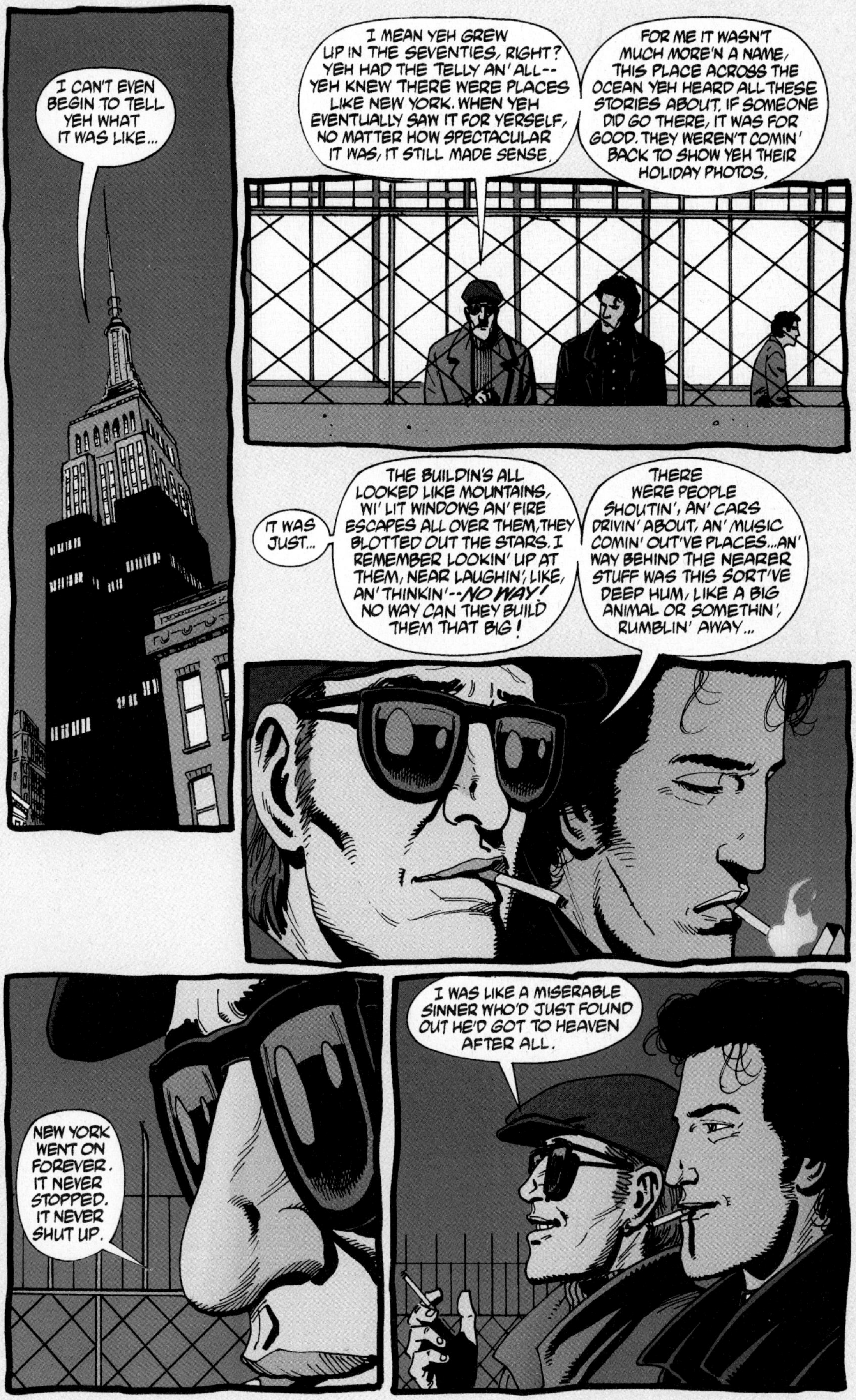
I CAN'T EVEN BEGIN TO TELL YEH WHAT IT WAS LIKE...
I MEAN YEH GREW UP IN THE SEVENTIES, RIGHT? YEH HAD THE TELLY AN' ALL-- YEH KNEW THERE WERE PLACES LIKE NEW YORK. WHEN YEH EVENTUALLY SAW IT FOR YERSELF, NO MATTER HOW SPECTACULAR IT WAS, IT STILL MADE SENSE.
FOR ME IT WASN'T MUCH MORE'N A NAME, THIS PLACE ACROSS THE OCEAN YEH HEARD ALL THESE STORIES ABOUT. IF SOMEONE DID GO THERE, IT WAS FOR GOOD. THEY WEREN'T COMIN' BACK TO SHOW YEH THEIR HOLIDAY PHOTOS.
IT WAS JUST...
THE BUILDIN'S ALL LOOKED LIKE MOUNTAINS, WI' LIT WINDOWS AN' FIRE ESCAPES ALL OVER THEM. THEY BLOTTED OUT THE STARS. I REMEMBER LOOKIN' UP AT THEM, NEAR LAUGHIN', LIKE, AN' THINKIN'--NO WAY! NO WAY CAN THEY BUILD THEM THAT BIG!
THERE WERE PEOPLE SHOUTIN', AN' CARS DRIVIN' ABOUT, AN' MUSIC COMIN' OUT'VE PLACES...AN' WAY BEHIND THE NEARER STUFF WAS THIS SORT'VE DEEP HUM, LIKE A BIG ANIMAL OR SOMETHIN', RUMBLIN' AWAY...
NEW YORK WENT ON FOREVER. IT NEVER STOPPED. IT NEVER SHUT UP.
I WAS LIKE A MISERABLE SINNER WHO'D JUST FOUND OUT HE'D GOT TO HEAVEN AFTER ALL.

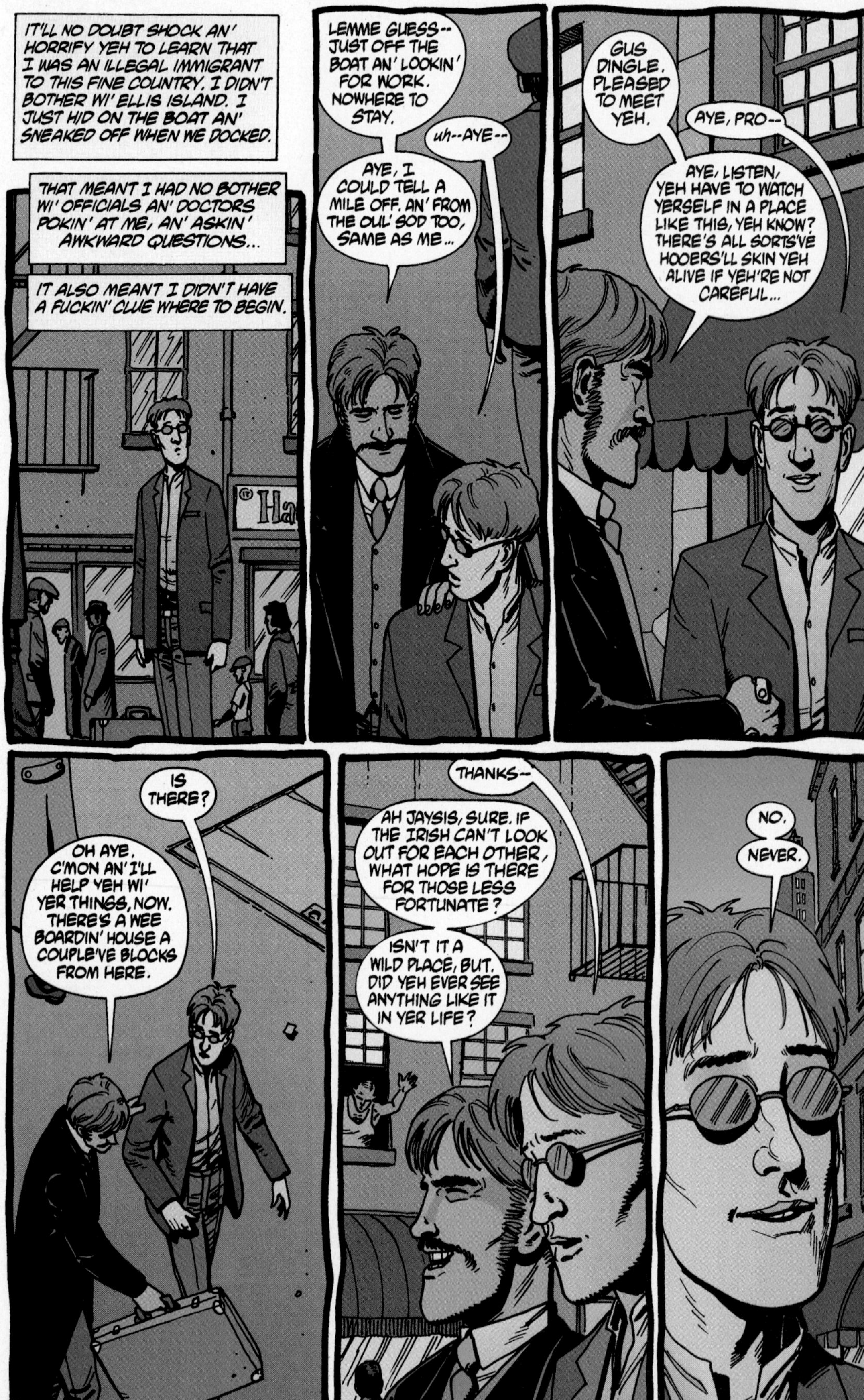
IT'LL NO DOUBT SHOCK AN' HORRIFY YEH TO LEARN THAT I WAS AN ILLEGAL IMMIGRANT TO THIS FINE COUNTRY. I DIDN'T BOTHER WI' ELLIS ISLAND. I JUST HID ON THE BOAT AN' SNEAKED OFF WHEN WE DOCKED.
THAT MEANT I HAD NO BOTHER WI' OFFICIALS AN' DOCTORS POKIN' AT ME, AN' ASKIN' AWKWARD QUESTIONS...
IT ALSO MEANT I DIDN'T HAVE A FUCKIN' CLUE WHERE TO BEGIN.
LEMME GUESS-- JUST OFF THE BOAT AN' LOOKIN' FOR WORK. NOWHERE TO STAY.
uh--AYE--
AYE, I COULD TELL A MILE OFF. AN' FROM THE OUL' SOD TOO, SAME AS ME...
GUS DINGLE. PLEASED TO MEET YEH.
AYE, PRO--
AYE, LISTEN, YEH HAVE TO WATCH YERSELF IN A PLACE LIKE THIS, YEH KNOW? THERE'S ALL SORTS'VE HOOERS'LL SKIN YEH ALIVE IF YEH'RE NOT CAREFUL...
IS THERE?
OH AYE. C'MON AN' I'LL HELP YEH WI' YER THINGS, NOW. THERE'S A WEE BOARDIN' HOUSE A COUPLE'VE BLOCKS FROM HERE.
THANKS--
AH JAYSIS, SURE. IF THE IRISH CAN'T LOOK OUT FOR EACH OTHER, WHAT HOPE IS THERE FOR THOSE LESS FORTUNATE?
ISN'T IT A WILD PLACE, BUT. DID YEH EVER SEE ANYTHING LIKE IT IN YER LIFE?
NO.
NEVER.

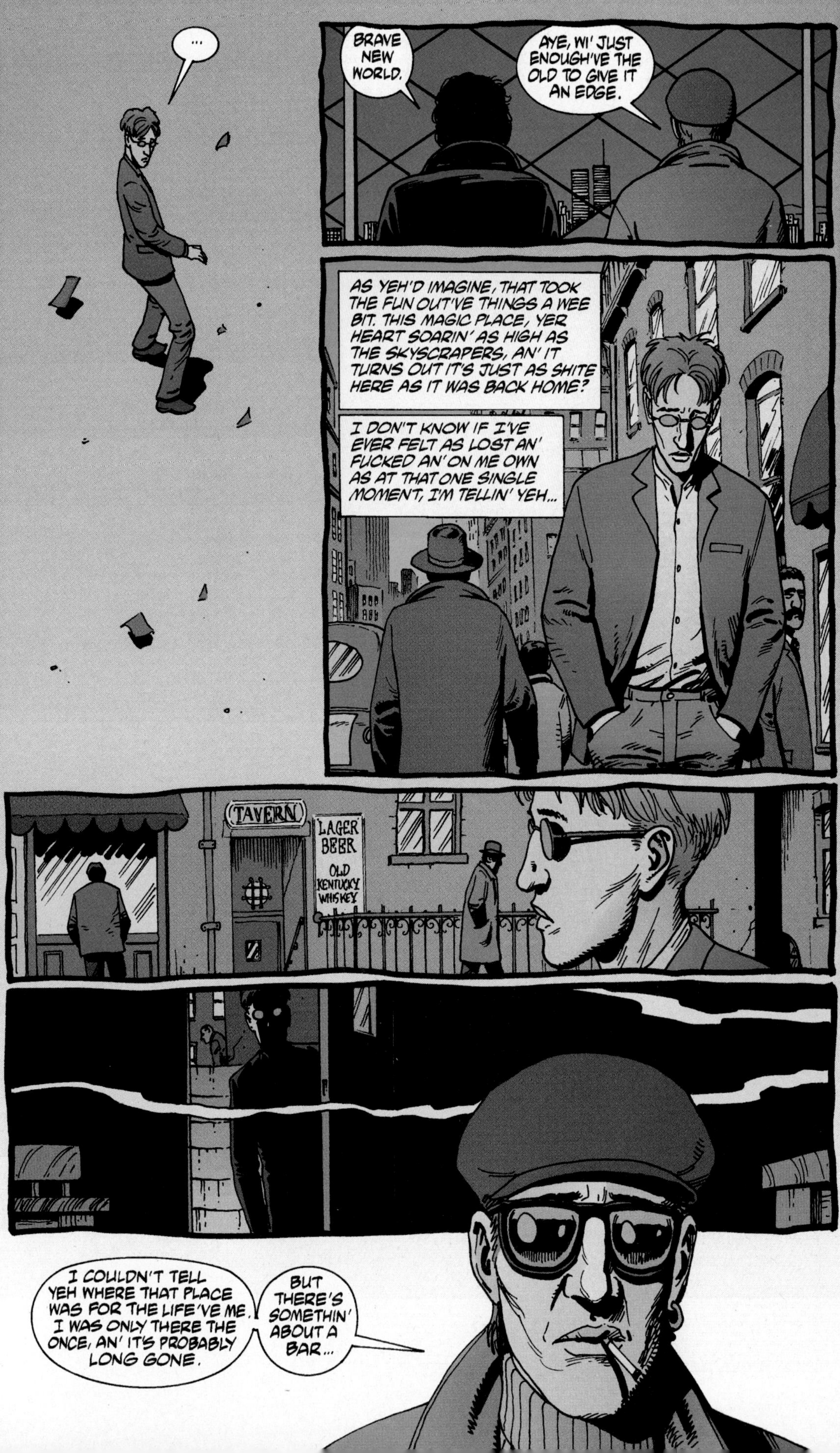
...
BRAVE NEW WORLD.
AYE, WI' JUST ENOUGH'VE THE OLD TO GIVE IT AN EDGE.
AS YEH'D IMAGINE, THAT TOOK THE FUN OUT'VE THINGS A WEE BIT. THIS MAGIC PLACE, YER HEART SOARIN' AS HIGH AS THE SKYSCRAPERS, AN' IT TURNS OUT IT'S JUST AS SHITE HERE AS IT WAS BACK HOME?
I DON'T KNOW IF I'VE EVER FELT AS LOST AN' FUCKED AN' ON ME OWN AS AT THAT ONE SINGLE MOMENT, I'M TELLIN' YEH...
TAVERN
LAGER BEER
OLD KENTUCKY WHISKEY
I COULDN'T TELL YEH WHERE THAT PLACE WAS FOR THE LIFE'VE ME. I WAS ONLY THERE THE ONCE, AN' IT'S PROBABLY LONG GONE.
BUT THERE'S SOMETHIN' ABOUT A BAR...

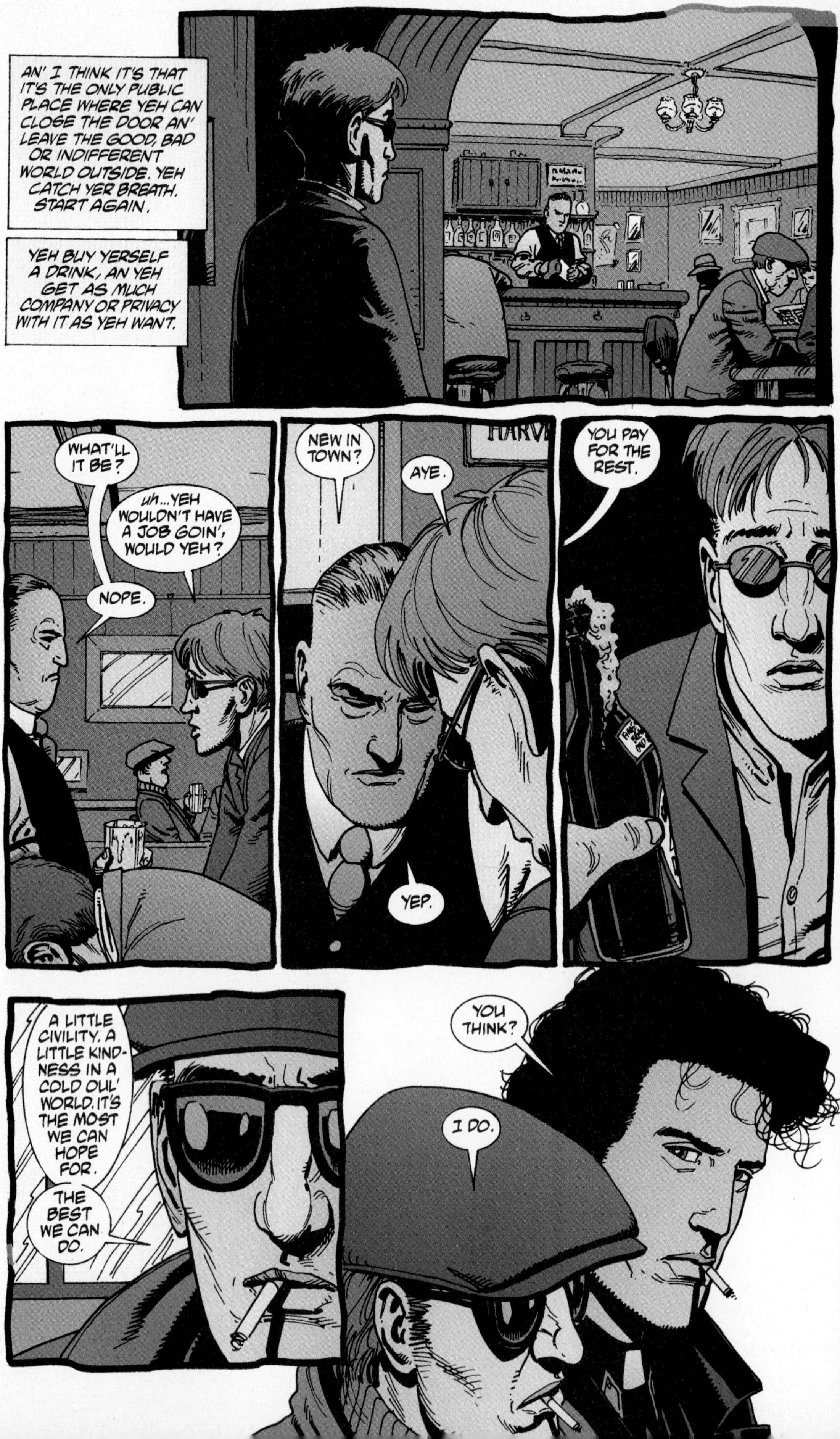
AN' I THINK IT'S THAT IT'S THE ONLY PUBLIC PLACE WHERE YEH CAN CLOSE THE DOOR AN' LEAVE THE GOOD, BAD OR INDIFFERENT WORLD OUTSIDE. YEH CATCH YER BREATH. START AGAIN.
YEH BUY YERSELF A DRINK, AN YEH GET AS MUCH COMPANY OR PRIVACY WITH IT AS YEH WANT.
WHAT'LL IT BE?
uh...YEH WOULDN'T HAVE A JOB GOIN', WOULD YEH?
NOPE.
NEW IN TOWN?
AYE.
YEP.
YOU PAY FOR THE REST.
A LITTLE CIVILITY. A LITTLE KINDNESS IN A COLD OUL' WORLD. IT'S THE MOST WE CAN HOPE FOR.
THE BEST WE CAN DO.
YOU THINK?
I DO.

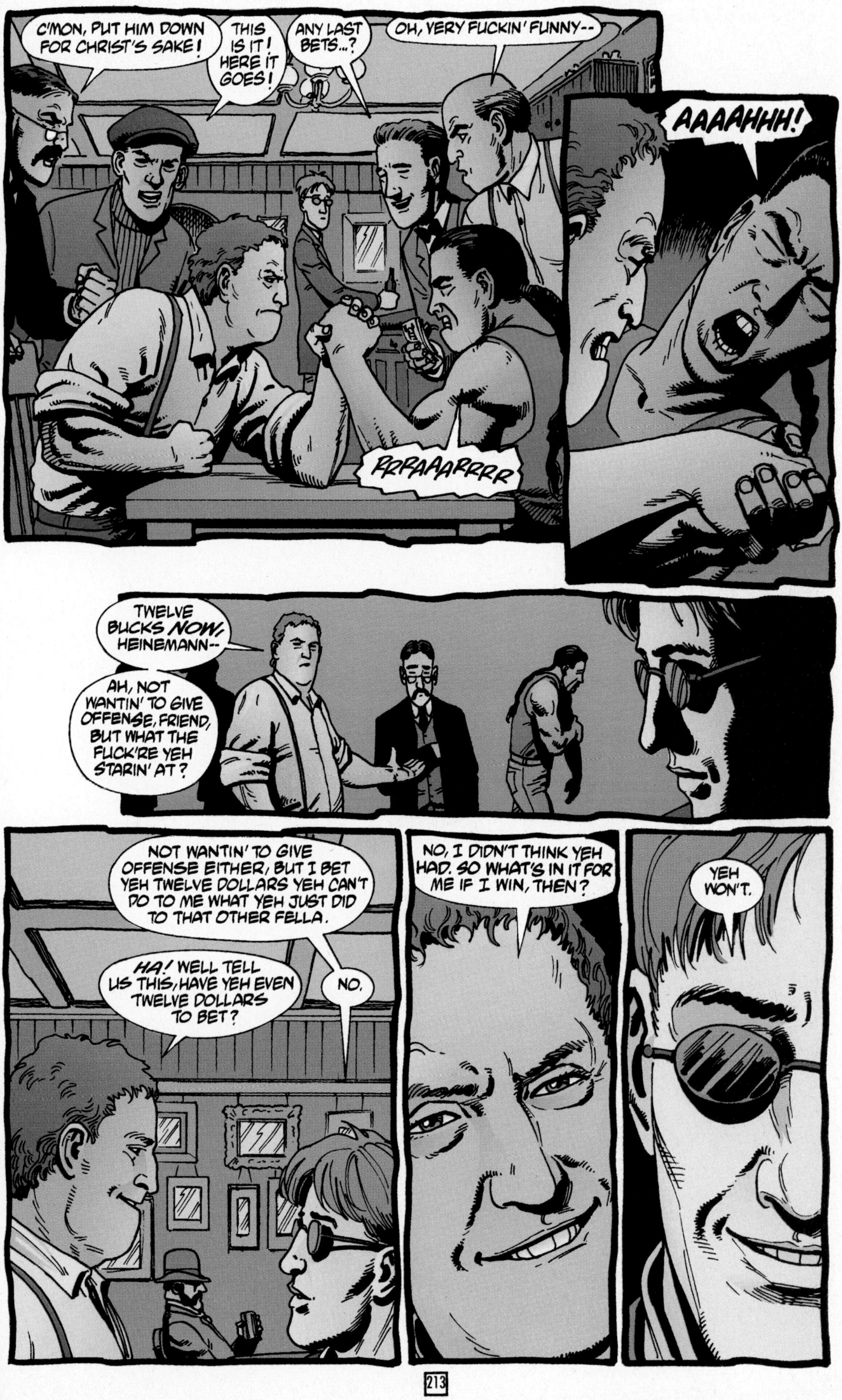
C'MON, PUT HIM DOWN FOR CHRIST'S SAKE!
THIS IS IT! HERE IT GOES!
ANY LAST BETS...?
OH, VERY FUCKIN' FUNNY--
RRRAAARRRR
AAAAHHH!
TWELVE BUCKS NOW, HEINEMANN--
AH, NOT WANTIN' TO GIVE OFFENSE, FRIEND, BUT WHAT THE FUCK'RE YEH STARIN' AT?
NOT WANTIN' TO GIVE OFFENSE EITHER, BUT I BET YEH TWELVE DOLLARS YEH CAN'T DO TO ME WHAT YEH JUST DID TO THAT OTHER FELLA.
HA! WELL TELL US THIS, HAVE YEH EVEN TWELVE DOLLARS TO BET?
NO.
NO, I DIDN'T THINK YEH HAD. SO WHAT'S IN IT FOR ME IF I WIN, THEN?
YEH WON'T.

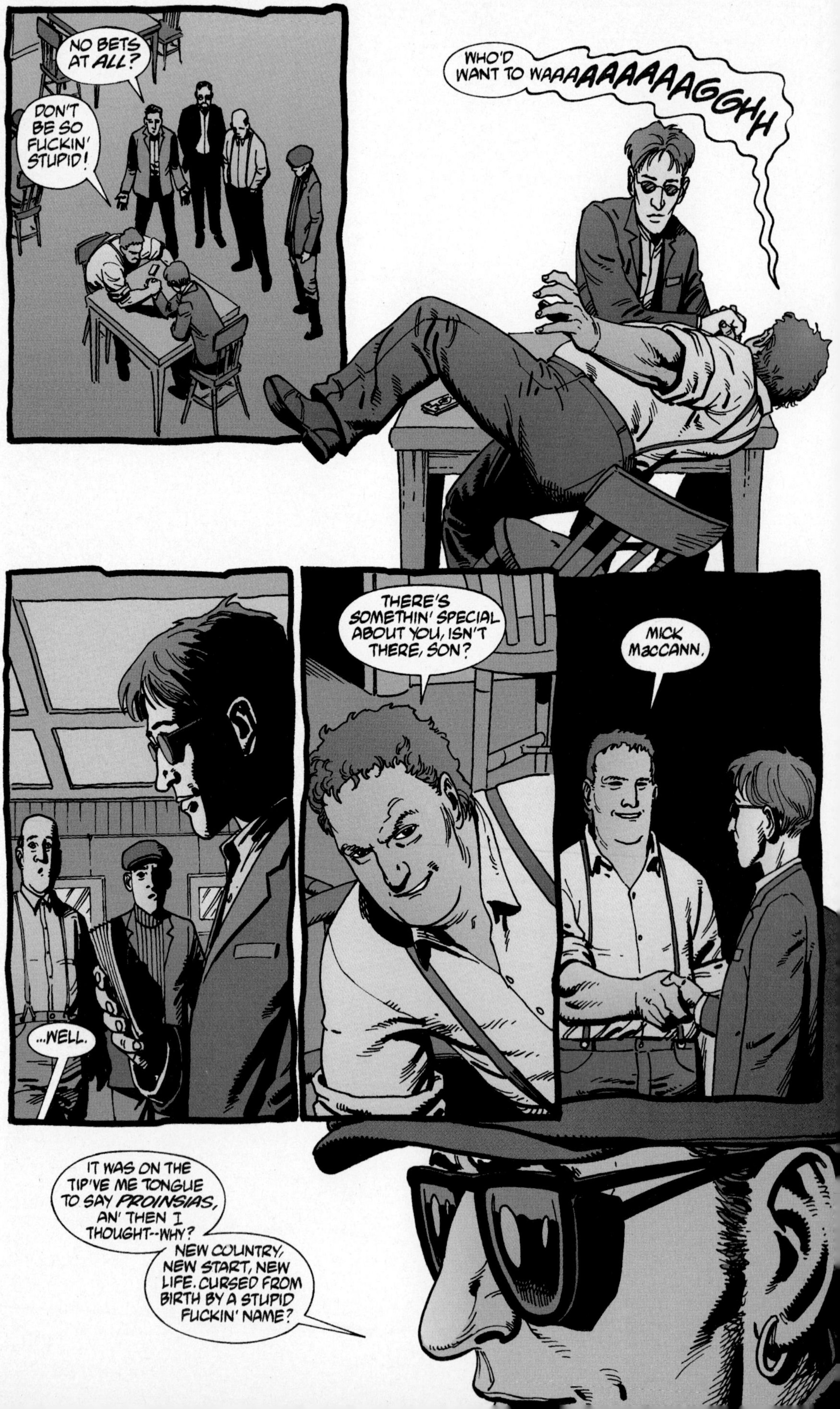
NO BETS AT ALL?
DON'T BE SO FUCKIN' STUPID!
WHO'D WANT TO WAAAAAAAAAGGHH
...WELL.
THERE'S SOMETHIN' SPECIAL ABOUT YOU, ISN'T THERE, SON?
MICK MacCANN.
IT WAS ON THE TIP'VE ME TONGUE TO SAY PROINSIAS, AN' THEN I THOUGHT--WHY?
NEW COUNTRY, NEW START, NEW LIFE. CURSED FROM BIRTH BY A STUPID FUCKIN' NAME?

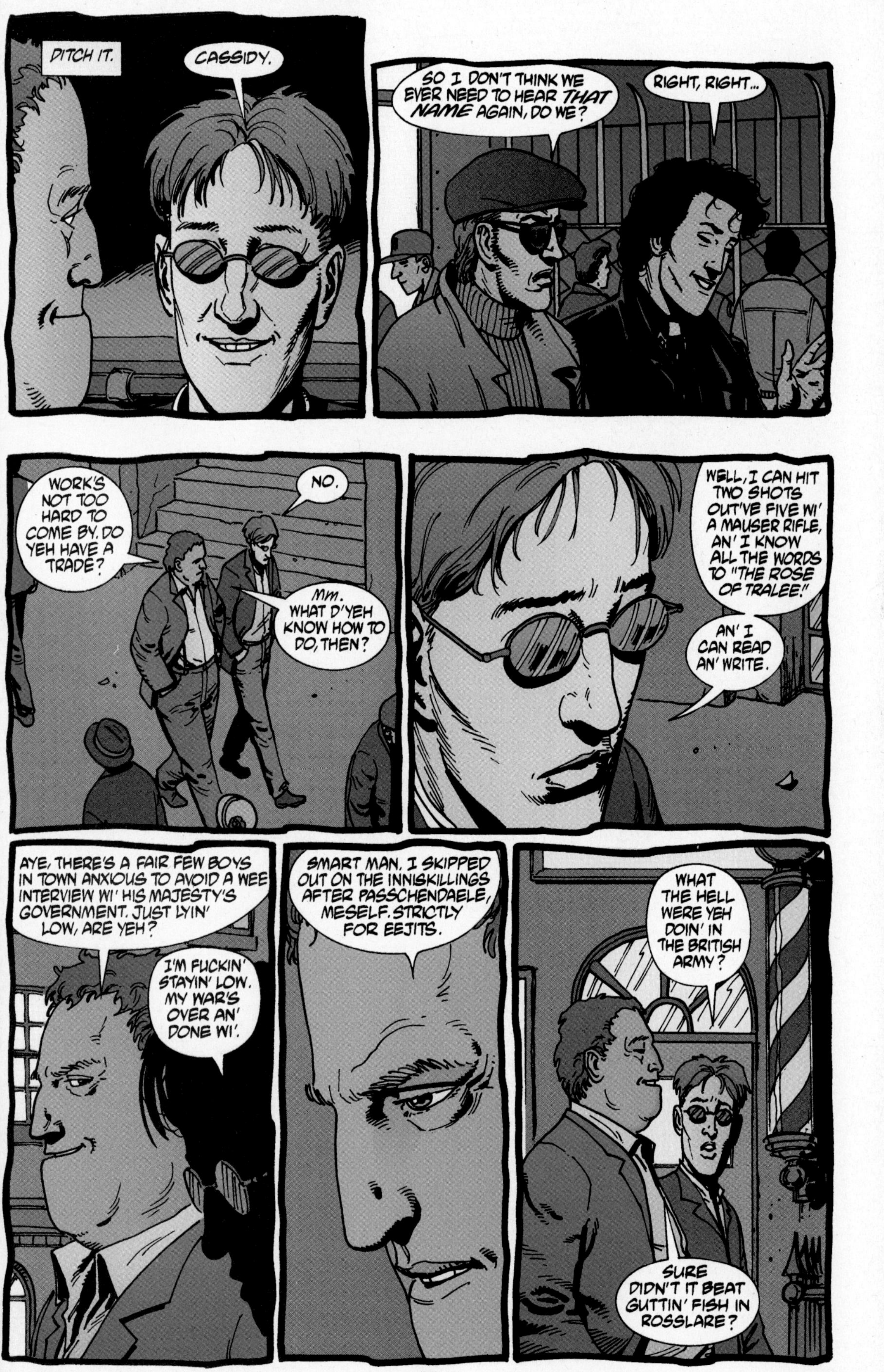

DITCH IT.
CASSIDY.
SO I DON'T THINK WE EVER NEED TO HEAR THAT NAME AGAIN, DO WE?
RIGHT, RIGHT...
WORK'S NOT TOO HARD TO COME BY. DO YEH HAVE A TRADE?
NO.
MM. WHAT D'YEH KNOW HOW TO DO, THEN?
WELL, I CAN HIT TWO SHOTS OUT'VE FIVE WI' A MAUSER RIFLE, AN' I KNOW ALL THE WORDS TO "THE ROSE OF TRALEE."
AN' I CAN READ AN' WRITE.
AYE, THERE'S A FAIR FEW BOYS IN TOWN ANXIOUS TO AVOID A WEE INTERVIEW WI' HIS MAJESTY'S GOVERNMENT. JUST LYIN' LOW, ARE YEH?
I'M FUCKIN' STAYIN' LOW. MY WAR'S OVER AN' DONE WI'.
SMART MAN. I SKIPPED OUT ON THE INNISKILLINGS AFTER PASSCHENDAELE, MESELF. STRICTLY FOR EEJITS.
WHAT THE HELL WERE YEH DOIN' IN THE BRITISH ARMY?
SURE DIDN'T IT BEAT GUTTIN' FISH IN ROSSLARE?

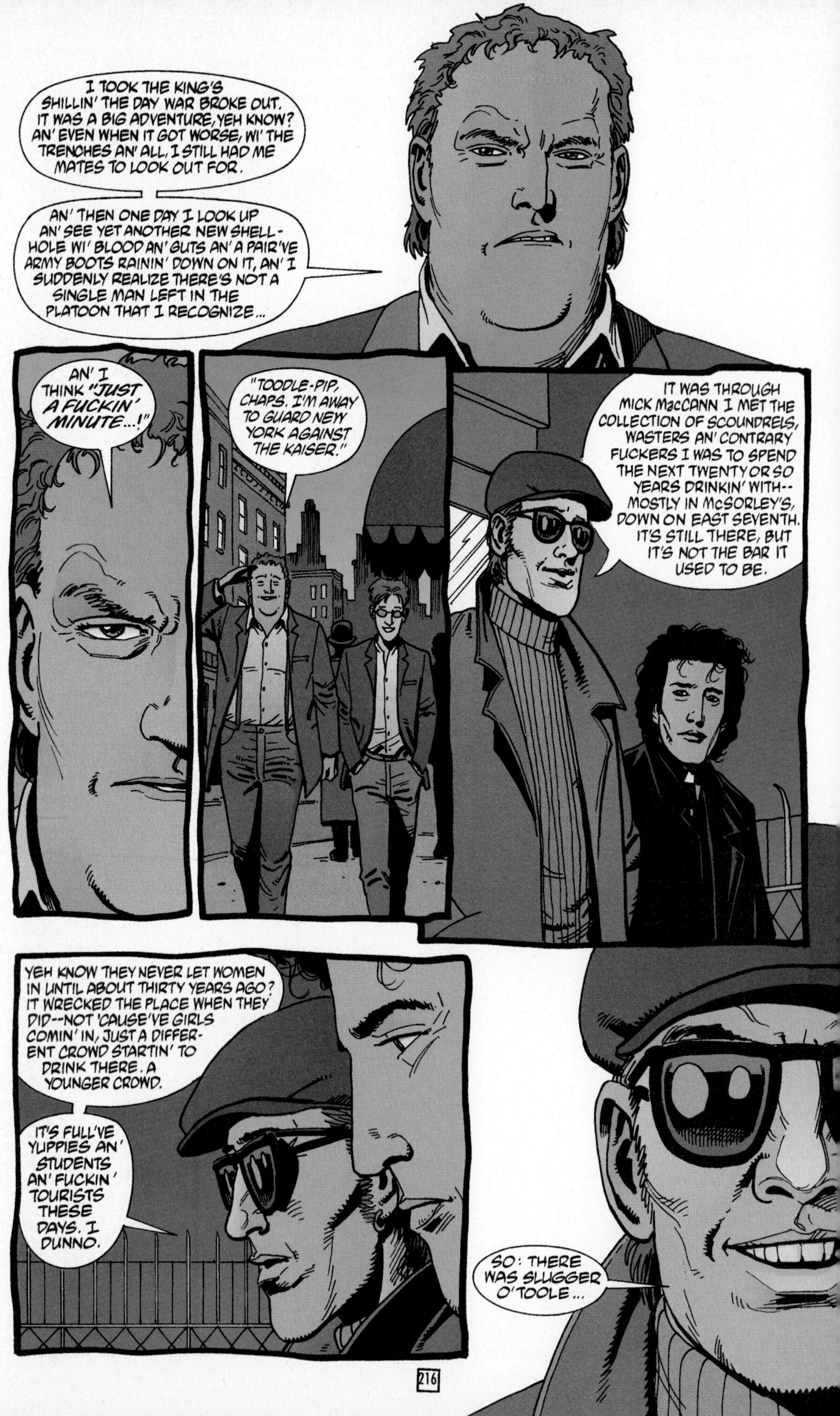
I TOOK THE KING'S SHILLIN' THE DAY WAR BROKE OUT. IT WAS A BIG ADVENTURE, YEH KNOW? AN' EVEN WHEN IT GOT WORSE, WI' THE TRENCHES AN' ALL, I STILL HAD ME MATES TO LOOK OUT FOR.
AN' THEN ONE DAY I LOOK UP AN' SEE YET ANOTHER NEW SHELL-HOLE WI' BLOOD AN' GUTS AN' A PAIR'VE ARMY BOOTS RAININ' DOWN ON IT, AN' I SUDDENLY REALIZE THERE'S NOT A SINGLE MAN LEFT IN THE PLATOON THAT I RECOGNIZE...
AN' I THINK "JUST A FUCKIN' MINUTE...!"
"TOODLE-PIP, CHAPS. I'M AWAY TO GUARD NEW YORK AGAINST THE KAISER."
IT WAS THROUGH MICK MacCANN I MET THE COLLECTION OF SCOUNDRELS, WASTERS AN' CONTRARY FUCKERS I WAS TO SPEND THE NEXT TWENTY OR SO YEARS DRINKIN' WITH-- MOSTLY IN McSORLEY'S, DOWN ON EAST SEVENTH. IT'S STILL THERE, BUT IT'S NOT THE BAR IT USED TO BE.
YEH KNOW THEY NEVER LET WOMEN IN UNTIL ABOUT THIRTY YEARS AGO? IT WRECKED THE PLACE WHEN THEY DID--NOT 'CAUSE'VE GIRLS COMIN' IN, JUST A DIFFERENT CROWD STARTIN' TO DRINK THERE. A YOUNGER CROWD.
IT'S FULL'VE YUPPIES AN' STUDENTS AN' FUCKIN' TOURISTS THESE DAYS. I DUNNO.
SO: THERE WAS SLUGGER O'TOOLE...

...WHO'D FIGHT ANY MAN IN THE ROOM SO LONG AS THEY DIDN'T MIND HIM SNEAKIN' UP AN' BLATTERIN' THEM ROUND THE HEAD WI' A BASEBALL BAT, AN' JOHNNY McGURK, THE BIGGEST HOOERMONGER I EVER KNEW, WHO ALWAYS HAD THE CLAP, AN' HOGAN AN' MALONE, WHO I'M STILL CONVINCED WERE UP EACH OTHER...

AN' MICKEY COOTE, THE CHAMPION'VE THE DOWNTRODDEN WORKERS --WHO'D NEVER DONE A HAND'S TURN IN HIS LIFE, AN' WHO MacCANN USED TO TAKE THE PISS OUT'VE SOMETHIN' SHOCKIN', AN' BARNEY McGEE AN' BILL TREACY, WHO WERE YER CLASSIC BOLD YOUNG REBEL MATERIAL, SO THANK JAYSIS THEY GOT NO NEARER IRELAND THAN THE STATEN ISLAND FERRY...

AN' YEA, VERILY, THE AIR IN McSORLEY'S WAS RENDERED THICK WITH EXPATRIATE BULLSHIT: EVERY FUCKIN' NIGHT.

LISTEN, LET ME TELL YEZ ABOUT THE LATEST FASCINATIN' DISCHARGE TO DRIP FROM ME OUL' FELLA. IMAGINE MUSHY PEAS WI' KETCHUP--

YEH DIRTY, DIRTY, DIRTY, DIRTY, DIRTY, DIRTY--

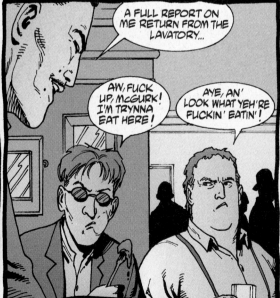

A FULL REPORT ON ME RETURN FROM THE LAVATORY...

AW, FUCK UP, McGURK! I'M TRYNNA EAT HERE!

AYE, AN' LOOK WHAT YEH'RE FUCKIN' EATIN'!

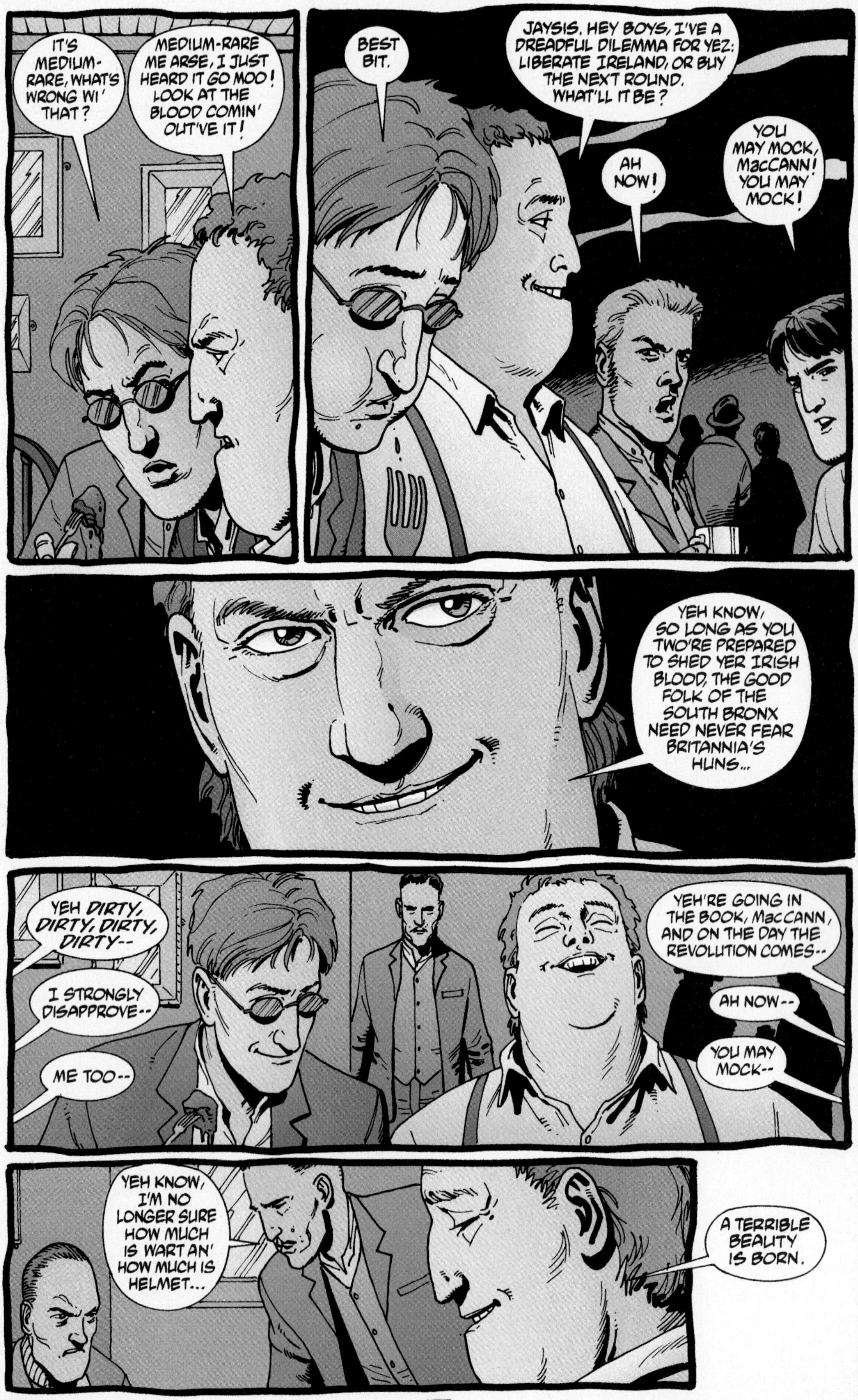
IT'S MEDIUM-RARE, WHAT'S WRONG WI' THAT?
MEDIUM-RARE ME ARSE, I JUST HEARD IT GO MOO! LOOK AT THE BLOOD COMIN' OUT'VE IT!
BEST BIT.
JAYSIS. HEY BOYS, I'VE A DREADFUL DILEMMA FOR YEZ: LIBERATE IRELAND, OR BUY THE NEXT ROUND. WHAT'LL IT BE?
AH NOW!
YOU MAY MOCK, MacCANN! YOU MAY MOCK!
YEH KNOW, SO LONG AS YOU TWO'RE PREPARED TO SHED YER IRISH BLOOD, THE GOOD FOLK OF THE SOUTH BRONX NEED NEVER FEAR BRITANNIA'S HUNS...
YEH *DIRTY, DIRTY, DIRTY, DIRTY*--
I STRONGLY DISAPPROVE--
ME TOO--
YEH'RE GOING IN THE BOOK, MacCANN, AND ON THE DAY THE REVOLUTION COMES--
AH NOW--
YOU MAY MOCK--
YEH KNOW, I'M NO LONGER SURE HOW MUCH IS WART AN' HOW MUCH IS HELMET...
A TERRIBLE BEAUTY IS BORN.

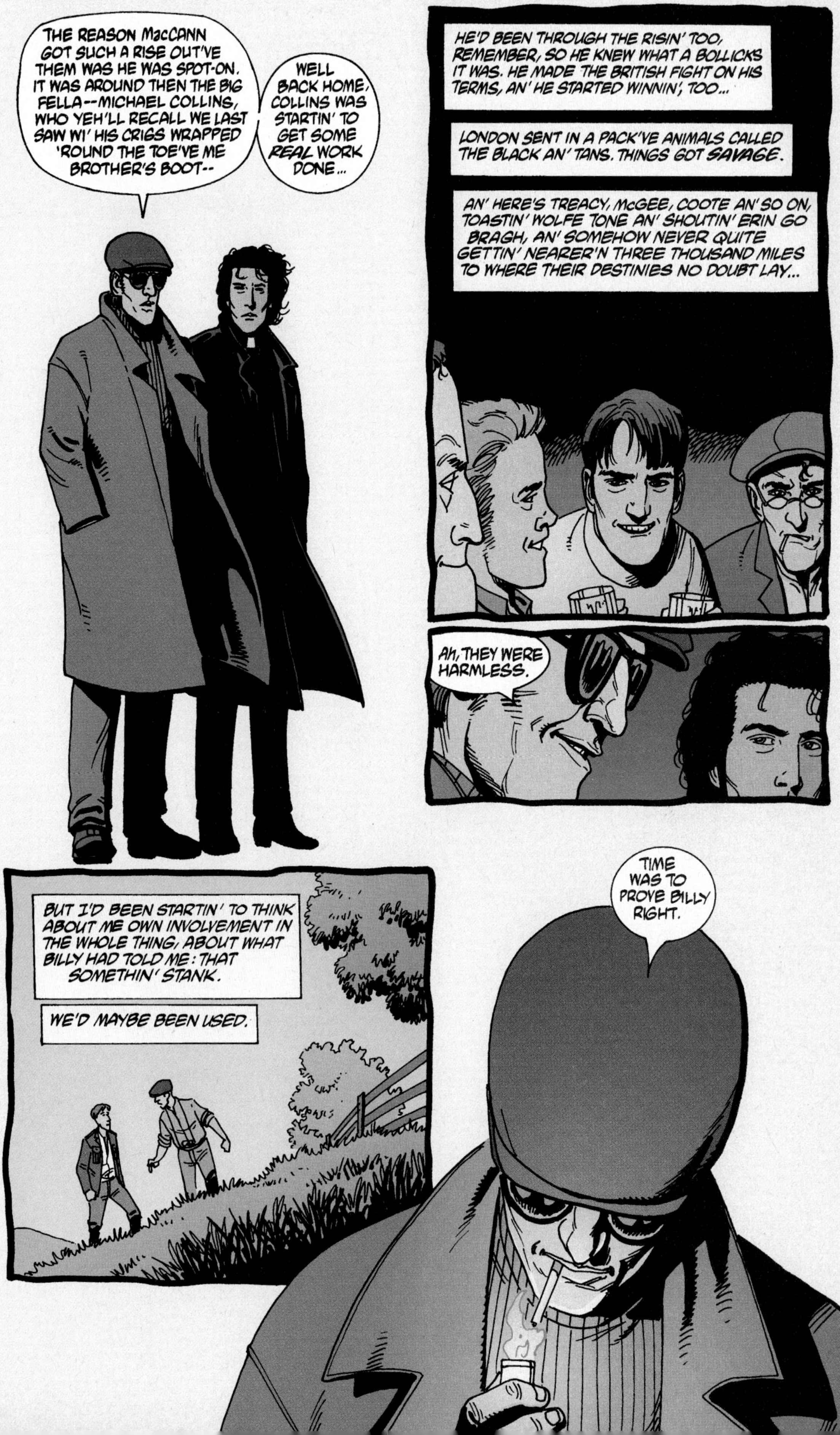
THE REASON MacCANN GOT SUCH A RISE OUT'VE THEM WAS HE WAS SPOT-ON. IT WAS AROUND THEN THE BIG FELLA--MICHAEL COLLINS, WHO YEH'LL RECALL WE LAST SAW WI' HIS CRIGS WRAPPED 'ROUND THE TOE'VE ME BROTHER'S BOOT--
WELL BACK HOME, COLLINS WAS STARTIN' TO GET SOME REAL WORK DONE...
HE'D BEEN THROUGH THE RISIN' TOO, REMEMBER, SO HE KNEW WHAT A BOLLICKS IT WAS. HE MADE THE BRITISH FIGHT ON HIS TERMS, AN' HE STARTED WINNIN', TOO...
LONDON SENT IN A PACK'VE ANIMALS CALLED THE BLACK AN' TANS. THINGS GOT SAVAGE.
AN' HERE'S TREACY, McGEE, COOTE AN' SO ON, TOASTIN' WOLFE TONE AN' SHOUTIN' ERIN GO BRAGH, AN' SOMEHOW NEVER QUITE GETTIN' NEARER'N THREE THOUSAND MILES TO WHERE THEIR DESTINIES NO DOUBT LAY...
Ah, THEY WERE HARMLESS.
BUT I'D BEEN STARTIN' TO THINK ABOUT ME OWN INVOLVEMENT IN THE WHOLE THING, ABOUT WHAT BILLY HAD TOLD ME: THAT SOMETHIN' STANK.
WE'D MAYBE BEEN USED.
TIME WAS TO PROVE BILLY RIGHT.

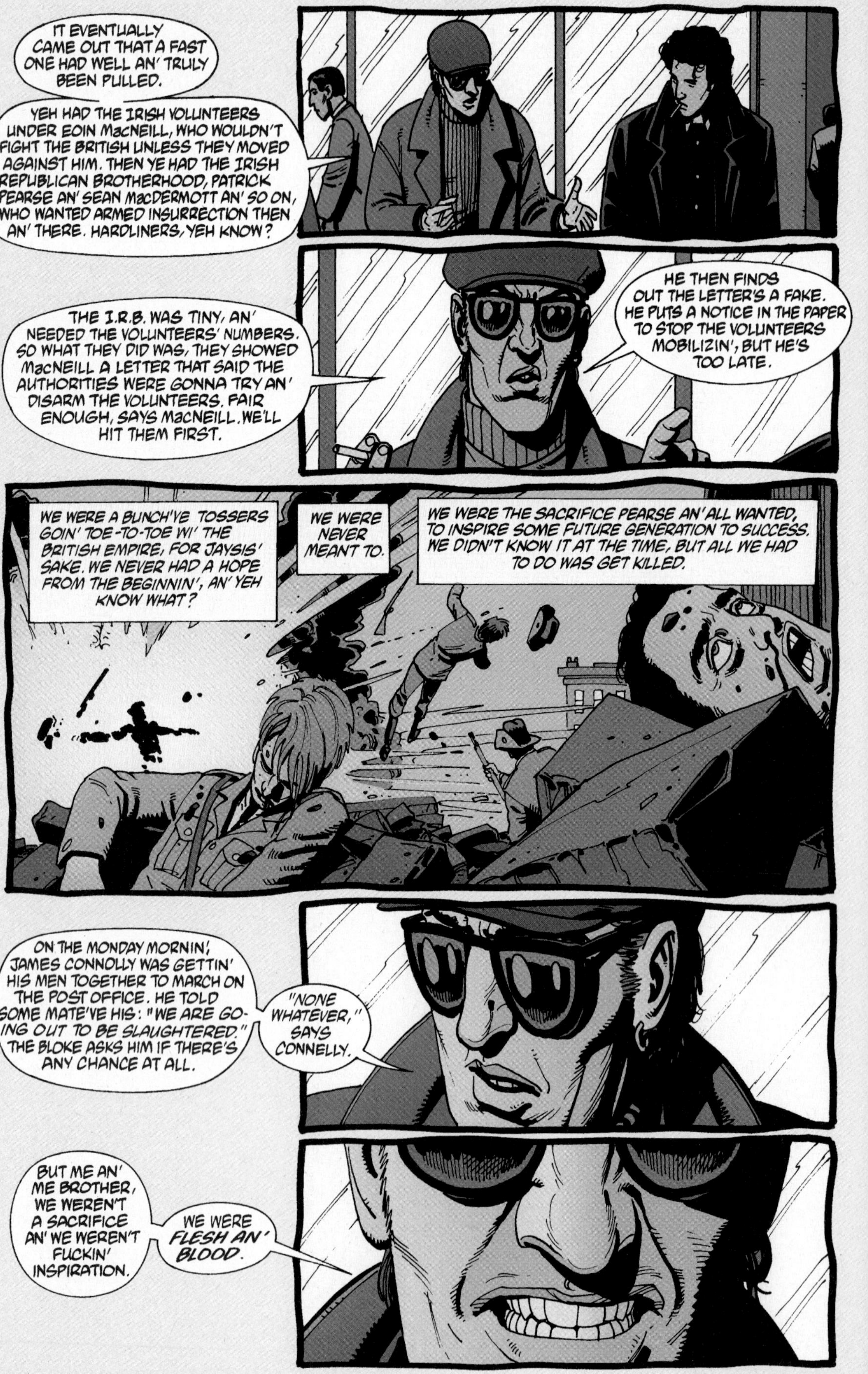
IT EVENTUALLY CAME OUT THAT A FAST ONE HAD WELL AN' TRULY BEEN PULLED.
YEH HAD THE IRISH VOLUNTEERS UNDER EOIN MacNEILL, WHO WOULDN'T FIGHT THE BRITISH UNLESS THEY MOVED AGAINST HIM. THEN YE HAD THE IRISH REPUBLICAN BROTHERHOOD, PATRICK PEARSE AN' SEAN MacDERMOTT AN' SO ON, WHO WANTED ARMED INSURRECTION THEN AN' THERE. HARDLINERS, YEH KNOW?
THE I.R.B. WAS TINY, AN' NEEDED THE VOLUNTEERS' NUMBERS. SO WHAT THEY DID WAS, THEY SHOWED MacNEILL A LETTER THAT SAID THE AUTHORITIES WERE GONNA TRY AN' DISARM THE VOLUNTEERS. FAIR ENOUGH, SAYS MacNEILL. WE'LL HIT THEM FIRST.
HE THEN FINDS OUT THE LETTER'S A FAKE. HE PUTS A NOTICE IN THE PAPER TO STOP THE VOLUNTEERS MOBILIZIN', BUT HE'S TOO LATE.
WE WERE A BUNCH'VE TOSSERS GOIN' TOE-TO-TOE WI' THE BRITISH EMPIRE, FOR JAYSIS' SAKE. WE NEVER HAD A HOPE FROM THE BEGINNIN', AN' YEH KNOW WHAT?
WE WERE NEVER MEANT TO.
WE WERE THE SACRIFICE PEARSE AN' ALL WANTED, TO INSPIRE SOME FUTURE GENERATION TO SUCCESS. WE DIDN'T KNOW IT AT THE TIME, BUT ALL WE HAD TO DO WAS GET KILLED.
ON THE MONDAY MORNIN', JAMES CONNOLLY WAS GETTIN' HIS MEN TOGETHER TO MARCH ON THE POST OFFICE. HE TOLD SOME MATE'VE HIS: "WE ARE GOING OUT TO BE SLAUGHTERED." THE BLOKE ASKS HIM IF THERE'S ANY CHANCE AT ALL.
"NONE WHATEVER," SAYS CONNELLY.
BUT ME AN' ME BROTHER, WE WEREN'T A SACRIFICE AN' WE WEREN'T FUCKIN' INSPIRATION.
WE WERE *FLESH AN' BLOOD*.

I DECIDED THEN THAT I'D NEVER BE USED AGAIN.

BILLY'S WAY WAS RIGHT. KEEP YER HEAD DOWN. WATCH OUT FOR FELLAS WI' GREAT CAUSES, AN GOALS TO STRUGGLE FOR.

OR AS MacCANN PUT IT--

WE ONLY GET ONE GO ON THIS MORTAL COIL, BOYS, SO BE SURE AN' MAKE THE MOST'VE YER TIME. AND IF YEZ DO DECIDE TO DIE FOR SOMETHIN', WELL JAYSIS : IT'D BETTER BE *FUCKIN'* WORTH IT.

AN' I SUPPOSE YOU THINK NOTHING'S WORTH DYING FOR, MacCANN?

AH, I CAN'T THINK OF ANYTHING OFFHAND, NO...

WHAT ABOUT YOUR COUNTRY? WHAT ABOUT IRELAND?

IRELAND, AYE...

WELL, YEH KNOW, WHEN I USED TO LOOK OUT THE WINDOW AN' SEE THE SHEEP GRAZIN' ON THE MOUNTAINS OF WHATYEHCALLIT AN' THE SUN RISIN' OVER LOUGH BOLLOCK, I ALWAYS WONDERED-- "HOW MUCH LONGER DO I HAVE TO STAY IN THIS GODFORSAKEN PLACE ANYWAY?"

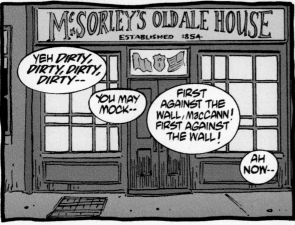

McSORLEY'S OLD ALE HOUSE
ESTABLISHED 1854

YEH *DIRTY, DIRTY, DIRTY, DIRTY--*

YOU MAY MOCK--

FIRST AGAINST THE WALL, MacCANN! FIRST AGAINST THE WALL!

AH NOW--

WE'RE IN AMERICA NOW. WE CAN LEAVE ALL THAT OUL' SHITE BEHIND US.

THAT'S WHAT MacCANN SAID.

SO ANYWAY, THE TWENTIES ROARED AN' THE THIRTIES WERE DEPRESSED, AN' THERE WAS STILL THESE NINE EEJITS SITTIN' ROUND A TABLE TALKIN' BOLLICKS. COOTE'S GLORIOUS DAY NEVER CAME. TREACY AN' McGEE NEVER MADE IT BACK TO THE FIGHT.

AN' THEN ONE DAY I FOUND THIS BOOK MacCANN WAS CARRYIN' AROUND WI' HIM, WHICH HE WAS IN THE HABIT'VE DOIN'...

WHAT'S THIS?

OH, HAVE YEH NEVER READ THAT? IT'S GOOD FUN.

BORROW IT IF YEH WANT.

ONE READ'VE THAT AN' EVERYTHING FELL INTO PLACE IN AN INSTANT. A LOT'VE IT WAS BOLLICKS, BUT THE ESSENTIAL TRUTHS WERE THERE: SUNLIGHT AN' BLOOD, OBVIOUSLY...

AN' LIVIN' FOREVER.

HOW OLD WOULD YEH SAY I LOOK?

ABOUT TWENTY-FIVE GOIN' ON NINETY.

YEH SHOULD SEE ME NAKED.

NO I FUCKING SHOULDN'T.

THE POINT IS I DON'T LOOK ME AGE. OH, TIME AN' SUBSTANCE-ABUSE HAVE TAKEN THEIR TOLL, BUT I'M NOT YER AVERAGE NINETY-SEVEN-YEAR-OLD.

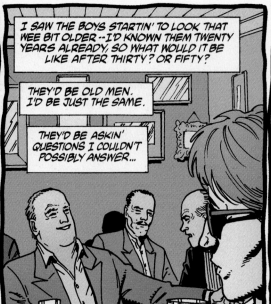

I SAW THE BOYS STARTIN' TO LOOK THAT WEE BIT OLDER -- I'D KNOWN THEM TWENTY YEARS ALREADY, SO WHAT WOULD IT BE LIKE AFTER THIRTY? OR FIFTY?

THEY'D BE OLD MEN. I'D BE JUST THE SAME.

THEY'D BE ASKIN' QUESTIONS I COULDN'T POSSIBLY ANSWER...

AN' AS WELL AS THAT...YEH KNOW...

I DIDN'T WANNA WATCH ME FRIEND GET OLD.

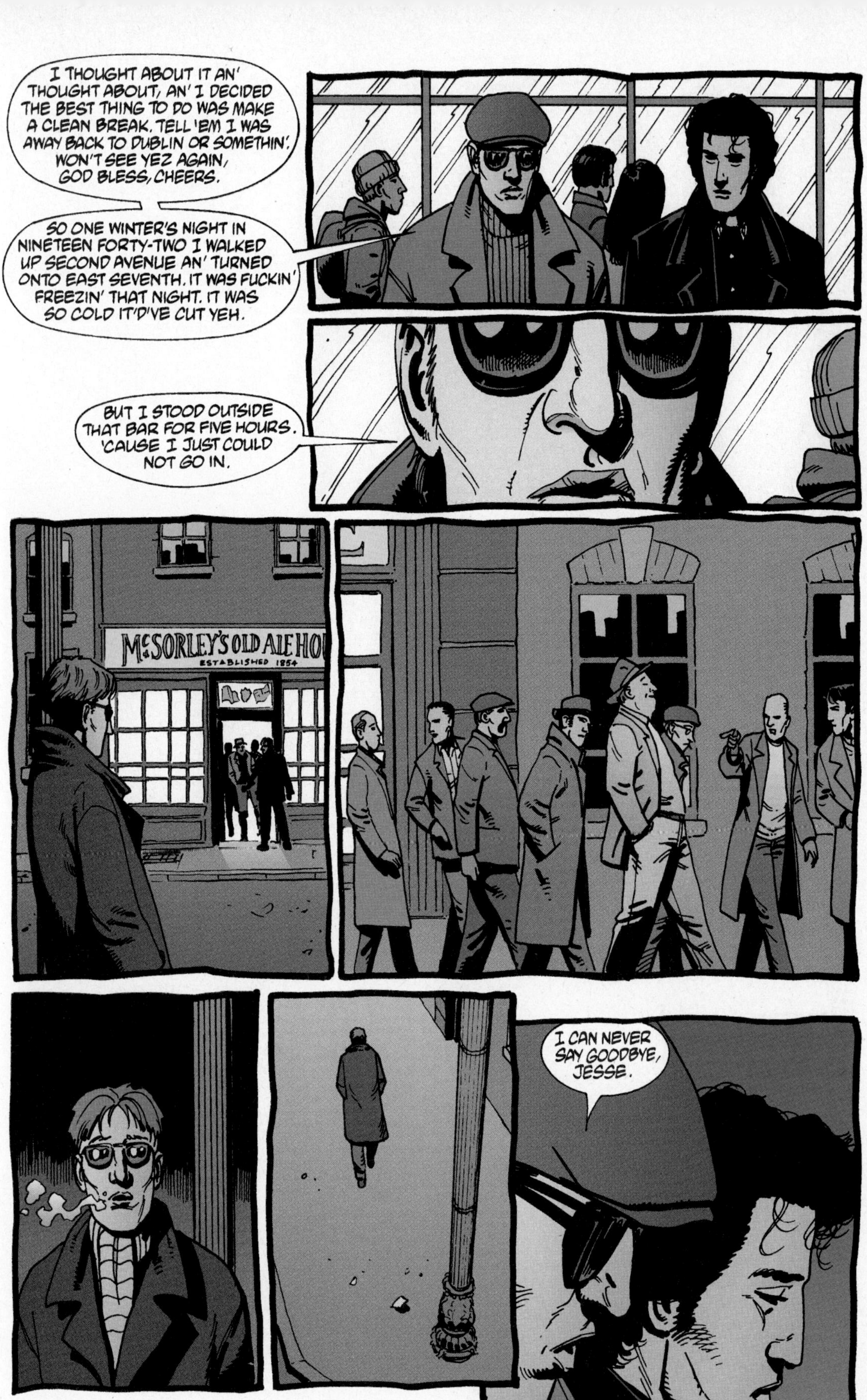
I THOUGHT ABOUT IT AN' THOUGHT ABOUT, AN' I DECIDED THE BEST THING TO DO WAS MAKE A CLEAN BREAK. TELL 'EM I WAS AWAY BACK TO DUBLIN OR SOMETHIN'. WON'T SEE YEZ AGAIN, GOD BLESS, CHEERS.
SO ONE WINTER'S NIGHT IN NINETEEN FORTY-TWO I WALKED UP SECOND AVENUE AN' TURNED ONTO EAST SEVENTH. IT WAS FUCKIN' FREEZIN' THAT NIGHT. IT WAS SO COLD IT'D'VE CUT YEH.
BUT I STOOD OUTSIDE THAT BAR FOR FIVE HOURS. 'CAUSE I JUST COULD NOT GO IN.
McSORLEY'S OLD ALE HOU
ESTABLISHED 1854
I CAN NEVER SAY GOODBYE, JESSE.

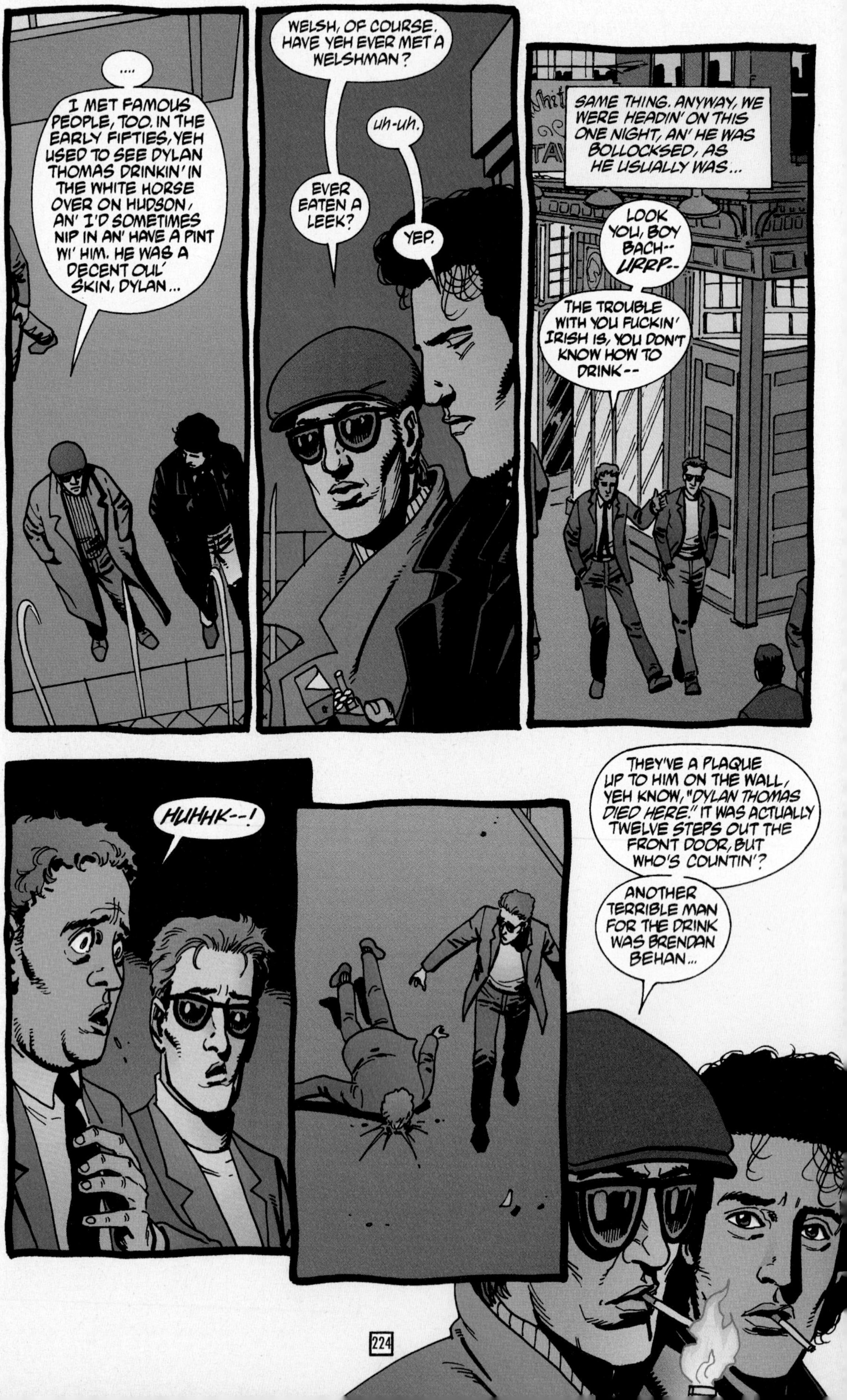
....
I MET FAMOUS PEOPLE, TOO. IN THE EARLY FIFTIES, YEH USED TO SEE DYLAN THOMAS DRINKIN' IN THE WHITE HORSE OVER ON HUDSON, AN' I'D SOMETIMES NIP IN AN' HAVE A PINT WI' HIM. HE WAS A DECENT OUL' SKIN, DYLAN...
WELSH, OF COURSE. HAVE YEH EVER MET A WELSHMAN?
uh-uh.
EVER EATEN A LEEK?
YEP.
SAME THING. ANYWAY, WE WERE HEADIN' ON THIS ONE NIGHT, AN' HE WAS BOLLOCKSED, AS HE USUALLY WAS...
LOOK YOU, BOY BACH-- URRP--
THE TROUBLE WITH YOU FUCKIN' IRISH IS, YOU DON'T KNOW HOW TO DRINK--
HUHHK--!
THEY'VE A PLAQUE UP TO HIM ON THE WALL, YEH KNOW, "DYLAN THOMAS DIED HERE." IT WAS ACTUALLY TWELVE STEPS OUT THE FRONT DOOR, BUT WHO'S COUNTIN'?
ANOTHER TERRIBLE MAN FOR THE DRINK WAS BRENDAN BEHAN...

...WHO I MET LOADS'VE TIMES. I FUCKIN' LOVED HIS PLAYS AN' ALL, AN' IT WAS WORTH IT KNOCKIN' AROUND WI' HIM, IF ONLY FOR A BIT'VE HIS WIT AN' WISDOM--

BASTARDS THEY LOT'VE THEM *BWUUUHH*

AN' I PONDERED THIS LONG, SAGE-LIKE ADVICE, AN' I DECIDED BRENDAN WAS--AS WHATSIZNAME SO BRILLIANTLY PUT IT--A DRINKER WI' A WRITIN' PROBLEM.

AH, HE WAS A GOOD SORT, YEH KNOW? WHEN HE WAS BEHAVIN' HIMSELF YEH COULDN'T WISH FOR BETTER COMPANY--BUT HE HAD THIS WEE ENTOURAGE OF PRICKS AN' HANGERS-ON, WHO'D FEED HIM DRINK JUST SO THEY COULD WATCH BRENDAN BE BRENDAN.

FUCKIN' BASTARDS, I'M TELLIN' YEH. NORMAN MAILER HAD THE SAME PROBLEM FOR A WHILE.

...WHERE WAS I?

I FIGURE THE EARLY SIXTIES.

AYE, THAT'S ABOUT RIGHT. JAYSIS, JESSE. THERE'S THAT MUCH...

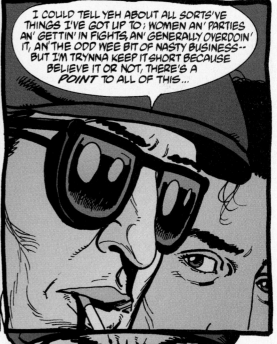

I COULD TELL YEH ABOUT ALL SORTS'VE THINGS I'VE GOT UP TO; WOMEN AN' PARTIES AN' GETTIN' IN FIGHTS, AN' GENERALLY OVERDOIN' IT, AN' THE ODD WEE BIT OF NASTY BUSINESS-- BUT I'M TRYNNA KEEP IT SHORT BECAUSE BELIEVE IT OR NOT, THERE'S A *POINT* TO ALL OF THIS...

OH AYE. ONE LAST WEE DRINKIN' STORY.

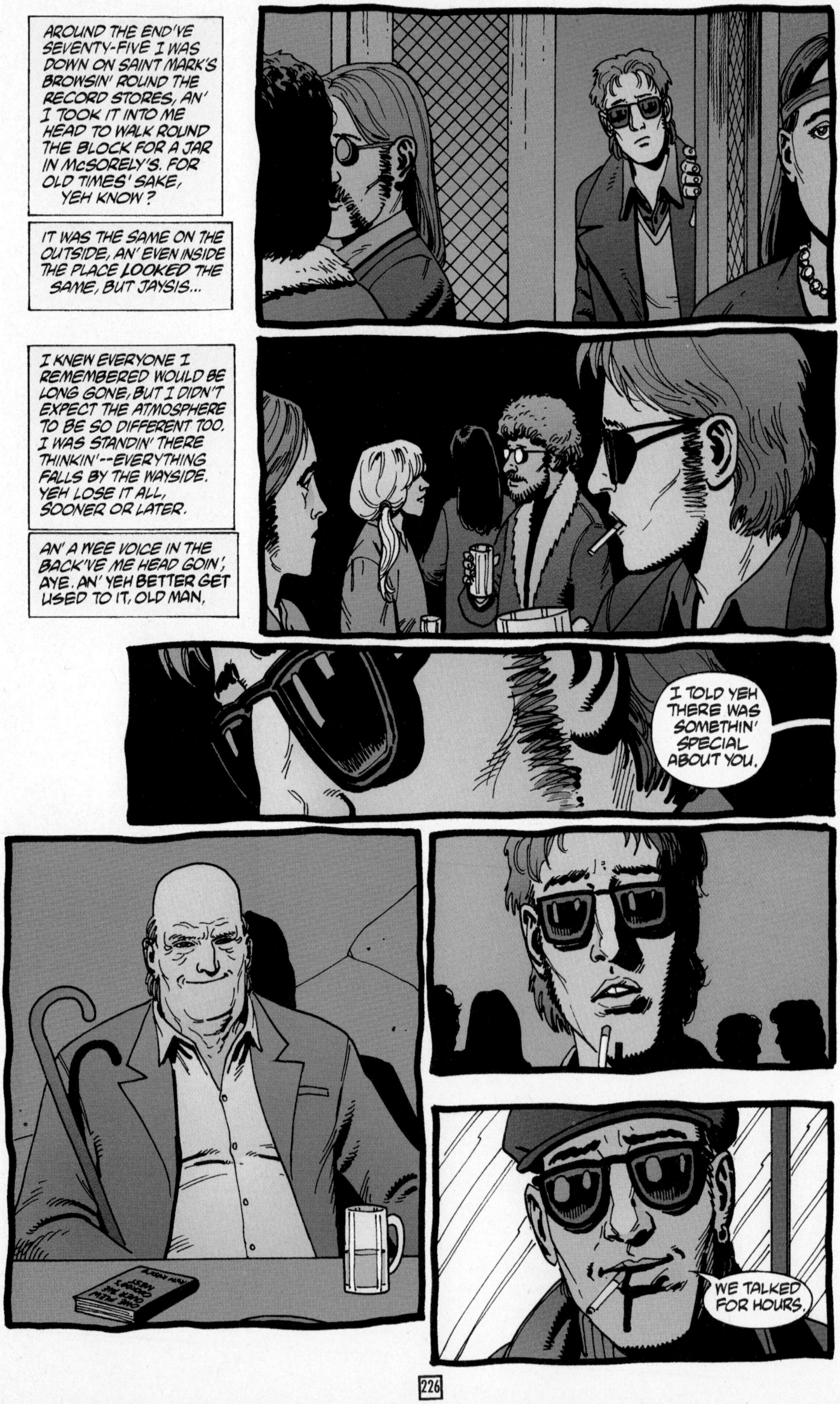
AROUND THE END'VE SEVENTY-FIVE I WAS DOWN ON SAINT MARK'S BROWSIN' ROUND THE RECORD STORES, AN' I TOOK IT INTO ME HEAD TO WALK ROUND THE BLOCK FOR A JAR IN McSORELY'S. FOR OLD TIMES' SAKE, YEH KNOW?
IT WAS THE SAME ON THE OUTSIDE, AN' EVEN INSIDE THE PLACE LOOKED THE SAME, BUT JAYSIS...
I KNEW EVERYONE I REMEMBERED WOULD BE LONG GONE, BUT I DIDN'T EXPECT THE ATMOSPHERE TO BE SO DIFFERENT TOO. I WAS STANDIN' THERE THINKIN'--EVERYTHING FALLS BY THE WAYSIDE. YEH LOSE IT ALL, SOONER OR LATER.
AN' A WEE VOICE IN THE BACK'VE ME HEAD GOIN', AYE. AN' YEH BETTER GET USED TO IT, OLD MAN.
I TOLD YEH THERE WAS SOMETHIN' SPECIAL ABOUT YOU.
WE TALKED FOR HOURS.

ABOUT EVERYTHING WE'D BEEN UP TO, AN' OLD TIMES, AN WHAT'D BECOME'VE EVERYONE. I DIDN'T SAY WHY I'D BARELY AGED A DAY, AN' HE DIDN'T ASK.

JOHNNY McGURK'S DICK EVENTUALLY FELL OFF, BY THE WAY.

I WALKED HIM TO HIS BUS, AN' WE SHOOK HANDS AN' WISHED EACH OTHER ALL THE BEST, AN' I WAS JUST WALKIN' AWAY WHEN I HEARD HIM SHOUT ME NAME:

MAKE THE MOST'VE IT, WHA'!

AN' AFTER THAT I NEVER HEARD FROM HIM AGAIN.

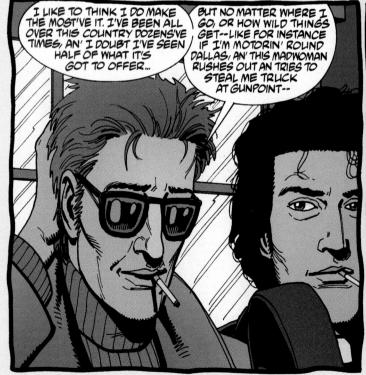

I LIKE TO THINK I DO MAKE THE MOST'VE IT. I'VE BEEN ALL OVER THIS COUNTRY DOZENS'VE TIMES, AN' I DOUBT I'VE SEEN HALF OF WHAT IT'S GOT TO OFFER...

BUT NO MATTER WHERE I GO, OR HOW WILD THINGS GET--LIKE FOR INSTANCE IF I'M MOTORIN' ROUND DALLAS, AN' THIS MADWOMAN RUSHES OUT AN TRIES TO STEAL ME TRUCK AT GUNPOINT--

I ALWAYS FIND ME WAY BACK HERE.

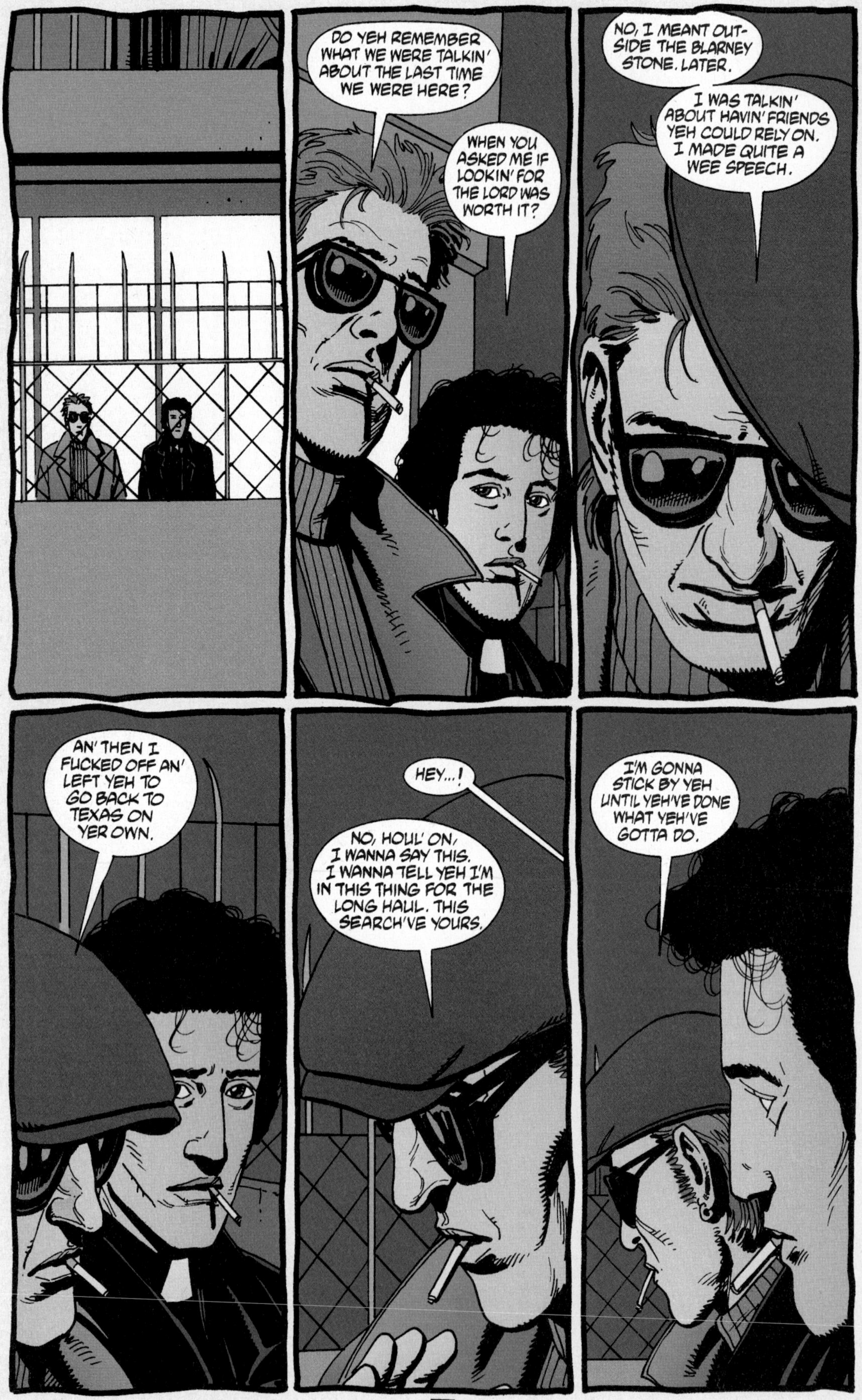
DO YEH REMEMBER WHAT WE WERE TALKIN' ABOUT THE LAST TIME WE WERE HERE?
WHEN YOU ASKED ME IF LOOKIN' FOR THE LORD WAS WORTH IT?
NO, I MEANT OUT-SIDE THE BLARNEY STONE. LATER.
I WAS TALKIN' ABOUT HAVIN' FRIENDS YEH COULD RELY ON. I MADE QUITE A WEE SPEECH.
AN' THEN I FUCKED OFF AN' LEFT YEH TO GO BACK TO TEXAS ON YER OWN.
HEY...!
NO, HOUL' ON, I WANNA SAY THIS. I WANNA TELL YEH I'M IN THIS THING FOR THE LONG HAUL. THIS SEARCH'VE YOURS.
I'M GONNA STICK BY YEH UNTIL YEH'VE DONE WHAT YEH'VE GOTTA DO.

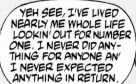

YEH SEE, I'VE LIVED NEARLY ME WHOLE LIFE LOOKIN' OUT FOR NUMBER ONE. I NEVER DID ANYTHING FOR ANYONE AN' I NEVER EXPECTED ANYTHING IN RETURN.

BUT YOU SAVED MY LIFE, JESSE.

THEY HAD ME IN THAT DESPERATE OUL' HOLE WI' THAT NO-DICK BASTARD GOODFELLA SHOOTIN' HOLES IN ME, AN' I DUNNO HOW MUCH MORE I COULD'VE TAKEN, MENTALLY OR PHYSICALLY. I MEAN, IN THEORY NOTHIN' CAN KILL ME BUT SUNLIGHT, BUT...

THERE WAS HUNDREDS'VE THE HOOERS, ALL ARMED TO THE BLEEDIN' TEETH, AN' THAT DICKLICKER STARR WAS USIN' ME AS A TRAP TO GET YEH TO COME TO HIM-- AN' YEH DIDN'T GIVE A FUCK.

YEH JUST WALKED IN ANYWAY, ALL ON YER OWN, AND YEH RISKED YER LIFE TO SAVE MINE.

AN' THE LAST TIME ANYONE DID A THING LIKE THAT FOR ME WAS ME BROTHER, AN' THAT WAS EIGHTY YEARS AGO.

...YOU AIN'T GOIN' MUSHY ON ME, ARE YOU, PROINSIAS?

WELL NOT ANY FUCKIN' MORE I'M NOT...!

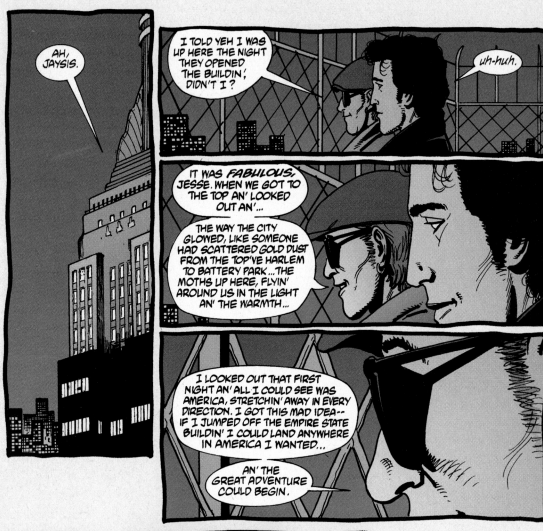

AH, JAYSIS.

I TOLD YEH I WAS UP HERE THE NIGHT THEY OPENED THE BUILDIN', DIDN'T I?

uh-huh.

IT WAS *FABULOUS*, JESSE. WHEN WE GOT TO THE TOP AN' LOOKED OUT AN'...

THE WAY THE CITY GLOWED, LIKE SOMEONE HAD SCATTERED GOLD DUST FROM THE TOP'VE HARLEM TO BATTERY PARK...THE MOTHS UP HERE, FLYIN' AROUND US IN THE LIGHT AN' THE WARMTH...

I LOOKED OUT THAT FIRST NIGHT AN' ALL I COULD SEE WAS AMERICA, STRETCHIN' AWAY IN EVERY DIRECTION. I GOT THIS MAD IDEA-- IF I JUMPED OFF THE EMPIRE STATE BUILDIN' I COULD LAND ANYWHERE IN AMERICA I WANTED...

AN' THE GREAT ADVENTURE COULD BEGIN.

THIS CITY, SHE'S AS BEAUTIFUL TONIGHT AS THE FIRST TIME I SAW HER.

I LOVE YEH, NEW YORK!

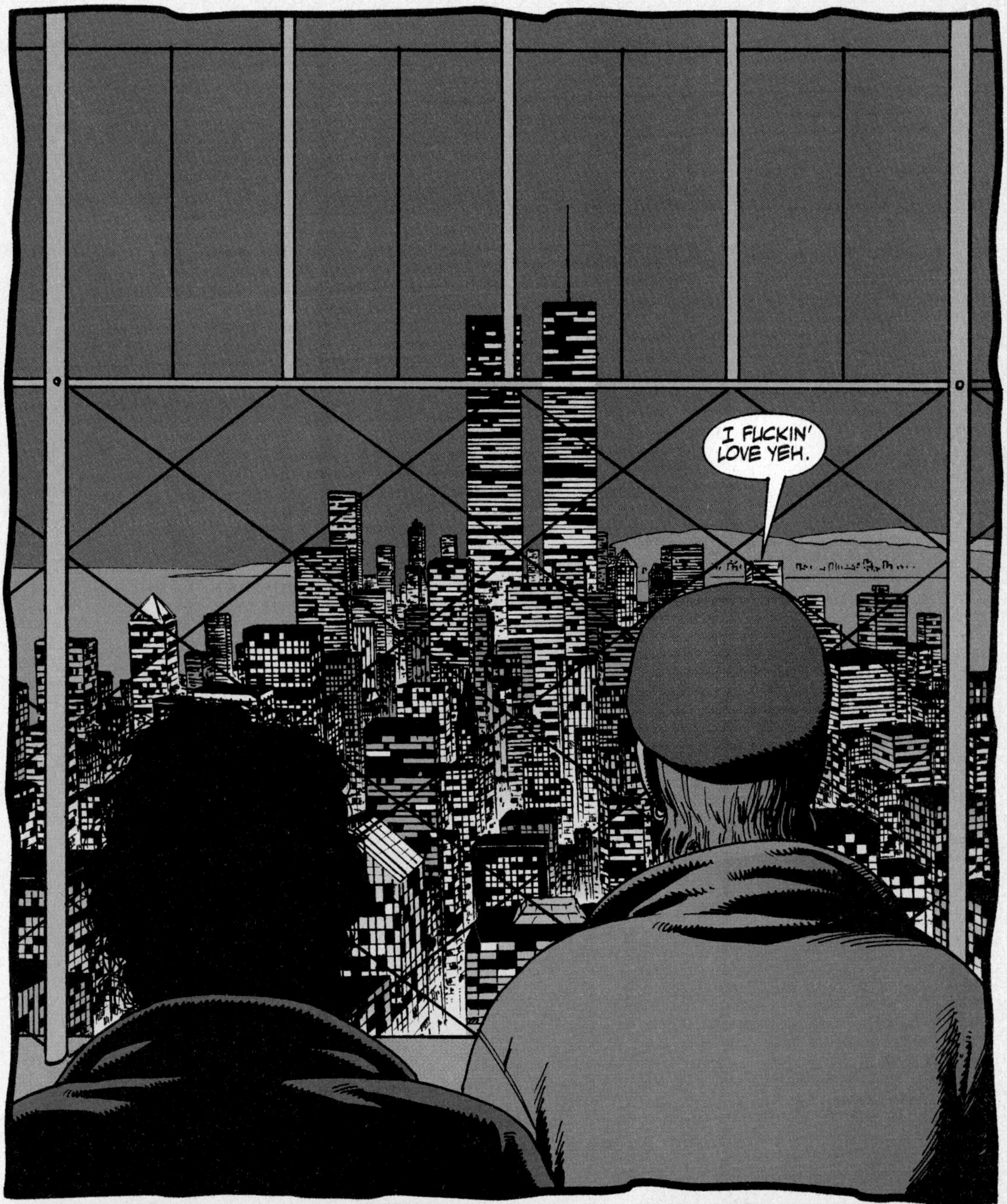
I FUCKIN' LOVE YEH.
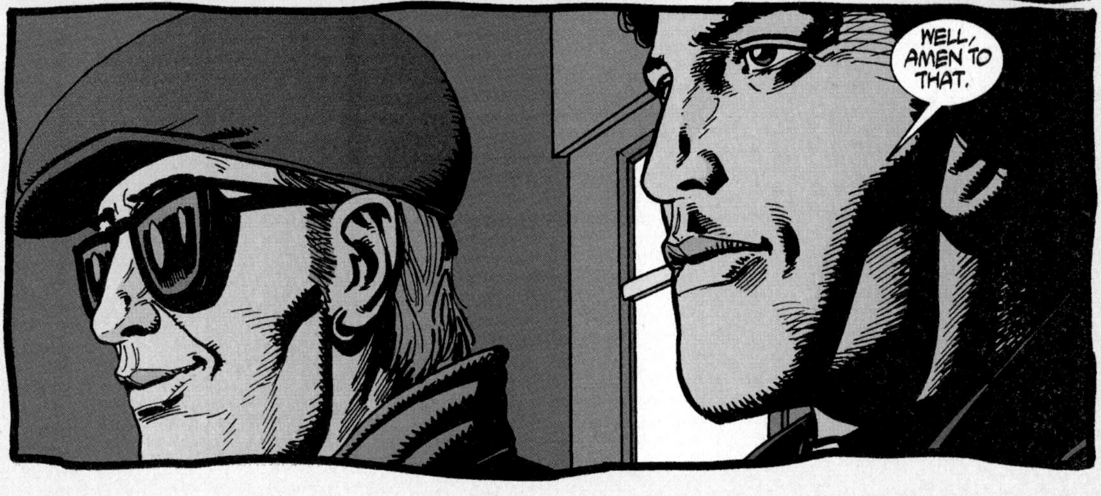
WELL, AMEN TO THAT.

look for these other vertigo books:

look for these other vertigo books:

GRAPHIC NOVELS

DHAMPIRE: STILLBORN
Nancy A. Collins/Paul Lee

MR. PUNCH
Neil Gaiman/Dave McKean

THE MYSTERY PLAY
Grant Morrison/Jon J Muth

TELL ME, DARK
Karl Wagner/Kent Williams

**VERTIGO VÉRITÉ:
SEVEN MILES A SECOND**
David Wojnarowicz/
James Romberger

COLLECTIONS

ANIMAL MAN
Grant Morrison/Chas Truog/
Tom Grummett/Doug Hazlewood

BLACK ORCHID
Neil Gaiman/Dave McKean

THE BOOKS OF MAGIC
Neil Gaiman/John Bolton/
Scott Hampton/Charles Vess/
Paul Johnson

**THE BOOKS OF MAGIC:
BINDINGS**
John Ney Rieber/Gary Amaro/
Peter Gross

**THE BOOKS OF MAGIC:
SUMMONINGS**
John Ney Rieber/Peter Gross/
Peter Snejbjerg/Gary Amaro/
Dick Giordano

**THE BOOKS OF MAGIC:
RECKONINGS**
John Ney Rieber/Peter Snejbjerg/
Peter Gross/John Ridgway

**DEATH: THE HIGH COST
OF LIVING**
Neil Gaiman/Chris Bachalo/
Mark Buckingham

DEATH: THE TIME OF YOUR LIFE
Neil Gaiman/Chris Bachalo/
Mark Buckingham/Mark Pennington

**DOOM PATROL: CRAWLING
FROM THE WRECKAGE**
Grant Morrison/Richard Case/
various

ENIGMA
Peter Milligan/Duncan Fegredo

**HELLBLAZER:
DANGEROUS HABITS**
Garth Ennis/William Simpson/
various

**HELLBLAZER:
FEAR AND LOATHING**
Garth Ennis/Steve Dillon

**HOUSE OF SECRETS:
FOUNDATION**
Steven T. Seagle/Teddy Kristiansen

**THE INVISIBLES:
SAY YOU WANT A REVOLUTION**
Grant Morrison/Steve Yeowell/
Jill Thompson/Dennis Cramer

JONAH HEX: TWO-GUN MOJO
Joe R. Lansdale/Tim Truman/
Sam Glanzman

PREACHER: GONE TO TEXAS
Garth Ennis/Steve Dillon

**PREACHER:
UNTIL THE END OF THE WORLD**
Garth Ennis/Steve Dillon

SAGA OF THE SWAMP THING
Alan Moore/Steve Bissette/
John Totleben

**SANDMAN MYSTERY THEATRE:
THE TARANTULA**
Matt Wagner/Guy Davis

THE SYSTEM
Peter Kuper

V FOR VENDETTA
Alan Moore/David Lloyd

VAMPS
Elaine Lee/William Simpson

WITCHCRAFT
James Robinson/
Peter Snejbjerg/Michael Zulli/
Steve Yeowell/Teddy Kristiansen

THE SANDMAN LIBRARY

**THE SANDMAN:
PRELUDES & NOCTURNES**
Neil Gaiman/Sam Kieth/
Mike Dringenberg/Malcolm Jones III

**THE SANDMAN:
THE DOLL'S HOUSE**
Neil Gaiman/Mike
Dringenberg/Malcolm Jones III/
Chris Bachalo/Michael Zulli/
Steve Parkhouse

**THE SANDMAN:
DREAM COUNTRY**
Neil Gaiman/Kelley Jones/
Charles Vess/Colleen Doran/
Malcolm Jones III

**THE SANDMAN:
SEASON OF MISTS**
Neil Gaiman/Kelley Jones/Mike
Dringenberg/Malcolm Jones III/
various

**THE SANDMAN:
A GAME OF YOU**
Neil Gaiman/Shawn McManus/
various

THE SANDMAN: BRIEF LIVES
Neil Gaiman/Jill Thompson/
Vince Locke

**THE SANDMAN:
FABLES AND REFLECTIONS**
Neil Gaiman/various artists

THE SANDMAN: WORLDS' END
Neil Gaiman/various artists

**THE SANDMAN:
THE KINDLY ONES**
Neil Gaiman/Marc Hempel/
Richard Case/various

THE SANDMAN: THE WAKE
Neil Gaiman/Michael Zulli/
Jon J Muth/Charles Vess

OTHER COLLECTIONS
OF INTEREST

CAMELOT 3000
Mike W. Barr/Brian Bolland

RONIN
Frank Miller

WATCHMEN
Alan Moore/Dave Gibbons

For the nearest comics shop carrying collected editions
and monthly titles from DC Comics, call 1-888-COMIC BOOK
ALL VERTIGO BACKLIST BOOKS ARE SUGGESTED FOR MATURE READERS